# Annotated Standards for Imposing Lawyer Sanctions

Second Edition

Ellyn S. Rosen, Editor



AMERICAN BAR ASSOCIATION
Center for Professional Responsibility

Cover and interior design by ABA Design.



Printed in the United States of America.

23 22 21 20 19    5 4 3 2 1

ISBN: 978-1-64105-383-9

Discounts are available for books ordered in bulk. Special consideration is given to courts, lawyer regulatory agencies, state bars, CLE programs, and other bar-related organizations. Inquire at Book Publishing, ABA Publishing, American Bar Association, 321 N. Clark Street, Chicago, Illinois 60654-7598.

www.shopABA.org

# Contents

# Acknowledgments for the Second Edition

Completion of this second edition of the *Annotated ABA Standards for Imposing Lawyer Sanctions* was a true collaboration. With special appreciation, recognition, and gratitude to the following volunteer authors, who helped bring it to timely completion with excellence:

**Mark Armitage**
Detroit, Michigan

**Alexander Bai**
Chicago, Illinois

**Nancy L. Cohen**
Denver, Colorado

**Hon. Daniel J. Crothers**
Bismarck, North Dakota

**Karen Daley**
Detroit, Michigan

**Dolores Dorsainvil**
Washington, D.C.

**Michael P. Downey**
St. Louis, Missouri

**Douglas J. Ende**
Seattle, Washington

**Ellen Fischer**
Chicago, Illinois

**Mary K. Foster**
Chicago, Illinois

**Arthur Garwin**
Chicago, Illinois

**Patrick Sean Ginty**
Chicago, Illinois

**Amanda Jones**
New Haven, Connecticut

**James A. Kawachika**
Honolulu, Hawaii

**Nicole Luth**
Spokane, Washington

**Jenny Mittelman**
Atlanta, Georgia

**Sari W. Montgomery**
Chicago, Illinois

**Wendy J. Muchman**
Chicago, Illinois

**Patricia Bartley Schwartz**
Wilmington, Delaware

**Paige Tungate**
St. Louis, Missouri

**Kathleen M. Uston**
Richmond, Virginia

**Maret Vessella**
Phoenix, Arizona

Yours was not an easy task. As chapter author and editor of this book, I am grateful for the time and care that each of you brought to this publication. A special thank you to Sue Hartley, Judicial Assistant to the Honorable Daniel J. Crothers of the North Dakota Supreme Court, for her editorial assistance and sharp eye. Appreciation also goes to Theresa M. Gronkiewicz and Martha Middleton. Their principal authorship of the previous edition is still evident in this publication. Continued dedication to the late Jeanne P. Gray, who served as Director of the Center for Professional Responsibility from 1982 until her passing in April 2013.

I would also like to express my gratitude to the members of the ABA Standing Committee on Professional Regulation and Center for Professional Responsibility Director, Tracy L. Kepler, who supported this project throughout its development and publication.

Finally, the Center for Professional Responsibility thanks Thomson Reuters (formerly the West Publishing Corporation) for its generous gift of the West Professional Responsibility Law Library, the resource for much of the research reflected in this work.

Ellyn S. Rosen,
Regulation and Global Initiatives Counsel
ABA Center for Professional Responsibility

# Acknowledgments for the First Edition

This inaugural edition of the *Annotated ABA Standards for Imposing Lawyer Sanctions* presents an authoritative and practical analysis of the cases and other legal authorities essential to understanding the application of the black letter Standards. The black letter Standards and Commentary were first adopted by the ABA House of Delegates in February 1986 and were last amended in February 1992. Since their adoption the Standards have served as a model comprehensive system for the imposition of lawyer disciplinary sanctions that leaves appropriate flexibility for courts and disciplinary agencies given the particular facts of each case of lawyer misconduct.

In February 2012, the ABA Standing Committee on Professional Discipline filed, and the ABA House of Delegates approved, Resolution 107 reaffirming the black letter Standards as policy of the Association and rescinding the House's adoption of the Commentary as such. The Committee determined and the House agreed that, unlike the Comments to the ABA Model Rules of Professional Conduct or the ABA Model Code of Judicial Conduct, the Commentary to the black letter Standards were more like annotations. By removing the Commentary from the Standards policy corpus this Annotation can and will be updated at regular intervals to ensure that the document remains most useful to the courts, profession, and the public.

This book is dedicated to the late Jeanne P. Gray, who served as Director of the Center for Professional Responsibility from 1982 until her untimely death in April 2013. Trailblazer in the area of professional responsibility law, leader, mentor, and friend, Jeanne's patience and wisdom shaped this book and all of those who produced it. Special appreciation is in order to Deputy Regulation Counsel Theresa M. Gronkiewicz and Special Consultant Martha Middleton, who served as the principal authors of this book, bringing it to completion with excellence and professionalism. Deputy Director of the Center for Professional Responsibility Ellyn S. Rosen and I served as editors. Special mention should also be made of Brett Gallagher, Kathleen E. Maher, and Center Senior Research Paralegal Natalia Vera.

I would also like to express my gratitude to the members of the ABA Standing Committee on Professional Discipline, who supported this project throughout its development and publication.

Finally, the Center for Professional Responsibility also thanks the West Publishing Corporation for its generous gift of the West Professional Responsibility Law Library, the resource for much of the research reflected in this work.

Arthur H. Garwin, Director
Center for Professional Responsibility

# Preface

*(Editor's Note: The Preface and Theoretical Framework appear here in the form in which they were originally published. They have not been annotated or otherwise updated for purposes of this publication. References in the Preface to "this report" are to the Report and Recommendation seeking approval of the Sanctions Standards submitted by the Joint Committee on Professional Sanctions to the ABA House of Delegates in December 1985.)*

## STANDARDS FOR IMPOSING LAWYER SANCTIONS

*AS APPROVED, FEBRUARY 1986*
*AND AS AMENDED, FEBRUARY 1992*

## *I. Preface*

### A. Background

In 1979, the American Bar Association published the Standards for Lawyer Discipline and Disability Proceedings. [The Standards for Lawyer Discipline and Disability Proceedings have been superseded by the ABA Model Rules for Lawyer Disciplinary Enforcement (MRLDE)][1] That book [the Standards] was a result of work by the Joint Committee on Professional Discipline of the American Bar Association. The Joint Committee was composed of members of the Judicial Administration Division and the Standing Committee on Professional Discipline of the American Bar Association. The task of the Joint Committee was to prepare standards for enforcement of discipline in the legal community.

The 1979 standards have been most helpful and have been used by numerous jurisdictions as a frame of reference against which to compare their own disciplinary systems. Many jurisdictions have modified their procedures to comport with these suggested standards, and the Standing Committee on Professional Discipline of the American Bar Association has assisted state disciplinary systems in evaluating their programs in light of the approved standards.

It became evident that additional analysis was necessary in one important area — that of appropriate sanctions for lawyer misconduct. The American Bar Association Standards for Lawyer Discipline and Disability Proceedings (hereinafter "Standards for Lawyer Discipline") do not attempt to recommend the type

1. Model Rules for Lawyer Disciplinary Enforcement (American Bar Association Standing Committee on Professional Discipline, 1989).

of discipline to be imposed in any particular case. The Standards merely state that the discipline to be imposed "should depend upon the facts and circumstances of the case, should be fashioned in light of the purpose of lawyer discipline, and may take into account aggravating or mitigating circumstances" (Standard 7.1) [See generally Rule 10, ABA MRLDE].

For lawyer discipline to be truly effective, sanctions must be based on clearly developed standards. Inappropriate sanctions can undermine the goals of lawyer discipline: sanctions which are too lenient fail to adequately deter misconduct and thus lower public confidence in the profession; sanctions which are too onerous may impair confidence in the system and deter lawyers from reporting ethical violations on the part of other lawyers. Inconsistent sanctions, either within a jurisdiction or among jurisdictions, cast doubt on the efficiency and the basic fairness of all disciplinary systems.

As an example of this problem of inconsistent sanctions, consider the range in levels of sanctions imposed for a conviction for failure to file federal income taxes. In one jurisdiction, in 1979, a lawyer who failed to file income tax returns for one year was suspended for one year,[2] while, in 1980, a lawyer who failed to file income tax returns for two years was merely censured.[3] Within a two-year period, the sanctions imposed on lawyers who converted their clients' funds included disbarment,[4] suspension,[5] and censure.[6] The inconsistency of sanctions imposed by different jurisdictions for the same misconduct is even greater.

An examination of these cases illustrates the need for a comprehensive system of sanctions. In many cases, different sanctions are imposed for the same acts of misconduct, and the courts rarely provide any explanation for the selection of sanctions. In other cases, the courts may give reasons for their decisions, but their statements are too general to be useful. In still other cases, the courts may list specific factors to support a certain result, but they do not state whether these factors must be considered in every discipline case, nor do they explain whether these factors are entitled to equal weight.

The Joint Committee on Professional Sanctions (hereinafter "Sanctions Committee") was formed to address these problems by formulating standards to be used in imposing sanctions for lawyer misconduct. The Sanctions Committee was composed of members from the Judicial Administration Division and the Standing Committee on Professional Discipline. The mandate given was ambi-

2. *In re Gold*, 396 N.E.2d 25 (1979).
3. *In re Oliver*, M.R. 2454, 79-CH-6 (1980).
4. *In re Smith*, 347 N.E.2d 133 (1976).
5. *In re DiBella*, 316 N.E.2d 771 (1974).
6. *In re Sherman*, 328 N.E.2d 553 (1975).

tious: the Committee was to examine the current range of sanctions imposed and to formulate standards for the imposition of appropriate sanctions.

In addressing this task, the Sanctions Committee recognized that any proposed standards should serve as a model which sets forth a comprehensive system of sanctions, but which leaves room for flexibility and creativity in assigning sanctions in particular cases of lawyer misconduct. These standards are designed to promote thorough, rational consideration of all factors relevant to imposing a sanction in an individual case. The standards attempt to ensure that such factors are given appropriate weight in light of the stated goals of lawyer discipline, and that only relevant aggravating and mitigating circumstances are considered at the appropriate time. Finally, the standards should help achieve the degree of consistency in the imposition of lawyer discipline necessary for fairness to the public and the bar.

While these standards will improve the operation of lawyer discipline systems, there is an additional factor which, though not the focus of this report, cannot be overlooked. In discussing sanctions for lawyer misconduct, this report assumes that all instances of unethical conduct will be brought to the attention of the disciplinary system. Experience indicates that such is not the case. In 1970, the ABA Special Committee on Evaluation of Disciplinary Enforcement (the Clark Committee), was charged with the responsibility for evaluating the effectiveness of disciplinary enforcement systems. The Clark Committee concluded that one of the most significant problems in lawyer discipline was the reluctance of lawyers and judges to report misconduct.[7] That same problem exists today. It cannot be emphasized strongly enough that lawyers and judges must report unethical conduct to the appropriate disciplinary agency.[8] Failure to render such reports is a disservice to the public and the legal profession.

Judges in particular should be reminded of their obligation to report unethical conduct to the disciplinary agencies. Under Rule 2.15 of the ABA Model Code of Judicial Conduct, a judge who receives information indicating a substantial likelihood that another judge or a lawyer has violated the applicable rules of professional conduct is obligated to take appropriate action. This action includes making a report of the violation to the appropriate authority when the violation raises a substantial question about the judge's fitness or the lawyer's honesty trustworthiness or fitness.[9] Frequently, judges take the position that there is no such need

7. Problems and Recommendations in Disciplinary Enforcement (Chicago: American Bar Association, Special Committee on Evaluation of Disciplinary Enforcement, 1970), at 167.

8. Lawyers have a duty to report ethical misconduct of other lawyers under Rule 8.3 of the Model Rules of Professional Conduct (American Bar Association, 1983) and under DR1-103 of the Model Code of Professional Responsibility (American Bar Association, 1981). Judges have a similar duty under the Model Code of Judicial Conduct, Canon 3(D)(2) (American Bar Association, 1990).

9. *Id.*, Code of Judicial Conduct.

and that errant behavior of lawyers can be remedied solely by use of contempt proceedings and other alternative means. It must be emphasized that the goals of lawyer discipline are not properly and fully served if the judge who observes unethical conduct simply deals with it on an ad hoc basis. It may be proper and wise for a judge to use contempt powers in order to assure that the court maintains control of the proceeding and punishes a lawyer for abusive or obstreperous conduct in the court's presence. However, the lawyer discipline system is in addition to and serves purposes different from contempt powers and other mechanisms available to the judge. Only if all lawyer misconduct is in fact reported to the appropriate disciplinary agency can the legal profession have confidence that consistent sanctions are imposed for similar misconduct.

Consistency of sanctions depends on reporting of other types as well. The American Bar Association Center for Professional Responsibility has established a "National Lawyer Regulatory Data Bank" which collects statistics on the nature of ethical violations and sanctions imposed in lawyer discipline cases in all jurisdictions. The information available from the Data Bank is only as good as the reports which reach it. It is vital that the Data Bank promptly receive complete, accurate and detailed information with regard to all discipline cases.

Finally, the purposes of lawyer sanctions can best be served, and the consistency of those sanctions enhanced, if courts and disciplinary agencies throughout the country articulate the reasons for sanctions imposed. Courts of record that impose lawyer discipline do a valuable service to the legal profession and the public when they issue opinions in lawyer discipline cases that explain the imposition of a specific sanction. The effort of the Sanctions Committee was made easier by the well-reasoned judicial opinions that were available. At the same time, the Sanctions Committee was frustrated by the fact that many jurisdictions do not publish lawyer discipline decisions, and that even published decisions are often summary in nature, failing to articulate the justification for the sanctions imposed.

[The Standards for Imposing Lawyer Sanctions were amended by the ABA House of Delegates on February 4, 1992. The amendments were proposed by the ABA Standing Committee on Professional Discipline as a result of its ongoing review of the courts' use of the Standards in lawyer disciplinary cases to assure their consistency with the developing case law.]

## B. Methodology

The Standards for Imposing Lawyer Sanctions have been developed after an examination of all reported lawyer discipline cases from 1980 to June 1984, where public discipline was imposed.[10] In addition, eight jurisdictions, which represent a variety of disciplinary systems as well as diversity in geography and population size, were examined in depth. In these jurisdictions—Arizona, California, the District of Columbia, Florida, Illinois, New Jersey, North Dakota, and Utah—all published disciplinary cases from January 1974 through June 1984, were analyzed. In each case, data were collected concerning the type of offense, the sanction imposed, the policy considerations identified, and aggravating or mitigating circumstances noted by the court.[11]

These data were examined to identify the patterns that currently exist among courts imposing sanctions and the policy considerations that guide the courts. In general, the courts were consistent in identifying the following policy considerations: protecting the public, ensuring the administration of justice, and maintaining the integrity of the profession. In the words of the California Supreme Court: "The purpose of a disciplinary proceeding is not punitive but to inquire into the fitness of the lawyer to continue in that capacity for the protection of the public, the courts, and the legal profession."[12] However, the courts failed to articulate any theoretical framework for use in imposing sanctions.

In attempting to develop such a framework, the Sanctions Committee considered a number of options. The Committee considered the obvious possibility of identifying each and every type of misconduct in which a lawyer could engage, then suggesting either a recommended sanction or a range of recommended sanctions to deal with that particular misconduct. The Sanctions Committee

10. See Appendix 3 for a listing of the actual number of reported cases from each jurisdiction. The differences in the number of reported cases among the jurisdictions is a function not only of the differences in lawyer populations, but in the operation of the state discipline systems. States differ dramatically in the sophistication of their disciplinary systems; most importantly for this study, states vary in the extent to which disciplinary orders are published. In those jurisdictions where disciplinary decisions are not published in the regional reporters, summaries in state bar publications or unreported cases (supplied by bar counsel) were examined. (To obtain copies of unreported decisions, contact the ABA Center for Professional Responsibility.) The states in which only reported cases were examined were: Alabama, Alaska, Arkansas, Colorado, Connecticut, Delaware, Georgia, Hawaii, Idaho, Indiana, Iowa, Kansas, Louisiana, Maryland, Minnesota, Mississippi, Missouri, Montana, Nebraska, Nevada, New Jersey, New Mexico, North Carolina, South Dakota, Ohio, Oklahoma, Oregon, Rhode Island, South Carolina, South Dakota, Utah, Vermont, Washington, West Virginia, and Wisconsin. In the following jurisdictions both reported and unreported cases were examined: Arizona, California, District of Columbia, Florida, Illinois, Kentucky, Massachusetts, New York, Pennsylvania, Tennessee, Virginia, and Wyoming. In the following jurisdictions, all data were collected from unreported decisions (supplied by bar counsel or taken from case summaries in bar publications): Maine, Michigan, New Hampshire, and Texas.

11. Because of the difficulty in getting complete factual statements, the report does not include cases which were the result of consent orders, or cases in which reciprocal discipline was imposed.

12. *Ballard v. State Bar of California*, 35 Cal. 3d 274, 673 P.2d 226 197 Cal. Rptr. 556, (1983).

unanimously rejected that option as being both theoretically simplistic and administratively cumbersome.[13]

The Sanctions Committee next considered an approach that dealt with general categories of lawyer misconduct and applied recommended sanctions to those types of misconduct depending on whether or not—and to what extent—the misconduct resulted from intentional or malicious acts of the lawyer. There is some merit in that approach; certainly, the intentional or unintentional conduct of the lawyer is a relevant factor. Nonetheless, that approach was also abandoned after the Sanctions Committee carefully reviewed the purposes of lawyer sanctions. Solely focusing on the intent of the lawyer is not sufficient, and proposed standards must also consider the damage which the lawyer's misconduct causes to the client, the public, the legal system, and the profession. An approach which looked only at the extent of injury was also rejected as being too narrow.

The Committee adopted a model that looks first at the ethical duty and to whom it is owed, and then at the lawyer's mental state and the amount of injury caused by the lawyer's misconduct. (See Theoretical Framework, p. 5, for a detailed discussion of this approach.) Thus, one will look in vain for a section of this report which recommends a specific sanction for, say, improper contact with opposing parties who are represented by counsel [Rule 4.2/DR 7-104(A)(1)],[14] or for any other specific misconduct. What one will find, however, is an organizational framework that provides recommendations as to the type of sanction that should be imposed based on violations of duties owed to clients, the public, the legal system, and the profession.

13. An example of the problems which would be encountered in such an approach will suffice to demonstrate why that approach was rejected. It is improper for a lawyer to neglect a legal matter entrusted to him (Rule 1.3/DR 6-101 (A)(3)). Sanctions which are imposed for violations of this ethical rule vary dramatically. Such conduct may be an intentional violation of the rule (as where a lawyer takes a client's money never intending to perform the services requested), or it may result from negligence (as where an overworked or inexperienced lawyer does not meet a deadline relating to some aspect of the representation). The Sanctions Committee felt that a listing of sanctions based merely on the type of lawyer misconduct would not adequately differentiate between conduct which has an extremely deleterious effect on the client, the public, the legal system, and the profession, and conduct which has only a minimal effect. In short, the Sanctions Committee concluded that an approach that reviewed each type of misconduct would result in nothing more than a general statement that the individual circumstances of a case dictate the type of sanction which ought to be imposed.

14. Although the House of Delegates of the American Bar Association adopted the Model Rules of Professional Conduct on August 2, 1983, as the ethical standards for the legal profession, references to the Code of Professional Responsibility are included here because some states' ethical standards still follow the Code in both form and substance.

To provide support for this approach, the Sanctions Committee has offered as much specific data and guidance as possible from reported cases.[15] Thus, with regard to each category of misconduct, the report provides the following:

- discussion of what types of sanctions have been imposed for similar misconduct in reported cases;
- discussion of policy reasons which are articulated in reported cases to support such sanctions; and,
- finally, a recommendation as to the level of sanction imposed for the given misconduct, absent aggravating or mitigating circumstances.

While it is recognized that any individual case may present aggravating or mitigating factors which would lead to the imposition of a sanction different from that recommended, these standards present a model which can be used initially to categorize misconduct and to identify the appropriate sanction. The decision as to the effect of any aggravating or mitigating factors should come only after this initial determination of the sanction.

The Sanctions Committee also recognized that the imposition of a sanction of suspension or disbarment does not conclude the matter. Typically, disciplined lawyers will request reinstatement or readmission. While this report does not include an in-depth study of reinstatement and readmission cases, a general recommendation concerning standards for reinstatement and readmission appears as Standard 2.10.

## *II. Theoretical Framework*

These standards are based on an analysis of the nature of the professional relationship. Historically, being a member of a profession has meant that an individual is some type of expert, possessing knowledge of high instrumental value such that the members of the community give the professional the power to make decisions for them. In the legal profession, the community has allowed the profession the right of self-regulation. As stated in the Preamble to the ABA Model Rules of Professional Conduct (hereinafter "Model Rules"), "[t]he legal profession's relative autonomy carries with it special responsibilities of self-government. The profession has a responsibility to assure that its regulations are conceived in the public interest and not in furtherance of parochial or self-interested concerns of the bar."[16]

15. While it is not possible to discuss in detail each of the 2,991 cases which have been examined in preparing this report, statistical summaries are available from the American Bar Association Center for Professional Responsibility.

16. Preamble to Model Rules, paragraph 11, *supra* n.8.

This view of the professional relationship requires lawyers to observe the ethical requirements that are set out in the Model Rules (or applicable standard in the jurisdiction where the lawyer is licensed). While the Model Rules define the ethical guidelines for lawyers, they do not provide any method for assigning sanctions for ethical violations. The Committee developed a model which requires a court imposing sanctions to answer each of the following questions:

1. What ethical duty did the lawyer violate? (A duty to a client, the public, the legal system, or the profession?)
2. What was the lawyer's mental state? (Did the lawyer act intentionally, knowingly, or negligently?)
3. What was the extent of the actual or potential injury caused by the lawyer's misconduct? (Was there a serious or potentially serious injury?) and
4. Are there any aggravating or mitigating circumstances?

In determining the nature of the ethical duty violated, the standards assume that the most important ethical duties are those obligations which a lawyer owes to clients. These include:

(a) the duty of loyalty which (in the terms of the Model Rules and Code of Professional Responsibility) includes the duties to:
    i. preserve the property of a client [Rule 1.15/DR9-102],
    ii. maintain client confidences [Rule 1.6/DR4-101], and
    iii. avoid conflicts of interest [Rules 1.7 through 1.13, 2.2, 3.7, 5.4(c) and 6.3/DR5-101 through DR 5-105, DR9-101];
(b) the duty of diligence [Rules 1.2, 1.3, 1.4/DR6-101(A)(3)];
(c) the duty of competence [Rule 1.1/DR6-101(A)(1) & (2)]; and
(d) the duty of candor [Rule 8.4(c)/DR 1-102(A)(4) & DR7-101(A)(3)].

In addition to duties owed to clients, the lawyer also owes duties to the general public. Members of the public are entitled to be able to trust lawyers to protect their property, liberty, and their lives. The community expects lawyers to exhibit the highest standards of honesty and integrity, and lawyers have a duty not to engage in conduct involving dishonesty, fraud, or interference with the administration of justice [Rules 8.2, 8.4(b)&(c)/DR 1-102(A)(3)(4)&(5), DR 8-101 through DR 8-103, DR 9-101(c)].

Lawyers also owe duties to the legal system. Lawyers are officers of the court, and must abide by the rules of substance and procedure which shape the administration of justice. Lawyers must always operate within the bounds of the law, and cannot create or use false evidence, or engage in any other illegal or improper conduct [Rules 3.1 through 3.6, 3.9, 4.1 through 4.4, 8.2, 8.4(d)(e)&(f)/DR7-102 through DR7-110].

Finally, lawyers owe duties to the legal profession. Unlike the obligations mentioned above, these duties are not inherent in the relationship between the professional and the community. These duties do not concern the lawyer's basic responsibilities in representing clients, serving as an officer of the court, or maintaining the public trust, but include other duties relating to the profession. These ethical rules concern:

(a) restrictions on advertising and recommending employment [Rules 7.1 through 7.5/DR2-101 through 2-104];
(b) fees [Rules 1.5, 5.4 and 5.6/DR2-106, DR2-107, and DR3-102];
(c) assisting unauthorized practice [Rule 5.5/DR3-101 through DR3-103];
(d) accepting, declining, or terminating representation [Rules 1.2, 1.14, 1.16/DR2-110]; and
(e) maintaining the integrity of the profession [Rules 8.1&8.3/DR1-101 and DR 1-103].

The mental states used in this model are defined as follows. The most culpable mental state is that of intent, when the lawyer acts with the conscious objective or purpose to accomplish a particular result. The next most culpable mental state is that of knowledge, when the lawyer acts with conscious awareness of the nature or attendant circumstances of his or her conduct both without the conscious objective or purpose to accomplish a particular result. The least culpable mental state is negligence, when a lawyer fails to be aware of a substantial risk that circumstances exist or that a result will follow, which failure is a deviation from the standard of care that a reasonable lawyer would exercise in the situation.

The extent of the injury is defined by the type of duty violated and the extent of actual or potential harm. For example, in a conversion case, the injury is determined by examining the extent of the client's actual or potential loss. In a case where a lawyer tampers with a witness, the injury is measured by evaluating the level of interference or potential interference with the legal proceeding. In this model, the standards refer to various levels of injury: "serious injury," "injury," and "little or no injury." A reference to "injury" alone indicates any level of injury greater than "little or no" injury.

As an example of how this model works, consider two cases of conversion of a client's property. After concluding that the lawyers engaged in ethical misconduct, it is necessary to determine what duties were breached. In these cases, each lawyer breached the duty of loyalty owed to clients. To assign a sanction, however, it is necessary to go further, and to examine each lawyer's mental state and the extent of the injuries caused by the lawyers' actions.

In the first case, assume that the client gave the lawyer $100 as an advance against the costs of investigation. The lawyer took the money, deposited it in a personal checking account, and used it for personal expenses. In this case, where the lawyer acted intentionally and the client actually suffered an injury, the most severe sanction—disbarment—would be appropriate.

Contrast this with the case of a second lawyer, whose client delivered $100 to be held in a trust account. The lawyer, in a hurry to get to court, neglected to inform the secretary what to do with these funds and they were erroneously deposited into the lawyer's general office account. When the lawyer needed additional funds he drew against the general account. The lawyer discovered the mistake, and immediately replaced the money. In this case, where there was no actual injury and a potential for only minor injury, and where the lawyer was merely negligent, a less serious sanction should be imposed. The appropriate sanction would be either reprimand or admonition.

In each case, after making the initial determination as to the appropriate sanction, the court would then consider any relevant aggravating or mitigating factors (Standard 9). For example, the presence of aggravating factors, such as vulnerability of the victim or refusal to comply with an order to appear before the disciplinary agency, could increase the appropriate sanction. The presence of mitigating factors, such as absence of prior discipline or inexperience in the practice of law, could make a lesser sanction appropriate.

While there may be particular cases of lawyer misconduct that are not easily categorized, the standards are not designed to propose a specific sanction for each of the myriad of fact patterns in cases of lawyer misconduct. Rather, the standards provide a theoretical framework to guide the courts in imposing sanctions. The ultimate sanction imposed will depend on the presence of any aggravating or mitigating factors in that particular situation. The standards thus are not analogous to criminal determinate sentences, but are guidelines which give courts the flexibility to select the appropriate sanction in each particular case of lawyer misconduct.

The standards do not account for multiple charges of misconduct. The ultimate sanction imposed should at least be consistent with the sanction for the most serious instance of misconduct among a number of violations; it might well be and generally should be greater than the sanction for the most serious misconduct. Either a pattern of misconduct or multiple instances of misconduct should be considered as aggravating factors (see Standard 9.22).

# Standards for Imposing Lawyer Sanctions

## Definitions

**"Injury" is harm to a client, the public, the legal system, or the profession which results from a lawyer's misconduct. The level of injury can range from "serious" injury to "little or no" injury; a reference to "injury" alone indicates any level of injury greater than "little or no" injury.**

**"Intent" is the conscious objective or purpose to accomplish a particular result.**

**"Knowledge" is the conscious awareness of the nature or attendant circumstances of the conduct but without the conscious objective or purpose to accomplish a particular result.**

**"Negligence" is the failure of a lawyer to heed a substantial risk that circumstances exist or that a result will follow, which failure is a deviation from the standard of care that a reasonable lawyer would exercise in the situation.**

**"Potential injury" is the harm to a client, the public, the legal system or the profession that is reasonably foreseeable at the time of the lawyer's misconduct, and which, but for some intervening factor or event, would probably have resulted from the lawyer's misconduct.**

# A. Purpose and Nature of Sanctions

## 1.1 Purpose of Lawyer Discipline Proceedings

**The purpose of lawyer discipline proceedings is to protect the public and the administration of justice from lawyers who have not discharged, will not discharge, or are unlikely properly to discharge their professional duties to clients, the public, the legal system, and the legal profession.**

## Annotation

### *The Basic Purposes of Discipline*

Although courts vary in expressing their views on the purposes of lawyer discipline, they are in accord on the basic objectives. Generally, courts agree that protecting the public, upholding the integrity of the legal system, assuring the fair administration of justice, and deterring other lawyers from similar misconduct are the primary purposes of lawyer discipline. *See, e.g., Gillette v. Edison*, 593 F. Supp. 2d 1063, 1066 (D.N.D. 2009) ("The purpose of disciplinary proceedings is for the North Dakota Supreme Court to determine, in the public interest, whether an attorney should continue to practice law"; quoting North Dakota Standards for Imposing Lawyer Sanctions, Standard 1.1, court held that state supreme court had jurisdiction and authority to discipline lawyer for alleged misconduct occurring in connection with litigation in Indian tribal court); *In re Wiederholt*, 24 P.3d 1219, 1226 (Alaska 2001) ("The purposes underlying both attorney disciplinary and reinstatement proceedings are to safeguard the public, maintain the integrity of the profession, and to protect the administration of justice from reproach."); *In re Buckalew*, 731 P.2d 48 (Alaska 1986) (court emphasized that its paramount concern was for the protection of the public, but also included purposes of deterring unethical conduct and educating other lawyers and the public); *In re Isler*, 315 P.3d 711, 718–19 (Ariz. 2014) (objectives of lawyer discipline are protection of the public and the courts and deterrence of respondents and other lawyers from committing misconduct); *In re Shepard*, 457 S.W.3d 280, 284 (Ark. 2015) (purpose of court exercising its authority to regulate the practice of law is "to protect the public and to maintain the integrity of the courts and the honor of the profession"); *Hugen v. People*, 199 P.3d 760, 767 (Colo. O.P.D.J. 2008) (citing Standard 1.1 in considering petition for readmission: "The purpose of attorney disciplinary proceedings is to protect the public and the administration of justice from attorneys who fail to uphold their professional duties to clients, the public, the legal system, and the legal profession."); *D'Attilo v. Statewide Grievance Comm'n*, 188 A.3d 727, 739 (Conn. 2018) (the attorney disciplinary process exists "within the broader framework of the relationship between attorneys and the judiciary. . . . This unique position as officers and commissioners of the court . . . casts attorneys in a special relationship with the judiciary and subjects them to its discipline") (citations omitted); *In re Koyste*, 111 A.3d 581, 589 (Del. 2015) ("the goals of lawyer discipline are to protect the public, to protect the administration of justice, to preserve confidence in the legal profession, and to deter other lawyers from similar misconduct") (citation omitted); *Iowa Supreme Ct. Att'y Disciplinary Bd. v. Buchanan*, 757 N.W.2d 251, 256 (Iowa 2008) (listing obligation to protect the public from further harm by lawyer and deter other lawyers from engaging in similar misconduct, the court noted, "Finally, we are also mindful that one of the underlying purposes of attorney discipline is 'to protect the integrity of and public confidence in our system of justice'") (citations omitted); *Att'y Grievance Comm'n v. McGlade*, 42 A.3d 534, 547 (Md. 2012) (court explained that "[t]he purpose of disciplinary proceedings is 'not to punish the lawyer, but to protect the public and the public's confidence in the legal profession.'") (citations omitted); *In re Cupples*, 952 S.W.2d 226, 232 (Mo. 1997) ("The purpose of disciplinary proceedings is to protect the public and the profession from persons unfit to practice law."); *In re Marshall*, 394 P.3d 208, at *1 (Table) (Nev. 2017) ("We must ensure that the discipline is sufficient to protect the public, the courts, and the legal profession.") (citations omitted); *In re Disciplinary Action Against Nassif*, 547 N.W.2d 541 (N.D. 1996) (citing Standard 1.1 of the North Dakota Standards for Imposing Lawyer Sanctions, court noted that since primary purpose of disciplinary process is protection of the public, disbarment of lawyer required due to his prior disciplinary history, pattern of gross incompetence, unacceptable office practices, inadequate recordkeeping, and mishandling and conversion of client funds); *State ex rel. Oklahoma Bar Ass'n v. Demopolos*, 352 P.3d 1210, 1213 (Okla. 2015) ("[p]rotecting the public and purification of the Bar are the primary purpose of the disciplinary proceedings rather than punishment of the offending attorney"); *In re Spilman*, 240 P.3d 702 (Okla. 2010) (court has constitutional duty to ensure that goals of lawyer discipline are carried out, including preservation of public trust and confidence in the bar by strict maintenance of the profession's integrity, protection of the public and the courts, and deterrence of similar behavior by both the disciplined lawyer and by other members of the bar); *In re Chastain*, 532 S.E.2d 264 (S.C. 2000) (citing Standard 1.1, court found that primary purpose of lawyer discipline proceedings is to protect the public from unscrupulous and indifferent lawyers); *In re Discipline of Reynolds*, 762 N.W.2d 341, 352 (S.D. 2009) ("The attorney disciplinary process is intended to: a) protect the public from further fraudulent, unethical or incompetent activities involving the lawyer; b) preserve the image and integrity of attorneys, the bar association and the legal profession as a whole; and, c) deter like conduct by other attorneys."); *In re Cottingham*, 423 P.3d 818, 827 (Wash. 2018) ("[o]ne primary purpose of the attorney disciplinary system is to protect the public and the severity of the sanction should be calculated to achieve these ends") (citations omitted); *Lawyer Disciplinary Bd. v. Blyler*, 787 S.E.2d 596, 611 (W. Va. 2016) ("[a]ttorney disciplinary proceedings are not designed solely to punish the attorney, but rather to protect the public, to reassure it as to the reliability and integrity of attorneys and to safeguard its interest in the administration of justice") (citations omitted); *Bd. of Prof'l Responsibility v. Custis*, 348 P.3d 823, 828–29 (Wyo. 2015) (protecting the public, maintaining the integrity of the legal system, ensuring the fair administration of justice, and deterring other lawyers from committing similar misconduct are purposes of the attorney disciplinary system).

For further discussion of the purposes of lawyer discipline, *see generally* Mary M. Devlin, *The Development of Lawyer Disciplinary Procedures in the United States*, 7 Geo. J. Legal Ethics 911 (1994) (examining history of lawyer discipline); Fred C. Zacharias, *The Purposes of Lawyer Discipline*, 45 Wm. & Mary L. Rev. 675, 677 (2003) (suggesting that "protecting the public" is too simplistic a characterization of the purpose of lawyer discipline; arguing that more precise identification of a wide variety of purposes of discipline would create better results).

- **Protection of the Public**

Protection of the public is commonly cited as the first and foremost purpose for imposing lawyer discipline. *See, e.g., In re Vance*, 421 P.3d 53 (Alaska 2018) (lengthy suspension not necessary to protect the public where the nature of misconduct coupled with mitigating factors warrants a suspension on low end of the possible range); *In re Hanlon*, 110 P.3d 937 (Alaska 2005) (three-year suspension imposed; rejecting argument that sanction effectively would end lawyer's legal career, court observed that respondent admitted that primary purpose of lawyer discipline is to protect the public; more severe sanction warranted to serve the interests of the public and bar); *In re Comstock*, No. 12-N-16765, 2015 WL 4238008, at *4 (Cal. Bar Ct. June 25, 2015) ("The purpose of attorney discipline is not to punish the attorney but to protect the public, the courts and the legal profession, and to maintain high professional standards for attorneys."); *Statewide Grievance Comm'n v. Ganim*, 87 A.3d 1078, 1092 (Conn. 2014) ("if a court disciplines an attorney, it does so not to mete out punishment to an offender, but so that the administration of justice may be safeguarded and the courts and the public protected from the misconduct or unfitness of those who are licensed to perform the important functions of the legal profession."); *In re Bria*, 86 A.3d 1118, at *5 (Table) (Del. 2014) (attorneys owe duties not only to clients but to the general public as well; "[m]embers of the public are entitled to be able to trust lawyers to protect their property, liberty, and their lives."); *In re Fry*, 806 S.E.2d 604, 606 (Ga. 2017) ("the primary purpose of a disciplinary action is to protect the public from attorneys who are not qualified to practice law due to incompetence or unprofessional conduct."); *In re Harrington*, 385 P.3d 905, 916 (Kan. 2016) ("the ultimate goal in disciplinary matters is to protect the public . . ."); *Att'y Grievance Comm'n of Maryland v. Barnett*, 102 A.3d 310, 319 (Md. 2014) ("[t]his Court sanctions a lawyer not to punish the lawyer, but instead to protect the public and public's confidence in the legal profession"); *In re Torre*, 127 A.3d 690, 696 (N.J. 2015) ("[t]he attorney disciplinary system is not designed to punish lawyers. Its goals are to protect the public and preserve the public's confidence in the bar. The imposition of discipline in a particular case, thus, is meant to foster continued faith in the legal profession as a whole.") (internal citations omitted); *In re Torres*, 374 P.3d 700, 701–02 (N.M. 2016) (where attorney's neglect was an isolated occurrence, public would be protected by a sanction of a public censure and a one-year deferred suspension); *In re Hann*, 848 N.W.2d 725 (N.D. 2014) (court imposed several conditions on disciplined attorney's return to practice of law in order to ensure that public protected); *Disciplinary Counsel v. Schuman*, 92 N.E.3d 850 (Ohio 2017) (primary purpose of attorney discipline is to protect the public, not to punish); *State ex rel. Oklahoma Bar Ass'n v. Bounds*, 415 P.3d 519, 520 (Okla. 2018) ("[p]rotection of the public and purification of the Bar are the primary purposes of disciplinary proceedings rather than to punish the accused lawyer."); *In re Conduct of Ramirez*, 408 P.3d 1065, 1071 (Or. 2018) ("our purpose is to protect the public and the administration of justice from lawyers who have not discharged properly their duties to clients, the public, the legal system, or the profession.") (internal citations omitted); *In re McMaster*, 795 S.E.2d 853, 855 (S.C. 2017) ("[t]he primary purpose of . . . suspension is the removal of an unfit person from the profession for the protection of the courts and the public, not punishment of the offending attorney.") (citations omitted); *In re Disciplinary Proceeding Against Jones*, 338 P.3d 842, 856–57 (Wash. 2014) (protecting the public from dishonest lawyers is part of the lawyer disciplinary process). *But see Office of Lawyer Disciplinary Counsel v. Plants*, 759 S.E.2d 220 (W. Va. 2014) (interim suspension for prosecutor/attorney accused of domestic violence denied; no conflict of interest found between his personal interests and his duties as a prosecutor).

- **License to Practice Law a Privilege**

Protection of the public squares with the notion that a license to practice law is neither a right nor an entitlement, but a privilege conferred on the lawyer primarily for the benefit of the public. *See, e.g., In re Shepard*, 457 S.W.3d 280, 283 (Ark. 2015) ("the practice of law is a privilege, not a right."); *Statewide Grievance Comm'n. v. Ganim*, 87 A.3d 1078, 1092 (Conn. 2014) (an attorney, as an officer of the court, "is continually accountable to it for the manner in which he exercises the privilege which has been accorded him. His admission is upon the implied condition that his continued enjoyment of the right conferred is dependent upon his remaining a fit and safe person to exercise it, so that when he . . . has become or is an unfit or unsafe person to be entrusted with the responsibilities and obligations of an attorney, his right to continue in the enjoyment of his professional privilege may and ought to be declared forfeited.") *In re Crossen*, 880 N.E.2d 352, 388 (Mass. 2008) ("The right to practice law is not one of the inherent rights of every citizen . . . [but] is a peculiar privilege granted and continued only to those who demonstrate special fitness in intellectual attainment and in moral character.") (citation omitted); *In re Reinstatement of Drain*, 376 P.3d 208 (Okla. 2016) (in reinstating a lawyer who had voluntarily resigned from the bar for personal reasons, court opined that those attorneys who resign and then seek reinstatement are not automatically entitled to the privileges and advantages of being a member of the bar); *Steele v. Bonner*, 782 N.W.2d 379, 384 (S.D. 2010) (regarding the practice of law, the court stated that "Certainly, it is in no sense an absolute right. It is in the nature of a franchise to the enjoyment of which no one is admitted as a matter of right, but only upon proof of fitness and qualifications which must be maintained if the privilege is to continue in enjoyment.") (citations omitted); *In re Discipline of Laprath*, 670 N.W.2d 41 (S.D. 2003) (holder of law license holds privilege to serve public, not absolute right); *Bd. of Prof'l Responsibility v. Barry*, 545 S.W.3d 408, 426 (Tenn. 2018) ("a license to practice law in this state is not a right but a privilege. The license to practice law in this State is a continuing proclamation by the Court that the holder is fit to be entrusted with professional and judicial matters, and to aid in the administration of justice as an attorney and as an officer of the Court.") (internal citations omitted). *But see Ala. State Bar v. McBrayer*, 20 So.3d 100, 105 (Ala. 2009) ("This Court has previously recognized 'that the right to engage in the practice of law in Alabama is a property right that may be denied only if the denial comports with the procedural due process of law guaranteed by the Alabama and United States Constitutions.'") (citation omitted).

- **Preservation of the Public's Trust and Confidence**

The privilege of practicing law carries with it the obligation to be worthy of the public's trust and confidence. Thus, lawyers are required to continually demonstrate good character in all endeavors. As the Court of Appeals of Maryland explained in *Maryland State Bar Association v. Agnew*:

> Few vocations offer as great a spectrum for good and honorable works as does the legal profession. The attorney is entrusted with the life savings and investments of his clients. He becomes the guardian of the mentally deficient and potential savior for the accused. He is a fiduciary, a confidant, an advisor, and an advocate. However, the great privilege of serving in all of these capacities does not come without

> the concomitant responsibilities of truth, candor and honesty. In fact, it can be said that the presence of these virtues in members of the bar comprises a large portion of the fulcrum upon which the scales of justice rest. Consequently, an attorney's character must remain beyond reproach.

318 A.2d 811, 814 (Md. 1974) (disbarment imposed on former Vice President Spiro Agnew following conviction for tax evasion). *See also In re Ivy*, 374 P.3d 374, 387 (Alaska 2016) (public confidence in the profession's ability to discipline itself is of the utmost importance) (citations omitted); *In re Buckalew*, 731 P.2d 48, 55 (Alaska 1986) ("[I]t is of the utmost importance that the public have confidence in the profession's ability to discipline itself—lest the privilege be withdrawn."); *Ligon v. Tapp*, 519 S.W.3d 315 (Ark. 2017) (the totality of the attorney's misconduct combined with prior discipline warranted disbarment to preserve the public's confidence in the legal profession); *In re Lee*, 95 A.3d 66 (D.C. 2014) (disbarment appropriate where attorney misappropriated funds, despite mitigating factors, in order for public to maintain confidence in the bar); *In re Addams*, 579 A.2d 190, 194 (D.C. 1990) ("It is . . . important that we reemphasize that the principal reason for discipline is to preserve the confidence of the public in the integrity and trustworthiness of lawyers in general.") (citation omitted); *In re Fry*, 806 S.E.2d 604 (Ga. 2017) (protection of public's confidence in the legal system is an important consideration in imposing discipline); *Att'y Grievance Comm'n v. Agbaje*, 93 A.3d 262, 285 (Md. 2014) ("the purpose of a sanction is not to punish but rather, to protect . . . the public's confidence in the legal profession.") (citations omitted); *In re Corbett*, 84 N.E.3d 837, 839 (Mass. 2014) ("[w]hile each case is unique, and every offending attorney must receive the sanction most appropriate in the circumstances, the common overarching factor for our consideration in all cases is the effect upon, and perception of, the public and the bar."); *In re Cammarano*, 98 A.3d 1184, 1187 (N.J. 2014) ("misconduct that breaches a fundamental and solemn trust is itself sufficient to trigger automatic disbarment.") (citations omitted); *In re Key*, 113 P.3d 340 (N.M. 2005) (court equally concerned with protection of the public as purpose of attorney discipline, as well as the public's perception of the profession and the legal system); *Disciplinary Counsel v. Calabrese*, 36 N.E.3d 151 (Ohio 2015) (court disbarred attorney, in part, to maintain public confidence in the legal profession); *In re Reinstatement of Blake*, 371 P.3d 465 (Okla. 2016) (a primary objective of the bar disciplinary system is to maintain confidence in the bar); *In re Discipline of Reynolds*, 762 N.W.2d 341, 352 (S.D. 2009) ("Only by providing high quality lawyering can the integrity of the legal profession remain inveterate and the confidence of the public and the Bar remain strong.") (citations omitted); *Petition of Pier*, 561 N.W.2d 297, 302 (S.D. 1997) ("Handling client funds requires trust and confidence—attributes essential to the attorney-client relationship."); *cf. In*

*re Disciplinary Proceeding Against Johns*, 847 N.W.2d 179 (Wash. 2014) (court dismissed disciplinary proceedings against attorney convicted of drunk driving incident in which his brother was killed, ruling that public confidence in the bar would not be shaken by the dismissal since attorney had already suffered consequences in criminal proceeding and underlying incident had nothing to do with his status as an attorney); *In re Disciplinary Proceeding Against Curran*, 801 P.2d 962, 974 (Wash. 1990) (conceding that purpose of maintaining public confidence in the bar is "not nearly as important as protecting the public from unworthy practitioners").

- **Continued Fitness**

Also inherent to the privilege of holding a license is the ability of the lawyer to maintain the standards established for fitness to practice law. *See, e.g., In re Buckalew*, 731 P.2d 48, 55 (Alaska 1986) ("[After admission,] the requirement of good character does not cease to exist. In fact, it continues to be one of the most important requisites of bar membership in this state."); *Statewide Grievance Comm'n v. Ganim*, 87 A.3d 1078, 1092 (Conn. 2014) (admission to the bar is conditioned upon an attorney "remaining a fit and safe person to exercise it, so that when he, by misconduct in any capacity, discloses that he has become or is an unfit or unsafe person to be entrusted with the responsibilities and obligations of an attorney, his right to continue in the enjoyment of his professional privilege may and ought to be declared forfeited."); *Office of Disciplinary Counsel v. Buffington*, No. SCAD-14-0000880, 2014 WL 3056353 (Haw. July 7, 2014) at *1 (attorney allowed to resign from the bar in lieu of discipline after engaging in misconduct that reflected adversely on her fitness as a lawyer); *Att'y Grievance Comm'n v. Greenleaf*, 91 A.3d 1066, 1073 (Md. 2014) (court protects the public by suspending or disbarring a lawyer who is unfit to continue to practice law); *In re Riehm*, 883 N.W.2d 223, 232 (Minn. 2016) (primary purpose of the lawyer disciplinary process is to "assess an attorney's fitness to practice law, including the attorney's personal integrity."); *In re Legato*, 161 A.3d 111, 116 (N.J. 2017) (although lawyer's criminal conduct occurred outside the practice of law, offenses revealed unfitness to continue as member of the bar; "the privilege to practice law is dependent on an attorney's ability to maintain a high moral character.") (citations omitted); *State ex rel. Okla. Bar Ass'n v. Drummond*, 393 P.3d 207, 215 (Okla. 2017) (while every criminal conviction does not prove an attorney is unfit to practice law, smuggling contraband into prison does; disbarment warranted); *In re Henry*, 841 N.W.2d 471, 475–76 (S.D. 2013) (a "license to practice law in South Dakota is a continuing proclamation by the Supreme Court that the holder is fit to be entrusted with professional and judicial matters and to aid in the administration of justice.") (citations omitted); *Lawyer Disciplinary Bd. v. Stanton*, 760 S.E.2d 453, 464 (W. Va. 2014) (court ruled that evidence not squarely within the purview of the disciplinary charges could be considered because of relevance to lawyer's fitness to practice law) (citations omitted).

- **Protection of Reputation**

Protecting the integrity and reputation of the courts and the bar are additional objectives of the lawyer disciplinary process. *See, e.g., In re Phillips,* 244 P.3d 549, 554 (Ariz. 2010) (another purpose of lawyer discipline "is to instill public confidence in the Bar's integrity"; six-month suspension warranted for supervisory and managerial breaches by managing partner who had full control of law firm's policies and practices and made decisions directly affecting the public, the profession, and the integrity of the legal system); *In re Vanderslice,* 166 A.3d 1244 (Del. 2015) (court disbarred lawyer where his misappropriation of funds caused a waste of judicial resources and denigrated the reputation of Delaware's legal profession); *Iowa Supreme Court Att'y Disciplinary Bd. v. Hedgecoth,* 862 N.W.2d 354 (Iowa 2014) (preserving the reputation of the bar is a factor to consider when determining an appropriate disciplinary sanction); *State ex rel. Counsel for Discipline v. Halstead,* 902 N.W.2d 701 (Neb. 2017) (one-year suspension for attorney who falsified guardianship petitions necessary to maintain the reputation of the bar); *In re Cammarano,* 98 A.3d 1184, 1187 (N.J. 2014) (court disbarred attorney who accepted a bribe while serving as an elected official, finding his conduct "wholly incompatible with the high standards expected of members of the bar and tarnish[ing] the repute of an honorable profession.") *In re Torres,* 374 P.3d 700 (N.M. 2016) (attorney discipline is meant to protect the public and the reputation of the profession). *But see Att'y Grievance Comm'n v. Reno,* 103 A.3d 565 (Md. 2014) (court rejected argument that damage to lawyer's reputation constituted mitigating factor, ruling that damage to a lawyer's image occurs in nearly every disciplinary proceeding).

- **Deterrence**

Deterrence, another stated purpose for discipline, has a twofold purpose, as aptly described in *Attorney Grievance Comm'n v. Shapiro,* 108 A.3d 394, 410 (Md. 2015). In that case, the Court of Appeal held that "[s]anctions protect the public in two ways: through deterrence of the type of conduct which will not be tolerated, and by removing those unfit to continue in the practice of law from the rolls of those authorized to practice law in this State . . . Therefore, the public interest is served when sanctions designed to effect general and specific deterrence are imposed on attorney who violates the disciplinary rules, and those sanctions demonstrate to members of the legal profession the type of conduct that will not be tolerated." Courts frequently proclaim the goal of deterring other members of the bar from engaging in similar misconduct when issuing sanctions upon an attorney. *See, e.g., In re Isler,* 315 P.3d 711, 718–19 (Ariz. 2014) (part of the purpose of attorney discipline is to deter the disciplined attorney, as well as other attorneys, from committing the same or similar misconduct); *In re Grandell*, 189 A.3d 1288 (Del. 2018) (an objective of the lawyer discipline system is to deter other lawyers from similar misconduct); *In re Murdter*, 131 A.3d 355 (D.C. 2016) (court rejected the Board of Professional Responsibility's lesser recommended sanction and imposed six-month suspension where attorney intentionally neglected criminal appellate cases; stronger sanction needed, even where attorney expressed remorse, to deter other attorneys from neglecting their cases); *Fla. Bar v. Adorno*, 60 So.3d 1016, 1035 (Fla. 2011) (rejecting public reprimand recommendation in favor of three-year suspension for significant abuse of the class-action mechanism; "[w]hen considering lawyer discipline, we must impose a discipline that is severe enough to deter other attorneys who might be prone to engage in similar conduct"); *In re Csehy*, 764 S.E.2d 540 (Ga. 2014) (court rejected proposed voluntary two-year suspension by attorney who pled nolo contendre to drug possession and use of a firearm during a crime, ruling it was not long enough to deter other attorneys from similar crimes); *Iowa Supreme Ct. Att'y Disciplinary Bd. v. Kingery*, 871 N.W.2d 109 (Iowa 2015) (goal of deterrence would not be diminished by imposing sixty-day suspension where attorney voluntarily stopped practicing law and other mitigating factors existed); *Comm'n on Prof'l Ethics & Conduct v. Baudino*, 452 N.W.2d 455, 459 (Iowa 1990) ("[o]ur purpose in imposing sanctions is to deter other lawyers from similar conduct; to assure the public that we will maintain the ethics of the profession; and to appropriately reflect our view of the attorney's fitness to practice law"; six-month suspension for failing to timely file income tax returns for three years and making false statement on client security questionnaire); *State ex rel. Counsel for Discipline of Nebraska Supreme Court*, 886 N.W.2d 530 (Neb. 2016) (need for deterrence must be considered when determining an appropriate sanction); *State ex rel. Okla. Bar Ass'n v. Hunt*, 394 P.3d 216 (Okla. 2017) (censure for attorney's conviction for driving while under the influence of alcohol served aim of deterrence for lawyer and the bar); *In re Obregon*, 145 A.3d 226 (Vt. 2016) (court denied disciplinary counsel's request for suspension of attorney who failed to file state income tax returns for a number of years; censure adequate to deter future misconduct); *Lawyer Disciplinary Bd. v. Munoz*, 807 S.E.2d 290, 291–92 (W. Va. 2017) ("[T]his Court must consider not only what steps would appropriately punish the respondent attorney, but also whether the discipline imposed is adequate to serve as an effective deterrent to other members of the Bar and at the same time restore public confidence in the ethical standards of the legal profession.") (citation omitted); *In re Disciplinary Proceedings Against Lemanksi*, 892 N.W.2d 305, 310 (Wis. 2017) (in issuing public instead of private reprimand, court reasoned that private admonishment would not sufficiently impress upon the attorney "the seriousness of his misconduct and the need for him to conform his conduct in the future to the Rules of Professional Conduct . . .").

- **Rehabilitation**

When applicable, rehabilitation can be another stated goal of lawyer discipline. *See, e.g., In re Scholl*, 25 P.3d 710, 712 (Ariz. 2001) ("[W]e view discipline as assisting, if possible, in the rehabilitation of an errant lawyer."); *In re Rivkind*, 791 P.2d 1037, 1040 (Ariz. 1990) (in considering the purpose of disciplinary proceedings, the court noted that "[o]n occasion, it is also appropriate for us to assist, if we can, in rehabilitating an errant attorney," especially when, as here, the lawyer "has taken very considerable and substantial steps" to rehabilitate and assist himself); *In re Rhode*, 191 A.3d 1124 (D.C. 2018) (court rejected disciplinary counsel's request for disbarment, finding attorney's ongoing rehabilitation from alcoholism merited suspension); *Fla. Bar v. Ross*, 140 So.3d 518, 523 (Fla. 2014) ("discipline must protect the public from unethical conduct, must be fair to a respondent, yet sufficient to sanction the misconduct and encourage reformation and rehabilitation. . . ."); *Iowa Supreme Court Disciplinary Bd. v. Kingery*, 871 N.W.2d 109 (Iowa 2015) (rehabilitative efforts, such as maintaining sobriety, can serve as a mitigating factor in determining sanctions); *In re Harris*, 868 A.2d 1011, 1020 (N.J. 2005) ("[a]nother goal of the process is to spur a disciplined attorney, who is redeemable, to comply with the high standards that our profession demands"; in this case respondent's tenure as a lawyer was marked by incompetence, deceit, and disloyalty to clients, and as a result the record did not allow for a finding that lawyer was professionally salvageable, and therefore disbarment imposed); *Geauga Cty. Bar Ass'n v. Snavely*, 75 N.E.3d 117 (Ohio 2016) (where attorney overcame addiction to heroin and was convicted for drug possession, court imposed two-year suspension with eighteen months stayed by probation, factoring in lawyer's attempts at rehabilitation, including hiring an ethics expert to help her with her law practice); *Petition of Pier*, 561 N.W.2d 297, 302 (S.D. 1997) (conditional reinstatement of disbarred lawyer allowed; court held that "[w]hile his misconduct was harmful to both the public and the bar, we now look to 'temper justice with mercy, believing that his professional life is redeemable'") (citation omitted); *In re Disciplinary Proceeding Against Juarez*, 24 P.3d 1040, 1063 (Wash. 2001) (reference to the purposes outlined in Standard 1.1 and former commentary; noting sanctions also imposed "to rehabilitate the offending lawyer where possible"); *In re Disciplinary Proceedings Against Lemanski*, 892 N.W.2d 305 (Wis. 2017) (court issued a public reprimand, finding a private reprimand would have no rehabilitative effect); *Bd. of Prof'l Responsibility v. Custis*, 348 P.3d 823, 836 (Wyo. 2015) ("[w]e view discipline as assisting, if possible, in the rehabilitation of an errant lawyer") (citations omitted).

Some courts emphasize that protection of the public is paramount to the goal of rehabilitation. *See, e.g., In re Hull*, 767 A.2d 197 (Del. 2001) (while not unsympathetic to lawyer's psychiatric conditions and rehabilitative efforts, court's role in fashioning remedy for lawyer misconduct must reflect primary responsibility to its citizens; rejecting one-year suspension recommendation as inadequate to protect the public and imposing two-year suspension for various misconduct); *Ky. Bar Ass'n v. Hill*, 476 S.W.3d 874 (Ky. 2015) (court rejected attorney's plea for a short suspension, ruling that a suspension of less than 180 days would harm public trust in the legal profession and that the longer suspension would provide a better assessment of the attorney's rehabilitation); *In re Cammarano*, 98 A.3d 1184 (N.J. 2014) (in matter where attorney as an elected official accepted a bribe, disbarment was the only appropriate sanction, even though court believed that attorney was capable of rehabilitation); *Office of Disciplinary Counsel v. Pozonsky*, 177 A.3d 830, 842–43 (Pa. 2018) (court rejected attorney's plea for suspension instead of disbarment despite acknowledging his rehabilitative efforts); *cf. People v. Hook*, 91 P.3d 1070 (Colo. O.P.D.J. 2004) (paramount objective of public protection best achieved by assuring lawyer's rehabilitation from alcoholism is closely monitored; stayed suspension pending completion of three-year probation with conditions crafted to assure lawyer's sobriety). For additional discussion of rehabilitation as a factor considered in mitigation, see Annotation to Standard 9.3.

- **Punishment Not an Objective**

It is a well-established principle that the punishment of lawyers is not the purpose of lawyer disciplinary sanctions. *See, e.g., Matter of Ferko*, No. 12-O-10827, 2014 WL 3889184, at *7 (Cal. Bar Ct. Aug. 6, 2014) ("The purpose of attorney discipline is not to punish the attorney, but to protect the public, the courts and the legal profession, to maintain high standards for attorneys, and to preserve public confidence in the profession."); *Chief Disciplinary Counsel v. Heberling*, No. HHDCV156061996S, 2017 WL 5921728, at *2 (Conn. Super. Ct. Oct. 23, 2017) ("A court disciplining an attorney does so not to punish the attorney, but rather to safeguard the administration of justice and to protect the public from the misconduct or unfitness of those who are members of the legal profession."); *In re Koyste*, 111 A.3d 581, 589 (Del. 2015) ("[t]his Court has consistently held that the purpose of lawyer discipline is not to punish lawyers.") (citations omitted); *Akinaka v. Disciplinary Bd.*, 979 P.2d 1077, 1084 (Haw. 1999) (only supreme court can disbar, suspend, or publicly censure a lawyer for ethical misconduct and "even these '[d]egrees of discipline must be disassociated with the concept of punishment for wrongdoing[.]'") (citation omitted); *In re Edmonds*, 21 N.E.3d 447, 463 (Ill. 2014) ("The purpose of attorney discipline is not punishment, but rather to protect the public, maintain the integrity of the legal profession, and protect the administration of justice from reproach"); *Att'y Grievance Comm'n v. Shuler*, 164 A.3d 209 (Md. 2017) (repeating often-stated goal that lawyer discipline is to protect the public and public confidence in legal profession, not to punish lawyer); *In re MacDonald*, 906 N.W.2d 238, 247 (Minn. 2018) (the goal of lawyer discipline is not to punish but to "deter future misconduct by the disciplined attorney as well as by other attorneys."); *In re Forck*, 418 S.W.3d 437 (Mo. 2014) (protection of the public and maintaining the integrity of the profession, not punishment, are purposes of discipline); *In re Richmond's Case*, 872 A.2d 1023, 1029 (N.H. 2005) (discipline "is not intended as a mode of inflicting punishment for an offense"); *Columbus Bar Ass'n v. Reed*, 50 N.E.3d 516, 520 (Ohio 2016) ("the goal of disciplinary proceedings is not to punish the errant lawyer, but to protect the public."); *In re McDonough*, 77 P.3d 306, 312 (Or. 2003) (court held that punishing lawyers for crime is left to criminal courts, but "[t]he objects of the proceedings here are to uphold the dignity and respect of the profession, protect the courts, preserve the administration of justice and protect clients") (citation omitted); *In re McKenna*, 110 A.3d 1126, 1150 (R.I. 2015) ("the purposes of discipline are not punishment of the attorney but protecting the public and maintaining the integrity of the profession."); *Petition of Pier*, 561 N.W.2d 297 (S.D. 1997) (in conditionally reinstating lawyer who was disbarred for stealing over $45,000 of client's money, court reaffirmed that purpose of disciplinary process is to protect public, not to punish the lawyer); *Matter of Disciplinary Proceeding Against Waechter*, 419 P.3d 827 (Wash. 2018) (while criminal justice system imposed punishment on attorney convicted of crimes, lawyer discipline system does not mete out punishment). *But see In re Csehy*, 764 S.E.2d 540, 541 (Ga. 2014) ("the purpose of lawyer discipline is to act as a penalty to the offender, a deterrent to others, and as an indication to laymen that the courts will maintain the ethics of the profession."); *Miss. Bar v. Ogletree*, 226 So.2d 79, 83 (Miss. 2015) ("the purpose of discipline is not simply to punish the guilty attorney, but to protect the public, the administration of justice, to maintain appropriate professional standards, and to deter misconduct.); *In re Vogel*, 482 S.W.3d 520, 533 (Tenn. 2016) ("This Court looks to the [ABA Standards] in determining the appropriate punishment for an attorney's misconduct."); *Lawyer Disciplinary Bd. v. Hall*, 765 S.E.2d 187 (W. Va. 2014)( (determining appropriate sanctions requires court to consider not only what steps would appropriately punish the respondent but also whether sanction would protect the public and safeguard its interest in the administration of justice).

Although disciplinary sanctions can be viewed as having a punitive effect, courts reject retribution and humiliation as reasons to impose lawyer discipline. *See, e.g., In Matter of Kaye*, No. 11-C-10329, 2014 WL 1324546, at *6 (Cal. Bar Ct. Apr. 1, 2014) (aim of discipline is not retribution but protection of the public and promoting confidence in the legal system); *State ex rel. Okla. Bar Ass'n v. Helton*, 394 P.3d 227, 243 (Okla. 2017) (dissent) (dissenting justice stated that distinction between intentional versus negligent violations of the rules of professional conduct make little difference because the goal of attorney discipline is not retribution but protecting the public); *In re Ortner*, 699 N.W.2d 865, 877 (S.D. 2005) (nine-month suspension imposed for corruption of judicial process by concealing private agreement between divorcing parties; court rejected disciplinary board's recommendation of public censure that was based on rationale that lawyer had already "experienced considerable public humiliation and notoriety, as well as personal grief and anguish"); *see also* Leslie C. Levin, *The Emperor's Clothes and Other Tales About the Standards for Imposing Lawyer Discipline Sanctions,* 48 Am. U. L. Rev. 1 (1998) (questioning assertion of most courts that punishment is not purpose of lawyer sanctions; arguing that many sanctions fit definitions of punishment and meet utilitarian justifications of criminal punishment: incapacitation, rehabilitation, and deterrence).

## *Constitutional and Civil Protections*

### • Double Jeopardy

Although lawyers are entitled to some procedural safeguards in the disciplinary process, the constitutional proscription against being punished twice for the same offense does not apply to disciplinary proceedings. In such cases, courts have held that the double jeopardy clause of the Fifth Amendment is not triggered since protection of the public rather than punishment is the primary objective of lawyer discipline. *See, e.g., Marinangeli v. Lehman,* 32 F. Supp. 2d 1 (D.D.C. 1998) (rejecting double jeopardy claim by lawyer contesting suspension before the Patent and Trademark Office and finding that although lawyer was subject of criminal sentence as well as disciplinary action in New York for underlying felony theft, administrative disciplinary proceeding not subject to double jeopardy clause; double jeopardy does not bar successive state and federal prosecutions); *In re Triem,* 929 P.2d 634 (Alaska 1996) (holding that double jeopardy is a substantive due process protection not extended to attorney grievances, so it does not preclude judicial review of a lawyer's conduct in a disciplinary complaint); *In re Fisher,* 202 P.3d 1186, 1199 (Colo. 2009) (rejecting respondent's argument that double jeopardy applies to regulatory discipline, court reiterated its holding that "double jeopardy concepts do not apply to attorney discipline proceedings") (citation omitted); *Miss. Bar v. Coleman,* 849 So.2d 867, 874 (Miss. 2002) ("The case law, in this jurisdiction and others, could not be clearer. Double jeopardy is triggered *only* in a criminal setting, and as such is inapplicable to disciplinary proceedings."); *In re Chastain,* 532 S.E.2d 264 (S.C. 2000) (holding that no double jeopardy clause protection afforded because disciplinary proceedings are not criminal in nature and noting that courts uniformly hold double jeopardy clause not implicated in disciplinary proceedings regardless of whether proceedings are characterized as civil, quasi-criminal, or special).

Courts further reason that the double jeopardy clause is not applicable because lawyer sanctions are remedial and not "punishment." *See, e.g., In re Caranchini,* 160 F.3d 420 (8th Cir. 1998) (rejecting contention that disbarment violates double jeopardy clause due to previously imposed Fed. R. Civ. P. 11 sanctions for same conduct, and finding that attorney discipline, including sanctions and disbarment, is not punishment for purposes of the double jeopardy clause; the court discussed a collection of cases); *In re Brown*, 906 P.2d 1184 (Cal. 1995) (lawyer discipline does not take traditional form of criminal sanctions, such as fines or incarceration, and is not punishment for purposes of Fifth Amendment Double Jeopardy analysis); *People v. Marmon*, 903 P.2d 651, 655 (Colo. 1995) ("In determining the proper disposition, therefore, our analysis begins and ends with the disciplinary sanction necessary to protect the public, and thus is not punishment for double jeopardy purposes. A contrary conclusion would lead to the absurd result that lawyers convicted of criminal offenses could never be disciplined."); *In re Gordon*, 132 A.D.3d 191 (N.Y. App. Div. 2016) (attorney disciplined by federal appellate court argued that reciprocal discipline by New York would constitute violation of Fifth Amendment; court ruled that reciprocal discipline was warranted, double jeopardy argument lacked merit, and issued a public censure); *State ex rel. Okla. Bar Ass'n v. Giger*, 93 P.3d 32, 37 (Okla. 2004) (Double jeopardy protections do not prohibit the imposition of all additional sanctions that may be described as punishment: "[They] protect only against the imposition of multiple *criminal* punishments for the same offense. Although to the suspended or disbarred lawyer, a disciplinary sanction may feel like punishment, it is not in law."); *In re Harding*, 104 P.3d 1220, 1224 (Utah 2004) (rejecting double jeopardy claim in successive judicial and lawyer discipline proceedings arising from misconduct of sitting judge, the court found no double jeopardy protection in judicial or lawyer discipline matters because both are matters of "appointment, oath and privilege," not criminal sanction); *In re Discipline of Babilis*, 951 P.2d 207, 214 (Utah 1997) (in dismissing analogy of disciplinary case to criminal proceeding, court stated that the "penalties available under the Standards for Imposing Lawyer Sanctions are not punishment for double jeopardy purposes"); *Matter of Disciplinary Proceeding Against Waechter*, 419 P.3d 827, 835 (Wash. 2018) (attorney facing fifteen disciplinary charges for the same underlying misconduct contended such a proceeding would punish him more than once for the same acts in violation of double jeopardy clause; the court stated that double jeopardy does not apply to disciplinary proceedings and that the attorney's argument, taken to its logical extreme, would produce absurd results). For further discussion of double jeopardy and the nature of disciplinary proceedings, see Annotation to Standard 2.1.

- **Self-Incrimination**

In contrast to claims of double jeopardy, the privilege against self-incrimination under the Fifth Amendment to the U.S. Constitution does apply in lawyer disciplinary proceedings. Lawyers have the right to remain silent and refuse to give testimony against themselves in a disciplinary proceeding without suffering a disciplinary sanction. In *Spevack v. Klein*, 385 U.S. 511, 516 (1967), the court said:

> We find no room in the privilege against self-incrimination for classifications of people so as to deny it to some and extend it to others. Lawyers are not excepted from the words 'No person . . . shall be compelled in any criminal case to be a witness against himself'; and we can imply no exception.

Following *Spevack*, courts have been in agreement that a lawyer cannot be sanctioned solely for invoking the Fifth Amendment privilege against self-incrimination. *See, e.g., Ziankovich v. Large*, No. 17-CV-02039-CMA-NYW, 2017 WL 4418535, at *4 (D. Colo. Oct. 5, 2017) (while the Colorado Supreme Court has interpreted the *Spevack* case narrowly, "applying only to disclosures that could be used in criminal prosecutions or could lead to such evidence," attorneys may invoke the privilege when appropriate in their own disciplinary proceedings) (citations omitted); *In re Mitchell*, No. 4:03-MC-004-A, 2003 WL 21746254, at *4 (N.D. Tex. July 3, 2003) (lawyer's exercise of Fifth Amendment privilege is not a basis for discipline; however, "[n]othing in *Spevack* suggests that a [court] cannot in a disciplinary proceeding draw appropriate inferences from the failure or refusal of a member of the bar of the court to make requested disclosures concerning conduct of that member in relation to or directed against the court"); *People v. Robnett*, 859 P.2d 872 (Colo. 1993) (court's rules recognize right of a lawyer to assert his or her privilege against self-incrimination in the context of a disciplinary proceeding); *In re Artis*, 883 A.2d 85, 103 (D.C. 2005) ("The Fifth Amendment 'protects against any disclosures that the witness reasonably believes could be used in a criminal prosecution or could lead to other evidence that might be so used'") (citations omitted); *In re Kapchan*, 86 A.D.3d 110, 112 (N.Y. 2011) ("[M]erely invoking one's Fifth Amendment right against self-incrimination should not serve as a separate ground for an interim suspension."); *Disciplinary Counsel v. Heiland*, 880 N.E.2d 467, 472 (Ohio 2008) (court acknowledged U.S. Supreme Court's holding in *Spevack* but found that lawyer's "right against self-incrimination was not violated, because his failure to cooperate stemmed from events occurring before he invoked his Fifth Amendment privilege"); *Disciplinary Proceedings Against Curtis*, 907 N.W.2d 91 (Wis. 2018) (attorney justified in asserting Fifth Amendment privilege in connection with charge that he improperly withheld funds from law firm's employee retirement plan while he introduced other evidence at disciplinary hearing that the plan's finances were in order; the rules allow a strategic use of the right against self-incrimination and is unaffected by assertions of innocence).

Courts have ruled that the Fifth Amendment does not relieve lawyers of their ethical obligations under the rules of professional conduct, such as the duty to communicate with clients and to protect client property and funds. *See, e.g., In re Wiest*, 719 F. App'x 485, 491 (6th Cir. 2017) (attorney had duty to inform client of attorney's misuse of client information, and court's inference that attorney's failure to communicate constituted deceitful intent did not violate Fifth Amendment); *Disciplinary Counsel v. Snaider*, 90 A.3d 286 (Conn. 2014) (court did not infringe on attorney's privilege against self-incrimination by ordering him to comply with Statewide Grievance Committee's request for bank records pertaining to his client trust accounts); *Agwara v. State Bar of Nevada*, 406 P.3d 488, 492-93 (Nev. 2017) (court rejected Fifth Amendment claim in connection with request for attorney's client trust records, ruling that such records, which are required to be maintained by members of the bar, may not be public records, but "they do have 'public aspects' in that the public at large has an interest in the integrity of the profession and clients in particular have an interest in how an attorney handles money which belongs to them.") (citations omitted).

It is also important to note that the scope of the Fifth Amendment privilege is limited to those disclosures that would subject a lawyer to a criminal prosecution and that attorneys need to follow proper procedures in order to invoke the privilege. *See, e.g., In re Shannon*, 876 P.2d 548, 566 (Ariz. 1994) ("Because the primary function of state bar disciplinary sanctions is remedial, the right against self-incrimination does not attach when disciplinary sanctions are the only penalties to which a respondent is exposed."); *In re Barber*, 128 A.3d 637 (D.C. 2015) (court found no Fifth Amendment violation where attorney was forced to take the witness stand; unlike a criminal trial, where defendant can make a blanket refusal, the attorney was required to invoke his right against self-incrimination on a question-by-question basis in disciplinary proceeding); *Ky. Bar Ass'n v. Sparks*, 480 S.W.3d 278 (Ky. 2016) (attorney could not refuse to file an answer to a disciplinary complaint on Fifth Amendment basis, particularly where privilege would have applied to only one count of a multicount complaint); *cf. In re Hill*, 545 A.2d 1019 (Vt. 1988) (in upholding assertion of Fifth Amendment privilege by convicted judge subpoenaed to testify in judicial disciplinary proceeding against another judge, court found she was not required to demonstrate she would be prosecuted or that an answer would result in her conviction, only that there was valid risk of further prosecution).

For further discussion on the application of the privilege against self-incrimination to disciplinary proceedings, *see generally* Geoffrey C. Hazard, Jr. & Cameron Beard, *A Lawyer's Privilege Against Self-Incrimination in Professional Disciplinary Proceedings*, 96 Yale L.J. 1060, 1069 (1987); Helen Chun Parker, *Attorneys Who Plead the Fifth: How the Self-Incrimination Provision Applies to New Jersey Attorney Disciplinary Proceedings*, 27 Rutgers L.J. 493 (1996); Andrea G. Nadel, Annotation, *Extent and Determination of Attorney's Right or Privilege Against Self-Incrimination in Disbarment or Other Disciplinary Proceedings—Post-*Spevack *Cases*, 30 A.L.R.4th 243 (1984 & Supp. 1992).

- **Res Judicata**

The doctrine of res judicata, in which a matter may not be raised again because it already has been judged, generally does not apply to disciplinary proceedings or preclude the imposition of sanctions in lawyer disciplinary cases. *See, e.g., In re Landerman*, 7 F. Supp. 2d 1202 (D. Utah 1998) (res judicata claim raised by lawyer who had been convicted of felony and previously disciplined by Utah Supreme Court, in response to court's order to show cause why he should not be disciplined, found frivolous and without merit; federal courts have absolute and unfettered power to admit and discipline members of their bar, independent of admission and discipline of lawyers in state courts); *In re Berryman*, 764 A.2d 760 (D.C. 2000) (disposition by probate division that right of survivorship in joint account and outstanding fees owed by deceased client entitled lawyer to retain estate funds did not give rise to res judicata bar in disciplinary action alleging commingling and intentional misappropriation from client's estate and subsequent disbarment of lawyer); *Fla. Bar v. Trazenfeld*, 833 So.2d 734 (Fla. 2002) (referee erred in concluding that res judicata barred disciplinary action against lawyer based on grievance committee's earlier finding of no probable cause on same underlying facts; collecting case law from various jurisdictions in support of position that doctrine of res judicata not applicable to bar grievance committee proceedings when no findings of guilt have been made and no final judgment entered); *In re Krasnoff*, 78 N.E.3d 657 (Ind. 2017) (attorney argued earlier rule to show cause proceeding created res judicata; court disagreed, explaining the purpose of a rule to show cause order is coercive in nature and designed to secure attorney cooperation, whereas a disciplinary proceeding bears on the attorney's continued fitness to practice); *In re Delk*, 444 S.E.2d 198 (N.C. 1994) (rejecting lawyer's overbroad interpretation of res judicata doctrine suggesting that failure of judge who presided over lawyer's criminal trial to order lawyer disbarred following his felony conviction for extortion and conspiracy was res judicata, court noted that question of disbarment not part of criminal action and could be decided at later time); *State ex rel. Okla. Bar Ass'n v. Giger*, 93 P.3d 32 (Okla. 2004) (doctrine of claim preclusion (known in common law as res judicata) did not bar bringing separate disciplinary proceeding to determine whether lawyer's petty larceny warranted independent disciplinary sanctions; claim preclusion, however, did prevent relitigation of whether petty larceny violated terms of previously imposed disciplinary probation when that issue had been decided on the merits in prior disciplinary case); *In re Bertoni*, 426 P.3d 64 (Or. 2018) (attorney unsuccessfully argued claim preclusion where prior suspension did not encompass the misconduct at issue in the present case); *In re Sullivan*, 121 A.3d 623, 627 (Pa. 2015) ("[o]ur jurisprudence on the principle that ethical discipline is distinct from criminal prosecution has been uniform for as far back as research is available."); *Napolitano v. Bd. of Prof'l Responsibility*, 535

S.W.3d 481 (Tenn. 2017) (court rejected res judicata assertion where former client's first complaint on the amount of the legal fee was dismissed and subsequent complaint detailed attorney's mishandling of trust account); *Acevedo v. Comm'n for Lawyer Discipline*, 131 S.W.3d 99, 106 (Tex. App. 2004) (neither res judicata nor collateral estoppel bars use of evidence from underlying malpractice claim brought by former client alleging breach of fiduciary duty against lawyer because ultimate factual issues of whether lawyer is subject to professional discipline for rule violations "were not 'actually litigated,' 'essential to the judgment,' or 'finally adjudicated'" in breach of fiduciary lawsuit) (citations omitted). *But see N. Carolina State Bar v. Tillett*, 794 S.E.2d 743 (N.C. 2016) (jurisdiction to sanction sitting judges rests solely with Judicial Standards Commission and the Supreme Court of North Carolina; to allow the state bar to seek to impose discipline would raise potential res judicata and collateral estoppel issues, as well as basic questions of fundamental fairness).

The principle that double jeopardy protection and the doctrine of res judicata are inapposite in lawyer disciplinary cases extends to matters of reciprocal discipline as well, although courts may decide not to impose reciprocal discipline on other grounds. *See, e.g., In re Iulo*, 766 A.2d 335 (Pa. 2001) (principles of res judicata and collateral estoppel do not preclude initiation of reciprocal discipline proceedings—though, in this instance, the imposition of reciprocal discipline would result in grave injustice since lawyer's disbarment ten years earlier in New Jersey was disclosed and known to bar examiners who gave lawyer permission to sit for Pennsylvania bar exam); *cf. In re Dunietz*, 756 A.2d 437, 438 (D.C. 2000) (imposing reciprocal discipline based on only one of two matters considered together by Maryland Court of Appeals because D.C. Court of Appeals previously had imposed sanctions in one of the matters; finding that while constitutional notions of double jeopardy "probably do not apply here, fundamental fairness surely dictates that a court may not discipline an attorney more than once for the same disciplinary violation"). *See also Chief Disciplinary Counsel v. Rozbicki*, 167 A.3d 351 (Conn. 2017) (res judicata and collateral estoppel arguments rejected by court in disciplinary proceeding where judges in underlying cases that led to attorney misconduct did not sanction attorney or refer matters to disciplinary authority); *In re Lee*, 95 A.3d 66 (D.C. 2014) (attorney accused of misconduct in handling of settlement check contended that discipline would be barred by res judicata since the adverse party in the civil suit abandoned its claim to any funds; court ruled that the issues raised in the disciplinary proceeding were not raised and decided in any prior litigation so res judicata did not apply); *Bennett v. Comm'n for Lawyer Discipline*, 489 S.W.3d 58 (Tex. App. 2016) (appellate court's decision not to sanction attorney for frivolous pleading does not bar a disciplinary action for the same conduct "because the two proceedings do not involve the same parties, issues, or behavior").

Jurisdictions generally give full faith and credit to a disciplinary judgment, noting that a modified version of the res judicata principle applies in reciprocal discipline proceedings in the sense that courts will defer to the final judgment of another jurisdiction rather than rehear the entire disciplinary matter. *See* MRLDE Rule 22 (Reciprocal Discipline and Reciprocal Disability Inactive Status), Model Rules for Lawyer Disciplinary Enforcement R. 22 (2007) (a final adjudication in another jurisdiction that a lawyer has been guilty of misconduct is conclusive proof of that misconduct and is not subject to relitigation). *See, e.g., In re Kersey,* 825 N.E.2d 994 (Mass. 2005) (in reciprocal discipline cases, court will not engage in reexamining inquiry; applicable rule of court implicitly adopts modified rule of res judicata adopting originating jurisdiction's discipline unless certain conditions apply—namely, that (1) imposition of the same discipline would result in grave injustice; (2) misconduct established does not justify the same discipline in Massachusetts; or (3) misconduct established is not adequately sanctioned by the same discipline in Massachusetts); *In re Bailey,* 786 N.E.2d 337 (Mass. 2003) (applying same rule as *Kersey* but also noting need for notice or opportunity to be heard and strength of proof establishing the misconduct); *In re Smith,* 925 P.2d 169, 173 (Utah 1996) (finding issues relating to Utah-licensed lawyer's right to counsel and court's jurisdiction in criminal prosecution in Wisconsin had been fully and fairly litigated rendering resolution of those issues res judicata, under full faith and credit doctrine, for disciplinary charge based on Wisconsin conviction; "[t]he rationale for full faith and credit, in addition to promoting consistency and judicial economy, is to protect fairly adjudicated decisions from after-the-fact alteration by courts that lack access to true adversarial proceedings").

### *Discipline for Conduct Not Involving the Practice of Law*

Lawyers who are not actively practicing law but rather are serving in such roles as corporate officers, public officials, or law professors do not lose their association with the legal profession because of their primary occupation or relinquish their role as officers of the court, subject to the court's disciplinary authority. The public expects that anyone admitted to the practice of law, regardless of daily occupational activities, will conform to minimum ethical standards of the legal profession. Lawyers can be subject to discipline for conduct that reflects adversely on their fitness to practice, even when that conduct takes place outside the context of practicing law. *See e.g., Romero-Barcelo v. Acevedo-Vila,* 275 F. Supp. 2d 177 (D.P.R. 2003) (noting that lawyers may be disciplined for improper conduct in connection with business activities, individual or personal activities, and activities as judicial officer; citing federal district court local rule that provides for the imposition of disciplinary sanctions for violations of the ABA Model Rules of Professional Conduct, whether or not the act or omission occurred in the course of client-lawyer relationship or judicial proceeding; court imposed public reprimand for lawyer's false statements against political opponent); *People v. Ritland*, 327 P.3d 914 (Colo. O.P.D.J. 2014) (three-year suspension where attorney seeking to adopt a baby falsely listed her husband as the birth father on the baby's birth certificate, repeated this falsehood in a subsequent petition, and counseled her husband to falsely aver that he was the birth father); *In re Bria*, 86 A.3d 1118 (Del. 2014) (six-months-and-one-day suspension for attorney's failure to pay state and federal taxes and false certification in annual registration statement); *In re Hickerson*, 792 S.E.2d 321 (Ga. 2016) (reciprocal discipline sanction of indefinite suspension where attorney testified falsely in a deposition in a divorce action involving third parties and filed pleadings containing false statements in a civil matter in which she was a defendant); *In re Mintz*, 317 P.3d 756 (Kan. 2014) (indefinite suspension for attorney who made false statements to police and attempted to conceal his actions after he found his companion's corpse); *Attorney Grievance Comm'n v. Katz*, 116 A.3d 999 (Md. 2015) (disbarment for attorney's repeated and willful failure to file income tax returns for more than a decade); *In re Brown*, 123 A.D.3d 108 (N.Y. 2014) (one-year suspension for attorney who co-purchased property from long-time family friend and her daughter that was deceptively secured on disproportionately favorable terms that allowed the attorney to make the purchase without any financial contribution); *Disciplinary Counsel v. Hale*, 26 N.E.3d 785 (Ohio 2014) (six-month suspension for attorney who, while serving as a municipal judge, dismissed his personal attorney's speeding ticket without the prosecutor's involvement); *In re Carpenter*, 95 P.3d 203, 208 (Or. 2004) (lawyer's dishonesty in creating an online account, representing himself as a local high school teacher, and posting messages indicating he had engaged in sexual conduct with students "jeopardizes the public's interest in the integrity and trustworthiness of lawyers" and demonstrated that the lawyer lacked "those characteristics that are essential to the practice of law"; public reprimand imposed); *In re Obregon*, 145 A.3d 226, 227 (Vt. 2016) (public reprimand for failing to file personal Vermont income tax returns for four years); *In re Disciplinary Proceeding Against McKean*, 64 P.3d 1226 (Wash. 2003) (six-month suspension for lawyer who loaned one client's money held in trust to another client with whom the lawyer was involved in a farming business venture; court cited commentary and case law on responsibility of lawyer, as fiduciary, to meet high standards of legal profession whether or not acting in capacity as lawyer); *see also* ABA Comm'n on Ethics & Prof'l Responsibility, Formal Op. 336 (1974) (lawyer must comply with disciplinary rules whether acting in a professional capacity or otherwise). *See generally* Barrie Althoff, *Big Brother Is Watching: Discipline for "Private" Conduct*, 2000 PROF. LAW. (SYMPOSIUM ISSUE) 81 (discussing distinction between "public" and "private" conduct and whether lawyers should be subject to professional discipline for conduct unrelated to practice of law); Patrick O'Rourke, *Discipline Against Lawyers for Conduct Outside the Practice of Law*, COLO. LAW., Apr. 2003, at 75 (discussing discipline imposed upon lawyers based on private conduct; cautioning lawyers not to draw artificial distinction between professional and personal conduct to avoid discipline).

Disciplinary sanctions may be imposed when a lawyer engages in criminal conduct not associated with the representation of a client. *See, e.g., In re Hoare*, 155 F.3d 937, 940 (8th Cir. 1998) (in imposing reciprocal disbarment based on felony conviction for alcohol-related vehicular homicide, court stated, "[o]ffending conduct need not involve direct questions of honesty or trustworthiness, nor have an immediate relation to the daily business conducted by an attorney, in order to warrant substantial discipline"); *People v. Saxon*, 2016 WL 8540133 (Colo. O.P.D.J. Nov. 7, 2016) (lawyer convicted of misdemeanor for stalking ex-girlfriend, disclosing that she worked as a prostitute to her family and friends, and encouraging her to commit suicide received three-year suspension from the practice of law); *In re Fry*, 806 S.E.2d 604 (Ga. 2017) (attorney disbarred for conviction on two counts of bribery); *Iowa Supreme Ct. Att'y Disciplinary Bd. v. Khowassah*, 890 N.W.2d 647 (Iowa 2017) (indefinite suspension with no possibility of reinstatement for a period of six months where attorney pled guilty to public intoxication and operating a motor vehicle while intoxicated); *In re Minter*, 367 P.3d 1238 (Kan. 2016) (attorney indefinitely suspended after pleading no contest to three drug-related felonies); *Att'y Grievance Comm'n v. Paul*, 187 A.3d 625 (Md. 2018) (three-month suspension for convictions of traffic offenses related to road rage incident); *In re Disciplinary Action Against Siders*, 903 N.W.2d 218 (Minn. 2017) (attorney who pled guilty to felony for soliciting a minor to engage in prostitution received an indefinite suspension without the right to petition for reinstatement for two years); *In re Treffinger*, 393 P.3d 1084 (Nev. 2017) (court ordered interim suspension and referred for formal discipline for attorney who pled guilty to felony possession of heroin); *In re Cohen*, 100 A.3d 529 (N.J. 2014) (indefinite suspension for attorney who pled guilty to possessing sexually explicit pornographic images of children on his computer); *Disciplinary Counsel v. Hillman*, 500 N.E.3d 539 (Ohio 2016) (one-year suspension fully stayed with conditions for attorney convicted of failing to file a federal personal income tax return); *State ex rel. Okla. Bar Ass'n v. Ijams*, 338 P.3d 639 (Okla. 2014) (eighteen-month suspension for attorney serving deferred and suspended sentences for misdemeanor violations that included eluding a police officer and driving while under the influence); *In re Harding*, 104 P.3d 1220 (Utah 2004) (disbarring convicted lawyer for use of various unlawful controlled substances while actively serving as judge); *In re Pope*, 101 A.3d 1284 (Vt. 2014) (two-year suspension for attorney who pled guilty to misdemeanor charge of identity theft).

Not every improper act by a lawyer outside the practice of law will necessarily result in the imposition of a disciplinary sanction. The primary consideration by courts in declining to sanction a lawyer in such circumstances focuses on the lawyer's fitness to practice. *See, e.g., Att'y Grievance Comm'n v. Shaw*, 732 A.2d 876 (Md. 1999) (noting that lawyers are disciplined for conduct outside the practice of law only when that conduct is dishonest or adversely reflects on profession; remanding for determination whether lawyer, on inactive status, was involved in practice of law or had client-lawyer relationship with guardian when she incompetently researched stock for disabled person's estate); *In re Haderlie*, 885 N.W.2d 78 (N.D. 2016) (court dismissed reciprocal discipline action where attorney received censure from another state's supreme court for misdemeanor convictions for driving while intoxicated and interfering with a police officer; court ruled that not all illegal conduct is disciplinable and lawyer's conduct was not prejudicial to the administration of justice since it did not involve his law practice); *see also* ABA Comm'n on Ethics & Prof'l Responsibility, Formal Op. 04–433 (2004) (interpreting Model Rule 8.3 to require report of misconduct committed by another licensed lawyer, including a nonpracticing lawyer, even if arising from purely personal activity, when misconduct reflects adversely on lawyer's fitness to practice); CT R Super Ct Gen, Sec. 2-32(2)(G) (disciplinary complaints against attorneys should be dismissed if "the complaint alleges personal behavior outside the practice of law which does not constitute a violation of the Rules of Professional Conduct").

## *Discipline for Conduct Preceding Bar Admission*

In some instances, lawyers have been disciplined for misconduct preceding their admission to the bar. *See, e.g., In re Bravo*, No. 11-C-18189, 2014 WL 642857, at *1 (Cal. Bar Ct. Feb. 14, 2014) (court issued public reproval and probationary conditions for one year for attorney's three alcohol-related driving offenses, two of which occurred prior to his bar admission); *In re Comm'n on Bar Admissions*, 166 So.3d 249 (La. 2015) (despite passing the Louisiana Bar Examination, petitioner denied admission for convictions of crimes that included forgery, theft, and passing worthless checks); *State ex rel. Neb. State Bar Ass'n v. Blackstone*, 517 N.W.2d 400 (Neb. 1994) (disbarment warranted for admitted conduct during period between taking bar exam and being admitted to bar, that included engaging in criminal acts not disclosed to bar prior to admission, consisting of presenting forged checks to bank with intent to defraud); *In re Mikus*, 131 P.3d 653 (N.M. 2006) (lawyer may be disciplined for acts committed prior to admission but not discovered until after admission; suspension warranted for lawyer who failed to supplement his bar application with information regarding his indictment); *In re Wong*, 275 A.D.2d 1 (N.Y. App. Div. 2000) (court's inherent power to regulate lawyers and obligation to protect the public provide authority to discipline lawyer for conduct occurring prior to admission and unrelated to the admission process; public censure warranted for improper sexual touching of ten-year-old girl during gymnastics practice, which occurred when lawyer was law student); *State ex rel. Okla. Bar Ass'n v.*

*Flanery*, 863 P.2d 1146, 1150 (Okla. 1993) (holding that lawyer's preadmission conduct of embezzling $71,000 from family members warranted disbarment because it went "to the heart of respondent's fitness to practice law"); *Office of Disciplinary Counsel v. Zdrok*, 645 A.2d 830 (Pa. 1994) (six-month suspension based, in part, on lawyer's preadmission conviction of nighttime loitering and prowling in violation of Pennsylvania criminal statute); *In re Brown*, 605 S.E.2d 509 (S.C. 2004) (disbarment and two-year suspension to run concurrently for various acts of misconduct including unauthorized practice of law after lawyer graduated from law school but before he was licensed; court held that nature and severity of misconduct and relation to time of admission are factors to be considered in assessing whether to impose discipline for preadmission misconduct); *see also Fla. Bd. of Bar Examiners re Question as to Whether Undocumented Immigrants Are Eligible for Admission to the Florida Bar*, 134 So.2d 432 (Fla. 2014) (advisory opinion holding that unauthorized immigrants are ineligible for admission to the Florida Bar).

Bar applicants who fail to provide full and truthful disclosure on their applications or who demonstrate a pattern of untruthfulness during the admission process often are denied admission to the bar. *See, e.g., Fla. Bd. of Bar Exam'rs re B.H.A.*, 626 So.2d 683 (Fla. 1993) (false or misleading explanation of prior arrest on bar application, falsification of responses on application for legal intern position, and false answer on law school application disqualified applicant from admission to bar, despite character witnesses and excellent work record); *In re Montesanti*, 2018 WL 4054334, at *2 (Ga. Aug. 27, 2018) (applicant's false statements on bar application about nonpayment of a judgment against him, and applicant's statements to professor that he intentionally made false statements because bar examiners were not entitled to the truth led to denial of bar admission); *In re Brathcher*, 53 N.E.3d 416 (Ind. 2016) (false description of citation for retail theft in bar application warranted eighteen-month suspension without automatic reinstatement); *Att'y Grievance Comm'n v. Van Dusen*, 116 A.3d 1013 (Md. 2015) (court ruled that a bar applicant engaged in criminal conduct must report it to bar examiners and the court; court disbarred attorney who was secretly videotaping female tenants while bar admission was pending); *In re La Tourette*, 720 A.2d 339 (N.J. 1998) (court holds that applicant lacked character and fitness to practice law, such that certification of his application for bar admission would be withheld); *In re McLaughlin*, 675 A.2d 1101 (N.J. 1996) (certification of good character and fitness withheld from admission candidate for lack of truthfulness and candor and insufficient appreciation for proper administration of justice); *In re DeMaria*, 154 A.D.3d 1161 (N.Y. App. Div. 2017) (court revoked attorney's New York law license for his nondisclosure of cheating on a bar examination in Canada); *In re Application of Callam*, 81 N.E.3d 448 (Ohio 2017) (revocation of law license with right to reapply after two years for failure to disclose circumstances surrounding surrender of insurance license on bar application); *In re Bitter*, 969 A.2d 71 (Vt. 2008) (applicant failed to demonstrate that he possessed necessary moral character to be admitted to the Vermont Bar by failing to disclose entire criminal history and prior academic probation on law school application; incomplete and evasive answers to those questions demonstrated pattern short of complete honesty, a lack of forthrightness borne out in his answers on his Vermont Bar application); *In re Martin,* 510 N.W.2d 687 (Wis. 1994) (applicant denied certification for admission due to failure to truthfully answer criminal history questions on law school and bar admission applications); *but see In re Nichols,* 895 N.W.2d 831 (Wis. 2017) (applicant conditionally admitted despite instance of plagiarism in law school and failing to report citations for underage drinking on his law school application).

## 1.2 Public Nature of Lawyer Discipline

**Upon the filing and service of formal charges, lawyer discipline should be public in cases of disbarment, suspension, and reprimand. Only in cases of minor misconduct, when there is little or no injury to a client, the public, the legal system, or the profession, and when there is little likelihood of repetition by the lawyer, should private discipline be imposed.**

# Annotation

Rule 16 (Access to Disciplinary Information) of the ABA Model Rules for Lawyer Disciplinary Enforcement (MRLDE) recommends that records of a disciplinary agency and its proceedings be made available to the public following the filing and service of formal charges against a lawyer. There are certain exceptions set forth in Rule 16, including disability proceedings, when the respondent lawyer has waived confidentiality, and the issuance of protective orders upon a showing of good cause. Model Rules for Lawyer Disciplinary Enforcement R. 16 (2007). Currently, forty-two jurisdictions open lawyer disciplinary proceedings to the public at various stages of the disciplinary process. Oregon and Arizona, for example, have open systems in which even initial complaints filed against lawyers that have been dismissed after investigation are available to the public. *See* Or. State Bar Bylaws, art. 8, § 8.102 (as amended Feb. 21, 2014) and Rule 70, Ariz. R. Sup. Ct. Most jurisdictions, however, open disciplinary proceedings to the public after a finding of probable cause and upon the filing and service of formal charges. Still, nearly a dozen jurisdictions, including New York's multiple disciplinary departments, retain systems that remain closed to the public until a recommendation of discipline is filed with the court or upon the issuance of the court's final ruling.

## *Public Sanctions Increase Public Trust and Confidence in the Profession*

ABA policy has long urged public access to disciplinary records and disciplinary proceedings, except for privileged or otherwise protected materials and communications and work product, upon a finding of probable cause and the filing of formal charges. *See* Model Rules for Lawyer Disciplinary Enforcement R. 16 (2007). Public trust in the legal profession is enhanced when the lawyer disciplinary process is open to the public and when disciplinary sanctions are made public. As the ABA Commission on Evaluation of Disciplinary Enforcement, commonly known as the McKay Commission, noted in its report, secrecy is the greatest single source of public distrust of lawyer disciplinary systems and does great harm to the reputation of the profession as a whole. *See* Commission on Evaluation of Disciplinary Enforcement, Am. Bar Ass'n, Lawyer Regulation for a New Century (1992) at 33.

Public discipline also enhances the integrity of the profession and demonstrates the court's interest in protecting the public. Rule 10 of the MRLDE states that the disposition of lawyer discipline should be public in cases of disbarment, suspension, probation, and reprimand. *See* Model Rules for Lawyer Disciplinary Enforcement R. 10(D) (2007). The Commentary to that Rule further explains that the purposes of lawyer discipline are best served if the rationale for the sanctions imposed is set forth in a written opinion available to the public and the legal profession.

Transparency, greater access to information about lawyer misconduct, and knowledge about how the disciplinary system works help increase the public's confidence in the effectiveness of the disciplinary system and the profession's ability to self-regulate. *See, e.g., In re Att'y F.*, 285 P.3d 322, 328 (Colo. 2012) (court rejected lawyer's objections to posting on state's disciplinary website, while appeal was pending, hearing board's recommended imposition of public censure on lawyer for knowing misrepresentation to opposing counsel and agreed with presiding disciplinary judge who stated that suppressing board's "disposition in a case pending resolution of an appeal would 'impair the goal of transparency and public accountability in our disciplinary system'"); *In re Requests for Investigation of Att'y E.*, 78 P.3d 300, 308 (Colo. 2003) (one of the main goals of revisions to Colorado's lawyer discipline rules was "to allow liberal disclosures of information so as to provide a visible attorney discipline process."); *In re Benson*, 774 A.2d 258, 262 (Del. 2001) (in rejecting the parties' agreed stipulation for private discipline and imposing public reprimand and public probation for lawyer's failure to timely file and pay appropriate employment tax obligations, among other violations, the court stressed that public discipline "serves as an important preventive measure," and "affords the Court the opportunity to inform not only other members of the Bar but the general public that the Court takes very seriously a lawyer's obligation to maintain orderly books and records and to fulfill tax obligations"); *Miss. Bar v. Ogletree*, 226 So.3d 79, 84 (Miss. 2015) (six-month suspension appropriate where the lawyer misappropriated client funds and commingled client funds with his own; "Worthy of most consideration when contemplating sanctions is vindicating 'in the eyes of the public the overall reputation of the bar.'"); *Miss. Bar v. Walls*, 797 So.2d 217 (Miss. 2001) (quoting *Hall v. Miss. Bar*, 631 So.2d 120 (Miss. 1993), court reaffirmed that disciplinary sanctions must be "sufficient to vindicate in the eyes of the public the overall reputation of the bar."); *In re Gallo*, 835 A.2d 682, 684 (N.J. 2003) (court remanded matter for full hearing, noting that lawyer's "scant admissions" at criminal plea hearing admitting to four acts of sexual contact with three clients and one pro se party opponent did not provide sufficient basis to determine full gravity of misconduct; the court said that the "[r]espondent and the grievants, as well as the public, are entitled to a disciplinary review process in which a full, undistorted picture is the basis for disciplinary sanctions").

In *In re Lassen*, 672 A.2d 988, 1001 (Del. 1996), the Supreme Court of Delaware captured well the important policy considerations, such as those identified in Standard 1.2, supporting the imposition of public discipline, noting that the "guiding principle in determining whether a sanction should be public or private remains the protection of the public." Rejecting the lawyer's suggestion that he receive a private admonition and voluntary permanent retirement as the sanction, the court determined that a three-year public suspension more adequately advanced the interests of the public and the lawyer disciplinary system. It stated:

> The egregiousness of Respondent's misconduct in light of his earlier offense is inexcusable and very disturbing to this Court. To shelter such conduct from the light of public scrutiny does violence to the policies underlying the lawyer disciplinary system and undermines public confidence in the profession which traditionally has been built on trust and self-regulation. Dispensing a non-public sanction in this case runs a substantial risk of damaging the reputation of the Bar and the Court with the community at large, and provides an improper message to practitioners that egregious misdeeds may be engaged in without fear of public opprobrium. Moreover, Respondent's proposed result here may result in a dangerous and sometimes unworkable precedent, and would be unfair to other publicly sanctioned lawyers.

672 A.2d at 1002.

### *Additional Purposes for Public Sanctions*

The imposition of public disciplinary sanctions also serves other purposes. Public identification of a disciplined lawyer enables victims who may have been unaware of the disciplinary process to seek redress. *See, e.g., In re Allen*, 188 P.3d 953 (Kan. 2008) (court agreed that the recommended sanction of a public indefinite suspension was warranted for lawyer who abandoned his solo immigration law practice, noting that after lawyer complied with the hearing panel's request that he provide the disciplinary administrator with list of client names who still may be owed unearned fees, disciplinary administrator wrote to ninety-seven abandoned clients, informing them of status of disciplinary case, offering assistance in finding legal counsel, and requesting claims for unearned fees). When a particularly prominent lawyer is disciplined for misconduct, public identification can show that the system does not play favorites. *See, e.g., In the Matter of Andrew Thomas*, et.al, PDJ 2011-9002 (Ariz. 2012) *available at* https://www.azcourts.

gov/pdj/Decisions/2012 (Maricopa County Attorney engaged in multiple acts of serious misconduct, resulting in disbarment; he disclosed confidential client information in a press release, , approved filing a motion that contained a false statement of material fact, made extrajudicial statements that he knew would be publicly disseminated and had a substantial likelihood of materially prejudicing an adjudicative proceeding, brought and continued a RICO lawsuit without a good-faith basis in law and fact, sued four judges concerning their decisions in various matters, sought damages against judges for carrying out their obligations and duties when judges were immune from suit by law, and charged a judge with crimes to compel recusal in a pending matter); *Fla. Bar v. Bailey*, 803 So.2d 683, 694 (Fla. 2001) (prominent criminal defense lawyer F. Lee Bailey disbarred for "multiple counts of egregious misconduct, including offering false testimony, engaging in ex parte communications, violating a client's confidences, violating two federal court orders, and trust account violations, including commingling and misappropriation."); *N.C. State Bar v. Nifong*, No. 06 DHC 35 (N.C. 2007), *available at* http://www.ncbar.gov/orders/06dhc35.pdf (lead prosecutor disbarred for misconduct during his prosecution of three Duke University lacrosse players falsely accused of rape, sexual assault, and kidnapping; numerous violations, including failure to make timely disclosure to the defense of all evidence or information known to him that tended to negate the guilt of the accused, including DNA evidence, and making material misrepresentations to judge presiding in criminal case and to disciplinary authority).

When disciplinary sanctions are public, lawyers themselves can observe whether the system is operating fairly and treating consistently lawyers who are disciplined for similar misconduct. Public sanctions also educate members of the legal profession and help deter misconduct. The preventive aspect of public discipline cannot be overlooked. *See, e.g., Fla. Bar v. Adams*, 198 So.3d 593, 599 (Fla. 2016) (permanent disbarment appropriate where attorneys conspired to improperly effect the arrest of opposing counsel for driving under the influence in the midst of a high profile civil trial; court stated "We can only hope that our unanimous decision to approve the referee's recommendation to permanently disbar these attorneys . . . will serve to warn other attorneys of the high standards of professional conduct we demand of all attorneys. And we hope in some small way, it will send a message to the public that this Court will not tolerate such outrageous misconduct on the part of attorneys admitted to practice law in Florida."); *Fla. Bar v. Rodriguez*, 959 So.2d 150, 162 (Fla. 2007) (in addition to two-year suspension, lawyer required to disgorge prohibited fee to clients' security fund; permitting respondent "to retain his ill-gotten gains would fail to provide a deterrent and could actually encourage misconduct by greedy lawyers"); *Iowa Supreme Ct. Att'y Disciplinary Bd. v. Newman*, 748 N.W.2d 786, 788–89 (Iowa 2008) (in rejecting private admonishment ordered by the Grievance Commission, the court stated that a "public reprimand is necessary to signal Iowa lawyers and the citizens of Iowa that forging a judge's signature is a serious ethical violation under *any* circumstances"); *Att'y Grievance Comm'n v. Shuler*, 164 A.3d 209, 226 (Md. 2017) (disbarment appropriate for repeatedly failing to act timely, misrepresenting legal information to client, and refusing to cooperate with disciplinary counsel's investigation; lawyer previously suspended for similar violations; court held that "[i]n arriving at the appropriate sanction, we are guided by our interest in protecting the public and the public's confidence in the legal profession. . . . The purpose of [disciplinary] proceedings is not to punish the lawyer, but should deter other lawyers from engaging in similar conduct. "); *Att'y Grievance Comm'n v. Goodman*, 43 A.3d 988, 998 (Md. 2012) (sanctioning an offending lawyer "protects the public interest 'because it demonstrates to members of the legal profession the type of conduct which will not be tolerated' . . . and the sanctions imposed have the goal also of 'deterring other lawyers from engaging in similar conduct'") (citations omitted); *Disciplinary Proceedings Against Toran*, 909 N.W.2d 411, 415 (Wis. 2018) (sixty-day suspension for attorney who failed to provide fee agreement, failed to hold advanced fees in trust, and failed to return advanced fees for work not performed; court stated that sixty-day suspension "is sufficient to impress upon him the seriousness of his misconduct, to protect other clients, and to deter other attorneys from engaging in similar misconduct."). *But see In re Iulo*, 766 A.2d 335, 340 (Pa. 2001) (while noting, "deterrence is a considerable factor in matters of reciprocal discipline," the court discharged petition for reciprocal discipline, finding that the imposition of reciprocal disbarment would be a grave injustice on lawyer convicted and disbarred in New Jersey for misappropriation of client funds, when misconduct was more a result of being an "inept bookkeeper" rather than a "self-interested thief").

## *When Private Discipline Is Appropriate*

While recognizing that the interests of the public and the profession are served through the imposition of public discipline, courts have considered instances when the imposition of private discipline is appropriate. Private admonitions may be imposed for cases of minor misconduct; when there is little or no injury to a client, the public, the legal system or the profession; and when there is little or no likelihood of repetition. *See* Annotation to Standard 2.6; *see also In re PRB* No. 2013-145, 165 A.3d 130 (Vt. 2017) (private admonition for attorney who failed to establish, maintain, and manage trust account, even though presumptive sanction was a public reprimand; no actual injury to any client, and attorney brought trust accounts and accounting procedures into compliance with the rules); *In re PRB* No. 2013-153, 96 A.3d 468 (Vt. 2014) (admonition for attorney who placed advanced fees in operating account, failed to reconcile trust account, and failed to maintain an accounting system in violation of the rules, because no injury to clients).

A private sanction informs a lawyer that his or her actions are unethical but does not unnecessarily stigmatize a lawyer from whom the public needs no protection. The following are examples of misconduct for which courts chose to impose private sanctions against the lawyers. *See, e.g., In re Todd,* 418 P.3d 1265, 1268 (Kan. 2018) (attorney entered into diversion agreement for failure to act promptly on client's request for a recalculation of jail time credit;diversion agreement provided that attorney would avoid discipline if he completed sixteen hours of CLE within one year, but he only completed fifteen, resulting in termination of diversionagreement; court, in rejecting public censure, noted lawyer's battle with cancer and stated that because ". . . of the circumstances before us, we regard even published censure as a disciplinary step beyond the one necessary. Rather than imposing any discipline as a court, we remand . . . for the imposition of an informal admonition . . ."); *An Unnamed Attorney v. Ky. Bar Ass'n,* 345 S.W.3d 851 (Ky. 2011) (court approved negotiated sanction of private reprimand for lawyer who deducted fee from settlement proceeds in automobile accident case without notifying chiropractor who had lien against proceeds, noting that publication of the redacted private reprimand educates the public and bar concerning the ramifications of this type of conduct); *Discipline of an Attorney,* 864 N.E.2d 1167 (Mass. 2007) (court stated that public interest best served by adopting the board's recommendation of private admonition for lawyer who made misleading statements to clients and entered into a contingent fee agreement that capped clients' obligation for out-of-pocket expenses); *In re Charges of Unprofessional Conduct in Panel File No. 41310,* 899 N.W. 2d 821 (Minn. 2017) (private admonition warranted where attorney stated in email to insurance adjuster that he had advised his then-former client that the client had already accepted the insurance company's settlement offer and that the client could not rescind the acceptance; misconduct was minimal and involved a single email that did not result in any real harm to the client); *In re Charges of Unprofessional Conduct in Panel File No. 39302,* 884 N.W.2d 661 (Minn. 2016) (attorney wrongly believed he could negotiate settlement in Minnesota without being licensed to practice law in that state and engaged in series of email communications with opposing lawyer involving attorney's family members; weight of the misconduct was minimal and the only harm was delay in the resolution of the debt, warranting only private admonition); *In re PRB, Docket No. 2007-046,* 989 A.2d 523 (Vt. 2009) (private admonition was the appropriate sanction for two lawyers who misled a potential witness as to whether they were recording a telephone conversation, in which the lawyers were motivated by a desire to help their client rather than personal gain and cooperated with disciplinary counsel, and there was no injury to the client, little damage to the public legal system, or the profession, and no likelihood of repetition). *But see People v. Lopez,* 845 P.2d 1153 (Colo. 1993), in which the court, rejecting private censure recommendation for lawyer who revealed client's confidences and made false response to grievance committee investigation, imposed public censure, reiterating:

> A private censure, because it does not inform the public about a lawyer's misconduct, "should be used only when the lawyer is negligent, when the ethical violation results in little or no injury to a client, the public, the legal system, or the profession, and when there is little or no likelihood of repetition."

*Id.* at 1156 (citation omitted); *In re Lassen,* 672 A.2d 988, 1002 (Del. 1996) (three-year suspension, not permanent retirement in exchange for private admonition, warranted for lawyer who engaged in numerous instances of dishonesty, including misrepresentations to bankruptcy court in connection with misallocation of personal charges to client's account, and charging fictitious billable hours to clients' accounts; "[d]ispensing a non-public sanction in this case runs a substantial risk of damaging the reputation of the Bar and the Court with the community at large, and provides an improper message to practitioners that egregious misdeeds may be engaged in without fear of public opprobrium").

## *Reporting of Private Discipline*

In an effort to further educate and deter other lawyers, the court or bar should publish reports of private admonitions, omitting the names of the disciplined lawyers to protect their anonymity, but describing the facts of the case and the misconduct warranting discipline. *See* Model Rules for Lawyer Disciplinary Enforcement R. 10 (2007); *see also Wilhelm v. Idaho State Bar,* 89 P.3d 870 (Idaho 2004) (both client and lawyer—"Defendant A"—appealed board's recommendation of private reprimand for lawyer whose client claimed lawyer overcharged him and failed to provide adequate itemization of legal fees; court imposed private reprimand in public opinion omitting lawyer's name, finding, inter alia, that lawyer did not seek to defraud client, but was at most negligent and unable to account with sufficient detail the work he did for client); *In re Anonymous,* 819 N.E.2d 376 (Ind. 2004) (private reprimand appropriate disciplinary sanction for violating disciplinary rules prohibiting lawyer from communicating with a represented party and using methods to obtain evidence that violate a person's legal rights); *Unnamed Attorney v. Ky. Bar Ass'n,* 345 S.W.3d 851 (Ky. 2011) (court approved the parties' agreement to a private reprimand with the order of private reprimand redacting the lawyer's name and any fact-specific identifying information; order was published by the court and the bar association so as to educate members of the public and the bar concerning misconduct and its ramifications); *Ky. Bar Ass'n v. Unnamed Attorney,* 191 S. W.3d 640 (Ky. 2006) (court published private reprimand issued to lawyer for assisting suspended attorney in activities constituting unauthorized practice of law "so that members of the bar may be informed as to the limitations upon the use of suspended attorneys in their law practice"); *In re Anonymous Member of S.C. Bar*, 699 S.E.2d 693, 694 (S.C. 2010) (while issuing a private admonition against lawyer for engaging in a sexual relationship with wife of a current client, a per se conflict of interest, the court issued a public discussion of the facts, stating that "for the benefit of the bar, we take this opportunity to address what we see as a treacherous area for attorneys").

## *Discipline by Consent*

"Discipline by consent" is a process that allows a lawyer to tender a conditional admission to allegations of misconduct in exchange for an agreed-upon recommendation for the form of discipline to be imposed. In cases where the parties petition for discipline on consent, the hearing panel and court generally must approve the jointly recommended form of discipline. The appropriate use of "discipline by consent," akin to a plea bargain or other forms of negotiated dispositions, allows the respondent lawyer to avoid the trauma and cost of a public proceeding and allows the disciplinary agency to preserve resources. While the consent agreement may call for a public sanction, a petition for discipline on consent also may result in a recommendation for imposition of a private sanction. *See generally* Model Rules for Lawyer Disciplinary Enforcement R. 21 (2007) (outlining procedure for lawyer discipline by consent). Discipline by consent also protects the public. The expedited consent process allows the public to be immediately protected from a lawyer who may continue to commit misconduct while formal proceedings are pending. *See* Model Rules for Lawyer Disciplinary Enforcement R. 21 cmt. (2007).

For other cases involving discipline by consent, *see, e.g., State ex rel. Counsel for Discipline of Supreme Court v. Feller*, 908 N.W.2d 628 (Nebraska 2018) (court accepted voluntary surrender of attorney's license to practice law where lawyer chose not to contest the truth of the allegations that he misappropriated client funds); *Disciplinary Counsel v. Smith*, 93 N.E. 3d 955 (Ohio 2017) (court found that the consent-to-discipline agreement supported an eighteen-month suspension with twelve months stayed with conditions where attorney admitted that he failed to timely file criminal appeal, made misrepresentations to the tribunal, and provided false statements in connection with the disciplinary matter); *Disciplinary Counsel v. Hubbell*, 43 N.E.3d 397 (Ohio 2015) (court approved a consensual discipline of a stayed six-month suspension with the condition that attorney engage in no further misconduct; sanction appropriate for attorney who initiated romantic relationship with client he was representing pro bono in custody dispute); *Disciplinary Counsel v. Simon*, 944 N.E.2d 660 (Ohio 2011) (court adopted consent-to-discipline agreement and stipulation of facts, imposing one-year stayed suspension for admitted misuse of client trust account and failure to respond to information requests during investigation); *In re Danielson*, 706 S.E.2d 1 (S.C. 2011) (discipline by consent agreement accepted and two-year suspension imposed for, inter alia, lawyer's neglect of client matters and failure to refund unearned fees).

Courts considering whether to grant petitions for discipline by consent may accept or reject all or part of the proposed agreed-upon discipline, impose a different sanction, or remand the matter for a full hearing. *See, e.g., In re Goff*, 837 So.2d 1201, 1207 (La. 2003) (formal charges filed against lawyer after court rejected proposed consent discipline of nine-month suspension, deferred in full; court instead imposed nine-month suspension with six months deferred, stating that "we would denigrate the seriousness of runner-based solicitation if we were to adopt a fully deferred suspension under the facts of this case"); *In re Disciplinary Action Against McDonagh*, 822 N.W.2d 468, 472 (N.D. 2012) (court rejected agreed-upon sanction of three-year suspension and imposed disbarment in stipulated discipline case for various misconduct, including knowing conversion of client property and intentional forgery of two title opinions; court disagreed with disciplinary counsel's argument that lawyer's cooperation and restitution outweighed the seriousness of his violations and the presumptive sanction of disbarment, noting that "[w]hile it is important to promote cooperation and restitution, the protection of the public and the profession is paramount"); *Disciplinary Counsel v. O'Malley*, 935 N.E.2d 5 (Ohio 2010) (court imposed two-year suspension with credit for time served under interim felony suspension rule following remand of case after rejection of consent recommendation for twelve-month suspension for elected county recorder convicted of downloading obscene photographs and stories from Internet to personal computers in his home; court found increased sanction warranted due to severity of crime as measured by duration of prison term and subsequent supervised release); *Lawyer Disciplinary Bd. v. Morgan*, 717 S.E.2d 898 (W. Va. 2011) (court agreed with stipulated facts and violations but disagreed with recommended disposition of public reprimand, instead imposing one-year suspension for admitted neglect, failure to communicate, and failure to refund unearned fees in four client matters); *Disciplinary Proceedings Against Ruppelt*, 898 N.W.2d 473, 479 (Wis. 2017) (court rejected stipulation for one-year suspension for conversion of trust account funds, dishonest billing practices, and efforts to conceal the misconduct; court imposed fifteen-month suspension, stating that while ". . . this court often imposes the disciplinary sanctions that parties jointly request, we are free to reject such agreements as circumstances require. . . . Although this court fully appreciates the efficiency attained through stipulations, we will not allow the goal of efficiency to take precedence over the necessity of effecting the core functions of the lawyer disciplinary system.").

While there are many practical reasons for discipline by consent, the abbreviated process can give rise to some concerns and a court should, at a minimum, require that a statement of the facts be made public when it is imposed. *See, e.g., In re Hughes*, 833 N.E.2d 459 (Ind. 2005) (public reprimand imposed upon stipulation as to facts and conditional agreement for discipline; court set forth relevant facts providing basis for sanction due to lawyer's use of improper letterhead omitting jurisdictional limitation of law license and assisting in the unauthorized practice of law); *In re Harris*, 818 So.2d 741 (La. 2002) (court approved joint petition for disbarment on consent, extensively setting forth underlying facts supporting numerous violations, including the unauthorized practice of law with court noting significant aggravating factors); *State ex rel. Counsel for Discipline v. Lauby*, 703 N.W.2d 132 (Neb. 2005) (entering order of disbarment upon consent, court articulated facts of underlying guilty plea to felony sexual assault charge, voluntary surrender of license, and knowing admission to rule violations).

Discipline by consent also can provide the basis for reciprocal discipline in another jurisdiction. *See, e.g., In re Gailliard*, 944 A.2d 1109, 1111 (D.C. 2008) (three-year suspension with reinstatement required appropriate reciprocal discipline for respondent who received indefinite suspension in agreement for discipline by consent in South Carolina for criminal conviction involving striking his teenage son with a truck; indefinite suspension not a sanction in District of Columbia, but suspension for a term of years with fitness requirement for reinstatement is "functionally equivalent discipline"); *In re Megwa*, 252 So.3d 449 (La. 2018) (reciprocal thirty-day suspension by consent followed by a term of probation for a period of eighteen months for failing to timely act on behalf of client and failing to communicate with the client and insurance company); *Matter of Ehrlich*, 2018 WL 4781402 (N.J. October 4, 2018) (three-month reciprocal suspension warranted for attorney who received three-month consensual suspension in Florida for failing to communicate with client, failing to ensure nonlawyer's conduct was compatible with lawyer's obligations, and engaging and assisting in the unauthorized practice of law); *In re Doria*, 165 A.D.3d 33 (N.Y. App. Div. 2018) (attorney entered into agreement for reprimand on consent in New Jersey for charging his client an unreasonable fee for unnecessary legal work; reciprocal public censure imposed in New York); *In re Saidel*, 22 A.D.3d 54 (N.Y. App. Div. 2005) (reciprocal suspension imposed on lawyer who was suspended from practice in Arizona following discipline by consent based upon his guilty plea there to two counts of endangerment, which were class 6 dangerous felonies).

## *Retirement or Resignation While Discipline Pending*

In some jurisdictions, lawyers may agree to retire or resign from the bar. Generally, acceptance of a lawyer's resignation during a time that he or she is subject to disciplinary proceedings is within the court's discretion. *See, e.g., In re Petitto*, 149 A.D.3d 534 (N.Y. App. Div. 2017) (attorney allowed to resign with pending disciplinary proceedings for alleged misappropriation of funds, neglect of legal matters, and failure to account for funds); *State ex rel. Okla. Bar Ass'n v. Knight*, 359

P.3d 1122, 1128 (Okla. 2015) (. . . "[A] lawyer's attempt to waive certain personal procedural and substantive rights and admit to unprofessional conduct in the context of a resignation pending discipline is limited by public interest requirements for making resignation effective."); *Disciplinary Proceedings Against Shepard,* 897 N.W.2d 44, 51 (Wis. 2017) ("The court does not grant an attorney's petition to voluntarily resign from the practice of law when a disciplinary action is pending to avoid the imposition of discipline for unprofessional conduct.").

For more on the process of discipline on consent, *see generally* Jennifer Gerarda Brown & Liana G.T. Wolf, *The Paradox and Promise of Restorative Attorney Discipline,* 12 Nev. L.J. 253 (2012) (noting advantages and disadvantages of negotiated settlements between the respondent and disciplinary counsel); Donald R. Lundberg, *Two Case Studies in the Exercise of Discretion in Lawyer Discipline Systems,* 2009 J. Prof. Law. 107 (2009) (examining discipline on consent within two lawyer discipline systems, one hypothetical system governed by the MRLDE and the other by Indiana's disciplinary system); Lawrence H. Averill, Jr., *The Revised Lawyer Discipline Process in Arkansas: A Primer and Analysis,* 21 U. Ark. Little Rock L. Rev. 13, 70–71 (1998) (describing subsection in Procedures of the Arkansas Supreme Court Regulating Professional Conduct of Attorneys at Law dealing with negotiated settlements of discipline proceedings that have reached formal status; lawyer/respondent may admit unethical conduct in exchange for agreed disciplinary sanction; process is distinct from voluntary surrender of license procedure; noting settlement agreement must set out facts, admitted rule violations, and sanction); David B. Rubin, *Representing Respondents in Attorney Ethics Proceedings,* 177 N.J. Law. 27 (1996) (discussing discipline on consent as option in defending ethics charge; noting that sixty-day cutoff date after time prescribed for filing answer to complaint saves both parties time and the expense of hearing preparation; suggesting "discipline by consent" is the equivalent of plea bargaining).

## 1.3 Purpose of These Standards

**These standards are designed for use in imposing a sanction or sanctions following a determination by clear and convincing evidence that a member of the legal profession has violated a provision of the Model Rules of Professional Conduct (or applicable standard under the laws of the jurisdiction where the proceeding is brought). Descriptions in these standards of substantive disciplinary offenses are not intended to create grounds for determining culpability independent of the Model Rules. The Standards constitute a model, setting forth a comprehensive system for determining sanctions, permitting flexibility and creativity in assigning sanctions in particular cases of lawyer misconduct. They are designed to promote: (1) consideration of all factors relevant to imposing the appropriate level of sanction in an individual case; (2) consideration of the appropriate weight of such factors in light of the stated goals of lawyer discipline; (3) consistency in the imposition of disciplinary sanctions for the same or similar offenses within and among jurisdictions.**

## Annotation

### *A Model for Imposing Sanctions*

The ABA Standards for Imposing Lawyer Sanctions ("Sanctions Standards") were developed as guidelines for use by courts and disciplinary agencies in imposing sanctions *following* a finding of lawyer misconduct. Since their promulgation, the Sanctions Standards have been so used by courts. Opinions in disciplinary cases reflect courts' general acceptance of and reliance upon the Sanctions Standards. *See, e.g., In re Schuler,* 818 P.2d 138, 139 (Alaska 1991) (in determining appropriate sanction, "we will refer to the ABA Standards and methodology as an appropriate model for determining sanctions for lawyer misconduct in this state") (citation omitted); *People v. Snyder,* 418 P.3d 550 (Colo. O.P.D.J. 2018) (the Standards and Colorado Supreme Court case law guide the imposition of discipline); *In re Beauregard,* 189 A.3d 1236 (Del. 2018) (court is guided by the ABA Standards for Imposing Lawyer Sanctions and precedent when determining appropriate discipline to impose); *In re Doughty,* 832 A.2d 724 (Del. 2003) (Sanctions Standards are model for determining appropriate discipline to further objectives of protecting public, advancing administration of justice, preserving confidence in legal profession, and deterring other lawyers from similar misconduct); *Fla. Bar v. Johnson,* 132 So.3d 32, 38 (Fla. 2013) (generally, court "will not second-guess the referee's recommended discipline as long as it has a reasonable basis in existing case law and the Florida Standards for Imposing Lawyer Sanctions"); *In re Buckner,*

421 P.3d 226, 246 (Kan. 2018) ("Although not mandated by this court's rules, this court historically looks to the American Bar Association Standards for Imposing Lawyer Sanctions . . . to guide our determination of the appropriate discipline to impose.") (citations omitted); *Grievance Adm'r v. Lopatin*, 612 N.W.2d 120, 123 (Mich. 2000) (court adopts Sanctions Standards to "further the purposes of attorney discipline, help to identify the appropriate factors for consideration in imposing discipline and establish a framework for selecting a sanction in a particular case"); *In re Disciplinary Action Against Kaiser*, 484 N.W.2d 102, 106 (N.D. 1992) ("We treat the Standards as guidelines for assigning a sanction for particular misconduct.") (citing North Dakota Standards for Imposing Lawyer Sanctions adopted in 1988 and based on ABA Sanctions Standards); *Bd. of Prof'l Responsibility v. Parrish*, 556 S.W.3d 153, 167 (Tenn. 2018) (in determining appropriate sanction, "the ABA Standards serve as guideposts, and they direct the court, in applying the Standards, to consider . . ."); *In re Discipline of Lundgren*, 355 P.3d 984 (Utah 2015) (while Utah Standards are derived from ABA Sanctions Standards, they are more general and streamlined); *In re Disciplinary Proceeding Against Cottingham*, 423 P.3d 818, 827 (Wash. 2018) (guided by ABA Standards, court suspended lawyer for eighteen-months for engaging in frivolous litigation with the intent to harass; "We apply the ABA Standards in all lawyer discipline cases.").

Courts have relied upon the Sanctions Standards to varying degrees. *See, e.g., United States v. Koubriti*, 305 F. Supp. 2d 723 (E.D. Mich. 2003) (based on a number of considerations, the court found the Sanctions Standards relevant and helpful in resolving that admonition was the appropriate discipline for U.S. Attorney General John Ashcroft for violation of court order prohibiting public comments during criminal trial; court considered the nature of the ethical duty violated and found that the Attorney General's conduct implicated duties owed to the legal system); *Romero-Barcelo v. Acevedo-Vila*, 275 F. Supp. 2d 177, 192 (D.P.R. 2003) (applying Standards "as a basic, but not conclusive guide"). *See also In re Stepovich*, 386 P.3d 1205, 1208 (Alaska 2016) ("In determining the appropriate sanction, we apply our independent judgment. And we exercise that independent judgment to 'determine sanctions on a case-by-case basis, guided but not constrained by the American Bar Association's Standards for Imposing Lawyer Sanctions and by the sanctions imposed in comparable disciplinary proceedings.'"); *In re Abrams*, 257 P.3d 167, 170 (Ariz. 2011) ("In assessing sanctions, the Court is guided by the American Bar Association's Standards for Imposing Lawyer Sanctions.") (citations omitted); *People v. Rider*, 109 P.3d 1075, 1079–80 (Colo. O.P.D.J. 2005) (Sanctions Standards "are the guiding authority for selecting the appropriate sanction to impose for lawyer misconduct"); *Disciplinary Counsel v. Serafinowicz*, 123 A.3d 1279 (Conn. 2015) (Connecticut courts consult Sanctions Standards in evaluating attorney misconduct and in determining appropriate discipline); *In re Bailey*, 821 A.2d 851 (Del. 2003) (to fulfill objectives of disciplinary system Sanctions Standards used as guide); *In re Finley*, 488 S.E.2d 74 (Ga. 1997) (court guided by Sanctions Standards when determining sanction); *Office of Disciplinary Counsel v. Au*, 113 P.3d 203, 217 (Haw. 2005) ("The ABA Standards are a useful reference when determining disciplinary sanctions.") (citation omitted); *In re Atanga*, 636 N.E.2d 1253, 1260 (Ind. 1994) (court relies heavily upon Sanctions Standards, finding they "provide a good measure of the proportionality of any particular sanction to the alleged misconduct"); *In re Holmes*, 416 P.3d 143 (Kan. 2018) ("although not mandated by our rules, this court and disciplinary panels 'historically' turn to the ABA Standards for Imposing Lawyer Sanctions to guide the discipline discussion."); *In re Frank*, 876 So.2d 57 (La. 2004) (court considers Sanctions Standards and relevant jurisprudence to determine baseline sanction); *Att'y Grievance Com'n. v. Davy*, 80 A.3d 322, 341 (Md. 2013) (court has "looked often" to the Sanctions Standards); *Gex v. Miss. Bar*, 656 So.2d 1124, 1131 (Miss. 1995) (Sanctions Standards "helpful guidelines" for setting sanctions, citing other Mississippi cases invoking Sanctions Standards); *In re Krigel*, 480 S.W.3d 294 (Mo. 2016) (Sanctions Standards, similar past cases, and the disciplinary rules determine appropriate sanction); *In re Richmond's Case*, 872 A.2d 1023 (N.H. 2005) (though court has not adopted Sanctions Standards, it looks to them for guidance); *In re Stein*, 177 P.3d 513 (N.M. 2008) (Sanctions Standards provide guidance to court although not formally adopted); *In re Bertoni*, 426 P.3d 64 (Or. 2018) (in determining appropriate sanction court initially looks to ABA Standards); *In re Discipline of Russell*, 797 N.W.2d 77, 90 (S.D. 2011) ("Although the court has not adopted the ABA Standards for Imposing Lawyer Sanctions, we do consult them for guidance.") *Bd. of Prof'l Responsibility v. Sheppard*, 556 S.W.3d 139 (Tenn. 2018) ("The ABA Standards provide 'guideposts' for attorney discipline but are not considered 'rigid rules that dictate a particular outcome.'"); *In re Connor*, 191 A.3d 970 (Vt. 2018) (when sanctioning lawyer misconduct, court looks to Sanctions Standards for guidance); *In re Disciplinary Proceeding Against McGrath*, 280 P.3d 1091, 1101 (Wash. 2012) ("We use the ABA *Standards* as a guide to determine the appropriate sanction for misconduct. The guidelines are not rigid but are designed to permit 'flexibility and creativity in assigning sanctions.'") (quoting Standard 1.3) (citations omitted); *Lawyer Disciplinary Bd. v. Scott*, 579 S.E.2d 550 (W. Va. 2003) (court citing Sanctions Standards and formally adopting the mitigating factors outlined in the Standards).

## *Consistency as Goal*

The Sanctions Standards are designed to promote consistency in the imposition of sanctions for the same or similar offenses within and among jurisdictions. Courts have echoed this purpose. *See, e.g., In re Vance*, 421 P.3d 53 (Alaska 2018) citing *In re Buckalew*, 731 P.2d 48, 52 (Alaska 1986) (court says Standards "combine clear, straight-forward guidelines which ensure a level of consistency necessary for fairness to the public and the legal system with the flexibility and creativity essential to secure justice to the disciplined lawyer"); *In re Pappas,* 768 P.2d 1161 (Ariz. 1988) (guided by principle that effective system of professional sanctions must have internal consistency and citing appropriateness of Standard 1.3, inter alia, in examining sanctions imposed in cases factually similar to respondent's case); *In re Malik,* 167 A.3d 1189 (Del. 2017) (court looks to Sanctions Standards to promote consistency and predictability in imposition of sanctions); *In re Disciplinary Proceeding Against Curran,* 801 P.2d 962, 973 (Wash. 1990) (Adoption of Sanctions Standards reflects the court's agreement with purpose they are meant to serve, creating consistency in imposing sanctions both within and between jurisdictions: "We believe . . . that inconsistencies within a jurisdiction are even more corrosive than inconsistencies between jurisdictions. We reviewed this case for that reason and the sanction we impose will reflect this commitment to consistency as well.").

Some commentators have registered concern regarding inconsistency in sanctions both within and among jurisdictions, suggesting that improper or inconsistent application of the Standards facilitates continued uneven imposition of discipline. *See* Fred C. Zacharias, *The Purposes of Lawyer Discipline,* 45 Wm. & Mary L. Rev. 675 (2003) (arguing that regulators' failure to focus on purposes of discipline has resulted in inconsistent case law and clouded messages to prosecutors and profession; noting that Sanctions Standards recognize multiple purposes of discipline but criticizing them as providing "limitless flexibility" for identifying sanctions and weighing aggravating and mitigating factors); Leslie C. Levin, *The Emperor's Clothes and Other Tales About the Standards for Imposing Lawyer Discipline Sanctions,* 48 Am. U. L. Rev. 1 (1998) (praising Sanctions Standards as "an important first attempt to provide consistency and fairness in the imposition of sanctions" but arguing that their voluntary nature of and lack of specificity "invite inconsistency in their application"); *see also* Michael Goldman, Note, *Discipline of McLendon and Discipline of Petersen: Adding Chaos to Confusion in Washington Legal Ethics,* 29 Gonz. L. Rev. 187, 203–04 (1994) (comparing analogous conversion cases that resulted in irreconcilable holdings: in one case, the court imposed a two-year suspension with conditions and, in the other, it disbarred the lawyer; the author argued that in the first case the court failed adequately to consider the aggravating and mitigating circumstances set out in the Sanctions Standards, while in the second, the court considered all four framework factors; the author noted: "In order to avoid a loss of public confidence in the bar, the judiciary must treat like cases alike and not construct paper walls where no real distinction between cases exists. Only by applying the ABA Standards in an equitable and comprehensive manner can the judiciary achieve the consistency and fairness the general public and bar deserve.").

## *Sanctions Must Reflect Individual Circumstances*

While the Sanctions Standards set forth a model for achieving consistency in the imposition of disciplinary sanctions, they also recognize that sanctions must reflect the unique facts and circumstances of each case, and therefore provide for consideration of aggravating and mitigating circumstances relating to each lawyer. *See Romero-Barcelo v. Acevedo-Vila*, 275 F. Supp. 2d 177 (D.P.R. 2003) (citing Standard 1.3, noting Sanctions Standards are adaptable, and recognizing that discipline must reflect each individual lawyer's circumstances and provide for consideration of aggravating and mitigating factors in each case); *In re Attorney F.*, 285 P.3d 322, 326 (Colo. O.P.D.J 2012) (quoting comment to Standard 1.3 "While these standards set forth a comprehensive model to be used in imposing sanctions, they also recognize that sanctions imposed must reflect the circumstances of each individual lawyer, and therefore provide for consideration of aggravating and mitigating circumstances in each case.") *In re Rumsey*, 71 P.3d 1150, 1159 (Kan. 2003) ("The discipline must be based on the specific facts and circumstances of each case, so other disciplinary actions provide little guidance."); *In re Mitchell*, 145 So.3d 305, 318 (La. 2014) ("The discipline to be imposed depends upon the facts of each case and the seriousness of the offenses involved considered in light of any aggravating and mitigating circumstances.") *Grievance Adm'r v. Bowman*, 612 N.W.2d 820, 823 (Mich. 2000) (ordering application of Sanctions Standards on remand and citing Standard 1.3, court stated that while finding of misconduct generally should result in a sanction, "in the rare case where the mitigating factors clearly outweigh the aggravating factors as well as the nature and harm of the misconduct, an order of no discipline may still be appropriate"); *In re Hulstrand*, 910 N.W.2d 436 (Minn. 2018) (sanction determination is tailored to the specific facts of each case); *Bd. of Prof'l Responsibility v. Sheppard*, 556 S.W.3d 139, 149 (Tenn. 2018) ("The purpose of the ABA Standards is to 'promote . . . consideration of all factors relevant to imposing the appropriate level of sanction in an individual case.'") (citation omitted). In *In re Discipline of Crawley*, 164 P.3d 1232, 1237 (Utah 2007), the Utah Supreme Court, citing its Standard 1.3 (modeled on the ABA standards), noted with approval that the Sanctions Standards permit flexibility and creativity in assigning sanctions and that district courts have embraced this approach. The court said:

> We are satisfied—indeed pleased—with the discretion currently being exercised by district courts in sanctioning attorneys for misconduct. It is a delicate and often difficult task to craft sanctions appropriate for individual attorneys, no two of which have engaged in the same misconduct under the same aggravating and mitigating circumstances.

*See also People v. Swarts*, 414 P.3d 1168, 1172 (Colo. O.P.D.J. 2018) ("[t]he court recognizes the Colorado Supreme Court's directive to exercise discretion in imposing a sanction and to carefully apply aggravating and mitigating factors, and is mindful that 'individual circumstances make extremely problematic any meaningful comparison of discipline ultimately imposed in different cases.'"); *In re Disciplinary Proceeding Against Petersen*, 846 P.2d 1330 (Wash. 1993) (dissenting Justice Robert Utter, questioning whether lawyer's mental state justified disbarment, noted that Sanctions Standards do not purport to recommend type of discipline to be imposed in any particular case; citing Standard 1.3, he stated that discipline imposed must reflect the circumstances of each individual lawyer, and therefore provide for consideration of aggravating and mitigating circumstances in each case). (See Annotation to Standard 9.0, Aggravation and Mitigation.)

## *Clear and Convincing Evidence*

When disciplinary proceedings are brought against lawyers alleged to have engaged in unethical conduct, disciplinary counsel in most jurisdictions have the burden of proving misconduct by "clear and convincing evidence." *See, e.g.*, Model Rules for Lawyer Disciplinary Enforcement R. 18(C) (2007). *See generally ABA/BNA Lawyers' Manual on Professional Conduct*, "Misconduct and Discipline: Procedure," pp. 101:2101–11 *et seq.* (canvassing standards of proof for disciplinary charges; noting majority of jurisdictions hold that disciplinary charges must be proved by clear and convincing evidence, minority of states use combination of that standard with "preponderance" language, while some use standard of "a fair preponderance").

"Clear and convincing" in the context of a disciplinary proceeding is a rigorous evidentiary standard, but one that falls short of the "beyond a reasonable doubt" requirement imposed in criminal cases. *See Sowell v. Dicara*, 127 A.3d 356, 370 (Conn. App. Ct. 2015) ("[C]lear and convincing proof denotes a degree of belief that lies between the belief that is required to find the truth or existence of the [fact in issue] in an ordinary civil action and the belief that is required to find guilt in a criminal prosecution.") (citation omitted, internal quotation marks omitted). In *In re Doughty*, 832 A.2d 724, 732 (Del. 2003), the Delaware Supreme Court noted that a presumption of knowledge—in this case that the respondent should have known he was required to maintain a bona fide office for the practice of law in Delaware and that his failure to do so constituted a knowing violation of a court rule—could not satisfy disciplinary counsel's burden of proving the element of knowledge by clear and convincing evidence. The Court held, "In the face of evidence to the contrary, a presumption of knowledge cannot satisfy the [disciplinary counsel's] burden of proving, by clear and convincing evidence, the element of knowledge." *See also In re Szymkowicz*, 124 A.3d 1078 (D.C. 2015) (procedural requirements in lawyer discipline cases are analogous to other contested cases; the burden of proof is on bar counsel to support factual findings by clear and convincing evidence); *Idaho State Bar v. Malmin*, 78 P.3d 371 (Idaho 2003) (conclusion of misconduct involving dishonesty, fraud, deceit, or misrepresentation requires proof by clear and convincing evidence of both a misrepresentation and intent to deceive); *In re Eliasen*, 913 P.2d 1163, 1167 (Idaho 1996) ("The burden of proof in formal proceedings is 'clear and undoubted preponderance of the evidence,' which is synonymous with 'clear and convincing evidence.'") (citations omitted); *In re Baca*, 253 P.3d 348 (Kan. 2011) (lawyer misconduct must be established by clear and convincing evidence); *In re Gates*, 2018 WL 5629020 (La. October 29, 2018) (court conducts independent review of record to determine whether misconduct has been proven by clear and convincing evidence); *Matter of Studtmann*, 427 P.3d 964, 977 (Kan. 2018) (clear and convincing evidence has been defined as "evidence that causes the factfinder to believe that 'the truth of the facts asserted is highly probable.'"); *In re Disciplinary Action Against Stoneburner*, 882 N.W.2d 200, 203 (Minn. 2016) ("Clear and convincing evidence requires more than a preponderance of the evidence, but less than proof beyond a reasonable doubt."); *Bd. of Prof'l Responsibility v. Mears*, 418 P.3d 829, 832 (Wyo. 2018) ("[t]o impose discipline, we must be satisfied that there is substantial, clear, convincing and satisfactory evidence supporting the findings . . ."). Other courts also have adopted the clear and convincing standard in disciplinary cases and have offered interpretations of it. In *In re Drakulich*, 908 P.2d 709 (Nev. 1995), for example, the Nevada Supreme Court said the evidence required in lawyer discipline matters is a higher degree of proof than that required in ordinary civil proceedings. It defined clear and convincing evidence as "satisfactory" proof that is

> so strong and cogent as to satisfy the mind and conscience of a common man, and so to convince him that he would venture to act upon that conviction in matters of the highest concern and importance to his own interest. It need not possess such a degree of force as to be irresistible, but there must be evidence of tangible facts from which a legitimate inference . . . may be drawn.

908 P.2d at 715 (citations omitted). *See also In re Disciplinary Action Against Ward*, 881 N.W.2d 226, 229 (N.D. 2016) (court gives due weight to recommendations of the Disciplinary Board, but does not act as "rubber stamp"; disciplinary counsel must prove each alleged violation by clear and convincing evidence); *In re Summer*, 105 P.3d 848 (Or. 2005) (to prove ethics violation based on criminal act that reflects adversely on lawyer's honesty, trustworthiness or fitness to practice law, lawyer need not be convicted of crime, and bar need only establish the criminal act by clear and convincing evidence rather than beyond a reasonable doubt); *In re Disciplinary Proceeding Against Jones*, 338 P.3d 842, 852 (Wash. 2014) (in attorney disciplinary proceedings misconduct must be proven by a clear preponderance of the evidence; "Clear preponderance 'requires more proof than simple preponderance,

but less than beyond a reasonable doubt.'"); *accord Romero-Barcelo v. Acevedo-Vila*, 275 F. Supp. 2d 177 (D.P.R. 2003); *In re Alexander*, 300 P.3d 536 (Ariz. 2013); *In re Morse*, 900 P.2d 1170 (Cal. 1995); *Fla. Bar v. Martocci*, 699 So.2d 1357 (Fla. 1997); *Idaho State Bar v. Clark*, 283 P.3d 96 (Idaho 2012); *In re Edmonds*, 21 N.E.3d 447 (Ill. 2014); *Matter of Wall*, 73 N.E.3d 170 (Ind. 2017); *Att'y Grievance Comm'n v. Levin*, 91 A.3d 1001 (Md. 2014); *Crosby v. Miss. Bar*, 2018 WL 3061961 (Miss. September 20, 2018); *In re Johnson*, 84 P.3d 637 (Mont. 2004); *State ex rel. Counsel for Discipline v. Wolfe*, 918 N.W.2d 244 (Neb. 2018); *In re Ramirez*, 408 P.3d 1065 (Or. 2018); *In re Jordan*, 809 S.E.2d 5409 (S.C. 2018); *Lawyer Disciplinary Bd. v. Sirk*, 810 S.E.2d 276 (W. Va. 2018).

The clear and convincing standard is equated with a high degree of probability that the alleged misconduct is true. *See, e.g., In re Alexander*, 300 P.3d 536, 540 (Ariz. 2013) (state bar meets burden of clear and convincing evidence if it shows that it is "highly probable" allegations are true); *People v. Distel*, 759 P.2d 654, 661 (Colo. 1988) ("clear and convincing evidence" standard of proof in attorney disciplinary proceedings requires proof that persuades trier of fact that truth of contention is highly probable and is evidence that is stronger than preponderance of the evidence); *Chief Disciplinary Counsel v. Rozbicki*, 2013 WL 1277298, at *6 (Conn. March 8, 2013) ("[The burden] is sustained if evidence induces in the mind of the trier a reasonable belief that the facts asserted are highly probably true, that the probability that they are true or exist is substantially greater than the probability that they are false or do not exist.") (citation omitted, internal quotation marks omitted); *In re Haley*, 411 P.3d 1216, 1224 (Kan. 2018) (clear and convincing evidence is "'evidence that causes the factfinder to believe that the truth of the facts asserted is highly probable") (citation omitted); *State ex rel. Okla. Bar Ass'n v. Godlove*, 318 P.3d 1086, 1088 (Okla. 2013) (noting clear and convincing evidence "is sufficient evidence, both in quality and quantity, so as to produce a firm conviction of the truth of the allegations") (citation omitted); *In re McGraw*, 414 P.3d 841 (Or. 2018) (defining "clear and convincing evidence" as evidence "establishing that the truth of the facts asserted is highly probable").

## *Facts Deemed Admitted*

In some circumstances, allegations are deemed established by clear and convincing evidence, such as when findings of fact are uncontested by either party or when a lawyer fails to file a timely answer to a disciplinary complaint. *See, e.g., In re Moak*, 71 P.3d 343 (Ariz. 2003) (charges proved by clear and convincing evidence when most facts were stipulated and, along with remaining findings, were set forth thoroughly in hearing officer's report, which neither lawyer nor state bar contested); *People v. Collins*, 348 P.3d 993 (Colo. O.P.D.J 2014) (regulation counsel not required to prove allegations by clear and convincing evidence since allegations were taken as true and proven upon lawyer's default for failing to timely file answer); *In re Labadie*, 2018 WL 5629072 (La. October 29, 2018) (when lawyer does not answer formal charges, Office of Disciplinary Counsel has no additional burden to prove allegations, but evidence may be required to prove legal conclusions if not readily apparent from facts deemed admitted); *In re Moran*, 95 N.E.3d 226 (Mass. 2018) (admissions contained in pleadings are considered established); *In re Hursey*, 719 S.E.2d 670 (S.C. 2011) (disciplinary counsel met burden of establishing misconduct by clear and convincing evidence after factual allegations deemed admitted when respondent found in default for failing to answer and appear at proceedings); *Lawyer Disciplinary Bd. v. Morgan*, 717 S.E. 898 (W. Va. 2011) (misconduct proved by clear and convincing evidence when parties have stipulated to facts).

In reciprocal disciplinary matters, facts proven in one jurisdiction are deemed proven for the purposes of discipline in a sister jurisdiction. In such situations, the burden of proof is on the respondent lawyer rather than on disciplinary counsel to demonstrate that reciprocal discipline is not appropriate. *See, e.g., In re Williams*, 398 F.3d 116, 119–20 (1st Cir. 2005) (imposing reciprocal disbarment following disbarment order from the Maine Supreme Judicial Court; "[w]hen all is said and done, the respondent attorney must carry the devoir of persuasion, by clear and convincing evidence, that imposition of reciprocal discipline is unwarranted.); *In re Silva*, 703 Fed.Appx 104 (3d Cir. 2017) (lawyers subject to reciprocal discipline in federal court bear burden of demonstrating by clear and convincing evidence the presence of a serious infirmity in the state proceeding); *In re Palmisano*, 70 F.3d 483, 486 (7th Cir. 1995) (respondent disbarred in state court contended that federal court should employ a "reasonable doubt" standard and therefore make an independent decision because Illinois had used a "clear and convincing evidence" standard; district court disagreed, holding that Illinois applied a standard at least as demanding as the federal approach and it was entitled to accept state's findings); *Miss. Bar v. Burtoff*, 2018 WL 5076927, at *1 (Miss. October 18, 2018) (though bar typically bears burden of proof by clear and convincing evidence, certified copy of the judgment of public reprimand is "conclusive evidence of the guilt of the offense or unprofessional conduct on which said sanction was ordered").

# B. Sanctions

## 2.1 Scope

**A disciplinary sanction is imposed on a lawyer upon a finding or acknowledgement that the lawyer has engaged in professional misconduct.**

## Annotation

### *Sui Generis Proceedings*

Disciplinary proceedings and the sanctions imposed upon lawyers are neither criminal nor civil in nature, but are sui generis. As the U.S. Court of Appeals for the Seventh Circuit stated in *In re Echeles*, 430 F.2d 347 (7th Cir. 1970):

> [I]t would be well to note that disbarment and suspension proceedings are neither civil nor criminal in nature but are special proceedings, sui generis, and result from the inherent power of courts over their officers. Such proceedings are not lawsuits between parties litigant but rather are in the nature of an inquest or inquiry as to the conduct of the respondent. They are not for the purpose of punishment, but rather seek to determine the fitness of an officer of the court to continue in that capacity and to protect the courts and the public from the official ministration of persons unfit to practice.

*Id.* at 349; *see, e.g., Ligon v. Stilley*, 371 S.W.3d 615 (Ark. 2010) (reiterating that lawyer disciplinary proceedings are sui generis by nature and neither civil nor criminal); *In re Parker*, No. 95-PM-17584, 1997 WL 652367 (Cal. Bar Ct. Oct. 7, 1997) (state bar disciplinary proceedings, including probation revocation proceedings, are sui generis); *Smith v. Mullarkey*, 121 P.3d 890, 892 (Colo. 2005) ("The district courts have no jurisdiction over Bar proceedings, including those relating to admission, discipline, and disbarment, because such proceedings are neither criminal nor civil, but rather sui generis."); *Disciplinary Counsel v. Sporn*, 157 A.3d 108 (Conn. App. 2017) (proceeding to disbar or suspend lawyer is neither civil nor criminal in nature but is a proceeding sui generis); *In re Benjamin*, 698 A.2d 434 (D.C. 1997) (given sui generis nature of disciplinary proceedings, lawyers are not afforded all protections extended to criminal defendants); *In re Mitchell*, 145 So.3d 305 (La. 2014) (disciplinary proceedings stem from court's inherent exclusive original jurisdiction and are neither civil nor criminal but sui generis); *State ex rel. Okla.*

*Bar Ass'n v. Patterson*, 28 P.3d 551, 554 (Okla. 2001); ("A bar disciplinary proceeding is sui generis."); *In re Barber*, 904 P.2d 620 (Or. 1995) (lawyer disciplinary proceedings are sui generis, being neither civil nor criminal in nature); *In re Discipline of Lajeunesse*, 416 P.3d 1122 (Utah 2018) (court's review of attorney disciplinary matters is sui generis, giving some deference to district court by retaining discretion to overrule based on court's constitutional regulatory authority); *cf. Favaloro v. Comm'n for Lawyer Discipline*, 994 S.W.2d 815 (Tex. App. 1999) (rejecting contention that disciplinary actions are quasi-criminal in nature and reiterating that they are civil actions).

As noted *supra § Constitutional and Civil Protections, Double Jeopardy*, in part, because disciplinary proceedings are sui generis, they do not trigger double jeopardy considerations. *See also In re Caranchini*, 160 F.3d 420, 424 (8th Cir. 1998) (lawyer discipline "is not 'punishment' for purposes of double jeopardy"; upholding disbarment order by federal court based on state court findings and judgment of disbarment proceedings arising from Rule 11 sanctions imposed against lawyer in four separate federal cases); *In re Triem*, 929 P.2d 634 (Alaska 1996) (double jeopardy does not preclude judicial review of a lawyer's conduct in a disciplinary complaint); *In re Fisher*, 202 P.3d 1186, 1199 (Colo. 2009) (court rejected respondent's argument that double jeopardy applied to disciplinary proceedings, noting that "[i]n fact, this court has specifically held double jeopardy concepts do not apply to attorney discipline proceedings"); *Miss. Bar v. Coleman*, 849 So.2d 867, 874 (Miss. 2002) ("The case law, in this jurisdiction and others, could not be clearer. Double jeopardy is triggered *only* in a criminal setting, and as such is inapplicable to disciplinary proceedings."); *In re Chastain*, 532 S.E.2d 264 (S.C. 2000) (supreme court reiterates that other courts uniformly have concluded that double jeopardy clause is not implicated in disciplinary proceedings because disciplinary proceedings, whether classified as civil, quasi-criminal, or special, are not criminal in nature). For more discussion of double jeopardy and the nature of disciplinary proceedings, see Annotation to Standard 1.1.

## *Jurisdiction of State's Highest Court*

Disciplinary proceedings are conducted and sanctions imposed under authority of a U.S. jurisdiction's highest court of appellate jurisdiction, except in jurisdictions such as New York, where each of the four intermediate appellate courts have authority to impose discipline on lawyers. *See, e.g., In re Creasy*, 12 P.3d 214 (Ariz. 2000) (court has the exclusive power to regulate the practice of law, which includes disciplining lawyers); *Dodrill v. Exec. Dir., Comm'n on Prof'l Conduct*, 824 S.W.2d 383, 386 (Ark. 1992) (court rejected contention that federal rather than state disciplinary process should have been pursued because lawyer's misconduct occurred in federal court, holding that "[t]he fact that federal disciplinary rules may also exist affects the exclusive jurisdiction of this court over the conduct of this state's attorneys not one iota"); *People v. Shields*, 905 P.2d 608 (Colo. 1995) (grievance committee recommendation as to discipline is advisory only, as the Colorado Supreme Court retains independent authority to determine appropriate discipline); *In re Enna*, 971 A.2d 110, 113 (Del. 2009) ("This Court has the 'inherent and exclusive authority' to discipline Delaware attorneys.") (citation omitted); *Iowa Supreme Ct. Bd. of Prof'l Ethics & Conduct v. Mulford*, 625 N.W.2d 672 (Iowa 2001) (Iowa Supreme Court's authority to discipline lawyer admitted to practice in state is not suspended merely because lawyer does not hold active license and is not actively practicing law); *In re Laudumiey*, 849 So.2d 515, 523 (La. 2003) ("Regardless of the recommendation of the disciplinary board, 'it is the ultimate duty of this court to determine under the broad discretion vested in it what action, if any is to be taken against an attorney charged with misconduct. . . .'"); (citation omitted); *Att'y Grievance Comm'n v. Clevenger*, 187 A.3d 81 (Md. 2018) (it is a long-established principle that court of appeals possesses "original and complete" jurisdiction over lawyer discipline); *In re Riehm*, 883 N.W.2d 223 (Minn. 2016) (court's constitutional authority to regulate the practice of law comes from separation of powers present in Minnesota Constitution); *In re Schaefer*, 31 P.3d 365 (Nev. 2001) (Nevada Supreme Court has final authority over lawyer discipline); *In re Gallant's Case*, 177 A.2d 1283 (N.H. 2017) (New Hampshire Supreme Court retains ultimate authority to determine whether suspension in disciplinary case is necessary); *State ex rel. Okla. Bar Ass'n v. Knight*, 421 P.3d 299 (Okla. 2018) (court's exclusive regulatory authority over the practice of law, licensure, ethics, and discipline is constitutionally vested, nondelegable power); *In re Poff*, 714 S.E.2d 313, 319 (S.C. 2011) (court has "sole authority to discipline attorneys and decide appropriate sanctions after a thorough review of the record"); *In re Discipline of Welker*, 100 P.3d 1197 (Utah 2004) (lawyer discipline cases come to district court as partial delegation of authority of Utah Supreme Court, in contrast to matters of general jurisdiction of district courts); *In re Disciplinary Proceeding Against Cottingham*, 423 P.3d 818 (Wash. 2018) (state supreme court is definitive authority for lawyer discipline in the state).

### *Sanctions Distinct from Other Penalties*

Disciplinary sanctions are separate and distinct from penalties that may be imposed solely for civil or criminal conduct, including contempt of court. *See, e.g., In re Slattery*, 767 A.2d 203, 207 (D.C. 2001) ("A finding by clear and convincing evidence that the conduct at issue was a criminal act that merits disciplinary sanction is something altogether different than a finding beyond a reasonable doubt that the conduct merits conviction and criminal penalty. The first is within our disciplinary province; the second is not."); *In re Treinen*, 131 P.3d 1282 (N.M. 2006) (criminal conviction is not prerequisite to lawyer discipline for criminal conduct; sentence of conditional discharge does not preclude imposition of discipline); *In re*

*Harris*, 49 P.3d 778 (Or. 2002) (state statute identifies lawyer disciplinary proceeding as within court's regulatory authority over those who practice in the courts, rather than as criminal law process).

## *Violation of Administrative Rules*

Disciplinary sanctions also may be imposed on lawyers who violate administrative rules or regulations applicable to members of the bar, such as failing to pay dues or to attend mandatory CLE programs. *See, e.g., People v. Clark*, 900 P.2d 129 (Colo. 1995) (one-year-and-one-day suspension for failure to comply with mandatory CLE requirements and continuing to practice law after administrative suspension, among other misconduct); *People v. Pernell*, 86 P.3d 429 (Colo. O.P.D.J. 2004) (disbarment for misconduct following administrative suspension for failing to comply with CLE requirements); *In re Fountain*, 878 A.2d 1167 (Del. 2005) (three-year suspension for failure to complete CLE requirements, in addition to other misconduct such as multiyear failure to maintain books and records, safeguard client property, and pay taxes); *In re Pitre*, 903 So.2d 1130 (La. 2005) (disbarment for representing clients while ineligible as result of failure to pay bar dues and failure to fulfill mandatory CLE requirements); *In re Domm*, 883 So.2d 966, 972 (La. 2004) (disbarment for several instances of misconduct, including lawyer's "long history of failing to pay his bar dues and the disciplinary assessment, and of failing to complete his MCLE requirements, [that] demonstrate that he has no respect for his obligations as a professional"); *In re Bull*, 788 N.W.2d 890 (Minn. 2010) (public reprimand and two-year probation for representing multiple clients while on administrative suspension for failure to complete CLE requirements).

## *Transfer to Disability Inactive Status*

A lawyer whose ability to practice law is impaired by a physical or mental condition should be transferred to disability inactive status; whether professional misconduct has been committed is not necessarily determinative. *See* Model Rules for Lawyer Disciplinary Enforcement R. 23 (2007); *see, e.g., In re Dixon*, 744 So.2d 618 (La. 1999) (court ordered transfer to disability inactive status but deferred actual transfer for supervised probation for lawyer who issued bad checks, misconduct that was directly related to and caused by his alcoholism and drug addiction; upon successful completion of probation conditions, transfer to disability inactive status to be set aside); *In re Bailey*, 235 So.3d 1091 (La. 2018) (lawyer placed on disability inactive status in Tennessee meets criteria for reciprocal disability inactive status as shown by medical records); *In re Dwyer-Jones*, 24 N.E.3d 566 (Mass. 2015) (applying principle of equivalency in practical application, court in Massachusetts placed respondent who was previously suspended in Maine, a jurisdiction without disability inactive status, on disability inactive status); *In re Shontz*, 224 P.3d 603 (Mont. 2009) (transfer to disability inactive status necessary because lawyer's health and well-being diminished to such an extent that he was unable to assist in his defense; disciplinary proceeding stayed indefinitely); *In re Disciplinary Action Against Balerud,* 679 N.W.2d 768 (N.D. 2004) (lawyer placed on disability inactive status after court agreed he was medically incapable of responding to the allegations and charges pending before him; disciplinary proceedings stayed for sixty days pending psychiatrist evaluation); *cf. In re Hornbeck,* 61 A.D.3d 1268 (N.Y. App. Div. 2009) (in reciprocal proceeding, indefinite suspension by reason of incapacity imposed on lawyer who was transferred to disability inactive status in originating jurisdiction based on finding that he posed a substantial threat to the public). *See generally* Tricia S. Heil, *From Gatekeeping to Disbarment and Back Again: Chemical Dependency and Mental Health Issues in Licensing and Discipline,* 64 TEX. B.J. 158 (2001) (outlining step by step the disability suspension process in Texas).

## 2.2 Disbarment

**Disbarment terminates the individual's status as a lawyer. Where disbarment is not permanent, procedures should be established for a lawyer who has been disbarred to apply for readmission, provided that:**

**(1) no application should be considered for five years from the effective date of disbarment; and**

**(2) the petitioner must show by clear and convincing evidence:**

**(a) successful completion of the bar examination, and**

**(b) compliance with all applicable discipline or disability orders or rules: and**

**(c) rehabilitation and fitness to practice law.**

# Annotation

### *Purpose of Disbarment*

Disbarment is the most severe sanction, terminating the lawyer's ability to practice law. *See, e.g., Ligon v. Rees*, 364 S.W.3d 7 (Ark. 2010) (court noting that the most severe sanction for misconduct is disbarment, which terminates the lawyer's privilege to practice law and removes the lawyer's name from the list of licensed attorneys); *People v. Mason*, 212 P.3d 141 (Colo. O.P.D.J. 2009) (the most severe sanction of disbarment is presumed when a lawyer violates a court order not to practice law while under suspension); *Fla. Bar v. Ratiner*, 238 So.3d 117 (Fla. 2018) (disbarment is an extreme form of discipline reserved for the most egregious misconduct and for those who have demonstrated rehabilitation is highly unlikely, which was the case in this matter); *In re Shepherd*, 91 So.3d 283, 287 n.5 (La. 2012) (court imposed permanent disbarment on lawyer for money-laundering scheme, noting that permanent disbarment is the most severe sanction that can be imposed, "having the effect of forever removing him from the bar of this state," and so court did not need to discuss lawyer's alleged further misconduct); *Att'y Grievance Comm'n v. Byrd*, 970 A.2d 870, 890 (Md. 2009) (in imposing disbarment on lawyer who flagrantly disobeyed court orders and bankruptcy court rules and filed false business reports, court concluded "that '[o]nly the most severe sanction of disbarment will provide the protection to the public that this [attorney grievance] procedure is supposed to provide'") (citation omitted); *In re Carey*, 89 S.W.3d 477, 502 (Mo. 2002) ("Disbarment should be reserved for those cases in which it is clear that the attorney should not be at the Bar."); *Office of Disciplinary Counsel v. Pozonsky*, 177 A.3d 830 (Pa. 2018) (court disbarred lawyer who misused his position as a judge to steal cocaine and was convicted of multiple crimes, holding that "only the sanction of disbarment—the most severe condemnation available to us—can fulfill our Court's duty to protect the public. . . ."); *In re Jordan*, 809

S.E.2d 409 (S.C. 2017) ("the primary purpose of disbarment . . . is the removal of an unfit person from the profession for the protection of the courts and the public, not punishment of the offending attorney") (citation omitted); *In re Disciplinary Proceeding Against Eugster*, 209 P.3d 435, 450 (Wash. 2009) ("Disbarment is the most severe sanction . . . historically reserved . . . for grievous acts of ethical misconduct.").

Disbarment protects the public from further practice and harm by the lawyer and upholds the integrity of the legal profession. *See In re Cardwell*, 50 P.3d 897, 904 (Colo. 2002) (purpose of disbarment is not retribution but "[s]afeguarding the public from unscrupulous lawyers"; contrasting this with deterrence, which is not the primary purpose of disbarment, though it "may also have a deterrent effect on other lawyer misconduct"); *In re Enna*, 971 A.2d 110, 113 (Del. 2009) (disbarment warranted for lawyer's conduct in pleading guilty to falsifying physical evidence; "[d]isciplinary proceedings are intended, 'to protect the public; to foster public confidence in the Bar; to preserve the integrity of the profession; and to deter other lawyers from similar misconduct'") (citation omitted); *Ky. Bar Ass'n v. Steiner*, 157 S.W.3d 209, 214 (Ky. 2005) (lawyer permanently disbarred for misappropriating client funds; "one purpose for disbarment of an attorney is to uphold the ideals and traditions of an honorable profession") (citation omitted); *Att'y Grievance Comm'n v. Braskey*, 836 A.2d 605 (Md. 2003) (disbarment appropriate for exacting unreasonable fee combined with trust account violations and misrepresentations; public is entitled to protection against this type of conduct, which brings legal profession into disrepute); *In re Richmond's Case*, 904 A.2d 684 (N.H. 2006) (disbarment satisfies goals of the discipline system by protecting the public and preserving the integrity of the legal profession; here, withholding client's documents, cashing in client's securities, and demanding client sign letter against client's interest warranted disbarment); *Bd. of Prof'l Responsibility v. Barry*, 545 S.W.3d 408 (Tenn. 2018) (finding hearing panel acted arbitrarily and capriciously in recommending suspension instead of disbarment, court disbarred lawyer noting responsibility to protect the public and the legal system).

## *Criminal Conduct*

Disbarment is the presumed sanction when a lawyer intentionally commits a serious crime as defined in the Model Rules for Lawyer Disciplinary Enforcement (MRLDE). As noted in MRLDE Rule 19(C):

> A "serious crime" is any felony or any lesser crime that reflects adversely on the lawyer's honesty, trustworthiness or fitness as a lawyer in other respects, or any crime a necessary element of which, as determined by the statutory or common law definition of the crime, involves interference with the administration of justice, false swearing,

misrepresentation, fraud, deceit, bribery, extortion, misappropriation, theft, or an attempt, conspiracy or solicitation of another to commit a "serious crime."

Under MRLDE Rule 19, the finding of guilt of commission of a serious crime provides the requisite proof needed for interim suspension of a lawyer, although a number of jurisdictions require an order of conviction. Regarding proceedings to impose a final disciplinary sanction, the order of conviction provides requisite proof against the lawyer. *See, e.g., In re Laudumiey*, 849 So.2d 515, 524 (La. 2003) ("In an attorney disciplinary proceeding based on the lawyer's criminal conviction, the issue of his guilt may not be relitigated. Because the lawyer's conviction, whether based on adjudication or guilty plea, is tantamount to a finding of his guilt beyond a reasonable doubt, the clear and convincing standard of proof that applies to disciplinary proceedings has already been satisfied."); *Att'y Grievance Comm'n v. Blair*, 188 A.3d 1009 (Md. 2018) (integrity of a conviction cannot be challenged in disciplinary proceedings).

A conviction is not, however, a necessary condition for initiating disciplinary proceedings against a lawyer based on criminal conduct. *See, e.g., People v. Chappell*, 927 P.2d 829 (Colo. 1996) (finding it unimportant that lawyer, who aided client in violating custody order that resulted in felony charge for client, was not herself charged or convicted of the offense). For more cases and discussion of disbarment for "serious criminal conduct," *see* Annotation to Standard 5.11.

Automatic disbarment is not included as an option within the Sanctions Standards, because it does not fit the paradigm of providing presumptive sanctions that are subsequently adjusted based on aggravating and mitigating factors. *See* Standards for Imposing Lawyer Sanctions pt. II, Theoretical Framework (ABA 1992); *see also Wilson v. Neal*, 964 S.W.2d 199 (Ark. 1998) (trial court erred in concluding that disbarment was required as matter of law for lawyer who was convicted on five counts of knowing conversion of federal government money and property; remanding for hearing regarding appropriate sanction in light of aggravating and mitigating factors); *In re Disciplinary Proceeding Against Smith*, 246 P.3d 1224, 1231 (Wash. 2011) (after rejecting mitigating evidence, court disbarred lawyer convicted of conspiracy to commit securities and wire fraud because disbarment was presumptive sanction when a lawyer engages in any "serious criminal conduct a necessary element of which includes . . . misrepresentation, fraud, extortion, misappropriation, or theft").

Some jurisdictions, however, have retained provisions for automatic, rather than presumptive, disbarment when a lawyer is convicted of a "serious crime" (New York) or a "crime of moral turpitude" (District of Columbia and Texas), or crimes involving "fraud, dishonesty, misrepresentation, deceit, or willful failure to account for money or property of a client" (Mississippi) or a crime of moral turpitude or involving specific intent to deceive or suborn a false statement (California). *See, e.g., In re Lesansky*, 17 P.3d 764 (Cal. 2001) (lawyer's conviction for attempting to commit lewd act on a child related to fitness and involved moral turpitude, and therefore warranted summary disbarment); *In re Gjerde*, 117 A.3d 1039 (D.C. 2015) (disbarment for conviction for conspiracy to commit mail fraud involves moral turpitude, and therefore, disbarment is mandatory); *In re Johnson*, 48 A.3d 170, 172 n.3 (D.C. 2012) (disbarment for conviction of extortion under the color of official right, a crime of moral turpitude per se; "[m]oreover, if an offense 'manifestly involve[s] moral turpitude by virtue of [its] underlying elements,' disbarment is mandatory without inquiry into the specific conduct that led to the conviction") (citation omitted); *In re Colson*, 412 A.2d 1160 (D.C. 1979) (first case to apply District of Columbia's automatic disbarment rule; former White House aide disbarred upon conviction for obstruction of justice); *Farris v. State*, 764 So.2d 411 (Miss. 2000) (felony conviction for conspiracy to defraud conservatorship triggered automatic disbarment); *In re Smith*, 263 A.D.2d 107 (N.Y. App. Div. 1999) (once lawyer was convicted of felony for role in bribery and kickback scheme with insurance adjusters, court in disciplinary proceeding was required to disbar him and did not have discretion to consider lesser sanction); *In re Birdwell*, 20 S.W.3d 685 (Tex. 2000) (felony conviction for conspiracy to defraud IRS involved moral turpitude and triggered mandatory disbarment). *But see In re Witherspoon*, 3 A.3d 496, 505 (N.J. 2010) (noting that the New Jersey disciplinary system "includes few bright line rules, because few indeed are the acts for which one sanction will be invariably appropriate"; detailing court's practice of making case-specific decisions in situations in which lawyers have been convicted of criminal offenses). *See also* Rhonda Richardson Caviedes, Commentary, *Remnants of an Attorney Disciplinary Sanction: Which Jurisdictions Impose Automatic Disbarment? What Offenses Warrant the Imposition of an Automatic Disciplinary Sanction?*, 26 J. LEGAL PROF. 195 (2002); Alexandra Sorota & Shelley Lambert, *Driving on the Wrong Side of the Road: How Lawyers Are Sanctioned for Vehicular Homicide in New York and the District of Columbia*, 15 GEO. J. LEGAL ETHICS 865, 879–80 (2002) (New York's automatic-disbarment approach protects public best; District of Columbia's system of case-by-case evaluation for moral turpitude, presence of which triggers automatic disbarment, succeeds better in administration of justice; neither model preserves confidence in legal profession); David Weinreb, *When Is a Felony a Felony? Automatic Disbarment in New York After In re Johnston*, 57 BROOK. L. REV. 269 (1991) (examines application of automatic-disbarment rule when lawyer is convicted of felony under laws of foreign jurisdiction, but licensing jurisdiction does not define conduct as felony); Rachna K. Dhanda, Note, *When Attorneys Become Convicted Felons: The Question of Discipline by the Bar*, 8 GEO. J. LEGAL ETHICS 723 (1995).

Similarly, acquittals, pardons, and reversals of conviction will not result in automatic readmission. The underlying conduct giving rise to a conviction still may be addressed in a disciplinary proceeding, even after criminal charges have been dropped. *See generally ABA/BNA Lawyers' Manual on Professional Conduct, "Misconduct and Discipline: Sanctions,"* Laws. pp. 101:3009 *et seq.* (citing cases and commentary on "automatic," "compulsory," or "summary" disbarment, as well as discussion on effect of reversals, acquittals, and pardons).

## *Presumption Against Readmission*

Even though disbarment is reserved for the most serious cases, a majority of jurisdictions allow for application for readmission after a period of time, typically five years. In the interest of protecting the public, however, the presumption should be against readmission. *See, e.g., In re Reinstatement of Wiederholt,* 24 P.3d 1219 (Alaska 2001) (in issue of first impression, court recognized a presumption against readmission after disbarment, naming other jurisdictions, including Arkansas, Florida, and Pennsylvania, that have explicitly recognized existence of a presumption against readmission and noting that purpose of the presumption mirrors that of the disciplinary process, namely protection of the public); *Redden v. Ark. State Bd. of Law Exam'rs,* 269 S.W.3d 359, 362 (Ark. 2007) (reaffirming court's presumption against readmission following a lawyer's disbarment; "[t]he protection of the public and the honor and integrity of the profession have long been the principal criteria in determining whether a person should be admitted or readmitted to the bar"); *Petition of Pier,* 561 N.W.2d 297, 300 (S.D. 1997) (reinstatement, with conditions including supervision of practice and mandatory malpractice insurance, following disbarment for stealing more than $45,000; "[m]indful of these principles, '[a] court should be slow to disbar, but it should be even slower to reinstate; it should endeavor to make certain that it does not again put into the hands of an unworthy petitioner that almost unlimited opportunity to inflict wrongs upon society possessed by a practicing lawyer'") (citation omitted).

## *Length of Time Before Readmission*

To ensure that disbarment is a more serious sanction than suspension, no lawyer should be considered for readmission until at least five years after the effective date of disbarment. *See, e.g., Disciplinary Counsel v. Evans,* 2018 WL 793993 (Conn. January 10, 2018) (lawyer who engaged in the practice of law while suspended was disbarred; court noted that pursuant to Standard 2.2 disbarment is not permanent, but respondent cannot apply for reinstatement for five years from the effective date of the sanction); *In re Oberhellman,* 873 S.W.2d 851 (Mo. 1994) (citing Standard 2.2 and holding that no petition for readmission would be considered until at least five years after effective date of disbarment); *see also Petition of Pier,* 561 N.W.2d 297 (S.D. 1997) (raising concern that readmission petition was filed a little more than five years from date of disbarment, court would be more confident with longer period of time to clearly establish rehabilitation before a disbarred lawyer applies for readmission).

The Sanctions Standards do not provide for permanent disbarment, which some jurisdictions do impose. At least seven jurisdictions—Alabama, Indiana, Kentucky, New Jersey, Nevada, Ohio, and Oregon—treat all disbarments as permanent, while other states, such as Arkansas, Florida, Kansas, Louisiana, Mississippi, and Tennessee, allow for disbarment to be permanent in some situations. *See, e.g., Fla. Bar v. Behm*, 41 So.3d 136 (Fla. 2010) (permanent removal from bar justified by lawyer's persistent assertion of belief that income from labor not taxable); *Ky. Bar Ass'n v. Steiner*, 157 S.W.3d 209, 210 n.1 (Ky. 2005) (while disbarment under the Sanctions Standards "anticipates a severe term of suspension for at least five (5) years," Kentucky recognizes permanent disbarment since its rule amendments of October 1, 1998); *In re Dillon*, 66 So.3d 434 (La. 2011) (ordering permanent disbarment of lawyer convicted of two federal counts of deprivation of rights under color of law after abusing his power as deputy city attorney to sexually assault two women); *In re Kirchberg*, 856 So.2d 1162, 1166 (La. 2003) (imposing permanent disbarment for felony conviction for mail fraud, runner-based solicitation, and illegal payments from physicians in exchange for referring clients for medical treatment; rejecting lawyer's argument that guideline illustrating types of misconduct warranting permanent disbarment did not apply because it referred to insurance fraud, not mail fraud, court held that "guidelines are illustrative in nature and do not constitute an exclusive list of conduct for which an attorney may be permanently disbarred"); *In re Pinkston*, 852 So.2d 966, 976 (La. 2003) (permanent disbarment under 2001 amendment to court rules "does not represent a new sanction which did not previously exist; rather, it is simply a procedural change to the rule which recognizes a power the court has always possessed"); *In re Discipline of Crowley*, 406 P.3d 958 (Table) (Nev. 2017) (noting that disbarment in Nevada is irrevocable, court instead suspended lawyer who engaged in an isolated instance of intentionally practicing law while suspended and who showed remorse); *Disciplinary Counsel v. Character*, 950 N.E.2d 177 (Ohio 2011) (lawyer's extensive record of serious misconduct involving multiple clients and more than 40 violations of the professional conduct rules warranted permanent disbarment and was in line with court's decision in similar cases of misconduct); David E. Johnson, *The Case for Permanent Disbarment*, 5 PROF. LAW. 22 (1994); Ronald D. Rotunda, *The Case Against Permanent Disbarment*, 5 PROF. LAW. 22 (1994); Charles W. Kettlewell, *Permanent Disbarment: The Ohio Experience*, 9 PROF. LAW. 17 (Nov. 1997) (permanent disbarment eliminates incentives for rehabilitation and restitution and has no deterrent effect; its only potential benefit is public relations; author suggests indefinite suspensions permitting petition for conditional reinstatement after two to five years); Ronald D. Rotunda & Mary M. Devlin, *Permanent Disbarment: A Market-Oriented Proposal*, 9 PROF. LAW. 2, 13 (Nov. 1997) (recommending that every lawyer seeking readmission after disbarment be required to obtain insurance and bonding: "[t]he requirement of bonding and malpractice insurance will not only protect the public, but it will also help protect the readmitted lawyer, because it is in the economic self-interest of the insurance carriers and bonding companies to monitor their policyholders, identify risks, and eliminate them"); *see* Brian Finkelstein, *Should Permanent Disbarment Be Permanent?*, GEO. J. LEGAL ETHICS 587 (2007).

## *Readmission Criteria*

MRLDE Rule 25 calls for "readmission" after disbarment and "reinstatement" after suspension. While some jurisdictions refer to reinstatement post disbarment and not readmission, this annotation adopts the language set out in the MRDLE. A lawyer who has been disbarred carries the burden of proving by clear and convincing evidence that he or she has been rehabilitated and is fit to practice law again. In several states, the rules concerning readmission explicitly provide for a clear and convincing evidence standard. *See In re Griffith*, 913 P.2d 695, 699 (Or. 1996) ("In a sense, a lawyer who is seeking reinstatement after disbarment must prove by clear and convincing evidence not only that he or she generally is of good moral character, but also that he or she has overcome and will not again be influenced by the specific character flaw that led to disbarment. Thus, the focus of the inquiry in a reinstatement case is on *reformation*.").

The clear and convincing evidence standard has been a significant determinant in many post-disbarment disciplinary readmission and reinstatement cases. *See, e.g., In re Reinstatement of Wiederholt*, 24 P.3d 1219, 1224 (Alaska 2001) (court adopts clear and convincing standard; "[t]he major consideration in reinstatement proceedings is whether the disbarred attorney has shown that those weaknesses that produced the earlier misconduct have been corrected"). In *In re Spence*, 523 S.E.2d 323 (Ga. 1999), the court found that a lawyer who had been disbarred for signing his client's name on a summary judgment affidavit established rehabilitation and fitness to practice law and was entitled to reinstatement. The court explained:

> We note that the evidence presented proved clearly, convincingly, and overwhelmingly that [respondent] is rehabilitated and fit to be readmitted to the practice of law; that [he] has stayed abreast of the law through his work as a paralegal and legal researcher and through reading slip opinions and that this work has allowed him to maintain the professional proficiency and legal skills necessary to resume a career as a competent attorney; that his character, standing and reputation in his community were excellent prior to his disbarment and have continuously remained so; that his conduct since disbarment has been exemplary in all respects; and that he has accepted full responsibility

> for and been extraordinarily repentant and remorseful for the conduct which resulted in his disbarment.

*Id.* at 324; *see also In re Cooke*, 42 A.3d 610, 615 (Md. 2012) ("Reinstatement follows only when the applicant has demonstrated, through clear and convincing evidence of his conduct over a period of time, that he has been rehabilitated and is legally competent."); *In re Disciplinary Action Against Montgomery*, 566 N.W.2d 426, 429 (N.D. 1997) ("[Proper scope of inquiry on a petition for reinstatement requires] petitioner to prove by clear and convincing evidence he currently has the requisite honesty and integrity to practice law, *in spite of* the misconduct committed in the past. The rule envisions a balancing of the evidence of the petitioner's current good character with the seriousness of the prior misconduct."); *Petition of Pier*, 561 N.W.2d 297 (S.D. 1997) (citing Standard 2.2 in noting that while presumption should be against reinstatement, a disbarred lawyer who has proven the following by clear and convincing evidence can be readmitted: (1) successful completion of the bar examination, (2) compliance with all applicable discipline or disability orders or rules, and (3) rehabilitation and fitness to practice); *cf. In re Reinstatement of Perry*, 243 P.3d 15 (Okla. 2010) (disbarred lawyer failed to present clear and convincing evidence for readmission to practice; lawyer engaged in unauthorized practice of law since being disbarred; after disbarment lawyer failed to comply with rule governing procedures following disciplinary actions and winding up of business of disciplined lawyers, failed to pay costs of prior disciplinary proceedings in timely manner as ordered, omitted numerous facts and misstated other facts in readmission questionnaire, underlying misconduct was serious, and lawyer demonstrated incompetence with respect to rules governing attorney trust accounts).

In considering whether the respondent has met his or her burden of proof, courts have stressed the fundamental importance of gauging whether an applicant has demonstrated that he or she has corrected whatever weaknesses led to the misconduct. *See, e.g., In re Arrotta*, 96 P.3d 213 (Ariz. 2004) (reinstatement denied because lawyer failed to meet his burden of showing that he understood the cause of the misconduct leading to his disbarment); *In re Borders*, 665 A.2d 1381, 1385 (D.C. 1995) (reinstatement for lawyer convicted of conspiracy to solicit bribes from criminal defendants in exchange for lenient treatment from a judge is denied because of lawyer's persistence in remaining silent about his misconduct, refusing to testify against judge in earlier proceedings, and "his inability or refusal to explain why he had become involved in the criminal conduct"); *State ex rel. Counsel for Dis. v. Smith*, 844 N.W.2d 318 (Neb. 2014) (disbarred lawyer reinstated subject to two years of probation with trust account monitor showing by clear and convincing evidence that he was worthy of readmission to practice); *In re Brandes*, 65 N.E.3d 678 (N.Y. 2016) (third petition for reinstatement denied; lawyer who practiced law while suspended did not meet burden of proof by clear and convincing evidence that he possessed the character and fitness to practice law); *In re Reinstatement of Clayborne*, 406 P.3d 578, 579 (Okla. 2017) (petitioner reinstated after disbarment for subornation of perjury conviction; court held that "evidence demonstrates more than just commendable conduct over a substantial period of time and does meet his heavy burden to show that he would act differently if faced with similar pressures and circumstances . . ."); *In re Nash*, 855 P.2d 1112, 1116 (Or. 1993) ("We are entitled to have a reasonable assurance that the misconduct which brought the petitioner before this court once before will not reoccur.") (citation omitted); *In re Moynihan*, 778 P.2d 521, 522 (Wash. 1989) ("The major consideration in reinstatement proceedings is whether the disbarred attorney has overcome those weaknesses which produced the earlier misconduct.").

Courts also often cite the criteria in Rule 25(E) of the MRLDE to decide whether a lawyer should be reinstated or readmitted. Those criteria are (1) full compliance with the terms and conditions of all prior disciplinary orders; (2) that the lawyer has neither engaged in nor attempted to engage in the unauthorized practice of law during the period of disbarment; (3) any physical or mental disability or infirmity existing at the time of the disbarment has been removed, and when alcohol or other drug abuse was a causative factor in the lawyer's misconduct, the lawyer has pursued appropriate rehabilitative treatment, has abstained from the use of alcohol or other drugs for at least one year and is likely to continue to abstain from alcohol or other drugs; (4) the lawyer recognizes the wrongfulness and seriousness of the misconduct resulting in the disbarment; (5) the lawyer has not engaged in any other professional misconduct since disbarment; (6) notwithstanding the conduct for which the lawyer was disciplined, the lawyer has the requisite honesty and integrity to practice law; (7) the lawyer has kept informed about recent developments in the law and is competent to practice; and (8) the lawyer must pass the bar examination and the character and fitness examination.

Many courts have used various formulations of these factors in reviewing readmission petitions. *See, e.g.*, *In re Reinstatement of Wiederholt*, 24 P.3d 1219 (Alaska 2001) (in petition for readmission by disbarred lawyer, court concluded that ten factors listed in *Petition of Pier*, 561 N.W.2d 297 (S.D. 1997), provide useful guidance in inquiry since Alaska has only one bar rule that addresses question of readmission and no cases that interpret the language); *Iowa Supreme Ct. Att'y Disciplinary Bd. v. Reilly*, 884 N.W.2d 761 (Iowa 2016) (court's opinion cites to MRLDE 25(e) and discusses, in context of granting provisional reinstatement, the myriad of factors that vary from jurisdiction to jurisdiction in determining whether a petitioner should be reinstated, noting that there is no clear consensus on how the factors should be weighted) (citations omitted); *In re Reinstatement of Dobbs*, 256 P.3d 52, 54 (Okla. 2011) (applicant for reinstatement must establish, by clear and convincing evidence, that "the applicant's conduct will conform to the high standards required of a member of the Bar" if reinstated; outlining factors considered upon such an application: (1) present moral fitness; (2) demonstrated consciousness of wrongful conduct and its impact on the profession; (3) extent of rehabilitation; (4) seriousness of original misconduct; (5) conduct after the resignation; (6) the time that has elapsed; (7) character, maturity, and experience at the time of discipline; (8) present competence in legal skills); *Petition of Pier*, 561 N.W.2d 297, 301 (S.D. 1997) (listing cases from other jurisdictions and summarizing requirements they have set out for reinstatement, deeming the following elements most relevant: "1. present moral fitness; 2. acceptance of wrongdoing with sincerity and honesty; 3. extent of rehabilitation; 4. nature and seriousness of the original misconduct and the disrepute it brought on the legal profession; 5. conduct following the discipline, including whether there has been any unauthorized practice of law; 6. time elapsed since the original discipline; 7. character, maturity and experience at the time of discipline and now; 8. current competency and qualifications to practice law; 9. restitution; and 10. proof that resumption of the practice of law within the state will not be detrimental to the integrity and standing of the bar or the administration of justice, or subversive of the public interest."

## *Disbarment on Consent and Reciprocal Disbarment*

Disbarment includes disbarment on consent and reciprocal disbarment. Generally, a lawyer who has been disbarred on consent should not be readmitted earlier than any other lawyer who has been disbarred. *See, e.g., In re Novick*, 619 A.2d 514 (D.C. 1993) (disbarment by consent was warranted for lawyer convicted of making false statement in connection with Department of Housing and Urban Development transaction; when lawyer is disbarred for any reason, he or she may apply for readmission after five years); *In re Vega*, 198 So.3d 1176 (La. 2016) (reciprocal discipline in form of disbarment following Texas resignation in lieu of discipline for failing to return unearned fees, neglect, improper supervision of nonlawyer employees, and violations of rules requiring cooperation with disciplinary authorities; resignation in lieu of discipline in Texas is equivalent to disbarment in Louisiana); *Matter of Martin*, 141 A. D.3d 77 (N.Y. 1st Dept. 2016) (reciprocal disbarment in New York for lawyer who was permanently disbarred in Florida for conversion). *But see, e.g.*, Ill. Sup. Ct. R. 767(a) (2011) (petition for reinstatement after disbarment on consent may be filed after three years, while a lawyer must wait five years to petition for reinstatement after involuntary disbarment). Whether a lawyer resigned or was disbarred on consent is a factor that can be considered if the lawyer applies for readmission or reinstatement.

While ABA policy does not provide for "resignations in lieu of disbarment," some jurisdictions permit it. *See, e.g., In re Maguire*, 725 A.2d 417, 424 (Del. 1999) (declining to accept lawyer's resignation during pendency of disciplinary hearing, but considering resignation letter in resolving underlying discipline proceeding disbarring lawyer; "[w]hether a resignation or retirement during the pendency of disciplinary proceedings is ultimately accepted depends on the Court's assessment of the impact that the resignation or retirement will have on public policy interests such as the integrity of the legal profession, the administration of justice, and the protection of the public."); *Office of Disciplinary Counsel v. Hurley*, 787 P.2d 688, 689–90 (Haw. 1990) (a resignation in lieu of discipline "is tantamount to disbarment for purposes of reciprocal discipline"); *State ex rel. Okla. Bar Ass'n v. Rich*, 162 P.3d 920 (Okla. 2007) (respondent's name stricken from Roll of Attorneys after acceptance of resignation in lieu of disbarment imposed in sister jurisdiction; further ordered that lawyer make no application for reinstatement for five years); *Rosas v. Comm'n for Lawyer Discipline*, 335 S.W.3d 311 (Tex. App. 2010) (reciting that sanctions for misconduct may include resignation in lieu of disbarment).

## 2.3 Suspension

**Suspension is the removal of a lawyer from the practice of law for a specified minimum period of time. Generally, suspension should be for a period of time equal to or greater than six months, but in no event should the time period prior to application for reinstatement be more than three years. Procedures should be established to allow a suspended lawyer to apply for reinstatement, but a lawyer who has been suspended should not be permitted to return to practice until he has completed a reinstatement process demonstrating rehabilitation, compliance with all applicable discipline or disability orders and fitness to practice law.**

## Annotation

Suspension includes suspension by consent and reciprocal suspension. Suspension is an intermediate level of discipline. *See In re Howard,* 765 A.2d 39, 46 (Del. 2000) (court imposed three-year suspension on lawyer whose only ethical violation was misdemeanor drug conviction to "serve as a benchmark for any future disciplinary cases" and "send a message to other Delaware lawyers and to the public that this Court takes very seriously a lawyer's fundamental duty to foster the public's confidence in our Bar and to maintain the integrity of the legal profession"); *In re Carey,* 89 S.W.3d 477 (Mo. 2002) (suspension an appropriate intermediate sanction when reprimand is insufficient to protect the public and maintain the integrity of the profession, and when court does not believe that the acts of respondent are such that he or she should not be engaged in practice of law); *Bd. of Prof'l Responsibility v. Powers,* 322 P.3d 1287 (Wyo. 2014) (affirming board report citing to Standard 2.3 defining suspension as "removal of lawyer from practice for a specified minimum period of time"; nine-month suspension for lack of competence, diligence, and communication hearing panel).

### *Maximum of Three Years*

Although jurisdictions impose suspensions for various time periods, Rule 10(A)(2) of the MRLDE recommends that suspension be for an appropriate fixed period of time not to exceed three years. *See, e.g., In re Melvin,* 807 A.2d 550 (Del. 2002) (eighteen-month suspension warranted for lawyer who pleaded guilty to misdemeanor criminal contempt of a protection from abuse order and misdemeanor hindering prosecution, particularly given recent amendment to Delaware Rules of Disciplinary Procedure Rule 8(a)(2) (amended effective May 7, 2002) reducing maximum length of disciplinary suspensions from five years to three years); *In the Matter of Coulter,* 816 S.E.2d 1 (Ga. 2018) (rejecting special referee's recommended four-year suspension for mishandling client funds, court disbarred lawyer and cited to Standard 2.3's recommendation that suspensions not exceed three years); Fla. Bar v. Scott, 39 So.3d 309, 318 (Fla. 2010) (noting that maximum length of a definite-term suspension under Florida rules is three years; imposing three-year suspension because misconduct fell "close to the dividing line on the continuum between disbarment and suspension"); *La. State Bar Ass'n v. Amberg*, 553 So.2d 448, 452 (La. 1989) (negligent handling of client's settlement funds causing injury to client warranted three-year suspension with reinstatement subject to special conditions; court stated that "[o]ur impression is that the suspension should be of maximum duration, i.e., three years, Standard 2.3, because the substantial aggravating factors are not offset by any appreciable mitigation"); *In re Disciplinary Proceeding Against McMullen*, 896 P.2d 1281, 1291 (Wash. 1995) (quoting with approval Standard 2.3 provision that suspension generally "should be for a period of time equal to or greater than six months" but no longer than three years).

A number of jurisdictions, however, do impose suspensions longer than three years when a lawyer's misconduct is egregious. *See, e.g., In re Rice*, 260 P.3d 1020, 1036 n.44 (Alaska 2011) (court rejected lawyer's reliance on Standard 2.3 that sanction, short of disbarment, should be suspension not exceeding three years and imposed four-year suspension, holding that "we are guided but not constrained by the ABA Standards; past cases . . . reflect our practice of at least contemplating the imposition of sanctions longer than three years despite the ABA Standards' guidelines"); *In re Cyrus*, 241 P.3d 890, 894 (Alaska 2010) (while Standard 2.3 suggests suspensions last from six months to three years before the lawyer may apply for reinstatement, here, lawyer's "pattern of neglecting his clients and delaying court matters, after previous discipline for the same conduct, is disconcerting" and warranted five-year suspension); *Office of Disciplinary Counsel v. Au*, 113 P.3d 203, 222 (Haw. 2005) (imposing five-year suspension for, inter alia, misrepresenting published opinion to judge and using nonlawyer runner for client referrals because, under the circumstances, disbarment would be "too severe a sanction, and yet a suspension of less than five years would be insufficient to reflect our concern for the protection of the public, the legal profession, and the courts"); *Sivasubramaniam v. Kentucky Bar Ass'n*, 487 S.W.3d 891 (Ky. 2016) (lawyer who previously practiced medicine suspended for five years for knowingly inflating medical bills and pleading guilty to signing false tax returns; court imposed a five-year suspension instead of disbarment, stressing seriousness of misconduct by noting that the conduct occurred prior to lawyer's admission to practice, an absence of prior discipline, and full repayment to government); *In re Frelix*, 134 A.D.3d 58 (N.Y.S. 2015) (lawyer who engaged in pattern of misconduct over five-year period of time, including neglect and disregarding court orders, suspended for five years); *Matter of Greene*, 2017 WL4341434 (N.H. September 29, 2017) (in matter with no precedent directly on point, court imposed five-year suspension instead of disbarment as reciprocal discipline based on indefinite suspension in

Massachusetts for repeated conflicts of interest and dishonest misconduct relating to real estate matters; lengthy suspension instead of more severe sanction of disbarment because all misconduct took place in Massachusetts and involved Massachusetts property and residents); *cf. People v. Rhodes,* 107 P.3d 1177, 1188 (Colo. O.P.D.J. 2005) (disbarment warranted for knowing misappropriation of client funds, with board member concurring but disapproving that, short of disbarment, greatest sanction available for client conversion is three years: "I am very troubled that no intermediate sanction is available (such as suspension for longer than three years) that would recognize both the seriousness of conversion of client funds and also that the public interest is served when lawyers acknowledge their misconduct, demonstrate remorse, and voluntarily make arrangements for restitution, as [respondent] has done here").

## *Minimum Suspension of Six Months*

While the MRLDE do not suggest a minimum length for suspensions, Standard 2.3 provides that suspensions should generally be for a period of time equal to or greater than six months. *See, e.g., People v. Fagan,* 423 P.3d 412, 417 n. 22 (Colo. O.P.D.J. 2018) (holding that "served suspension of six months typically is viewed as a baseline sanction to be adjusted upward or downward in consideration of aggravating and mitigating factors," court cited to Standard 2.3 in footnote 22 in support; nine-month suspension imposed for abandoning client's case and not responding to regulatory counsel); *Statewide Grievance Comm'n v. Pinsky,* No. CV010452000S, 2001 WL 1614892 (Conn. Super. Ct. Nov. 28, 2001) (one-year suspension for, inter alia, lawyer who failed to bring personal injury action within statute of limitations; citing former comment to Standard 2.3); *In re Disciplinary Proceeding Against Poole,* 125 P.3d 954, 968 (Wash. 2006) (citing Standard 2.3 and noting that while court has "departed from the rule on occasion," here six-month suspension warranted); *In re Disciplinary Proceeding Against McKean,* 64 P.3d 1226 (Wash. 2003) (citing Sanctions Standard 2.3 that suspension should generally be no less than six months; imposing six-month suspension followed by six months of probation with conditions).

Nonetheless, some courts have imposed suspensions lasting less than six months, citing various reasons for departing from Standard 2.3. *See, e.g., In re Miranda,* 823 P.2d 1278, 1282 (Ariz. 1992) (recognizing general rule under Standard 2.3 that suspension should be for a period of at least six months, but imposing three-month suspension followed by two-year probation because lawyer had been heavily counseled by retained attorney, a past state-bar president, had good reputation for competence, provided service to underrepresented community, and longer suspension would be "merely inappropriate"); *In re Rosenau,* 132 A.3d 1174 (D.C. 2016) (thirty-day suspension for lawyer who failed to disclose to mediator that his client was dead) ; *In re O'Brien,* 26 A.3d 203 (Del. 2011) (court imposed three-month suspension, noting that the language of Standard 2.3, particularly use of the word "generally," supports case-by-case determination as to length of a suspension); *Iowa Supreme Ct. Att'y Disciplinary Bd. v. Waterman*, 890 N.W.2d 327 (Iowa 2017) (court suspended lawyer for thirty days after lawyer self-reported sexual relationship with client); *In re Chase*, 121 P.3d 1160 (Or. 2005) (thirty-day suspension appropriate for repeated failure to pay child support and knowing violation of circuit court's support order); *Cohn v. Bd. of Prof'l Responsibility*, 151 S.W.3d 473, 489 (Tenn. 2004) (court rejecting censure recommendation, citing Sanctions Standard 2.3 and imposing ninety-day suspension; "we have determined a suspension is justified, but we decline to order the ABA recommended suspension of six months," imposing, instead, "a suspension of ninety days" on bankruptcy lawyer who, over seven years, collected post-confirmation attorney's fees from debtor clients by improperly using creditor's procedure); *In re Wenk*, 678 A.2d 898 (Vt. 1996) (court's acceptance of Standard 2.3's recommendation regarding length of suspension does not foreclose imposition of suspension of less than six months); *see also In re Disciplinary Proceeding Against Poole*, 125 P.3d 954 (Wash. 2006) (Madsen, J., dissenting) (opposing six-month suspension and arguing instead for no more than sixty-day suspension; stating court repeatedly had deviated from Sanctions Standard 2.3 guideline and citing similar cases imposing sixty-day suspensions).

Some courts have implied, for example, that the six-month minimum suspension suggested by Standard 2.3 might have an unduly harsh impact on solo practitioners. *See In re Ford*, 128 P.3d 178, 186 (Alaska 2006) ("[Respondent] is a single practitioner and a suspension of ninety days will likely result in significant hardship. But we acknowledge that a 60-day suspension might be perceived as a 'vacation.' A suspension shorter than ninety days would be unlikely to deter [respondent] from future misconduct; a suspension longer than ninety days would be out of line with suspensions we have imposed for comparable violations." A ninety-day suspension was imposed for the lawyer's knowing violation of a court order); *see also In re Triem*, 929 P.2d 634 (Alaska 1996) (while recognizing that the Sanctions Standards disfavor suspensions of less than six months, court imposed ninety-day suspension because of significant impact on solo practitioner in a small community); *In re Davis*, 889 P.2d 621 (Ariz. 1995) (60-day suspension imposed because any suspension for sole practitioner is devastating and six-month suspension for sole practitioner is tantamount to disbarment).

## *Impact of Aggravating and Mitigating Factors on Length of Suspension*

Courts determine the appropriate length of suspension after examining any aggravating and/or mitigating factors. *See, e.g., In re Cummings*, 211 P.3d 1136 (Alaska 2009) (imposing three-month suspension on judge based on six-month baseline set forth in Standard 2.3, and consideration of aggravating and mitigating factors); *In re Moak*, 71 P.3d 343 (Ariz. 2003) (noting that presumptive suspension period is six months under Standard 2.3, court ordered suspension for six months and one day due to substantial aggravators including pattern of misconduct and multiple serious offenses); *In re Steiner*, 817 A.2d 793 (Del. 2003) (imposing three-year suspension after weighing aggravating factors including pattern of misconduct and further acts of similar knowing misconduct and also finding lawyer's addiction not a mitigating factor); *In re Benenati*, 136 A.D.3d 108 (N.Y. App. Div. 2015) (three-month suspension for deliberate misappropriation and misuse of notary stamp due to significant mitigation); *In re Lopez*, 252 P.3d 312 (Or. 2011) (while similar cases warranted suspensions from thirty days to six months, court imposed nine-month suspension in light of aggravating factors, including substantial experience in the practice of law, vulnerability of the victims, prior disciplinary offenses, multiple offenses, and pattern of misconduct); *In re Palmisano*, 177 A.3d. 1105 (Vt. 2017) (two-year reciprocal suspension despite only six-month suspension and two years of probation in originating jurisdiction, citing Standard 2.3 and highlighting that there were only aggravating factors). For more on the application of aggravating and mitigating factors in lawyer sanctions, see Annotation to Standard 9.0 (Aggravation and Mitigation).

## *Reinstatement*

If a lawyer's misconduct is serious enough to warrant a suspension from practice longer than six months, courts should not grant reinstatement until the lawyer demonstrates rehabilitation, compliance with all applicable discipline or disability orders and rules, and fitness to practice law. *See, e.g., In re Favata*, 119 A.3d 1283 (Del. 2015) (suspension of six months and one day for prosecutorial misconduct; while not citing to Sanctions Standards court noted that suspension of six months or less allows reinstatement without lawyer having to demonstrate rehabilitation); *Ky. Bar Ass'n v. Leadingham*, 317 S.W.3d 589 (Ky. 2010) (imposing 181-day suspension because suspensions for a period longer than 180 days require reinstatement proceedings, and reinstatement necessary given severity of underlying misconduct). *But see In re Hongisto*, 998 A.2d 1065, 1071 (Vt. 2010) ("[A] six-month suspension should not be applied for the sole purpose of triggering the reinstatement process—the individual's violations must, on their own, merit a sanction of six months. A six-month suspension is a serious sanction and should not be imposed solely to require a demonstration of rehabilitation and compliance before returning to practice.").

Courts have concluded that while it may be possible in some cases for a lawyer to show rehabilitation in less than six months, it is preferable to suspend a lawyer for at least six months to ensure effective rehabilitation. *See, e.g., In re Shannon*, 876 P.2d 548, 567 (Ariz. 1994) (citing former commentary to Standard 2.3, court noted that six-month suspension aids in ensuring rehabilitation and carries with it "pain" to the lawyer, which "is a necessary element of any suspension because it serves as both a general and specific deterrent to future misconduct"); *Fla. Bar v. Roberto,* 59 So.3d 1101, 1106 (Fla. 2011) (rejecting referee's recommendation of probation for one year, court imposed a one-year rehabilitative suspension on lawyer who had sexual relations with clients during the course of representation, concluding that "any sanction less than a suspension that requires Respondent to prove rehabilitation would not be consistent with the seriousness of the rule violations found in this case"); *In re Thomson,* 464 S.E.2d 818 (Ga. 1996) (rejecting thirty-day suspension, court reasoned that six-month suspension is generally the minimum time necessary to protect clients and ensure rehabilitation and compliance with reinstatement requirements); *In re Woolbert,* 672 N.E.2d 412 (Ind. 1996) (one-year suspension without automatic reinstatement preferable to ensure effective demonstration of rehabilitation); *Cleveland Bar Ass'n. v. Briggs,* 728 N.E.2d 1049, 1051 (Ohio 2000) (Cook, J., dissenting) (recommending one-year suspension rather than majority decision to stay entire one-year suspension in favor of supervised probation in case of lawyer who filed false incorporation papers and undertook a legal matter she was not competent to handle; quoting former commentary to Standard 2.3 "that '[i]f a lawyer's misconduct is serious enough to warrant a suspension from practice, the lawyer should not be reinstated until rehabilitation can be established. . . . [I]t is preferable to suspend a lawyer for at least six months in order to ensure effective demonstration of rehabilitation.'"); *cf. In re Bucknam,* 628 A.2d 932 (Vt. 1993) (citing former commentary to Standard 2.3, court noted that suspensions less than six months serve merely as fines and do not ensure rehabilitation; court instead imposed public reprimand for lawyer who misrepresented case status, attempted to alter fee agreement, failed to supply accounting of expenses, and otherwise bullied clients regarding fee payment). *But see Att'y Grievance Comm'n v. Garfield,* 797 A.2d 757, 770 (Md. 2002) (court rejected recommended two-year suspension and imposed indefinite suspension, with right to reapply in thirty days, for multiple offenses, including client neglect: "[W]e can see also some benefit to the potential of his return as a rehabilitated attorney. Our sanction, therefore, takes cognizance of the particular circumstances in this case, but also gives due regard to our obligation to protect the public, by ensuring that Respondent does not reenter the practice of law until he demonstrates and provides relative assurance that he is capable of doing so successfully.").

The MRLDE draw a distinction, for reinstatement purposes, between suspensions of six months or less, and suspensions exceeding six months. A lawyer who has been suspended for six months or less should be reinstated automatically (i.e., without having to establish rehabilitation) while lawyers suspended for more than six months do not qualify for automatic reinstatement; they must petition for and be granted reinstatement by the court. *See generally* MRLDE R. 10, R. 24, R. 25. *See In re Mitchell,* 901 F.2d 1179 (3d Cir. 1990) (relying on Standard 2.3 and noting application for reinstatement following a suspension greater than six months is not automatically granted; petition must demonstrate rehabilitation by clear and satisfactory evidence, either by certified copy of another court's finding of rehabilitation or by other means); *see also In re Johnson,* 298 P.3d 904 (Ariz. 2013) (respondent who had been suspended for six months and one day granted reinstatement after proving by clear and convincing evidence that he had "identified weaknesses that produced the misconduct and took the necessary steps to overcome those weaknesses. . . ."); *In re Howard,* 912 S.W.2d 61 (Mo. 1995) (citing Standard 2.3 and suspending lawyer indefinitely with leave to apply for reinstatement after six months).

## • Reinstatement Criteria

Standard 2.3 recommends that jurisdictions establish procedures for suspended lawyers to apply for reinstatement. Rule 25(E) of the MRLDE sets out the following criteria that lawyers suspended more than six months must meet before being reinstated:

- full compliance with the terms and conditions of all prior disciplinary orders;
- the lawyer has neither engaged in nor attempted to engage in the unauthorized practice of law during the period of suspension;
- any physical or mental disability or infirmity existing at the time of suspension has been removed; if alcohol or other drug abuse was a causative factor in the lawyer's misconduct, the lawyer has pursued appropriate treatment, has abstained from the use of alcohol or other drugs for a stated period of time, generally not less than one year and is likely to continue to abstain from alcohol or other drugs;
- the lawyer recognizes the wrongfulness and seriousness of the misconduct resulting in the suspension;
- the lawyer has not engaged in any other professional misconduct since suspension;
- notwithstanding the conduct for which the lawyer was disciplined, the lawyer has the requisite honesty and integrity to practice law; and
- the lawyer has kept informed about recent developments in the law and is competent to practice.

The reinstatement requirement is seen as a more effective means of protecting the public. *See, e.g., In re Disciplinary Matter of Shea,* 273 P.3d 612, 615 n.1 (Alaska 2012) (lawyer suspended for twenty-five months required to petition for reinstatement to comply with Alaska bar rule stating he demonstrate that resumption of practice would not be "subversive of the public interest"; rule applied to all lawyers suspended for more than two years); *Statewide Grievance Comm'n v. Johnson*, No. CV054012328S, 2011 WL 1087470, at *3 (Conn. Super. Ct. Mar. 3, 2011) (applicant's motion for reinstatement denied as court has "an obligation to the public to protect it against the possibility of any future misconduct"; here, no evidence that applicant had complied with her financial obligations to make restitution and that she had secured a suitable and willing mentor); *In re Howard*, 765 A.2d 39, 46 (Del. 2000) (lawyer suspended for three years following misdemeanor drug convictions that reflected a pattern of criminal behavior; "three-year suspension will also serve to protect the public . . . by postponing [lawyer's] opportunity to seek reinstatement . . . [to] . . . give [him] further time to establish himself as a recovered addict"); *Ky. Bar Ass'n v. Leadingham*, 317 S.W.3d 589, 591 (Ky. 2010) (Kentucky Supreme Court Rules provide that suspensions for a period longer than 180 days require reinstatement before a disciplined lawyer may resume practice; noting that lawyer's misconduct warranted 181-day suspension because lawyer "needs to be investigated and evaluated by the Character and Fitness Committee, for not only the protection of the public, but for Respondent's own welfare").

- **Other Conditions to Reinstatement**

In some instances, courts have added other reinstatement criteria or granted reinstatement with conditions attached to the order. *See, e.g., In re Sather*, 3 P.3d 403 (Colo. 2000) (imposing six-month suspension for knowingly mishandling client funds and knowingly deceiving a client; also requiring that lawyer undergo reinstatement proceedings normally reserved for lawyers suspended longer than one year, as well as proceeding to be reinstated from disability status); *Statewide Grievance Comm'n v. Palmieri*, No. CV020472045S, 2003 WL 963240 (Conn. Super. Ct. Feb. 25, 2003) (one-year suspension with requirement that lawyer take and pass the Multistate Professional Responsibility Examination (MPRE) or an ethics course at an accredited law school and perform 250 hours of community service); *In re Moorman*, III, 237 S.3d 492 (La. 2018) (lawyer with mental health issues who was suspended for three years retroactive to interim suspension reinstated with conditions, including continued counseling, appointment of practice monitor, and enrollment in ethics school); *In re Discipline of Janklow*, 709 N.W.2d 28 (S.D. 2006) (reinstatement to occur without further proceedings, subject to conditions including compliance with terms of lawyer's criminal probation, promptly advising of any probation violation, and reporting any moving violations of traffic laws for two years following probation; suspension arose out of lawyer's conviction for, inter alia, second-degree manslaughter while driving recklessly); *In re Hongisto*, 998 A.2d 1065, 1071 (Vt. 2010) (two six-month suspensions to be served concurrently, "with the added condition that, at the time that respondent applies for reinstatement, she must provide the Professional Responsibility Board with a detailed explanation for her lack of participation over the course of these proceedings"); *In re Disciplinary Proceeding Against DeRuiz*, 99 P.3d 881 (Wash. 2004) (two six-month suspensions, to be served consecutively, with reinstatement subject to payment of restitution and 18 months of probation, conditioned on professional office practice or management counseling and periodic audits or reports). *But see In re Boykins*, 999 A.2d 166, 175 (D.C. 2010) (agreeing with recommendation of two-year suspension but rejecting board's recommendation that respondent cooperate with a practice monitor prior to reinstatement; finding practice monitor not appropriate in this case because lawyer's actions "go well beyond the specific practice deficiencies that justified the use of a practice monitor").

## 2.4 Interim Suspension

**Interim suspension is the temporary suspension of a lawyer from the practice of law pending imposition of final discipline. Interim suspension includes:**

**(a) suspension upon conviction of a "serious crime" or,**

**(b) suspension when the lawyer's continuing conduct is or is likely to cause immediate and serious injury to a client or the public.**

# Annotation

### *Purposes of Interim Suspension*

Rule 19 of the MRLDE states that the court should place a lawyer on interim suspension immediately upon proof that the lawyer has been found guilty of a "serious crime." Rule 20 of the MRLDE provides for interim suspension of a lawyer upon the court's receipt of sufficient evidence demonstrating that the lawyer committed a violation of the Model Rules of Professional Conduct or is under a disability and "poses a substantial threat of serious harm to the public." Interim suspension is necessary in such cases both to protect members of the public and to maintain public confidence in the legal profession pending final determination of the appropriate discipline to be imposed. *See, e.g., Wood v. Supreme Ct. Comm'n on Prof'l Conduct,* 38 S.W.3d 310 (Ark. 2001) (interim suspension provides a means to preclude lawyer from practicing while further action is taken by disciplinary authorities); *Office of Disciplinary Counsel v. Plants,* 759 S.E.2d 220 (W. Va. 2014) (court has long recognized that interim suspension is extraordinary procedure to be used in only "the most extreme cases of lawyer misconduct"; court denied petition for interim suspension of prosecutor personally charged with domestic battery who was responsible for pursuing such cases as part of his job, finding no immediate substantial threat of harm existed because circuit court appointed special prosecutor for such matters and disqualified the respondent from handling them; court's opinion discusses range of violations that have justified interim suspension) (citation omitted). *But see Att'y Grievance Comm'n v. Downey,* 990 A.2d 1070, 1078 (Md. 2010) (noting the rule in Maryland permits, but does not require, interim suspension for conviction of a crime, the court denied the petition; relying on comments of the criminal sentencing judge characterizing the nature of lawyer's conviction as "just a regulatory compliance issue" and other circumstances that did not indicate a need to protect the public with lawyer's interim suspension).

Public confidence in the profession is strengthened when expedited procedures are available in such instances of lawyer misconduct. As explained in the

Commentary to Rule 19 of the MRLDE, it is difficult for the public to understand why a lawyer who has been convicted of stealing funds from a client can continue to handle client funds.

## *Lawyer Convicted of a Serious Crime*

A "serious crime" is defined in MRLDE Rule 19 (see also Annotation to Standard 2.2), which speaks in terms of a finding of guilt rather than a conviction. Rule 19, as originally adopted, referred to convictions. The Rule was amended in 1999 to provide for interim suspension upon a finding of guilt because of the often-significant delay between entry of the finding of guilt and entry of the ultimate judgment of conviction. Many courts still use the conviction to trigger interim suspension. *See, e.g., Att'y Grievance Comm'n v. Protokowicz*, 607 A.2d 33 (Md. 1992) (interim suspension warranted for conviction of breaking and entering and cruelly killing a cat by microwaving it); *In re Leibowitz*, 72 A.D.3d 1190, 1191 (N.Y. App. Div. 2010) (interim suspension of lawyer convicted of the federal offense of disclosure of classified information, a "serious crime," was proper; given the nature of the lawyer's offense, "allowing him to continue to practice is not 'consistent with the maintenance of the integrity and honor of the profession, the protection of the public [or] the interest of justice'") (citation omitted); *In re Baroni*, 152 A.D.3d 35 (N.Y App. Div. 2018) (crimes including conspiring to obtain by fraud, knowing conversion, and intentionally misapplying property of organization receiving federal benefits in effort to punish mayor for not supporting governor's re-election campaign were serious crimes meriting interim suspension); *In re Disciplinary Action Against Wolff*, 792 N.W.2d 499 (N.D. 2010) (lawyer's conviction for issuing a bank check with insufficient funds, a class C felony under North Dakota law, warranted an interim suspension).

Often, an interim suspension order does not recite details of the specific circumstances warranting the interim suspension. Rather, that is revealed in the final disciplinary order. *See, e.g., In re Smith*, 794 P.2d 601 (Ariz. 1990) (interim suspension upon conviction of federal felonies of aiding and abetting a mail fraud and aiding and abetting the sale of an unlicensed security); *In re Steiner*, 817 A.2d 793 (Del. 2003) (suspension of three years, retroactive to date of interim suspension, based on indictment on two counts of first-degree vehicular assault, a felony, and one count of driving under the influence); *In re Melvin*, 807 A.2d 550 (Del. 2002) (imposing eighteen-month suspension when lawyer pleaded guilty to misdemeanor criminal contempt of a protection order and hindering prosecution; basis of interim suspension had been indictment on felony charge of tampering with physical evidence); *In re Riddle*, 700 N.E.2d 788 (Ind. 1998) (interim suspension and, ultimately, disbarment of prosecutor, *pendente lite*, for ghost employment scam).

## *Lawyer Is Likely to Cause Immediate and Serious Injury*

As noted above, an interim suspension also may be warranted when sufficient evidence demonstrates that the lawyer has committed misconduct or is incapacitated and poses a substantial threat of serious harm to the public. *See Office of Disciplinary Counsel v. Fernandez,* No. SCAD-11-0000032, 2011 WL 1523482, at *1 (Haw. Apr. 18, 2011) (disciplinary counsel presented sufficient evidence demonstrating that lawyer "committed a violation of the Hawai'i Rules of Professional Conduct and poses a substantial threat of serious harm to the public," warranting an interim suspension pending the outcome of the disciplinary proceedings); *In re Tousant,* 851 So.2d 1048 (La. 2003) (interim suspension and subsequent disbarment of lawyer who had nineteen complaints pending against her alleging numerous violations of rules of professional conduct; lawyer was found to pose a substantial threat of serious harm to the public; court noting lawyer's complete and total disregard for welfare of clients); *In re Collie,* 749 S.E.2d 522 (S.C. 2013) (lawyer who persistently refused to comply with court rule and orders to provide current email address and maintain and monitor a working email account posed threat of serious harm to public and administration of justice and received interim suspension); *In re Discipline of Trujillo,* 24 P.3d 972, 980 (Utah 2001) (court reversed the denial of the petition for interim suspension and remanded the matter for application of the appropriate standard—that applied for issuing preliminary injunctions—"weighing the harm to the attorney in the event the interim suspension is granted against the harm to the public in the event the interim suspension is denied").

The Commentary to Rule 20 of the MRLDE provides that "[i]nterim suspension is also appropriate when the lawyer's continuing conduct is causing or is likely to cause serious injury to a client or the public." Two examples of such situations are a lawyer abandoning the practice of law and a lawyer engaged in ongoing trust-fund conversion.

For examples of client abandonment leading to an interim suspension, *see In re Brady,* 923 P.2d 836 (Ariz. 1996) (interim suspension and then disbarment of lawyer who mishandled or abandoned ten client cases when he left the country); *In re Callahan,* 64 So.3d 766, 767 (La. 2011) (noting that lawyer facing disbarment had been placed on interim suspension for "threat of harm to the public" following conduct that, inter alia, constituted abandonment of client matters); *In re Aubrey,* 928 So.2d 524 (La. 2006) (disbarment after interim suspension for abandonment of law practice, among other misconduct); *Lawyer Disciplinary Bd. v. Grafton,* 712 S.E.2d 488, 491 (W. Va. 2011) (court noting that while instant disciplinary proceeding was pending, lawyer received an interim suspension for "effectively abandon[ing] his clients and his law practice, posing a substantial threat of irreparable harm to his clients and the public").

For interim suspensions imposed for ongoing conversion of funds, *see In re Maguire,* 725 A.2d 417 (Del. 1999) (disbarment, following interim suspension when lawyer had record of repeated professional misconduct and Lawyer's Fund for Client Protection had paid $39,840 in claims by clients that were attributable to either his defalcations or inability to refund unearned fees); *In re Martin*, 883 So.2d 392 (La. 2004) (disbarring lawyer serving interim suspension for threat of harm to public for, inter alia, intentional conversion of client funds); *In re Morphis*, 831 So.2d 934 (La. 2002) (lawyer, who had been placed on immediate interim suspension for threat of harm when Office of Disciplinary Counsel first determined lawyer was mishandling large amounts of client funds, disbarred for commingling and converting in excess of $2.5 million in client funds); *In re Kennedy*, 87 A.D.3d 107, 110 (N.Y. App. Div. 2011) (concluding that lawyer's "admitted conversion and/or misappropriation of escrow funds, his failure to maintain a ledger for his escrow account, and his inability or unwillingness to account for numerous escrow account transactions, presents a continuous pattern of misconduct which constitutes an immediate threat to the public interest, warranting interim suspension"); *In re Murdock*, 968 P.2d 1270 (Or. 1998) (temporarily suspending salaried law firm associate who knowingly embezzled more than $9,000; finding lawyer's continued practice of law was likely to result in substantial harm to public, notwithstanding special master's conclusion that bar failed to establish risk of harm by preponderance of evidence).

### *Due Process Considerations*

Interim suspensions function similarly to civil temporary restraining orders, except that they do not automatically expire. MRLDE R. 20 cmt. Although due process does not require a hearing prior to imposing an interim suspension when a lawyer is found guilty of a serious crime or upon evidence that a lawyer poses a substantial threat of serious harm, an opportunity to show cause as to why it should not be imposed should be available. *See, e.g., People v. Varallo*, 913 P.2d 1 (Colo. 1996) (procedural due process is implicated anytime a lawyer's license is even temporarily suspended, but an interim suspension does not require a full evidentiary hearing; notice and opportunity to be heard to protect due process rights; interim suspension analogous to a preliminary injunction); *In re Richardson*, 692 A.2d 427 (D.C. 1997) (temporary suspension of lawyer subject to reciprocal disciplinary proceeding, without evidentiary hearing, does not violate due process); *In re Ellis*, 680 N.E.2d 1154 (Mass. 1997) (full evidentiary hearing before single justice not required before temporary suspension; appropriate for disciplinary counsel to rely on indictments, search warrants, and other documents to support request for interim suspension); *In re Disciplinary Proceeding Against Poole*, 193 P.3d 1064 (Wash. 2008) (lawyer's due process rights were not violated when bar association filed petition for interim suspension following lawyer's failure to produce client's billing file, knowing that another disciplinary matter was already before the court; association was authorized to seek order suspending lawyer pending compliance with the request and association advised lawyer that it would open a new grievance if lawyer failed to comply).

A lawyer should be given an opportunity to be heard about what constitutes a "serious crime." *See Hayes v. Ala. State Bar,* 719 So.2d 787, 790 (Ala. 1998) (court reversed disciplinary board's order granting "Petition for Determination of Serious Crimes" and imposing an interim suspension on nine lawyers who pleaded guilty to various misdemeanor charges involving deceptive conduct; lawyers should have been given "a meaningful opportunity to be heard" on whether their crimes constituted "serious crimes").

Further, as the Commentary to Rule 20 of the MRLDE explains, because an interim suspension can be imposed ex parte following efforts to notify a lawyer, a lawyer suspended without a hearing should be afforded an opportunity to challenge the suspension order on an expedited basis.

## *Length of Interim Suspension*

An interim suspension remains in effect until it is lifted by the court, or until the court imposes a final disciplinary sanction. Interim suspensions typically are followed by a suspension or disbarment. *See, e.g., In re Horwitz,* 881 P.2d 352 (Ariz. 1994) (disbarment effective to date lawyer was placed on interim suspension following negligent homicide convictions); *In re Brewster,* 587 A.2d 1067 (Del. 1991) (disbarring, as final sanction following interim suspension, for federal felony conviction for bank fraud); *In re Christie,* 574 A.2d 845 (Del. 1990) (three-year suspension following interim suspension for repetitive pedophilia); *In re Locklair,* 795 S.E.2d 9 (S.C. 2016) (disbarment with effective date retroactive to date of interim suspension for pattern of misconduct including neglect, failing to refund unearned fees, failing to cooperate with disciplinary authorities, and committing criminal acts). Interim suspension is not a precondition for disbarment. *See, e.g., In re Disciplinary Proceeding Against Kronenberg,* 117 P.3d 1134, 1141 n.9 (Wash. 2005) (disbarment not precluded because bar did not move for interim suspension prior to hearing; court noting that "[w]e have never held that an interim suspension is a prerequisite to disbarment and we decline to do so here").

In calculating the length of a subsequent suspension, courts may take into account the amount of time a lawyer has spent on interim suspension. *See, e.g., In re Schuler,* 818 P.2d 138 (Alaska 1991) (approving stipulated two-year suspension effective from date interim suspension was imposed for misdemeanor theft, court reasoned that practical effect would be suspension in excess of three years and two months; noting that if length of suspension had been calculated from date of issuance of opinion, rather than date of interim suspension, suspension would be in excess of five years and eight months); *In re Arrick,* 882 P.2d 943 (Ariz. 1994) (finding committee recommendation of one-year suspension essentially moot in light of fact that lawyer had been on interim suspension for a full four years; court concluded that the four-year interim suspension was sufficient, allowed lawyer to apply for reinstatement, and imposed two-year probation with conditions upon reinstatement); *People v. Gritchen*, 908 P.2d 70 (Colo. 1995) (denying motion for retroactive suspension in favor of two-year suspension when lawyer had been on interim suspension since 1994 for soliciting child prostitution; two-year suspension rather than three-year suspension appropriate because of length of lawyer's interim suspension); *Iowa Supreme Ct. Att'y Disciplinary Bd. v. Wright*, 857 N.W.2d 510 (Iowa 2014) (holding that "when we order an attorney's temporary suspension pending the outcome of a disciplinary proceeding for the same misconduct, we should give credit for the time served for the temporary suspension if the time served equals or exceeds the appropriate sanction"; court considered time respondent served on interim suspension when issuing sanction for practicing while suspended and trust account violations in one matter, but respondent still subject to additional suspension for misconduct in another matter); *Disciplinary Counsel v. Jacobs*, 14 N.E.3d 984 (Ohio 2014) (lawyer placed on interim suspension following conviction for filing false tax return; final discipline of two-year suspension ordered with credit for time served under interim suspension); *In re Disciplinary Proceeding Against Curran*, 801 P.2d 962, 974–75 (Wash. 1990) (conviction on two counts of vehicular homicide resulting from driving while intoxicated warranted six-month suspension rather than two-year suspension, when lawyer already had spent eighteen months on interim suspension; reasoning that "[t]his suspension was as real to him as a suspension ordered after completion of disciplinary proceedings"). *But see In re Higgins*, 884 P.2d 1094 (Ariz. 1994) (finding retroactive suspension makes no sense when lawyer ceased practice for only three months and, although he was given an interim suspension, was placed on probation shortly thereafter pursuant to stipulation; imposing continued probation for additional term of two years).

Both Rules 19 and 20 of the MRLDE provide for dissolution or modification of an interim suspension. For example, Paragraph D(1) of MRLDE 19, interim suspension for a lawyer found guilty of a crime, provides that in "the interest of justice, the court may terminate an interim suspension at any time upon a showing of extraordinary circumstances . . ." MRLDE 20 provides that the respondent may move to dissolve or modify an interim suspension order. Neither rule addresses explicitly the staying of an interim suspension order, but some jurisdictions have provided for such action. *See In re Discipline of Trefflinger*, 393 P.3d 1084 (Nev. 2017) (court entered interim suspension, but then stayed it with conditions for a lawyer who conditionally pled guilty to one count of possession of heroin without intent to sell and was placed into a diversion program, the successful completion of which would result in the dismissal of charges and no final conviction; citing Standard 2.4 and MRLDE 19, court affirmed that interim suspensions appropriate for conditional guilty pleas, but noted that rule was silent as to what constitutes "good cause shown" to set-aside or stay interim suspension; court created three-step test for making good cause determination consisting of: (1) looking to the danger that the lawyer poses to the public, clients, and the courts due to the nature of the crime; (2) determining whether there is a substantial likelihood of significant final discipline; and (3) considering the nature of harm that an interim suspension will cause to the lawyer and existing clients). *See also, Tapp v. Supreme Ct. Comm'n on Prof'l Conduct,* 428 S.W.3d 492 (Ark. 2013) (based on petition for writ of certiorari, request by lawyer to vacate interim suspension order during pendency of disbarment proceedings and replace with order imposing "reasonable conditions" denied; court references four-factor test in determining whether interim suspension was proper and should not be vacated: (1) will public suffer irreparable harm unless interim suspension is ordered; (2) does threatened injury to public outweigh harm to respondent caused by interim suspension; (3) is interim suspension adverse to the public interest; and (4) is there a substantial likelihood that the underlying misconduct will result in significant discipline.)

## 2.5 Reprimand

**Reprimand, also known as censure or public censure, is a form of public discipline which declares the conduct of the lawyer improper, but does not limit the lawyer's right to practice.**

# Annotation

### *Value of Public Sanction*

A public sanction serves the useful purpose of publicly identifying lawyers who have violated ethical standards and, if accompanied by a published opinion, educates members of the bar as to these standards. Publicity also enhances the effect of the discipline and emphasizes the concern of the court with all lawyer misconduct, not only serious ethical violations. *See, e.g., People v. Smith,* 769 P.2d 1078 (Colo. 1989) (private censure forgone and public censure imposed because private discipline did not inform the public of the lawyer's neglect and dishonesty). In *In re Doughty,* 832 A.2d 724 (Del. 2003), the court publicly reprimanded a lawyer for negligent violation of recordkeeping requirements, stating:

> [A] public sanction affords the Court the opportunity to underscore how serious the Court considers a lawyer's obligation to maintain orderly books and records. . . . A public sanction also serves as an important preventive measure in cases such as this in which the violations could be readily repeated without prompt detection. A public sanction puts clients on notice of past problems and allows them to take any steps deemed necessary to protect their own interests.

*Id.* at 736–37; *see also In re Wall,* 38 P.3d 640, 650 (Kan. 2002) (quoting Standard 2.5 and citing its former commentary in imposing published censure for, inter alia, lack of diligence; stating in response to lawyer's suggestion that his name be omitted from published opinion: "No precedent is cited in support of that type of opinion. We reject the suggestion."). In *Clark's Case,* 619 A.2d 220 (N.H. 1992), the court, in imposing public reprimand for failure to timely respond to disciplinary committee requests, stated:

> At some point, a respondent's repeated disregard of the duty to cooperate with the committee must be made public, both to correct the misconduct that private discipline seems insufficient to deter and to ensure that the committee obtains the information that it requires to investigate disciplinary matters. We conclude that the respondent's misconduct has reached that point. A profession whose reason for being is, in

> large part, the resolution of all manner of disputes within the society in which it serves, will be ill equipped to that task if it cannot with fairness and dispatch resolve disputes within its own ranks. The respondent's conduct in this case is an impediment to such an objective.

*Id.* at 221; *see also In re Friessen*, 991 P.2d 400 (Kan. 1999) (citing Standard 2.5, court imposed public censure upon a lawyer who negotiated unauthorized settlement of $2,400 and asked if client would accept $500); *In re Howes*, 940 P.2d 159, 171 (N.M. 1997) (quoting Standard 2.5, court imposed public censure on assistant U.S. attorney who improperly communicated with a represented defendant, citing former commentary to Standard 2.5 that public discipline "serves the useful purpose of identifying lawyers who have violated ethical standards and, if accompanied by a published opinion, educates members of the bar as to those standards."); *State ex rel. Okla. Bar Ass'n v. Strickland*, 256 P.3d 76, 79 (Okla. 2011) (concluding public censure, rather than private reprimand, was appropriate sanction for lawyer convicted of failing to file annual tax return; believing the lawyer's hard-learned lesson from failing to fulfill tax obligations would deter other lawyers from following in the same path, the court entered "a public censure in this case 'not for the purpose of punishing [this] attorney, but . . . to safeguard the interests of the public, the courts and the legal profession'") (citation omitted); *State ex rel. Okla. Bar Ass'n v. Murdock*, 236 P.3d 107, 113 (Okla. 2010) (the "Court's interest in explaining its expectations of professional legal practice may necessitate a more public form of discipline than that offered by private reprimand"; public censure for two counts of criminal sexual battery charges reduced to misdemeanor of Outraging Public Decency following lawyer's *Alford* plea); *In re Disciplinary Proceedings Against Bowe*, 800 N.W.2d 367, 372 (Wis. 2011) (concluding public reprimand was appropriate sanction for lawyer's repeated misrepresentations before a court in a divorce matter; "[a]lthough we are persuaded a suspension is not necessary to protect the public and the judicial system in this instance, [respondent] is admonished that a public reprimand should not be interpreted as indicating this court is untroubled by her misconduct").

## *Circumstances Appropriate for Reprimand*

A reprimand is appropriate in cases when a lawyer's conduct, although violating ethical standards, is not serious enough to warrant suspension or disbarment. *See, e.g., People v. Dalton*, 367 P.3d 126 (Colo. O.P.D.J. 2016) ( despite knowing violation of rule requiring lawyer to explain basis of fee in writing when lawyer had not previously represented client, court imposed public censure; because Sanctions Standards do not speak directly to failure to set forth fee in writing, court looked to related precedent and Standard 7.3, which states that reprimand is appropriate for single instance of charging excessive or improper fee as being most closely analogous to the current matter); *Iowa Supreme Ct. Att'y Disciplinary Bd. v. Smith*, 904 N.W.2d 154 (Iowa 2017) (respondent's request for private admonition for failing to reconcile trust accounts every month, and because no actual harm to clients occurred, rejected by court; holding that a public reprimand was appropriate, the court cited the potential for harm in respondent's conduct and held that public reprimand, not suspension, was consistent with precedent for minor trust account violations); *Bd. of Prof'l Responsibility v. Baker*, 326 P.3d 162 (Wyo. 2014) (reprimanding lawyer for complicity in client's not disclosing income to Social Security Administration, court cited to Standard 2.5's statement that reprimand demonstrates that the conduct of a lawyer is inappropriate but does not warrant limitations on practice; court also noted rationale underlying Standard 2.5 of educating the bar and enhancing the effect of discipline).

The types of misconduct that fall within Standard 2.5 may be described as "lesser misconduct." Rule 9(B) of the MRLDE provides the following definition of lesser misconduct:

> Lesser misconduct is conduct that does not warrant a sanction restricting the respondent's license to practice law. Conduct shall not be considered lesser misconduct if any of the following considerations apply:
>
> (1) the misconduct involves the misappropriation of funds;
>
> (2) the misconduct results in or is likely to result in substantial prejudice to a client or other person;
>
> (3) the respondent has been publicly disciplined in the last three years;
>
> (4) the misconduct is of the same nature as misconduct for which the respondent has been disciplined in the last five years;
>
> (5) the misconduct involves dishonesty, deceit, fraud, or misrepresentation by the respondent;
>
> (6) the misconduct constitutes a "serious crime" as defined in Rule 19(C); or
>
> (7) the misconduct is part of a pattern of similar misconduct.

Thus, courts have imposed reprimands when a lawyer has engaged in negligent misconduct. *See, e.g., People v. Dillings*, 880 P.2d 1220 (Colo. 1994) (accepting stipulation to public censure for negligent false statements made during discovery in lawyer's personal injury action); *In re Elgart*, 999 A.2d 853, 859 (Del. 2010) (imposing public reprimand on lawyer who mishandled insurance proceeds in client's personal injury case and failed to disclose information to the Office of Disciplinary Counsel; noting that lawyer's negligence resulted from poor record-keeping and Sanctions Standards support public reprimand as the appropriate sanction for "lawyer misconduct involving diligence, competence and obligations to disciplinary authorities"); *In re Carpenter*, 808 P.2d 1341 (Kan. 1991) (negligence by prosecutor in failing to determine results of inquiry to hospital as to whether rape victim had gonorrhea before asserting that fact at trial warranted public censure); *In re Klemp*, 418 P.3d 733 (Or. 2018) (lawyer acted negligently when engaging in improper communication with unrepresented party because she did not know of party's confusion regarding her role; multiple aggravating factors did not dissuade the court from imposing a reprimand); *Garland v. Bd. of Prof'l Responsibility*, 536 S.W.3d 811 (Tenn. 2017) (lawyer acted negligently when failing to keep client apprised of status of adoption matter and not promptly responding to client's requests for information; public censure supported by "substantial and material evidence"); *Bd. of Prof'l Responsibility v. Jolley*, 805 P.2d 862, 863 (Wyo. 1991) (public censure of lawyer who, in attempt to obtain release of incarcerated criminal defendant client, swore at a justice of the peace over the telephone when he refused to release client and threatened that, unless his client was released from jail, he or his client would sue the county, demand a jury trial, and "cause everyone as much trouble and expense" as possible; lawyer also omitted from bar application that his prior arrest for assault and battery included assault with attempt to commit rape). *But see Fla. Bar v. Adorno*, 60 So.3d 1016, 1033 (Fla. 2011) (concluding public reprimand recommended by referee was an inappropriate sanction for lawyer whose "actions in breaching the essential obligation to his clients were intentional and not negligent"; imposing three-year suspension as lawyer's actions, including lawyer's breach of his fiduciary obligations to thousands of putative class members, were deliberate and knowing).

Reprimand also may be appropriate when there has been little or no injury as a result of a lawyer's misconduct or when there is little threat of future injury. *See, e.g., In re Brown*, 392 P.3d 474 (Alaska 2017) (public censure and not suspension appropriate for experienced lawyer who knowingly disregarded court order in handling criminal appeal and neglected matter, because of lesser degree of injury to client; no likelihood client would suffer adverse ruling on merits despite delay caused by misconduct); *People v. Peters*, 82 P.3d 389 (Colo. O.P.D.J. 2003) (public censure of lawyer who used shortcut system of obtaining process server's signature on blank affidavits and having completed affidavits notarized in his absence; suspension unnecessary to protect public because substantial remedial measures were taken); *State ex rel. Counsel for Discipline v. Wintroub*, 800 N.W.2d 269 (Neb. 2011) (public reprimand was appropriate sanction for lawyer's misconduct in obtaining a loan from a client who did not suffer any economic injury—due to the fact that the client had been reimbursed in full with interest before disciplinary action was filed; lack of economic injury was also considered in mitigation).

Some courts have opted to impose a reprimand, even when the misconduct does not fit the definition of "lesser misconduct," because a suspension appears too severe and a private reprimand too lenient. *See, e.g., Romero-Barcelo v. Acevedo-Vila*, 275 F. Supp. 2d 177 (D.P.R. 2003) (quoting Standard 2.5, court found public reprimand warranted for false statements in Federal Elections Commission complaint accusing political rival of receiving illegal campaign contributions because misconduct caused harm and, while not rising to seriousness of disbarment or suspension, deserved public reprimand); *In re Fink*, 22 A.3d 461, 475 (Vt. 2011) (lawyer's failure to put contingent fee agreement in writing and attempt to charge unreasonable contingent fee for his services warranted public reprimand with probationary period rather than disciplinary counsel's recommendation of suspension; balancing all relevant circumstances, suspension was inappropriate as some misconduct was based on negligence, and private reprimand was inappropriate as there was actual injury to the public and potential injury to the client). In *In re Wenk*, 678 A.2d 898 (Vt. 1996), the Vermont Supreme Court said that a public reprimand was adequate to protect the public from further misconduct by a lawyer who knowingly deceived client as to the status of pending litigation. The court stated:

> Had there been any evidence of actual injury in this case, we would not hesitate to recommend . . . suspen[sion]. However, the majority is mindful of the Supreme Court's position that suspension of lawyers for a period of less than six months is inappropriate. We feel that a suspension of that duration would be far too severe in this case. In this case the injury is speculative and was at least partially a product of respondent's medical disability. In such circumstances, we feel that a suspension would serve merely a punitive function.

*Id.* at 901.

## *Additional Conditions*

A reprimand is not always sufficient to protect the public; courts may also attach conditions to that sanction. When a lawyer lacks competence in one area of practice or neglects client matters, for example, the court can impose a reprimand and require the lawyer to attend CLE courses, take and pass the MPRE, or meet other conditions. *See, e.g., In re Hohn*, 832 P.2d 192 (Ariz. 1992) (public censure and completion of CLE courses in creditor's rights and ethics ordered for lawyer who improperly filed *lis pendens* in attempt to circumvent requirements for provisional remedies); *In re Elgart*, 999 A.2d 853 (Del. 2010) (public reprimand, eighteen-month probation period, and additional requirement that disciplined lawyer complete twelve hours of CLE in law office management ordered for lawyer whose misconduct stemmed in part from negligent recordkeeping); *In re Brown*, 778 S.E.2d 790 (Ga. 2015) (in case involving petition for consensual discipline, court imposed public reprimand and order to consult with State Bar's law practice management section after failing to properly handle funds relating to the sale of property in a divorce matter); *In re Eddings*, 795 S.E.2d 183 (Ga. 2016) (rejecting Bar's recommendation for disbarment, court reprimanded lawyer whose wife was his firm's financial manager and stole, without his knowledge, $2.3 million from his trust account; court, noting that lawyer was victim of an elaborate scam, including a bank unwittingly helping wife cover up theft, also ordered lawyer to participate in Bar's law practice management program, take and pass MPRE, and make full restitution to victims within five years); *Lutes v. Ky. Bar Ass'n*, 338 S.W.3d 278 (Ky. 2011) (approving negotiated sanction of a public reprimand with conditions including successful completion of bar association's seven-hour Ethics and Professionalism Enhancement Program, as well as passing score on the ethics exam given at the end of the program; noting that failure to comply with the conditions within one year of the order would result in the reprimand becoming a thirty-day suspension); *In re Disciplinary Action Against Nassif*, 504 N.W.2d 311 (N.D. 1993) (public reprimand and obtaining a passing score on the MPRE was appropriate sanction for previously disciplined lawyer whose recent misconduct involved neglect and lack of diligence); *In re Disciplinary Action Against Johnson*, 872 N.W.2d 300 (N.D. 2015) (public reprimand and completion of CLE relating to conflicts of interest for lawyer who hired paralegal who previously worked for opposing counsel's office and failed to properly screen the paralegal from a case).

## 2.6 Admonition

**Admonition, also known as private reprimand, is a form of non-public discipline which declares the conduct of the lawyer improper, but does not limit the lawyer's right to practice.**

# Annotation

### *Private Sanction*

Admonition is the least serious of the formal disciplinary sanctions and is the only private sanction. This sanction is also sometimes called a private reprimand or private censure. *See, e.g., In re Mulhall,* 768 P.2d 1173, 1177 n.3 (Ariz. 1989) (noting Arizona's informal reprimand is equivalent of Standard 2.6 "admonition, also known as private reprimand").

A private sanction under Standard 2.6 is only appropriate in limited situations, and thus courts have rejected various arguments by lawyers wishing to avoid public sanctions in favor of a private admonition. *See, e.g., People v. Bergner,* 873 P.2d 726, 728 (Colo. 1994) (imposing public censure over lawyer's objections that public discipline would adversely affect his ability to participate in certain religious and charitable organizations and activities; reasoning that "[w]hile these concerns may prove accurate, the gravity of the respondent's misconduct, when coupled with the fact of his prior discipline, requires the imposition of a public censure"); *In re Lassen,* 672 A.2d 988, 1000 (Del. 1996) (rejecting proffer of voluntary permanent retirement sanction in exchange for private admonition; private admonition under Standard 2.6 is inappropriate in this case for several reasons, including that the concept of admonition "implies advice to correct" and thus does not apply to one permanently retiring from law practice); *Long v. Ethics & Discipline Comm'n of the Utah Supreme Ct.,* 256 P.3d 206, 221 (Utah 2011) (lawyer received public reprimand and nonpublic admonition in two separate matters related to charging of unreasonable fees; in rejecting lawyer's argument that nonpublic admonitions were warranted in both matters as they involved violations of the same rules, court concluded that ordering a public reprimand in one case and a nonpublic admonition in another was "not inconsistent . . . because each case involves different facts and circumstances" and the level of injury suffered in each case was different); *In re Disciplinary Proceedings Against Shepherd,* 897 N.W.2d 44 (Wis. 2017) (lawyer on interim suspension argued private sanction appropriate for multiple violations involving three clients and practicing law while suspended, because he suffered from depression, planned to leave the practice of law, and public sanction would "exacerbate his feelings of shame and sense of failure"; court upheld referee's rejection of offer of private sanction in exchange for resignation, finding that while depression played a role in the misconduct, the referee took that into consideration at mitigation in determining public reprimand appropriate).

## *Minor Misconduct*

Admonition should be used only in cases of minor misconduct, when there is little or no injury to a client, the public, the legal system, or the profession, and when there is little or no likelihood of repetition. *See, e.g., In re Charge of Unprofessional Misconduct*, 899 N.W.2d 821 (Minn. 2017) (court held private admonishment appropriate for lawyer who, in one instance, revealed confidential information regarding a former client to insurance adjuster; conduct was isolated, court determined it to be not serious, and there was minimal, if any, harm to the client); *In re PRB Docket No. 2007-046*, 989 A.2d 523, 531 (Vt. 2009) (private admonition for two lawyers who falsely denied they were recording a telephone conversation with a potential witness; private discipline was appropriate given that "there was no injury to the client, little damage to the public trust, the legal system, or the profession, and nothing in the record suggest[ed] a likelihood of repetition"); *In re PRB*, 165 A.3d 130 (Vt. 2017) (while presumptive sanction was reprimand for lawyer who did not maintain and reconcile trust account records for nine months and who failed to categorize IOLTA transactions by client or matter, private admonition imposed due to significant mitigation including lawyer hired accountant, took remedial measures, and no injury to any client); *Lawyer Disciplinary Bd. v. Beveridge*, 459 S.E.2d 542 (W. Va. 1995) (when lack of organization and management were root causes of lawyer's difficulties, court found most effective sanction was admonition coupled with six months of supervised practice and payment of costs); *cf. Toth v. Disciplinary Bd.*, 562 N.W.2d 744 (N.D. 1997) (in dismissing the complaint against lawyer, court noted that admonition is generally a sanction imposed for lesser misconduct; court finding inconsistency between board's issuance of admonition and finding of misrepresentation, of the most serious charges brought against a lawyer); *In re Farrar*, 949 A.2d 438, 440 (Vt. 2008) (despite the presence of several mitigating factors, court determined that public reprimand and not private admonition was appropriate given the nature of respondent's offense—the "serious offense" of commingling client and personal funds in a lawyer's trust account; "[p]rivate reproval should be used only 'in cases of minor misconduct, when there is little or no injury to a client, the public, the legal system, or the profession, and when there is little likelihood of repetition by the lawyer'"; "we cannot characterize respondent's acts as minor").

An admonition is inappropriate in cases of more serious misconduct. *See, e.g., People v. Blundell*, 901 P.2d 1268 (Colo. 1995) (respondent's prolonged course of disturbing conduct constituted serious error in professional judgment, not simple negligence; thus public, not private, censure warranted); *People v. Wilder*, 860 P.2d 523, 523 (Colo. 1993) (holding that "[t]he seriousness of the respondent's misconduct, which involved at least a reckless disregard of his obligation not to withhold material information from the fact finder in a legal proceeding, precludes a private sanction"); *In re Blase*, 920 P.2d 931, 938 (Kan. 1996) (quoting Standard 2.6 in rejecting panel's recommendation of "formal reprimand" as a "middle ground" between published censure and informal admonition for active involvement in illegal check-kiting scheme; imposing public censure); *State ex rel. Okla. Bar Ass'n v. Strickland*, 256 P.3d 76 (Okla. 2011) (public censure, rather than private reprimand, for lawyer convicted of failing to file an annual tax return, who also had a history of not filing tax returns; noting that such conduct is serious and should be addressed publicly in order to deter other lawyers from committing similar acts).

### *Little or No Injury/Recidivism Unlikely*

As noted above, one criterion for an admonition is that the degree of injury or potential injury must be little or none. When greater actual injury occurs, a more severe sanction than an admonition under Standard 2.6 is indicated. *See, e.g., People v. Brady*, 923 P.2d 887 (Colo. 1996) (because $15,000 injury suffered by clients from respondent's misconduct could not be characterized as "little," private discipline not appropriate); *In re Goldstein*, 990 A.2d 404 (Del. 2010) (imposing public rather than private reprimand for lawyer who committed misconduct during the course of handling ten closings for a private money lender; while lawyer's actions were negligent, misconduct caused actual injury to all 10 borrowers, including $85,000 in damages connected with loan documents that violated federal law). A sanction of public reprimand rather than private admonition also is warranted when the potential injury from a lawyer's misconduct is greater than little or none. *See, e.g., People v. Bertagnolli*, 861 P.2d 717, 721 (Colo. 1993) (imposing public censure and finding private sanction would be "unduly lenient" when lawyer's conduct in misleading arbitrators as to witness's mistaken testimony went "beyond mere negligence"; although misconduct caused no actual harm, "it cannot be said that the potential for harm was negligible"); *People v. Lopez*, 845 P.2d 1153, 1155 (Colo. 1993) (public rather than private censure appropriate when unlawful disclosure of client confidence created "a very real potential for injury"); *In re Fink*, 22 A.3d 461 (Vt. 2011) (public rather than private reprimand warranted for lawyer's knowing and negligent misconduct in failing to put contingent fee agreement in writing and in attempting to charge an unreasonable fee; concluding that while there was no actual harm to the client, there was potential for significant injury to the client had the lawyer not been dismissed from the case and subsequently collected the excessive fee); *In re Anderson*, 769 A.2d 1282 (Vt. 2000) (private admonition is an insufficient sanction for lawyer who delayed in reporting another lawyer's mishandling of a shared client trust account and failed to monitor the trust account for irregularities; injury to the public, although intangible, was still significant and required a public reprimand). *But see United States v. Koubriti*, 305 F. Supp. 2d

723, 763–64 (E.D. Mich. 2003) (imposing a formal judicial admonishment under Standard 6.2, the "most modest among the range of disciplinary measures," for Attorney General John Ashcroft's inadvertent public statements in violation of a court order; reasoning that "while the Attorney General's comments created a real potential for prejudice and interference with these proceedings, the Court already has observed that no actual prejudice resulted from these remarks").

Another criterion in the admonition calculus is whether a lawyer is likely to repeat the misconduct. When recidivism is likely, an admonition is not indicated. *See, e.g., People v. Cabral*, 888 P.2d 245 (Colo. 1995) (because of prior discipline, it cannot be assumed that repetition of misconduct is unlikely, and private discipline is inappropriate); *In re Lassen*, 672 A.2d 988, 999 (Del. 1996) (finding the "principal aggravating factor is that Respondent's conduct at issue here is in the nature of a repeat offense," making private admonition under Standard 2.6 inappropriate; public reprimand and three years' suspension warranted for serious misconduct including false billings and misrepresentations to the court).

The three criteria—minor misconduct; little or no injury to a client, the public, the legal system, or the profession; and little or no likelihood of repetition—are considered together. Thus, even when rehabilitative efforts might reduce the likelihood of repeated misconduct, if the injury or potential injury was serious, a private admonition is not warranted. *See, e.g., People v. Wallace*, 837 P.2d 1223 (Colo. 1992) (suspension for three months upon conviction for assaulting girlfriend; reasoning that private sanction not appropriate because, although lawyer's rehabilitation in treatment program for batterers may reduce the chances that such an incident of violence will be repeated, misconduct actually caused serious injury on more than one occasion); *People v. Senn*, 824 P.2d 822 (Colo. 1992) (public rather than private censure appropriate when intoxicated lawyer discharged pistol above wife's head; reasoning that although evidence of lawyer's rehabilitation and reconciliation with wife may reduce chances of repeated incidents, misconduct went beyond mere negligence and posed a significant danger of serious injury).

## *Balancing Public Protection and Lawyer's Reputation*

Relying on the above criteria should help protect the public while, at the same time, avoiding damage to a lawyer's reputation when future ethical violations seem unlikely. To enhance the preventive nature of lawyer discipline, the court or disciplinary agency should publish description of cases where admonitions are imposed without disclosing the lawyer's name. For example, in *Wilhelm v. Idaho State Bar*, 89 P.3d 870 (Idaho 2004), the Idaho Supreme Court ruled on a challenge by the lawyer's client, "Defendant A," that the lawyer had failed to produce an adequate itemization of fees charged to handle a criminal matter. Applying Standard 2.6, the court found that, although the lawyer's billing practices were in disarray, he did not seek to defraud his client or try to cover up any wrongdoing and that at worst he was negligent. The court concluded that a private reprimand was appropriate because there was little or no likelihood of repetition. *See also An Unnamed Attorney v. Ky. Bar Ass'n,* 345 S.W.3d 851, 852 n.1 (Ky. 2011) (private reprimand for lawyer who deducted fee from settlement proceeds in automobile accident case without notifying chiropractor who had lien against proceeds; court redacted lawyer's name and any fact-specific identifying information, stating that "[t]hough the reprimand is private, the parties and the Court believe other members of the bar will benefit from a published redacted opinion disapproving the attorney's actions).

In contrast, the U.S. District Court in *United States v. Koubriti,* 305 F. Supp. 2d 723, 764 n. 25 (E.D. Mich. 2003), did name Attorney General John Ashcroft in imposing an admonition. While the court recognized that admonitions generally are a private form of discipline, Attorney General Ashcroft was named because his statements in violation of a court order had been widely reported in the media, the defendants' motion was part of the public record in the case, the possibility of contempt proceedings against the attorney general was frequently reported in the news, and the position of attorney general is a highly visible and public office. The court concluded that "[u]nder these circumstances, the Court's resolution of this matter necessarily and unavoidably is, and should be, available for public scrutiny." *See also In re Gerber,* 868 N.W.2d 861 (N.D. 2015) (lawyer who was licensed in Minnesota and not North Dakota admonished by court for improperly holding himself out as a lawyer while working as lobbyist in North Dakota branch of Minnesota firm; court, while noting the purposes of a private admonition, stated that "although this Court has recognized an admonition is intended to be a non-public form of discipline . . . we have acknowledged that any form of discipline this court imposes will be de facto public") (citation omitted). For further discussion of this case, see Annotation to Standard 6.2.

## 2.7 Probation

**Probation is a sanction that allows a lawyer to practice law under specified conditions. Probation can be imposed alone or in conjunction with a reprimand, an admonition or immediately following a suspension. Probation can also be imposed as a condition of readmission or reinstatement.**

# Annotation

## *Little Likelihood of Public Harm*

Probation is a sanction that should be imposed when a lawyer's right to practice law needs to be monitored or limited rather than suspended or revoked. Probation is appropriate when a lawyer can perform legal services but has problems that require supervision, such as improper maintenance of books and records, lack of timely communication with clients, mental or physical disabilities, or alcohol and chemical dependency. By imposing probation, courts allow a lawyer to continue to practice, but require the lawyer to meet certain conditions that will protect the public and assist the lawyer to meet ethical obligations. *See, e.g., In re Redondo,* 861 P.2d 619, 623 (Ariz. 1993) (court's "carefully crafted disposition" included suspension followed by "a lengthy term of *supervised* probation," which court said would protect the public from the lawyer and at the same time give him an opportunity to cure his significant problems before he was allowed to practice on an unsupervised basis again); *In re Reardon,* 759 A.2d 568, 577 (Del. 2000) ("Probation, as a rehabilitative sanction, is justified . . . when it appears that the conduct at issue is capable of being corrected. And, if it is not corrected, suspension or revocation, as the case may be, should follow."); *In re Jordan,* 623 N.E.2d 1372 (Ill. 1993) (court expanded probation to apply in cases when no disability proven); *In re LaHatte,* 851 So.2d 1024 (La. 2003) (record did not demonstrate that respondent's commingling and conversion of third-party funds was a direct result of his impaired state of mind caused by alcoholism, although court accepted his condition as a factor to be considered in mitigation; two-year suspension with all but six months deferred and four-year probation subject to conditions, including continuing participation in recovery programs and retaining a certified public accountant (CPA) to monitor his trust and operating accounts). In *Louisiana State Bar Association v. Longenecker,* 538 So.2d 156 (La. 1988), the Louisiana Supreme Court vacated suspension and imposed a two-year probation on a lawyer who suffered alcoholic psychosis at time of misconduct, but had been in recovery. The court said:

> It is highly unlikely that the profession or the public will be endangered by the continuation of respondent's license to practice law under

> probationary guidelines and supervision. Indeed, conditions of probation not only will insure that respondent will practice according to acceptable standards, but also may provide valuable public service (such as counseling to attorneys undergoing alcohol-related problems).

*Id.* at 164.

Probation is also an appropriate sanction when there is little likelihood that the respondent will harm the public during rehabilitation. *See* MRLDE R. 10(A)(3); *see also In re Levine*, 847 P.2d 1093, 1121 (Ariz. 1993) (finding probation under Standard 2.7 appropriate for lawyer who brought frivolous and harassing actions in wake of breakup of law firm because "imposition of terms of probation that incorporate respondent's rehabilitative efforts, including the mentoring program and counseling, will sufficiently reduce the likelihood that respondent will engage in future misconduct and will provide a means to provide restitution to the victims of his previous misconduct"); *In re Taylor*, 802 So.2d 1287 (La. 2002) (accepting consent discipline of deferred suspension, followed by supervised probation for two instances of neglect when lawyer no longer practicing law moved out of state, and presented little risk of future harm to the public); *Bd. of Prof'l Responsibility v. Daniel*, 549 S.W.3d 90 (Tenn. 2018) (in misappropriation case, court suspended lawyer for three years, with one year of active suspension followed by two years of probation, finding Board acted arbitrarily and capriciously by probating the entire suspension; court reiterated that probation appropriate where little likelihood that lawyer will harm public during period of rehabilitation). *But see In re Wright*, 76 P.3d 1018 (Kan. 2003) (rejecting panel recommendation of three-year suspension with five-year probation subject to conditions and disbarring lawyer who caused actual injury by intentionally writing forty-seven checks for his own use from account of great aunt for whom he held power of attorney and from entity account for which he served as secretary/treasurer); *In re Key*, 113 P.3d 340 (N.M. 2005) (suspending lawyer for duration of federal probation and rejecting probation based on argument that continued practice by lawyer convicted of felony tax offense would in no way endanger public; court concerned not only with public protection but equally with public perception of profession and with protecting profession and legal system).

### *Probation in Conjunction with Other Sanctions*

The need for probation can arise in a variety of situations. *See, e.g., In re Zawada*, 92 P.3d 862, 871 (Ariz. 2004) (six-month-and-one-day suspension followed by one-year, bar-supervised probation for prosecutorial misconduct; reasoning that censure or even the imposition of probation without suspension "would undermine the disciplinary process applicable to all lawyers, would contravene the presumptive discipline suggested by the ABA *Standards*, and would be grossly disproportionate to discipline imposed in other cases in which serious misconduct was found"); *In re Holmes*, 855 So.2d 736 (La. 2003) (accepting consent discipline for one-year-and-one-day suspension, with all but six months deferred, subject to eighteen-month probation with conditions for neglecting client matter resulting in dismissal of lawsuit); *In re Dumaine*, 818 So.2d 756 (La. 2002) (suspension of one year with six months deferred, plus one-year supervised probation, when lawyer's neglect and failure to communicate with clients was more negligent than intentional); *State ex rel. Okla. Bar Ass'n v. Smith*, 246 P.3d 1090, 1096 (Okla. 2011) (lawyer's misconduct resulted from an addiction to pain medication and her "conduct in confronting her addiction and seeking treatment, her self-reporting to the Bar and her forthrightness and cooperation throughout the disciplinary process serves as an example to other lawyers who are addicted"; concluding that under those circumstances public censure with a deferred suspension of one year, subject to ten agreed probationary conditions, was appropriate to serve as a deterrent and "to encourage a permanent change of lifestyle"); *In re Disciplinary Proceeding Against Christopher*, 105 P.3d 976 (Wash. 2005) (imposing eighteen-month suspension followed by three-year period of probation for falsifying court documents and forging secretary's signature).

Probation can be imposed either alone or with a sanction of reprimand, admonition, or suspension (actual or stayed). *See, e.g., In re La Paglia*, 843 P.2d 1271 (Ariz. 1992) (imposing censure for lack of diligence, in addition to two-year probation with terms including a law office audit, law office management counseling, continued therapy, and requirement that lawyer inform state bar in writing within ten days of his return to private practice); *In re Elinoff*, 22 P.3d 60 (Colo. 2001) (imposing three-year suspension, with one-year suspension while on probation, for lawyer's attempted bribe of two police officers); *In re Pearson*, 888 N.W.2d (Minn. 2016) (public reprimand plus one-year unsupervised probation for minor bookkeeping violations); *In re PRB Docket No. 2014.133*, 136 A.3d 564 (Vt. 2015) (lawyer who engaged in minor violation of rules regarding trust account maintenance admonished and placed on probation for one year to be monitored).

There are, nonetheless, cases in which courts have found probation inappropriate in light of other discipline imposed. *See, e.g., In re Blair*, 840 So.2d 1191 (La. 2003) (imposing three-month suspension because conduct of lawyer who prepared will with legacy in favor of his wife was negligent and not due to improper motive; declining board's recommendation to suspend for six months with six months' supervised probation and requirement of successful completion of ethics school program offered through state bar association); *In re Obert*, 89 P.3d 1173 (Or. 2004) (setting aside stayed suspension with two-year probation in favor of 30-day suspension; court disfavors probationary terms unless stipulated; when misconduct warrants lengthy probation, concrete suspension period is preferable due to uncertainties in probation monitoring process); *In re Schaffner*, 918 P.2d 803

(Or. 1996) (finding probation not indicated when 120-day suspension justified for knowing neglect of client's case and for failure to cooperate with disciplinary investigation).

## *Probation as Deterrent*

Courts sometimes note that a supervised probationary period imposed with a sanction of reprimand or admonition can help ensure that the lawyer's misconduct will not recur and may be more effective than unsupervised suspension. *See, e.g., In re Piatt,* 951 P.2d 889, 892 (Ariz. 1997) (public censure with one-year probation for sexual extortion and harassment; conditions included participation in membership assistance program of state bar, counseling at lawyer's expense, and supervision by practice monitor; court said a public censure and publication of opinion would get the lawyer's attention: "And supervised probation with counseling is more likely than unsupervised suspension to ensure that this behavior will never happen again. The prospect that noncompliance will lead to revocation of probation, suspension or disbarment is likely to be a powerful incentive to change.").

## *Probation as Condition of Reinstatement*

Probation also can be imposed as a condition of readmission following disbarment or as a condition of reinstatement following a period of suspension. *See, e.g., In the Reinstatement Matter Involving Wiederholt,* 295 P.3d 396 (Alaska 2013) (court reinstated disbarred lawyer with probationary condition of three years of mentoring; court held that Standard 2.7 clearly contemplated supervision of and mentoring of reinstated lawyer as a condition of reinstatement, but not requirement that lawyer advise future clients that he had been disbarred); ( *In re Moak,* 71 P.3d 343 (Ariz. 2003) (probation or conditions of reinstatement may be appropriate upon reinstatement from suspension, leaving that for consideration when lawyer applies for reinstatement); *In re Bailey,* 821 A.2d 851 (Del. 2003) (ordering six-month-plus-one-day suspension despite stipulation between disciplinary counsel and lawyer that sanction should be a public reprimand and three years of public probation; if lawyer seeks reinstatement following suspension, panel of board should determine at that time whether further probation is appropriate and, if appropriate, whether conditions should attach); *In re Bailey,* 478 S.E.2d 131 (Ga. 1996) (indefinite suspension lifted only upon compliance with conditions, including a finding from lawyer impairment program that lawyer is fit to resume practice, payment of restitution, and successful completion of state bar's ethics school); *In re Dunn,* 717 So.2d 639 (La. 1998) (imposing one-year supervised probationary period as condition to reinstatement, including restitution or proof of good faith efforts at restitution, psychological treatment and medication with quarterly reports, six hours of CLE in management of small or solo firm, and supervision by probation monitor with more than ten years' experience); *In re Coleman*, 793 N.W.2d 296 (Minn. 2011) (indefinite suspension for lawyer who committed misconduct related to mishandling client matters, misconduct similar to that for which lawyer had been disciplined in the past; upon order of reinstatement, lawyer subject to two years of supervised probation and such other conditions as the court may then impose).

## *Probation Conditions*

Courts impose a variety of conditions on lawyers as part of the sanction of probation. Conditions of probation can include the following.

- **Regular Reports of Caseload Status**

Requiring quarterly or semiannual reports of a lawyer's caseload status is a condition of probation that often is imposed after a lawyer has been disciplined for neglect or poor recordkeeping. *See, e.g., In re Doughty*, 832 A.2d 724 (Del. 2003) (public reprimand with two-year probation for recordkeeping violation includes requirement of quarterly reports of compliance with recordkeeping and tax-filing rules in first year and semiannual reports in second year, along with an audit at end of first year); *In re Clothier*, 344 P.3d 370 (Kan. 2015) (lawyer whose mental disability caused misconduct and who made significant progress in rehabilitation and treatment placed on probation for three years, a condition of which was that lawyer obtain practice supervisor who, in addition to other duties, must audit lawyer's client files every six months and report audit results; continued counseling and monitoring by lawyer assistance program also required); *In re Applebaum*, 803 N.W.2d 914 (Minn. 2011) (appointing supervising attorney and requiring quarterly written reports inventorying status of reprimanded lawyer's active client files as condition of two-year probationary period for, inter alia, failing to diligently pursue a client matter, to adequately communicate case status to the client, and to maintain and return the client's file).

- **Supervision by Lawyer**

As an extra measure of protection for clients, a court may require that a disciplined lawyer practice under the supervision of another lawyer for the term of the probation. *See, e.g., In re Reardon*, 759 A.2d 568 (Del. 2000) (requiring lawyer to consult with a lawyer/practice monitor designated by disciplinary counsel within ten days of start of probation; lawyer to implement any suggestions of practice monitor to improve office practices and procedure and permit office monitor to supervise through periodic checks with lawyer and staff); *In re Solomon*, 745 A.2d 874 (Del. 1999) (assigning an experienced family-law lawyer as practice monitor to write required reports, advise board of any problems facing disciplined lawyer, work with that lawyer to avoid future problems, and have discretion as to how many active cases lawyer can handle at any given time); *In re Smith*, 887 So.2d 449 (La. 2004) (lawyer to establish effective calendaring system and obtain assistance of the bar's loss prevention counsel, practice assistance counsel, and probation monitor in creation of proper law office management program); *In re Dumaine*, 818 So.2d 756 (La. 2002) (appointing practice monitor who is a lawyer to review files on a periodic basis to ensure full compliance with professional obligations); *State ex rel. Counsel for Discipline v. Pierson*, 798 N.W.2d 580 (Neb. 2011) (two-year probation under supervision of a monitoring lawyer to oversee disciplined lawyer's probation plan, office management, and compliance with professional obligations); *In re Disciplinary Proceeding Against Juarez*, 24 P.3d 1040 (Wash. 2001) (imposing eighteen-month suspension followed by twelve-month probation conditioned upon practicing law only under supervision of another lawyer licensed to practice in the state; finding supervision requirement appropriate although lawyer argued requirement was unfair and unworkable); *Bd. of Prof'l Responsibility v. Abraham*, 376 P.3d 483 (Wyo. 2016) (lawyer who neglected criminal matters causing three appeals to be dismissed was suspended for six months with the suspension stayed and a six-month period of probation imposed; conditions of probation include implementing detailed law office practices and procedures and arranging for practice monitor who will make monthly written reports to disciplinary counsel).

- **Periodic Audits of Trust Accounts**

Trust account audits are conditions of probation especially appropriate in cases in which lawyers have improperly handled client funds. *See, e.g., In re Gray*, 152 A.3d 581 (Table) (Del. 2016) (in unpublished decision, court placed lawyer on probation for trust account, bookkeeping, and tax-related violations after random audit revealed improprieties; books and records must be pre-certified by CPA and lawyer must file certifications with court and disciplinary counsel); *In re Dal Santo*, 953 N.E.2d 468 (Ind. 2011) (suspension of 180 days stayed subject to completion of eighteen months of probation for trust-account-related misconduct with conditions requiring that all trust accounts be monitored and audited); *In re Lucas*, 825 So.2d 1090 (La. 2002) (lawyer to retain certified public accountant at own expense to help create bookkeeping system and audit trust account and make quarterly reports to disciplinary agency and probation monitor); *In re Cannain*, 930 P.2d 1162 (N.M. 1997) (term of probation for short-term misuse of client funds, including commingling and improper advancement of costs, was two audits of accounts during probationary period); *In re Miller*, 210 A.D.2d 869 (N.Y. App. Div. 1994) (terms of probation included semiannual reports from CPA confirming that lawyer who commingled properly maintained client trust account); *In re Disciplinary Proceeding Against Poole*, 125 P.3d 954 (Wash. 2006) (periodic audits of trust account for backdating invoice and failing to account for the distribution of a judgment award).

- **Attendance at CLE Programs**

Attendance at CLE programs is often a condition of probation, although the courses and hours required vary widely. *See, e.g., Columbus Bar Ass'n v. McCord*, 79 N.E.3d 503 (Ohio 2016) (lawyer who improperly designated fee as earned upon receipt and failed to file tax returns placed on probation with a stayed one-year suspension, a condition of probation being completion of six hours of CLE in law office management); *In re Goldberg*, 952 N.E.2d 200 (Ind. 2011) (two-year probationary period included condition that lawyer complete three CLE hours on trust account management and six CLE hours on law office management); *In re Dumaine*, 818 So.2d 756 (La. 2002) (lawyer required to attend ethics school and submit evidence of attendance); *In re Houston*, 985 P.2d 752 (N.M. 1999) (requiring successful completion of fifteen fifty-minute CLE hours in ethics and/or in law practice management during period of probation). *But see In re Wahlder*, 728 So.2d 837 (La. 1999) (deleting probation condition ordered by board requiring lawyer's staff to attend workshop on efficient office management; finding condition unnecessary because lawyer has ultimate responsibility for actions of his staff).

The court order imposing this probation condition often is tailored to include courses that address the specific problem giving rise to the misconduct. *See, e.g., In re Vorv*, 172 A.3d 911 (D.C. 2017) (lawyer who mishandled matter in attempt to delay client's removal from country suspended for thirty days, with suspension stayed and probation for one year, with conditions including completion of ten hours of CLE in immigration law); *In re Dal Santo*, 953 N.E.2d 468 (Ind. 2011) (several violations of rules related to proper use and maintenance of client trust accounts warranted eighteen-month probationary period, including condition that lawyer complete three CLE hours on trust account management); *In re Cicardo*, 877 So.2d 980 (La. 2004) (when lawyer used client trust account funds for law office operation, court mandated successful completion of state bar's ethics school during first year of probation plus, during second year, eight additional hours of CLE in area of law practice management or maintenance of client trust accounts, including any "trust accounting school" established by state bar's practice assistance and improvement committee); *In re Disciplinary Proceeding Against Longacre*, 122 P.3d 710 (Wash. 2005) (thirty additional hours of CLE courses in criminal law and procedure imposed on lawyer who failed to communicate plea offers and sentencing implications to client); *In re Disciplinary Proceeding Against McKean*, 64 P.3d 1226 (Wash. 2003) (lawyer who entered business arrangement with client and used trust account for own business purposes precluded from law practice until he demonstrated familiarity in managing trust accounts to disciplinary counsel's satisfaction and completed ten hours of live CLE credits on conflicts of interest).

- **Participation in Substance Abuse Treatment Programs**

When the lawyer's abuse of alcohol or other substances bears a causal connection to the misconduct, a frequently ordered condition of probation is participation in a substance abuse treatment program. *See, e.g., In re Rhode*, 2018 WL 4136542 (D.C. August 30, 2018) (lawyer convicted of fleeing the scene of an accident that he caused by driving drunk was suspended from the practice of law for two years, with a requirement to show fitness before reinstatement; suspension stayed for three years of probation; as a condition of probation, lawyer, who had shown long-standing period of recovery, required to continue participation in substance abuse treatment program); *Fla. Bar v. Boland*, 702 So.2d 229 (Fla. 1997) (two-year suspension with probation, including rehabilitation for alcoholism, warranted in case of multiple offenses of incompetent representation); *Disciplinary Counsel v. Blair*, 944 N.E.2d 1161 (Ohio 2011) (two-year suspension with 18-month stayed probationary period for lawyer whose chronic depression and alcohol abuse resulted in misappropriation of funds belonging to an incompetent ward and filing of false statements concerning wards' assets; probation conditions included compliance with lawyer assistance program contract and alcohol and mental-health counseling); *Cincinnati Bar Ass'n v. Baas*, 681 N.E.2d 421 (Ohio 1997) (probation requiring continued treatment for alcoholism imposed for repeated neglect of client matters and failure to return unearned fees).

Courts also can require random drug screening as a condition of probation. *See, e.g., In re Hueben*, 362 P. 3d 809 (Kan. 2015) (lawyer convicted of driving under the influence, her third offense, and refusing breathalyzer test, suspended for two years, with suspension suspended and two years probation imposed, a condition of which was submitting to random screens for drugs and alcohol); *In re Allred*, 27 P.3d 977 (N.M. 2001) (requiring lawyer to abstain from alcohol use and submit to and pay for random drug screens for the presence of alcohol within eight hours of a request for testing; lawyer also required to provide disciplinary counsel with a telephone number at which he can always be reached or at which he will receive messages in sufficient time to submit to a random drug screen within eight hours of a request); *State ex rel. Okla. Bar Ass'n v. Smith*, 246 P.3d 1090 (Okla. 2011) (lawyer required to submit to random drug testing as part of probation with a public reprimand and one-year deferred suspension for misconduct including arrest for felony offense of attempting to obtain a controlled substance by forgery or fraud, and relapses following inpatient drug treatment program).

- **Periodic Physical or Mental Examinations and Treatment**

Treatment and periodic exams, either physical or mental, often are appropriate when the lawyer's physical or mental condition caused the misconduct. *See, e.g., In re La Paglia*, 843 P.2d 1271 (Ariz. 1992) (lawyer to continue with psychotherapy and any medication recommended by specified doctor and psychiatrist in consultation with director of lawyer assistance program); *In re McNeely*, 174 A.3d 865 (D.C. 2017) (terms of probation include remaining in therapy and executing release so that psychologist or psychiatrist can report noncompliance); *In re Works*, 43 P.3d 816 (Kan. 2002) (lawyer to continue treatment for depression with specified doctor throughout probation period and must take medication as prescribed, when lawyer's mental disability was factor in failure to handle two personal injury cases); *In re Perkins*, 946 P.2d 998 (Kan. 1997) (continued treatment for depression required as term of probation for failing to handle estate matters competently and diligently); *In re LaMartina*, 38 So.3d 266 (La. 2010) (suspension for one year and one day, fully deferred, subject to two-year probation with condition that lawyer submit to an examination by a licensed mental-health-care professional within thirty days of the judgment and comply with all recommended treatment during probationary period); *In re Robinson*, 819 So.2d 280 (La. 2002) (one-year suspension, with eleven months deferred, for violation of court's preliminary injunction against further contact with surgeon to whom lawyer had sent numerous inappropriate personal communications; active period of suspension followed by one-year probation with conditions including mental-health exam and compliance with any ordered treatment, notification to disciplinary counsel regarding exam and provision of medical records upon request, appointment of probation monitor to ensure compliance with treatment, and deferred period of suspension to become active upon failure to comply with any probation conditions); *In re Allred*, 27 P.3d 977 (N.M. 2001) (lawyer to follow treatment plan of evaluating psychologist, including attending counseling as recommended, and execute a form for release of information pertaining to treatment and progress to disciplinary counsel); *In re Zamora*, 21 P.3d 30 (N.M. 2001) (requiring, among other conditions, that lawyer successfully complete a long-term, inpatient treatment program; continue with appropriate outpatient treatment; and satisfy requirements of written monitoring agreement outlining program for recovery, including regular meetings with monitor; regular participation in twelve-step recovery program and random drug testing and screening).

- **Passing a Bar or Professional Responsibility Examination**

Courts may also require as a condition of probation that a lawyer successfully pass the bar examination or the MPRE. *See, e.g.*, *In re Pautler*, 47 P.3d 1175 (Colo. 2002) (where deputy district attorney deceived murder suspect to obtain surrender, finding that three-month stayed suspension and twelve-month probation with conditions, including retaking MPRE, was reasonable); *Fla. Bar v. Doltie*, 606 So.2d 1158 (Fla. 1992) (one-year probation, a term of which was passing the ethics portion of the bar exam, for failing to attend hearing on client's behalf, overcharging, and prior disciplinary history); *In re Brooks*, 803 N.W.2d 391 (Minn. 2011) (lawyer suspended for ninety days was reinstated and placed on one-year probation, during which time the lawyer was required to successfully complete the professional responsibility portion of the state bar examination or face automatic resuspension); *State ex rel. Neb. State Bar Ass'n v. Kinney*, 740 N.W.2d 607 (Neb. 2007) (court held that disbarred lawyer met his burden of establishing good moral character to warrant readmission, conditioned upon his successfully passing the state bar exam); *In re Application of Sandler*, 588 N.E.2d 779 (Ohio 1992) (applicant's license to practice law was immediately revoked with option to reapply for admission provided that he undergo another character and fitness exam in which he successfully demonstrates his character, fitness, and moral qualifications to practice law, and successfully retake the Ohio bar examination).

- **Limitations on Practice**

Courts place a variety of limitations on a lawyer's practice as a condition of probation to address the underlying issue that gave rise to the misconduct and to help prevent such misconduct from reoccurring. *See, e.g., In re Zawada*, 92 P.3d 862 (Ariz. 2004) (requiring prosecutor who improperly argued, among other things, that mental health experts in general create excuses for criminals to take fifteen hours of continuing education addressing effective use of psychological testimony and not to participate in cases involving mental-health component until completion of this education requirement); *In re Higgins*, 884 P.2d 1094 (Ariz. 1994) (lawyer must decline representation in domestic relations matters as condition of probation); *In re Elgart*, 999 A.2d 853 (Del. 2010) (prohibition against serving as managing attorney at any firm during eighteen-month probationary period for lawyer who failed to distribute insurance proceeds to client and failed as a managing attorney to properly supervise other lawyers and staff in handling client funds); *In re Foraone*, 722 A.2d 1 (Del. 1998) (lawyer who knowingly assisted unscrupulous client to take advantage of innocent third parties in real estate transactions and to defraud the state and county of real estate transfer taxes barred from representing parties in mortgage assumption or payment takeover transactions during eighteen-month probation); *In re Works*, 43 P.3d 816 (Kan. 2002) (practice shall consist of criminal defense cases and cases related to criminal defense—i.e., driver's license suspension cases, drug-tax cases—and no representation of clients in civil matters, including domestic relations cases); *In re Allred*, 27 P.3d 977 (N.M. 2001) (lawyer can work for other licensed attorneys, either as employee or on contract basis, but shall have no direct contract with any client; employing lawyers must agree to submit quarterly reports on lawyer's performance).

- **Restitution and/or Payment of Disciplinary Costs**

Restitution is a common condition of probation when a lawyer has mishandled funds. *See, e.g., In re Fuchs*, 905 A.2d 160 (D.C. 2006) (imposing reciprocal suspension stayed by a period of probation and ordering lawyer to pay restitution, a condition of probation in originating jurisdiction); *In re Faraone*, 722 A.2d 1 (Del. 1998) (six-month suspension followed by a year-and-a-half probation, including restitution to defrauded third parties and to defrauded taxing authorities; also requiring restitution to third parties at any later date should they suffer quantifiable injury resulting from foreclosure of their former home due to lawyer's misconduct); *In re Christians*, 978 P.2d 910 (Kan. 1999) (lawyer who failed to file client's bankruptcy ordered to serve eighteen months' probation in addition to restitution consisting of $95 collected filing fee, $400 attorney's fee, and $52 for client's lost wages); *In re Yates*, 923 So.2d 618 (La. 2006) (six-month suspension followed by supervised probation for one year, including $2,000 restitution to client); *In re Pepper*, 876 So.2d 772 (La. 2004) (ordering one-year probation subject to restitution in the amount of $600 plus legal interest); *In re Dumaine*, 818 So.2d 756 (La. 2002) (conditions of probation to include rendering accounting and refunding any unearned fees); *In re Disciplinary Proceeding Against DeRuiz*, 99 P.3d 881 (Wash. 2004) (imposing two six-month suspensions, to be served consecutively, with reinstatement subject to eighteen months' probation and payment of restitution).

Courts also commonly require lawyers placed on probation to repay the costs of the disciplinary proceeding leading to the sanction. *See, e.g., In re Augenstein*, 870 P.2d 399 (Ariz. 1994) (ordering restitution of $1,700 to one client and $2,547.71 to another individual, plus costs of proceeding of $801.98, together with interest at the legal rate from date of judgment); *In re Cassalia*, 843 P.2d 654 (Ariz. 1992) (lawyer to pay all costs of disciplinary proceeding to state bar prior to termination of probation, including cost of retaining practice monitor); *In re Moore*, 769 So.2d 1180 (La. 2000) (lawyer placed on probation to pay all costs of proceedings); *In re Roberts-Hohl*, 866 P.2d 1167 (N.M. 1994) (payment of costs and restitution ordered as conditions of probation rather than preconditions to reinstatement); *Akron Bar Ass'n v. DeLoach*, 956 N.E.2d 811 (Ohio 2011) (six-month suspension stayed subject to two years of monitored probation, including condition that lawyer pay all costs of disciplinary proceedings).

- **Other Conditions as Are Appropriate for the Misconduct**

In addition to the above-mentioned conditions of probation, courts are free to impose any other condition or conditions as may be appropriate to address the given misconduct. *See, e.g., In re Phillips*, 244 P.3d 549 (Ariz. 2010) (six-month suspension warranted for managing partner who violated ethics rules regarding supervision of other firm lawyers and employees with twenty-one conditions of probation imposed, including submitting to state bar audit program, ensuring that nonlawyer staff does not give legal advice to clients, and not basing bonuses to legal administrators, in whole or in part, on number of clients retained, amount of fees generated or refunded, or number of clients who cancel); *In re Baxter*, 940 P.2d 37 (Kan. 1997) (requiring certification of legal malpractice insurance coverage of at least $1 million with a $10,000 deductible); *In re Brooks*, 803 N.W.2d 391 (Minn. 2011) (lawyer suspended for, inter alia, failing to diligently represent client, communicate with client, return client's file, and refund retainer subsequently placed on one-year probation requiring that he ensure prompt responses to correspondence, telephone calls, and other communications from clients, courts, and others); *State ex rel. Okla. Bar Ass'n v. Smith*, 246 P.3d 1090 (Okla. 2011) (requiring that lawyer arrested for attempting to obtain a controlled substance by forgery or fraud, with a history of relapses, be monitored and supervised by partners in her law firm, who were required to report any violation of the conditions of probation); *In re McCarty*, 665 A.2d 885 (Vt. 1995) (when lawyer failed to return client property after termination of representation and did not comply with client's reasonable request for details regarding outstanding bill, court required, as condition of probation, that lawyer provide to client the requested information and, if client continued to dispute charges, lawyer must submit to fee arbitration). *But see In re Haws*, 801 P.2d 818 (Or. 1990) (withdrawing conditions of probation when they were imprecise and did not track charges against lawyer).

## *Termination of Probation*

Probation may be terminated by the court after the respondent lawyer has filed an affidavit of compliance with all conditions of probation and the court is satisfied that the need for probation no longer exists. Probation should not exceed two years but may be renewed for an additional period of two years by consent or after a hearing to determine if there is a continued need for supervision. *See* MRLDE Rule 10. *See, e.g., In re Plener*, 55 So.3d 786 (La. 2011) (conditional admission granted subject to monitored two-year probationary period; disciplinary counsel required to file a report with the court within thirty days of expiration of the probation period recommending that the conditional admission be terminated or extended); *In re Becker*, 902 N.W.2d 921 (Minn. 2017) (court agreed with joint recommendation by disciplinary counsel and lawyer to terminate probation after successful completion of conditions); *In re Miller*, 210 A.D.2d 869 (N.Y. App. Div. 1994) (citing Standard 2.7 in ordering that after two-year suspension period, stayed upon probation with conditions, lawyer may apply for termination, with supporting documentation that conditions have been met, and may have a hearing).

## *Violations of Probation*

In the event that a lawyer is alleged to have violated conditions of probation, a hearing may be needed to determine whether a violation has occurred. The disciplinary agency has the burden of establishing any such violation by clear and convincing evidence. *In re Phillips*, 244 P.3d 549 (Ariz. 2010), for example, sets out the procedure when a lawyer fails to comply with terms of probation. The court wrote:

> In the event that [lawyer] fails to comply with any of the foregoing conditions and the State Bar receives information thereof, bar counsel

> shall file with the imposing entity a Notice of Non-Compliance. . . . The Hearing Officer shall conduct a hearing within thirty (30) days after receipt of said notice, to determine whether the terms of probation have been violated and whether an additional sanction should be imposed. In the event there is an allegation that any of these terms has been violated, the burden of proof shall be on the State Bar of Arizona to prove noncompliance by a preponderance of the evidence.

*Id.* at 561. *But see In re Smith,* 887 So.2d 449 (La. 2004) (adding as condition of probation that any violation of any probation terms shall result in summary revocation of probation).

Upon a finding that a lawyer has violated probation conditions, the court may extend the probation, impose a more severe sanction, or other discipline. *See, e.g., In re Steiner,* 817 A.2d 793 (Del. 2003) (finding series of probation violations due to lawyer's continued alcohol consumption, in flagrant violation of zero-tolerance orders, should be weighed in aggravation; imposing three-year suspension); *In re Castaldo,* 952 N.E.2d 202 (Ind. 2011) (revoking twenty-four-month probation for violations of the conditions, including material breaches of the lawyer assistance program's monitoring agreement and failure to attend a trust account management course; ordering that ninety-day stayed suspension become executory, that reinstatement not be automatic, and that lawyer fulfill the duties of a suspended lawyer); *In re Mitchell,* 946 P.2d 999 (Kan. 1997) (indefinite suspension for lawyer who violated conditions of probation when he was arrested and incarcerated for disorderly conduct; conditions had included abstaining from alcohol and remaining in treatment facility); *In re Warner,* 215 So.3d 221 (La. 2017) (revocation of probation granted for lawyer who violated terms of probation by not making himself available to disciplinary counsel, failing to pay annual licensing fee, failing to fulfill CLE requirements, and being the subject of additional disciplinary complaints); *In re Pepper,* 876 So.2d 772 (La. 2004) (violation of probation conditions or other misconduct during probation may be grounds for making deferred portion of suspension executory or imposing additional discipline); *In re Forck,* 418 S.W.3d 437 (Mo. 2014) (citing Standard 2.7 court extended period of probation instead of imposing stayed suspension after respondent committed additional misconduct; lawyer maintained sobriety and unlikely to harm public during extended period of probation).

## 2.8 Other Sanctions and Remedies

**Other sanctions and remedies which may be imposed include:**

**(a) restitution,**

**(b) assessment of costs,**

**(c) limitation upon practice,**

**(d) appointment of a receiver,**

**(e) requirement that the lawyer take the bar examination or professional responsibility examination,**

**(f) requirement that the lawyer attend continuing education courses, and**

**(g) other requirements that the state's highest court or disciplinary board deems consistent with the purposes of lawyer sanctions.**

## Annotation

### *Other Sanction Options*

The court or disciplinary authority may impose other sanctions and remedies when it is deemed necessary to fulfill the goals of the disciplinary process. *See, e.g., In re Zang,* 803 P.2d 419 (Ariz. 1990) (court has power to order restitution to those financially injured by professional misconduct); *Fla. Bar v. Abrams,* 919 So.2d 425 (Fla. 2006) (noting the court's responsibility to order appropriate sanctions and relying on Florida Standard 2.8 in upholding an order for payment of restitution to victims plus costs of the proceeding); *In re Disciplinary Proceeding Against Juarez,* 24 P.3d 1040 (Wash. 2001) (citing Standard 2.8 providing for sanctions, including assessment of costs, limitation of practice, and any other reasonable requirement; imposing eighteen-month suspension followed by probation conditioned on supervision by another lawyer and assessment of costs and expenses associated with disciplinary proceeding).

Courts often are creative and flexible in approaching cases where there is some misconduct but a severe sanction is not required. In cases of minor incompetence, for example, a sanction requiring the lawyer to attend CLE courses or limiting the lawyer's practice to handling certain types of cases, with a stayed suspension, may better protect the public than a period of suspension from practice.

#### • Restitution

When a lawyer has misappropriated client funds or failed to perform professional services for which the lawyer has been paid, courts often order restitution. *See, e.g., In re Brady,* 923 P.2d 836 (Ariz. 1996) (disbarring and ordering restitution totaling $12,850 to five clients whom lawyer either abandoned or for whom he knowingly failed to perform services); *In re Cardenas,* 791 P.2d 1032 (Ariz. 1990) (citing Standard 2.8 for proposition that restitution is a proper sanction for lawyer misconduct; ordering restitution to victim of $20,000 with interest at rate of 10 percent per annum); *People v. Mascarenas*, 103 P.3d 339 (Colo. O.P.D.J. 2003) (restitution of $8,228.60 to client's mother because lawyer improperly gave her legal advice and coercively procured lien on her property to secure fee; also ordering reimbursement of $277.57 to a client for interest charged and compounded monthly on a bill lawyer did not present to client for more than seven-month period); *In re Pennington*, 713 S.E.2d 261 (S.C. 2011) (disbarring lawyer and ordering restitution to clients and third parties based on several instances of mishandling client funds, as well as failure to remit funds owed to third parties, to refund unearned fees, and to protect client interests upon lawyer's initial suspension); *Bd. of Prof'l Responsibility v. Reguli*, 489 S.W.3d 408 (Tenn. 2015) (relying on Standard 2.8, court upheld order requiring lawyer to make restitution of unearned fee, finding that otherwise lawyer would gain windfall at the expense of client).

Restitution as a disciplinary sanction should be distinguished from civil judgments against lawyers. *See Fla. Bar v. Walton*, 952 So.2d 510, 516 (Fla. 2006) (rejecting referee's recommendation that lawyer pay attorney's fees and costs to opposing counsel, court reiterated established policy of not awarding restitution to third parties in disciplinary matters; "[d]isciplinary actions cannot be used as a substitute for what should be addressed in private civil actions against attorneys. We cannot and should not turn restitution as a condition to practicing our profession into a judgment for a third party") (citation omitted). In *In re Disciplinary Proceeding Against Anschell*, 9 P.3d 193 (Wash. 2000), the Washington Supreme Court found that the board erred in including, in its restitution order, $68,483.63, the entire amount of a client's legal malpractice judgment against the lawyer. Reinstating the hearing officer's original restitution order of $4,000 to one client, $190 to another, and $9,090 plus attorney's fees to another client, the court said:

> An order of restitution and a civil judgment are distinct remedies and should not be conflated. . . . A civil judgment is subject to collection by resort to independent legal processes and may include monetary awards far greater, and significantly different, than those granted by restitution (i.e., treble damages and compensation for emotional distress). We believe it is improper to include such judgments in an attorney discipline restitution order.

*Id.* at 206; *see also In re Disciplinary Proceedings Against Mutschler*, 804 N.W.2d 680, 684 (Wis. 2011) (restitution inappropriate regarding lawyer's representation of two clients on whose cases the lawyer and his firm performed substantial work; court said that whether that work was appropriate and fulfilled his contractual obligation to the clients would require an extensive evidentiary hearing or trial and extensive fact-finding, which is not consistent with the focus of disciplinary proceedings on whether an attorney violated the rules of professional conduct and should receive some form of discipline; "[t]here are other venues for resolving such monetary issues").

Courts have found that restitution can help a lawyer understand the impact of his or her misconduct and begin to make amends. *See, e.g., People v. Flores,* 804 P.2d 192, 195 (Colo. 1991) (ordering restitution of $300 plus statutory interest under Standard 2.8(a); "[r]estitution forces a conscious acknowledgment by the respondent of the connection between the misconduct and the adverse impact on a client"); *In re Disciplinary Proceedings Against Jennings,* 801 N.W.2d 304, 316 (Wis. 2011) (noting, within the context of a reinstatement proceeding, a lawyer's "continuing effort toward restitution, to the extent he is financially able, is necessary to demonstrate [the lawyer's] attitude and understanding of the ethical standards required of members of the bar").

In states where disbarment is permanent, however, courts have found that such demonstration is unnecessary and have declined to order restitution as a disciplinary sanction. *See, e.g., Ky. Bar Ass'n. v. Chesley,* 393 S.W.3d 584, 602 (Ky. 2013) (observing that the rules do not allow for any conditions to be imposed with permanent disbarment; permanently disbarred attorney is no longer subject to court's direct supervision, thus a remedy for injured clients "is more appropriately addressed" in civil action); *In re Errico,* 2018 WL 5095817, at *2 (Table) (Nev. October 10, 2018) ("when disbarment is permanent, as it is in Nevada, imposing additional forms of discipline does not further the purpose of attorney discipline—the public and profession are fully protected because the attorney is permanently removed from the practice of law, making rehabilitation irrelevant").

Courts have found restitution inappropriate if a lawyer's conduct did not enrich the lawyer or cause a client's financial loss. *See, e.g., In re Carnow,* 501 N.E.2d 128 (Ill. 1986) (granting readmission petition of public official disbarred for participation in extortion plan; mere fact of involvement in misconduct insufficient ground for requiring restitution payment when official gained no benefit and caused no loss to public entity); *In re Disciplinary Proceeding Against Longacre,* 122 P.3d 710 (Wash. 2005) (declining to order $9,000 in restitution, the amount the lawyer allegedly received from client's father to represent client, when lawyer gave value in representing client and documentation of costs to hire new counsel was absent); *cf. In re Disciplinary Proceedings Against Mutschler,* 804 N.W.2d 680, 683 (Wis. 2011) (rejecting clients' request for restitution in the amount of a $13,500 flat fee, court agreed with office of lawyer regulation's finding that while the clients were unsatisfied with the results, the lawyer performed a substantial amount of work on their behalf, "which meant that the amount of any restitution award was unclear and could not be easily and reasonably ascertained").

A restitution order may involve not only repayment to clients, but also reimbursement of monies distributed from a jurisdiction's client protection fund. *See, e.g., People v. Mitchell,* 124 P.3d 917 (Colo. O.P.D.J. 2005) (full restitution to former clients and Colorado Attorney's Fund for Client Protection in amount to be determined at future date); *People v. Calbo,* 122 P.3d 1101 (Colo. O.P.D.J. 2005) (ordering reimbursement of $20,500 to Colorado Attorneys' Fund for Client Protection and restitution to any unpaid clients including $3,000 to a specific client); *In re McCann,* 894 A.2d 1087 (Del. 2005) (lawyer to pay costs of proceeding, costs of client-protection-fund audits, past and current federal and state income taxes, past and current payroll tax obligations, and repay to clients all unearned fees); *In re Glover,* 704 S.E.2d 347 (S.C. 2011) (ordering full reimbursement to Lawyers' Fund for Client Protection for amounts paid to the lawyer's clients as a result of misconduct).

Often restitution is ordered as a condition of reinstatement or readmission. *See, e.g., In re Rubenstein,* 875 P.2d 783 (Ariz. 1994) (ordering restitution, prior to reinstatement, in the amount of $1,348.25); *People v. Hassan,* 45 P.3d 1283 (Colo. O.P.D.J. 2002) (reimbursement of client funds with interest as condition of reinstatement following eighteen-month suspension for conversion); *In re Scimeca,* 962 P.2d 1080 (Kan. 1998) (ordering restitution to all complainants prior to filing reinstatement petition); *In re Walker,* 713 S.E.2d 264 (S.C. 2011) (prohibiting lawyer from filing for reinstatement until, inter alia, full restitution is made to the parties affected by lawyer's misappropriation of funds from his trust accounts to the Lawyers' Fund for Client Protection, and until he has satisfied all judgments against him arising from his practice of law). For further discussion of restitution as a condition of reinstatement or as a probation condition, see Annotation to Standard 2.10 (Readmission and Reinstatement) and Annotation to Standard 2.7 (Probation).

- **Assessment of Costs**

In many instances, including but not limited to cases where probation is imposed, courts have assessed the costs and expenses of the disciplinary proceeding against the disciplined lawyer. *See, e.g., In re Brown,* 392 P.3d 474 (Alaska 2017) (ordering that censured lawyer pay $1,000 in costs and attorney's fees incurred by bar association in pursuing the disciplinary case); *In re Peasley,* 90 P.3d 764 (Ariz. 2004) (assessment of costs and expenses is one of permissible sanctions; court sustained disbarred lawyer's objections to statement of costs, in part, and reduced amount of costs after deducting expense of computer software program purchased by the bar to scan 4,800 pages of murder trial transcripts and two consulting expert witnesses who were not called to testify nor disclosed; court rejected lawyer's argument that only 40 percent of costs should be assessed because bar only proved two of five counts against him); *People v. Flores,* 804 P.2d 192 (Colo. 1991) (ordering suspended lawyer to pay costs of proceeding in amount of $338.37 within 90 days of opinion); *People v. Schofield,* 119 P.3d 1103 (Colo. O.P.D.J. 2005) (ordering disbarred lawyer to pay costs of disciplinary proceeding); *In re Richards*, 986 P.2d 1117 (N.M. 1999) (suspended lawyer to pay costs of action in amount of $1,704.98 by date certain; any balance remaining after that date to bear interest at a rate of 15 percent per annum); *Long v. Bd. of Prof'l Responsibility*, 435 S.W.3d 174 (Tenn. 2014) (rule requiring assessment of costs against disciplined lawyer, including expenses of hearing panel, does not violate due process). *But see State ex rel. Okla. Bar Ass'n v. Wilcox*, 227 P.3d 642 (Okla. 2009) (in denying application for costs, court considered the manner in which bar litigated disciplinary matter, including a delay of four years to litigate case, some of which was not justified, assertion of some rule violations not supported by the facts, misstated facts, a deplorable record as well as a majority of the charges not being proven; public reprimand imposed for proven misconduct).

- **Limitation upon Practice**

If a lawyer's misconduct arises from a lack of a particular skill or from an inability to function well in a specific type of legal practice, courts can craft corresponding limitations upon the lawyer's future practice to minimize the risk that the lawyer will repeat the misconduct. *See, e.g., In re Reardon*, 759 A.2d 568, 580 (Del. 2000) (imposing permanent restrictions on law practice including not accepting any civil matters, except court-appointed guardian cases, and not accepting representation in any felony criminal cases; reasoning that such a sanction "serves the critical goal of protecting the public by ensuring that [the lawyer] be restricted permanently from accepting client matters outside his sphere of expertise").

In some instances, the restriction or limitation is imposed only during the specific period of a lawyer's discipline. *See, e.g., In re Elgart*, 999 A.2d 853 (Del. 2010) (public reprimand and eighteen-month probation for failure to distribute insurance proceeds to a client and failure to make disclosures to disciplinary counsel, including lawyer's prior private admonition for failing as managing attorney to properly supervise other lawyers and staff in handling client funds; sanction included prohibition against serving as a managing attorney at any firm during the probationary period); *In re Garrett*, 835 A.2d 514 (Del. 2003) (lawyer prohibited from any contact with clients, prospective clients, witnesses, or prospective witnesses if acting as paralegal, legal assistant, or law clerk when working under supervision of another bar member during three-year suspension).

In other situations, courts impose a permanent limitation on certain aspects of practice. *See, e.g., In re Davis*, 974 A.2d 170 (Del. 2009) (one-year suspension for misconduct related to a series of real estate transactions in which lawyer, as purchaser, falsely notarized the transactions, failed to pay transfer taxes on one transaction, and restated the purchase price on two other transactions; court held that in the event of reinstatement the lawyer was subject to permanent restrictions on his future practice of law, including prohibiting him from, inter alia, acting as lawyer, settlement agent, or notary for any transaction documents in any real estate closing in which the lawyer is a party to the transaction); *In re Solomon*, 745 A.2d 874 (Del. 1999) (lawyer who failed to safeguard client's property, act with reasonable diligence, and explain matters was required, among other conditions and limitations, to close solo law practice, never again have responsibility for financial recordkeeping requirements, have no access to funds or check-writing privileges, and have no duties regarding office management); *In re Reinstatement of Nemec*, 799 N.W.2d 370, 372 (N.D. 2011) (reinstatement of suspended lawyer conditioned on a limitation of the practice of law to association with an experienced supervising lawyer; petitioner's long history of alcohol addiction necessitated further precautions "to ensure that the public is protected upon [petitioner's] return to the practice of law").

- **Appointment of a Receiver**

Courts may appoint a receiver to handle recordkeeping and financial obligations of a law practice when a lawyer is placed on interim suspension, suspension, disability inactive status, or is disbarred. *See generally* MRLDE Rule 28 and ABA Center for Professional Responsibility, *Chart of State by State Caretaker Rules when Lawyer Disappears, Dies, or is Declared Incompetent* (last updated May 2015), http://www.americanbar.org/content/dam/aba/administrative/professional_responsibility/chart_state_by_state_caretaker_rules.authcheckdam.pdf. *See In re Carucci*, 132 A.3d 1161 (Table) (Del. 2016) (receiver appointed for lawyer transferred to disability inactive status; at time receiver assumed control, balance in trust and operating accounts had been depleted and lawyer had failed to maintain proper books and records, among other misconduct); *In re McCann*, 894 A.2d 1087 (Del. 2005) (disbarring lawyer who, inter alia, failed to keep proper records and to pay personal and payroll taxes but falsely certified he was in compliance with requirements and ordering disciplinary counsel to petition court for appointment of receiver); *In re Lessoff*, 150 A.D.3d 159 (N.Y. App. Div. 2017) (rejecting lawyer's motion to resign from bar after conviction for grand larceny of $743,327 in settlement funds; court disbarred lawyer and appointed receiver to protect interests of lawyer and his clients); *In re Bernstein*, 78 A.D.3d 94, 98 (N.Y. App. Div. 2010) (disbarring lawyer following convictions for criminal tax fraud and grand larceny stemming from theft from escrow accounts and appointing a lawyer receiver to inventory the disbarred lawyer's client files "and to take such action as seems indicated to protect the interests of his clients").

*See also In re Fountain*, 878 A.2d 1167 (Del. 2005) (suspension for multiyear failure to maintain proper books and records, safeguard client funds, and timely file and pay taxes; appointing a receiver to protect the interest of clients and former clients when lawyer's inability to correct accounting deficiencies poses ongoing risk of harm); *In re Shamers*, 873 A.2d 1089 (Del. 2005) (granting disciplinary counsel's application for leave to petition the court for a receiver of law practice when lawyer's inability to correct escrow accounting deficiencies poses ongoing risk of harm); *In re Rosabianca,* 131 A.D.3d 215 (N.Y. App. Div. 2015) (disbarring lawyer who continued to practice law and accept escrow funds for real estate transactions after suspension and appointing receiver to inventory all client files and accounts after lawyer had wired $1.5 million from trust account to an Italian banking or investment firm; receiver authorized to make transfers and withdrawals from lawyer's bank and trust accounts); *In re Siskin,* 78 A.D.3d 112 (N.Y. App. Div. 2010) (following suspension for nonresponsiveness to disciplinary committee's inquiry into mishandling of escrow accounts, court ordered disbarment and appointed receiver to inventory and manage lawyer's client files).

The appointment of a receiver also can protect the public in the event a lawyer fails to abide by the conditions of discipline imposed. *See, e.g., In re Hull,* 767 A.2d 197 (Del. 2001) (if lawyer fails to comply with requirements or to arrange with other members of bar to protect interest of clients during suspension, disciplinary counsel shall immediately file petition for appointment of receiver for her law practice).

- **Bar Examination or Professional Responsibility Examination Requirement**

The requirement that a lawyer retake the bar examination or a professional responsibility examination is a specific remedy available under Standard 2.8. Most typically, the court requires successful completion of the Multistate Professional Responsibility Examination (MPRE). *See, e.g., Statewide Grievance Comm'n v. Schaffer,* No. CV030196758, 2004 WL 303654 (Conn. Super. Ct. Feb. 2, 2004) (application for readmission conditioned on passing score on MPRE); *In re Miller,* 210 A.D.2d 869 (N.Y. App. Div. 1994) (citing Standard 2.8 in ordering that lawyer take and pass the MPRE).

Requiring a lawyer to take and pass the MPRE helps ensure that the lawyer is aware of ethical obligations in the practice of law. *See Idaho State Bar v. Malmin,* 78 P.3d 371, 379 (Idaho 2003) (when lawyer neglected client, failed to provide accounting, and made false statements, sitting for MPRE is appropriate sanction "because the test should help [the lawyer] understand the ethical standards to which she is held").

Courts often impose this requirement in addition to other sanctions. *See, e.g., In re Stepovich,* 386 P.3d 1205, 1216 (Alaska 2016) (previously disciplined lawyer suspended for twelve months for naming himself contingent beneficiary of client's will; court found requiring lawyer to take and pass MPRE as condition of reinstatement appropriate in light of lawyer's defense that he "was not aware of Rule 1.8 or the seriousness of the conflict of interest created by his conduct"); *People v. Sheffer,* 35 P.3d 466 (Colo. O.P.D.J. 1999) (two-year suspension plus additional reinstatement requirement that lawyer satisfactorily complete the MPRE); *Statewide Grievance Comm'n v. Palmieri*, No. CV020472045S, 2003 WL 963240, at *7 (Conn. Super. Ct. Feb. 25, 2003) (court incorporated in its disposition that taking and passing the MPRE or an ethics course at an accredited law school, prior to reinstatement, is an appropriate means to accomplish the goal of rehabilitation, "an important element of the ultimate sanction in a professional discipline case, especially one in which the respondent is eventually going to return to the practice of law."); *Statewide Grievance Comm'n v. DeLucia*, No. CV02080512, 2003 WL 1900869 (Conn. Super. Ct. Mar, 28, 2003) (imposing one-year suspension with conditions, including psychiatric treatment, in addition to requiring lawyer to provide proof of having achieved a passing grade on the MPRE); *In re Marcantonio*, 491 S.E.2d 49 (Ga. 1997) (imposing thirty-month suspension for various infractions, including improper handling of client funds, and requiring lawyer to pass the MPRE as condition of reinstatement); *In re Albrecht*, 779 N.W.2d 530 (Minn. 2010) (minimum two-year suspension and respondent required to successfully complete and obtain passing score on MPRE as condition of reinstatement); *In re Richmond's Case*, 872 A.2d 1023 (N.H. 2005) (six-month suspension plus, under Standard 2.8, lawyer must surrender client files for inventory by court-appointed lawyer, reimburse committee for costs of investigating and prosecuting matter, and satisfactorily complete the MPRE); *In re Richards*, 986 P.2d 1117 (N.M. 1999) (imposing one-year suspension, six months deferred, with conditions, including that lawyer successfully complete the MPRE); *In re Galvin*, 87 A.D.3d 1223 (N.Y. App. Div. 2011) (application for readmission following two-year suspension conditioned on passing score on the MPRE and completion of six hours of CLE in ethics and professionalism in addition to traditional CLE requirements).

If a lawyer has been suspended, especially for an extended period of time, a court may require that the lawyer retake the entire bar examination. *See, e.g.*, *People v. Cain*, 957 P.2d 346 (Colo. 1998) (requiring lawyer to pass bar examination before reinstatement when he was suspended for almost eight years); *Daly v. Miss. Bar*, 83 So.3d 1262 (Miss. 2011) (while original order imposing a three-year suspension conditioned petition for reinstatement on passage of the Mississippi bar exam, petitioner had been prohibited from sitting for the examination until the court granted reinstatement; granting reinstatement to the practice of law on the condition that the lawyer pass the state bar examination); *Emil v. Miss. Bar*, 690 So.2d 301 (Miss. 1997) (indefinite suspension for soliciting business and sharing legal fees, reinstatement contingent on proof of passing all sections of bar examination).

### • Continuing Education Requirement

Courts often require lawyers to complete additional hours of CLE, particularly when a lawyer has demonstrated lack of competence in a certain area of the law.

*See In re Disciplinary Proceeding Against Longacre*, 122 P.3d 710 (Wash. 2005) (imposing thirty hours of additional CLE courses with sixty-day suspension for, inter alia, failure to render competent representation).

The CLE requirement is frequently coupled with a requirement to retake the MPRE. *See, e.g., In re Breen*, 830 P.2d 462 (Ariz. 1992) (reinstatement conditioned on passing bar ethics examination and successfully completing twelve hours of CLE in ethics or course in ethics at accredited college of law); *People v. Vincent*, 35 P.3d 140 (Colo. O.P.D.J. 1999) (when lawyer commingled client funds with personal and operating funds, failed to promptly pay vendor bills, and was dishonest, court ordered, inter alia, completion of thirty-five hours of attendance at CLE programs—twenty hours that were to focus on accounting requirements, segregation of client funds, and Model Rules of Professional Conduct—and proof of successful completion of the MPRE, in addition to suspension); *Statewide Grievance Comm'n v. Sideleau*, No. CV010384234S, 2003 WL 21154114 (Conn. Super. Ct. Mar. 22, 2003) (eighteen-month suspension for lawyer who committed multiple acts of misconduct plus requirement that he pass either the MPRE or a course on legal ethics offered by an accredited law school or other acceptable entity); *Statewide Grievance Comm'n v. Pinsky*, No. CV010452000S, 2001 WL 1614892 (Conn. Super. Ct. Nov. 28, 2001) (ordering lawyer to take and pass the MPRE and to take and complete one CLE class in professional responsibility prior to automatic reinstatement after one-year suspension); *In re Tigue*, 900 N.W.2d 424 (Minn. 2017) (permanently prohibiting lawyer from being an authorized signatory on client trust account and ordering two-year suspension with reinstatement conditioned on successful completion of professional responsibility portion of bar exam and satisfaction of CLE requirements); *In re Ganley*, 549 N.W.2d 368 (Minn. 1996) (requiring successful completion of a trust account CLE or other similar session regarding the maintenance and handling of trust accounts and client funds in addition to successful completion of the professional responsibility portion of the bar examination); *In re Galvin*, 87 A.D.3d 1223 (N.Y. App. Div. 2011) (conditions for termination of two-year suspension included a passing score on the MPRE, completion of six credit hours of CLE in ethics and professionalism, and completion of the traditional CLE requirements for all lawyers); *Lawyer Disciplinary Bd. v. Aleshire*, 736 S.E.2d 70 (W. Va. 2012) (lawyer's egregious misconduct, including his unresponsiveness to two clients causing them to suffer actual monetary damages, required three years' suspension, restitution, that he pass the MPRE, and that he complete an additional twelve hours of CLE prior to petitioning for reinstatement).

- **Other Requirements Consistent with Purposes of Lawyer Sanctions**

A jurisdiction's highest court or a disciplinary board may impose other requirements that are consistent with the purposes of lawyer discipline. *See, e.g., People v. Rotenberg*, 911 P.2d 642 (Colo. 1996) (lawyer publicly censured for driving while intoxicated; imposing additional conditions including continued psychotherapy and Antabuse regimen, monthly written reports regarding treatment, and records of random urinalysis tests); *People v. Egbune*, 58 P.3d 1168 (Colo. O.P.D.J. 1999) (ordering lawyer to bring an interpleader action to determine the rightful apportionment of $6,122 in disputed fees, which lawyer took as contingent fee from settlement funds knowing prior lawyer claimed an interest in funds). Such requirements can be imposed along with other conditions. *See, e.g., In re Pelletier*, 84 A.3d 960 (Del. 2014) (Delaware Court suspended New Jersey lawyer for one year for unauthorized practice of law in Delaware and also prohibited lawyer from acting pro hac vice in any Delaware matter and from providing advice to any Delaware clients during period of suspension); *In re Kingsley*, 950 A.2d 659 (Table) (Del. 2008) (disbarring lawyer not admitted to practice in Delaware who violated prior court orders and engaged in the unauthorized practice of law by preparing wills, trusts, deeds, and powers of attorney for accountant's Delaware clients; court also prohibited lawyer from, providing advice to any Delaware clients on matters of Delaware law, ordered lawyer to refrain in all respects from identifying his law firm address as being in Delaware, and directed that he request the Philadelphia Estate Planning Council no longer list his law firm address in Delaware); *In re Burchett*, 630 N.E.2d 205 (Ind. 1994) (when lawyer converted funds through forgery to support drug habit, court imposed six-month suspension with fifty hours of service in a drug and/or alcohol rehabilitation program and fifty hours with a community service organization); *Disciplinary Counsel v. Blair*, 944 N.E.2d 1161 (Ohio 2011) (two-year suspension with eighteen-month stayed probationary period for lawyer who misappropriated client funds and filed false statements concerning those funds; probation conditions included supervision by an appointed lawyer monitor and completion of twelve hours of CLE in law-office management and other requirements related to lawyer's substance addiction); *In re Discipline of Reynolds*, 762 N.W.2d 341, 356 (S.D. 2009) (concluding that three-year suspension was warranted for serious misconduct, including a pattern of unresponsiveness to the disciplinary board, neglect of client matters, and failure to communicate with clients, to "allow a once very competent attorney time to identify to himself his professional flaws and attempt to cure them"; conditions to reinstatement included that lawyer take and pass the MPRE, successfully complete a law office management course, have a complete psychological evaluation and submit the results to the board, and that upon readmission he agree to file monthly reports on the status of all open files for two years); *In re Discipline of Ortner*, 699 N.W.2d 865 (S.D. 2005) (upon reinstatement lawyer to submit affidavit stating he has reviewed Rules of Professional Conduct along with pledge to abide by rules, pass MPRE, reimburse state bar, and maintain professional malpractice insurance with proof).

Fee disgorgement is another requirement a court or disciplinary board may impose when a lawyer has overstepped ethical boundaries in taking a fee. *See, e.g., In re Frye*, No. 15-10242, 570 B.R. 21 (Banktcy. D. Vt. 2017) (failing to timely and fully disclose fees as per Bankruptcy Code warranted disgorgement of half of fees paid, despite finding that lawyer provided competent service at a below-market rate); *In re Nguyen*, 447 B.R. 268 (B.A.P. 9th Cir. 2011) (bankruptcy court did not abuse discretion in imposing sanctions related to incompetent and negligent representation of debtor clients, including fee disgorgement, monetary sanctions, permanent injunctive relief, and a temporary suspension from bankruptcy practice in the district; failure to apply each criterion of the Sanctions Standards when determining sanctions was not an abuse of discretion); *In re Wimmershoff*, 3 P.3d 417 (Colo. 2000) (ordering public censure plus $1,000 refund to client when lawyer charged unreasonable fee, failed to explain basis of fee, and violated rules on contingent fee agreements); *In re Edwards*, 668 S.E.2d 791 (S.C. 2008) (in reciprocal discipline proceeding court imposed sanction similar to that imposed by bankruptcy court, two-year suspension and disgorgement of fees paid by twenty-four clients); *Cohn v. Bd. of Prof'l Responsibility*, 151 S.W.3d 473, 486 (Tenn. 2004) (affirming disgorgement order for $13,996.73 in post-confirmation work for improper collection of attorney's fees in bankruptcy cases when lawyer engaged in surreptitious and improper filing of proof of claim; holding orders of disgorgement in bankruptcy case are "sanctions upon an attorney, not a modification of a debtor's discharge"). *But see In re McDermitt*, No. 05-11710, 2006 WL 1582390 (Bankr. D. Vt. May 30, 2006) (vacating disgorgement order when no proof of pecuniary loss as result of lawyer's procedural oversights and tardiness in filings); *Fla. Bar v. Dove*, 985 So.2d 1001 (Fla. 2008) (disapproving referee's recommendation that respondent disgorge her fees as part of sanction for misconduct, including false statements to court in adoption case; finding that disgorgement inapplicable in case where lawyer provided inadequate services to client).

## 2.9 Reciprocal Discipline

**Reciprocal discipline is the imposition of a disciplinary sanction on a lawyer who has been disciplined in another jurisdiction.**

# Annotation

### *Purpose of Reciprocal Discipline*

A lawyer who has been disciplined in one U.S. jurisdiction is subject to reciprocal discipline in any other U.S. jurisdiction in which the lawyer is admitted. The purposes of reciprocal discipline are to prevent a lawyer admitted to practice in more than one jurisdiction from avoiding the effect of discipline by simply practicing in another jurisdiction, to prevent relitigation of misconduct that already has been established in another jurisdiction, and to protect the public from lawyers who commit such misconduct. *See, e.g., People v. Bode,* 119 P.3d 1098 (Colo. O.P.D.J. 2005) (citing former commentary to Standard 2.9; finding that Colorado has interest in reciprocal discipline to prevent the misconduct that resulted in suspension by other jurisdiction); *In re Powell,* 548 S.E.2d 615 (Ga. 2001) (rejecting recommendation of public reprimand in reciprocal discipline case in favor of disbarment when lawyer who pleaded guilty to eight misdemeanor counts of prostitution voluntarily surrendered license to practice law in West Virginia as part of plea agreement); *In re Wilson-Lindsay,* 492 S.E.2d 671 (Ga. 1997) (reciprocal disbarment of lawyer disbarred by consent in D.C. Court of Appeals); *In re Schwedler,* 895 N.W.2d 409, 411 (Wis. 2017) ( six-month suspension by USPTO subject to reciprocal discipline in Wisconsin; court observed that "USPTO, a federal agency with its own licensing and disciplinary proceedings, is appropriately considered 'another jurisdiction' for purposes of our reciprocal discipline rule. . . ."); *In re Edwards,* 668 S.E.2d 791, 794 (S.C. 2008) (rejecting lawyer's claim that reciprocal discipline rule not applicable to bankruptcy court's order imposing sanctions, court noted provisions of rule authorizing imposition of reciprocal discipline on a lawyer disciplined in another jurisdiction "does not require that the other jurisdiction be located outside the borders of this State"). *But see Disciplinary Counsel v. Lapine,* 942 N.E.2d 328, 332 (Ohio 2010) (concluding that the U.S. Securities and Exchange Commission was not a "jurisdiction" for purposes of reciprocal discipline, nor did a settlement agreement between the SEC and the lawyer, which did not include any affirmative findings of misconduct, constitute an "order of discipline upon which reciprocal discipline could be based); *In re Kern,* 816 S.E.2d 574, 577 (S.C. 2018) (in matter of first impression, court determined that Securities and Exchange Commission was not a "jurisdiction" for purposes of reciprocal discipline despite findings of fact made in agency's order; lawyer suspended for eighteen months based on "ample evidence [independent of agency's order] that lawyer committed professional misconduct by providing false information in statements to others").

## *Procedure*

Rule 22 of the MRLDE sets forth model procedures for the prompt initiation and resolution of reciprocal disciplinary proceedings. The Model Rule provides that a certified copy of a final adjudication imposing discipline on a lawyer in another jurisdiction constitutes conclusive evidence that the lawyer committed the misconduct. With few exceptions, a majority of jurisdictions impose reciprocal discipline equal to that issued by the originating jurisdiction. *See, e.g., People v. Distel*, 76 P.3d 473 (Colo. O.P.D.J. 2003) (imposing disbarment in reciprocal discipline action after lawyer disbarred in Arizona for conversion, trust account violations, neglect, and misstatements to tribunal; final adjudication in another jurisdiction conclusively established grounds for discipline in Colorado); *Chief Disciplinary Counsel v. Burbank*, 2018 WL 3060237 at *1 (Conn. 2018) (court declined to depart from majority view that "most courts extend the reciprocity doctrine to include a practice of imposing a disciplinary sanction that normally will be the same in operative length and severity as that imposed in the first jurisdiction. An inappropriately lenient or severe sanction, however, will not be copied") (citations omitted); *Statewide Grievance Comm'n v. Tartaglia*, No. CV030828136S, 2003 WL 22904558 (Conn. Super. Ct. Nov. 24, 2003) (Connecticut decisional law requires the court to exercise its discretion, on a case-by-case basis, when presented with a request for reciprocal discipline); *In re Drager*, 846 A.2d 992 (D.C. 2004) (held in reciprocal attorney discipline cases, there is a general presumption that discipline in the District of Columbia should mirror the sanction imposed by the first jurisdiction); *In re Berger*, 737 A.2d 1033 (D.C. 1999) (in consolidated appeals of reciprocal discipline, court adhered to strong presumption in favor of imposing identical sanction in a reciprocal discipline proceeding; imposing sixty-day suspension, identical to the sanction imposed by Maryland, against one respondent and two-year suspension, identical to that imposed by New Jersey, against the other, with requirement that as condition of reinstatement both respondents prove by clear and convincing evidence their fitness to return to the practice of law); *In re Rickabaugh*, 661 N.W.2d 130 (Iowa 2003) (lawyer should be suspended indefinitely with no possibility of reinstatement for three years; concluding that prior disbarment order in Nebraska was essentially an identical sanction for purposes of Iowa's Rules of Discipline); *In re Walters*, 45 So.3d 1016 (La. 2010) (imposing reciprocal nine-month suspension for gross negligence; court noted that only under extraordinary circumstance should there be significant variance from sanction imposed by the other jurisdiction); *Att'y Grievance Comm'n v. Kourtesis*, 87 A.3d 1231, 1237 (Md. 2014) (court will often impose identical discipline in reciprocal cases, but "[w]hen our cases . . . clearly demonstrate that we would apply a different sanction—had the conduct occurred or the case originated here—we need not follow the original jurisdiction's determination") (citations omitted); *Att'y Grievance Comm'n v. Thaxton*, 1 A.3d 470, 482 (Md. 2010) (in reciprocal disciplinary proceedings, court "generally treat[s] the factual findings and conclusions of law from the original jurisdiction as conclusive evidence of an attorney's misconduct"; lawyer's admitted misconduct in disciplinary case before the D.C. Court of Appeals, including misappropriation of settlement funds and interference with the administration of justice, considered conclusive evidence of misconduct in Maryland case); *Miss. Bar v. Beal*, 167 So.3d 180 (Miss. 2014) (reciprocal two-year suspension warranted for lawyer's knowing abandonment of clients in another jurisdiction to their financial detriment); *State ex rel. Counsel for Discipline v. Murphy*, 814 N.W.2d 107, 108 (Neb. 2012) (denying lawyer's request for private reprimand and imposing reciprocal discipline of public reprimand, court reiterated that "in a reciprocal discipline proceeding, a judicial determination of attorney misconduct in one jurisdiction is generally conclusive proof of guilt and is not subject to relitigation in the second jurisdiction); *In re Fitzgerald*, 153 A.D.3d 315, 318 (N.Y. App. Div. 2017) (court "generally defers to the sanction determination made in the State where the misconduct occurred" in reciprocal cases) (citation omitted); *In re Reciprocal Discipline of Rokahr*, 681 N.W.2d 100 (S.D. 2004) (recognizing South Dakota rule of employing identical sanction imposed by foreign jurisdiction unless (1) the procedure in the other jurisdiction was so lacking in notice or opportunity to be heard as to constitute a due process violation, (2) there was such an infirmity of proof establishing the misconduct that the court could not reasonably rely upon them, or (3) the misconduct justifies substantially different discipline; court declined to impose reciprocal discipline where its own disciplinary proceedings reached contrary factual conclusions); *In re Discipline of Welker*, 100 P.3d 1197 (Utah 2004) (in reciprocal discipline proceeding, the Rules of Lawyer Discipline and Disability do not allow Utah to impose a sanction more severe than that imposed in the other state); *In re Disciplinary Proceedings Against Maloney*, 686 N.W.2d 148 (Wis. 2004) (in discipline proceeding lawyer was subject to identical sanction imposed upon him by the foreign jurisdiction based upon Wisconsin's ethics rules); *cf. Att'y Grievance Comm'n v. Sabghir*, 710 A.2d 926 (Md. 1998) (in reciprocal disbarment of lawyer disbarred in New York for fraud and misappropriation, court held that lawyer sanctioned in one state may not collaterally attack factual finding of those proceedings in reciprocal discipline proceeding).

### *Due Process and Variance from Original Sanction*

Although a hearing is not necessary for reciprocal discipline to be imposed, a court must provide the lawyer or disciplinary counsel with an opportunity to raise a due process challenge or to show that a sanction different from the sanction imposed in the other jurisdiction is warranted. *See Selling v. Radford*, 243 U.S.

46 (1917) (seminal decision identifying factors that bar reciprocal discipline when a court finds (1) absence of due process in the prior disciplinary procedure, (2) substantial infirmity in the proof of lack of private and professional character, or (3) some other grave reason sufficient to indicate that reciprocal disbarment or other reciprocal discipline is inconsistent with principles of right and justice). In *In re McTighe*, 131 F. Supp. 2d 870 (N.D. Tex. 2001), for example, the court explained that, in reciprocal discipline cases, federal effect is given to a state court's disciplinary order unless one or more of those factors is present. In that case, involving a lawyer who was suspended for six months by the U.S. Court of Appeals for the 10th Circuit for making frivolous arguments and deceiving the court, the court determined that none of the factors was present, and thus also suspended the lawyer for six months. *See also In re Walden*, 709 Fed. Appx. 644 (U.S.C.A 11th Cir. 2017) (affirming district court's reciprocal disbarment of lawyer disbarred in Alabama, finding that although federal disbarment does not automatically result from state disbarment, the three factors enumerated in *Selling* were not present); *Stanley v. Ligon*, 285 S.W.3d 649, 654 (Ark. 2008) (in granting lawyer's petition for writ of mandamus, court held that professional conduct committee did not have authority to impose five years' reciprocal suspension on lawyer whose accreditation to represent claimants before the Social Security Administration was suspended for five years and canceled with the Department of Veteran Affairs; finding the committee exceeded its authority since neither governmental agency is vested with the authority to regulate the practice of law, respondent "was never disbarred or suspended 'from the practice of law in any other state' as expressly required" by the disciplinary procedural rules); *People v. Romo-Vejar*, 138 P.3d 1218 (Colo. O.P.D.J. 2006) (court to impose same discipline as originating jurisdiction unless misconduct warrants substantially different discipline; public censure and one-year probation for lawyer who negligently dealt with client funds as imposed by Arizona Supreme Court was reciprocally appropriate, rather than six-month suspension, when misconduct was negligent, involved only one client, and caused only potential harm; court determined to forgo probation in Colorado as lawyer had successfully completed one-year probation in Arizona at time of reciprocal discipline); *People v. Chastain*, 109 P.3d 1072 (Colo. O.P.D.J. 2005) (identical sanction reciprocally appropriate for lawyer disbarred by the South Carolina Supreme Court, unless improper to do so based on lack of due process, infirm proof, or grave injustice); *In re Peters*, 149 A.3d 253, 258 (D.C. 2016) (rejecting seven-year reciprocal suspension and ordering three-year suspension; court stated that seven-year suspension "would be a longer period than standard disbarment and far longer than allowed in an ordinary suspension case originating in the District of Columbia"); *In re Tluscik*, 219 P.3d 1220, 1223 (Kan. 2009) (in reciprocal discipline proceedings, indefinite suspension imposed on lawyer who failed to cooperate and participate in proceedings rather than the disbarment by way of default imposed in Missouri,

with the court noting the differences in the burden of proof in each jurisdiction warranted a different sanction; the Missouri disbarment order concluded that there was "probable cause" to believe the ethical violations alleged had occurred, a lesser standard than "clear and convincing" proof that Kansas rules required); *In re Walters*, 45 So.3d 1016, 1018–19 (La. 2010) ("In determining the appropriate measure of reciprocal discipline, we are not required to impose the same sanction as that imposed by the state in which the misconduct occurred. Nevertheless, only under extraordinary circumstances should there be a significant variance from the sanction imposed by the other jurisdiction."); *Att'y Grievance Comm'n v. Peters-Hamlin*, 136 A.3d 374, 391 (Md. 2016) (court declined to impose reciprocal seven-year suspension, instead ordering disbarment in light of lawyer's conduct, which it found was "infected with fraud, deceit and dishonesty without any compelling extenuating circumstances"; exceptional circumstances existed and warranted increased sanction); *Att'y Grievance Comm'n v. Zodrow*, 19 A.3d 381, 391 (Md. 2011) (disbarment, rather than suspension for one year and one day as ordered by the Colorado Supreme Court, was appropriate sanction for lawyer's conduct involving intentional dishonesty, fraud, and deceit; concluding that the current state of law in Maryland warranted substantially different discipline from that imposed by Colorado and noting that "[t]he purpose of that Rule is to ensure that all attorneys of this Bar are subject to similar sanctions for similar misconduct, regardless of whether the misconduct takes place in this State or another jurisdiction"); *Bd. of Prof'l Responsibility v. Blatt*, 133 P.3d 965, 967 (Wyo. 2006) (in reciprocal disciplinary proceeding, court approved thirty-day suspension rather than six-month suspension that Pennsylvania had imposed, noting that lawyer's six-month suspension had served its purpose and he "has suffered the shame and humility of being punished for the exercise of very poor judgment" and "has fully acknowledged his poor decisions, and has made full restitution as required by the Pennsylvania Supreme Court").

## *Increased Sanction May Be Warranted*

In reciprocal discipline matters, courts have the discretion to rely on precedent or the specific facts of the case to impose a harsher sanction for the same or similar misconduct than that imposed by the originating jurisdiction. Commonly notice is given to the respondent lawyer of the intent to impose such different discipline. *See, e.g., People v. Andrews*, 74 P.3d 969 (Colo. O.P.D.J. 2003) (although knowing misappropriation would warrant disbarment in Colorado, under Colorado Rules of Procedure, absent notice, hearing board can impose no greater sanction than that imposed by another jurisdiction; imposing reciprocal discipline of six-month suspension with requirement of reinstatement proceeding); *In re Jacoby*, 945 A.2d 1193 (D.C. 2008) (rejecting lawyer's assertions that the court lacked authority to impose, the disciplinary board lacked authority to recommend, and bar counsel lacked standing to request greater discipline in reciprocal case; court imposed a sixty-day suspension based on limited precedent that simple assault conviction arising from domestic violence incident warranted a substantially different discipline in the District of Columbia from the public censure imposed in New Jersey); *Att'y Grievance Comm'n v. Poverman*, 103 A.3d 667 (Md. 2014) (indefinite suspension with right to apply for reinstatement after no less than one year, rather than public reprimand as imposed in Delaware, was consistent with Maryland precedent for lawyer who made knowing misrepresentations in registration statement); *Att'y Grievance Comm'n v. Katz*, 55 A.3d 909, 916 (Md. 2012) (in determining that the appropriate reciprocal sanction in Maryland was an indefinite suspension, with the right to apply for reinstatement after lawyer is readmitted in four other jurisdictions, rather than the six months' suspension imposed by Virginia for lawyer's willful failure to file income tax returns, court noted that although the identical discipline "may not result in a 'grave injustice' . . . [respondent's] conduct warrants 'substantially different discipline in this state'"; court has discretion to impose discipline consistent with sister jurisdiction or to order a different or more serious alternative based on the existence of exceptional circumstances).

### *Comparable Discipline When Identical Discipline Not Available*

When identical discipline is not available, courts have imposed a comparable sanction. *See, e.g., People v. Bode*, 119 P.3d 1098 (Colo. O.P.D.J. 2005) (three-year reciprocal suspension appropriate for a seven-year suspension imposed by the U.S. Patent and Trademark Office (PTO) when Colorado rules did not allow for suspensions exceeding three years and the PTO stayed the final four years of suspension, placing lawyer on probation during that period); *Att'y Grievance Comm'n v. Kourtesis*, 87 A.3d 1231 (Md. 2014) (lawyer indefinitely suspended with disciplinary proceedings held in abeyance in District of Columbia due to disability; reciprocal remedy unavailable in Maryland, which, instead, transferred lawyer to disability inactive status relying on factual findings of incapacity from District of Columbia proceeding); *Att'y Grievance Comm'n v. Thaxton*, 1 A.3d 470, 484 (Md. 2010) (noting that one-year suspension with six months' stayed, the sanction imposed by the D.C. Court of Appeals for lawyer's misconduct involving misappropriation of settlement funds and interference with the administration of justice, was not within Maryland's "spectrum of sanctions" and ordering an indefinite suspension upon concluding it was the functional equivalent to the D.C. court's sanction).

## 2.10 Readmission and Reinstatement

**In jurisdictions where disbarment is not permanent, procedures should be established to allow a disbarred lawyer to apply for readmission. Procedures should be established to allow a suspended lawyer to apply for reinstatement.**

## Annotation

Readmission occurs when a disbarred lawyer is returned to practice; reinstatement occurs when a suspended lawyer is returned to practice. Some courts use the terms "readmission" and "reinstatement" interchangeably. Disbarment on consent has the same effect, for readmission purposes, as disbarment. *In re Reinstatement of Wiederholt*, 24 P.3d 1219, 1223 n.10 (Alaska 2001) (noting that Standard 2.10 uses the term "readmission" to refer to the return of a disbarred lawyer to the practice of law and the term "reinstatement" to refer to the return to practice of a suspended lawyer while Alaska Bar Rule 29(a) uses the word "reinstatement" to cover both situations); *In re Reinstatement of Blevins*, 59 P.3d 510, 511 (Okla. 2002) ("In regard to a reinstatement application, a petitioner that has resigned his membership in the [Oklahoma Bar Association] pending a bar disciplinary proceeding has the same burden as an individual that has been disbarred by this Court.").

### *Readmission Following Disbarment*

Because the purpose of lawyer discipline is not punishment, readmission after disbarment may be appropriate. In *In re Ellis*, 930 N.E.2d 724 (Mass. 2010), the Supreme Judicial Court of Massachusetts noted:

> A fundamental precept of our system is that persons can be rehabilitated. . . . The test is whether at the present time, in spite of his previous misconduct, the petitioner has rehabilitated himself sufficiently to inspire public confidence, that is, whether he currently possesses the necessary moral character and legal acumen to be admitted to the bar of the Commonwealth.

*Id.* at 726. The presumption, however, should be against readmission. *See, e.g., In re Reinstatement of Wiederholt*, 182 P.3d 1047, 1048 (Alaska 2008) (denying readmission despite disbarred lawyer's "persuasive showing" that he met requirements for readmission and accepting disciplinary board's finding that lawyer "lacks insight into the reasons for the conduct that led to his disbarment" and was unconvinced that readmission "would not be detrimental to the administration of justice or subversive of the public interest"); *Adams v. Ark. State Bd. of Law Exam'rs*, 538 S.W.3d 836 838 (Ark. 2018) ("Once a lawyer has lost his or her license to practice law, whether through surrender or disbarment, there is a presumption against readmission. The protection of the public and the honor and integrity of the profession have long been the principal criteria in determining whether a person should be admitted or readmitted to the bar."); *Fla. Bar v. Clement*, 662 So.2d 690, 699 (Fla. 1995) (reiterating presumption against readmission and quoting commentary to Rule 2.2 of the Florida Standards for Imposing Lawyer Sanctions: "[a] former member who has been disbarred may only be admitted again upon full compliance with the rules and regulations governing admission to the bar"); *In re Fletcher*, 997 N.E.2d 1196, 1200 (Mass. 2013) (court denied reinstatement finding disbarred lawyer had fallen considerably short of demonstrating that she had led a "sufficiently exemplary life to inspire public confidence, once again, in spite of [her] previous actions" and that she also lacked necessary competence in the law).

Lawyers should not be considered for readmission until at least five years after the effective date of disbarment. *See, e.g.*, *In re Horwitz*, 881 P.2d 352 (Ariz. 1994) (lawyer disbarred for negligent homicide involving use of cocaine may not apply for readmission for five years from date of disbarment; noting difference between disbarment and five-year suspension lies in greater opprobrium attached to disbarment, even if practical effect is not more severe); *Grievance Adm'r v. August*, 475 N.W.2d 256, 262 (Mich. 1991) (vacating readmission order of lawyer disbarred for attempt to influence judge assignment; interpreting five-year rule as "temporal milepost . . . fixing the minimum time after which a disbarred attorney may be declared rehabilitated," but rejecting implication that passage of five years guarantees eligibility for reinstatement; remanding for consideration of nature of offense and lapse of time since misconduct); *In re Oberhellmann*, 873 S.W.2d 851 (Mo. 1994) (lawyer disbarred for intentionally deceiving court may not apply for readmission until at least five years after effective date of disbarment); *State ex rel. Okla. Bar Ass'n v. Lewis*, 257 P.3d 998, 1000 (Okla. 2011) (noting that "[b]ecause resignation pending disciplinary proceedings is tantamount to disbarment," lawyer could not make an application for reinstatement for five years following the effective date of resignation). *But see In re Laudumiey*, 849 So.2d 515 (La. 2003) (five-year minimum period for seeking readmission is a rule of procedure that does not vest any substantive rights in the lawyer; the procedural nature of the rule is illustrated by court's prior decisions in which it held that the minimum period for applying for readmission may be extended or otherwise modified at court's discretion).

Some jurisdictions have imposed longer periods prior to application for readmission, some shorter. *Compare Statewide Grievance Comm'n v. Schaffer*, No. CV030196758, 2004 WL 303654 (Conn. Super. Ct. Feb. 2, 2004) (disbarring and prohibiting from applying for readmission for a period of three years), *with In re Salat*, 131 So.3d 841 (La. 2014) (in determining disbarred lawyer was permanently enjoined from applying for readmission, court declared it "always had the unfettered authority to refuse readmission to disbarred attorneys, including the right to do so on a permanent basis").

## *Demonstrating Moral Fitness and Rehabilitation by Clear and Convincing Evidence*

After a requisite waiting period, a lawyer seeking to be readmitted to practice after disbarment must prove fitness to practice. A primary consideration in granting readmission is whether the traits leading to the original misconduct have been corrected. In *In re Arrotta,* 96 P.3d 213 (Ariz. 2004), the Arizona Supreme Court explained the rationale for this requirement:

> [W]e cannot fulfill our duty to protect the public unless, before granting reinstatement, we are confident that a lawyer will avoid the pitfalls that caused his earlier serious misconduct. To show rehabilitation, an applicant must first establish by clear and convincing evidence that he has identified just what weaknesses caused the misconduct and then demonstrate that he has overcome those weaknesses.

*Id.* at 217. The court in *Arrotta* collected cases from other jurisdictions similarly stressing the fundamental importance of gauging whether the lawyer has demonstrated correction of weaknesses that led to misconduct. *See also In re Hart,* 822 P.2d 264 (Wash. 1992) (denying petition for reinstatement by lawyer/trustee who had been disbarred for misuse of estate assets; lawyer's willingness to take shortcuts and elevate expedience over respect for the law persuaded court that lawyer had not overcome weaknesses that produced earlier misconduct). Although a lawyer must identify and overcome the weakness that caused the misconduct, he or she need not necessarily establish what was or might have been the underlying cause of the identified weakness that led to the misconduct. *See, e.g., In re Poliquin,* 135 A.3d 1282, at *9 (Table) (Del. 2016) (conditionally reinstating petitioner who had been suspended for misconduct related to ADHD and substance abuse, finding "it is not the specific underlying mental condition or diagnosis that is critical, but whether steps to address the conduct leading to the discipline have been addressed in an appropriate manner").

Courts also have emphasized the importance of considering the seriousness of the lawyer's prior misconduct against evidence of rehabilitation. *See, e.g., In re Reinstatement of Wiederholt,* 89 P.3d 771 (Alaska 2004) (holding seriousness of previous misconduct can outweigh otherwise sufficient showing; lawyer failed to establish current moral fitness by clear and convincing evidence given severity of multiple acts of misconduct, lack of remorse, attempt to rationalize behavior, and display during hearing of many traits that led to disbarment). *But see In re Reinstatement of Wiederholt,* 295 P.3d 396 (Alaska 2013) (disbarred lawyer's fifth petition for reinstatement granted; after eighteen years, court found that, despite serious nature of the misconduct, sufficient time had elapsed and petitioner's character, maturity, experience, and approach to life had changed dramatically between the time of discipline and present); *Iowa Supreme Ct. Att'y Disc. Bd. v. Reilly*, 884 N.W.2d 761 (Iowa 2016) (lawyer disbarred for egregious misconduct including converting nearly $100,000 in settlement funds from a minor due to a gambling addiction conditionally readmitted after ten years, despite seriousness of misconduct, upon showing dedication to recovery, acceptance of responsibility and remorse for the harm he caused, current position of responsibility, and that he poses no threat to the public). *See also In re Robbins*, 836 P.2d 965 (Ariz. 1992) (court considered exhaustive list of elements in a readmission action; burden of showing, by clear and convincing evidence, that lawyer is rehabilitated, competent, and no longer poses threat to members of public is same whether applicant was disbarred or resigned in lieu of disbarment); *In re Williams*, 8 A.3d 666, 668 (Me. 2010) (disbarred lawyer bears "burden to present 'clear and convincing evidence demonstrating the moral qualifications, competency, and learning in law required for admission to practice law in this State,' as well as evidence establishing that 'reinstatement will not be detrimental to the integrity and standing of the Bar, the administration of justice, or to the public interest'") (citations omitted); *In re Ellis*, 930 N.E.2d 724, 726 (Mass. 2010) (a disbarred lawyer "bears the heavy burden of establishing that he presently meets . . . moral and competency qualifications" sufficient for reinstatement; in making reinstatement determinations, court weighs "the circumstances concerning the petitioner's misconduct against his subsequent actions that show rehabilitation"); *In re Disciplinary Action Against Montgomery*, 566 N.W.2d 426, 429 (N.D. 1997) (lawyer seeking reinstatement must prove "by clear and convincing evidence he currently has the requisite honesty and integrity to practice law, *in spite of* the misconduct committed in the past" and "[t]he rule envisions a balancing of the evidence of the petitioner's current good character with the seriousness of the prior misconduct"); *Petition of Pier*, 561 N.W.2d 297, 300 (S.D. 1997) (while acknowledging that "the more culpable the misconduct, the greater the burden to prove worthiness for reinstatement," court readmitted lawyer who had been disbarred for stealing more than $45,000 in client funds after surveying criteria used by the ABA and in other jurisdictions and noting that he plainly confessed his misconduct, evidenced sincere remorse and fitness to practice, repaid what he took, with interest, had widespread community support for readmission and, in his work as a paralegal during his disbarment, properly avoided the unauthorized practice of law); *cf. Statewide Grievance Comm'n v. Toro*, No. CV030478961S, 2008 WL 5219433 (Conn. Super. Ct. Nov. 14, 2008) (relying on criteria set forth in Sanctions Standards to evaluate eligibility for readmission, including demonstration of rehabilitation, fitness to practice law, and compliance with discipline orders, though Sanctions Standards not officially adopted in Connecticut).

## *Reinstatement Following Suspension*

Reinstatement occurs when a suspended lawyer is returned to practice. A lawyer who has been suspended for six months or less should be reinstated at the end of the period of suspension by filing an affidavit stating that he or she has fully complied with terms of the suspension order and has paid any required fees and costs. *See* MRLDE R. 24.

When a lawyer has been suspended for more than six months, reinstatement may be appropriate when the lawyer can show rehabilitation. Application for reinstatement should not be permitted until the expiration of the ordered period of suspension and generally not until at least six months after the effective date of suspension. A lawyer should not be reinstated unless he or she can show by clear and convincing evidence criteria set forth in Rule 25(E) of the MRLDE (see Annotation to Standards 2.2. and 2.3). *See Wotan v. People*, 35 P.3d 516 (Colo. O.P.D.J. 2000) (court granted lawyer's reinstatement petition following one-year suspension, considering such rehabilitation factors as lawyer's state of mind and professional ability, conduct since original discipline was imposed, professional competence, candor and sincerity, personal and community service, and recognition of the seriousness of previous misconduct); *In re Reinstatement of Dobbs*, 256 P.3d 52 (Okla. 2011) (significant consideration is given to evidence that the applicant would not repeat the past behavior—namely, whether the lawyer had been disciplined in the past for similar conduct and whether the past behavior had been corrected and rehabilitation demonstrated); *In re Hunter*, 704 A.2d 1154, 1159 (Vt. 1997) (lawyer suspended for three years not to be reinstated until he has demonstrated, by clear and convincing evidence, that "(1) he has the moral qualifications, competency, and learning required for admission to practice law in this state; (2) the resumption of his practice will be neither detrimental to the integrity and standing of the bar or the administration of justice nor subversive to the public interest; and (3) he has been rehabilitated").

## *Conditional Readmission/Reinstatement*

Conditional readmission and conditional reinstatement may be appropriate when supervision of a lawyer returning to practice is necessary or when an articulated requirement will help ensure that the lawyer meets his or her ethical obligations. *See, e.g., In re Reinstatement of Nemec*, 799 N.W.2d 370 (N.D. 2011) (reinstatement conditioned on association with an experienced supervising lawyer and active participation in Alcoholics Anonymous; given that petitioner's long history of alcohol addiction contributed to several instances of professional misconduct, including failure to competently and diligently represent clients).

Conditions that can be imposed include probation (see Annotation to Standard 2.7) or other sanctions or remedies (see Annotation to Standard 2.8). In addition to probation, for example, limits can be placed upon a lawyer's practice or a lawyer may be required to make restitution as a condition of readmission or reinstatement. *See, e.g., People v. Huntzinger,* 967 P.2d 160 (Colo. 1998) (imposing as specific condition of reinstatement payment of court-ordered $460 in attorney's fees plus interest; whether amount was discharged in bankruptcy irrelevant since purpose of payment is rehabilitative rather than payment of debt or restitution as such; collecting cases from various jurisdictions on imposing restitution after lawyer is discharged in bankruptcy); *People v. Rivers,* 933 P.2d 6 (Colo. 1997) (restitution of $200 plus statutory interest imposed as a condition of reinstatement); *People v. Andersen,* 58 P.3d 537 (Colo. O.P.D.J. 2000) (prior to submission of any petition for readmission, lawyer required to pay $3,400 plus statutory interest); *In re Fountain,* 878 A.2d 1167 (Del. 2005) (upon reinstatement, lawyer may not practice as solo practitioner or not in any office-sharing arrangement that would amount to solo practice; lawyer to have no responsibility for financial recordkeeping or check issuing from operating or escrow accounts); *In re Baker,* 649 So.2d 850 (Miss. 1995) (granting petition for reinstatement on condition lawyer pay restitution of $1,500); *In re Carlton,* 993 P.2d 736 (N.M. 2000) (imposing indefinite suspension, with three years' probation with conditions prior to and following reinstatement); *In re Disciplinary Proceedings Against Jennings,* 801 N.W.2d 304, 316 (Wis. 2011) (reinstatement conditioned on lawyer's continued compliance with restitution obligations to an employee stock ownership trust, his family, his former law firm, a malpractice insurance provider, and a fiduciary services company that paid restitution to lawyer's injured client; "we determine that a continuing effort toward restitution, to the extent he is financially able, is necessary to demonstrate [respondent's] attitude and understanding of the ethical standards required" of lawyers). *But see Toledo Bar Ass'n. v. Hales,* 899 N.E.2d 130 (Ohio 2008) (court acknowledged that paying restitution would further suspended lawyer's rehabilitation but declined to order it due to discharge of debt in bankruptcy).

## *Prerequisites for Reinstatement*

Courts often will order CLE or an examination to demonstrate proficiency as a precondition to readmission or reinstatement. *See, e.g., Statewide Grievance Comm'n v. Schaffer,* No. CV030196758, 2004 WL 303654 (Conn. Super. Ct. Feb. 2, 2004) (any application for readmission conditioned on achieving a passing score on the MPRE); *In re Hearin,* 897 So.2d 579 (La. 2005) (thirty-six hours of CLE prior to seeking reinstatement ordered for lawyer who violated numerous ethics rules); *In re Carlton,* 993 P.2d 736 (N.M. 2000) (imposing indefinite suspension, with many reinstatement conditions including passing the MPRE, a minimum of sixteen hours of CLE in professional ethics and/or law office management, a fee accounting, and relinquishing client file); *In re Crockett,* 120 A.D.3d 878 (N.Y. App. Div. 2014) (suspended lawyer who converted and mishandled client funds demonstrated cause for concern relative to her knowledge, ethics, and practice; lawyer ordered to complete, prior to applying for reinstatement, four hours of CLE in ethics and professionalism, four hours of CLE in law practice management, and four hours of CLE in New York practice, in addition to regular CLE requirements); *In re Galvin*, 87 A.D.3d 1223 (N.Y. App. Div. 2011) (application for readmission conditioned on passing score on the MPRE and completion of six hours of CLE in ethics and professionalism in addition to traditional CLE requirements).

Prerequisites to readmission/reinstatement also may include a combination of conditions designed to ensure a lawyer's fitness and compliance with ethics rules. *See, e.g.*, *In re McGrath*, 259 P.3d 437 (Alaska 2011) (prior to filing for reinstatement, suspended lawyer ordered to pay costs incurred by the bar in pursuing disciplinary case and $1,000 in attorney's fees, make full restitution to client protection fund, complete six hours of CLE in legal ethics and twelve hours in law office management courses, obtain training in establishing and handling client funds and trust accounts, and implement approved plan for his law practice financial procedures); *Iowa Supreme Ct. Att'y Disc. Bd. v. Turner*, 918 N.W.2d 130 (Iowa 2018) (prior to any application for reinstatement, lawyer, who suffered from depression and ADHD and was suspended for one year, ordered to provide evaluation by licensed mental health professional verifying fitness to practice law); *In re Crews*, 159 S.W.3d 355 (Mo. 2005) (prior to filing for reinstatement, lawyer required to obtain no less than $250,000 in malpractice insurance; complete fifteen hours of CLE credits in office management, civil procedure, and ethical practice; prepare and submit an office management plan; and pass the MPRE); *In re Carlton*, 993 P.2d 736 (N.M. 2000) (prior to any reinstatement application, suspended lawyer required to pass MPRE, complete sixteen-hours of CLE in ethics and/or law office management, pay costs, reimburse fees, provide client with accounting and file, document he has received appropriate treatment for health and personal problems, provide certification of fitness from psychotherapist, and obtain certification from New Mexico lawyer in good standing that his financial records are current and he opened IOLTA account).

# C. Factors to Be Considered in Imposing Sanctions

**3.0 Generally**
**In imposing a sanction after a finding of lawyer misconduct, a court should consider the following factors:**
- **(a) the duty violated;**
- **(b) the lawyer's mental state;**
- **(c) the potential or actual injury caused by the lawyer's misconduct; and**
- **(d) the existence of aggravating or mitigating factors.**

## Annotation

### *Jurisdictions Using Method*

Numerous jurisdictions have adopted the Sanctions Standards, modeled their own version on them, or are guided by them and follow Standard 3.0's methodology in deciding appropriate lawyer discipline. Alaska, Oregon, and Washington were the first states to embrace the Sanctions Standards in 1986. The Alaska Supreme Court reiterated its analysis for determining the appropriate discipline:

> We use "a three-step analysis" when determining sanctions in attorney discipline cases. The first step requires us to address "(1) the duty violated; (2) the lawyer's mental state; and (3) the extent of the actual or potential injury." In the second step we "examine recommended sanctions under the ABA standards for misconduct found in the first step." In the third step we "determine how aggravating or mitigating factors affect the recommended sanctions."

*In re Disciplinary Matter of Stepovich*, 386 P.3d 1205, 1208–09 (Alaska 2016) (citations omitted). *See also In re Abrams*, 257 P.3d 167 (Ariz. 2011) (court guided by Sanctions Standards, considers the four factors listed in Standard 3.0 in determining appropriate discipline); *People v. Tolentino*, 285 P.3d 340, 343 (Colo. 2012) ("The American Bar Association Standards for Imposing Lawyer Sanctions ('ABA Standards') and Colorado Supreme Court case law guide the imposition of sanctions for lawyer misconduct. In imposing a sanction after a finding of lawyer misconduct, the

Court must consider the duty violated, the lawyer's mental state, the actual or potential injury caused by the lawyer's misconduct, and the existence of aggravating and mitigating evidence pursuant to ABA Standard 3.0."); *Chief Disciplinary Counsel v. Rivera*, 2017 WL 660011, at *4 (Conn. January 4, 2017) ("Courts considering sanctions against attorneys measure the defendant's conduct against the rules. Although the rules define misconduct, they do not provide guidance for determining what sanctions are appropriate. . . . Connecticut courts reviewing attorney misconduct, therefore, have consulted the American Bar Association's Standards for Imposing Lawyer Sanctions . . . Although the [ABA] standards have not been officially adopted in Connecticut, they are used frequently by the Superior Court in evaluating attorney misconduct and in determining discipline. This court is, thus, guided by the ABA standards in determining the appropriate sanctions."); *Burton v. Mottolese*, 835 A.2d 998, 1033 (Conn. 2003) (Sanctions Standards "provide that, after a finding of misconduct, a court should consider (1) the nature of the duty violated, (2) the lawyer's mental state, (3) the potential or actual injury stemming from the lawyer's misconduct; and (4) the existence of aggravating or mitigating factors."); *In re Vanderslice*, 116 A.3d 1244, at *10 (Table) (Del. 2015) ("In determining the appropriate sanction, the Board considers the ABA Standards for Imposing Lawyer Sanctions and the four factor analysis under those standards: (a) the ethical duties violated by the lawyer; (b) the lawyer's mental state; (c) the extent of actual or potential injury caused by the lawyer's misconduct; and (d) aggravating and mitigating factors."); *Fla. Bar v. Helinger*, 620 So.2d 993 (Fla. 1993) (court considers four factors under Standard 3.0 of the Florida Standards for Imposing Lawyer Sanctions in determining appropriate discipline); *In re Freeman*, 506 S.E.2d 872, 873 (Ga. 1998) (in determining appropriate level of discipline to impose, "this Court looks to the ABA Standards for guidance, and considers, among other things, the duty violated, the lawyer's mental state, the injury caused by the lawyer's misconduct, and the extent of aggravating and mitigating factors"); *Office of Disciplinary Counsel v. Au*, 113 P.3d 203 (Haw. 2005) (after finding of misconduct, court should consider four factors in ABA Sanctions Standard 3.0); *In re Welling*, 715 N.E.2d 377 (Ind. 1999) (in determining appropriate sanction, court considers the duty violated, the lawyer's mental state, the actual or potential injury caused by the lawyer's misconduct, and the existence of aggravating or mitigating factors); *In re Najim*, 405 P.3d 1223, 1235 (Kan. 2017) ("This court and disciplinary panels have historically turned to the ABA Standards for Imposing Lawyer Sanctions for guidance. ABA Standard § 3.0 provides four factors to consider in assessing punishment: (1) the ethical duty violated by the lawyer; (2) the lawyer's mental state; (3) the actual or potential injury resulting from the misconduct; and (4) the existence of aggravating and mitigating circumstances."); *La. State Bar Ass'n v. Boutall*, 597 So.2d 444, 446–47 (La. 1992) (citing Standard 3.0 in noting that "[t]he court, in determining the penalty to be imposed in a disciplinary proceeding, should consider the duty violated, the lawyer's mental state, the actual or potential injury caused by the misconduct, and the existence of aggravating or mitigating factors"); *Bd. of Overseers of the Bar v. Prolman*, 2018 WL 4090648, at *10 (Maine 2018) (Maine Bar "Rule 21(c) incorporates the framework and methodology of the ABA Sanction Standards, thereby requiring that framework to be explicitly applied after a finding of lawyer misconduct. . . . the court abused its discretion by imposing a sanction on Prolman without applying the ABA Sanction Standards to Prolman's violations of the Maine Rules of Professional Conduct."); *Att'y Grievance Comm'n v. Zuckerman*, 872 A.2d 693 (Md. 2005) (ABA Standards create organizational framework calling for four questions to be considered); *In re Ehler*, 319 S.W.3d 442, 451 (Mo. 2010) (reaffirming that the court looks to the Sanctions Standards "for guidance when imposing attorney discipline but considers the ABA Standards advisory"); *In re Discipline of Lerner*, 197 P.3d 1067, 1077 (Nev. 2008) ("The American Bar Association Standards for Imposing Lawyer Sanctions suggest an analysis of four factors to be considered in determining an appropriate disciplinary sanction: the duty violated, the lawyer's mental state, the potential or actual injury caused by the lawyer's misconduct, and the existence of aggravating or mitigating factors."); *In re O'Meara's Case*, 54 A.3d 762, 769 (N.H. 2012) ("We look to the *Standards* for guidance. Under the *Standards*, we consider: (a) the duty violated; (b) the lawyer's mental state; (c) the potential or actual injury caused by the lawyer's misconduct; and (d) the existence of aggravating or mitigating factors."); *In re Estrada*, 143 P.3d 731, 743 (N.M. 2006) ("In imposing a sanction after a finding of lawyer misconduct, a court should consider the following factors: (a) the duty violated; (b) the lawyer's mental state; and (c) the potential or actual injury caused by the lawyer's misconduct; and (d) the existence of aggravating or mitigating factors. *ABA Standards* § 3.0."); *In re Disciplinary Action Against Edin*, 697 N.W.2d 727 (N.D. 2005) (guided by Standard 3.0 of the North Dakota Standards for Imposing Lawyer Sanctions, the court considers the duty violated, lawyer's mental state, potential or actual injury and aggravating or mitigating factors); *In re McGraw*, 414 P.3d 841 (Or. 2018) (court's determination of an appropriate sanction includes consideration of the four factors of Standard 3.0); *In re O'Leary*, 818 A.2d 676 (R.I. 2003) (court applies the four Standard 3.0 factors); *In re Discipline of Light*, 615 N.W. 2d 164 (S.D. 2000) (although not adopting Sanctions Standards, the court held that the appropriate approach is to consider them for guidance and evaluate conduct under the four Standard 3.0 factors); *Lockett v. Bd. of Prof'l Responsibility*, 380 S.W.3d 19, 26 (Tenn. 2012) ("This Court uses the ABA Standards as a guidepost for determining the appropriate level of discipline for attorney misconduct," considering the duty violated, the lawyer's mental state, the potential or actual injury caused by the lawyer's misconduct and the existence of aggravating or mitigating factors); *Long v. Ethics & Discipline Comm'n of the Utah Supreme Ct.*, 256 P.3d 206 (Utah 2011) (court applies four factors identical to Standard 3.0 in determining appropriate discipline, as outlined in Utah Standards for Imposing Lawyer Sanctions); *In re PRB,* 121 A.3d 675, 677 (Vt. 2015) (The ABA Standards for Imposing Lawyer Discipline have been adopted for consideration of "four factors to consider when determining an appropriate sanction in a disciplinary proceeding: (1) the duty violated; (2) the lawyer's mental state; (3) actual or potential injury caused by the misconduct; and (4) aggravating or mitigating factors."); *In re Disciplinary Proceeding Against Day,* 173 P.3d 915 (Wash. 2007) (disciplinary board conducts a two-step process for determining appropriate discipline recommendation: first, it determines the presumptive sanction with reference to duty violated, lawyer's mental state and harm caused, followed by determination of whether to modify presumptive sanction by applying aggravating and mitigating factors); *Lawyer Disciplinary Bd. v. Sims,* 574 S.E.2d 795 (W. Va. 2002) (Rule 3.16 of the West Virginia Rules of Lawyer Disciplinary Procedure enumerates four factors to be considered in imposing sanctions; those factors mirror Standard 3.0); *Bd. of Prof'l Responsibility v. Shreve,* 341 P.3d 370, 560 (Wyo. 2013) (Standard 3.0 factors considered in report and recommendation for disbarment).

When determining lawyer discipline, federal courts also apply the four factors outlined in Standard 3.0, often whether or not they have expressly adopted the Sanctions Standards. *See, e.g., In re Warburgh,* 644 F.3d 173 (2d Cir. 2011) (noting that Second Circuit's Committee on Admissions and Grievances considers the four factors of Standard 3.0 in recommending discipline); *In re Sealed Appellant,* 194 F.3d 666, 673 (5th Cir. 1999) (ABA Standard 3.0 cited for guidance, stating "the Louisiana Supreme Court has looked to the ABA Standards for Imposing Lawyer Sanctions. We do likewise."); *In re Bellows-Fairchild,* 322 B.R. 675 (Bankr. D. Or. 2005) (noting the court previously adopted the ABA Sanctions Standard and applying the four factors outlined in Standard 3.0 to permanently enjoin lawyer from appearing before the bankruptcy court in Oregon); *Frye v. Pena,* No. CIV 97-10 TUC RMB,1997 WL 659817 (D. Ariz. Oct. 2, 1997) (finding that lawyer engaged in misconduct by filing multiple frivolous lawsuits in bad faith and solely to harass, court cited Standard 3.0 in determining that disbarment was appropriate); *Haye v. Ashcroft,* No. Civ.A. 3:01CV414, 2004 WL 1936204 (D. Conn. Aug. 27, 2004) (in imposing sanction, court should consider four factors under Standard 3.0); *In re Doud,* 2017 WL 2704071 (D. Mich. June 23, 2017) (Standard 3.0 cited for factors considered when imposing discipline); *Matter of Hawk,* 2016 WL 7157977 (D. Ga. December 6, 2016) (following Georgia Supreme Court in using ABA Standard 3.0); *Romero-Barcelo v. Acevedo-Vila,* 275 F. Supp. 2d 177, 212 (D.P.R. 2003) (concluding public reprimand appropriate for lawyer who made false statements in complaint against challenger filed with Federal Elections Commission, court held that "[a]lthough not mandatory, the ABA Standards provide a useful touchstone in deciding the sanction to be applied" and that the "Standards suggest that a court imposing sanctions consider '(a) the duty violated; (b) the lawyer's mental state;

(c) the actual or potential injury caused by the lawyer's misconduct; and (d) the existence of aggravating or mitigating factors'"); *cf. In re Nguyen*, 447 B.R. 268, 277 (B.A.P. 9th Cir. 2011) (ruling that it was not reversible error and would no longer constitute an abuse of discretion if a bankruptcy court failed to apply each criterion of the Sanctions Standards in imposing sanctions for attorney misconduct; noting that the Sanctions Standards "were developed primarily for nonfederal, nonbankruptcy courts by unelected and nonjudicial parties [and] are ill-adapted to federal bankruptcy proceedings").

## *Applying the Factors*

*In re Hertach*, 109 P.3d 1218 (Kan. 2005), is a case that exemplifies how courts apply the four factors in Standard 3.0 when determining sanctions in disciplinary cases. In *Hertach*, the lawyer was charged with thirty-four counts of bribery (thirteen later dismissed based on the statute of limitations) arising from a secret and silent partnership he entered into with the county sheriff to operate a private jail annex. The lawyer pleaded guilty to two misdemeanor counts of participation in a prohibited contract and accepted joint and several responsibility to pay $750,000 in restitution. Following his conviction, disciplinary proceedings were initiated. The disciplinary panel found all charges were proven, and unanimously recommended disbarment.

The Supreme Court of Kansas examined the evidence using Standard 3.0. First, the court considered the nature of the duty violated, whether the duty was to the client, the public, the legal system, or the profession. It concluded the respondent lawyer violated his duty owed to the public. The court's second inquiry focused on the lawyer's culpability: whether his conduct was "intentional, knowing, or negligent." *Id.* at 1223. The court upheld the disciplinary panel's finding that the respondent intentionally violated his duty to the public, noting his agreement to keep the partnership secret, the complicated money-laundering scheme funneling profits through several corporations and back to the sheriff, and the respondent's efforts to destroy any paper trail regarding these corporations. In assessing the third factor under Standard 3.0, examination of actual or potential injury, the court found ample evidence that serious injury resulted from the respondent's misconduct. It found monetary injury to the public, which incurred the cost of taking legal action to terminate the contract and to appoint a receiver.

Finally, the court affirmed the disciplinary panel's findings regarding evidence in aggravation and mitigation. The court held that the lawyer engaged in bad faith obstruction of the disciplinary proceedings by not filing a written answer to the disciplinary complaint for six months, refused to acknowledge his wrongful conduct, showed indifference to making restitution, engaged in deceitful conduct motivated by greed, demonstrated a pattern of misconduct through the ongoing nature of the prohibited contracts, had substantial experience in the practice of law, and engaged in illegal conduct. In mitigation, the court found that the respondent had no prior disciplinary record, self-reported his misconduct the day criminal charges were filed, had good character and reputation before the misconduct, and already had been sanctioned by serving a 12-month jail term. Upon completing its analysis under Standard 3.0, the court unanimously agreed with the disciplinary panel's conclusions and recommendations and imposed disbarment. *See also People v. Tolentino*, 285 P.3d 340, 343–44 (Colo. O.P.D.J. 2012) (providing extensive discussion of each factor); *In re Vanderslice*, 116 A.3d 1244, at *10 (Table) (Del. 2015) (same).

## *Duty Violated*

The first step in the Standard 3.0 analysis, identifying the ethical duty the lawyer violated, requires the court to determine whether the duty breached was owed to a client, the public, the legal system, or the profession. Courts generally hold that the most important ethical duties are those owed to clients. *See, e.g., People v. Rhodes*, 107 P.3d 1177 (Colo. O.P.D.J. 2005) (most important duty that lawyer violated was that owed to his clients; failure to act with integrity in handling client property was egregious, warranting disbarment); *In re Ehler*, 319 S.W.3d 442 (Mo. 2010) (lawyer's knowing violation of several duties owed to her clients, including duties of safekeeping property, candor, competence, and diligence, warranted imposition of disbarment); *State ex rel. Neb. State Bar Ass'n v. Veith*, 470 N.W.2d 549 (Neb. 1991) (lawyer disbarred for knowingly commingling and misappropriating trust funds, one of the most serious violations of duty a lawyer owes to clients). For representative cases imposing discipline for violations of various aspects of a lawyer's duty to clients, see Annotation to Standard 4.0.

Lawyers also owe duties to the public. An example of when lawyers violate their duties to the public is when they commit a criminal act that reflects adversely on their honesty, trustworthiness, or fitness as a lawyer in other respects, or in cases in which their conduct involves dishonesty, fraud, deceit, or misrepresentation. *See In re King*, 646 So.2d 326 (La. 1994) (disbarment is suitable when a lawyer violates his or her duty to the public by serious criminal conduct involving false swearing, misrepresentation or fraud; suspension can be the proper sanction in some cases); *In re Smith*, 236 P.3d 137 (Or. 2010) (respondent violated his duties to the public when he engaged in criminal conduct and made misrepresentations to further that conduct; ninety-day suspension warranted). Violations of a lawyer's duties to the public are examined in depth in the discussion of Annotation to Standard 5.0.

Lawyers, as officers of the court, owe a duty to the legal system not to engage in conduct prejudicial to the administration of justice or conduct that involves dishonesty, fraud, deceit, or misrepresentation to a court. *See, e.g., In re Peasley*, 90 P.3d 764, 773 (Ariz. 2004) (by deliberately presenting false testimony in the prosecution of two defendants in a capital case, prosecutor violated "one of the most important duties of a lawyer," his duty as a prosecutor to seek justice); *In re Jensen*, 191 P.3d 1118 (Kan. 2008) (court imposed public censure on respondent for violating his duty to the legal system by telling a witness subpoenaed by the other party's lawyer in a child custody case that witness's testimony might not be required at hearing and that respondent would contact witness if he needed to appear in court); *In re Page*, 955 P.2d 239 (Or. 1998) (respondent violated her duty to the legal system when she knowingly filed altered documents with the court); *In re Jones*, 951 P.2d 149 (Or. 1997) (lawyer who filed documents containing false statements violated his duty to the legal system); *Bd. of Prof'l Responsibility v. Custis*, 295 P.3d 334 (Wyo. 2012) (respondent breached numerous duties he owed to the legal system when he presented a monetary inducement to victim's mother as a "quid pro quo" to persuade her to change her sentencing recommendation). Violations of duties owed to the legal system are explored in Annotation to Standard 6.0.

Other duties that lawyers owe as professionals do not always involve their basic responsibilities in representing clients or serving as officers of the court. As stated in Standard 7.0, addressing violations of duties owed as a professional, discipline can be appropriate in cases involving false or misleading communications about the lawyer or the lawyer's services, improper communications of the lawyer's fields of practice, improper solicitations of professional employment from a prospective client, unreasonable or improper fees, unauthorized practice of law, improper withdrawal from representation, or failure to report professional misconduct. *See, e.g., People v. Duggan*, 282 P.3d 534 (Colo. O.P.D.J. 2012) (respondent violated his duty to the legal profession when he failed to respond to a lawful demand for information during investigation); *In re Weaver*, 281 P.3d 502 (Kan. 2012) (among the duties violated, lawyer violated duties to the legal profession by failing to maintain his personal integrity when he distributed false and misleading advertising material); *In re Roswold*, 249 P.3d 1199 (Kan. 2011) (lawyer violated his duty to the legal profession and was suspended for one year for failing, as local counsel, to ensure out-of-state lawyer complied with pro hac vice rules); *In re Broome*, 815 So.2d 1 (La. 2002) (suspension for one year and one day for directly soliciting prospective clients who already were represented by Department of Justice, and making statements designed to mislead prospective clients to believe lawyer was working with Department of Justice); *In re Coffey's Case*, 880 A.2d 403, 414 (N.H. 2005) (lawyer "knowingly engaged in conduct that violated his duties as a professional with the intent to benefit himself" when he charged excessive fees and took real estate in exchange for his legal services that was worth substantially more than the amount the client owed); *In re Disciplinary Action Against McCray*, 825 N.W.2d 468 (N.D. 2012) (respondent admitted that suspension is generally appropriate when a lawyer knowingly engages in conduct that is a violation of a duty owed to the profession); *State ex rel. Okla. Bar Ass'n v. Leigh,* 914 P.2d 661 (Okla. 1996) (respondent's violation of duty to profession included use of legal stationery that identified him as a certified public accountant (CPA) and tax lawyer after he had failed to pass the CPA exam); *In re Obert,* 282 P.3d 825 (Or. 2012) (charging a clearly excessive fee violates duty owed to legal profession); *Bd. of Prof'l Responsibility v. Metler,* 273 P.3d 507 (Wyo. 2012) (misconduct of the sort engaged in by respondent, which essentially involved misleading communications about the lawyer or the lawyer's services, is addressed in Standard 7.0). Annotation to Standard 7.0 discusses discipline for violations of duties owed to the profession.

Courts often find violations of multiple duties by lawyers. *See, e.g., People v. Staab,* 287 P.3d 122 (Colo. O.P.D.J. 2012) (respondent violated duty to his clients by not exercising reasonable diligence, providing inadequate communication and making a false statement to his longtime client; lawyer also neglected his duties to the legal system by ignoring court orders, and violated duties to the profession by failing to take appropriate measures upon termination of his representations); *People v. Rhodes,* 107 P.3d 1177 (Colo. O.P.D.J. 2005) (lawyer disbarred for knowingly and intentionally misappropriating clients' funds and thereby violating duties to the public, the legal profession, and most importantly to his clients); *In re Bailey,* 821 A.2d 851, 866 (Del. 2003) (respondent violated his ethical duty to his clients, to the lawyers and employees of the firm, to the legal system, and to the legal profession when, as managing partner, he failed "to exercise even a modicum of diligence with respect [to the firm's] recordkeeping and tax obligations"); *In re Ortman,* 709 S.E.2d 784 (Ga. 2011) (lawyer convicted of aggravated battery suspended for one year and was held to have violated duty owed to the public and the legal profession not to engage in illegal conduct); *In re Lund,* 19 P.3d 110 (Kan. 2001) (lawyer suspended for one year for misconduct that included disregarding court orders, violating his duty to the legal system, and failing to maintain personal integrity, violating his duty to the legal profession); *In re Deshotels,* 863 So.2d 507 (La. 2003) (court accepted disciplinary board's finding that lawyer's failure to cooperate in disciplinary process, neglect of clients' matters, and disobedience of court orders constituted violations of duties owed to his clients, the public, the legal system, and the profession); *In re Fairbairn,* 802 N.W.2d 734 (Minn. 2011) (although client suffered no harm, misappropriation of client funds constituted breach of duty to the public and legal profession); *Cincinnati Bar Ass'n v. Farrell,* 895 N.E.2d 800 (Ohio 2008) (lawyer's illegal act of securing a loan with false information and forgery of his wife's signature constituted a breach of duty to the public, the legal profession, and the judicial system); *In re Lopez,* 252 P.3d 312 (Or. 2011) (respondent violated the duties that he owed to his clients when he mishandled their property, failed to represent them competently, and failed to provide them with complete and accurate information; he violated his duty as an officer of the court when he failed to obtain required court approval to settle certain claims and to deduct his fee from those settlement proceeds; and he violated his duty to the legal profession when he aired an illegal advertisement); *In re Disciplinary Proceeding Against Preszler,* 232 P.3d 1118 (Wash. 2010) (respondent breached his ethical duty to the legal system by knowingly violating bankruptcy court rules and breached his ethical duty to the profession by failing to properly manage a nonlawyer assistant); *In re Disciplinary Proceeding Against Eugster,* 209 P.3d 435, 447 (Wash. 2009) (court noting that "[a] single act of misconduct may violate more than one ethical duty," thereby impacting the sanction to be imposed); *Lawyer Disciplinary Bd. v. Martin,* 693 S.E.2d 461 (W. Va. 2010) (lawyer who served as executor of estate violated duties owed to client, public, legal system, and the profession by failing to diligently represent an estate, not providing an accurate accounting, and taking fee advances that were subsequently not earned).

## *Mental State*

Evaluation of a lawyer's mental state, or mens rea, under Standard 3.0 requires a determination as to whether, at the time of misconduct, the lawyer acted intentionally, knowingly, or negligently. These three mental states address the degree of the lawyer's culpability for disciplinary purposes. *See, e.g., In re Phillips,* 244 P.3d 549, 555 (Ariz. 2010) (lawyer's mental state at the time of a violation is important, as it affects the appropriate discipline imposed; "[i]ntentional or knowing conduct is sanctioned more severely than negligent conduct because it threatens more harm"); *In re Van Dox,* 152 P.3d 1183, 1186 (Ariz. 2007) (a lawyer's mental state affects the sanction for ethical violations; "[i]ntentional or knowing conduct threatens more harm to the public, the legal system, and the profession than does negligent conduct, and is accordingly sanctioned more severely"); *People v. Varallo,* 913 P.2d 1 (Colo. 1996) (lawyer's mental state is decisive element in determining level of discipline); *In re Davenport,* 49 P.3d 91, 103 n.17 (Or. 2002) ("As this court recently explained in *In re Flannery,* 47 P.3d 891 (Or. 2002), a determination that an accused lawyer acted 'knowingly' for purposes of a particular rule violation does not preclude the conclusion that the lawyer acted 'intentionally' for purposes of the sanction analysis."); *In re Disciplinary Proceeding Against Preszler,* 232 P.3d 1118 (Wash. 2010) (severity of the presumptive sanction depends on both lawyer's state of mind at time of the conduct and gravity of the harm caused); *In re Disciplinary Proceeding Against Cohen,* 67 P.3d 1086, 1093 (Wash. 2003) (Court asserted that mental state important because of presumptive sanction to be considered: "When the misconduct is 'knowingly,' the presumptive sanction or starting point in determining the appropriate sanction is suspension. With negligent acts, the presumptive sanction is less than suspension."); *In re Disciplinary Proceeding against Eugster,* 209 P.3d 435, 448 (Wash. 2000) ("[w]hen assessing a lawyer's mental state for purposes of imposing sanctions, we look to his state of mind relative to the consequences of his misconduct rather than the duty violated."). *See generally*

Nancy J. Moore, *Mens Rea Standards in Lawyer Disciplinary Codes*, 23 GEO. J. LEGAL ETHICS 1 (2010) (discusses use of *scienter* standards in the ABA Model Rules of Professional Conduct, including failure of certain rules to contain a state-of-mind requirement).

- **Intentional Misconduct**

Acting with intent constitutes the most culpable mental state under the Sanctions Standards and arises when a lawyer acts with a conscious objective or purpose to accomplish a particular result. *See, e.g., In re Schuler*, 818 P.2d 138 (Alaska 1991) (in criminal cases where intent is an element of the offense, conviction is conclusive proof that the lawyer acted with intent as defined in the Sanctions Standards; lawyer suspended for two years for conviction of class A misdemeanor concealment of merchandise as result of shoplifting cassette tapes); *People v. Pautler*, 35 P.3d 571 (Colo. O.P.D.J. 2001) (planned course of deception extended beyond knowing conduct to intentional when deputy district attorney made conscious choice to represent to a murder suspect that he was a public defender who would assist the suspect in his effort to surrender); *In re Cairns*, 132 A.3d 1160 (Del. 2016) (driving a car while intoxicated clearly reflects a knowing state of mind); *In re Gemmer*, 679 N.E.2d 1313 (Ind. 1997) (intent to commit clearly illegal act of converting funds of veterans' organization for which lawyer served as "quartermaster" constituted most culpable of mental states); *In re Frosch*, 643 N.E.2d 902 (Ind. 1994) (misuse of client funds by drawing some hundred checks on client trust account for payment of lawyer's personal obligations demonstrated intent, the most culpable state of mind); *Att'y Grievance Comm'n v. Culver*, 808 A.2d 1251, 1260 (Md. 2002) (when indefinitely suspending lawyer who failed to reduce contingency fee modification to writing and disbursed settlement proceeds to himself, court reiterated principle that "[c]learly, one who acts with deliberation and calculation, fully cognizant of the situation and, therefore, fully intending the result that is achieved is more culpable than one who, though doing the same act, does so unintentionally, negligently or without full appreciation of the consequences") (citations omitted); *In re Andres*, 857 A.2d 803 (Vt. 2004) (lawyer's failure to attend pretrial conference and abandonment of client's case was intentional and warranted a two-month suspension under Standard 3.0); *In re Disciplinary Proceeding Against Smith*, 246 P.3d 1224, 1231 (Wash. 2011) (disbarment warranted for lawyer who "possessed the requisite intent necessary to engage in the criminal conspiracy that gave rise to his ethical violations," resulting in his criminal conviction for conspiracy to commit securities and wire fraud).

Courts will find that intent is established even when a lawyer says that he or she was ignorant of the law, playing a practical joke, or making a truthful statement that nonetheless was misleading. *See, e.g., Fla. Bar v. Forrester*, 818 So.2d 477, 484 (Fla. 2002) (sixty-day suspension, followed by one year of probation, warranted for concealing a document during deposition and making an intentional misrepresentation regarding the document's whereabouts; respondent's truthful reply of "I'm not seeing it" to question regarding location of exhibit was intended to mislead because she in fact knew where document was located and failed to disclose that information); *Att'y Grievance Comm'n v. Nwadike*, 6 A.3d 287 (Md. 2010) (despite careless recordkeeping, lawyer's misuse of funds in attorney trust account for personal expenses, failure to deposit a refund check, and commingling of funds constituted intentional misappropriations); *Att'y Grievance Comm'n v. Braskey*, 836 A.2d 605 (Md. 2003) (no reasonable basis in record to support hearing judge's conclusion that lawyer was not acting dishonestly; lawyer did not put client money in trust account and then engaged in a deliberate course of misrepresentation about those funds in correspondence to client's nieces resulting in disbarment); *In re Carpenter*, 95 P.3d 203 (Or. 2004) (court rejected lawyer's claim that he intended a practical joke when he posted message on Internet site falsely identifying himself by name of local high school teacher and implying that teacher had engaged in illegal sexual activity with students; lawyer acted with conscious objective to harm teacher, even if lawyer contemplated action only for a few moments and did not consider potential effect of his actions; two dissenting justices favored no sanction); *In re Gatti*, 8 P.3d 966 (Or. 2000) (public reprimand imposed on lawyer who acted intentionally by misrepresenting his identity and making false statements; court rejected lawyer's argument that his mental state should be viewed as negligent because he believed, relying on letters to him from disciplinary counsel regarding similar conduct by government lawyers, that he was acting ethically).

- **Knowing Misconduct**

The next most culpable mental state, knowledge, occurs when a lawyer "acts with conscious awareness of the nature or attendant circumstances" of the conduct, but "without the conscious objective or purpose to accomplish a particular result." Standards for Imposing Lawyer Sanctions pt. II, Theoretical Framework (ABA 1992); *see, e.g.*, *In re Van Dox*, 152 P.3d 1183, 1188 (Ariz. 2007) (definition of knowledge in the Sanctions Standards "clarifies that merely knowing one performs particular actions is not the same as consciously intending by those actions to engage in unethical conduct"); *In re Roose*, 69 P.3d 43, 48 (Colo. 2003) (court explained distinction between knowledge and intent as critical to decision as to which sanction to impose and noted that intent "may not be presumed from proof of [knowledge] but must be separately proved by clear and convincing evidence"); *People v. Rider*, 109 P.3d 1075 (Colo. O.P.D.J. 2005) (lawyer admitted that he acted knowingly in misappropriating $148,000 from estate of an ill and elderly woman while acting as her conservator, yet continued misconduct for eight years, deceiving client, court, and client's beneficiary and executor and abusing the trust that he knew others placed in him); *In re Grandell*, 189 A.3d 1288, at *4 (Table) (Del. 2018) ("willful ignorance" in context of lawyer ethics can support a finding of a knowing violation); *In re Bailey*, 821 A.2d 851, 863 (Del. 2003) (holding that there was substantial evidence to support board's conclusion that respondent knew that client trust funds were invaded to satisfy a personal debt, court cited Delaware ethics rule that "'knowing' misconduct denotes 'actual knowledge of the fact in question'"); *Att'y Grievance Comm'n v. Sheridan*, 741 A.2d 1143 (Md. 1999) (repeated invasions of client trust account were circumstantial evidence that lawyer knew or should have known that he was acting unethically); *State ex rel. Neb. Bar Ass'n v. Zakrzewski*, 560 N.W.2d 150, 156 (Neb. 1997) (knowing misconduct includes that which is so carelessly and recklessly negligent as to lead only to the conclusion that it was done knowingly; lawyer's failure to investigate constituted extreme carelessness resulting in court's finding that lawyer knowingly made false statement of fact in affidavit); *In re Disciplinary Action Against McKechnie*, 670 N.W.2d 864 (N.D. 2003) (lawyer who failed to file appeal when he had conscious awareness of filing deadline knowingly failed to perform services); *In re Disciplinary Action Against LaQua*, 548 N.W.2d 372 (N.D. 1996) (noting that knowledge may be inferred from circumstances surrounding lawyer's conduct and does not require evil intent, only the non-coerced exercise of free will, court rejected assertion that lawyer did not act knowingly due to a mental block); *In re Worth*, 82 P.3d 605, 615 (Or. 2003) (among other misconduct, respondent's knowing misrepresentation to the bar that he had obtained client's sentencing transcript when he knew, in fact, that he had not, warranted ninety-day suspension; trial court improperly imposed requirement of "willful" mental state, which is synonymous with "intentional," when the appropriate mental state was the less egregious "knowing"); *In re Fink*, 22 A.3d 461, 475 (Vt. 2011) (lawyer's failure to put a contingent fee agreement in writing was done knowingly because he "knew that having a written agreement was a requirement of the rules and that he did not have one with [his client]"); *In re Disciplinary Proceeding Against Boelter*, 985 P.2d 328 (Wash. 1999) (in fee dispute, lawyer acted knowingly when he falsely stated in fee collection letter that he would have to reveal tape recording of client's confidential statement that client had lied to IRS; no such tape recording existed and lawyer would not necessarily have been compelled to reveal confidential information); *In re Disciplinary Proceeding Against Dann*, 960 P.2d 416, 420 (Wash. 1998) (lawyer who misrepresented to clients which lawyers and firm employees worked on their cases violated conduct rules with knowledge; i.e., he had "conscious awareness of the nature or attendant circumstances of the conduct, but without the conscious objective or purpose to accomplish a particular result").

- **Negligent Misconduct**

The least culpable mental state is negligence. Negligence occurs when a lawyer lacks awareness of a "substantial risk that circumstances exist or that a result will follow, which failure is a deviation from the standard of care that a reasonable lawyer would exercise in the situation." STANDARDS FOR IMPOSING LAWYER SANCTIONS pt. II, Theoretical Framework (ABA 1992); *see, e.g., In re Reardon*, 759 A.2d 568 (Del. 2000) (because negligence is the least culpable mental state, it is not as strong a predictor of future misconduct as prior acts of knowing or intentional misconduct); *In re Stanford*, 50 So.3d 151, 156 (La. 2010) (lawyer's endorsement of client's name on a settlement check and release, and failure to properly deposit settlement check and render appropriate accounting were negligent because the lawyer "sincerely believed he was acting appropriately" and conduct was a product of inexperience and lack of dishonest motive); *In re Pryor*, 864 So.2d 157 (La. 2004) (failure to communicate promptly with clients was negligent result of poor office management skills rather than intentional misconduct; two-year suspension, eighteen months deferred, with supervised probation following active portion of suspension); *Att'y Grievance Comm'n v. Stolarz*, 842 A.2d 42 (Md. 2004) (failing to list loan from bank as one of client's obligations and not making payment on loan from client's settlement funds was negligent, resulting in remand of case for dismissal with admonition).

Courts recognize that the distinction between negligent and knowing behavior can be difficult to discern. *See, e.g., Att'y Grievance Comm'n v. Glenn*, 671 A.2d 463, 487 (Md. 1996) ("The line between knowing conduct and gross negligence in this case is a thin one and difficult to draw. Based on the record, we find that Respondent knew, or should have known, that when he wrote checks on the attorney trust account, the balance would be insufficient to satisfy his obligations."); *In re Fink*, 22 A.3d 461, 474 (Vt. 2011) (because the "line" between negligent and knowing conduct "is difficult to discern and involves factual determinations," court gave deference to the panel's assessment of lawyer's mental state); *In re Disciplinary Proceeding Against Stansfield*, 187 P.3d 254, 262 (Wash. 2008) ("The line between negligent acts and acts with knowledge can be fine and difficult to discern, yet the difference between the presumptive sanction of reprimand or suspension is great.").

Courts also attempt to distinguish between negligent acts that warrant discipline and isolated errors of judgment that do not warrant disciplinary sanction. *See, e.g., Florida Bar v. Neale*, 384 So.2d 1264, 1265 (Fla.1980) (noting the "rights of clients should be zealously guarded by the bar, but care should be taken to avoid the use of disciplinary action . . . as a substitute for what is essentially a malpractice action"); *In re Disciplinary Action Against Ward*, 881 N.W.2d 226 (N.D. 2016) (clear and convincing evidence did not support finding of violation when attorney's conduct, "at best, [was] nothing more than an isolated instance of ordinary negligence."); *In re Gygi*, 541 P.2d 1392, 1396 (Or. 1975) (stating "we are not prepared to hold that isolated instances of ordinary negligence are alone sufficient to warrant disciplinary action"); *Cte. on Legal Ethics v. Mullins*, 226 S.E.2d 427, 430 (1976) (stating "[c]harges of isolated errors of judgment or malpractice in the ordinary sense of negligence would normally not justify the intervention of the ethics committee"; overruled on other grounds); *Cte. on Legal Ethics v. Cometti,* 430 S.E.2d 320, 330 (W. Va. 1993).

## *Mental State Versus Motivation*

In contrast to evaluating a lawyer's mental state under Standard 3.0 for purposes of determining a presumptive sanction, a lawyer's motivation or the lack thereof is evaluated as an aggravating or mitigating factor. Compare the mental state determination under Standard 3.0 with analyses under Standards 9.22(b) (dishonest or selfish motive as aggravating factor), 9.32(b) (absence of dishonest or selfish motive as mitigating factor), and 9.32(i) (mental disability or chemical dependency as mitigating factor). *See, e.g., In re Att'y D.,* 57 P.3d 395 (Colo. 2002) (distinguishing between "mental state" in Standard 3.0 and "motivation" in Standard 9.32(b), court said both are material to the propriety of a sanction, but mental state refers to respondent's intent or awareness with respect to either his conduct or a result of his conduct while "absence of a dishonest or selfish motive" refers to lawyer's motive for his conduct, without regard to any awareness on his part whether that conduct is specifically proscribed); *Att'y Grievance Comm'n v. Nwadike,* 6 A.3d 287, 300 (Md. 2010) (respondent intentionally made misrepresentations and misappropriated client and third-party funds, and also acted with selfish or dishonest motive given "the duration, frequency, and egregiousness of her mishandling of her attorney trust account"); *In re Discipline of Corey,* 274 P.3d 972 (Utah 2012) (lack of motive to injure client irrelevant to intent inquiry as the latter focuses on whether lawyer intended to benefit himself or another through his misconduct). *But see Statewide Grievance Comm'n v. Axelrod,* No. 00044406S 2001 WL 1571407, at *2 (Conn. Super. Ct. Nov. 26, 2001) (citing Standard 3.0, court found respondent's mental state at time of misconduct was affected by his having been fired, attempting to practice law as a solo practitioner for the first time, and complicated by his family history, which does not excuse the misconduct "but does suggest that his dishonesty was an aberrational situational response to unusual financial pressures").

## *Injury*

The Sanctions Standards distinguish the various levels of actual or potential injury caused by a lawyer's misconduct, noting that the extent of the injury is defined by the "type of duty violated and the extent of actual or potential harm." Standards for Imposing Lawyer Sanctions pt. II, Theoretical Framework (ABA 1992); *see, e.g., In re Vanderslice,* 116 A.3d 1244, at *12 (Table) (Del. 2015) ("The level of injury can range from 'serious' injury to 'little or no' injury; a reference to 'injury' alone indicates any level of injury greater than 'little to no' injury."); *In re Froelich,*

838 A.2d 1117, 1122 (Del. 2003) (court imposed reprimand rather than suspension for lawyer's failure to properly maintain trust account records, stating that "[w] hile [respondent's] oversights and misrepresentations clearly implicated his ethical duty to the legal profession and his duty of candor to this Court," his carelessness resulted in "little potential for actual injury"); *In re Richardson*, 1 P.3d 328 (Kan. 2000) (lawyer disbarred for scheme with law partner in which he invested client funds in real estate, stocks, and bonds in their own names, used client funds to pay for expenses associated with management of such investments, and such misconduct caused overwhelming injury in the loss of millions of dollars); *In re Disciplinary Action Against LaQua*, 548 N.W.2d 372, 377 (N.D. 1996) (finding clear and convincing evidence that lawyer's failure to make timely distribution of residue of estate and failure to close estate for nineteen years caused serious injury to beneficiary, court held that "[i]njury is defined as 'harm to a client, the public, the legal system, or the profession which results from a lawyer's misconduct'"); *In re Gustafson*, 41 P.3d 1063 (Or. 2002) (for purposes of determining appropriate sanction for lawyer's misconduct, actual or potential injury may range from serious to slight); *In re Disciplinary Proceeding Against Anschell*, 69 P.3d 844 (Wash. 2003) (failure to take action resulting in client's deportation order and missed opportunity to appeal resulted in extremely serious injury). *But see Statewide Grievance Comm'n v. Bartinik*, No. 564475 2004 WL 1155079, at *4 (Conn. Super. Ct. May 7, 2004) (although lawyer's poor judgment created "inexcusable byproducts, such as unnecessary litigation, additional attorney's fees, and uncertainty for the litigants," misconduct did not cause substantial injury to litigants).

- **Actual Injury**

When analyzing the injury caused by a lawyer's misconduct, courts will often distinguish between actual and potential injury. An actual injury arising from a lawyer's misconduct can be inflicted on the client or others, the public, the legal system, or the profession. *See, e.g., People v. Parsley*, 109 P.3d 1060 (Colo. O.P.D.J. 2005) (serious actual injury to lender with little recourse to recover funds when lawyer defaulted on personal loan obtained by false pretenses; lawyer's use of his status to obtain loan undermined confidence in profession and thus caused injury to legal profession); *People v. Franklin*, 106 P.3d 1087 (Colo. O.P.D.J. 2005) (client suffered actual injury when lawyer failed to account for entrusted funds, failed to return $9,900 when requested, and gave client insufficient funds check in partial repayment); *Fla. Bar v. Pearce*, 631 So.2d 1092, 1094 (Fla. 1994) (repeated failure to file tax returns was serious offense that adversely reflected on practice of law and profession, and even though no client was harmed, under Florida Standards for Imposing Lawyer Sanctions, "injury encompasses not only harm to a client, but also harm to 'the public, the legal system, or the profession, which results from a lawyer's misconduct.'"); *In re Miller*, 112 P.3d 169 (Kan. 2005) (lawyer's misconduct caused actual injury to client's mother by depriving her of life insurance benefits for one year after client's death); *In re Beauchamp*, 70 So.3d 781 (La. 2011) (lawyer's misconduct in handling client matters caused significant actual injury to several clients, who lost their legal fees and/or had their cases delayed and to whom no restitution was made, and to the disciplinary system, which had to expend additional resources to gather information from lawyer when she failed to answer complaints); *In re Poirrier*, 854 So.2d 311 (La. 2003) (abandoning client's personal injury matter caused actual harm via dismissal of lawsuit, deprivation of client's right to pursue claim, and lawyer's failure to cooperate in disciplinary investigation impaired operation of process).

- **Potential Injury**

The injury resulting from the lawyer's misconduct need not be actually realized. Courts also examine the potential for injury caused by the lawyer's misconduct. *See In re Cimino*, 3 P.3d 398 (Colo. 2000) (status as corporate counsel while simultaneously being a creditor of the corporation created potential for injury to client corporation); *In re O'Brien*, 26 A.3d 203, 207 (Del. 2011) (adopting Board on Professional Responsibility's conclusion that lawyer's violation of conflict-of-interest rules created "significant potential for injury"); *In re Johanning*, 111 P.3d 1061 (Kan. 2005) (potential for injury existed in that outcomes of cases might have been different had lawyer provided diligent representation); *In re Francis*, 79 P.3d 1285, 1288 (Kan. 2003) (knowing failure to follow up on problem with settlement check caused "at least potential, if not actual, injury"); *In re Howes*, 940 P.2d 159 (N.M. 1997) (while no evidence that government lawyer's inappropriate contacts with defendant resulted in actual injury to either defendant or the legal process in general, the potential for injury was obvious); *In re Disciplinary Action Against McDonald*, 609 N.W.2d 418 (N.D. 2000) (potential for very serious miscarriage of justice when intentionally falsified evidence could have provided basis for taking of mineral interests; breach extremely serious even though falsified evidence was immaterial to litigation's actual outcome); *In re Knappenberger*, 108 P.3d 1161 (Or. 2005) (potential injury in communication with represented employees was foreseeable result that employees would reveal privileged information or become intimidated by employer).

- **Both Actual and Potential Injury**

The same misconduct can result in a finding of both actual and potential harm. *See, e.g., In re Rice*, 260 P.3d 1020 (Alaska 2011) (lawyer's delay in providing an accounting caused potential harm to clients and actual harm to the reputation of the legal profession); *People v. Segall*, 111 P.3d 580 (Colo. O.P.D.J. 2005) (serious harm and potential harm to clients in neglect of divorce and child-custody matters, including, inter alia, owing clients thousands of dollars in unearned attorney's fees, costing one client $14,144 in child support and potentially harming parent-child relationship by neglecting to assert other clients' rights as to allocation of parental responsibility); *In re Potter*, 112 P.3d 216 (Kan. 2005) (actual and potential injury to clients from failure to file actions and failure to return documentation and unearned fees); *Grievance Adm'r v. Lopatin*, No. 92-224-GA, at *7 (Mich. Att'y Discipline Bd. Aug. 15, 2001), *available at* http://www.adbmich.org/download/92o-224.pdf (emphasizing harm to legal system as identified in Sanctions Standards' definition of injury and noting, although no proof of any actual harm to a party, lawyer's ex parte communication with judge caused serious potential harm to opposing party as well as "significant actual injury to the legal system in the form of diminished confidence in the impartial administration of justice"). *See also In re Lopez*, 252 P.3d 312, 316 (Or. 2011) (concluding that lawyer caused both actual and potential injury to his clients, court noted that lawyer's failure to communicate with clients and to diligently pursue their cases exposed them to potential economic injury as well as "ascertainable injury 'measured in terms of time, anxiety, and aggravation' to the client") (citation omitted); *In re Knappenberger*, 108 P.3d 1161 (Or. 2005) (actual and potential injury caused as result of conflict of interest in divorce case; actual injury included legal fees incurred by both parties in resolving conflict and potential injury was risk of misusing confidential information); *In re McDonough*, 77 P.3d 306 (Or. 2003) (lawyer's driving while intoxicated and driving with suspended license caused actual injury to one party, potential injury to public every time he drove while intoxicated, actual injury to legal system by undermining the orders that had suspended his driving privileges and by demonstrating an indifference to the law, and potential injury to legal profession by damaging public's confidence in lawyers); *In re Disciplinary Proceeding Against Lopez*, 106 P.3d 221 (Wash. 2005) (misconduct caused actual injury to client due to the delay in appeal and potential injury to client because appeal was subjected to possible dismissal); *In re Disciplinary Proceeding Against Juarez*, 24 P.3d 1040 (Wash. 2001) (suspension from practice of law for eighteen months, with probation conditioned upon lawyer's return to practice under supervision of another lawyer was appropriate to preserve integrity of legal profession and to maintain public confidence when lawyer lacked diligence in one personal matter and in managing two client matters that caused actual or serious potential injury to his clients).

### *Existence of Aggravating and Mitigating Factors*

The final step in the four-part analysis under Standard 3.0 is consideration of relevant aggravating or mitigating factors that may justify an upward or downward departure from the baseline sanction. *See, e.g., Briggs v. McWeeny*, 796 A.2d 516 (Conn. 2002) (trial court did not abuse discretion in ordering lawyer's disqualification as sanction for attempting to subvert the discovery process by failing to disclose discoverable material after appropriately weighing aggravating and mitigating factors of the Sanctions Standards); *In re Johanning*, 111 P.3d 1061, 1065 (Kan. 2005) (pursuant to Standard 3.0, "[a]ggravating circumstances are any considerations or factors that may justify an increase in the degree of discipline to be imposed" and "[m]itigating circumstances are any considerations or factors that may justify a reduction in the degree of discipline to be imposed"; one-year suspension, stayed in favor of eighteen months' probation, in light of aggravating factors, including prior discipline, pattern of misconduct and vulnerability of victims, and mitigating factors including lack of dishonest or selfish motive, cooperation with disciplinary proceedings, good character and reputation, and genuine remorse); *In re Disciplinary Proceeding Against Scannell*, 239 P.3d 332 (Wash. 2010) (consideration of aggravating and mitigating factors is second stage of two-stage process to determine appropriate sanction; disbarment was presumptive sanction and then ultimate sanction for several instances of misconduct, given multiple aggravating factors and no mitigating factors); *In re Disciplinary Proceeding Against Romero*, 94 P.3d 939 (Wash. 2004) (adhering to principle that presumptive sanctions may be increased due to aggravating factors). For detailed discussion of aggravating and mitigating factors, see cases under Annotation to Standard 9.0.

## *Additional Factors Sometimes Considered*

Some jurisdictions have created their own lists of factors that incorporate elements of Standard 3.0 and include one or two additional components to guide the court in determining an appropriate sanction. *See, e.g., In re Ryan*, 824 N.E.2d 687 (Ind. 2005) (adding to four factors outlined in Standard 3.0, namely, consideration of court's duty to preserve profession's integrity and risk to public in allowing lawyer to continue to practice); *Att'y Grievance Comm'n v. Kreamer*, 946 A.2d 500 (Md. 2008) (examining nature of the misconduct, the lawyer's state of mind, actual or potential injury, duty of court to preserve the integrity of profession, risk to the public in allowing the respondent to practice, and any mitigating or aggravating factors).

Other states analyze lawyer discipline cases based on a more extensive set of factors. *See McIntyre v. Miss. Bar*, 38 So.3d 617, 625 (Miss. 2010) (listing nine areas of inquiry, four of which derive from the Sanctions Standards: "(1) [t]he nature of the misconduct involved; (2) the need to deter similar misconduct; (3) the preservation of dignity and reputation of the legal profession; (4) the protection of the public; (5) sanctions imposed in similar cases; (6) the duty violated; (7) the lawyer's mental state; (8) the actual or potential injury resulting from the misconduct; and (9) the existence of aggravating or mitigating factors"; citing cases using this analysis) (citations omitted); *Rosas v. Comm'n for Lawyer Discipline*, 335 S.W.3d 311 (Tex. App. 2010) (Texas Rule of Disciplinary Procedure 3.10 provides that to determine appropriate sanction, court must consider (1) the nature and degree of the misconduct for which the attorney is being sanctioned, (2) the seriousness of and circumstances surrounding the professional misconduct, (3) the loss or damage to the client, (4) the damage to the profession, (5) the assurance that those who seek legal services in the future will be insulated from the type of professional misconduct found, (6) the profit to the attorney, (7) the avoidance of repetition, (8) the deterrent effect on others, (9) the maintenance of respect for the legal profession, (10) the conduct of the respondent during the course of committee action, (11) the trial of the case, and (12) other relevant evidence concerning the attorney's personal and professional background).

In 1983, prior to adoption of the Sanctions Standards, the Washington Supreme Court adopted a notable list of sanctioning factors, known as the *Noble* factors. In *In re Disciplinary Proceeding Against Noble,* 667 P.2d 608 (Wash. 1983), the court, in an attempt to provide an objective standard in lawyer disciplinary matters, identified five factors for the board to consider when determining the appropriate sanction for lawyer misconduct: the purposes of attorney discipline, the proportionality of the sanction to the misconduct, the effect of the sanction on the lawyer, whether the record supports the board's recommendation, and the extent of agreement among board members.

There have been several significant cases applying the *Noble* factors since the original decision. For example, in *In re Disciplinary Proceeding Against Schwimmer,* 108 P.3d 761 (Wash. 2005), the court ruled that it would use the Sanctions Standards as a basic, but not conclusive, guide, coupled with an evaluation of the sanction under the *Noble* factors if raised by a lawyer being disciplined. In *In re Disciplinary Proceeding Against Kuvara,* 66 P.3d 1057 (Wash. 2003), the court retained the *Noble* factors of proportionality and degree of unanimity, but discarded the remaining three factors as duplicative of the Sanctions Standards' analysis.

## *Consideration of Precedent*

Courts also often look to their own precedent, under the principle of stare decisis, to assess whether the recommended discipline is consistent with that imposed in similar cases. *See, e.g., In re Van Dox,* 152 P.3d 1183, 1190 (Ariz. 2007) ("When sanctioning lawyers, in addition to the guidance provided by the *ABA Standards,* 'we look to other, similar cases in determining whether the sanction imposed is proportionate to the misconduct charged.'") (citation omitted); *In re Peasley,* 90 P.3d 764, 773 (Ariz. 2004) (finding no cases with similar fact pattern when prosecutor presented false testimony in two criminal trials to secure murder conviction and death-penalty sentence, court relied upon other cases in state and other jurisdictions, concluding that sanction of disbarment was proportional to discipline imposed in other cases involving serious misconduct); *People v. Ra'shadd,* 110 P.3d 388 (Colo. O.P.D.J. 2005) (Sanctions Standards and Colorado Supreme Court case law are guiding authority for sanction selection); *Matter of Najim,* 405 P.3d 1223, 1235 (Kan. 2017) (holding "prior cases may have some effect on the decision of this court with reference to [disciplinary] sanctions imposed.... Although we do consider respondent's individual case, we also may turn to these other cases for some guidance, i.e., they may provide supportive, but not conclusive, authority."); *Att'y Grievance Comm'n v. Zuckerman*, 872 A.2d 693 (Md. 2005) (referring to Sanctions Standards along with Maryland cases as precedent); *Disciplinary Counsel v. Travis*, 804 N.E.2d 969 (Ohio 2004) (adding consideration of sanctions imposed in similar cases to the four factors enumerated in Sanctions Standards); *In re McGraw*, 414 P.3d 841 (Or. 2018) (court's determination of an appropriate sanction includes consideration of Supreme Court cases and the four factors of Standard 3.0); *In re Leisure*, 113 P.3d 412 (Or. 2005) (court relies on Sanctions Standards for preliminary analysis of duty violated, mental state, actual or potential injury, and aggravating or mitigating circumstances and then reviews applicable case law).

While the jurisdictional precedent approach may help to provide more consistent sanctions within a jurisdiction, the broader goal of providing uniformity in sanctions across jurisdictions may suffer when sanctions suggested by the Sanctions Standards are ignored in favor of local precedent. *See generally* Sarah A. Hirsh, Note, *The Illusive Consistency: A Case for Adopting the ABA Standards for Imposing Lawyer Sanctions in In re Martin*, 40 S.D. L. REV. 300 (1995) (citing pervasive problem of inconsistent sanctions within and among jurisdictions; suggesting application of Sanctions Standards to South Dakota disciplinary actions would result in more consistency and proportionality in sanctions); Cynthia A. Kelly, *Lawyer Sanctions: Looking Back Through the Looking Glass*, 1 GEO. J. LEGAL ETHICS 469 (1988) (statistical analysis of sanctions imposed in conversion cases in various jurisdictions and demonstrating need for uniform sanctioning standards); John D. Fabian & Brian Reinthaler, *An Examination of the Uniformity (or Lack Thereof) of Attorney Sanctions*, 14 GEO. J. LEGAL ETHICS 1059 (2001) (analyses of four major state jurisdictions' uniformity in imposing sanctions for perjury and false statements revealed that adoption of uniform standards will result in greater uniformity among individuals who have engaged in similar acts of misconduct in different jurisdictions but also recognizing discord as result of courts' inherent authority to evaluate the lawyer misconduct on a case-by-case basis). *See also* Leslie C. Levin, *The Emperor's Clothes and Other Tales About the Standards for Imposing Lawyer Discipline Sanctions*, 48 AM. U. L. REV. 1 (1998) (applauding Sanctions Standards as important step in providing consistency in lawyer sanctions but recommending mandatory standards to promote greater consistency).

# 4.0 Violations of Duties Owed to Clients

## Annotation

The duties addressed in this chapter arise out of the basic relationship between the lawyer and the client. For example, lawyers must preserve and keep safe the property of clients (Model Rules of Professional Conduct Rule 1.15), maintain client confidences (Model Rule 1.6), and avoid conflicts of interest and other conduct that impairs their independent professional judgment (Model Rules 1.7–1.13, 3.7, 5.4(c), and 6.3). In addition, lawyers must be competent to perform the services requested by clients (Model Rule 1.1), act in accordance with the objectives of representation by clients (Model Rule 1.2), and be diligent in performing those services (Model Rule 1.3). Lawyers also must be candid with the client during the course of the professional relationship and exercise independent professional judgment (Model Rules 1.4 and 2.1).

### 4.1 Failure to Preserve the Client's Property

**Absent aggravating or mitigating circumstances, upon application of the factors set out in 3.0, the following sanctions are generally appropriate in cases involving the failure to preserve client property:**

**4.11 Disbarment is generally appropriate when a lawyer knowingly converts client property and causes injury or potential injury to a client.**

## Annotation

### *Knowing Conversion*

Although Standard 4.11 should be applied when courts find a "knowing" conversion, some courts use the mens rea of "intentional" to support disbarment. Others use the terms "intentional" and "knowing" interchangeably. Regardless of the terminology used, the focus is on deliberate conduct. See *In re Discipline of Corey*, 274 P.3d 972, 977–978 (Utah 2012) (lawyer's conversion of client's settlement funds for the operational needs of his law firm was "knowing and intentional"; "Generally our rule is that 'intentional misappropriation of client's funds will result in disbarment unless the lawyer can demonstrate truly compelling mitigating circumstances.'") (citation omitted); *but see In re Discipline of Barrett*, 391 P.3d 1031 (Utah 2017) (presumption of disbarment does not apply where lawyer misappropriates firm funds because same policy concerns do not arise where no client money is affected).

Some courts have established a bright-line rule that disbarment is the only appropriate discipline when a lawyer knowingly converts client funds. In the seminal case of *In re Wilson*, 409 A.2d 1153 (N.J. 1979), the Supreme Court of New Jersey noted that it is commonplace for lawyers' work to involve possession of their clients' funds, whether it be a real estate closing, the establishment of a trust, the purchase of a business, the investment of funds, the receipt of proceeds of litigation, or any one of a multitude of other situations. The court said that there are few more egregious acts of which a lawyer can be guilty than misappropriation of those funds and that "[r]ecognition of the nature and gravity of the offense suggests only one result disbarment." *Id.* at 1155.

Similarly, in *Carter v. Ross*, 461 A.2d 675 (R.I. 1983), the respondent acknowledged misappropriating $33,890.34 of funds belonging to an estate for which he served as lawyer. He used the money to reimburse another client whose funds the lawyer had converted to his own use to pay personal and business expenses. Citing *Wilson*, the Rhode Island Supreme Court imposed disbarment: "We, like our New Jersey colleagues, are convinced that continuing public confidence in the judicial system and the bar as a whole requires that the strictest discipline be imposed in misappropriation cases." *Id.* at 676. (For a discussion of the establishment of the "*Wilson* rule" and its evolution, see James R. Zazzali, *The Whys and Hows of Permanent Disbarment: New Jersey's Wilson Rule*, 21 Geo J. Legal Ethics 311 (2008)).

Other jurisdictions have followed the *Wilson* decision, advocating the presumption of disbarment as appropriate for lawyers who knowingly use or borrow client monies without clients' consent. *See, e.g., In re LaLonde*, 834 P.2d 146 (Ariz. 1992) (citing Standard 4.11, inter alia, court imposed another disbarment on lawyer, already disbarred for a murder conviction, for settling cases without consent and converting settlement funds from fourteen clients, notwithstanding numerous mitigating factors, including full restitution, expression of remorse, and cocaine addiction); *Fla. Bar v. Korones*, 752 So.2d 586 (Fla. 2000) (lawyer serving as personal representative for estate of his uncle misappropriated $123,752 in funds from estate for personal use, filed a false accounting with beneficiaries, and paid his son so that he would not report the lawyer to the bar; disbarment warranted despite lawyer's remorse, financial and familial difficulties, health problems, good reputation, and restitution to the beneficiaries); *Fla. Bar v. Clement*, 662 So.2d 690 (Fla. 1995) (American with Disabilities Act did not prevent the court from imposing disbarment on lawyer suffering from bipolar disorder who knowingly misappropriated client funds); *In re Stochel*, 34 N.E.3d 1207 (Ind. 2015) (citing Standard 4.11, court held disbarment appropriate where lawyer embezzled more than $230,000 from receivership and covered up theft for nearly a decade); *In re Veith*, 843 P.2d 729 (Kan. 1992) (in reciprocal proceeding, court imposed disbarment, under Standard 4.11, noting findings that lawyer knowingly transferred money from client trust account to business account); *In re Grady*, 782 So.2d 570 (La. 2001) (lawyer disbarred, under Standard 4.11, inter alia, for misconduct including placing client funds in account that he treated as his personal account and issuing client a worthless check; although lawyer ultimately made restitution to the client, he deprived client of her funds for a period of several months and required her to obtain services of another lawyer to recover the money); *Att'y Grievance Comm'n v. Whitehead*, 950 A.2d 798, 805 (Md. 2008) (finding that lawyer "clearly knew what he was doing," the court disbarred lawyer for withdrawing $600,000 of assets from conservatorship of an adult disabled ward without court approval to purchase investment property for himself and his business partner, even though money was repaid); *Att'y Grievance Comm'n v. Watson*, 855 A.2d 1213, 1219 (Md. 2004) (court reiterated that its "application of the general rule has been consistent: 'disbarment will inevitably follow any unmitigated misappropriation of client, or any third party's funds[.]'") (citation omitted); *Att'y Grievance Comm'n v. Cockrell*, 499 A.2d 928, 935 (Md. 1985) ("[W]hen an attorney is found to have betrayed the high trust imposed in him by appropriating to his own use funds of others entrusted to him, then, absent the most compelling extenuating circumstances, disbarment should follow as a matter of course."); *In re Farris*, 472 S.W.3d 549 (Mo. 2015) (citing Standard 4.11, court held disbarment is presumptive sanction for lawyer who knowingly misappropriated $93,000 belonging to clients and/or their medical creditors); *In re Harris*, 396 P.3d 745 (Nev. 2017) (citing Standard 4.11, court disbarred lawyer for misappropriation of more than $425,000 of client funds; lawyer also demonstrated indifference to the disciplinary process); *In re Carroll*, 503 A.2d 750, 751 (N.H. 1985) (lawyer's conviction for theft and magnitude of debt owed to his victims, other gamblers, relatives, friends, and the government "militate against permitting the respondent to practice law. . . . Ordinarily, the misuse of a client's funds justifies disbarment."); *N.C. State Bar v. Leonard*, 632 S.E.2d 183 (N.C. 2006) (lawyer who misappropriated client funds is disbarred after court noted that the "Bar does not need to show he intentionally used the property entrusted to him for his own purposes; instead it is sufficient to show that 'defendant fraudulently or knowingly and willfully misapplied the property for purposes other than those for which he received it as agent or fiduciary'") (citation omitted); *In re Disciplinary Action Against McDonagh*, 822 N.W.2d 468 (N.D. 2012) (disbarment warranted for lawyer who, inter alia, knowingly converted funds when he deposited client funds into the law firm's operating account and used the funds to pay operating expenses); *In re Maroney*, 927 P.2d 90 (Or. 1996) (citing Standard 4.1, inter alia, court ruled disbarment warranted for lawyer's purposeful conversion of client funds for his own use, failure to account for those funds, and failure to promptly return money to client); *Bd. of Prof'l Responsibility v. Barry*, 545 S.W.3d (Tenn. 2018) (under Standard 4.11, disbarment presumptive sanction for knowing conversion of client funds and hearing panel acted arbitrarily and capriciously in departing from presumptive sanction in the absence of mitigating factors and presence of five aggravating factors).

In *In re Discipline of Grimes*, 297 P.3d 564 (Utah 2012), the Utah Supreme Court reversed the district court's order of suspension partly stayed by a period of probation, finding that the presumptive sanction of disbarment must be imposed on a lawyer who took his client's retainer of $7,070, spent the retainer for personal use, and failed to take any action in his client's case. The court noted that although evidence in mitigation and aggravation was presented, the district court failed to make factual findings weighing that evidence or make any explicit finding that the mitigating circumstances presented by the lawyer were truly compelling. The court instead held that the district court had erred in its reliance on *In re Discipline of Crawley*, 164 P.3d 1232 (Utah 2007), to depart from the presumptive sanction of disbarment. *Crawley* involved two lawyer discipline cases where the district court, recognizing that the Sanction Standards permit flexibility, exercised its discretion in tailoring the presumptive sanction of suspension through the use of probation. The court in *Grimes*, however, made clear:

> As a practical matter, probation cannot coexist with disbarment. Because a disbarred lawyer does not have the right to practice law, the concept of probation has no possible application where the presumptive sanction is disbarment unless the mere availability of probation were a sufficient basis on which to depart from the presumptive sanction.

297 P.3d at 568. The court determined that none of the mitigating factors presented by the lawyer in *Grimes*, including his financial distress as a result of earning only $13,000 over thirteen months to support his wife and five children and the severe illness of a son, was sufficiently compelling to justify the downward departure from disbarment. *See also In re Discipline of Johnson*, 48 P.3d 881 (Utah 2001) (in knowing misappropriation of client funds, downward departure from presumptive sanction of disbarment appropriate only when lawyer demonstrated truly compelling mitigating circumstances); *In re Disciplinary Proceeding against Schwimmer*, 108 P.3d 761, 766 (Wash. 2005) (citing Standard 4.11, inter alia, court rejected conclusion that lawyer "merely knowingly misused client funds," concluding instead that he intentionally misappropriated client funds and finding disbarment presumptive sanction for such misconduct). *Cf. Iowa Supreme Ct. Att'y Disciplinary Bd. v. Nelsen*, 807 N.W.2d 259 (Iowa 2011) (long policy of imposing disbarment for conversion of client funds includes lawyer's knowing participation in aiding and abetting clients in scheme to defraud bank and court-appointed receiver by converting funds owed to the bank even though lawyer received no personal gain nor was convicted of a crime); *N.C. State Bar v. Ford*, 94 DHC 4 (N.C. Disciplinary Hearing Comm'n Sept. 16, 1994) (North Carolina Bar's Disciplinary

Hearing Commission disbarred lawyer for gross negligence in handling and overseeing client's trust account, finding that lawyer's failure to oversee account and monitor secretary who issued checks on it by signing lawyer's name, resulting in balance falling below amount owed to clients, constituted misappropriation of client funds). For a general discussion of the *Ford* case, see Michael J. Dayton, Note, *A New Standard for Disbarments: Misappropriation Through Gross Negligence—* North Carolina State Bar v. Ford, 21 N.C. Cent. L.J. 343 (1995).

While some courts eventually impose lesser sanctions after finding compelling extenuating circumstances, many opt for disbarment when purposeful misappropriation is established. *See, e.g., People v. Young*, 864 P.2d 563, 564 (Colo. 1993) (citing Standard 4.11, court held that knowing conversion of clients' funds warranted disbarment even absent prior disciplinary history and despite cooperation and making restitution; "[w]hen a lawyer knowingly converts client funds, disbarment is 'virtually automatic,' at least in the absence of significant factors in mitigation") (citation omitted); *People v. Radosevich*, 783 P.2d 841, 842 (Colo.1989) (citing Standard 4.11, the court said, "[o]ur previous cases involving the conversion of client funds treat this type of misconduct very seriously because it destroys the trust essential to the attorney-client relationship, severely damages the public's perception of attorneys, and erodes public confidence in our legal system"); *In re Benge*, 783 A.2d 1279 (Del. 2001) (disbarment under Standard 4.11, inter alia, warranted for lawyer's misconduct, including taking unauthorized fees and failing to comply with recordkeeping requirements for estate escrow account); *In re Cloud*, 939 A.2d 653, 662 (D.C. 2007) (court found that lawyer's testimony made clear that his failure to repay client funds was "knowing and deliberate" and therefore supported board's finding that lawyer had engaged in misappropriation that was at least reckless and that disbarment was appropriate); *In re Quist*, 483 S.E.2d 569 (Ga. 1997) (disbarment generally appropriate, under Standard 4.11, when a lawyer knowingly converts client funds, as in this case, where the lawyer converted retainer fees paid by bankruptcy client and presented insufficient funds check to bankruptcy trustee when ordered to disgorge fee); *In re Murphy*, 224 So.3d 947 (La. 2017) (disbarment is presumptive sanction for misappropriation where lawyer failed to refund $7,150 in unearned fees; amount of money misappropriated was not a consideration in determining sanction); *In re Toner*, 85 A.D.3d 55 (N.Y. App. Div. 2011) (reciprocal disbarment imposed for knowing conversion of client funds when lawyer deposited funds received from his cousin for the purpose of paying a judgment entered against her into lawyer's business account and drew two checks to pay his mortgage); *In re Disciplinary Action Against Buresh*, 726 N.W.2d 210, 214 (N.D. 2007) (in imposing disbarment under North Dakota Standard 4.11, inter alia, the court reiterated that "[a] lawyer's conversion of a client's funds to his own use is impossible to condone and is one of the least excusable acts of misconduct for which a lawyer can be disciplined") (citation omitted); *State ex rel. Okla.*

*Bar Ass'n v. Gray*, 948 P.2d 1221 (Okla. 1997) (disbarment warranted for lawyer who knowingly engaged in acts of dishonesty toward his law firm by misappropriating fees and costs belonging to it); *In re Palmisano*, 683 A.2d 1348 (Vt. 1996) (lawyer's conversion of funds he was to hold in trust on behalf of several clients compelled disbarment under Standard 4.11, inter alia); *Bd. of Prof'l Responsibility v. Shifrar*, 286 P.3d 1027 (Wyo. 2012) (lawyer's knowing conversion of probate estate's funds warranted disbarment).

The District of Columbia Court of Appeals, in *In re Addams*, 579 A.2d 190, 191 (D.C. 1990), reaffirmed that the presumptive sanction of disbarment is imposed for misappropriation, holding that "in virtually all cases of misappropriation, disbarment will be the only appropriate sanction unless it appears that the misconduct resulted from nothing more than simple negligence." The court noted that a per se rule would be inequitable since there may be circumstances in which disbarment would not be appropriate for misappropriation of client funds. Twenty years later in *In re Hewett*, 11 A.3d 279 (D.C. 2011), the court reevaluated its rule of imposing disbarment as a presumptive sanction for misappropriation of client funds and held that a stayed six-month suspension was a sufficient sanction for a lawyer who knowingly withdrew funds from a ward's bank account while serving as conservator of the ward's estate and treated the funds as his own. The court stated: "[W]e determine, for the first time, that the presumptive rule of disbarment established in [*Addams*] should not be imposed as a sanction for intentional misappropriation." *Id.* at 281. Although the lawyer's unauthorized withdrawal of monies from the ward's account for attorney's fees before receiving court approval was found to be a purposeful act and not a result of simple negligence, the court, quoting *Addams*, reiterated that it was appropriate to consider the surrounding circumstances regarding the misconduct and to evaluate whether the mitigating factors are highly significant and whether they substantially outweigh any aggravating factors such that the presumption of disbarment is rebutted. In distinguishing the sanction imposed in *Addams* from the one before it, the court concluded that the purpose for spending down the amount of monies maintained in the ward's account benefited the client, who otherwise would have lost Medicare benefits.

## *Knowing Misappropriation with Substantial Mitigating Factors*

Even with a knowing conversion, some courts will not impose disbarment when there are substantial mitigating factors. Often such cases result in suspension, especially when there is no evidence of actual injury to the client. *See, e.g., In re Rooney*, 709 N.W.2d 263 (Minn. 2006) (among numerous mitigating factors considered in imposing eighteen-month suspension instead of disbarment for knowing misappropriation of client funds, the court considered that the lawyer's clients suffered no harm from the misappropriations); *Disciplinary Counsel v. Edwards*, 981 N.E.2d 857 (Ohio 2012) (imposing two-year suspension, stayed entirely, instead of presumptive sanction of disbarment, for lawyer who misappropriated $69,500 from clients' personal injury settlements to cover subrogated interests, court stated that presumptive sanction may be tempered by extenuating circumstances or mitigating factors, such as here, where there was no actual harm to clients or subrogees).

And while at least one court imposed suspension due to numerous mitigating factors, it also found that disbarment could be appropriate for cases involving a lawyer's gross negligence in dealing with client property. In *Chefsky v. State Bar*, 680 P.2d 82 (Cal. 1984), the California Supreme Court, noting that misappropriation is a serious offense involving moral turpitude, held that even absent knowing conversion a lawyer could be disbarred for gross negligence in dealing with client property. The court imposed suspension, stayed entirely by a period of probation, rather than disbarment because, inter alia, the lawyer's violations occurred within a relatively short time period, the last of which was more than five years earlier and appeared to have been aberrant behavior, he had practiced law for nearly twenty years with no disciplinary record, he was ill during much of the time in question, and he was attempting to relocate his practice. *See also In re Dahlin*, Nos. 05-O-00754; 05-O-01987, 2011 WL 9375629 (Cal. Bar Ct. Oct. 4, 2011) (court reiterating that a lawyer's actions constituting gross carelessness and negligence in misappropriation of client funds will not preclude finding of moral turpitude warranting disbarment).

In other cases, involving knowing misappropriation where there is significant mitigation, courts have imposed sanctions less than disbarment. *See, e.g., In re Fischer*, 89 P.3d 817, 822 (Colo. 2004) (rejecting disciplinary board's recommendation of disbarment, finding that board "overemphasized the notion of a 'presumption of disbarment' . . . and undervalued the importance of other factors in determining the needs of the public," including significant facts in mitigation warranting suspension for one year and one day); *Fla. Bar v. Cramer*, 643 So.2d 1069 (Fla. 1994) (lawyer's misuse of trust account to deceive the IRS constituted dishonest and deceitful behavior, but court followed referee's recommendation of ninety-day suspension because lawyer had serious health problems, none of his clients was injured by his conduct, and he fully cooperated with the bar). In *In re Boohaker*, 927 So.2d 268 (La. 2006), the court imposed an 18-month suspension with all but six months deferred for commingling client funds and failing to render an accounting to the client. However, two justices dissented, one of whom asserted that disbarment was the appropriate sanction:

> In essence, [the lawyer] commingled $300,000.00 collected on behalf of his client and converted his client's funds for his personal use. His failure to properly handle his client's funds caused those funds to be

lost through [lawyer's] bankruptcy, which caused the client a substantial actual loss. This was not an isolated incident, as [he] has a prior disciplinary history which include a 1988 reprimand for a similar misconduct.

*Id.* at 270; *see also In re Emmons*, 68 N.E.3d 1068 (Ind. 2017) (although under Standard 4.11 disbarment is presumptive sanction for misappropriation of client funds, court found combination of mitigating factors warranted decrease in sanction to three-year suspension); *In re Scheurich*, 871 So.2d 1104, 1106 (La. 2004) (suspending lawyer for three years for converting to own use more than $14,000 in funds withheld to pay third-party medical providers for services rendered to clients; court stated that "[a]lthough respondent paid all outstanding amounts to the medical providers after institution of these proceedings, his clients were exposed to the danger of being required to pay the providers for the unsatisfied balances on their accounts"); *In re Rooney*, 709 N.W.2d 263 (Minn. 2006) (citing Standard 4.1, court ruled that even though knowing misappropriation usually warrants disbarment, the Sanctions Standards expressly contemplated consideration of both aggravating and mitigating circumstances, resulting in a less severe sanction of eighteen-month suspension due to numerous mitigating factors for lawyer who misappropriated $27,700 in client funds in seventeen separate instances during one year); *In re Belz*, 258 S.W.3d 38, 46 (Mo. 2008) (citing Standards 4.1 and 4.12, inter alia, court ordered suspension for lawyer with bipolar disorder who misappropriated client funds, stating that "in a rare but appropriate case a sanction other than disbarment may be appropriate for intentional misappropriation where mental illness is shown to have played a role in the misconduct and other substantial mitigating factors are also present"); *Cleveland Bar Ass'n v. Harris*, 772 N.E.2d 621 (Ohio 2002) (while presumption of permanent disbarment exists in cases of misappropriation, lesser penalty may be in order when there are sufficient mitigating factors and board recommends it; here, court adopted board's recommendation of indefinite suspension, noting also that respondent was an honorably discharged veteran, a member of the bar for twenty-seven years, never disciplined for professional misconduct, and active in his church, inter alia); *Bd. of Prof'l Responsibility v. Sheppard*, 2018 WL 3829229 at *7 (Tenn. August 13, 2018) (court imposed sixty-day suspension followed by two years of probation after finding that hearing panel, which did not specify whether it relied on Standard 4.11 or 4.12, did not abuse its discretion in recommending such sanction for conversion because of numerous mitigating factors present; court found that "hearing panel was at liberty to recommend suspension as the proper sanction for Mr. Sheppard upon adequate consideration of aggravating and mitigating factors and of sanctions imposed in similar cases," and because both Standards 4.11 and 4.12 apply when knowing misconduct causes injury or potential injury, that such injury occurred in this case does not require disbarment); *In re Disciplinary Proceedings Against Tasker,* 9 P.3d 822 (Wash. 2000) (while disbarment is usual result when lawyers use clients' funds for their own personal use or mishandle trust funds, it is not inevitable result, and in this case misuse of client funds that were or should have been held in trust account resulted in two-year suspension due to mitigating factors such as three-and-a-half-year delay in filing formal charges, lawyer demonstrated interim rehabilitation and lack of financial loss suffered by clients); *contra In re McMillin,* 521 S.W.3d 604 (Mo. 2017) (citing *Belz,* court found mitigating factors of chemical dependency, major depression, anxiety, and personality disorder did not warrant decrease in presumptive sanction of disbarment because aggravating factors overwhelmed mitigation).

For a comparison of the use of a bright-line standard versus a case-by-case approach to disciplining lawyers for purposeful misappropriation of client funds, *see generally* David Luty, Note, *In the Matter of Mitigation: The Necessity of a Less Discretionary Standard for Sanctioning Lawyers Found Guilty of Intentionally Misappropriating Client Property,* 32 Hofstra L. Rev. 999 (2004).

## *Injury or Potential Injury to Client*

The second element of Standard 4.11 is "injury or potential injury to a client." In *People v. Edwards,* 240 P.3d 1287 (Colo. O.P.D.J. 2010), citing Standards 4.1 and 4.11, inter alia, the Colorado Supreme Court found in disbarring a lawyer for converting client funds, inter alia, that he caused injury by failing to return an unearned retainer to his client after doing little or no work. The client testified she was forced to borrow substantial sums of money to hire another lawyer to represent her and that she attempted with little success to represent herself in court, causing her case to be delayed. *See also People v. Adkins,* 57 P.3d 750 (Colo. O.P.D.J. 2001) (citing Standard 4.11, inter alia, court found the lawyer's knowing conversion of some $130,000 in estate funds for her own business and/or personal purposes caused undeniably serious potential monetary injury, warranting disbarment); *In re Fountain,* 913 A.2d 1180 (Del. 2006) (citing Standard 4.11, inter alia, and imposing disbarment, the court noted that lawyer's clients suffered financial injury as a result of lawyer's conversion of unearned retainers and Medicaid reimbursement check); *In re Weaver,* 281 P.3d 502 (Kan. 2012) (lawyer who caused serious injury after taking money from thousands of vulnerable loan-modification clients, giving most of the money to nonlawyers and then doing nothing on his clients' behalf, was disbarred under Standard 4.11); *Ky. Bar Ass'n v. Edwards,* 377 S.W.3d 557, 563 (Ky. 2012) (permanent disbarment warranted for lawyer who took "advantage of a highly vulnerable, disabled client" adjudged incompetent when he wrote $78,000 in checks from her account, described as "loans," and sold her property without court approval); *In re Humphrey,* 15 So.3d 960 (La. 2009) (multiple acts of misconduct, including lawyer's refusal to comply with court order to turn over a piece of artwork of a renowned local artist she was to hold in trust, caused serious to potentially serious injury under Standard 4.11, inter alia, requiring disbarment); *Rayburn v. Bd. of Prof'l Responsibility*, 300 S.W.3d 654 (Tenn. 2009) (affirming order of disbarment under Standard 4.11, inter alia, court found injury to clients as a result of lawyer's misuse of client funds when he knowingly and repeatedly deprived his clients of funds to which they were entitled, causing one client to incur considerable expense to recover funds lawyer withheld for more than four years); *In re Disciplinary Proceeding Against Simmerly*, 285 P.3d 838, 851 (Wash. 2012) (in imposing disbarment, the court affirmed findings that lawyer's misappropriation of client funds caused potential injury to some clients and actual injury to others, as well as harm to the administration of justice, including the disciplinary process, which is "harmed every time a trust account is misused"); *cf. People v. Heaphy*, 2015 WL 11081955 (Colo. O.P.D.J. September 9, 2015) (citing Standard 4.11, court found disbarment appropriate sanction for lawyer who knowingly misappropriated more than $14,000 of client trust funds even though client suffered no actual injury).

**4.12 Suspension is generally appropriate when a lawyer knows or should know that he is dealing improperly with client property and causes injury or potential injury to a client.**

## Annotation

Courts commonly reserve suspension for lawyers who engage in misconduct that does not amount to knowing misappropriation or conversion of client property but, rather, deal with it improperly. In *In re Konopka*, 596 A.2d 733 (N.J. 1991), the court imposed a six-month suspension for a lawyer who engaged in careless bookkeeping practices and stressed that disbarment should be imposed only if knowing misappropriation of client funds was established by clear and convincing evidence. Rejecting the disciplinary panel's finding that the lawyer "knowingly" misappropriated clients' funds, the court relied on evidence that established the lawyer never reconciled his trust account and did not use his trust account for venal purposes. In his concurring opinion, Justice Gary Stein suggested revisiting the steadfast rule of disbarment for knowing misappropriations of client funds and the court's decision in *Wilson* (*infra* at § Standard 4.11, Knowing Conversion):

> To the extent *Wilson* precludes us from considering the entire record in misappropriation cases, I am no longer satisfied that it is necessary for the Court to follow its mandate unreservedly. I believe the *Wilson* rule should continue to guide the Court in determining the discipline to be imposed in the vast majority of misappropriation cases. Those determinations, however, would in my view better reflect the collective wisdom of the Court and better serve the interests of the bar and the public if they were tempered by a recognition that under special circumstances discipline short of disbarment may occasionally be appropriate in knowing misappropriation cases.

*Id.* at 752.

The most common cases under Standard 4.12 involve lawyers who commingle client funds with their own or fail to remit client funds promptly. *See, e.g., Office of Disciplinary Counsel v. Au*, 113 P.3d 203 (Haw. 2005) (citing 4.12, inter alia, court imposed five-year suspension for lawyer whose misconduct included mishandling client funds and client trust account, holding that although misconduct did not appear to have caused actual harm to lawyer's clients, it did cause potentially serious injury to them and seriously harmed the integrity of the legal system); *In re Emmons*, 68 N.E.3d 1068 (Ind. 2017) (although under Standard 4.11 disbarment is the presumptive sanction for misappropriation of client funds, court found combination of mitigating factors warranted decrease to three-year suspension); *Iowa Supreme Ct. Att'y Disciplinary Bd. v. Morse*, 887 N.W.2d 131 (Iowa 2016) (court imposed thirty-day suspension where lawyer used $1400 of client's trust funds toward his fees rather than pay for trial transcript as the client had directed); *In re Caskey*, 866 So.2d 226, 227 (La. 2004) (citing Standard 4.12, court ordered six-month suspension for lawyer who retained attorney's fees in his client trust account for several months, resulting in improper commingling of his funds with those of his clients, and stated that "it is undisputed that there is no evidence of conversion of client funds, nor is there any evidence respondent's conduct caused any harm to his clients"); *Att'y Grievance Comm'n v. McLaughlin*, 974 A.2d 315 (Md. 2009) (indefinite suspension, rather than disbarment, appropriate for misconduct including operation of law practice from single checking/escrow account resulting in the commingling of lawyer's personal funds with client and third-party funds; court found that lawyer lacked dishonest motive, repaid clients, and felt genuine remorse); *In re Discipline of Brohawn*, 396 P.3d 745 (Table) (Nev. 2017) (citing Standards, court imposed six months and a day suspension on lawyer who knowingly failed to return $4,935 in unearned funds, resulting in injury to clients); *Maddux v. Bd. of Prof'l Responsibility*, 409 S.W.3d 613 (Tenn. 2013) (citing Standard 4.12, court imposed nine-month suspension where lawyer's conduct caused potential injury when lawyer represented interests of Client A over interests of Client B by giving Client A $35,000 over which Client B had a claim); *In re Disciplinary Proceeding Against McKean*, 64 P.3d 1226, 1233 (Wash. 2003) (citing Standard 4.12, court imposed six-month suspension followed by six months of probation on lawyer who, inter alia, commingled client money held in trust with his own money, noting "Lawyers sometimes forget that the dangers of commingling are not merely that the lawyer will squander the money 'borrowed' from a trust account and not be able to restore it, but that the commingled funds might be subject to attachment by a lawyer's creditors, thus preempting the lawyer's ability to do so") (citation omitted); *but see In re Farrar*, 949 A.2d 438 (Vt. 2008) (although presumptive sanction was suspension under Standard 4.12 for lawyer's acknowledged practice of commingling client and personal funds in his trust account, court found public reprimand appropriate when lawyer lacked dishonest motive, made full and free disclosure, and expressed remorse).

## *Knowledge Not Required for Suspension*

Lawyers who do not have knowledge that they are dealing improperly with clients' property may nonetheless face suspension if proven that they should have known they are doing so and the client suffers injury or potential injury. This scenario frequently occurs, but is not limited to, when lawyers fail to oversee their employees' actions in regard to client funds and the employee commingles or wrongfully uses those monies. *See, e.g.*, *In re Bailey*, 821 A.2d 851 (Del. 2003) (in imposing six-month suspension court agreed with finding that when lawyer instructed the bookkeeper to transfer funds from escrow account to operating account, he knew or should have known of firm's financial difficulties due to repeated overdrafts in operating account); *Ky. Bar Ass'n v. Lococo*, 199 S.W.3d 182 (Ky. 2006) (citing Standard 4.12, inter alia, court ordered six-month suspension for lawyer whose secretary, without lawyer's consent or knowledge, erroneously wrote and distributed $10,000 check to client from funds that had been ordered withheld to pay Medicaid and client's doctors); *Att'y Grievance Comm'n v. Zuckerman*, 872 A.2d 693 (Md. 2005) (indefinite suspension imposed in case of first impression addressing appropriate sanction when misappropriation was based upon lawyer's ineffectual accounting procedures and theft of funds by an employee that would have been revealed had lawyer timely reviewed bank statements); *Att'y Grievance Comm'n v. Powell*, 614 A.2d 102 (Md. 1992) (citing Standard 4.12, inter alia, court imposed indefinite suspension for unintentional misappropriation resulting from disorganization and inefficiency of practice; lawyer claimed three checks were mis-deposited by his secretary, who at that time was a temporary employee hired from a temporary secretarial service agency); *Disciplinary Counsel v. Ball*, 618 N.E.2d 159, 162 (Ohio 1993) (relinquishment of significant aspects of probate practice to secretary who misappropriated client funds during ten-year period warranted six-month suspension because lawyer should have known of misconduct had he had "any semblance of supervisory control over the work delegated"); *In re Marshall*, 498 S.E.2d 869 (S.C. 1998) (six-month suspension and restitution for office manager's embezzlement of client trust funds since lawyer should have noticed the many warning signals and could have mitigated damages had office manager been properly monitored); *In re Discipline of Bates*, 391 P.3d 1039 (Utah 2017) (five-month suspension warranted where lawyer unwittingly deposited $16,000 belonging to client into operating account and then transferred $20,000 from operating account to payroll account, leaving the operating account with a negative balance and exhausting client's $16,000); *In re Disciplinary Proceeding Against Marshall*, 157 P.3d 859, 874 (Wash. 2007) (in rejecting lawyer's argument that "he did not realize that he improperly inflated his costs by $41,000," court emphasized that Standard 4.12 applies "where a lawyer should know he is dealing improperly with client funds" and imposed eighteen-month suspension for this and other misconduct).

**4.13 Reprimand is generally appropriate when a lawyer is negligent in dealing with client property and causes injury or potential injury to a Client.**

## Annotation

Reprimands should be reserved for lawyers who are merely negligent in dealing with clients' property but still may have caused injury or potential injury to a client. Reprimand is appropriate, for example, for lawyers who negligently fail to follow established trust account procedures or fail to return client property. *See, e.g., In re Riggs,* 869 P.2d 170 (Ariz. 1994) (sloppy and inadequate office and financial management practices supported finding that conduct was negligent rather than intentional and warranted censure, along with one-year probation); *In re Hickox,* 889 P.2d 47, 49 (Colo. 1995) (imposing public censure on lawyer who engaged in multiple offenses, including failure to provide appropriate accounting for funds collected on client's behalf, court held that "respondent's predominant mental state was one of negligence, and given the absence of actual harm that has been demonstrated . . . public censure is a sufficient disciplinary sanction"); *People v. Romo-Vejar,* 138 P.3d 1218 (Colo. O.P.D.J. 2006) (approving reciprocal discipline and imposing public censure for lawyer who negligently transferred portion of funds held to satisfy workers' compensation lien from trust account to operating account); *In re Black,* 156 P.3d 641, 651 (Kan. 2007) (published censure warranted for county attorney who failed to safeguard funds and keep proper records of funds paid to county attorney by participants in informal traffic diversion program; finding the potential for injury was substantial, court rejected lawyer's argument that conduct not wrongful, noting lawyer "fails to grasp that keeping other people's cash in an unlocked desk drawer, identified by a sticky note, and failing to get receipts for the delivery of the cash to the proper recipient or otherwise maintain a record of cash distributions falls woefully short of the professional fiduciary standard" imposed on a lawyer); *In re Glatman,* 47 A.D.3d 230, 232 (N.Y. App. Div. 2007) (in reciprocal proceeding, censure, the equivalent to the public reprimand, imposed by other jurisdiction, was appropriate sanction for mishandling of escrow account as "result of either inadvertence or poor accounting practices, as opposed to an intent to steal funds"); *Lawyer Disciplinary Bd. v. Chittum,* 689 S.E.2d 811 (W. Va. 2010) (public reprimand warranted for lawyer who, among other misconduct, commingled personal and client funds in his "Attorney at Law Trust Account" and paid personal expenses out of trust account; court affirmed findings that there was no actual injury to any client, no intent to convert clients' entrusted funds for his own use, and lawyer's conduct was negligent); *Bd. of Prof'l Responsibility v. Asay,* 374 P.3d 295 (Wyo. 2016) (citing Standard 4.13, court imposed public censure on lawyer who knew or should have known he was improperly using client funds when directing staff to apply the funds to prior billing statements).

## *Injury or Potential Injury*

As Standards 4.11 and 4.12 do, Standard 4.13 calls for actual injury or potential injury for a reprimand to be imposed. *See, e.g., In re Froelich,* 838 A.2d 1117 (Del. 2003) (court held that public reprimand was appropriate when the lawyer acted negligently with regard to books and records, including misdirection of wire transfer of real estate settlement, there was little potential for actual injury, no misappropriation of funds, and disclosure and reconciliation were swift); *In re Stockwell,* 101 P.3d 1211 (Kan. 2004) (censure imposed under Standard 4.13 because lawyer caused injury to the trust by failing to transfer earnest money to the trust's interest bearing account and caused potential injury by failing to timely distribute trust assets to the beneficiaries); *In re Anderson,* 769 A.2d 1282, 1285 (Vt. 2000) ("Notwithstanding the fact that here there is no actual pecuniary injury to a client, lawyer misconduct in handling and protecting client trust accounts does injure both the public at large and the profession by increasing public suspicion and distrust of lawyers.").

## *Negligent Oversight of Staff*

Reprimand or censure also can be appropriate when a lawyer has negligently trained or supervised his or her office staff concerning proper procedures for handling client funds and that staff mishandles those funds. In *In re White-Steiner,* 198 P.3d 1195 (Ariz. 2009), for example, the Arizona Supreme Court, citing Standard 4.13, inter alia, imposed a sanction of censure combined with two years' probation on a lawyer who improperly managed a client trust account that resulted in the firm's trust account being overdrawn by $44.27. The court held that the lawyer's conduct in improperly dealing with client trust accounts and failing to supervise those responsible for maintaining the firm's trust accounts was negligent and violated rules governing trust accounts and the safekeeping of client property. *See also In re Osborne,* 713 A.2d 312 (D.C. 1998) (lawyer censured for commingling his personal funds with his clients' funds and for failing to supervise a nonlawyer staff member to assure compliance with ethical obligations); *In re Eddings,* 795 S.E.2d 183, 185 (Ga. 2016) (citing Standard 4.13, court rejected recommendation of disbarment and imposed public reprimand where $ 2.3 million was stolen from lawyer's trust account by his wife, the law firm's financial manager; court found no intentional conduct by lawyer and he was a "victim of an elaborate con perpetrated by his wife . . . a con that even bank officials unwittingly helped [the wife] commit and in one case even helped her cover up"); *State ex rel. Okla. Bar Ass'n v. Hill,* 281 P.3d 1264 (Okla. 2012) (public censure for lawyer who failed to timely return client funds and failed to properly supervise his staff, which allowed them to access law office's operating and trust accounts for personal use and, in so doing, secretarial staff used rubber stamp to forge attorney's signature and cash various checks); *In re Discipline of Light*, 615 N.W.2d 164, 167 (S.D. 2000) (citing Standard 4.13, court imposed public censure for lawyer who improperly managed a trust account; lawyer said he trusted that his staff and associate were managing it correctly and arguing that "in the 'real world' he believed [reconciling statements monthly] was commonly not done."); *In re Anderson*, 769 A.2d 1282 (Vt. 2000) (citing Standard 4.13, inter alia, court ruled that public reprimand warranted for lawyer who ignored reports of law partner misusing client trust account and delayed reporting partner to disciplinary authorities, noting misconduct was not minor nor isolated incident).

## *Negligence with Deceptive Conduct*

Although a reprimand or censure is generally appropriate for lawyers who are negligent in dealing with the attorney trust account or client property, the sanction will be increased and suspension imposed if the lawyer engaged in deceptive conduct or obstruction of the disciplinary process. *See, e.g., In re Skagen*, 149 P.3d 1171 (Or. 2006) (lawyer who failed to prepare trust account ledger, never reconciled his monthly bank statements, and kept track of client fund balances in his head was negligent in handling of trust account and failing to bring trust account into compliance with rules; citing Standard 4.13 reprimand generally applicable, court instead imposed one-year suspension because of lawyer's repeated actions in obstructing the bar's investigation).

**4.14 Admonition is generally appropriate when a lawyer is negligent in dealing with client property and causes little or no actual or potential injury to a client.**

## Annotation

Admonition should be reserved for cases in which a lawyer's negligence in maintaining client property poses little or no risk of injury to a client. An admonition would be appropriate, for example, when a lawyer's sloppy bookkeeping practices make it difficult to determine the state of a client trust account, but when all client funds are actually properly maintained. Imposing an admonition in such a case can serve as a warning to a lawyer to improve his or her accounting procedures, thus preventing any actual injury to a client. *See, e.g., In re Anonymous,* 876 N.E.2d 333 (Ind. 2007) (although lawyer was negligent in supervising firm's trust account, he took immediate and effective action to protect clients and rectify the situation once misappropriations of his nonlawyer employee, his wife, came to his attention and he cooperated fully with the commission; court imposed private reprimand); *In re Disciplinary Action Against Becker,* 504 N.W.2d 303 (N.D. 1993) (admonition instead of public reprimand recommended by disciplinary board where no practical injury to the profession and little or no actual injury to client as a result of lawyer's negligence in failing to safeguard client's jewelry valued under $5,500 stolen from lawyer's car; restitution provided via legal services totaling approximately $6,420); *In re PRB,* 165 A.3d 130 (Vt. 2017) (while presumptive sanction under Standard 4.13 was public reprimand, admonition imposed under Standard 4.14 for lawyer who failed to establish, maintain, and manage trust account due to mitigating factors of no actual injury to client and lawyer's remedial measures to bring trust accounts and accounting procedures into compliance with rules of professional conduct).

## 4.2 Failure to Preserve the Client's Confidences

**Absent aggravating or mitigating circumstances, upon application of the factors set out in 3.0, the following sanctions are generally appropriate in cases involving improper revelation of information relating to representation of a client:**

**4.21 Disbarment is generally appropriate when a lawyer, with the intent to benefit the lawyer or another, knowingly reveals information relating to representation of a client not otherwise lawfully permitted to be disclosed, and this disclosure causes injury or potential injury to a client.**

## Annotation

Clients retain lawyers expecting that the information they share will remain confidential, unless otherwise authorized by the client or law. As a result, disbarment is warranted when a lawyer knowingly abuses that trust and knowingly reveals confidential client information improperly with the intent of achieving personal benefit and causing injury or potential injury to the client. Because the violation of a client's confidence poses such a serious threat to the foundation of trust underlying the client-lawyer relationship, injury or potential injury to the client need not be serious; any injury to a client can be sufficient to impose disbarment. In *In re Diaz*, 288 P.3d 486 (Kan. 2012), a lawyer who served as a deputy staff judge advocate assigned to the Joint Task Force in Guantanamo Bay, Cuba, was convicted and dismissed from naval service for surreptitiously disclosing classified information regarding individual detainees. In determining that disbarment was the appropriate disciplinary sanction, the court found that the lawyer's conduct caused potential serious injury to the public and the United States as well as to particular persons. "Simply put, the disclosure of the classified information about which team was assigned to each detainee could increase the chances of their individual members being publicly identified. Given the nature of their work, such identification could put them at personal risk by any Guantanamo Bay detainee's supporters around the world." *Id.* at 494. *See also In re Smith*, 991 N.E.2d 106 (Ind. 2013) (citing Standard 4.21, disbarment imposed upon lawyer who published book that revealed confidential information about former client and lover for personal gain; noting lawyer's dishonesty, misrepresentations, and financial motivation as aggravating factors).

There are few reported cases, however, in which a court has disbarred a lawyer solely for revealing, or threatening to reveal, client confidences. Often, such misconduct is included with other serious violations warranting disbarment. *See, e.g., In re Wiederholt*, 877 P.2d 765, 775 (Alaska 1994) (disbarment, under Standard 4.21, warranted for forging a client's endorsement and threatening to reveal client confidences with the intent to benefit the lawyer where lawyer threatened to expose client if he did not accede to lawyer's demands in dispute over fees; court noted that "the injury to the client and the lawyer-client relationship here is the same as if client confidences were, in fact, revealed"); *In re Bailey*, 786 N.E.2d 337 (Mass. 2003) (reciprocal disbarment imposed for multiple violations including conversion of client property and revealing and threatening to reveal client confidences in a letter lawyer sent, ex parte, to judge presiding over client's case after the client sought to terminate the representation); *In re Ghobashy*, 185 A.D.2d 23 (N.Y. App. Div. 1993) (disbarment warranted for lawyer who regularly engaged in a pattern of professional misconduct including revealing confidences of four immigration clients and deliberately making false prejudicial statements about such clients to governmental agencies).

In at least two cases, courts specifically stated that disbarment was the presumptive sanction for such misconduct, but then imposed suspension instead. *See, e.g., In re Murphy*, 936 P.2d 1269 (Ariz. 1997) (lawyer used confidential client information to client's disadvantage when he used his knowledge of clients' sales difficulties to make last-minute demand for personal guarantees before investing in clients' business deal and arranging for other clients to invest; court acknowledged that presumptive sanction was disbarment but imposed suspension because it was lawyer's first disciplinary complaint in twenty-six years of practice); *In re Huffman*, 983 P.2d 534 (Or. 1999) (lawyer who was suing former client for attorney's fees sent letter to former client's new lawyer, which included information about former client's assets, divorce, and possible participation in criminal activity; court acknowledged that lawyer acted intentionally and that disclosure injured former client by exposing him to embarrassment and possible criminal investigation and further noted that lawyer was motivated by self-interest, refused to acknowledge that his conduct was wrongful, and only mitigating factor was lack of prior disciplinary record; court concluded that presumptive sanction was disbarment, but imposed two-year suspension after reviewing prior case law and finding conduct was a single act and not extended course of conduct).

In other cases, courts also imposed suspension instead of disbarment when the lawyer's knowing revelation of confidential client information was an isolated incident or involved a single client, notwithstanding the serious harm caused. *See, e.g., In re Disciplinary Proceeding Against Eugster*, 209 P.3d 435, 449 (Wash. 2009) (in rejecting disbarment recommendation and imposing eighteen months' suspension for lawyer who knowingly filed a guardianship petition against his client and disclosed client's personal and financial information and stated that client was delusional, notwithstanding that lawyer "knew his action might benefit himself financially," the court noted misconduct isolated to a single client and a single legal action).

At least one commentator has suggested that less severe sanctions are being imposed because courts disregard "potential injury to a client as grounds for disbarment. *See* Leslie C. Levin, *The Emperor's Clothes and Other Tales About the Standards for Imposing Lawyer Discipline Sanctions,* 48 Am. U. L. Rev. 1 (1998) (citing *Att'y Grievance Comm'n v. Driscoll,* BV No. 30, 1996 Md. LEXIS 133, at *34 (Oct. 8, 1996)); *In re Nomura,* No. SB-96-0005-D, 1996 Ariz. LEXIS 8, at *12–13 (Ariz. Disciplinary Comm'n Jan. 26, 1996) (declining to impose a suspension because, inter alia, client suffered only potential rather than actual injury; finding censure with a period of probation more likely to achieve goals of lawyer discipline).

**4.22 Suspension is generally appropriate when a lawyer knowingly reveals information relating to the representation of a client not otherwise lawfully permitted to be disclosed, and this disclosure causes injury or potential injury to a client.**

## Annotation

In many cases involving disclosure of client confidences, courts will impose the less severe sanction of suspension even when lawyers acted knowingly to benefit themselves, causing injury or potential injury to the client, and even in the absence of mitigating factors warranting a downward departure from the presumptive sanction. *See, e.g., In re Phillips*, 107 P.3d 615 (Or. 2005) (lawyer's knowing disclosure of clients' names and addresses to financial services company selling primarily insurance products was for his own personal advantage in collecting approximately $810,000 in commissions, violating duty under Standard 4.22 to preserve client's secrets and warranting three-year suspension). *See also People v. Isaac*, 2016 WL 6124510, at *6 (Colo. O.P.D.J. September 22, 2016) (applying Standard 4.22, lawyer suspended for publishing "embarrassing" confidential information about clients who criticized him online and attacking ethics probe into his actions as "reminiscent of Stalinist Russia [and] Nazi Germany").

An appropriate case for a suspension might involve a lawyer who knowingly reveals confidential information to the opposing party in litigation, thus weakening the client's position. *See, e.g., People v. Fain*, 229 P.3d 302 (Colo. O.P.D.J. 2010) (one-year-and-one-day suspension for lawyer who, after his services were terminated, inter alia, forwarded to opposing counsel and client's family an email lawyer sent to client that falsely accused client of committing perjury, judge tampering, engaging in a criminal enterprise for financial gain, and included confidential information learned about client during the client-lawyer relationship); *In re Hilson*, 863 N.E2d 483 (Mass. 2007) (lawyer suspended indefinitely for revealing client confidences in deposition). In *Fla. Bar v. Lange*, 711 So.2d 518 (Fla. 1998), a one-year suspension was imposed on a lawyer who knowingly divulged information about a government witness, a former client, relating to uncharged murders that the former client had confessed to committing. In rejecting the lawyer's argument that the crime-fraud exception applied, the court in *Lange* said:

> In a flagrant disregard for [his former client's] privacy, respondent knowingly offered intricate, damaging information about him at the conflict hearing when a simple, general statement of conflict would have sufficed. Moreover, respondent divulged [his former client's] secrets without obtaining a waiver from him before disclosing to both opposing counsel and the court this privileged information. The infor-

> mation, although conceivably helpful to his present client as impeachment evidence against [the former client], was injurious to [the latter], especially since he was never charged with or convicted of such crimes.

*Id.* at 522.

*See also Fla. Bar v. Knowles*, 99 So.3d 918, 924 (Fla. 2012) (one-year suspension instead of recommended ninety days warranted for lawyer who, after client retained new counsel contacted assistant state attorney assigned to client's criminal case and disclosed that client would lie in an upcoming immigration hearing and sent confidential client paperwork to the prosecutor; court noted that lawyer "improperly turned on her client and breached her client's confidences"). In *In re Disciplinary Proceeding Against Botimer*, 214 P.3d 133 (Wash. 2009), a lawyer was suspended for six months for disclosing a former client's confidential information to trial counsel for the former client's son, with whom the former client was engaged in litigation, and sending a letter to the IRS stating that, contrary to his advice, the client failed to correctly state her income and pay gift tax and illegally invested her grandchildren's trust property. Rejecting the lawyer's argument that he was fulfilling a legal duty to disclose under federal law, the court found that the applicable federal tax code does not create a duty to do more than advise a client of past mistakes.

A lawyer's improper disclosure of confidential information learned during a consultation with a prospective client can also result in a suspension. In *Disciplinary Counsel v. Cicero*, 982 N.E.2d 650 (Ohio 2012), a case of first impression, the Ohio Supreme Court imposed a one-year suspension on a lawyer who twice disclosed confidential information to a third party after a prospective criminal client met with him to discuss federal drug charges. Shortly after each meeting, the lawyer sent emails to a state university football coach alerting him about a possible association between the prospective client and team members and that university football memorabilia had been seized by federal agents from the prospective client's home. Rejecting the recommended six months' suspension, the court determined that the severity of the misconduct as well as aggravating factors, including the harm caused to the prospective client and the university football program and the lawyer's selfish motive, warranted a longer period of suspension.

Courts are willing to impose substantial suspensions when aggravating factors are present. *See, e.g., In re Gonzalez*, 132 A.D.3d 1 (N.Y. App. Div. 2015) (one-year suspension for lawyer instead of recommended six months because lawyer intentionally made prejudicial statements to immigration authorities about client, intended to cause arrest and deportation of former client, failed to meet his income tax obligations for six years, and received two prior admonitions); *In re Vogel*, 482 S.W.3d 520 (Tenn. 2016) (under Standard 4.22, one-year suspension imposed on lawyer who engaged in sexual relationship with client, then copied judge hearing client's criminal case on letter to client that contained confidential information; because misconduct included the exploitation of particularly vulnerable client, a heavier sanction was necessary).

### *Disclosures to the Media*

Disclosures of confidential client information to the press are also grounds for suspension. *See, e.g., In re Harding,* 223 P.3d 303 (Kan. 2010) (city attorney suspended for ninety days for, among other misconduct, disclosing confidential information, some of which surfaced in the newspaper, that was obtained via client-lawyer relationship with city; while lawyer had practiced law for thirty-two years without any disciplinary action, enjoyed respect of peers, acknowledged his wrongful conduct, and apologized to city, he knowingly violated his duty to city, causing actual injury to city and to reputations of some city council members, and his conduct was motivated by anger and selfishness); *In re Lackey,* 37 P.3d 172 (Or. 2002) (former judge advocate for Oregon National Guard suspended for one year for disclosing client confidence when he sent a memorandum to the media revealing that an internal audit of Oregon National Guard showed that many senior employees had erroneously received overpayments during the previous year).

### *Motive Not Determinative*

While lawyers' bad motives in revealing client confidences may result in disbarment, courts have held that a lawyer's motive is not determinative under Standard 4.22. In particular, a lawyer's "good" motive for revealing confidential client information will not preclude a court from suspending a lawyer. For example, in *In re Disciplinary Proceeding Against Schafer,* 66 P.3d 1036 (Wash. 2003), a lawyer was suspended for six months for disclosing to multiple parties, including the FBI, the IRS and three newspapers, inappropriate dealings a client had with another lawyer who had served as an estate's personal representative before that lawyer became a judge. While it was clear that the lawyer's primary motive was to expose judicial corruption, ultimately resulting in the judge's removal from the bench, the court found that no exception excused the lawyer's revealing client confidences and secrets, and that it was not reasonable to believe that any of the disclosures were necessary to report suspected judicial or lawyer misconduct. The court stated:

> Erosion of [the] privilege through willful breaches of a client's trust by an attorney is undoubtedly harmful to society because these breaches weaken the public perception that people can seek assistance and rely on an attorney as an expert and counselor "free from the consequences or the apprehension of disclosure."

*Id.* at 1042 (citation omitted).

**4.23 Reprimand is generally appropriate when a lawyer negligently reveals information relating to representation of a client not otherwise lawfully permitted to be disclosed and this disclosure causes injury or potential injury to a client.**

## Annotation

Reprimand is imposed when a lawyer negligently breaches a client's confidence. Even when the client is not actually harmed, the potential for harm to the client and damage to the professional relationship are so significant that a public sanction should be imposed. For example, a reprimand would be appropriate for a lawyer who negligently leaves a client's documents in a conference room following a meeting or in a public place, or who discusses a client's matter in a public place. *See, e.g., Disciplinary Counsel v. Shaver,* 904 N.E.2d 883 (Ohio 2009) (public reprimand warranted for lawyer who improperly disposed of client files by placing boxes of client files inside and outside trash receptacle). A lawyer who plays a more direct role in disclosing a client's confidential information by, for instance, turning over documents to opposing counsel or the media, also might be reprimanded if he or she acted negligently or even recklessly. *See, e.g., In re Holley,* 285 A.D.2d 216, 221 (N.Y. App. Div. 2001) (in case of first impression, court imposed public censure on lawyer who turned over a sealed court document to legal affairs editor of a magazine without first determining whether it was restricted; court found lawyer's conduct not only negligent but also reckless; "[r]espondent's act of casually turning over a document to a journalist without first determining whether it was restricted or not and knowing that it would be subject to the possibility of widespread dissemination, was a critical lapse in professional and moral responsibility").

Despite Standard 4.23's mens rea of negligent revelation, in some instances, even if a lawyer acts knowingly in disclosing a client's confidential information, a court may find that a public reprimand is warranted if the lawyer was not fully aware of the resulting injury or potential for injury to the client. For example, in *In re Pressly,* 628 A.2d 927 (Vt. 1993), the court found that the lawyer acted knowingly in disclosing to opposing counsel that his client was opposed to her husband having unsupervised visits with their nine-year-old daughter because she suspected that the daughter had been sexually abused by the father. Citing Standards 4.2 and 4.23, inter alia, the court held that public reprimand was appropriate because the lawyer was negligent (not knowing) with respect to the potential injury to his client caused by the disclosure, when the client suffered emotional distress as a result. "[W]e agree with the Board that a suspension would be too harsh. On the other hand, a private admonition would unduly depreciate the violation." *Id.* at 931. *See also In re Goebel,* 703 N.E.2d 1045, 1049

(Ind. 1998) (public reprimand appropriate when lawyer knowingly revealed confidential information under threat of grievous bodily harm or death; court noted that it rarely before had dealt with revelation of confidential information as an isolated incident, and in this instance lawyer did so "for his own interest of self-preservation").

The Nevada Supreme Court addressed the revelation of confidential information in the context of a prospective client. In *In re Beguelin*, 417 P.3d 1118 (Table) (Nev. 2017), the court reprimanded a lawyer for revealing confidential information he gained during consultation with a prospective client. The prospective client consulted with the lawyer about possibly filing for divorce and told the lawyer that her husband was verbally abusive. The husband was a friend and sometimes client of the lawyer, and because of that the lawyer declined to represent the wife. After the consultation the lawyer contacted the husband and told him of the consultation with the wife. The husband then telephoned the wife at work and yelled at her. *Id.* at 1118. The court held that instead of suspension, the mitigating factors warranted imposition of a reprimand.

## *Electronic Disclosure of Client Confidences*

A growing issue today and no doubt in the years to come is the disclosure of confidential client information online or that is available in electronic format. While a negligent disclosure through email would likely be grounds for a reprimand, it is possible that a lawyer who fails to protect confidential client information on his or her computer network also may be deemed to be negligent, warranting a reprimand. *See generally* Bill Piatt & Paula deWitte, *Loose Lips Sink Attorney-Client Ships: Unintended Technological Disclosure of Confidential Communications*, 39 St. Mary's L.J. 781 (2008). *See also* Am. Bar Ass'n, Cybersecurity Legal Task Force, Resolution 118 (2013), *available at* http://www.americanbar.org/content/dam/aba/administrative/law_national_security/resolution_118.authcheckdam.pdf (policy urging, inter alia, that lawyers and law firms comply with provisions of the Model Rules of Professional Conduct as well as state and federal laws and court rules relating to safeguarding client information, data privacy, and cybersecurity).

The revelation of client confidences in response to a client's online criticism of the lawyer has resulted in reprimands. *See, e.g., In re Skinner*, 758 S.E.2d 788 (Ga. 2014) (attorney reprimanded for posting confidential information about a client in response to a negative review about a divorce matter, including the name of the client, the name of the client's employer, the fee paid by the client, and the disclosure that the client had a boyfriend); *In re Tsamis*, Comm'n No. 2013PR00095 (Ill. 2013) (although not citing to the Standards, reprimand imposed for isolated revelation of information in response to a negative review). *But see People v. Isaac*, 2016 WL 6124510 (Colo. O.P.D.J. September 22, 2016) (citing Standard 4.22 as providing the basis for suspension instead of reprimand because lawyer's conduct was knowing; court suspended lawyer for six months for posting online responses to negative client reviews, including pieces of information relating to those clients' cases such as the nature of the matters, details of the representation, how the lawyer was paid, and criminal allegations against one of the clients).

**4.24 Admonition is generally appropriate when a lawyer negligently reveals information relating to representation of a client not otherwise lawfully permitted to be disclosed and this disclosure causes little or no actual or potential injury to a client.**

## Annotation

Maintaining a client's confidence is so fundamental to the professional relationship that, generally, a public rather than a private sanction should be imposed (see Annotation to Standard 4.23). Still, some courts have imposed the lesser sanction of private admonition when lawyers have negligently revealed information relating to representation of a client not otherwise lawfully permitted to be disclosed, and the disclosure causes little or no actual or potential injury to a client. *See In re Koeck*, D.C. Ct. App. Bd. on Prof'l Responsibility, No. 14-BD-061 (2016) (whistleblower lawyer admonished for helping a fired in-house lawyer leak detrimental information about the fired lawyer's employer to law enforcement and journalists); *In re Anonymous*, 932 N.E.2d 671, 675 (Ind. 2010) (private reprimand appropriate for lawyer who referred prospective client to her law firm and later disclosed to a mutual friend, who expressed concern for client, that client had filed for divorce and client's husband had accused client of threatening to harm him during an altercation; pointing out that no exception allowed disclosure by lawyer of information contained in public records, the court stated that "[a] n attorney has a duty to prospective, current, and former clients to scrupulously avoid revelation of such information, even if, as may have been the case here, the attorney is motivated by personal concern for the client."); *In re Discipline of Two Att'ys*, 660 N.E.2d 1093 (Mass. 1996) (lawyers' conduct, although it harmed neither client, involved use of clients' secrets and representation of differing interests, warranting informal admonition; lawyers' use of information concerning purchase of property by one client to advance interests of another client, who was judgment creditor of seller, was detrimental to interests of purchaser clients because it placed their acquisition of property at greater risk; although the creditor client materially benefitted from the lawyers' actions and the purchaser clients were not harmed, the lawyers are not absolved of the imposition of discipline); *In re Charges of Unprofessional Conduct*, 899 N.W.2d 821 (Minn. 2017) (private admonition for lawyer who in one instance revealed confidential information regarding a former client to insurance adjuster; conduct was isolated, court determined it was not serious, and there was minimal, if any, harm to the client).

## 4.3 Failure to Avoid Conflicts of Interest

**Absent aggravating or mitigating circumstances, upon application of the factors set out in Standard 3.0, the following sanctions are generally appropriate in cases involving conflicts of interest:**

**4.31 Disbarment is generally appropriate when a lawyer, without the informed consent of client(s):**

- **(a) engages in representation of a client knowing that the lawyer's interests are adverse to the client's with the intent to benefit the lawyer or another, and causes serious or potentially serious injury to the client; or**
- **(b) simultaneously represents clients that the lawyer knows have adverse interests with the intent to benefit the lawyer or another, and causes serious or potentially serious injury to a client; or**
- **(c) represents a client in a matter substantially related to a matter in which the interests of a present or former client are materially adverse, and knowingly uses information relating to the representation of a client with the intent to benefit the lawyer or another, and causes serious or potentially serious injury to a client.**

## Annotation

Disbarment is an appropriate sanction when a lawyer, without a client's consent and with the intent to benefit the lawyer or another, engages in conduct that constitutes a conflict of interest either by knowingly representing a client whose interests are adverse to the lawyer's interests; representing multiple clients who have adverse interests; or representing one client in a matter substantially related to a matter in which the interests of a former or current client are materially adverse and uses information relating to that representation. In each instance, the lawyer's conduct causes serious or potentially serious injury to a client.

### *Lawyer's Interests Adverse to Client's Interests*

Courts generally disbar lawyers who intentionally exploit the client-lawyer relationship by acquiring an ownership, possessory, security, or other interest adverse to a client without the client's informed consent. *See, e.g., In re Wade,* 846 P.2d 826, 830 (Ariz. 1993) (disbarment imposed on lawyer who showed "a propensity to insert himself into his clients' business dealings" by entering into a real estate business transaction with his client; court considered fact that lawyer's long-term relationship with his client made the client more vulnerable); *In re Baggette,* 26 So.3d 98 (La. 2009) (finding dishonest motive, court imposed disbarment under Standard 4.31 on lawyer who took $600,000 loan from elderly client and entered into agreement to purchase client's interest in successions without properly disclosing terms of either transaction); *In re O'Meara's Case*, 54 A.3d 762, 770 (N.H. 2012) (disbarment under Standard 4.31, inter alia, for lawyer who selfishly allowed his own pecuniary interest in collecting a "lucrative fee" to materially limit his representation by a series of actions, including threatening to withdraw on the morning of a scheduled mediation unless his client agreed to pay him $2 million); *In re Wolterbeek's Case*, 886 A.2d 990, 996 (N.H. 2005) (rejecting consent petition for two-year suspension, court noted that the "harshest sanction" of disbarment was warranted for lawyer who, inter alia, engaged in a course of deceptive conduct during a span of several years motivated by self-interest by acquiring an interest in client's foreclosed property without full and complete disclosure to client); *Toledo Bar Ass'n v. Cook*, 868 N.E.2d 973, 999 (Ohio 2007) (lawyer disbarred permanently under Standard 4.31(a), inter alia, for falsifying deed to elderly client's farm, transferring the property to herself, giving the farm to her client's church, and then taking charitable deductions for the gift; court rejected lawyer's assertions that she obtained client's informed consent to self-dealings and lawyer's claim that she "actually helped her client by seeing that her charitable deduction did not go unused."); *In re Hassenstab*, 934 P.2d 1110, 1118 (Or. 1997) (citing former commentary to Standard 4.31, court said lawyer "intentionally exploit[ed] the lawyer-client relationship" for his personal benefit when he engaged in criminal sexual offenses with clients, warranting disbarment); *In re Discipline of Laprath*, 670 N.W.2d 41 (S.D. 2003) (among misconduct warranting disbarment, lawyer engaged in multiple conflicts of interest for her personal benefit, including serving as lawyer and guardian for her disabled ex-husband and charging excessive fees, taking a client to the bank to borrow funds for her fees and mortgage estate property, and initiating guardianship proceedings over a client's objection and requesting that she be appointed guardian); *In re Disciplinary Proceeding Against Osborne*, 386 P.3d 288 (Wash. 2016) (disbarment under Standard 4.31 where lawyer revised client's will to make himself residual beneficiary of $600,000 without client's consent, then appointed himself personal representative of the estate after client died); *In re Disciplinary Proceeding Against Miller*, 66 P.3d 1069, 1077 (Wash. 2003) (disbarment under Standard 4.31, inter alia, for multiple instances of misconduct that caused serious harm to client, including preparation of client's will naming lawyer as beneficiary, arranging for client to put lawyer's name on client's certificate of deposit, and then using that interest as collateral for personal line of credit without giving client appropriate disclosures; court found that lawyer "acted knowing his actions would harm [his client], and with the intent to benefit himself"). *But see In re Ungar*, 25 So.3d 101 (La. 2009) (Jeannette Theriot Knoll, J., dissenting) (from the majority's imposition of a three-year suspension, noting that deviating from the baseline sanction of disbarment, under Standard 4.31, inter alia, diminished the severity of lawyer's egregious self-dealing that included advocating against his clients when he negotiated a class-action settlement agreement, proposing an agreement that provided an $11 million fee to be shared with out-of-state co-counsel, and employing coercive tactics in an effort to secure his clients' approval of the settlement agreement).

- **Business Transaction with a Client**

A lawyer who enters into a business transaction with a client knowing that the terms of the arrangement are adverse to the client's interests may face disbarment. *See, e.g., People v. Calvert*, 280 P.3d 1269, 1290 (Colo. O.P.D.J. 2011) (disbarment warranted for misconduct including urging one client to assign deed in trust to lawyer's company, without client's informed consent, to secure lawyer's interest in loans made to another client; hearing board noted that "[a] less severe sanction would undermine the seriousness of Respondent's wrongdoing in the eyes of both the profession and the public"). In *People v. Barbieri*, 61 P.3d 488 (Colo. O.P.D.J. 2000), a lawyer was disbarred under Standard 4.31(a) for engaging in business transactions with a client for the lawyer's own benefit and that of his company without making the required disclosures to the client and knowing that his personal financial interests would become adverse when the transactions were consummated. The court summed up a lawyer's problem with such transactions this way:

> By acquiring a financial interest adverse to one's client, a lawyer places himself or herself in the position of choosing between the best course of action for the client and benefiting the lawyer's personal financial position. It is not the lawyer's choice to make; rather, it is the client's choice. The Rules of Professional Conduct mandate that when faced with such a choice, the client must be fully informed, must have sufficient opportunity to reflect upon the proposed transaction . . . and must evidence his or her consent in writing.

*Id.* at 493. *See also Fla. Bar v. Doherty*, 94 So.3d 443 (Fla. 2012) (disbarment for lawyer who was legal and financial advisor to elderly client and entered into business transaction with client without making appropriate disclosures when he agreed to sell annuities to client that would earn lawyer commissions); *In re Rankin*, 351 P.3d 1274 (Kan. 2015) (lawyer disbarred where evidence established flagrant pattern of misrepresentation, exploitation of vulnerable victim, and conflicts of interest—including loan from a client and transferring a client's assets into business in which the attorney was an owner—all of which resulted in a substantial loss of the client's property); *In re Peterson*, 718 N.W.2d

849 (Minn. 2006) (disbarment imposed on lawyer who, inter alia, entered into impermissible business transaction with client when he purchased automobile from client at less than market value); *In re Coffey's Case,* 880 A.2d 403 (N.H. 2005) (disbarment warranted for lawyer who knowingly entered into transaction with elderly and mentally ill client that resulted in lawyer's acquisition of an interest in the client's real property for substantially less than the fair market value of the property); *In re Brown,* 956 P.2d 188 (Or. 1998) (lawyer disbarred for entering into transaction with clients to purchase shopping center and failing to disclose that he was structuring the transaction so that he would eventually have full ownership and claim stepped-up depreciation on his own taxes, knowing that his clients wanted and expected to share equally in ownership of the shopping center); *In re Jordan,* 674 S.E.2d 149 (S.C. 2009) (lawyer disbarred for, inter alia, entering into a business transaction with client without disclosing the conflicts of interest; client agreed to sell a parcel of real estate to lawyer and to finance the transaction). *But see In re Williams,* 971 N.E.2d 92, 95 (Ind. 2012) (while court found Standard 4.31(a), inter alia, applied where lawyer's personal interests conflicted with client's when he entered into a business transaction with client and unilaterally raised his fee, issued checks from frail, elderly client's account and paid himself "an inordinate amount [for] unproductive and nonprofessional work," it imposed suspension for no less than two years without automatic reinstatement since lawyer essentially withdrew from the practice two decades earlier; dissenting justice would have imposed disbarment).

- **Loan from a Client**

A lawyer who obtains a loan from a client without fully disclosing the terms of the loan and without advising the client to seek independent counsel may face disbarment. *See, e.g., People v. Johnson,* 35 P.3d 168 (Colo. O.P.D.J. 1999) (disbarment warranted for lawyer who, aware that the client had received a bequest from the estate that was subject of representation, obtained two loans from a client totaling $50,000, failed to advise client to seek independent counsel regarding loan, and did not obtain client's written consent); *In re Baggette,* 26 So.3d 98 (La. 2009) (lawyer disbarred for borrowing $600,000 from elderly client and entering into agreement to purchase the client's interest in successions of two deceased individuals without disclosing to client in writing the terms of both transactions, giving client reasonable opportunity to seek advice of independent counsel, and obtaining client's written consent to the transactions); *Att'y Grievance Comm'n v. Parker,* 884 A.2d 104 (Md. 2005) (disbarment warranted for lawyer who took $70,000 loan from client, gave client a sham mortgage to secure the loan, and then repaid the loan from commissions he claimed from client's sale of parcels of farm property to which he was not entitled); *In re Wyant,* 533 N.W.2d 397 (Minn. 1995) (lawyer who, over a period of years, took more than $1.4 million in loans from clients to either his law firm, himself, or to a corporation in which he was part owner was disbarred, notwithstanding that his partner solicited a majority of the loans); *In re Disciplinary Action Against Crary*, 638 N.W.2d 23 (N.D. 2002) (disbarment for lawyer who, while representing 85-year-old client who had suffered stroke and was dependent upon lawyer for personal needs, drafted codicil to client's will naming lawyer's wife as a beneficiary, took $3,500 loan from client, and advised client to cash in investments to purchase annuities from company for which lawyer was agent and received commissions from purchases); *In re Disciplinary Proceeding Against Miller*, 66 P.3d 1069 (Wash. 2003) (disbarment appropriate for multiple acts of misconduct including loan from client at interest rate less than bank rate, and note not payable until client reached the age of 115; lawyer's claim that loan had been forgiven by client not supported by evidence).

## *Simultaneously Representing Clients with Adverse Interests*

Disbarment is also appropriate in cases involving simultaneous multiple representations of clients with adverse interests when a lawyer engages in such conduct with the intent to benefit the lawyer or another and causes serious or potentially serious harm to a client. *See, e.g., Office of Disciplinary Counsel v. Smith*, No. 26374, 2004 WL 1948420 (Haw. Aug. 30, 2004) (lawyer's obligations in representing client in estate planning matters conflicted with professional and personal relationship with another client and warranted disbarment); *In re Beckner*, 778 N.E.2d 806 (Ind. 2002) (disbarment for misconduct including lawyer's representation of corporation in which he was director and lawyer during corporation's purchase of healthcare facility that lawyer also represented and for which lawyer also served as director); *Att'y Grievance Comm'n v. Kent*, 653 A.2d 909 (Md. 1995) (disbarment, under Standard 4.31(b), inter alia, warranted for lawyer who engaged in conflicts of interest by simultaneously representing both the defendant charged with murder and alleged accomplice who had agreed to testify as state's principal witness; lawyer held several secret meetings with accomplice-client, successfully convincing him not to testify against defendant-client but was not successful in convincing court to have accomplice's guilty plea withdrawn resulting in the imposition of two consecutive life sentences); *In re Gelbwaks*, 260 A.D.2d 47 (N.Y. App. Div. 1999) (disbarment warranted for lawyer whose misconduct included convincing a client to personally guarantee a loan in which lawyer represented both the debtor and the loan guarantor at closing; debtor later defaulted on the $190,000 loan); *In re Disciplinary Proceeding Against Marshall*, 217 P.3d 291, 309 (Wash. 2009) (disbarment for lawyer who engaged in violations including multiple conflicts of interest, one of which involved representation of two clients in breach of contract action where lawyer, to his own benefit, subsequently agreed to represent third client in same lawsuit).

## *Current Client's Interests Adverse to Those of Former Client*

Disbarment may be warranted if a lawyer knowingly uses information relating to a representation of a former client with the intent to benefit the lawyer or another in the course of representing a current client in a substantially related matter whose interests are materially adverse to the former client and causes serious or potentially serious injury. *See, e.g., In re Benge*, 783 A.2d 1279 (Del. 2001) (disbarment, under Standard 4.31, inter alia, for knowingly advising beneficiary of potential legal challenges to will lawyer drafted for former client); *In re White*, 11 A.3d 1226 (D.C. 2011) (disbarment warranted for misconduct including lawyer's agreement to act as co-counsel in representing client in federal age-discrimination lawsuit against governmental entity shortly after lawyer's tenure with human rights office where she supervised the investigation of client's age-discrimination claim and reviewed a draft "no probable cause" letter sent to client; court noting lawyer's willingness to share confidential information about the proceedings conducted by her former employer threatened to give client in the federal litigation an unfair advantage and tainted the judicial process); *In re Disciplinary Proceeding Against Anschell*, 69 P.3d 844 (Wash. 2003) (lawyer failed to disclose to client that he had previously represented the man she married in securing a letter of immunity from the immigration office in exchange for information about the client and their sham marriage; disbarment warranted). *But see In re Stauffer*, 956 P.2d 967, 977 (Or. 1998) (court cited Standard 4.31, inter alia, as possible sanction for lawyer's multiple conflicts of interest in representing current clients against former client in matters significantly related to his prior representation of former client; finding lawyer engaged in "a staggering amount of unnecessary litigation," using courts as "mere tools in his efforts to pursue his attorney's fees claims" against his former client, but imposed two-year suspension in light of court's precedent); *In re McKee*, 849 P.2d 509 (Or. 1993) (lawyer's simultaneous representation in dissolution of marriage proceeding of husband and wife he knew were not in agreement as to child custody and property division issues caused actual injury to both clients, and subsequent representation of husband in slander of title action against wife in a matter substantially related to the dissolution met the criteria for disbarment under Standard 4.31(c); but lack of evidence that information lawyer obtained from wife benefited husband in later lawsuit warranted eighteen-month suspension).

## *What Constitutes "Serious Injury"?*

Disbarment is appropriate under Standard 4.31 when a lawyer's conflict of interest causes "serious or potentially serious injury" to a client. *See, e.g., In re Beckner*, 778 N.E.2d 806, 811 (Ind. 2002) (in disbarring lawyer, court found various business transactions by lawyer involved "deliberate, preconceived schemes to deprive clients and third parties of substantial sums for his own benefit and the benefit of his family"); *In re Hodge*, 407 P.3d 613 (Kan. 2017) (holding Standard 4.31 applicable, court disbarred lawyer for business transaction with client where terms were not fair and reasonable to the client, lawyer knew of client's significant financial problems, and knew client did not have funds to seek advice of independent counsel; significant injury included lost opportunities to take advantage of bankruptcy code protections); *In re Hutton*, 25 So.3d 767 (La. 2009) (lawyer caused serious harm when he gave his former sister-in-law an assignment of life insurance benefits to sign and misled her into signing the assignment, paying her only $25,000, without disclosing that the value of the life insurance policy was in excess of $800,000; disbarment warranted); *In re Guirard*, 11 So.3d 1017, 1030 (La. 2009) (lawyer's egregious compensation plan for nonlawyer employees created conflicts between clients and employees who received bonuses for "signing up" clients and were paid based on successful settlements, thereby depriving clients "of the benefit of a thoughtful, individualized and professional legal analysis of their cases") (citation omitted); *Stark Cnty. Bar Ass'n v. Hare*, 791 N.E.2d 966 (Ohio 2003) (egregious misconduct by lawyer while representing both the birth mother and the adoptive parents who were victimized vulnerable clients, jeopardizing the adoption process and warranting disbarment); *In re Crews*, 698 S.E.2d 785, 795 (S.C. 2010) (disbarment warranted for lawyer's "egregious, predatory behavior, taking advantage of and causing great detriment to his clients" for, inter alia, multiple conflicts of interest in numerous business transactions with clients using powers of attorney given to lawyer by two clients to sell, buy, encumber, or convey clients' real estate properties, naming himself primary and residual beneficiary in one client's will, and using client's credit card for personal use); *In re Disciplinary Proceeding Against Anschell*, 69 P.3d 844 (Wash. 2003) (lawyer's conflicts of interest caused serious or potentially serious harm to immigration client who was arrested after deportation hearing in which lawyer conceded client entered into a fraudulent marriage and failed to disclose to client that he had previously represented the man she married in securing a letter of immunity from the immigration office in exchange for information about the client and the sham marriage). *But see In re Kiczales*, 36 A.D.3d 276, 280 (N.Y. App. Div. 2006) (rejecting the recommendation of thirty months' suspension and imposing five-year suspension, court found lawyer allowed his own financial interests to affect his professional judgment when he solicited money in exchange for secretly providing information to assist opposing party in settling case with lawyer's client; court stated "such misconduct 'strikes at the heart of the attorney-client relationship, that is, the trust that clients place in their attorneys to pursue their legal interests'") (citation omitted); but for mitigating factors, totality of lawyer's misconduct warranted disbarment).

When a lawyer enters into a business transaction with a client, the client may incur "serious injury" if he or she is required to expend significant amounts of money to rectify the problem. In disbarring a lawyer who entered into a business transaction with a client, the court in *People v. Barbieri*, 61 P.3d 488 (Colo. O.P.D.J. 2000), found that the lawyer's misconduct resulted in a loss to the client of no less than $168,000, and the client was also required to spend more than $76,000 in legal fees and costs attempting to recover the funds loaned to the lawyer. "Under these facts, [the client] suffered serious harm," the court noted. *Id.* at 493.

**4.32 Suspension is generally appropriate when a lawyer knows of a conflict of interest and does not fully disclose to a client the possible effect of that conflict, and causes injury or potential injury to a client.**

## Annotation

As with conflicts of interest warranting disbarment under Standard 4.31, those warranting suspension under 4.32 similarly can take the form of a conflict between a lawyer and the client, between or among current clients, or between a former client and a present client. The distinction between conflicts warranting disbarment and those warranting suspension generally turns on the seriousness of the injury that the client incurs and may also involve the extent to which the lawyer benefited, regardless of intent. *See, e.g., Ligon v. Rees*, 364 S.W.3d 28 (Ark. 2010) (lawyer engaged in multiple conflicts of interests warranting a one-year suspension when, among other misconduct, he agreed to represent driver of vehicle involved in collision in unrelated matter while representing the passenger of driver's vehicle in personal injury claim against driver and his employer, dismissed driver-client from lawsuit he filed without disclosure to personal injury client, provided financial assistance to personal injury client, and obtained general release of liability from personal injury client; serious misconduct resulted in or was likely to result in substantial prejudice to both clients); *Fla. Bar v. Herman*, 8 So.3d 1100 (Fla. 2009) (eighteen-month suspension under Florida Standard 4.32, inter alia, for lawyer who formed company in direct competition with client's company without disclosing his adverse interests); *In re Rasley*, 918 N.E.2d 302 (Ind. 2009) (two lawyers disciplined for engaging in different conflicts of interest: one suspended for 120 days for representing seller in litigation against buyer who had purchased real estate property financed by lawyer and on which lawyer held a mortgage, and the other suspended for thirty days for concurrent representation of seller and his partner-lawyer-mortgagor in litigation against buyer); *In re Wolterbeek's Case*, 886 A.2d 990, 993 (N.H. 2005) (comparing Standards 4.32 with 4.31, court stated that "[t]he critical distinction between suspension and disbarment is whether the conflict of interest is between the lawyer and the client and whether the lawyer acts with the intention to benefit himself," noting disbarment warranted in this case because lawyer's acts in deceiving client strongly suggest he intended to benefit himself at the client's expense); *In re Disciplinary Proceeding Against Haley*, 138 P.3d 1044 (Wash. 2006) (one-year suspension under Standard 4.32 for agreements lawyer made with client without the requisite disclosure of potential conflicts and failure to advise client to seek independent representation, including agreement to finance lawsuit settlement in exchange for release of any malpractice rights against lawyer and his firm).

## *Lawyer's Interest Adverse to Current Clients*

Regarding conflicts of interest between a lawyer and a current client, suspension is appropriate when a lawyer knows that his or her interests may be or are likely to be adverse to that of the client but does not fully disclose the conflict, resulting in injury or potential injury to the client. In *In re Polevoy*, 980 P.2d 985 (Colo. 1999), citing Standard 4.32, the court suspended a lawyer for one year and one day for drafting wills for a client that named the lawyer a residuary beneficiary and directed her to care for the client's pets. After the lawyer was appointed temporary guardian of her client, she used estate funds to pay herself but euthanized her client's cats due to a "lack of funds" shortly before she sold client's home for $35,000. The court, in suspending the lawyer, stated that "[t]he conflicts of interest in this case were obvious. As the residuary beneficiary and as the lawyer and guardian, who expected to get paid for her work, [the lawyer's] own financial interests were directly adverse to [the client's] interests, including that of preserving the lives of her pets." *Id. at 988. See also People v. Miller*, 354 P.3d 1136 (Colo. O.P.D.J. 2015) (six-month suspension for attorney who drafted and entered into management agreement giving him complete control over his family's corporation and its assets, without obtaining the board of directors' consent and concealing the agreement; Standard 4.32 cited); *In re Cutright*, 910 N.E.2d 581 (Ill. 2009) (two-year suspension for, inter alia, representing one client in drafting loan forgiveness documents in favor of another client without making appropriate disclosures); *In re Meek*, 289 P.3d 95 (Kan. 2012) (forty-month suspension stayed after twelve months by a period of probation for lawyer who was convicted of unlawfully possessing hydrocodone and engaged in conflict of interest by obtaining prescription pain medication from his clients); *In re Griffing*, 236 So.3d 1213 (La. 2017) (Assistant United States Attorney suspended under Standard 4.32, inter alia, for intimate relationship with FBI agent called as witness in her case; although no indication agent's testimony was influenced or colored by their relationship, AUSA admitted failure to disclose it during prosecution of two city councilmen and a sheriff); *In re Grevemberg*, 838 So.2d 1283 (La. 2003) (one-year suspension, under Standard 4.32, for lawyer's knowing conflict of interest in drafting will for client naming lawyer's wife residuary legatee); *In re DeSousa*, 36 A.D.3d 121, 125 (N.Y. App. Div. 2006) ("substantial evidence of overreaching" by the lawyer when he acquired interest in elderly client's assets by transferring assets into vehicles benefitting him without disclosing ramifications to client); *In re Phillips*, 107 P.3d 615 (Or. 2005) (three-year suspension, under Standard 4.32, inter alia, for sending insurance agents to review clients' trusts while failing to disclose that lawyer and his law firm by receiving commission had a financial interest in the agents' sale to clients of any insurance products); *In re Disciplinary Proceeding Against Hall*, 329 P.3d 870 (Wash. 2014) (two-year suspension for attorney who named himself as alternate trustee and health care representative and gave himself power of attorney without fully explaining to client the legal effects of these roles, including the ways in which these roles could conflict with his own interests and have adverse effect on client interests).

- **Business Transactions with Clients**

A frequent ground for suspension under Standard 4.32 arises when a lawyer knowingly enters into a business transaction with a client without making necessary disclosures regarding the potential conflicts of interest. *See, e.g., In re Elgin*, 918 A.2d 362 (D.C. 2007) (lawyer who allowed personal and financial interests to conflict with client's when he used client's credit card, with authorization, to charge personal and business expenses, failed to pay the charges, and did not disclose to client collection lawsuit filed against her by credit card company suspended for six months with restitution ordered); *Florida Bar v. Parrish*, 241 So.3d 66 (Fla. 2018) (three-year suspension under Florida Standard 4.32 where attorney improperly entered into business transactions with clients by obtaining security interest in a Lamborghini to cover legal fees, loaning money to clients to fund payment of back taxes, accepting mortgage on several parcels to secure the loan, and negotiating potential settlement agreement creating a new entity in which the attorney would be part owner); *Iowa Supreme Ct. Att'y Disciplinary Bd. v. Powell*, 901 N.W.2d 513 (Iowa 2017) (six-month suspension increased to two years where attorney obtained loan from estate client and withdrew loan proceeds from the trust account before agreement he drafted was executed; suspension increased due to significant aggravating factor of repeated misconduct over a decade); *Iowa Supreme Ct. Att'y Disciplinary Bd. v. Johnston*, 732 N.W.2d 448 (Iowa 2007) (three-month suspension for numerous conflicts of interest in representing parties with competing interests, including acquiring ownership rights in property that was the subject of clients' litigation); *In re Biscanin*, 390 P.3d 886 (Kan. 2017) (two-year suspension stayed after six months under Standard 4.32 where lawyer "held" $10,000 for a client, agreed to pay interest for period of time money held, and executed promissory note; conduct constituted financial transaction that formed business relationship with client outside the course of the representation); *In re Odo*, 375 P.3d 320 (Kan. 2016) (one-year suspension for attorney who represented both the lending company from which he received profits and clients in the loan transactions; Standard 4.32 cited); *In re Curry*, 16 So.3d 1139 (La. 2009) (three lawyers suspended for six months with three months deferred for, inter alia, entering into an improper business transaction with client by changing terms of fee agreement during the representation, placing them in a better position than original agreement); *In re Disciplinary Action Against Giese*, 662 N.W.2d 250 (N.D. 2003) (ninety-day suspension for obtaining warranty deed from client; although lawyer advised client to seek independent counsel when contract for deed was signed, lawyer did not advise client to seek independent counsel when she executed warranty deed; *In re Discipline of Mattson*, 651 N.W.2d 278 (S.D. 2002) (two-year suspension under Standard 4.32, inter alia, for lawyer who took advantage of 90-year-old uncle by engaging in an egregious course of conduct to enrich himself and his wife, including series of inter vivos transactions resulting in lawyer and his wife receiving more than half the estate, a "gift" of more than $325,000); *In re Disciplinary Proceeding Against McKean*, 64 P.3d 1226 (Wash. 2003) (six-month suspension under Standard 4.32, followed by six-months of probation, for misconduct including entering into a farming business arrangement with clients to shield clients from creditors and obtaining a 51 percent interest in company lawyer formed to operate farm, without sufficiently informing the clients of the risks inherent in having their lawyer as a business associate). *Compare In re Spencer*, 330 P.3d 538, 550 (Or. 2014) (thirty-day suspension under Standard 4.32 for lawyer who represented client in legal matter and also served as client's real estate broker, thereby entering into business transaction with client absent informed consent in writing; suspension limited because case involved "a single violation" and "the accused's misconduct did not involve nondisclosure or lack of consent . . .") with *In re Ramirez*, 408 P.3d 1065 (Or. 2018) (court distinguished *Spencer* in imposing longer one-year suspension because of multiple and repeated misconduct over a long time).

- **Loans from Clients**

A lawyer who obtains a loan from a client or loans money to a client without making proper disclosures may also be suspended. *See, e.g., People v. Culter*, 277 P.3d 954 (Colo. O.P.D.J. 2011) (lawyer knowingly entered into improper business transaction with clients when he took loans from clients without full disclosure warranting six-month suspension, under Standard 4.32, inter alia; suspension stayed upon successful completion of three-year probation); *In re Timpone*, 804 N.E.2d 560 (Ill. 2004) (forty-two-month suspension until further order of court for lawyer who, inter alia, obtained unsecured loan from client within weeks of completing post-decree work that generated the funds); *Iowa Supreme Ct. Att'y Disciplinary Bd. v. Lynch*, 901 N.W.2d 501 (Iowa 2017) (six-month suspension for attorney who borrowed money from clients without advising them to obtain independent counsel, did not obtain written informed consent, and continued representation without disclosing perilous financial situation; while misconduct caused serious economic harm to clients, only six-month suspension because no prior discipline, lengthy history of community service and pro bono work, misconduct self-reported, and lawyer cooperated in investigation); *In re Clark*, No. BD-2001-097, 2002 WL 32254600 (Mass. St. Bar. Disp. Bd. Jan. 18, 2002) (reciprocal discipline of three-year suspension with restitution ordered for lawyer who failed to discuss his conflict of interest with two elderly clients from whom lawyer borrowed $58,000 without fully disclosing terms of the loan in writing and obtaining their consent);

*State ex rel. Okla. Bar Ass'n v. Clausing*, 224 P.3d 1268, 1277 (Okla. 2009) (imposing one-year suspension on lawyer who violated his fiduciary duties as trustee when he made unauthorized withdrawals of trust funds as personal loans, court noted that lawyer's conduct did not cause "grave economic harm"); *In re Sheehan*, 985 A.2d 1017 (R.I. 2009) (eighteen-months suspension for taking $50,000 loan from client secured by mortgage on encumbered property that lawyer subsequently sold without notice to client, utilizing a forged mortgage release document; suspension to run consecutive to two-year suspension for other misconduct); *In re Disciplinary Proceeding Against Holcomb*, 173 P.3d 898 (Wash. 2007) (six-month suspension under Standard 4.32 for lawyer who obtained twenty-four unsecured loans from a client totaling $52,300 without benefit of promissory notes, interest payments, or disclosure of lawyer's dire financial situation).

- **Sexual Relationship Between Lawyer and Client**

Other types of inappropriate relationships or transactions with clients give rise to conflicts of interest justifying suspension. *See, e.g.*, *In re Stanton*, 376 P.3d 693 (Alaska 2016) (stipulated three-year suspension under Standard 4.32 for sexting and inappropriate physical contact with client in child custody matter); *Chief Disciplinary Counsel v. Zelotes*, 98 A.3d 852 (Conn. 2014) (five-month suspension for concurrent conflict where lawyer had intimate relationship with client during her divorce case; Sanctions Standards not cited); *Fla. Bar v. Roberto*, 59 So.3d 1101 (Fla. 2011) (one-year suspension under Florida Standard 4.32 for lawyer's sexual relationship with two criminal clients and providing financial assistance to them, impairing the exercise of his professional judgment, and creating a conflict of interest); *Iowa Supreme Ct. Att'y Disciplinary Bd. v. Marzen*, 779 N.W.2d 757 (Iowa 2010) (indefinite suspension of no less than six months for lawyer who, inter alia, entered into sexual relationship with client after representing her in a mental-health-commitment hearing; finding lawyer exploited client-lawyer relationship for own sexual gratification, taking advantage of an extremely vulnerable client); *In re Pattison*, 121 P.3d 423 (Kan. 2005) (lawyer suspended for one year after becoming personally and romantically involved with mother of four children for whom he was appointed to serve as guardian *ad litem*; lawyer caused potential injury to the legal system and the children); *In re Fuerst*, 157 So.3d 569 (La. 2014) (six-month suspension where lawyer filed divorce petition on behalf of client and during six-month waiting period to file rule to show cause why the divorce should not be granted, engaged in sexual relationship with client; lawyer negligently violated duties owed to client and the legal profession, and although no apparent harm, the potential for harm existed); *State ex rel. Neb. State Bar Ass'n v. Freese*, 611 N.W.2d 80 (Neb. 2000) (eighteen-month suspension warranted for lawyer's numerous violations, including sexual relationship with client while representing client and her husband in personal injury case and subsequent representation of client in dissolution of marriage proceedings); *In re Vogel*, 482 S.W.3d 520 (Tenn. 2016) (finding Standard 4.32 applies, attorney suspended for one year after knowingly disclosing confidential information to a judge about his client, and in another matter engaging in sexual relationship with a client during the representation).

### *Conflicts Between Current Clients*

Suspension may be an appropriate sanction when a lawyer knows of a conflict of interest between clients, does not fully disclose the possible effect of the multiple representations, and the lawyer's conduct causes injury or potential injury to one or more of those clients. *See In re Katz*, 981 A.2d 1133 (Del. 2009) (three-month suspension for lawyer who, before agreeing to represent borrower-clients, knowingly failed to provide them with timely written disclosures that he also represented lender; citing Standard 4.32, court found the lawyer knew of concurrent conflict but made no effort to disclose it to lender and made untimely disclosures to borrowers, or in the case of one borrower, no disclosure at all, resulting in injury or potential injury to all clients); *In re Hoffman*, 883 So.2d 425 (La. 2004) (three-month suspension for lawyer who, at a minimum should have obtained informed consent of his clients—three siblings/legatees—to a disbursement of aggregate settlement that benefited all of them; lawyer knew or should have known of the conflict of interest among his clients, but he did not fully disclose the possible effect of the multiple representations, resulting in serious actual harm to two of the three clients); *In re Montoya*, 266 P.3d 11, 14 (N.M. 2011) (one-year suspension with three-year probationary term for lawyer's "numerous, well-documented ethical lapses," including concurrent conflicts of interest in representing woman whose boyfriend died, their child, and woman's daughter in recovering life insurance proceeds, workers' compensation benefits, and wrongful death proceeds); *Dayton Bar Ass'n v. Parisi*, 965 N.E.2d 268 (Ohio 2012) (lawyer's representation of client's niece in guardianship proceedings against elderly client with diminished capacity while acting as client's attorney-in-fact under a power of attorney created impermissible conflict of interest warranting six-month fully stayed suspension); *In re Conduct of Gatti*, 333 P.3d 994 (Or. 2014) (ninety-day suspension under Standard 4.32 for lawyer who allocated lump-sum settlement proceeds among jointly represented clients without first seeking to secure the clients' written informed consent to method used to divide settlement proceeds); *Cody v. Bd. of Prof'l Responsibility*, 471 S.W.3d 420 (Tenn. 2015) (180-day suspension where attorney represented two clients in the same civil lawsuit: a childcare center and the former director of the center, who was accused of stealing from the center and against whom the center's receiver had obtained a judgment); *In re Disciplinary Proceeding Against Botimer*, 214 P.3d 133 (Wash. 2009) (six-month suspension for lawyer who simultaneously represented three parties—a mother, her son, and his wife—on various business and estate matters that involved all three in their capacities either as lessors and lessees, or as a potential beneficiary to another's estate, without obtaining informed consent in writing); *In re Disciplinary Proceeding Against Egger*, 98 P.3d 477 (Wash. 2004) (six-month suspension for lawyer who arranged for a long-term client to make a loan to another client but failed to disclose and get written consent to potential conflict of interest from the lending client about lawyer's dual representation).

## *Former Client Conflicts*

Suspension is appropriate when a lawyer knows or should know that the interests of a current client are materially adverse to the interests of a former client in a substantially related matter, and such a conflict causes injury or potential injury to the former or subsequent client. *See In re Balocca*, 151 P.3d 154 (Or. 2007) (ninety-day suspension for lawyer who obtained confidences or secrets from former bankruptcy client relating to his finances such that lawyer's subsequent representation of the girlfriend of the former client in paternity case filed by him created conflict of interest since former client's financial status was relevant to custody and child-support issues).

Suspension may be appropriate even when the former client is deceased and the interests of the deceased client are adverse to those of a current client in a substantially related matter. *See, e.g., In re Hostetter*, 238 P.3d 13, 20 (Or. 2010) (suspension of 150 days for lawyer who, inter alia, represented a borrower in obtaining a series of loans, and after borrower died, lawyer represented the lender in collecting the outstanding loans from deceased client's estate; noting that this was a matter of first impression in Oregon and that no jurisdiction appeared to have directly addressed the issue, court held that "an attorney is prohibited from engaging in a former-client conflict of interest even when the former client is deceased, as long as the former client's interests survive his or her death and are adverse to the current client during the subsequent representation").

## *Lawyer Must Act Knowingly*

Suspension under Standard 4.32 is appropriate when a lawyer knows of the conflict and fails to reveal it. *See, e.g., People v. Bath*, 410 P.3d 859 (Colo. 2018) (two-year suspension where respondent disbursed settlement funds even though he knew of pending medical lien, advanced substantial living expenses to client during the representation, and made negligent misrepresentations about intentions to pay the lien); *In re Ramirez*, 408 P.3d 1065 (Or. 2018) (one-year suspension where attorney attempted to settle a potential legal malpractice claim with client, but did not explain what client's potential malpractice claims might be or advise client of desirability of seeking independent legal counsel to review settlement agreement; attorney acted knowingly and his interests were directly adverse to the client's when he settled the potential malpractice claim).

A lawyer need not necessarily be aware that his or her conduct violates a disciplinary rule, as long as he or she knows the essential facts giving rise to a violation. *See, e.g., In re Disciplinary Matter Involving Stepovich,* 386 P.3d 1205 (Alaska 2016) (in determining whether conduct is negligent or knowing, question is not whether the attorney knew of a particular ethics rule, but whether the attorney had knowledge of nature of his conduct and knew it created conflict of interest; one-year suspension appropriate because the attorney knew will he drafted identified himself as the contingent beneficiary, creating an obvious conflict of interest); *In re Cimino,* 3 P.3d 398 (Colo. 2000) (in rejecting lawyer's claims that his mental state was merely negligent rather than knowing conflict of interest, court considered lawyer's role as creditor for loan made to corporation while simultaneously representing the corporation as legal counsel regarding the debt and imposed thirty-day suspension, citing Standard 4.32); *In re Schenck,* 194 P.3d 804 (Or. 2008) (one-year suspension under Standard 4.32, inter alia, for lawyer who drafted wills for two sisters who had conflicting interests and who drafted a will that included a $1,000 gift to his wife; suspension appropriate even when lawyer was not aware his conduct violated a disciplinary rule because he was consciously aware of facts giving rise to the violation); *In re Disciplinary Proceeding Against Holcomb,* 173 P.3d 898, 909 (Wash. 2007) (noting that court's "definition of 'knowledge' includes the requirement that the lawyer *should have known* that a conflict existed" and, therefore, affirming finding that respondent acted knowingly when he requested loans from his client); *In re Disciplinary Proceeding Against Gillingham,* 896 P.2d 656 (Wash. 1995) (given obvious nature of conflict and potential for serious injury to client, sixty-day suspension under Standard 4.32 appropriate when lawyer knew or should have known of facial and obvious conflict of interest inherent in drafting will for a client in which he was named a substantial beneficiary).

A lawyer's knowledge can be inferred from the circumstances. For example, in *In re Hostetter,* 238 P.3d 13, 28 (Or. 2010), a lawyer was suspended for representing a lender in a collection action against the estate of a deceased debtor who the lawyer originally had represented in obtaining the loans. The lawyer knew that deceased client-borrower had received loans from his current client, and that the lender was seeking to enforce his rights arising out of the very documents that the lawyer had drafted on behalf of the now deceased client in the prior representation. The lawyer testified that he was aware that his lender-client's interest was "in getting as much as possible pursuant to the promissory notes and even some loans under which there were no notes" and, therefore, was consciously aware of the nature or attendant circumstances of the conduct underlying the violations in the debtor client's matter.

## *Intent to Cause Injury Not Required*

A lawyer need not act with the objective to cause a particular injury in order to warrant a suspension under Standard 4.32. *See, e.g., People v. Fisher,* 237 P.3d 645 (Colo. O.P.D.J. 2010) (suspension for lawyer who engaged in a conflict of interest when he entered into a loan transaction with his client even though he acted without the conscious objective to cause particular injury to his client); *In re Disciplinary Proceeding Against Carpenter,* 155 P.3d 937, 944 (Wash. 2007) (two-month suspension imposed against lawyer who knowingly violated disciplinary rules when he represented codefendants in a lawsuit and then represented one of them against the other in a later indemnification suit without obtaining consent or a waiver; lawyer knew he was representing the client against a former client in a substantially related matter involving some of the same facts and circumstances and whose interests were materially adverse; while no actual harm, "there was a substantial possibility of injury" to the former client).

## *Intent to Benefit Lawyer or Another Not Required*

Unlike disbarment under Standard 4.31, under Standard 4.32 suspension may be warranted regardless of whether the lawyer was acting with the intent to benefit himself or another. *See, e.g., In re Caliguiri,* 50 A.D.3d 90 (N.Y. App. Div. 2008) (one-year suspension warranted for lawyer who reviewed client insurance company's confidential file secretly obtained by lawyer's wife who was employed by client and provided advice to neighbor-lawyer adverse to client in medical malpractice case notwithstanding no evidence of financial benefit or venal motive); *In re Disciplinary Proceeding Against Egger,* 98 P.3d 477 (Wash. 2004) (six-month suspension for failure to obtain written consent to potential conflict of interest between two current clients regarding a loan transaction; finding Standard 4.32 not limited to instances in which lawyer is acting in his own self-interest); *cf. In re Disciplinary Proceeding Against Anschell,* 69 P.3d 844, 856 (Wash. 2003) (suspension was presumptive sanction for lawyer who failed to disclose prior representation of adverse witness while representing client in deportation proceeding that disclosed sham marriage between witness and client absent any indication that misconduct was intended to benefit the lawyer or another although "serious or potentially serious harm" to the client occurred rather than only "injury" under Standard 4.32; disbarment imposed due to lack of diligence in another matter and prior discipline).

## *Suspension Reduced to Public Censure Due to Mitigation*

In some cases, even when a suspension is the presumptive sanction under Standard 4.32, a court may reduce the sanction to a reprimand (or public censure) when mitigating factors are present (see Annotation to Standard 9.32). *See, e.g., People v. Vsetecka,* 893 P.2d 1309 (Colo. 1995) (citing Standard 4.32, court nonetheless imposed a public censure on lawyer whose misconduct included representing two clients after it had become clear that conflict existed, citing mitigating factors of absence of previous discipline in lawyer's twenty-two years of practice and his cooperation in disciplinary proceedings); *In re Whalen*, 888 P.2d 395, 398 (Kan. 1995) (suspension under Standard 4.32 appropriate when lawyer, acting as trust officer, made a "knowing, conscious act" to transfer assets from a trust administered by the bank on client's behalf to a trust of which lawyer was both settlor and individual trustee, without knowledge or consent of any other employee of the bank; public censure imposed due to several mitigating factors, most significantly a lack of selfish motive as lawyer "believed that he was 'doing the right thing'"); *In re Leuenberger*, 93 P.3d 786 (Or. 2004) (suspension under Standard 4.32 was presumptive sanction for lawyer who violated conflict of interest and disclosure rules when he requested that trial court satisfy sanction judgments, for which he was jointly liable with his clients, from proceeds of foreclosure on clients' property; but public reprimand imposed because of mitigating factors); *In re Howser*, 987 P.2d 496 (Or. 1999) (suspension is appropriate sanction for lawyer's conflict of interest in representing borrower in lawsuit brought by former client for whom law firm prepared wills in which borrower is named as one of the beneficiaries, but public reprimand imposed in light of mitigating factors, including exemplary record of service, lack of prior discipline, and lack of selfish motive).

**4.33 Reprimand is generally appropriate when a lawyer is negligent in determining whether the representation of a client may be materially affected by the lawyer's own interests, or whether the representation will adversely affect another client, and causes injury or potential injury to a client.**

## Annotation

Courts generally will impose a reprimand (or public censure) when a lawyer engages in a conflict of interest and has been negligent in deciding whether the representation may be affected by the lawyer's own interest or whether it will adversely affect another client. The conflicted representation also must cause injury or potential injury to a client. *See In re Walker,* 24 P.3d 602 (Ariz. 2001) (imposing public censure under Standard 4.33 rather than recommended suspension on lawyer who attempted to enter into a consensual sexual relationship with a client, court finding that lawyer's actions were aberrational and arose out of negligence); *People v. Gonzales,* 922 P.2d 933 (Colo. 1996) (lawyer agreed to represent plaintiff in auto injury case and then negligently agreed to represent the driver of the other car in filing for bankruptcy, without advising either of the effect such representation would have on his ability to exercise independent professional judgment on each client's behalf; citing Standard 4.33, inter alia, public reprimand imposed because conflicting representation resulted in no actual harm); *In re Haitbrink,* 375 P.3d 296 (Kan. 2016) (citing hearing panel's consideration of Standard 4.33, public censure for lawyer who acted negligently by including in fee agreements a provision that the client would hold the firm and any attorneys harmless from any claim, suit, action, or demand arising out of or in relation to the agreement); *Att'y Grievance Comm'n v. Ruddy,* 981 A.2d 637 (Md. 2009) (reprimand for lawyer, appointed personal representative of his aunt's estate, who failed to make provision for the collection of interest on a loan he received from aunt that was in default at the time he undertook the representation); *In re Kalla,* 811 N.W.2d 576 (Minn. 2012) (conflict of interest arose in lawyer's simultaneous representation of two clients in lawsuit against lender for issuing usurious loans when one client was broker for loan transaction of other client and potentially liable to that client as a third-party defendant, warranting sanction of public reprimand and two years' probation; lawyer did not cure conflict by subsequently withdrawing his representation of broker-client); *In re Weier,* 994 S.W.2d 554 (Mo. 1999) (public reprimand for lawyer who failed to disclose his financial interest as a shareholder in corporation that leased a medical device owned by partnership of urologists represented by lawyer; case fit squarely into Standard 4.33 analysis in that lawyer engaged in a single instance of negligent misconduct involving conflict of interest resulting in no discernible harm to clients); *Johnston v. Johnston,* 872 N.W.2d 300 (N.D. 2015) (reprimand under Standard 4.33 for lawyer who disregarded a conflict of interest involving a paralegal who previously worked for an opposing law firm; instead of screening the paralegal from the case against the other side, the lawyer put the paralegal primarily in charge of the matter); *Disciplinary Counsel v. Jacobs*, 846 N.E.2d 1260 (Ohio 2006) (public reprimand for lawyer who represented husband and wife prior to their separation and then continued to represent each one on other matters while their divorce was pending without disclosing the conflict of interest); *In re Disciplinary Proceeding Against Stansfield*, 187 P.3d 254 (Wash. 2008) (two reprimands imposed on lawyer who represented driver charged with vehicular homicide and deceased victim's estate; lawyer violated rule governing conflicts of interest and acted negligently in doing so, causing actual harm to client and potential harm to the legal system); *Bd. of Prof'l Responsibility v. Jones*, 358 P.3d 498 (Wyo. 2015) (public reprimand under Standard 4.33 where respondent, before undertaking representation of two clients in a boundary dispute adverse to a former client, did not tell them of his prior relationships, inform them of how this would limit his representation, or get their written consent; reprimand was proper because respondent admitted negligence and clients were injured as a result); *Bd. of Prof'l Responsibility v. Abraham*, 221 P.3d 960 (Wyo. 2009) (public censure for lawyer who failed to immediately withdraw from representing a client in a criminal case after that client allegedly made statements to the police implicating another of the lawyer's clients who he was representing in divorce proceedings).

Even when the presumptive sanction is public reprimand for negligently undertaking a representation resulting in a conflict of interest, courts may impose suspension or disbarment when other violations or aggravating factors are present. *See, e.g., In re Rumsey*, 71 P.3d 1150 (Kan. 2003) (reprimand is presumptive sanction for lawyer who allowed client's mother, who was paying legal fees, to influence his independent professional judgment in representing client-daughter, causing potential harm to client by affecting her ability to discharge debt in bankruptcy due to numerous other violations and several aggravating factors; lawyer suspended for one year); *In re Obert*, 89 P.3d 1173 (Or. 2004) (reprimand is presumptive sanction for lawyer who was retained by couple to locate birth father of her son from a previous relationship and also unknowingly represented the birth father in three criminal matters; lawyer suspended for thirty days due to ethics rules violations involving another client); *In re Disciplinary Proceeding Against Scannell*, 239 P.3d 332 (Wash. 2010) (reprimand is presumptive sanction for a lawyer who represented both a husband and wife charged with stealing computers from husband's employer and from one of his coworkers; record showed the lawyer informed clients of some of the conflicts inherent in joint representation and the wife gave informed consent to most significant conflict suggested that lawyer's failure to obtain consent in writing was an honest mistake, albeit one showing that he was not familiar with ethical rules; lawyer disbarred for additional misconduct including intentionally failing to cooperate in disciplinary proceedings with the intent to frustrate and delay those proceedings); *In re Disciplinary Proceeding Against McKean,* 64 P.3d 1226 (Wash. 2003) (reprimand is presumptive sanction under Standard 4.33 for lawyer's conflict of interest while representing estate in loaning funds to farming company that lawyer formed with another client; lawyer acted negligently in determining whether his financial interest in company created a conflict of interest, never informed estate's heirs of the loans, did not obtain written consent after full disclosure, and it was not reasonable for him to believe his representation of estate would not be adversely affected; lawyer ultimately suspended under Standard 4.32, inter alia, for entering into the business venture with client).

Courts may also impose a reprimand in cases involving conflicts of interest arising out of a subsequent representation. For instance, in *In re Whalen,* 888 P.2d 395 (Kan. 1995), the court found that public censure under Standard 4.33 was appropriate for a lawyer who undertook representation of former client's sons in a matter adverse to the interests of the former client, with whom he neither consulted nor obtained consent to carry on his representation of her sons.

**4.34 Admonition is generally appropriate when a lawyer engages in an isolated instance of negligence in determining whether the representation of a client may be materially affected by the lawyer's own interests, or whether the representation will adversely affect another client, and causes little or no actual or potential injury to a client.**

## Annotation

Admonition is an appropriate sanction when the lawyer, in an isolated instance, is negligent in determining whether a conflict exists and causes little or no injury or potential injury to a client. *See, e.g., In re Anonymous,* 655 N.E.2d 67 (Ind. 1995) (lawyer's representation of former union trustee in potential action against company, also lawyer's client, without obtaining either party's consent, warranted private admonition; misconduct was based on single, isolated incident, evidence showed conduct was not intentional but negligent, and lawyer caused no real harm to either client); *An Unnamed Attorney v. Ky. Bar Ass'n,* 186 S.W.3d 741 (Ky. 2006) (conduct of lawyer in committing to represent husband and wife by conducting private investigation into shooting death of wife's former husband for the sake of ruling each spouse out in pending criminal investigation, without first fully explaining to clients the potential conflict and consequences of representing clients with divergent interests, warranted private reprimand, especially since lawyer's investigation uncovered facts implicating one of the spouses in the possible murder, which gave rise to conflict); *In re Discipline of an Attorney,* 864 N.E.2d 1180 (Mass. 2007) (admonition appropriate for lawyer's conflict of interest in recording discharge of mortgage on behalf of client-mortgagor without consulting with former client-mortgagee for whom the lawyer drafted the discharge document given isolated event, lawyer not motivated by self-interest, and extent of harm to mortgagee was not established).

## 4.4 Lack of Diligence

**Absent aggravating or mitigating circumstances, upon application of the factors set out in Standard 3.0, the following sanctions are generally appropriate in cases involving a failure to act with reasonable diligence and promptness in representing a client:**

**4.41 Disbarment is generally appropriate when:**

**(a) a lawyer abandons the practice and causes serious or potentially serious injury to a client; or**

**(b) a lawyer knowingly fails to perform services for a client and causes serious or potentially serious injury to a client; or**

**(c) a lawyer engages in a pattern of neglect with respect to client matters and causes serious or potentially serious injury to a client.**

## Annotation

Lack of diligence can take a variety of forms. Some lawyers simply abandon their practices, leaving clients completely unaware that they have no legal representation and sometimes leaving clients without any legal remedy. Other lawyers knowingly fail to perform services for a client or engage in a pattern of misconduct, demonstrating by their behavior that they either cannot or will not conform to required ethical standards. When lawyers engage in such conduct and cause "serious or potentially serious injury," disbarment is the presumptive sanction. Courts may consider that a lawyer who abandons a client, knowingly fails to perform services for a client, or engages in a pattern of neglect with regard to a client matter "betray[s] the trust that his clients placed in him when they sought his assistance and the public trust with which he was endowed when he was admitted to the Bar. . . ." *Att'y Grievance Comm'n v. Kwarteng*, 984 A.2d 865, 870 (Md. 2009) (quoting *Att'y Grievance Comm'n v. Tinsky*, 835 A.2d 542, 547 (Md. 2003) (disbarring a lawyer who accepted fees to represent clients in two criminal cases, entered his appearance in those two cases, then failed to appear at scheduled trials and, without notice to the court or to his clients, closed his law office). Indeed, the obligation to diligently pursue a client's interests is one of the "most important ethical duties [as one] that a lawyer owes to the client." *In re Conduct of Sousa*, 915 P.2d 408, 413 (Or. 1996).

Oftentimes, cases that proceed on a default basis due to the lawyer's failure to participate in the disciplinary proceedings involve charges establishing a pattern of neglect, inattention to clients' matters, and failure to communicate with clients. *See, e.g., People v. Williamson*, 2016 WL 3964666 at *6 (Colo. O.P.D.J. 2016) (appropriate sanction was disbarment where a lawyer missed deadlines, failed to attend hearings, failed to respond to client requests for return of files, and caused serious injury by having two clients' cases dismissed, while also having an "apparent lack of concern for [the disciplinary] proceeding"); *Att'y Grievance Comm'n v. Garrett*, 46 A.3d 1169 (Md. 2012) (disbarment the appropriate sanction for lawyer's more than eighty serious ethics violations and default in disciplinary proceedings, including his acceptance of fees from multiple clients, abandonment of those clients without producing any meaningful work for them, and his misappropriation of the fees they gave him); *In re Sousa*, 915 P.2d 408 (Or. 1996) (misconduct including a continuous pattern of neglect, failure to act on clients' matters, and failure to respond to the bar's investigation warranted disbarment).

### *Abandonment of Law Practice*

Absent significant mitigating circumstances, disbarment is warranted for a lawyer who effectively abandons his or her practice without protecting the clients' interests. *See, e.g., People v. Nelson*, 40 P.3d 840 (Colo. O.P.D.J. 2002) (lawyer's misconduct including knowing abandonment of client in an immigration matter resulting in severe injury to client who was deported, his neglect of clients' matters, and failure to communicate with them warranted sanction of disbarment); *In re McCoy*, 767 A.2d 191 (Del. 2001) (Standard 4.41, inter alia, compelled conclusion that disbarment was only appropriate sanction for lawyer whose violations were numerous and extended over a long period of time, including effectively abandoning his law practice without taking any steps to protect his clients, ultimately causing serious or potentially serious injury to his clients); *Fla. Bar v. Irish*, 48 So.3d 767 (Fla. 2010) (citing Florida Standards for Imposing Lawyer Sanctions, court disbarred lawyer and found lawyer's various misconduct demonstrated lack of diligence, inter alia, when lawyer abandoned his practice, seriously injured his clients by missing scheduled court dates, hearings, and a deposition and vacated his office without informing his clients); *In re Boyer*, 26 So.3d 139 (La. 2010) (court disbarred lawyer for essentially abandoning law practice when he neglected his clients' matters, failed to communicate with his clients, and failed to return unearned fees, causing both actual and potential harm to his clients); *Att'y Grievance Comm'n v. Fox*, 11 A.3d 762 (Md. 2010) (while not citing Sanctions Standards, court disbarred lawyer who abandoned his clients in their actions to recover damages following traffic accidents and misrepresented his involvement in their case). *But see, e.g., In re Disciplinary Proceeding Against Wickersham*, 310 P.3d 1237 (Wash. 2013) (despite finding disbarment the presumptive sanction under Standard 4.4 for a lawyer who abandoned his practice for five months, court imposed three-year suspension after taking into account mitigating and aggravating factors, along with cases involving similar conduct).

## *Knowing Failure to Perform Services*

Disbarment under Standard 4.41(b) is the presumptive sanction when a lawyer knowingly fails to perform services on behalf of a client, or multiple clients, resulting in serious or potentially serious injury. For example, in *People v. Ward*, 2017 WL 1046462 (Colo. O.P.D.J. 2017), a lawyer was disbarred for failing to act with diligence in court proceedings resulting in being sanctioned by the courts eleven times and filing bankruptcy petitions for clients knowing that she was being suspended for two years for a prior disciplinary matter and would not be able to complete work, in addition to misleading the clients about their cases and her disciplinary status. The presiding disciplinary judge found Standard 4.1(b) applicable to the lawyer's misconduct, inter alia, and ordering disbarment held that the lawyer lacked fitness to continue to practice law in the state. *See also In re Hamer*, 808 S.E.2d 647 (Ga. 2017) (disbarment warranted where lawyer knowingly failed to provide services to clients and failed to advance one client's matter for several months to benefit the lawyer); *In re Schambach*, 826 So.2d 539 (La. 2002) (disbarment warranted for lawyer who accepted a $2,000 fee from his client but did little, if any, work on the client's legal matter during a twelve-year period, made no effort to account for his fee or refund the unearned portion of it, and, after being suspended, failed to give notice of his suspension to client, nor moved to withdraw from representation); *In re Disciplinary Action Against Karlsen*, 778 N.W.2d 522 (N.D. 2008) (disbarment under Standard 4.41, inter alia, warranted for misconduct that included neglect of clients' immigration matters).

A lawyer's neglect of a client matter may warrant disbarment when the client suffers a very serious and perhaps irreparable injury, such as deportation. *See In re Disciplinary Proceeding Against Anschell*, 69 P.3d 844 (Wash. 2003) (citing Standard 4.41(b), court ordered disbarment for lawyer who failed to take action in client's immigration case or to withdraw from representation when the client allegedly disappeared, resulting in order of deportation and missed the deadline for appealing that order). Disbarment may also be warranted where the lawyer's neglect could have caused serious injury, but the client was saved from harm by other circumstances; a potentially serious injury can suffice for disbarment even with no actual harm. *See, e.g., In the Matter of Barton*, 813 S.E.2d 590 (Ga. 2018) (lawyer disbarred for failing to take any action on behalf of one client, who reported the issue to the court and was assisted in locating substitute counsel, and for failing to appear in a criminal matter without notice to court or client, but ultimately reaching a plea agreement with the prosecutor later without prejudice to the client).

As set forth in the *Definitions* to the black letter Standards, *supra*, "knowledge" is defined as "the conscious awareness of the nature or attendant circumstances of the conduct but without the conscious objective or purpose to accomplish a particular result." Knowing disregard can be found when the facts in a case show that a lawyer was made aware of his or her obligations but ignored them. *See In re*

*Bourcier*, 939 P.2d 604 (Or. 1997) (court disbarred lawyer who acted knowingly in failing to communicate with client regarding his appeal of a criminal conviction).

### *Pattern of Neglect*

Disbarment may also be appropriate when a lawyer who engages in a "pattern of neglect" with regard to client matters resulting in serious or potentially serious injury. *See People v. Blase*, 106 P.3d 1057, 1062 (Colo. O.P.D.J. 2005) (disbarment warranted for lawyer's pattern of neglect regarding ten clients, failure to communicate with clients, abandonment of practice without protecting client interests, and misappropriation of client property; court stated that "[t]he totality of the facts demonstrates that Respondent effectively deserted, rejected, and relinquished her professional responsibilities"). In *In re Disbarment of Taylor*, 60 V.I. 356 (V.I. 2014), the court assessed each grievance separately, finding that although disbarment was not the appropriate sanction for any one instance of neglect, when taken cumulatively, the appropriate suspension would exceed seven years. Given the pattern of conduct demonstrated by multiple grievances for similar neglect, the court ultimately determined that disbarment was appropriate overall. *See also People v. Braham*, 409 P.3d 655 (Colo. 2017) (disbarment warranted for failure to appear for hearings, mishandling bankruptcy case resulting in dismissal, never filing a bankruptcy petition for two other clients, and aggravating factors of abandoning multiple cases, demonstrating a pattern of neglect); *In re Spiller*, 788 A.2d 114 (Del. 2001) (disbarment warranted under Standard 4.41(c) for lawyer's pattern of neglect involving hundreds of matters in which he failed to prepare, record, and/or notarize documents on behalf of clients and others in residential real estate settlements, which resulted in damages to clients in excess of $645,000); *In the Matter of Briley-Holmes*, 815 S.E.2d 59, 65 (Ga. 2018) (disbarment and voluntary surrender of license of lawyer with a "disturbingly excessive pattern of misconduct extending over a period of several years, including seven cases of abandonment"); *In re Rawls*, 936 N.E.2d 812, 816 (Ind. 2010) (disbarment of lawyer who demonstrated a pattern of neglecting clients' cases, "resulting in adverse dispositions, suspension of one client's driver's license, a missed opportunity to settle, and undue delay," warranted severe discipline); *In re Swokowski*, 796 N.W.2d 317 (Minn. 2011) (court disbarred lawyer for repeatedly failing to take action on behalf of his clients and ignoring their attempts to communicate with him about their cases); *In re McMillin*, 521 S.W.3d 604 (Mo. 2017) (disbarment warranted for misappropriation of client funds and a pattern of neglect and failing to advance matters while ignoring client communications); *In re Ehler*, 319 S.W.3d 442 (Mo. 2010) (disbarment warranted under Standard 4.41(c), inter alia, for lawyer who engaged in a pattern of neglect by failing to respond to client's repeated requests for information about the status of her case, failing to promptly deliver money owed to client and her ex-husband after the sale of the marital residence, and failing to give a client the interrogatories he was to complete, which resulted in a default judgment being entered against the client); *Hoover v. Bd. of Prof'l Responsibility*, 395 S.W.3d 95 (Tenn. 2012) (disbarment for lawyer engaged in a pattern of neglect in five client matters that included failure to file appellate brief, resulting in dismissal of appeal, and filing a frivolous action, resulting in Rule 11 sanctions); *Sneed v. Bd. of Prof'l Responsibility*, 301 S.W.3d 603 (Tenn. 2010) (pattern of failure to update clients with status of cases, failure to advise clients of potential conflicts of interest, and engaging in unauthorized practice of law, coupled with unwillingness to abide by ethics rules, despite years of disciplinary action taken against him, resulted in permanent disbarment).

## *Effect of Extent of Injury*

The primary distinction between misconduct warranting disbarment and misconduct warranting suspension in cases under Standard 4.4 is the extent to which the client is injured. For disbarment, "serious" or "potentially serious" injury is required, while suspension requires only "injury" or "potential injury." *See, e.g., In the Matter of Briley-Holmes*, 815 S.E.2d 59, 63 (disbarring lawyer for lack of diligence with regard to seven clients, which "caused at least three clients serious injury as two had their cases dismissed and a third suffered arrest and a period of incarceration" as a result). Despite this distinction, courts sometimes find reasons to impose a suspension or reprimand even though "serious injury" has been established. In *In re Christof*, No. 04-1290, 2006 WL 6319082, (Ariz. Disp.Com. Feb. 7, 2006), for example, the Arizona Disciplinary Commission found clear and convincing evidence that three clients suffered "serious injury" or "serious potential injury." One client had a default judgment entered against her and incurred significant legal fees in an unsuccessful attempt to get the default set aside. The second client lost child support and had to incur additional legal fees to correct the problem caused by the lawyer. The third client was significantly delayed in her effort to establish paternity and recover child support at a time when she was raising her young son without support or other assistance from the father of the child. The court, nonetheless, imposed a two-year suspension rather than disbarment based upon a proportionality analysis of sanctions imposed in factually similar cases. *People v. Costa*, 56 P.3d 130 (Colo. O.P.D.J. 2002), is another example of how the assessment of serious injury to a client can result in a sanction less than disbarment. In *Costa*, a reciprocal discipline matter, the Colorado Supreme Court imposed disbarment for violations resulting in "serious injury" caused by a lawyer's misconduct, including neglect of client matters, failure to communicate with clients, and material misrepresentations to the court in New Mexico. On the same facts, the Supreme Court of New Mexico, in the originating matter, had imposed a reprimand, a sanction that the Colorado Supreme Court found "would result in grave injustice" and was contrary to its law. *Id.* at 136; *see also People v. Doering*,

35 P.3d 719, 722 (Colo. O.P.D.J. 2001) (in default proceeding, lawyer suspended for one year and one day for neglecting the legal matters of three clients, one of whom "suffered serious injury" resulting from going forward with negotiations and performing under a construction contract without benefit of legal representation and, as a result, experienced significant difficulty on the project; despite acknowledgment of serious injury to one of the clients, court cited only Sanctions Standard 4.42, not Standard 4.41); *In re Rumsey*, 71 P.3d 1150 (Kan. 2003) (lawyer knowingly failed to perform services for client by not providing promised strategy letter and failed to diligently pursue workers' compensation claims in Missouri and Kansas, causing client to lose potential cause of action and monetary recovery for her injury, a serious or potentially serious injury; one-year suspension instead of disbarment imposed based on variance in recommended sanctions for lawyer's multiple violations and a list of aggravating and mitigating circumstances); *In re Disciplinary Proceeding Against Shepard*, 239 P.3d 1066 (Wash. 2010) (disbarment is presumptive sanction, under Standard 4.41, for lawyer's misconduct arising from his involvement with "living trust mill" company, causing serious or potentially serious harm to his clients and to the legal profession when lawyer performed no real legal work beyond mailing out a form letter, lawyer made no effort to ensure that trusts were executed properly or that clients understood how they worked, and his negligence enabled his business associate to exploit elderly and vulnerable clients; but mitigating factors warranted a two-year suspension rather than disbarment).

**4.42 Suspension is generally appropriate when:**
**(a) a lawyer knowingly fails to perform services for a client and causes injury or potential injury to a client; or**
**(b) a lawyer engages in a pattern of neglect causes injury or potential injury to a client.**

## Annotation

Suspension should be imposed when a lawyer knows that he or she is not performing the services he or she was retained to complete or when a lawyer engages in a pattern of neglect resulting in injury or potential injury to a client. Frequently, the lawyer's neglect also involves the lawyer's failure to communicate with the client, to respond to the client's request for information or to return files and unearned fees or costs. *See, e.g., In the Matter of Johnson*, 815 S.E.2d 55 (Ga. 2018) (citing Standard 4.42, court suspended lawyer for six months for neglecting six separate matters and failing to communicate with the clients). Further, in many cases, the lawyer's neglect requires the client to seek alternate counsel to handle the matter at additional cost. In *People v. Staab*, 287 P.3d 122 (Colo. O.P.D.J. 2012), for example, the court, citing Standard 4.42, imposed a suspension of one year and one day on a lawyer who failed to exercise reasonable diligence and promptness by neglecting two clients' matters and failing to take appropriate measures upon termination of representation, among other misconduct. *See also In re Bankston*, 791 So.2d 1263 (La. 2001) (lawyer suspended for a year and a day for misconduct that included failure to communicate with the client about an adverse court order authorizing seizure of the client's automobile, in addition to failure to refund unused court costs of $334, and account for unearned fees); *In re DeJean*, 782 So.2d 566 (La. 2001) (one-year suspension for neglecting legal matter and failing to communicate with client, which caused delay of the client's matter but no permanent harm and lawyer agreed to take steps to improve his calendaring system to avoid such problems in the future); *In re Disciplinary Action Against Balerud*, 719 N.W.2d 329 (N.D. 2006) (lead counsel who missed meetings, including a scheduled mediation, was repeatedly late for court, disorganized at trial, and repetitious in questioning witnesses suspended for six months and one day); *Sneed v. Bd. of Prof'l Responsibility*, 37 S.W.3d 886 (Tenn. 2000) (rejecting lawyer's argument that he could not be disciplined for "negligent conduct," court suspended lawyer for six months for, inter alia, failing to apply for appellate court review of one client's criminal case despite telling client he had, and neglect of a federal court case resulting in dismissal of another client's case for failure to comply with discovery and other court orders; indefinite suspension imposed to allow lawyer to complete law office management and legal ethics courses); *Bd. of Prof'l Responsibility v. Cannon*, 189 P.3d 857

(Wyo. 2008) (two-month suspension under Standard 4.42 for several instances of failing to diligently pursue client matters, including failure to file domestic matter in timely manner and failure to pursue divorce to completion after filing petition so that client had to obtain alternate counsel).

## *Knowing Failure to Perform Services*

Like Standard 4.41(b), Standard 4.42(a) requires that the lawyer knowingly fail to perform services for a client. *See In re Sisk*, 54 A.3d 257 (Del. 2012) (in rejecting disciplinary board's recommendation of public reprimand, court noted that lawyer's conduct was knowing rather than negligent and imposed a six-month-and-one-day suspension for neglect of several clients' matters, including five-year delay in completing qualified domestic relations order); *In re Hult*, 410 P.3d 879 (Kan. 2018) (indefinite suspension for knowingly violating duty to immigration clients and failing to provide diligent representation, resulting in actual and serious injury to clients; court noted hearing panel's careful study of Standard 4.42, inter alia); *In re Discipline of Brohawn*, 413 P.3d 836 (Table) (Nev. 2018) (eighteen-month suspension pursuant to Standard 4.42, inter alia, for lawyer who knowingly accepted fees without performing legal work); *In re LaBahn*, 67 P.3d 381 (Or. 2003) (sixty-day suspension under Standard 4.42(a) for lawyer who knowingly neglected legal matter by failing to serve defendant in client's case, failing to file proof of service with court within statute of limitations, and failing to inform client for more than one year that court had dismissed his case); *In re Parker*, 9 P.3d 107 (Or. 2000) (four-year suspension for lawyer's "knowing" mental state in neglecting his law practice established by evidence in the record that his secretary sent him all his mail and telephone messages daily and repeatedly reminded him of obligations; mitigating factors warranted suspension rather than disbarment); *In re Disciplinary Proceeding Against Marshall*, 157 P.3d 859 (Wash. 2007), *aff'd* 217 P.3d 291 (Wash. 2009) (suspension presumptive sanction, under Standard 4.42(a), inter alia, for various misconduct including lawyer's failure to get authorization from clients to pursue an appeal; eighteen-month suspension imposed).

## *Pattern of Neglect*

A pattern of neglect warranting suspension under Standard 4.42(b) often emerges as a result of a lawyer's poor law-office management skills requiring the courts to, in addition to imposing a suspension, add a term of probation to monitor the lawyer's law practice. *See, e.g., In re Brady*, 387 P.3d 1 (Alaska 2016) (referencing Standard 4.42, court suspended lawyer for six months for failing to conduct pretrial discovery, meet court-imposed deadlines, file timely responsive pleadings, or pay sanctions, as a result of failing to control his work load overall); *In re Fox*, 66 A.3d 548, 555 (D.C. 2013) (without citing Standard 4.42, court imposed two-year suspension, the final year of which was stayed in favor of eighteen-months of probation, where "appointment of a practice monitor provides a thoughtful, targeted response to respondent's 'sloppy recordkeeping and a failure to communicate that resulted in his abandonment of his client's matters'"); *In re Beauchamp*, 821 So.2d 1281 (La. 2002) (one-year-and-one-day suspension, deferred in full by a period of probation, for lawyer for lack of diligence, failure to communicate, and failure to expedite litigation in multiple client matters; lawyer's actions were due to negligence and poor law-office management, and caused actual harm to clients by delaying their legal matters); *In re Holley*, 797 So.2d 46 (La. 2001) (under Standard 4.42, six-month suspension, with all but sixty days deferred followed by one-year probation, for lawyer who neglected clients' matters; misconduct was more negligent than intentional, as lawyer had just started practicing law by himself, was overwhelmed by running the law office, failed to establish efficient office procedures, and lacked necessary support staff and calendaring system); *Bd. of Prof'l Responsibility v. Abraham*, 376 P.3d 483 (Wyo. 2016) (six-month suspension with probation where a lawyer received a total of seventeen client complaints mostly resulting from lack of diligence).

It is worth noting that where a pattern of neglect has been established, a suspension may be warranted even if the conduct is negligent rather than knowing. *See Bd. of Prof'l Responsibility v. Hiatt*, 422 P.3d 940 (Wyo. 2018) (where attorney performed no work on a matter for three months and failed to return client communications, but only a negligent mental state was proven, a thirty-day suspension was imposed over a reprimand due to aggravating factors of refusal to acknowledge wrongdoing, obstructing disciplinary proceedings, and prior similar discipline for neglect); *In re Jones*, 487 N.W.2d 599 (N.D. 1992) (thirty-day suspension imposed for negligently failing to complete work where lawyer already had two private reprimands for similar conduct).

Under Standard 4.42(b), the conduct found to constitute a pattern of neglect resulting in suspension is wide ranging. It includes lawyers who neglect client matters during a single time period to those who neglect only one matter, but do so for many years. *See, e.g., Fla. Bar v. Petersen*, 2018 Fla. Lexis 1378 (Fla. 2018) (after considering Florida Standard 4.42, inter alia, three-year suspension for failing to prosecute a case for two years, resulting in dismissal, with court noting that the more severe suspension was given based on a pattern of neglect); *In re Disciplinary Action Against Britton*, 484 N.W.2d 110, 112 (N.D. 1992) (repetition of the same sort of misconduct as lawyer has previously engaged in indicated "an intractable pattern of neglect"; court concluded that respondent's misconduct warranted two-year suspension under Standard 4.42(b), inter alia); *Disciplinary Counsel v. Ranke*, 956 N.E.2d 288 (Ohio 2011) (indefinite suspension imposed for lawyer who never filed a criminal appellate brief despite four extensions of time, resulting in the client's appeal being dismissed, with aggravating factors of prior public censure for similar neglect); *In re Knappenberger*, 135 P.3d 297, 301 (Or. 2006) (one-year suspension under Standard 4.42 for lawyer's failure to finalize a domestic relations order for more than eight years supported finding that lawyer engaged in "a course of neglectful conduct"); *In re Blais,* 817 A.2d 1266 (Vt. 2002) (five-month suspension under Standard 4.42 appropriate for misconduct consisting of five instances of neglecting client matters); *In the Matter of the Suspension of Maynard,* 2018 WL 2938633 (V.I. June 8, 2018) (suspending lawyer for eighteen months for failure to prosecute an estate administration matter for more than a decade, demonstrating a pattern of neglect); *In re Disciplinary Proceeding Against Kagele,* 72 P.3d 1067 (Wash. 2003) (eight different instances of failure to act diligently and promptly to pursue client matters established pattern of neglect warranting one-year suspension under Standard 4.42(b)).

A lawyer also may be found to have engaged in a pattern of neglect if the lawyer fails to properly supervise his or her employees. *See, e.g., People v. Smith,* 74 P.3d 566 (Colo. O.P.D.J. 2003) (solo practitioner with large-volume practice, about half of it devoted to domestic relations law, failed to properly supervise his paralegal, who was allowed to oversee client's divorce case during period of tweny-seven months; pattern of neglect established and nine-month suspension under Standard 4.42(b) imposed).

### *Misleading Clients About Neglectful Representation*

Lawyers who not only neglect client matters but also mislead clients about the status of their cases or fail to make any effort to keep clients informed of the status of their matters may face long periods of suspension. *See, e.g., People v. Yost,* 729 P.2d 348 (Colo. 1986) (citing Standard 4.42, inter alia, court said that respondent not only knew of his neglect of legal matters but attempted to mislead his clients and the grievance committee with false documents; three-year suspension warranted); *People v. Muhr,* 370 P.3d 677 (Colo. O.P.D.J. 2016) (after considering Standard 4.42, inter alia, lawyer suspended for one year and one day for allowing a client's statute of limitations to expire before settling the case or filing suit and directing staff to provide a settlement check to the client nonetheless, misleading the client to believe that her case had been settled); *In re Daniels,* 159 P.3d 995 (Kan. 2007) (one-year suspension under Standard 4.42, inter alia, for lawyer's misconduct in connection with his representation of client in case involving the death of her daughter, including lawyer's failure to file suit on behalf of client until after statute of limitations expired and providing false information to client regarding status of her case); *In re Butler,* 921 P.2d 401 (Or. 1996) (lawyer's effort to mislead his client regarding the status of legal matter, saying that he was working on case when he knew that court had dismissed it, aggravated his misconduct under Standard 4.42, which included failing to avoid dismissal of client's case on limitations grounds and failing to keep client fully apprised of status of case; one-year suspension warranted).

## *Injury or Potential Injury Warranting Suspension*

"Injury or potential injury" under Standard 4.42 may include a client suffering monetary losses or incurring additional costs when forced to hire another lawyer to handle the matter. *See, e.g., People v. Schmeiser,* 35 P.3d 560 (Colo. O.P.D.J. 2001) (one-year suspension for neglecting case and allowing critical deadlines to pass, resulting in clients being exposed to interest and penalties from taxing authorities and having to secure replacement counsel with attendant increase in attorney's fees); *In re Hult,* 410 P.3d 879 (Kan. 2018) (indefinite suspension warranted for lawyer's misconduct in handling multiple client matters, including neglect and misrepresentation, causing serious financial injury by failing to refund attorney's fees and failing to satisfy a malpractice action judgment); *In re Renfroe,* 800 So.2d 371 (La. 2001) (lawyer's neglect of client matter resulted in actual harm of additional time and expense for client in obtaining alternate counsel and warranted six-month suspension); *Nevin v. Bd. of Prof'l Responsibility,* 271 S.W.3d 648 (Tenn. 2008) (six-month suspension for lawyer who failed to discharge his duties with reasonable diligence and caused both actual injury and potential injury; lawyer's failure to document his transactions involving client trust-account funds ultimately led to his owing $25,000 to client for whom he was appointed conservator, and his misconduct with regard to four-year-old child for whom he was appointed guardian *ad litem* resulted in loss of child's home).

"Injury" also may include a delay incurred by the client in receiving a settlement or property to which he or she is entitled, as well as missed opportunities to resolve a legal matter resulting in the client's needless worry, frustration, and anxiety. *See, e.g., In re Thompson,* 911 A.2d 373 (Del. 2006) (three-year suspension and public reprimand for lawyer whose misconduct included failure to make timely filings in divorce matter resulting in substantial delay before client was awarded the equity of her marital home); *In re Koch,* 198 P.3d 910, 917 (Or. 2008) (although lawyer's clients did not suffer any monetary loss or lost opportunity, her "repeated failure to respond to her clients' reasonable requests did result in injuries to her clients, 'measured in terms of time, anxiety, and aggravation, in attempting to coax cooperation from the accused'" (citation omitted); 120-day suspension imposed); *In re Redden,* 153 P.3d 113 (Or. 2007) (sixty-day suspension when lawyer's sustained neglect resulted in client's lost opportunity to enter into favorable settlement; citing Standards 4.4 and 4.42(a)); *In re Walwyn,* 531 S.W.3d 131 (Tenn. 2017) (finding that misconduct fits neatly under Standard 4.42, court suspended lawyer for failing to file a notice of appeal for more than three years, initially due to lack of calendaring but then due to knowing delay while "searching" for a substitute appellate lawyer; lawyer's belief that the client would always be able to file late was not reasonable).

In addition to considering the injury suffered by a client, courts may consider the injury to the legal system or the profession caused by a lawyer's neglect of client matters. *See People v. Powell,* 37 P.3d 545 (Colo. O.P.D.J. 2001) (lawyer suspended for one year and a day for failure to keep clients reasonably informed about the status of a legal matter and properly comply with reasonable requests for information; his abandonment of one client's case and his failure to update home and business addresses injured not only the client but also the profession as a whole); *In re Weybright*, 656 N.E.2d 1142, 1145 (Ind. 1995) (three-year suspension warranted for lawyer who abandoned clients' cases without taking steps reasonably practical to protect their interests, caused monetary losses, needless anxiety, legal harm, great inconvenience, and "greatly damage[d] the perception of the legal profession as a whole and tarnish[ed] an image of professionalism and dedication a majority of practitioners strive to foster and uphold"); *In re Disciplinary Proceeding Against Lopez*, 106 P.3d 221 (Wash. 2005) (lawyer's failure to file opening brief in client's criminal appeal caused actual and potential injury to client by subjecting appeal to potential dismissal and injury to the legal system by having the court issue eight notices and/or orders to motivate lawyer to take action on client's behalf; sixty-day suspension appropriate).

Standard 4.42 has also been applied to judicial misconduct, where there may be injury to the legal system caused by a judge's neglect. In *In re Estelle*, the Alaska Supreme Court suspended a trial judge for forty-five days without pay for failing to decide matters in a timely manner and for signing pay affidavits incorrectly asserting that no matters were pending longer than six months. 336 P.3d 692 (Alaska 2014). The court found that the judge acted recklessly by being aware of his pending caseload but disregarding the risk that the pay affidavits were incorrect, specifically causing "actual injury to the public's perception of the integrity of the judiciary." *Id.* at 697.

## *Abandonment of Practice*

Under Standard 4.42, there is no specific provision for imposing suspension in the case of abandonment of practice, as there is for imposing disbarment under Standard 4.41(a). Nonetheless, several courts have addressed abandonment under Standard 4.42, and imposed suspension as the sanction. In *People v. Carvell*, 62 P.3d 167 (Colo. O.P.D.J. 2000), the court stated:

> To find abandonment rather than merely neglect, there must be proof that the attorney—during a given time period—was required to accomplish specific professional tasks for the client, failed to accomplish those tasks, and failed to communicate with the client. The proof must objectively indicate that the attorney has deserted, rejected and/or relinquished the professional responsibilities owed to the client.

*Id.* at 170–71. Citing Standard 4.42, the court imposed suspension for one year and one day since lawyer abandoned one client when he neglected client's divorce case at a critical stage of the court proceedings, depriving client of having a meaningful final orders hearing. *See also In re Vaughan,* 801 So.2d 1058 (La. 2001) (three-year suspension under Standard 4.42, inter alia, for abandoning law practice without informing client, resulting in client being deprived of legal counsel and files in a contested child-support matter); *In re Romero,* 22 P.3d 215 (N.M. 2001) (indefinite suspension under Standard 4.42 warranted for pattern of neglect when lawyer abandoned six clients in their personal injury matters by failing to file or prosecute claims, communicate with clients, respond to requests for information, and return clients' files).

**4.43 Reprimand is generally appropriate when a lawyer is negligent and does not act with reasonable diligence in representing a client, and causes injury or potential injury to a client.**

## Annotation

Most courts impose a reprimand (or public censure) when a lawyer has been negligent in failing to act with reasonable diligence or timely refund unearned fees. For example, in *In re Elgart*, 999 A.2d 853 (Del. 2010), a lawyer was publicly reprimanded for failing to disburse insurance proceeds to personal injury client until seven years after the funds were received by the firm. The court found that the mistake was due to the lawyer's negligence and poor recordkeeping. *See also In re Beardsley*, 658 N.E.2d 591, 592 (Ind. 1995) (during administration of estate, which was open seventeen years, lawyer did not keep co-executors informed of status, failed to return phone calls, refused to meet with them, and allowed a former employee, who subsequently died, to handle duties associated with processing the estate with little supervision; although no indication that clients were harmed by lawyer's misconduct, potential for harm existed and clients were "fortunate that no actual harm occurred"); *In re Wall*, 38 P.3d 640 (Kan. 2002) (lawyer who let statute of limitations on client's personal injury claim expire caused significant potential injury to client who was seriously injured in a car accident; public censure rather than a more serious sanction imposed because client appeared to have a malpractice action against lawyer); *In re Thomson*, 698 S.E.2d 625 (S.C. 2010) (public reprimand warranted for lawyer who failed to promptly respond to client's request for information and refund unearned fees); *In re Andres*, 749 A.2d 618 (Vt. 2000) (public reprimand, under Standard 4.43, inter alia, for neglect of one client's matter resulting in loss of client's right to pursue appeal of an adverse decision and in another client's matter, lawyer filed a series of motions to continue child-support case instead of diligently pursuing the matter); *Bd. of Prof'l Responsibility v. Abraham*, 149 P.3d 456 (Wyo. 2006), *aff'd* 221 P.3d 960 (Wyo. 2009) (public censure under Standard 4.43 appropriate sanction for lawyer who failed to diligently pursue three separate cases).

A frequent basis for reprimand is a lawyer's failure to timely file pleadings in one or more cases. *See Disciplinary Bd. v. Landon*, 600 N.W.2d 856 (N.D. 1999) (citing North Dakota Standard 4.43, court reprimanded lawyer and ordered restitution where lawyer failed to respond to a motion for summary judgment or a subsequent motion to vacate or alter and the client's case was dismissed); *Cleveland Metro Bar Ass'n v. Ranke*, 937 N.E.2d 84, 88 (Ohio 2010) ("repeated failures to respond to discovery requests, motions to exclude and to dismiss, and the dismissal of a case without the client's consent demonstrate a pattern of neglect"; public censure warranted); *In re Scholes*, 54 A.3d 520, 524 (Vt. 2012) (lawyer's conduct in not filing bankruptcy petitions for three clients until more than twenty months had passed in each client's case warranted public reprimand; court stated that "[i]n these three cases, there does not appear to be any financial injury, but there is the very real anxiety felt by the clients who wanted to move their bankruptcy petitions to conclusion."); *Bd. of Prof'l Responsibility v.Johnson*, 355 P.3d 1234 (Wyo. 2015) (lawyer was publicly censured for failing to appear for hearings, proposing a plea agreement without reviewing discoverable material that would have exonerated the client, and failing to communicate with the client; court approved board's recommendation, which cited Standard 4.43); *Bd. of Prof'l Responsibility v. Keenan*, 148 P.3d 1 (Wyo. 2006) (stipulated public censure under Standard 4.43 for failure to diligently pursue three legal matters for clients, including failure to file petition lawyer had drafted, draft orders as assigned by judge, and pursue a matter after obtaining default judgment).

A lawyer's negligence may be due to being understaffed, taking on more work than he or she can handle, or mental-health issues. *See, e.g., In re Young*, 84 A.D.3d 29, 32 (N.Y. App. Div. 2011) (rejecting hearing panel's recommendation of a six-month suspension, court determined public censure appropriate "in light of the nonvenal nature of respondent's misconduct" and that neglect of client's matter attributed to attention deficit disorder); *In re Cohen*, 8 P.3d 953, 964 (Or. 2000) (public reprimand instead of suspension warranted for lawyer who "aggressively and successfully address[ed] his mental health problems and the deficiencies in his office practices that led to his misconduct," notwithstanding repeated instances of neglect; court noting only actual injury to client was that of anxiety and frustration); *In re McCarty*, 649 A.2d 764 (Vt. 1994) (public reprimand under Standard 4.43 for lawyer who neglected at least two clients after his two associates left the practice at the same time; lawyer did not purposely fail to meet client needs, but also did not take any action to alleviate the situation by obtaining additional help or voluntarily withdrawing from noncritical matters and, instead, simply reacted to emergencies rather than review pending matters to set priorities).

In imposing a public reprimand rather than a more severe sanction, a court may take into consideration the fact that the lawyer remediated the injury to the client by returning unearned fees. *See, e.g., In re Wilson*, 672 N.E.2d 931 (Ind. 1996) (approving agreement to reprimand for neglect when lawyer in two cases failed to act with reasonable promptness and diligence, inter alia, but did not retain any unearned fees; citing Standard 4.43 recommendation of public reprimand for negligent misconduct); *In re Schneider*, 404 P.3d 338 (Kan. 2017) (noting hearing panel's thorough consideration of Standard 4.43, court imposed public censure for failure to properly handle client's bankruptcy petition and failure to timely respond to motions and discovery requests; lawyer demonstrated remorse, cooperation, and restitution, including taking actions to improve diligence through improved calendaring); *In the Matter of Thomas*, 159 A.D.3d 35 (N.Y. App. Div. 2018) (lawyer received a less severe sanction of censure due to mitigation evidence and no evidence of client harm; Sanctions Standards not cited).

**4.44 Admonition is generally appropriate when a lawyer is negligent and does not act with reasonable diligence in representing a client, and causes little or no actual or potential injury to a client.**

## Annotation

Admonition will be imposed when a lawyer's failure to act diligently in representing a client is due to the lawyer's negligence, resulting in little or no actual or potential damage to the client. *See In re Baldwin*, 685 N.E.2d 1069 (Ind. 1997) (citing Standard 4.4, admonishment and reprimand for lawyer, hired by client to collect past-due rent, who silently retained garnished funds in his trust account, depriving his client of the relief sought for an extended period and forcing his client to take affirmative steps to learn the status of the matter; lawyer delivered to his client all funds due and admitted his misconduct). *But see, e.g., In re Bristol*, 142 P.3d 905 (N.M. 2006) (rejecting hearing committee recommendation that lawyer receive a private, informal admonition under the Sanctions Standards when lawyer's acts and omissions contributed to the revocation of a client's discharge in bankruptcy; public censure instead); *In re Scholes*, 54 A.3d 520, 524 (Vt. 2012) ("In distinguishing neglect cases in which admonition is imposed and those in which the sanction is public reprimand, hearing panels have looked at the number of clients involved, the duration of the neglect, the injury to the client, and the aggravating and mitigating factors"; imposing public reprimand where the neglect involved three clients and lasted several years, even though no financial injury but "very real anxiety" for the clients whose cases were lingering; admonition is typically imposed "where the delay was short and one or a very few client matters [were] involved").

## 4.5 Lack of Competence

**Absent aggravating or mitigating circumstances, upon application of the factors set out in Standard 3.0, the following sanctions are generally appropriate in cases involving failure to provide competent representation to a client:**

**4.51 Disbarment is generally appropriate when a lawyer's course of conduct demonstrates that the lawyer does not understand the most fundamental legal doctrines or procedures, and the lawyer's conduct causes injury or potential injury to a client.**

## Annotation

Disbarment should be imposed on a lawyer who engages in multiple instances of incompetent behavior as well as on a lawyer whose course of conduct demonstrates that he or she cannot or will not master the knowledge and skills necessary for competent practice. *See, e.g., Fla. Bar v. Springer,* 873 So.2d 317, 322 n.1 (Fla. 2004) (disbarment warranted for lawyer's multiple instances of failing to provide competent representation, failing to act with reasonable diligence, failing to keep client reasonably informed, and misrepresenting to client the status of the client's matter; court held that lawyer "did more than just venture ill-prepared into a new area of the law" but "simply totally failed to perform, or incompetently performed, the basic tasks of his profession which he accepted and agreed to complete").

Disbarment may be appropriate when a lawyer demonstrates a lack of competence, in one case or several, while also violating other ethics rules. For example, a lawyer's lack of competence combined with a failure to keep clients informed as to the status of their cases, respond to their requests for information, or diligently handle their matters can result in disbarment. *See, e.g., People v. Varallo,* 61 P.3d 38 (Colo. O.P.D.J. 2002) (disbarring a lawyer for a pattern and practice of incompetence and neglect, including failing to communicate with and ultimately abandoning six members of an Armenian family that he represented in an immigration matter who faced removal from this country); *In re Powell,* 893 N.E.2d 729 (Ind. 2008) (citing Standard 4.51, inter alia, court held disbarment appropriate sanction for lawyer's misconduct, which included failing to take action in cases, failing to keep clients informed about status of their cases, failing to respond to clients' requests for information, accepting a settlement without a client's approval, giving clients erroneous legal advice, failing to appear at hearings in clients' cases, missing deadlines in clients' cases, and misrepresenting extent of professional experience); *In re Hawver,* 339 P.3d 573 (Kan. 2014) (disbarment under Standard 4.51 appropriate for lawyer who, in capital murder case, demonstrated lack of competence by, inter alia, failing to obtain training about how to handle capital murder trials and by failing to: file required notice of alibi, challenge constitutional validity of death penalty, conduct investigations for the guilt and penalty phases of trial, and death/life qualify jury); *In re Bishop*, 240 P.3d 956 (Kan. 2010) (citing Standard 4.51, inter alia, court found disbarment warranted for misconduct that included failure to seek to have a client's debt to an unlisted creditor discharged in bankruptcy while client's bankruptcy case remained open, failure to diligently and promptly represent the client when the creditor filed lawsuit against client to collect debt, and filing answer to creditor's collection action asserting that the debt had been discharged in bankruptcy when the lawyer believed it had not been); *In re Disciplinary Action Against Keller*, 652 N.W.2d 308 (N.D. 2002) (disbarring lawyer for misconduct in four client matters involving nine complaints, including unauthorized practice of law, charging excessive fees, dishonesty concerning amounts lawyer paid himself from client's account, failure to comply with order to produce records to conservator of estate, as well as incompetent handling of client's property-tax matter by failing to correct error after wrong lot was reassessed and sold for unpaid taxes).

**4.52 Suspension is generally appropriate when a lawyer engages in an area of practice in which the lawyer knows he or she is not competent, and causes injury or potential injury to a client.**

## Annotation

### *Incompetence in an Area of Law*

In order to protect the public, a suspension should be imposed when a lawyer practices in areas of the law in which a lawyer knows that he or she is not competent. *See In re Bradley*, 875 So.2d 67 (La. 2004) (lawyer suspended for eighteen months after accepting a criminal case despite knowing that he had not practiced criminal law for twenty years and had not kept abreast of either the substantive or procedural changes in criminal law); *see also In re Richmond's Case*, 872 A.2d 1023, 1029 (N.H. 2005) (lawyer suspended for six months; numerous errors in conducting stock offerings and inadequately preparing the appropriate forms "demonstrate his lack of knowledge about securities law practice"); *In re Ramirez*, 408 P.3d 1065, 1071 (Or. 2018) (lawyer suspended for one year pursuant to Standard 4.52, inter alia, for conduct including failure to competently represent plaintiff in collection matter by making same mistake three times in trying to foreclose on collateral property; court found that lawyer had a "conscious awareness" he lacked competence to handle matter).

Suspension probably will be imposed when the evidence shows that the lawyer failed to understand relevant legal doctrines or procedures or failed to adequately prepare for a case. *See People v. Bontrager*, 407 P.3d 1235, 1277 (Colo. O.P.D.J. 2017) (under Standard 4.52, lawyer suspended for nine months for incompetent representation and filing frivolous claims in multiple oil and gas cases, resulting in multiple sanctions by judges; "Regardless of whether Respondent agreed with these judicial rulings, they were certainly enough to give a reasonable lawyer conscious awareness that continued pursuit of those claims might subject him to disciplinary sanctions. Thus, we conclude that Respondent should have known that he was pursuing frivolous claims and providing incompetent representation for his five clients."); *In re Eadie*, 36 P.3d 468, 480 (Or. 2001) (suspending lawyer for three years for misconduct including incompetence when records from two cases revealed lawyer failed to understand relevant legal documents or procedures and demonstrated lack of skill and preparation; court noted that "incompetence often is found where there is a lack of basic knowledge or preparation, or a combination of those factors") (citation omitted). *But see In re Sylvester*, 144 P.3d 697 (Kan. 2006) (public reprimand imposed rather than a ninety-day suspension, as recommended by the hearing panel, on lawyer who primarily practiced criminal law for lack of competence and diligence in handling a client's patent application and failure to keep the client informed that the application had been abandoned; court took into consideration that the United States Patent and Trademark Office had suspended the lawyer's license to practice and required him to retake the patent bar exam before his license could be reinstated).

## *Conditions to Reinstatement*

When a lawyer is suspended for incompetence, some courts will attach conditions to the suspension, such as a requirement that the lawyer complete classes in legal ethics, law practice management, or other subjects. *See, e.g., In re Wolfram*, 847 P.2d 94 (Ariz. 1993) (lack of competent investigation and preparation of defense, among other misconduct, warranted suspension and additional twenty-four hours of CLE); *Sneed v. Bd. of Prof'l Responsibility*, 37 S.W.3d 886 (Tenn. 2000) (lawyer's suspension would not end until he completed courses provided by the Board of Professional Responsibility); *In re Disciplinary Proceeding Against Longacre*, 122 P.3d 710 (Wash. 2005) (requiring lawyer who was suspended for sixty days for incompetent representation of a criminal client to obtain thirty hours of CLE credit in the area of criminal law and procedure).

## *Extension of Probation*

When a lawyer is already on probation with a corresponding stayed suspension, some courts will extend the period of probation instead of activating the stayed suspension where the lawyer is found to have engaged in additional misconduct involving lack of competence. *See, e.g., In re Forck*, 418 S.W.3d 437 (Mo. 2014) (probation would be extended instead of stayed suspension being imposed for lawyer who failed to, inter alia, provide competent representation in estate matters; court found negligent state of mind for sanction purposes even where lawyer knowingly advertised that he and his firm had expertise in estate planning law; court explained that evidence showed lawyer only did so, despite inexperience in this area of law, upon urging from experienced counsel).

**4.53 Reprimand is generally appropriate when a lawyer:**

**(a) demonstrates failure to understand relevant legal doctrines or procedures and causes injury or potential injury to a client; or**

**(b) is negligent in determining whether he or she is competent to handle a legal matter and causes injury or potential injury to a client.**

## Annotation

### *Failure to Understand Relevant Legal Doctrines*

Reprimand is appropriate for a lawyer who demonstrates that he or she does not understand relevant legal doctrines or procedures; resulting in injury or potential injury to a client. *See In re Dillon*, 176 A.3d 716 (Table) (Del. 2017) (lawyer reprimanded under Standard 4.53, inter alia, for misconduct including failure to understand requirements of procedures regarding perfection of service on parties and timely filing of motions to extend time for obtaining service; lawyer failed to locate defendants in seventeen matters and to timely file requests for extensions of time to do so, resulting in dismissals without prejudice of four of those matters and causing potential injury to clients); *In re Myers*, 127 P.3d 325 (Kan. 2006) (public censure for lawyer who failed to provide competent representation of couple in estate planning, created trust documents that failed to accomplish goals of estate plan, which included preserving assets if wife required nursing home care, and encouraged clients' daughter to appeal denial of wife's application for Medicaid benefits, despite well-established law contradicting the appellate claims; finding that conduct caused actual injury); *In re Disciplinary Proceeding Against Kagele*, 72 P.3d 1067 (Wash. 2003) (as to lawyer's lack of competence in filing a complaint that contained numerous errors and in failing to review the complaint with the clients prior to filing, reprimand was presumptive sanction under Standard 4.53; ultimately suspension and reprimand imposed for all lawyer's misconduct including pattern of neglect). *But see People v. Beecher*, 350 P.3d 310 (Colo. O.P.D.J. 2014) (finding that both Standards 4.53 and 6.22 applied, disciplinary judge followed recommendation in Sanctions Standards that ultimate sanction ought to be consistent with that for most serious misconduct and suspended lawyer for six months with reinstatement required; lawyer's conduct that fell under Standard 4.53 was incompetent advice to client in criminal matter not to appear for bond-returnable pretrial conference when condition of client's pretrial supervision was requirement to appear; disciplinary judge rejected lawyer's claim that advice to client to not appear was to protect client in event client's abusive ex-husband appeared).

## *Negligence in Determining Competence*

A reprimand is also the appropriate sanction when a lawyer is negligent in determining whether he or she is competent to handle a client's matter and that negligence injures or potentially injures the client. *See In re Polsley*, 61 P.3d 715 (Kan. 2003) (public censure for lawyer found negligent in determining whether he was competent to handle an estate case and a legal malpractice matter against the estate's former lawyer). In *State ex rel. Counsel for Discipline v. Orr*, 759 N.W.2d 702 (Neb. 2009), the Nebraska Supreme Court publicly reprimanded a lawyer, a general practitioner, who negligently determined that he was competent to represent a client who wanted to franchise coffee shops. The court held:

> As a lawyer who has been practicing law for 40 years, [respondent] should have been aware that he was not competent to represent franchisors, and he was warned by another attorney that franchise law was a specialized area. At the very least, [he] should have done the research necessary to become competent in the area of franchise law. The fact that [he] did little or no research into state or federal franchising law until long after he first received notice that there was a problem with the franchising documents is inexcusable.

*Id.* at 709; *see also State ex rel. Counsel for Discipline v. Pinard-Cronin*, 743 N.W.2d 649 (Neb. 2008) (public reprimand for lawyer whose practice focused on juvenile and family law but who accepted a personal injury case and failed to timely serve the defendant, resulting in the action being dismissed after the statute of limitations had run, failed to respond to telephone calls from the client, and failed to inform client that his lawsuit had been dismissed).

**4.54 Admonition is generally appropriate when a lawyer engages in an isolated instance of negligence in determining whether he or she is competent to handle a legal matter, and causes little or no actual or potential injury to a client.**

## Annotation

While a reprimand might be the appropriate discipline for a lawyer who is negligent in evaluating his or her competence to handle a legal matter (see Annotation to Standard 4.53(b)), a lawyer may be admonished rather than publicly disciplined when the misconduct is an isolated incident. In *In re Curtis*, 908 P.2d 472 (Ariz. 1995), a lawyer was retained to lift a bankruptcy stay against a contractor so that the lawyer's client could pursue a claim against the Contractor's Recovery Fund. The lawyer failed to investigate the elements of the claim, determine what evidence was needed to support it, and request that information from the client. "If Respondent was not competent to handle the claim he had the duty to become competent or not take the case," the court said. *Id.* at 477. Both the hearing board and disciplinary commission recommended suspension, but the court, citing Standard 4.54, inter alia, suggested that admonition was the more appropriate sanction. Because Arizona disciplinary rules do not provide for admonition, however, the court decided upon censure.

**4.6 Lack of Candor**
**Absent aggravating or mitigating circumstances, upon application of the factors set out in Standard 3.0, the following sanctions are generally appropriate in cases where the lawyer engages in fraud, deceit, or misrepresentation directed toward a client:**

**4.61 Disbarment is generally appropriate when a lawyer knowingly deceives a client with the intent to benefit the lawyer or another, and causes serious injury or potentially serious injury to a client.**

## Annotation

### *Deception Regarding Status of Case*

Disbarment is appropriate when a lawyer knowingly abuses the fiduciary relationship by deceiving a client with the intent to benefit himself, herself, or another, and causes serious injury or potentially serious injury to a client. For example, a lawyer may face disbarment for deceiving clients about the status of their legal matters. *See People v. Essay*, 35 P.3d 590, 592 (Colo. O.P.D.J. 2001) (finding lawyer engaged in "prohibited conduct knowing that it violated his responsibilities as an attorney and with the intent to benefit himself at the expense of his clients," court imposed disbarment for knowing misrepresentations in five separate matters in which lawyer told clients he was in settlement discussions and would soon resolve their cases, in some instances for very large amounts of money, when he had, in fact, taken little if any action; in several cases, while clients were in his office, lawyer fabricated telephone conferences with a judge and opposing counsel, intending the clients to believe that he was working on their cases when he was not; in one matter, two elderly sisters paid the lawyer a monthly amount for his fees, and he knowingly converted this amount to his own use); *State ex rel. Counsel for Discipline v. Thew*, 794 N.W.2d 412 (Neb. 2011) (lawyer who engaged in a series of ethical breaches including neglecting client matters, making false and misleading statements to clients, and creating false documents to hide his procrastination was disbarred); *In re Disciplinary Proceeding Against Marshall*, 217 P.3d 291, 310 (Wash. 2009) (lawyer disbarred under Standard 4.61, inter alia, for misconduct including attempting "to squeeze his clients for additional fees" and "bully his clients into settling their claims"; lawyer sought additional fees from clients after entering into flat-fee agreement and told clients that despite their reluctance to sign settlement agreement their claims had been dismissed when in fact the trial court had never directed clients to sign agreement nor did any order of dismissal appear in the docket). *But see People v. Muhr*, 370 P.3d 677, 698 n. 126 (Colo. O.P.D.J. 2016) (concluding Standard 4.61 was not applicable although lawyer deceived client with intent to benefit himself when lawyer concealed mistake in allowing statute of limitations on client's matter to expire; there was no finding that lawyer seriously or potentially seriously harmed her client, and client's malpractice lawyer acknowledged that client's injuries were "minimal to moderate").

Other types of misrepresentations warranting disbarment may include a lawyer's knowing deception about the status of law license, handling client trust funds, or the legal services provided by the lawyer. *See, e.g., In re Collins*, 403 P.3d 1076 (Alaska 2017) (citing Standard 4.61, inter alia, court disbarred lawyer who misappropriated settlement funds and advanced fees in two matters and represented client in a third matter when lawyer was suspended); *People v. Auer*, 332 P.3d 136 (Colo. O.P.D.J. 2014) (citing Standard 4.61, inter alia, and disbarring lawyer, a certified public accountant, for falsely holding himself out as licensed Colorado lawyer repeatedly, establishing multiple law offices, drafting legal documents, offering legal advice, and misrepresenting to clients his licensure status in the state); *People v. Corbin*, 82 P.3d 373 (Colo. O.P.D.J. 2003) (disbarring lawyer under Standard 4.61 for ignoring suspension order, filing twelve applications for trademarks, and misrepresenting to clients that he was still authorized to practice law); *People v. Poll*, 65 P.3d 483 (Colo. O.P.D.J. 2003) (citing Standard 4.61, inter alia, court found disbarment warranted for lawyer who neglected clients' case, including falsely telling them that an order of sanctions against them could be appealed and that he had filed an appeal); *In re Hamer*, 808 S.E.2d 647 (Ga. 2017) (disbarment appropriate under Standard 4.61, inter alia, for lawyer who knowingly failed to provide services to a client, engaged in pattern of neglect, knowingly deceived client with the intent to benefit himself, and dealt improperly with client property); *In re Weaver*, 281 P.3d 502 (Kan. 2012) (disbarment warranted, under Standard 4.61, inter alia, for lawyer who assisted in the unauthorized practice of law by associating with a loan modification company, engaged in dishonest predatory conduct by assuring clients he offered a nationwide network of lawyers for mortgage assistance, falsely guaranteed refund of fees if clients' loans were not modified, and falsely advertised other legal services; conduct caused actual serious injury to vulnerable clients in dire financial straits); *In re Wolterbeek's Case*, 886 A.2d 990, 993 (N.H. 2005) (citing Standard 4.61, inter alia, disbarment imposed on lawyer who deceived client for his own personal gain by acquiring from bank three mortgages held on client's property and presenting client with quitclaim deed transferring title of property to company owned by lawyer without full disclosure); *In re Disciplinary Action Against Keller*, 652 N.W.2d 308 (N.D. 2002) (citing Standard 4.61, inter alia, court imposed disbarment for lawyer's multiple violations, including failing to inform clients that his law license was suspended and numerous acts of dishonesty involving client trust funds, misinformation regarding clients' legal matters, and the amounts lawyer paid himself from client's account). *But see People v. Edwards*, 240 P.3d 1287 (Colo. O.P.D.J. 2010) (court finding that Standard 4.61 was not applicable since there was no allegation that lawyer intended to benefit himself or another when he misrepresented to client that he was unable to continue with client's matter because he was called to military duty when in fact lawyer was suspended from the practice of law; disbarment imposed for other misconduct).

## *Deception Regarding Settlement Funds*

Many cases citing Standard 4.61 as grounds for disbarment also involve a lawyer's misappropriation of client funds for his or her own benefit. *See People v. Haines*, 179 P.3d 1021 (Colo. O.P.D.J. 2006) (lawyer disbarred for misappropriating $70,000 in settlement proceeds of one of estate's claims; without giving co-counsel or client an opportunity to exercise their respective rights under the contingency agreement; lawyer's conduct was deceitful even if she could claim administrative fees for estate work earned on an hourly basis outside of the contingency fee agreement); *In re Stochel*, 34 N.E.3d 1207 (Ind. 2015) (lawyer disbarred for stealing hundreds of thousands of dollars from receivership and tens of thousands of dollars from former law partner and that partner's clients; in receivership case, court found the lawyer covered up theft for nearly a decade, deceived the court, later defied its orders, and actively obstructed the disciplinary process). *See In re Brown*, 766 N.E.2d 363 (Ind. 2002) (disbarment warranted for misconduct in three client matters, including forgery of a client's signature and theft of a client's portion of settlement from her case; lawyer engaged in a series of transactions aimed at stealing his client's funds without detection); *In re Disciplinary Action Against Buresh*, 726 N.W.2d 210 (N.D. 2007) (disbarment under Standard 4.61, inter alia, appropriate for lawyer who repeatedly and blatantly lied to client when she inquired about the status of her settlement funds and deceived her into believing her funds were forthcoming, with promises that the check had been mailed, to buy himself time to replenish his trust account after lawyer misused client's funds to cover his own financial crisis); *In re Hunter*, 769 A.2d 1286 (Vt. 2000) (lawyer's repeated misuse of client funds for his own benefit and lying to clients, other lawyers, and the court to cover up his misconduct warranted disbarment when lawyer previously had received maximum sanction short of disbarment for other less serious misconduct, some of which occurred while last disciplinary action was pending, indicating that the last sanction or its threat was inadequate to deter continuing misconduct). *But see In re Cohen*, 406 P.3d 958 (Nev. 2017) (although Standard 4.61 applicable when lawyer sought and obtained reimbursement for expenses that he did not actually incur during the course of representing insurance client and fraudulently billed client for four years, court found that mitigating factors warranted suspension); *Napolitano v. Bd. of Prof'l Responsibility*, 535 S.W.3d 481 (Tenn. 2017) (finding Standard 4.61 incorrectly applied by hearing panel because lawyer not charged with or found to have deceived client, but failed to maintain funds in trust account as required and converted those funds).

**4.62 Suspension is generally appropriate when a lawyer knowingly deceives a client, and causes injury or potential injury to the client.**

## Annotation

### *Misrepresentation Regarding Nature and Extent of Legal Services Performed*

Suspension is appropriate when a lawyer knowingly deceives a client, although not necessarily for his or her own benefit, and the client is injured. The most common cases are those in which a lawyer misrepresents the nature or the extent of services performed. *See In re Hanlon,* 110 P.3d 937, 941 (Alaska 2005) (lawyer suspended for three years under Standard 4.6, inter alia, for neglecting a client matter, knowingly providing misleading information to client, and then fabricating a "settlement" from the lawyer's own funds in attempt to avoid malpractice liability; disciplinary committee noted suspension was more appropriate than disbarment, considering several factors including that harm to client did not amount to "serious injury or potential serious injury"); *In re Henry,* 2017 WL 2874461 (Bankr. D. Alaska July 5, 2017) (citing Standard 4.62, lawyer suspended from practicing in Bankruptcy Court for one year for attempting to conceal failure to timely file client's bankruptcy petition; lawyer filed petition more than nineteen months after client completed and signed paperwork and knew at time of filing the documents were no longer accurate and were inadequate to satisfy client's bankruptcy obligations); *see also People v. Miller,* 354 P.3d 1136 (Colo. O.P.D.J. 2015) (six-month suspension under Standard 4.62, inter alia, when lawyer serving as shareholder and director of his family's corporation engaged in conflict of interest by acting both as counsel to the corporation and as an interested party in two transactions; lawyer failed to obtain necessary consent from corporation to enter into transactions and concealed them from board of directors to obtain personal benefit); *People v. Smith,* 136 P.3d 279 (Colo. O.P.D.J. 2006) (suspension of one year and one day for failing to actively assert client's interests in probate matter, failing to diligently handle a real estate matter, and leading clients to believe all was well with the case, with the result that clients lost their house, uprooted their children, suffered stress, and had to pay another lawyer to settle the matter); *Fla. Bar v. Broome,* 932 So.2d 1036 (Fla. 2006) (one-year suspension instead of public reprimand recommended by referee for lawyer whose misconduct included deceit in promising a client several times to either pay him by a certain date money she owed him from a judgment he obtained against her for return of fees or to begin paying him, when she must have known at the time she would be unable to do so); *In re Ware,* 112 P.3d 155 (Kan. 2005) (imposing one-year suspension under Standard 4.62 on in-house counsel who failed to defend against employment discrimination claim, made intentional false entries in case-tracking system to prevent company from discovering her inaction, and falsely accused her secretary of errors in tracking system); *In re Crews*, 159 S.W.3d 355, 361 (Mo. 2005) (lawyer suspended indefinitely for misconduct that included providing differing explanations to client, court, and disciplinary panel as to why he failed to defend against a summary judgment motion and prepare an acceptable brief for the court of appeals; court found that "[w]hile Respondent may not have intentionally set out to abuse the professional relationship between himself and his clients, Respondent committed misconduct when attempting to shroud his substandard actions with the varying explanations that he proffered").

A lawyer's failure to disclose information or to correct a false impression created by nondisclosure of a material fact also constitutes deception, warranting suspension under Standard 4.62. *See In re Ungar*, 25 So.3d 101, 112 (La. 2009) (lawyer suspended for three years for intentionally withholding information from his clients regarding a class-action settlement in order to facilitate collecting an excessive fee; dissenting opinion stated that disbarment was the appropriate sanction under Standard 4.61 because lawyer's actions were "deliberate, dishonest, deceitful, and motivated by self-interest"). Similarly in *In re Brandt*, 10 P.3d 906 (Or. 2000), the Oregon Supreme Court cited Standard 4.62, inter alia, in suspending one lawyer for one year and a second lawyer for thirteen months (due to a prior admonition) for failing to disclose to client that, under the settlement agreement the lawyers agreed to, they would represent the opposing party in any future litigation and would be indemnified fully by the opposing party for any claim that their client could possibly have brought against them. The court found that such undisclosed facts were material to the client's decision whether to rely on lawyers' advice in recommending acceptance of proposed settlement.

### *Deception Regarding Status of Case*

Additionally, a lawyer may be suspended for deceiving a client about the status of his or her case. While in some instances a lawyer may be disbarred, in other instances, courts impose the less severe sanction of suspension after finding evidence of injury or potential injury to a client, rather than serious injury or potentially serious injury, as required for disbarment under Standard 4.61. One of the most common and egregious forms of deception by lawyers involves misrepresentations to the client that his or her case has been filed or is pending when in fact a lawyer has allowed the statute of limitations to expire. *See, e.g., People v. Bendinelli*, 329 P.3d 300 (Colo. O.P.D. J. 2014) (under Standard 4.62, inter alia, lawyer suspended for sixty days, all stayed, in favor of one-year probation, when in course of representing client on a loss of consortium claim lawyer failed to keep his client reasonably informed about the status of case and failed to obtain client's informed consent in writing to settle an aggregate claim; lawyer also signed client's name to settlement agreement without her authority and knowingly misrepresented facts of her case with the intent that client rely on those misrepresentations and agree to dismiss claim that had already settled); *People v. Eaton*, 240 P.3d 1282 (Colo. O.P.D.J. 2010) (lawyer suspended for two years for misconduct that included representing to client that she was still pursuing the client's claim and that a trial date would be set, even though the lawyer had missed the statute of limitations by failing to file a return of service under a court order); *In re Bishop*, 179 P.3d 1096 (Kan. 2008) (clear and convincing evidence supported finding that client paid lawyer to prepare and file a qualified domestic relations order; lawyer knowingly failed to perform services for client and, for years, knowingly lied about that conduct; indefinite suspension imposed); *In re Romero*, 22 P.3d 215 (N.M. 2001) (indefinite suspension under Standard 4.62 for knowing deception when lawyer gave false account of status of cases to her clients and their health-care providers, stating that cases remained pending when they had been dismissed or were not filed within the statute of limitations); *In re Disciplinary Action Against Summers*, 821 N.W.2d 758 (N.D. 2012) (six-month-and-one-day suspension, under North Dakota Sanctions Standard 4.62, for lawyer's dishonesty in advising client that lawyer was waiting for court to schedule hearing on his motion to enforce child visitation after the court had already dismissed the motion); *In re Obert*, 89 P.3d 1173 (Or. 2004) (lawyer's failure to disclose to criminal client the dismissal of his appeal, which was due to lawyer's negligence in failing to file notice of appeal in a timely manner, warranted suspension); *In re Disciplinary Proceeding Against Cohen*, 67 P.3d 1086 (Wash. 2003) (lawyer suspended after he knowingly deceived his clients by failing to inform them that their case was dismissed until two months after dismissal and after he had collected a fee of nearly $12,000). *But see People v. Schroeder*, 410 P.3d 854 (Colo. O.P.D.J. 2018) (citing Standard 4.62, disciplinary judge ordered lawyer disbarred for failing to be diligent in three collection matters, making misrepresentations to client, commingling funds, failing to disburse funds owed to his client, and converting client funds for his own use).

When injury to the client is minimal, a court may decide on a less severe sanction than suspension. In *People v. Johnston*, 955 P.2d 1051 (Colo. 1998), for example, a lawyer was publicly censured rather than suspended for misrepresenting the status of a case in a memorandum to the client by failing to inform the client that the case had been dismissed. In imposing the less severe sanction, the court noted that in addition to the mitigating factors such as the absence of a dishonest or selfish motive, full and free disclosure in the disciplinary proceedings, and the presence of remorse, any actual harm to the client was in the cost of hiring a new lawyer to pursue an appeal of the dismissal order, and the lawyer had refunded the fee he had collected from the client.

## *Deception Regarding Attorney's Fees*

A lawyer's deceptive conduct regarding the fees owed or due the lawyer may be grounds for suspension. An obvious deception occurs when a lawyer knowingly submits a false or inaccurate invoice to a client. *See In re Benett,* 14 P.3d 66 (Or. 2000) (six-month suspension under Standard 4.62, inter alia, for lawyer who, among other misconduct, acted dishonestly in not making complete refund of fees owed to clients, forcing clients to litigate the fee dispute despite lawyer's acknowledgment that he knew he was not entitled to charge his clients additional fees for disputing his bill); *Bd. of Prof'l Responsibility v. Casper,* 318 P.3d 790 (Wyo. 2014) (lawyer suspended for thirty days for excessively billing legal fees and then improperly seeking to collect those fees by filing a "lien statement" with court against a property owned by client's ex-husband); *cf. In re Disciplinary Proceeding Against Poole,* 125 P.3d 954, 966 (Wash. 2006) (while court reversed board's reliance on Standard 4.62 in favor of Standard 4.64, six-month suspension nonetheless imposed on lawyer whose misconduct included creating an invoice, backdating it, and providing it to opposing counsel; court noted that Standard 4.6 failed to completely address situation in which a lawyer knowingly falsifies a document with the intent to deceive, but his or her act causes no injury to the client, as it found here; suspension appropriate because lawyer acted knowingly and intentionally in fabricating the invoice, in addition to four aggravating factors against a lack of mitigating factors and comparison of respondent's misconduct with that of lawyers in other discipline cases).

A lawyer who does not misrepresent the amount of fees owed or the amount of work completed on the client's behalf may nonetheless face suspension for making a knowing misrepresentation regarding the nature of the fees. *See In re Sather,* 3 P.3d 403, 416 (Colo. 2000) (six-month suspension for lawyer who knowingly misrepresented fees paid by a client as "non-refundable"; lawyer "knew that, despite the fee agreement's boldface and repeated language to the contrary, he misrepresented the nature of the advance fee to [his client] as 'non-refundable' because fees are always subject to refund in the event they are unreasonable or unearned"); *cf. In re Smith,* 887 So.2d 449, 456 (La. 2004) (one-year suspension fully deferred warranted under Standard 4.62, inter alia, when client was not harmed but lawyer engaged in negligent misconduct in dealings with his clients, including inadequate explanation of fee arrangement and case status; "the main cause of respondent's negligent misconduct was his lack of detail, clarity, and organization in dealing with his clients and running his law office").

**4.63 Reprimand is generally appropriate when a lawyer negligently fails to provide a client with accurate or complete information, and causes injury or potential injury to the client.**

## Annotation

Reprimand is justified when a lawyer is merely negligent in failing to provide a client with accurate or complete information and injury or potential injury to a client is established regarding fees owed or the status of a client's case. *See, e.g., In re Otlowski*, 976 A.2d 172 (Table) (Del. 2009) (lawyer negligent in filing annual report with the court stating inaccurately that he had pre-certification review of escrow account not realizing that his accountant failed to reconcile account and that he was victim of theft by a dishonest employee, his daughter, who embezzled funds from his escrow account; public reprimand under Standard 4.63, inter alia); *Iowa Supreme Ct. Att'y Disciplinary Bd. v. Taylor*, 814 N.W.2d 259 (Iowa 2012) (public reprimand warranted for lawyer who was negligent in providing misleading information to client about the reasons client's case was dismissed on appeal when client persisted in requesting status information about client's case); *In re Friesen*, 991 P.2d 400 (Kan. 1999) (relying on Standard 4.63, court imposed public reprimand on lawyer who failed to follow client's instruction to dismiss her case and instead settled case, signed client's name to check, and presented a blank release asking if she would accept $500 in settlement when he and opposing lawyer agreed to settle for $2,400); *Bd. of Prof'l Responsibility v. Jones*, 358 P.3d 498 (Wyo. 2015) (public censure under Standard 4.63 warranted when lawyer failed to fully inform clients he was materially limited from representing them in dispute against current client and did not obtain their informed consent to act as intermediary in resolving the real property dispute).

### *Misrepresentation Regarding Attorney's Fees*

A lawyer's negligent misrepresentations regarding attorney's fees owed may be the basis for a public reprimand. *See In re Discipline of Light*, 615 N.W.2d 164 (S.D. 2000) (lawyer took over a wrongful-death case from another lawyer in the firm and, after finding an unsigned contingency fee agreement in the file, sent the client a new contingency fee agreement without advising the client that the terms of the new agreement were more favorable to the lawyer than the original; reprimand appropriate sanction because the lawyer acted negligently in failing to determine that the client's interests may be materially affected by the lawyer's own interests and that such information needed to be disclosed to the client); *see also Bd. of Prof'l Responsibility v. Mulligan*, 162 P.3d 468 (Wyo. 2007) (public censure for misrepresenting to client that lawyer had performed legal services in perfecting appeal, including research and brief preparation; lawyer billed client hourly rate of $250 when work was actually performed by independent associate counsel at the rate of $85 per hour).

In addition to providing inaccurate information, a lawyer may be publicly reprimanded for providing incomplete information. In some instances, the lawyer's failure to provide complete information may result from poor recordkeeping. *See Cox's Case*, 813 A.2d 429 (N.H. 2002) (citing Standard 4.63, court found reprimand appropriate sanction for failing to comply with client's request for billing information and to provide a full, detailed, and accurate account of all money that lawyer handled for the client; client's requests could have been easily resolved had lawyer maintained appropriate trust accounting).

### *Misrepresentation Regarding Status of Case*

Although a lawyer who knowingly deceives a client about the status of his or her case, resulting in injury to the client, is often subject to suspension or, in some instances, disbarment, a lesser sanction of a public reprimand may be imposed when mitigating circumstances are found. *See, e.g., People v. Kram*, 966 P.2d 1065 (Colo. 1998) (after lawyer failed to file a response to a motion for summary judgment resulting in dismissal of the case, lawyer told client that the motion had been resolved in her favor and met with her on numerous occasions for the stated purpose of preparing for trial; while presumptive sanction under Standard 4.62 is suspension, public censure warranted due to the fact that the lawyer had severe personal and emotional problems and, during the time of the misconduct, was experiencing a number of serious traumatic events, including his wife's health problems); *cf. In re Wilks*, 99 A.3d 228 (Del. 2014) (reprimand with two-year probation warranted when lawyer intentionally failed to provide client with accurate information about their matter and allowed statute of limitations to toll without preserving their rights in personal injury claim).

**4.64 Admonition is generally appropriate when a lawyer engages in an isolated instance of negligence in failing to provide a client with accurate or complete information, and causes little or no actual or potential injury to the client.**

## Annotation

Admonition is the appropriate sanction for a lawyer who, in an isolated instance, is negligent in providing a client with accurate or complete information and no actual or potential injury to the client has occurred. Although admonitions frequently do not appear in reported cases, *People v. Gray*, 35 P.3d 611 (Colo. O.P.D.J. 2001), provides insight into the type of conduct that might warrant an admonition. In *Gray*, an inexperienced lawyer was asked by a lawyer named Mark Field, who was facing a six-month suspension, to take over his law practice under the name of "Field & Associates, Attorneys at Law," during the lawyer's suspension. The clients were notified of this arrangement. The suspended lawyer continued to work at the law firm as a paralegal, bookkeeper, and secretary. By sending out communications on this letterhead, the inexperienced lawyer made a false or misleading communication about herself and her services, the court said, noting that in light of the fact that the inexperienced lawyer's misconduct was negligent, involved only one client, and caused little or no actual harm to the client, the profession, or the legal system, the presumptive sanction was a private admonition. Additional misconduct involving a technical conversion of funds, however, increased the sanction to a public censure. *See also In re Welcome*, 60 V.I. 240 (V.I. 2013) (admonition under Standard 6.64 appropriate for lawyer who prepared, but negligently did not send, letter responsive to client's requests for information and that explained reasons lawyer would have to terminate client-lawyer relationship).

# 5.0 Violations of Duties Owed to the Public

## Annotation

The most fundamental duty a lawyer owes to the public is the duty to maintain standards of personal integrity upon which the community relies. The public expects lawyers to be honest and to abide by the law; public confidence in the integrity of officers of the court is undermined when lawyers engage in illegal or other dishonest conduct. Standard 5.0 provides recommended disciplinary sanctions for lawyers who commit criminal acts that reflect adversely on their honesty, trustworthiness, or fitness as a lawyer and who engage in conduct involving dishonesty, fraud, deceit, misrepresentation, or other conduct that reflects adversely on their fitness to practice law. *See, e.g., In re Pohland*, 377 P.3d 911, 915 (Alaska 2016) ("[t]he public expects lawyers to be honest and to abide by the law"; this lawyer's misconduct, which took place while she was employed by the Alaska Department of Law, "violated a basic professional obligation a lawyer owes to the public"; lawyer disbarred after pleading guilty to shoplifting and also being convicted of official misconduct for, in part, tipping off her friend about an investigation into the friend's conduct); *People v. Kintzele*, 409 P.3d 680 (Colo. O.P.D.J. 2017) (citing Standard 5.11, lawyer disbarred after conviction for attempted murder of wife); *Statewide Grievance Comm'n v. Schaffer*, No. CV030196758, 2004 WL 303654, at *10 (Conn. Super. Ct. Feb. 2, 2004) (citing then existing commentary to Standard 5.0, the court disbarred lawyer with significant disciplinary history who, inter alia, violated duties of an escrow agent when he used his client trust account to receive funds from third parties for the purchase of Ferrari automobiles from his client and disbursed funds to his client without receiving any documentation or confirmation that the third parties received their automobile; lawyer "violated fundamental duties of this profession," is not "a safe and fit person to be entrusted with the responsibilities and obligations of an attorney," and "cannot be trusted to protect the interests of his clients, the public, and the administration of justice"); *Statewide Grievance Comm'n v. Small*, No. CV 940541637S, 1999 WL 195814, at *4 (Conn. Super. Ct. Mar. 18, 1999) (court rejected lawyer's argument that drunk driving resulting in negligent homicide did not reflect adversely on lawyer's fitness to practice law, and imposed a five-year suspension, noting that "[s]uch conduct, when committed by an officer of the court, constitutes a failure to maintain personal integrity, reflects upon one's fitness to practice law, and brings the bench and the bar into disrepute"); *In re Disney*, 922 S.W.2d 12, 15 (Mo. 1996) (in imposing six-month suspension under Sanction 5.0, court stated that "[q]uestions of honesty go to the heart of fitness to practice law" and "[m]isconduct involving subterfuge, failing to keep promises, and untrustworthiness undermine public confidence in not only the individual but in the bar"); *Disciplinary Counsel v. Dann*, 979 N.E.2d

1263, 1268 (Ohio 2012) ("The integrity of the profession can be maintained only if the conduct of the individual attorney is above reproach. He should refrain from any illegal conduct. Anything short of this lessens public confidence in the legal profession—because obedience to the law exemplifies respect for the law.") (citations omitted); *cf. In re Jaffee*, 15 P.3d 533, 537 (Or. 2000) (in disbarring lawyer for, inter alia, conviction for criminal interference with girlfriend's arrest and disrespecting law enforcement by giving false information during a traffic stop, court recognized that not every criminal act reflects adversely on a lawyer's fitness to practice law, and noted that "[t]here must be some rational connection other than the criminality of the act between the conduct and the actor's fitness to practice law") (citation omitted).

Misconduct warranting discipline under Standard 5.0 most often involves illegal acts directly implicating aspects of the lawyer's fitness to practice law. Comment 2 to Rule 8.4 of the ABA Model Rules of Professional Conduct describes to some extent the types of illegal conduct that may result in the imposition of discipline for violation of the rule. While offenses involving fraud or the willful failure to file income tax returns do adversely reflect on fitness to practice, other criminal acts carry no such implication. Comment 2 notes: "Traditionally, the distinction was drawn in terms of offenses involving 'moral turpitude.' . . . Although a lawyer is personally answerable to the entire criminal law, a lawyer should be professionally answerable only for offenses that indicate lack of those characteristics relevant to law practice. Offenses involving violence, dishonesty, breach of trust, or serious interference with the administration of justice are in that category. A pattern of repeated offenses, even ones of minor significance when considered separately, can indicate indifference to legal obligation." MODEL RULES OF PROF'L CONDUCT R. 8.4 cmt. 2. Every violation of the law, however, does not necessarily result in the imposition of disciplinary sanctions. As the Supreme Court of Arizona explained in *In re Horwitz*, 881 P.2d 352 (Ariz. 1994):

> With due respect to Thomas More, who we fear is an exception to the rule, we do not equate the practice of law with the path leading to sainthood. An occasional violation of the law of a type not involving moral turpitude does not necessarily reflect on a lawyer's professional fitness. On the other hand, the public has a right to expect that lawyers will, in general, live as law-abiding citizens.

*Id.* at 356. The court, in *Horwitz*, determined that any lesser sanction than disbarment, considering the lawyer's many years of extensive alcohol and drug abuse along with his conviction on two counts of negligent homicide, "would be an inappropriate statement of what the bar and this court should and would tolerate." *Id.* at 361.

In *In re Diaz*, 288 P.3d 486, 493 (Kan. 2012), the court cited Standard 5.0 to support a disbarment sanction for violations of duties owed to the public, finding Standard 5.11 applicable to a lawyer who engaged in serious criminal conduct, including four felony convictions for revealing classified government information concerning Guantanamo Bay detainees, constituting "theft—of his country's classified information." The court considered the potential injury to the public, the United States, and the possibility of serious injury to particular persons. *See also In re Davenport*, 49 P.3d 91 (Or. 2002) (lawyer's misrepresentations and criminal act of giving false testimony under oath in bankruptcy proceeding violated duty to public to maintain personal integrity, warranting a two-year suspension after consideration of several Sanctions Standards, including Standard 5.1, and case law); *In re Gustafson*, 968 P.2d 367, 377 (Or. 1998) ("[b]y misrepresenting facts to the court, the accused violated her duty to the public to maintain her personal integrity," warranting a six-month suspension; discussion of Sanctions Standards included Standards 5.1 and 5.2); *In re Disciplinary Proceedings Against Elliott*, 790 N.W.2d 508, 513 (Wis. 2010) (lawyer who engaged in pattern of converting client and third-party funds and multimillion-dollar check-kiting scheme to cover thefts "is not fit to be licensed as a lawyer in the state of Wisconsin" and is disbarred).

### *Practicing Law During Suspension*

Practicing law during a period of license suspension can also result in the imposition of sanctions under Standard 5.0 for failure to maintain personal integrity. *See, e.g.*, *In re Davis*, 43 A.3d 856 (Del. 2012) (lawyer defied order of suspension when he engaged in the unauthorized practice of law by continuing to meet with clients and prospective clients and by performing title services; disbarment under Standard 5.11, inter alia); *In re Jones*, 99 So.3d 20, 23 (La. 2012) (citing Sanctions Standards generally, court imposed two-year suspension for misconduct including lawyer's "refusal to stop practicing law while suspended"); *In re Koliha*, 9 P.3d 102, 105 (Or. 2000) (lawyer who practiced law while suspended for failure to pay bar dues violated "her duty to public and as a professional to refrain from unauthorized practice"; citing Standard 5.0, inter alia, in imposing one-year suspension); *In re Devers*, 974 P.2d 191 (Or. 1999) (disbarment for, among other misconduct, lawyer's unauthorized practice of law during administrative and disciplinary suspensions; citing Standard 5.0 among other Standards).

### *The Integrity of Public Officials*

Standard 5.0 also identifies the appropriate sanctions for public officials who engage in conduct prejudicial to the administration of justice or who state or imply an ability to influence improperly a government agency. Lawyers serving as public officials also have a duty to avoid using their public position to obtain a special advantage for themselves or their clients. Comment 5 to Rule 8.4 of the

ABA Model Rules of Professional Conduct highlights the heightened responsibilities of lawyers serving this role: "Lawyers holding public office assume legal responsibilities going beyond those of other citizens. A lawyer's abuse of public office can suggest an inability to fulfill the professional role of lawyers." *See, e.g.*, *In re Peasley*, 90 P.3d 764, 772, 779 (Ariz. 2004) (disbarment warranted for lawyer who violated his duties to the public and the court, and his responsibilities as a prosecutor "to seek justice" when he presented false testimony in two capital murder cases, causing "incalculable injury to the integrity of the legal profession and the justice system"); *In re Gelof*, 142 A.3d 506, at *6, 8 (Table) (Del. 2016) (in "unprecedented" matter, court upheld hearing panel's application of Standard 5.2 and imposed thirty-day suspension on deputy attorney general who convinced courthouse security officer to draw his gun on colleagues as part of practical joke; court "takes very seriously a lawyer's fundamental duty to foster public confidence in our Bar and to maintain the integrity of the legal profession. . . . Respondent's 'practical joke' caused actual harm to the Superior Court's administration of justice by diverting the court's resources to handle the aftermath of Respondent's misconduct."); *In re Gorecki*, 802 N.E 2d 1194, 1195 (Ill. 2003) (four-month suspension warranted for former county state's attorney whose recorded false statements indicating that another public official could be bribed into providing jobs under the guise of payments made in the form of "campaign contributions" constituted serious misconduct; Sanctions Standards not cited); *Ky. Bar Ass'n v. Dixon*, 373 S.W.3d 444, 451 (Ky. 2012) (public reprimand appropriate sanction for elected county attorney who agreed to cash third-party checks for client with whom he had long-standing friendship; court found that although lawyer was pawn in client's money-laundering scheme, as an elected official, he was "responsible under the law for giving 'legal advice to the fiscal court' and opposing 'all unjust or illegally presented claims'") (citation omitted); *In re Rome*, 856 So.2d 1167, 1172 (La. 2003) (assistant district attorney convicted of malfeasance in office for converting funds received as payment of traffic fines and costs was permanently disbarred with the court noting, "It requires no citation of authority to conclude the baseline sanction for such misconduct is unquestionably disbarment"; Sanctions Standards cited generally); *In re Magid*, 655 A.2d 916, 919 (N.J. 1995) (in a case of first impression, court imposed public reprimand on prosecutor convicted of simple assault, cautioning that suspension would be imposed in future for any pattern of abusive behavior; court stated that "[a]ttorneys who hold public office are invested with a public trust and are thereby more visible to the public" and "are held to the highest of standards"); *Disciplinary Counsel v. Dann*, 979 N.E.2d 1263, 1269 (Ohio 2012) (six-month suspension appropriate for state's attorney general who solicited improper compensation and filed false financial disclosure statements resulting in criminal conviction; court noted that lawyer's misconduct caused "incalculable harm to the public perception of the attorney general's office and those government agencies, departments, and institutions that the attorney general advises and represents"); *Disciplinary Counsel v. Engel*, 969 N.E.2d 1178, 1182 (Ohio 2012) (six-month suspension for chief legal counsel of state agency who intercepted and disbursed confidential emails from inspector general's office about pending law-enforcement and ethics investigations; finding lawyer acted recklessly and "worked to undermine public trust not only in the legal system, but in state government as a whole"); *State ex rel. Okla. Bar Ass'n v. Clark*, 276 P.3d 1012 (Okla. 2012) (prosecutor's conviction for embezzlement warranted disbarment; court finding that lawyer "disregarded his responsibilities as a lawyer . . . [and] . . . ignored the best interest of his clients"); *cf. Office of Disciplinary Counsel v. Cappuccio*, 48 A.3d 1231, 1240, 1241 (Pa. 2012) (although not relying on the Sanctions Standards, court noted the "broader public trust reposed in judges, prosecutors and the like" and considered chief deputy district attorney's position as a public official a significant aggravating factor in imposing disbarment following prosecutor's conviction for supplying minors with alcohol and marijuana while serving as a church youth-group leader, even though the misconduct did not occur while the respondent was acting in his official capacity; court stated that "any sanction short of disbarment in these circumstances threatens the integrity of the legal system, undermines our very serious duty to protect the public, and fails to give appropriate weight to Respondent's status as a public official").

## *Prosecutors' Special Obligations*

All prosecutors take an oath to ensure that justice is done in each case and owe concomitant special duties to the public and the justice system. *See* Model Rules of Prof'l Conduct R. 3.8, Special Responsibilities of a Prosecutor (2013); ABA Criminal Justice Standards 3-1.2(c), The Function of the Prosecutor (1993) ("The duty of the prosecutor is to seek justice, not merely to convict."); *see also Connick v. Thompson*, 131 S. Ct. 1350, 1362 (2011) (prosecutors who violate their ethical obligations are subject to professional discipline since "[p]rosecutors have a special 'duty to seek justice, not merely to convict.'") (citation omitted); *Imbler v. Pachtman*, 424 U.S. 409, 429 (1976) (disciplinary sanctions should be applied to deter prosecutorial misconduct that otherwise would go unpunished; "a prosecutor stands perhaps unique, among officials whose acts could deprive persons of constitutional rights, in his amenability to professional discipline by an association of his peers"); *Berger v. United States*, 295 U.S. 78, 88 (1935) (prosecutors have special obligations as representatives "not of an ordinary party to a controversy, but of a sovereignty whose obligation to govern impartially is as compelling as its obligation to govern at all; and whose interest, therefore, in a criminal prosecution is not that it shall win a case, but that justice shall be done"); *United States v. Lopez-Avila*, 678 F.3d 955, 956 (9th Cir. 2012) ("Prosecutors, as servants of the law, are subject to constraints and responsibilities that do not apply to other lawyers. . . . Their job is not just to win, but to win fairly, staying within the rules."). In *In re Doe,* 801 F. Supp. 478 (D.N.M. 1992), state disciplinary proceedings were initiated against a federal prosecutor for communicating directly with a represented defendant. The federal prosecutor removed the disciplinary proceedings to federal court. In granting the motion to remand, the court held, inter alia, that the prosecutor was not authorized by his position to ignore state codes of ethics nor was he entitled to prosecutorial immunity from state bar disciplinary proceedings. The court stated:

> Recognizing a Government lawyer's role as a shepherd of justice, we must not forget that the authority of the Government lawyer does not arise from any *right* of the Government, but from *power* entrusted to the Government. When a Government lawyer, with enormous resources at his or her disposal, abuses this power and ignores ethical standards, he or she not only undermines the public trust, but inflicts damage beyond calculation to our system of justice. This alone compels the responsible and ethical exercise of this power.

*Id.* at 480. In the disciplinary proceeding following the removal action, in *In re Howes,* 940 P.2d 159, 170 (N.M. 1997), the Supreme Court of New Mexico publicly censured the prosecutor, noting his communication with a represented defendant violated "one of the most elementary premises of the adversary system." *See also In re Howes,* 52 A.3d 1, 21 (D.C. 2012) (in second discipline case against this prosecutor, court stated that in prosecutor misconduct cases determining the "appropriate disciplinary sanction has heightened significance . . . because the prosecutor's violation of ethical rules is compounded by his additional duty to the public"; prosecutor disbarred for numerous instances of misusing federal witness vouchers and not revealing information to the court and opposing counsel); *Fla. Bar v. Cox,* 794 So.2d 1278, 1285 (Fla. 2001) ("[A] prosecutor has responsibilities beyond that of an advocate, and has a higher duty to assure that justice is served."); *State v. Rogan,* 984 P.2d 1231, 1244 (Haw. 1999) (in case where deputy prosecutor's remarks during closing argument were an appeal to racial prejudice that had no objectively legitimate purpose and were sufficiently egregious to bar retrial, court stated that "the prosecution must serve the truth-seeking and fairness functions of trial and to pursue and present relevant evidence, regardless of which side it benefits"; "unlike any other advocate, the prosecutor must always be mindful of his or her primary obligation to seek justice while at the same time fulfilling his or her obligation to seek convictions"); *State v. Torres,* 744 A.2d 699, 708 (N.J. Super. Ct. App. Div. 2000) ("A prosecutor is not simply another lawyer who happens to represent the State. Because of the overwhelming power vested in his office, his obligation to play fair is every bit as compelling as his responsibility to protect the public.").

## *Unfounded Charges*

Prosecutors can be disciplined for bringing unfounded charges. *See, e.g., In re Leonhardt,* 930 P.2d 844 (Or. 1997) (disbarment warranted under Standards 5.11(a) and (b) and 5.21, inter alia, for numerous disciplinary violations including institution of criminal charges when prosecutor knew that charges not supported by probable cause). *But see In re Disciplinary Proceedings Against Lucareli,* 611 N.W.2d 754 (Wis. 2000) (dismissing disciplinary proceeding against prosecutor for filing criminal charge against lawyer representing defendant in underlying sexual assault case, when such charges against lawyer were unsupported by probable cause; court held that board failed to show that prosecutor knew charges against lawyer were not supported by probable cause).

## *Obligation to Disclose Exculpatory Evidence or Other Material Information*

A prosecutor's obligation to turn over exculpatory evidence to the defense is a well-established constitutional and ethical requirement. *See* Rule 3.8(d) of the ABA Model Rules of Professional Conduct. *See also Giglio v. United States,* 405 U.S. 150 (1972) (prosecutors obligated to disclose material impeachment evidence affecting the credibility of a witness); *Brady v. Maryland,* 373 U.S. 83, 87 (1963) (prosecutor's withholding evidence favorable to defendant and "material either to guilt or to punishment" violates defendant's due process rights). *But see United States v. Ruiz,* 536 U.S. 622 (2002) (prosecutor not required to disclose impeachment information prior to entering into a plea agreement with the defendant).

Failure to disclose exculpatory evidence or withholding other material information has resulted in a range of disciplinary sanctions against prosecutors. *See Fla. Bar v. Cox,* 794 So.2d 1278, 1286 (Fla. 2001) (although disbarment presumptive sanction, one-year suspension warranted for prosecutor who improperly withheld material information by concealing identity of confidential informant; citing Florida Standard 5.2, court found that the "public clearly deserves protection from a prosecutor who determines on her own when and how to follow the rules" and "[t]he public expects and deserves fairness and candor from attorneys, especially from a prosecutor who has the power and responsibility derived from representing the government"); *Comm'n on Prof'l Ethics & Conduct v. Ramey,* 512 N.W.2d 569 (Iowa 1994) (prosecutor indefinitely suspended with no possibility of reinstatement for three months for false statements and failure to disclose exculpatory evidence); *In re Jordan,* 91 P.3d 1168 (Kan. 2004) (public censure under Standard 5.23, inter alia, for prosecutor whose misconduct included failure to disclose to defense counsel that victim used cocaine approximately one month after crimes committed and that she expected expert witness to testify regarding victim's blood alcohol concentration at time of crime; court found prosecutor recklessly interfered with the administration of justice resulting in two mistrials and dismissal of cases); *In re Jordan*, 913 So.2d 775 (La. 2005) (in case of first impression in Louisiana on issue of prosecutor's failure to disclose evidence to a defendant in a capital murder case that tended to negate guilt of accused or mitigated offense, court imposed three-month suspension but deferred it due to mitigating factors); *N.C. State Bar v. Nifong*, No. 06 DHC 35 (N.C. Disciplinary Hearing Comm'n 2007), *available at* http://www.ncbar.gov/orders/06dhc35.pdf (disbarring prosecutor in "The Duke Lacrosse Case" for numerous violations, including failure to make timely disclosure to the defense of all evidence or information known to him that tended to negate the guilt of the accused, including DNA evidence, and making material misrepresentations to judge presiding in criminal case and to disciplinary authority); *N.C. State Bar v. Hoke & Graves*, No. 04 DHC 15 (2004), *available at* http://www.ncbar.gov/orders/volume%206/06019087.pdf (because of mitigating evidence, public reprimand warranted for two prosecutors in the attorney general's office who failed to provide witness statements and tape recording in investigation files); *Disciplinary Counsel v. Wrenn*, 790 N.E.2d 1195 (Ohio 2003) (respondent breached his duties as an officer of the court and his public responsibility as assistant prosecutor when, before defendant's guilty plea, he failed to disclose results of DNA tests in child sexual abuse case that, while not entirely exculpatory, were favorable to defendant and prompted a significant change in victim's account of crime; six-month stayed suspension warranted when no aggravating factors); *In re Grant*, 541 S.E.2d 540 (S.C. 2001) (public reprimand by consent for prosecutor who failed to fully disclose exculpatory material and impeachment evidence regarding statements given by state's key witness in murder prosecution; accused pleaded guilty to voluntary manslaughter as a result of misconduct; decision does not cite Sanctions Standards). *But see In re Seastrunk*, 236 So.3d 509, 519 (La. 2017) (in matter of first impression, court dismissed disciplinary charges against prosecutor alleging improper failure to disclose inconsistent witness statements and statements regarding witness's past possession of a gun; addressing relationship between Louisiana Rule of Professional Conduct 3.8(d) and prosecutor's *Brady* obligations, court found duties in Rule and *Brady* to be "coextensive" and rejected disciplinary counsel's argument that Rule 3.8(d) imposed a broader obligation; court cited similar precedent in other jurisdictions, including the Ohio case of *Disciplinary Counsel v. Kellogg-Martin*, explaining, "[a]s these other courts have found, under conflicting standards, prosecutors would face uncertainty as to how to proceed, as they could find themselves in compliance with the standard enumerated in Brady, but in potential violation of the obligation set forth in Rule 3.8(d) . . . we decline to impose inconsistent disclosure obligations on prosecutors . . ."); *Disciplinary Counsel v. Kellogg-Martin*, 923 N.E.2d 125 (Ohio 2010) (rejecting recommended one-year suspension with six months stayed, court dismissed complaint filed against prosecutor who failed to disclose two reports before defendant pleaded guilty to reduced charges; relying on the contours of the *Brady* rule, the court determined that the scope of a prosecutor's ethical obligation is not broader than the constitutional duty and therefore disclosure was not legally required prior to defendant's guilty plea; one dissenting justice found prosecutor's misconduct severe enough to warrant the recommended sanction).

For additional discussion regarding a prosecutor's duty to disclose, *see also* Kevin C. McMunigal, *The (Lack of) Enforcement of Prosecutor Disclosure Rules*, 38 HOFSTRA L. REV. 847 (2010); Christina Parajon, Comment, *Discovery Audits: Model Rule 3.8(d) and the Prosecutor's Duty to Disclose*, 119 YALE L.J. 1339, 1342–43 (2010); Joseph R. Weeks, *No Wrong Without a Remedy: The Effective Enforcement of the Duty of Prosecutors to Disclose Exculpatory Evidence*, 22 OKLA. CITY U. L. REV. 833 (1997).

- **Proof of Intent**

A violation of the professional conduct rule governing a prosecutor's duty to timely disclose exculpatory evidence is not dependent upon a finding that the conduct was "intentional." *See, e.g., In re Jordan*, 913 So.2d 775 (La. 2005) (prosecutor's knowing failure to disclose *Brady* evidence in capital murder case warranted three-month suspension, deferred due to mitigating factors); *In re Disciplinary Action Against Feland*, 820 N.W.2d 672, 681 (N.D. 2012) ("the reach of [the professional responsibility rule] is not limited to a prosecutor's intentional failure to disclose exculpatory evidence, but also applies to a knowing or negligent failure to disclose"; finding prosecutor's negligent failure to disclose exculpatory evidence warranted admonition); *Lawyer Disciplinary Bd. v. Hatcher*, 483 S.E.2d 810, 818 (W. Va. 1997) (court held that a prosecutor who "knowingly fails to make a timely disclosure" of evidence or information to the defense "runs risk of violating" professional conduct rules but dismissed complaint because charges that prosecutor "knowingly" withheld information were not proven by clear and convincing evidence). *But see In re Att'y C.*, 47 P.3d 1167 (Colo. 2002) (as a matter of first impression, court held that when a prosecutor is aware of exculpatory evidence before any critical stage of the proceeding, he or she must disclose that evidence before proceeding takes place; court reversed public censure against assistant district attorney who failed to disclose exculpatory evidence to defense until after preliminary hearing because prosecutor lacked intent to withhold evidence and rule was unclear as to prosecutor's obligation to disclose prior to any critical stage of proceeding).

## *Good Motives No Excuse*

Good motives do not excuse prosecutorial misconduct. In *In re Pautler*, 47 P.3d 1175 (Colo. 2002), for example, a deputy district attorney received a three-month suspension, stayed entirely by a period of probation, for purposefully deceiving a murder suspect when, during a telephone negotiation between the suspect and law-enforcement agents, he posed as a public defender to encourage the suspect's surrender. The court found such purposeful deception intolerable and held that the prosecutor violated the duties he owed the public, the legal system, and the profession. The court noted the lawyer's "role of prosecutor makes him an instrument of the legal system, a representative of the system of justice. The fact that he lied for what he thought was a good reason does not obscure the fact that he lied—in an important circumstance and about important facts." *Id.* at 1183. Refusing to craft an exception for prosecutors who face situations constituting a threat of "imminent public harm," the court stated:

> [W]e are adamant that when presented with choices, at least one of which conforms to the Rules, an attorney must not select an option that involves deceit or misrepresentation. The level of ethical standards to which our profession holds all attorneys, especially prosecutors, leaves no room for [deception]. . . . [The prosecutor] cannot compromise his integrity, and that of our profession, irrespective of the cause.

*Id.* at 1180–81; *see also In re Howes*, 52 A.3d 1, 22 (D.C. 2012) (disbarment imposed notwithstanding prosecutor justifying his actions based on "moral reasons"; court said failure to disbar would "endorse respondent's reasoning that honorable ends justify unlawful means," failing to deter others from adopting similar attitudes); *cf. People v. Reichman*, 819 P.2d 1035 (Colo. 1991) (public censure for prosecutor who filed false criminal complaint and other false documents, thereby deceiving court in effort to protect undercover officer in identity rehabilitation; court finding respondent's responsibility as prosecutor to enforce laws granted him no license to ignore those laws or ethics rules and his motives do not excuse ethical violations but are mitigating factors; decision does not cite Sanctions Standards).

## *Sanctions Against Prosecutors*

Prosecutorial misconduct and professional regulators' response to it have attracted legal commentary and recent focus among courts. *See, e.g., United States v. Lopez-Avila*, 678 F.3d 955, 965, 966 (9th Cir. 2012) (court expressed concern over prosecutor's use of misleadingly edited transcript to impeach defendant as well as the government's failure to acknowledge and take responsibility for misconduct; court remanded so that district court could consider dismissal of indictment to prevent future misconduct as well as disciplinary options); *see also* Ellen Yaroshefsky & Bruce A. Green, *Prosecutors' Ethics in Context: Influences on Prosecutorial Disclosure, in* LAWYERS IN PRACTICE: ETHICAL DECISION MAKING IN CONTEXT 289 (Leslie Levin & Lynn Mather eds., 2012); Stephanos Bibas, *Prosecutorial Regulation Versus Prosecutorial Accountability*, 157 U. PA. L. REV. 959 (2009); ANGELA J. DAVIS, ARBITRARY JUSTICE: THE POWER OF THE AMERICAN PROSECUTOR 150–51 (2007); Ellen Yaroshefsky, *Wrongful Convictions: It Is Time to Take Prosecution Discipline Seriously*, 8 UDC/DCSL L. REV. 275 (2004); Bruce A. Green, *Prosecutorial Ethics as*

*Usual,* 2003 U. ILL. L. REV. 1573 (2003); Fred C. Zacharias, *The Professional Discipline of Prosecutors,* 79 N.C. L. REV. 721, 745, 778 (2001). *But see* Monroe H. Freedman, *Professional Discipline of Prosecutors: A Response to Professor Zacharias,* 30 HOFSTRA L. REV. 121 (2001).

Disbarment of prosecutors for dishonest behavior is relatively rare, but such sanctions have been imposed. *See, e.g., In re Peasley,* 90 P.3d 764, 778–79 (Ariz. 2004) (prosecutor disbarred, although under Standard 6.11, for suborning perjured testimony to establish crucial fact in prosecution of two capital murder defendants; court noting misconduct "could not have been more harmful to the justice system"); *In re Howes,* 52 A.3d 1, 21 n.26 (D.C. 2012) (disbarment for assistant U.S. attorney who intentionally distributed more than $42,000 worth of witness vouchers in several felony prosecutions to ineligible individuals and intentionally failed to disclose voucher payments to courts and opposing counsel, resulting in substantial reduction of sentences for at least nine convicted felons; court stated that "[h]ere, as demonstrated in the *Standards,* disbarment is an appropriate sanction where respondent, in a governmental position, intentionally used his access to exploit public resources and call into question the federal and state judicial processes in which he participated"); *Disciplinary Counsel v. Phillips,* 843 N.E.2d 775, 777 (Ohio 2006) (in disbarring prosecutor for multiple criminal convictions, including bribery and attempting to obstruct justice arising from his offer to fix criminal cases, court noted that prosecutor, while "serving in that noble position of trust . . . betrayed his principal duty as a prosecutor—to see that justice is done in each case"; Sanctions Standards not cited). *But see In re Parshall,* 878 A.2d 1253 (D.C. 2005) (reciprocal discipline of eighteen-month suspension rather than reprimand imposed by originating jurisdiction upon consideration of mitigating factors for prosecutor who intentionally misled federal court by submitting a false status report and forged court order).

## 5.1 Failure to Maintain Personal Integrity

**Absent aggravating or mitigating circumstances, upon application of the factors set out in Standard 3.0, the following sanctions are generally appropriate in cases involving commission of a criminal act that reflects adversely on the lawyer's honesty, trustworthiness, or fitness as a lawyer in other respects, or in cases with conduct involving dishonesty, fraud, deceit, or misrepresentation:**

**5.11 Disbarment is generally appropriate when:**

**(a) a lawyer engages in serious criminal conduct a necessary element of which includes intentional interference with the administration of justice, false swearing, misrepresentation, fraud, extortion, misappropriation, or theft; or the sale, distribution or importation of controlled substances; or the intentional killing of another; or an attempt or conspiracy or solicitation of another to commit any of these offenses; or**

**(b) a lawyer engages in any other intentional conduct involving dishonesty, fraud, deceit, or misrepresentation that seriously adversely reflects on the lawyer's fitness to practice.**

# Annotation

A lawyer who engages in any of the acts listed in Standard 5.11 has violated one of the most basic professional obligations to the public: the pledge to maintain personal honesty and integrity. *See People v. Sims*, 190 P.3d 188, 190 (Colo. O.P.D.J. 2008) (Disbarment was warranted for lawyer convicted in California for first-degree murder. "Respondent specifically violated her duty to uphold the laws of the state and failed to maintain the standards of personal integrity upon which the community relies. The entry of default established that Respondent engaged in her misconduct (committed murder) with malice aforethought and caused serious harm to the victim and the public."). Courts generally find that when a lawyer breaches this duty to the public, discipline is warranted even when the lawyer has not been charged with or convicted of a crime. In *In re Slattery*, 767 A.2d 203 (D.C. 2001), for example, the court disbarred a lawyer who misappropriated more than $10,000 from a bank account held in the name of a fraternal organization finding, inter alia, that the lawyer committed a criminal act that reflected adversely on the lawyer's honesty, trustworthiness, or fitness. In rejecting the lawyer's challenge to the court's jurisdiction to impose discipline, the court held that there was no requirement in the disciplinary rules that the lawyer "actually have been convicted of a crime for the rule to apply. . . . [A]n attorney is not immune from bar discipline . . . merely because a complainant or prosecuting authority has chosen not to bring criminal charges." *Id.* at 207; *see also In re Egbune*, 971 P.2d 1065 (Colo. 1999) (lawyer accused but not criminally convicted of making unwanted sexual advances to client was found to have committed a criminal act by violating the third-degree sexual assault statute; rejecting lawyer's assertion that he had a right to be tried by a jury with proof beyond a reasonable doubt, the court noted that a discipline proceeding was not a criminal proceeding, standards of proof differed, and, therefore, the lawyer had no Sixth Amendment right to a jury trial); *Fla. Bar v. Karahalis*, 780 So.2d 27 (Fla. 2001) (reciprocal proceeding resulting in disbarment for lawyer who received four-year suspension from another jurisdiction for engaging in serious criminal conduct involving bribery of congressman, citing Florida Standard 5.11; court noted that it previously had found:

> [B]ribery is a particularly noxious ethical failure under the Code of Professional Responsibility, because it not only involves a breach of the individual attorney's public trust as a member of the legal profession, but also represents an attempt by the offending lawyer to induce a third party to engage in fraudulent and corrupt practices. Such conduct strikes at the very heart of the attorney's responsibility to the public and profession (citation omitted).

780 So.2d at 29.

Some courts have held that uncharged criminal conduct that is so closely related to the practice of law and poses an immediate threat of harm to the public warrants immediate interim suspension pending a final determination of what ultimate discipline should be imposed. *See, e.g.*, Model Rules for Lawyer Disciplinary Enforcement (MRLDE) R. 20 (2007); *see also In re Kapchan*, 86 A.D.3d 110 (N.Y. App. Div. 2011) (lawyer who participated in mortgage fraud scheme and testified under grant of immunity immediately suspended pending conclusion of disciplinary proceedings); *In re Disciplinary Action Against McDonagh*, 822 N.W.2d 468, 471 (N.D. 2012) (lawyer who engaged in various misconduct, including forging documents and misappropriating client funds, placed on interim suspension pending final resolution of disciplinary proceedings; ultimately disbarment was imposed); *In re Murdock*, 968 P.2d 1270, 1272 (Or. 1998) (finding lawyer's continued practice "likely to result in substantial harm to the public," court imposed temporary suspension during pendency of charges that lawyer embezzled funds from his law firm); *In re Dickey*, 718 S.E.2d 739 n.1 (S.C. 2011) (upon receiving complaint that lawyer created a fictitious medical record in conjunction with an automobile-accident case, the court ordered the lawyer's interim suspension).

When misconduct leading to felony convictions directly involves the practice of law, courts, absent significant mitigating evidence, almost always impose disbarment. *See, e.g., People v. Dunsmoor*, 79 P.3d 1061 (Colo. O.P.D.J. 2003) (citing

Standard 5.11, court imposed disbarment on lawyer convicted of embezzling funds from longshoreman union's employee pension plan and money laundering, noting that conduct was knowing and willful); *Fla. Bar v. Cueto,* 834 So.2d 152, 157 (Fla. 2002) (lawyer's participation in and conviction for participating in illegal kickback scheme involving settlement of injury cases with county adjuster warranted disbarment, even though referee had recommended three-year suspension; court said that "[a]fter reviewing the existing case law and the Florida Standards for Imposing Lawyer Sanctions, we conclude that the recommended discipline has no reasonable basis in existing case law and that disbarment is the appropriate sanction"); *Fla. Bar v. Wolis,* 783 So.2d 1057 (Fla. 2001) (felony conviction for obstruction of justice in connection with false testimony during Securities and Exchange Commission investigation of client's company, with predicate acts involving preparation and filing of false reports to Securities and Exchange Commission that potentially could have resulted in personal gain, warranted disbarment); *In re Jackson,* 27 So.3d 273 (La. 2010) (city attorney assigned to prosecute driving while intoxicated (DWI) cases agreed to represent client in DWI and then, in his capacity as city attorney, dismissed the charges against his client; conviction for fixing traffic cases warranted disbarment under Standard 5.11(a), inter alia); *In re Mithun,* 776 So.2d 426, 428 (La. 2001) (lawyer who attempted to bribe assistant district attorney to influence outcome of case disbarred after conviction, with court stating that "[t]hese crimes clearly reflect on respondent's moral fitness to practice law," misconduct that "strikes at the very heart of the integrity of the legal profession"); *In re Disciplinary Action Against Wolff,* 788 N.W.2d 594 (N.D. 2010) (citing North Dakota Standard 5.11 in imposing disbarment for lawyer convicted of attempted possession of controlled substance following his solicitation of client to provide him with cocaine); *In re Disciplinary Proceeding Against Vanderveen,* 211 P.3d 1008, 1017 (Wash. 2009) (imposing disbarment under Standard 5.11(b) on lawyer who pleaded guilty to willful failure to file a currency report, a felony, after receiving two $10,000 cash payments as his legal fee, court noted conduct was dishonest and "injurious to the reputation of the legal profession").

Courts have also held that misconduct that occurs outside the lawyer's practice warrants discipline under Standard 5.0 when the conduct adversely reflects on the lawyer's honesty, trustworthiness, or fitness as a lawyer. *See, e.g., People v. Jackson,* 943 P.2d 450 (Colo. 1997) (citing Standards 5.11(a) and (b) and case law in supporting disbarment for fraudulent conduct in connection with sale of lawyer's residence and residence of lawyer's brother); *In re Freebery,* 947 A.2d 1121 (Del. 2008) (disbarment for lawyer's conduct in failing to disclose a $2.3 million loan on personal mortgage application, a federal felony offense to which she pleaded guilty); *Att'y Grievance Comm'n v. Gore,* 845 A.2d 1204, 1214 (Md. 2004) (willful failure to file returns or pay sales taxes on behalf of restaurant lawyer owned and misappropriation of those funds warranted disbarment; court concluding that "[t]hrough his actions, [respondent] has demonstrated himself unfit to continue to be authorized to practice law in this State" and "placed himself and his business above the law"); *Fla. Bar v. Irish,* 48 So.3d 767, 772 (Fla. 2010) (disbarment under Florida Standard 5.11(a) warranted for lawyer convicted of six felony offenses involving the sale and delivery of illegal drugs; court noted that "[d]isbarment is the presumed sanction for a single felony conviction"); *Iowa Supreme Ct. Bd. of Prof'l Ethics & Conduct v. Bell,* 650 N.W.2d 648, 652 (Iowa 2002) (lawyer disbarred for misappropriating law association's funds while serving as its treasurer; court noting the fact that conversion "did not involve client funds does not diminish the seriousness of the violation"); *In re Brown,* 674 So.2d 243, 249 (La. 1996) (in imposing disbarment, court stated that "gravity of the [lawyer's negligent homicide conviction] reflects heavily on respondent's fitness to practice law" and "[a]ny sanction less than disbarment would certainly deprecate the seriousness of the offense"); *In re Finneran,* 919 N.E.2d 698, 707 (Mass. 2010) (citing Standard 5.11, inter alia, court disbarred former speaker of Commonwealth's House of Representatives after his guilty plea to federal charges of obstruction of justice for giving false testimony in federal voting-rights lawsuit; court rejected lawyer's argument that lesser sanction appropriate because crime did not involve practice of law or representation of client); *In re Labovitz,* 681 N.E.2d 268 (Mass. 1997) (disbarment warranted under Standard 5.11(a) for thirteen felony convictions involving multiple counts of bankruptcy fraud; court rejected lawyer's claim that case was governed by so-called private-citizen exception because ethical violations occurred while conducting personal business and not in practice of law); *Grievance Adm'r v. Deutch,* 565 N.W.2d 369, 378 (Mich. 1997) (in reversing hearing board's dismissal of charges against two lawyers convicted of drunk driving and remanding cases for consideration of sanction, noting that it had repeatedly rejected the idea that a lawyer has a duty to act professionally only during business hours or while at work, the court said, "[a] lawyer is a professional 'twenty-four hours a day, not eight hours, five days a week'") (citations omitted); *In re Pugh,* 710 N.W.2d 285, 289 (Minn. 2006) (disbarment warranted for lawyer convicted of thirty-two felony counts related to misappropriation of more than $1 million entrusted to his real estate closing business; rejecting lawyer's argument that sanction should be lighter because his misconduct did not involve the practice of law, court noted that it has "held in the past that a lawyer's ethical obligations are not limited to actions occurring in the practice of law, but extend to business dealings unconnected with the practice of law").

Courts also have found that lawyers acting outside the practice of law at times assume fiduciary duties analogous to those of practicing lawyers, and serious violations of those duties often warrant serious disciplinary action. *See In re Mayne,* 783 N.W.2d 153 (Minn. 2010) (lawyer disbarred upon conviction of felony financial exploitation of a vulnerable adult for misappropriating about $60,000 from elderly father's bank accounts for her personal use while acting as father's attorney-in-fact; although not acting in her capacity as a lawyer when she engaged in misconduct, lawyer had fiduciary duty as father's attorney-in-fact similar to client-lawyer fiduciary duty).

## *Intentional Versus Knowing*

In *In re Freebery*, 947 A.2d 1121 (Del. 2008), the court disbarred a lawyer convicted for making a false statement to a bank by failing to disclose a $2.3 million loan on a mortgage application, a federal felony offense. Rejecting the lawyer's contention that a knowingly false statement does not constitute fraud, the court found that respondent acted intentionally, and not merely knowingly, when she purposely omitted information about the loan to ensure that the bank would rely on the erroneous application in granting the mortgage. The court noted that an intentional act was an element of the federal crime of which the lawyer was convicted, a critical distinction since recommendations suggested by the Sanctions Standards are based on the mental state that forms the basis of a lawyer's misconduct; in other words, the more culpable mental states generally receive more severe sanctions. *See also In re Vanderslice*, 116 A.3d 1244 (Table) (Del. 2015) (court determined that lawyer's actions in his attempts to withhold earned fees from his partners were "intentional" based on the attempts made by the lawyer to conceal his actions); *In re Disciplinary Action Against McDonagh*, 822 N.W.2d 468, 471 (N.D. 2012) (citing North Dakota Standard 5.11, court imposed disbarment for forgery of two title opinion documents and repeated lies about land commission check; noting that under the Sanctions Standards the "difference between 'knowledge' and 'intent' is a 'conscious objective or purpose to accomplish a particular result'"; court finding that forgery was intended to deceive bank in order to obtain line of credit).

One court made clear in its opinions that the mens rea necessary for assessing whether professional discipline is appropriate is distinguishable from the intent necessary to establish an element of a crime. *See, e.g., In re Thompson*, 991 P.2d 820 (Colo. 1999) (disbarring lawyer under Standard 5.11(b) for knowing misappropriation of approximately $15,000 received from clients that should have been turned over to his law firm; unlike prosecutions under theft statute, intent to permanently deprive another of property is not an element of knowing misappropriation for attorney discipline purposes).

## *Criminal Prosecution or Conviction Unnecessary*

As noted above, courts have held that lawyers can be disbarred for criminal conduct even when criminal charges have not been filed or convictions obtained. *See, e.g., In re Ivy*, 374 P.3d 374 (Alaska 2016) (despite a lack of a prior disciplinary record or convictions arising from her dishonesty, disbarment warranted for lawyer who lied during an ethics proceeding and in a civil trial); *People v. Odom*, 941 P.2d 919 (Colo. 1997) (citing Standard 5.11 generally, court found disbarment appropriate for lawyer who committed but was not charged with crime of concealing automobile in which former client had taken security interest following settlement in legal malpractice action); *People v. Rishel*, 50 P.3d 938 (Colo. O.P.D.J. 2002) (finding conduct met criteria under both Standards 5.11(a) and (b), court ruled disbarment appropriate for lawyer who, as member of group, pooled funds to buy baseball season tickets, obtained funds from other members for purported purpose of purchasing season tickets, but then converted them for his own use); *In re Tenenbaum*, 918 A.2d 1109, 1134 (Del. 2007) (lawyer's sexual assault of former client who reported the criminal conduct twenty-two years later warranted disbarment under Standard 5.11(b); although not convicted, lawyer's criminal conduct "meets the general language and intent of Standard 5.0" and is conduct that reflects adversely on lawyer's fitness even if it arguably does not involve dishonesty); *Fla. Bar v. Hall*, 49 So.3d 1254, 1259 (Fla. 2010) (citing Florida Standards 5.11(b) and (f), the equivalent of Standard 5.11(b) under the ABA Sanctions Standards, court disbarred lawyer who was found to have engaged in fraudulent conduct in her personal affairs by filing a forged document in order to place cloud on property owners' title, despite a "not guilty" finding in criminal matter arising out of same conduct; noting severity of the lawyer's fraud, the court pointed out that it did "not look favorably on those who use their standing as an officer of the court to deliberately harm others—especially when they intentionally hurt members of the public for their own personal gain. Further, in the instant case, [the property owners] were seniors and [one] was suffering from Alzheimer's disease. Respondent was preying upon this vulnerable couple"); *In re Arabia*, 156 P.3d 652 (Kan. 2007) (lawyer's multiple rule violations, including committing a criminal act by providing false information to police during death investigation, warranted disbarment under Standard 5.11, inter alia); *In re Williams*, 85 So.3d 583, 591 (La. 2012) (relying on Standard 5.11 and finding that lawyer knowingly violated his duties to the public and the profession when he shot and killed his friend, court imposed permanent disbarment notwithstanding that lawyer's guilty plea and criminal sentence were vacated by the appellate court; court noting that "[t]he fact that an attorney has not been convicted of a crime does not preclude the [disciplinary authority] from proving the attorney committed a criminal act"); *Att'y Grievance Comm'n v. Spery*, 810 A.2d 487 (Md. 2002) (lawyer's misappropriation of partnership funds was fraudulent criminal conduct falling under Standard 5.11, warranting disbarment); *Att'y Grievance Comm'n v. Childress*, 692 A.2d 465 (Md. 1997) (a lawyer may be disciplined for engaging in criminal acts that do not result in a conviction, requiring only proof by clear and convincing evidence of a rule violation, not beyond a reasonable doubt); *In re Disciplinary Proceeding Against Kronenberg*, 117 P.3d 1134, 1141 n.9 (Wash. 2005) (citing Standard 5.11, inter alia, court found disbarment appropriate for lawyer representing accused child rapist who bribed victim with $3,000 and a one-way ticket to leave the state and then violated a court order by failing to divulge to prosecutors information related to witness's whereabouts; court held that the absence of a criminal prosecution was irrelevant to lawyer discipline "because the interest sought to be protected is different" and, citing former commentary to Standard 5.11, said that the lawyer's duty to the public was breached regardless of whether a criminal charge had been brought against the lawyer).

## *Felonies as Serious Criminal Conduct*

Courts have often concluded that conviction of a felony constitutes evidence of serious criminal conduct that will lead to disbarment. *See, e.g., People v. Zarlengo,* 367 P.3d 1197 (Colo. 2016) (disbarment was more appropriate than suspension due to the seriousness of the disbarred lawyer's felony theft); *People v. Littlefield,* 893 P.2d 773 (Colo. 1995) (citing both Standards 5.11(a) and 5.11(b) in imposing disbarment upon lawyer who pleaded guilty to felony menacing arising out of incident with office landlord in which lawyer pointed shotgun at landlord and fired shot that hit rear of landlord's vehicle); *In re Freebery,* 947 A.2d 1121 (Del. 2008) (disbarring lawyer who pleaded guilty to felony concealment of $2.3 million loan obligation on mortgage application, court noted that Delaware had disbarred lawyers convicted of felonies, without exceptions); *In re Funk,* 742 A.2d 851, 855 (Del. 1999) (disbarring upon conviction of serious crime, i.e., felony possession of firearm by unlawful drug user; aggravating factors included prior disciplinary history "reflecting a pattern of unethical conduct"); *In re Wheeler,* 871 A.2d 476, 479 (D.C. 2005) (disbarment required when lawyer convicted in another jurisdiction of misapplication of entrusted property; court analogized offense to felony theft, noting it "is a crime of moral turpitude *per se* warranting disbarment"); *In re Tolen,* 265 P.3d 546 (Kan. 2011) (disbarment under Standard 5.11, inter alia, for lawyer convicted of thirty-six charges of criminal sodomy and one charge of victim tampering); *In re Hattier,* 894 So.2d 1123 (La. 2005) (disbarment upon felony conviction for fraudulent concealment of assets in lawyer's own bankruptcy case); *In re Mmahat,* 736 So.2d 1285 (La. 1999) (disbarment warranted for lawyer who was bank board chairman following conviction of multiple felonies for making sham loans to shell corporations and swapping loans with other banks to conceal bank's weak financial position); *State ex rel. Counsel for Discipline v. Boose,* 759 N.W.2d 110, 113 (Neb. 2009) (in reciprocal proceeding, disbarment warranted for lawyer's conviction for failing to report county-commissioner-client's felonious self-dealing activity in land transaction involving the county, notwithstanding three-year suspension imposed by originating jurisdiction; court stated that lawyer's failure to uphold the laws of the United States "is a grievous breach of professional ethics . . . violates basic notions of honesty and endangers public confidence in the legal profession"); *In re Disciplinary Proceedings Against Elliott,* 790 N.W.2d 508 (Wis. 2010) (revocation of license appropriate sanction for lawyer who engaged in lengthy pattern of converting client or third-party funds for his own benefit, resorted to multimillion-dollar check-kiting scheme to continue his theft of others' money and never provided response when asked for information by the Office of Lawyer Regulation; Sanctions Standards not cited); *Bd. of Prof'l Responsibility v. Neilson,* 816 P.2d 120 (Wyo. 1991) (disbarment warranted under Standards 5.11(a) and (b) for conviction of five felonies involving preparation and use of forged instruments as trial evidence). *But see In re Key,* 113 P.3d 340 (N.M. 2005) (court rejected recommended sanction of probation emphasizing its policy that lawyers should not be allowed to practice law while on probation under a criminal sentence; presumptive sanction is disbarment under Standard 5.11(a) when lawyer engages in serious criminal conduct, here a felony conviction for filing false tax returns and involvement in tax shelter scam, but imposing suspension based on mitigating factors; court listing cases in which court had consistently disbarred or suspended lawyers convicted of criminal acts).

## *Misdemeanors as Serious Criminal Conduct*

Crimes other than felonies also can qualify as serious criminal conduct under Standard 5.11(a). *See, e.g., People v. Boyle,* 942 P.2d 1199 (Colo. 1997) (lawyer engaged in serious misconduct including, inter alia, misdemeanor conviction for aiding and abetting alien entry into United States by willfully making misleading statements); *In re Hertach,* 109 P.3d 1218 (Kan. 2005) (disbarment warranted notwithstanding misdemeanor criminal conviction for intentional conduct involving dishonesty and fraud through participation in prohibited silent partnership with sheriff to develop and run a private jail annex for the county without disclosure); *In re Disciplinary Action Against Wolff,* 788 N.W.2d 594 (N.D. 2010) (citing North Dakota Standard 5.11(a), court disbarred lawyer who pleaded guilty to misdemeanor attempted possession of a controlled substance after initially being charged with felony conspiracy to unlawfully possess a controlled substance); *In re Kimmell,* 31 P.3d 414, 419 n.7 (Or. 2001) (rejecting argument that shoplifting a jacket should not be considered "serious crime" under Standard 5.11(a), court observed that Sanctions Standards do not differentiate among degrees or kinds of theft; court nonetheless imposed six-month suspension because this theft did not violate fiduciary duty).

## *Specific Criminal Conduct Under Standard 5.11(a)*

A lawyer who engages in any of the criminal acts listed in Standard 5.11(a) is subject to disbarment. In addition to cases cited above for other propositions, the following cases illustrate the specific crimes to which courts have applied Standard 5.11(a).

• **Intentional Interference with the Administration of Justice**

The types of serious criminal conduct under Standard 5.11(a) that involve an element of intentional interference with the administration of justice include offenses involving obstruction of justice or bribery. *See, e.g., In re Bankston,* 810 So.2d 1113 (La. 2002) (disbarring Louisiana state senator under Standard 5.11(a) upon conviction for accepting bribe in form of sham condominium rental in exchange for using legislative office to protect individual holding video-poker license from unfavorable legislation); *In re Mithun,* 776 So.2d 426, 428 (La. 2001) (in imposing disbarment under Standard 5.11 on lawyer who attempted to bribe assistant district attorney in attempt to influence the outcome of client's criminal case, court noted such conduct "strikes at the very heart of the integrity of the legal profession"); *In re Finneran,* 919 N.E.2d 698 (Mass. 2010) (federal obstruction of justice conviction of former speaker of state's house of representatives for giving false testimony in federal voting rights lawsuit fell under Standard 5.11(a), inter alia, as criminal conduct involving intentional interference with the administration of justice); *In re Andrade,* 736 N.W.2d 603, 606 (Minn. 2007) (disbarment warranted for lawyer convicted of felony attempted theft by swindle after telling client he needed $50,000 to bribe high-ranking police official to get pending drug charges dismissed; court noting lawyer's "misconduct calls into question the very integrity of the judicial system, a system the attorney has sworn to uphold"); *Disciplinary Counsel v. Atkin,* 704 N.E.2d 244, 245 (Ohio 1999) (permanent disbarment warranted for lawyer convicted of numerous criminal offenses, including falsely representing to client that he could bribe a federal judge and then receiving $550,000 from the client for that purpose; court noting that "[s]uggestions by an attorney, however untrue, that a judge might be bribed weakens the public's respect for the judicial system and the faith of the people in a rule of law over men, and are intolerable"; Sanctions Standards not cited). *But see, e.g., In re Elinoff,* 22 P.3d 60, 64 (Colo. 2001) (although disbarment under Standard 5.11(a) was presumed sanction for felony conviction involving attempt to bribe two police officers, court imposed three-year suspension with one year suspended by probation in light of cases presenting similar facts and mitigating factors; court stated that "[bribery] is a crime that strikes at the heart of a lawyer's duty to uphold the administration of justice").

Similarly, courts have held that intentional witness tampering interferes with the administration of justice and can result in disbarment. *See, e.g., In re Conway,* 526 A.2d 658 (N.J. 1987) (lawyer's conviction involving crimes of conspiracy and witness tampering was a purposeful, knowing, and corrupt subversion of the criminal justice system constituting per se evidence of professional unfitness mandating disbarment); *In re Disciplinary Proceeding Against Kronenberg,* 117 P.3d 1134, 1140 (Wash. 2005) (disbarring lawyer who gave rape victim $3,000 and a one-way ticket to Oklahoma so victim would leave town and not testify as prosecution witness in child rape case; reaffirming long-held principle "that '[a]ttempting to tamper with a witness represents a flagrant disregard for the very principles upon which our legal system is grounded and renders an attorney unfit to practice law") (citation omitted). *But see In re Mintz,* 317 P.3d 756 (2014) (indefinite suspension appropriate in lieu of disbarment where lawyer, who tampered with a crime scene and intentionally misled the police in an investigation into the circumstances of the death of his mistress, rectified the damage caused by the false information provided to the police by ultimately reporting his transgressions to the police; disbarment not warranted because lawyer's dishonesty arose from a personal matter and his desire to hide the affair from his wife, not from his conduct in the practice of law, and lawyer had a prior unblemished career).

- **False Swearing**

While Standard 6.0 (Violations of Duties Owed to the Legal System) provides the recommended discipline for false statements, fraud, and misrepresentation to a court, such misconduct also is often analyzed under Standard 5.11(a) as involving a serious criminal conduct, an element of which is false swearing. *See, e.g., People v. Kiely,* 968 P.2d 110 (Colo. 1998) (citing only Standard 5.11(a) and imposing disbarment as appropriate reciprocal discipline following conviction on federal felony count of false statement on credit application); *People v. Vivarttas,* 139 P.3d 707, 710 (Colo. O.P.D.J. 2006) (citing both Standards 5.11 and 6.11, inter alia, court imposed disbarment on lawyer who testified falsely and presented false documents in her petty theft/shoplifting trial, noting that "lawyer who does not abide by an oath to tell the truth poses a serious danger to the public"); *In re Swindall,* 468 S.E.2d 372 (Ga. 1996) (disbarment warranted under Standard 5.11(a) for lawyer convicted of nine counts of perjury in relation to his testimony before a grand jury notwithstanding that three of the convictions were reversed on appeal); *In re Lehman,* 901 N.E.2d 1097, 1099 (Ind. 2009) (citing Standards 5.11(a) and (b) in disbarring respondent who pleaded guilty to filing false tax return, court reasoned that "[r]espondent pled guilty to a federal felony involving false swearing and misrepresentation, he acted out of a selfish motivation, and he has a substantial disciplinary history"); *In re Disciplinary Proceeding Against Whitney,* 120 P.3d 550 (Wash. 2005) (disbarment warranted under Standards 5.11 and 6.11, inter alia, for testifying falsely under oath while acting as guardian *ad litem* for children in family law dispute and failing to cooperate with disciplinary investigation; aggravating factors included dishonest or selfish motive, bad faith obstruction of disciplinary proceedings, and vulnerability of victim/clients). *But see People v. Lindquist,* 2016 WL 7373880 (Colo. O.P.D.J. 2016) (disbarment was the presumptive sanction under Standard 5.11(a) for lawyer's conduct in purposefully altering an exhibit during a divorce proceeding and later relying on that falsified exhibit before an appellate tribunal; court imposed three-year suspension because lawyer's misconduct was a departure from her regular course of conduct on behalf of her clients); *In re Disciplinary Proceeding Against Dornay*, 161 P.3d 333 (Wash. 2007) (disbarment presumptive sanction under both Standard 5.11 and Standard 6.11 for making materially misleading statements under oath in divorce proceedings and concealing fact that lawyer was having affair with husband in those proceedings; court imposed lesser sanction of three-year suspension in light of significant mitigating factors).

- **Misrepresentation and Fraud**

Serious criminal conduct that includes elements of misrepresentation and fraud warrants disbarment under Standard 5.11(a). *See, e.g., Cambiano v. Ligon*, 44 S.W.3d 719 (Ark. 2001) (citing Standard 5.11, court affirmed disbarment as the appropriate sanction for lawyer convicted of aiding and abetting the filing false currency transactions report and false representations to the bank and the Internal Revenue Service in an attempt to shield his drug-dealer-client's assets); *People v. Hilgendorf*, 895 P.2d 544, 545 (Colo. 1995) (disbarment warranted upon convictions for false statements to federal banks involving overvaluation of land and failure to disclose debts on loan applications; court cited cases of disbarment following convictions of "comparably serious crimes," including mail fraud, bank fraud, and bankruptcy fraud); *People v. Pilgrim*, 802 P.2d 1084 (Colo. 1990) (disbarment warranted for lawyer's convictions of serious offenses against the United States based on his conspiracy to impede the ability of the IRS to collect revenues by creating fraudulent trust agreements for the purpose of reducing clients' tax liabilities); *People v. Barringer*, 61 P.3d 495 (Colo. O.P.D.J. 2001) (citing Standard 5.11(a), court imposed disbarment for numerous misrepresentations and dishonest actions including affixing client's signature to settlement without authorization and impersonating a notary); *In re Brewster*, 587 A.2d 1067 (Del. 1991) (disbarment under Standard 5.11(a) warranted for felony bank fraud conviction for making misrepresentations about collateral to secure a series of loans and altering stock certificates); *Att'y Grievance Comm'n v. Wingerter*, 929 A.2d 47 (Md. 2007) (disbarment warranted for in-house counsel's misprision of a felony conviction arising from his failure to report company's participation in conspiracy to commit immigration fraud and his actions in concealing the fraud); *In re Otis*, 782 N.E.2d 502 (Mass. 2003) (disbarment warranted upon felony conviction for conspiracy to commit bankruptcy fraud); *Disciplinary Counsel v. Stern*, 834 N.E.2d 351, 352–53 (Ohio 2005) (lawyer's conviction of four federal criminal charges, including bank fraud and money laundering, was "harmful to the legal profession, which is and ought to be a high calling dedicated to the service of clients and the public good," and warranted permanent disbarment; Sanctions Standards not cited); *State ex rel. Okla. Bar Ass'n v. Golden*, 201 P.3d 862, 866 (Okla. 2008) (lawyer's participation in health-care fraud scheme by concealing his client's transfer of funds from employees' pension fund to client's various companies led to conviction for misprision of a felony and disbarment; court stating that lawyer's misconduct "was egregious, was an abuse of trust, brought great disrepute to the legal profession, and actively concealed great harm to many people and to the health care system as exhibited by the $5,719,340.22 order of restitution" imposed in lawyer's criminal sentence); *In re Disciplinary Proceeding Against Smith*, 246 P.3d 1224 (Wash. 2011) (disbarment warranted for lawyer who pleaded guilty to crime of conspiracy to commit federal securities fraud and wire fraud; sole mitigating factor of no prior disciplinary record not sufficient to justify departure from presumptive sanction). *But see In re Pennington*, 921 A.2d 135 (D.C. 2007) (in reciprocal proceeding, court rejected disbarment sanction imposed in originating jurisdiction; two-year suspension with reinstatement conditioned upon showing of fitness for lawyer who falsified settlement documents to conceal mishandling of clients' personal injury claims and deceived clients; court noted that District of Columbia deviated from standard in that intentionally dishonest conduct would not warrant presumptive disbarment unless it involved misappropriation of client funds).

- **Extortion**

Extortion is also considered serious criminal conduct warranting a lawyer's disbarment under Standard 5.11(a). *See, e.g., Ky. Bar Ass'n v. Reynolds*, 378 S.W.3d 310 (Ky. 2012) (lawyer's conviction for conspiring with county sheriff to extort funds from clients referred to him by the sheriff was serious criminal conduct that interfered with the administration of justice and warranted disbarment under Standard 5.11(a)); *In re King*, 33 So.3d 873 (La. 2010) (Standard 5.11, inter alia, supported disbarment sanction for former district judge who required his staff to campaign on his behalf or risk the loss of employment, who was charged criminally with public salary extortion, and pleaded guilty to one felony count of public payroll fraud); *Lawyer Disciplinary Bd. v. Blevins*, 671 S.E.2d 658, 664 (W. Va. 2008) (disbarment warranted for lawyer's criminal acts that included soliciting the services of a known felon to extort money through violence and intimidation of individuals, some of whom were former clients who owed lawyer money; rejecting lawyer's claim that he was merely "role-playing" and that no harm resulted from his conduct, court stated that "[t]here does not exist in the Rules of Professional Conduct a 'no harm, no foul' Rule").

- **Misappropriation or Theft**

The recommended discipline for conversion of funds is set forth under Standard 4.1, Failure to Preserve Client Property, but courts also often cite Standard 5.11 when considering the appropriate sanction for misappropriation and conversion. *See, e.g., People v. Allbrandt*, 913 P.2d 532 (Colo. 1996) (disbarment warranted under Standard 5.11(a) for lawyer who knowingly converted for his personal use $445,000 in securities investment scheme operated out of law office); *People v.*

*Brown*, 840 P.2d 348 (Colo. 1992) (disbarment warranted under Standard 5.11 for deputy public defender whose numerous offenses included conviction of embezzlement of public property by soliciting and converting funds from his indigent clients, using cocaine, and submitting false information and fabricated evidence); *In re Garrett*, 909 A.2d 103, 105 (Del. 2006) (disbarring lawyer who intentionally misappropriated client funds, court, relying on Standard 5.11(a), noted that "in every prior Delaware disciplinary matter in which an attorney has intentionally misappropriated client funds, the attorney has been disbarred"); *In re Hill*, 655 N.E.2d 343, 345 (Ind. 1995) (citing Standard 5.11, inter alia, in determining that lawyer's criminal conversion of estate funds mandated the most severe sanction of disbarment, the court held that "[m]isappropriation of client funds is a grave transgression" and "demonstrates a conscious desire to accomplish an unlawful act, denotes a lack of virtually all personal characteristics we deem important to law practice, threatens to bring significant misfortune on the unsuspecting client and severely impugns the integrity of the profession"); *Iowa Supreme Ct. Att'y Disciplinary Bd. v. Carroll*, 721 N.W.2d 788 (Iowa 2006) (lawyer who served as president of nonprofit arts council disbarred for misappropriating council's funds and unauthorized use of council's credit card following second-degree theft charges); *Att'y Grievance Comm'n v. Olujobi*, 984 A.2d 237 (Md. 2009) (disbarment warranted for lawyer who, as trustee for divorcing parties' property estate, failed to turn over sale proceeds; Sanctions Standards not referenced but court applied comparable analysis); *In re Leon*, 524 N.W.2d 723 (Minn. 1994) (disbarment warranted under Standard 5.11 for law firm associate who regularly and purposely circumvented firm's billing procedures to misappropriate law firm and client funds); *In re Disciplinary Action Against Buresh*, 726 N.W.2d 210 (N.D. 2007) (court finding that lawyer's actions in misappropriating client's share of proceeds from sale of family farm constituted a crime warranting disbarment under North Dakota Standard 5.11); *In re Jordan*, 674 S.E.2d 149 (S.C. 2009) (disbarment warranted for lawyer who made unauthorized transfer of $2.3 million in client funds from trust accounts to himself for his own benefit, for which lawyer pleaded guilty to federal wire fraud); *In re Disciplinary Proceedings Against Koch*, 787 N.W.2d 814 (Wis. 2010) (revocation of license when lawyer converted more than $2.4 million in subrogated funds collected on behalf of client and lost it gambling).

Other types of misappropriation are also subject to presumptive disbarment under Standard 5.11(a). *See, e.g., People v. Carlson*, 2016 WL 8290617 (Colo. O.P.D.J. 2016) (citing Standard 5.11, inter alia, disbarment warranted for multiple acts of misrepresentation, the most serious of which involved converting funds belonging to others; lawyer also neglected two cases, leading to their dismissal, lied about the cases' status to the affected clients, and neglected to pay medical costs he was obligated to pay); *People v. Lavenhar*, 934 P.2d 1355 (Colo. 1997) (disbarment warranted for multiple acts of misconduct, the most serious of which was knowing conversion of $28,000 check mistakenly sent by Enron Corp., with whom lawyer as sublessee of law office space had disagreement; lawyer placed on disability inactive status after misconduct occurred and did not participate in all disciplinary proceedings; court finding that long-standing personality disorder with antisocial aspects not amenable to treatment cannot be considered mitigating factor); *Iowa Supreme Ct. Att'y Disciplinary Bd. v. Polsley*, 796 N.W.2d 881, 886 (Iowa 2011) (revoking licenses of lawyers, a married couple, after conviction for conversion of Social Security checks mistakenly sent to trust account of one lawyer's mother for which lawyer served as trustee); *In re Basile*, 714 So.2d 687 (La. 1998) (disbarment warranted for lawyer, a relapsing alcoholic and drug addict who pleaded guilty to attempted misdemeanor theft, failed to appear for arraignment on charges of prostitution and felony theft, and was arrested on multiple felony theft charges stemming from her purchase of goods through fraudulent use of her father's credit card); *In re Pugh*, 710 N.W.2d 285 (Minn. 2006) (disbarment warranted under Standard 5.11(a) after federal conviction for criminal conversion of $1 million in funds of real estate closing company owned by lawyer); *In re Abell*, 697 A.2d 340 (Vt. 1997) (disbarment warranted under Standard 5.11 for managing partner's embezzlement of $408,260 from his law firm). *But see People v. Barnthouse*, 948 P.2d 534 (Colo. 1997) (finding disbarment presumptive sanction under Standard 5.11(a) for theft of four pairs of eyeglass frames, a felony, but imposing suspension of a year and a day in view of precedent); *In re Summer*, 105 P.3d 848 (Or. 2005) (finding disbarment under Standard 5.11(a) presumptive sanction for attempted theft by deception in attempt to recover twice from separate insurers for client's injuries, but imposing 180-day suspension as consistent with state's prior case law involving similar misconduct); *and In re Kimmell*, 31 P.3d 414, 420 (Or. 2001) (citing Standard 5.11 for lawyer's theft of jacket from store but imposing six-month suspension, court drawing "distinction between lawyer theft that results in a violation of a fiduciary duty and lawyer theft that does not").

- **Sale, Distribution, or Importation of Controlled Substances**

Felony drug convictions result in a baseline sanction of disbarment under Standard 5.11(a). *See, e.g., Ala. State Bar v. Quinn*, 926 So.2d 1018, 1024 (Ala. 2005) (although lawyer was convicted of contributing to the delinquency of a minor, his smoking marijuana with a group of minors and "giving away" a marijuana "blunt" to a minor established a criminal act under Alabama Sanctions Standard 5.11(a), distribution of a controlled substance warranting disbarment); *People v. Ebbert*, 925 P.2d 274 (Colo. 1996) (disbarment on consent warranted upon felony convictions for possession of cocaine and contributing to delinquency of minor); *Fla. Bar v. Irish*, 48 So.3d 767 (Fla. 2010) (disbarment warranted for lawyer convicted of six felony offenses involving trafficking, sale, and delivery of illegal drugs and who also misused client funds to support his drug habit); *Fla. Bar v. Liberman*, 43

So.3d 36 (Fla. 2010) (lawyer convicted of felony trafficking in Ecstasy is disbarred); *In re Swearingen*, 501 S.E.2d 200 (Ga. 1998) (disbarment warranted for lawyer upon guilty plea to felony possession of cocaine with intent to distribute); *In re Brown*, 953 P.2d 1367 (Kan. 1998) (disbarment warranted for lawyer upon federal felony convictions for conspiracy and possession of cocaine with intent to distribute); *In re Alexander*, 37 So.3d 999 (La. 2010) (adhering to baseline sanction of disbarment under Standard 5.11(a) as it expressly applies to the sale, distribution, or importation of controlled substances, and ordering disbarment of lawyer convicted of distribution of controlled substance); *Att'y Grievance Comm'n. v. Dechowitz*, 747 A.2d 657 (Md. 2000) (in imposing disbarment on lawyer convicted of possession with intent to distribute marijuana, court drew distinction between conduct involving mere possession of illegal substances, often resulting in suspension, and that involving sale/distribution of narcotics; Sanctions Standards not cited); *In re Disciplinary Action Against Wolff*, 788 N.W.2d 594, 599 (N.D. 2010) (citing North Dakota Standard 5.11(a), court disbarred lawyer convicted of attempted possession of controlled substance after he solicited client to provide him with cocaine); *In re Discipline of Harding*, 104 P.3d 1220 (Utah 2004) (disbarment warranted for former judge who resigned from the bench rather than face impeachment following conviction for unlawful possession and use of controlled substances; court considered totality of circumstances including lawyer's continual public maintenance of innocence and malignment of his accusers despite full knowledge of culpability); *In re Discipline of Pendleton*, 11 P.3d 284 (Utah 2000) (in imposing disbarment, court relied not only upon the fact of lawyer's criminal conviction for methamphetamine possession but also upon other serious criminal conduct involving the possession, use, procurement, and distribution of methamphetamine and which at times involved clients); *Lawyer Disciplinary Bd. v. Askin*, 507 S.E.2d 683, 686 (W. Va. 1998) (in imposing disbarment based on criminal-contempt conviction arising from lawyer's refusal to testify in federal trial about cocaine transactions with defendants, two of whom had been his clients, court noted that the criminal contempt conviction "offends the essence of the integrity of the legal system"; Sanctions Standards not cited); *cf. In re Petition for Reinstatement of Madden*, No. 12-345, 2012 WL 2355572 (Ark. June 21, 2012) (disbarred lawyer denied reinstatement as a result of misprision of a felony conviction arising from his failure to report knowledge of a drug transaction, sale of an ounce of cocaine, between his former client and a law firm secretary because state's rules prohibited readmission after felony conviction of a "serious crime" as defined in state supreme court procedures regulating professional conduct).

- **Intentional Killing of Another**

Disbarment is considered the appropriate sanction when a lawyer is convicted of murder, with the courts often citing Sanctions Standard 5.11(a). *See, e.g., People v. Kintzele*, 409 P.3d 680, 683 (Colo. 2017) (citing Standard 5.11, court held that "disbarment is the only condign sanction" for attempted second-degree murder of the lawyer's wife where lawyer nearly killed his wife by brutally attacking her with a hatchet and a kitchen knife); *People v. Sims*, 190 P.3d 188 (Colo. O.P.D.J. 2008) (applying Standard 5.11(a), court held that respondent's conviction in California for first-degree murder warranted disbarment); *In re Weber*, 183 A.D.2d 349 (N.Y. App. Div. 1992) (automatic disbarment required for lawyer convicted of first-degree murder in Illinois, which is a felony in New York).

**• Attempt or Conspiracy or Solicitation of Another to Commit Any of These Offenses**

When a lawyer conspires with another to commit a criminal offense or solicits another to do so, the lawyer can be disciplined under Standard 5.11(a). *See, e.g., In re Mendenhall*, 959 N.E.2d 254 (Ind. 2012) (citing Standard 5.11(a), court imposed permanent disbarment on lawyer convicted as guilty but mentally ill of several violent felonies including attempted murder after lawyer beat his victim when gun malfunctioned); *In re Grand*, 778 So.2d 580 (La. 2001) (disbarment warranted for, among other misconduct, conviction of misprision of felony under federal law for concealing conspiracy to commit mail fraud by a medical provider); *In re Walker*, 713 S.E.2d 264 (S.C. 2011) (disbarment appropriate for respondent who pleaded guilty to solicitation of a felony when he attempted to hire a hit man to kill another member of the bar by paying with a postdated check, and in light of other misconduct relating to numerous client matters, including trust account violations).

Lawyers can be disbarred under Standard 5.11(a) not only when they conspire with another to commit a criminal offense or solicit another to do so, but also when they help clients violate the law. *See, e.g., People v. Sugar*, 360 P.3d 1041 (Colo. 2015) (disbarment under Standard 5.11 warranted for lawyer who pleaded guilty to felony conspiracy to defraud after assisting more than 150 clients in evading taxes, thus defrauding the federal government of millions of dollars); *In re Allison*, 481 S.E.2d 211 (Ga. 1997) (court relying on Standard 5.11, inter alia, imposed disbarment for lawyer's dishonesty in aiding client's use of fictitious names in connection with loan and other legal documents).

## *Multiple Acts of Misconduct*

Cases in which lawyers are disbarred often involve multiple acts of criminal misconduct, falling under Standard 5.11(a). *See, e.g., In re Woltman*, 875 P.2d 781, 782 (Ariz. 1994) (court imposed disbarment on lawyer, under Standard 5.11, inter alia, for misconduct that included conversion of client funds, finding lawyer's multiple acts of misconduct "so egregious that virtually every standard is applicable"); *In re Lopez*, 980 P.2d 983 (Colo. 1999) (disbarment warranted on consent under Standard 5.11(a) following criminal convictions for fraud, perjury, and forgery); *People v. Andersen*, 58 P.3d 537 (Colo. O.P.D.J. 2000) (disbarment warranted under Standard 5.11(a), inter alia, for knowing conversion of client funds, felony forgery for using law firm employer's signature stamp to negotiate stolen trust account checks, and felony theft of automobile); *In re Enna*, 971 A.2d 110, 113–14 (Del. 2009) (in imposing disbarment, court relied on lawyer's stipulation that "he was convicted of multiple misdemeanors and two felonies, including falsifying evidence, terrorizing, assault, violation of condition of release, and violation of protection from abuse order"); *In re Blair*, 40 A.3d 883 (D.C. 2012) (lawyer's federal convictions for obstruction of justice and witness tampering are crimes involving moral turpitude and therefore mandate disbarment); *Fla. Bar v. Wolis*, 783 So.2d 1057 (Fla. 2001) (in-house counsel who was named in sixty-four-count federal indictment alleging multiple securities laws violations and pleaded guilty to one count felony obstruction of justice charge was disbarred); *In re Sniadecki*, 924 N.E.2d 109 (Ind. 2010) (lawyer's multiple criminal acts, including forgery of documents and false affidavit under oath stating lawyer provided clients written notice of his suspension, warranted disbarment under Standard 5.11, inter alia); *In re Farrell*, 21 P.3d 552, 560 (Kan. 2001) (relying on Standard 5.11(a) and finding that lawyer's conduct "amounted to 'criminal acts directly involved with the practice of law' and 'involved felonious conduct interfering with the administration of justice, false swearing, misrepresentation, fraud, and acts adversely reflecting on the lawyer's fitness to practice law,'" court imposed disbarment); *In re Richard*, 50 So.3d 1285, 1289 (La. 2010) (lawyer who forged a medical record at his client's request and was convicted of criminal mischief as result of a violent physical altercation with his father was disbarred; board noted that lawyer "has a 'demonstrated propensity to engage in criminal activity,' which leads to the conclusion that he lacks the requisite good moral character and fitness necessary to practice law"); *In re Harrington*, 710 So.2d 243 (La. 1998) (disbarment warranted upon conviction for conspiracy to induce illegal aliens into the United States, transporting illegal aliens, and obstruction of justice by bribery in attempt to induce false testimony regarding lawyer's role in the matter); *In re Concemi*, 662 N.E.2d 1030, 1033 (Mass. 1996) (disbarment under Standard 5.11(a) warranted for lawyer convicted of thirty-five felony counts of conspiracy to defraud bank, bank fraud, and making false statements to federally insured bank; disbarment or indefinite suspension is "the usual sanction imposed for a felony conviction"); *Lawyer Disciplinary Bd. v. Robinson*, 736 S.E.2d 18 (W. Va. 2012) (disbarment warranted for lawyer with history of violent behavior for numerous acts of misconduct, including conviction for beating his client with a baseball bat and throwing propane tank through windshield of car driven by lawyer's wife, conduct that adversely reflected on lawyer's fitness to practice).

## *Misconduct Under Standard 5.11(b)*

When intentional acts by a lawyer do not involve the serious criminal conduct set forth in Standard 5.11(a), disbarment may still be warranted under Standard 5.11(b), when the conduct involves dishonesty, fraud, deceit, or misrepresentation and has a serious adverse reflection on the lawyer's fitness to practice law.

For a discussion of the distinction between subsections (a) and (b) of Standard 5.11, see *In re Hertach,* 109 P.3d 1218 (Kan. 2005). There, the court applied Standard 5.11(b) and disbarred the lawyer convicted of a misdemeanor for conspiring to defraud the county by participating in a prohibited silent partnership with the sheriff to develop and run a private jail annex. Agreeing with the lawyer's argument that he was not convicted of any of the crimes included within Standard 5.11(a), the court found that, nonetheless, disbarment was appropriate under Standard 5.11(b) because the lawyer engaged "in 'intentional conduct involving dishonesty, fraud, deceit, or misrepresentation that seriously adversely reflects on the lawyer's fitness to practice.' Conviction or even the charging of a crime with these elements is not necessary for this provision to apply." *Id.* at 1225.

In some instances, courts have applied both Standards 5.11(a) and 5.11(b) to discipline a lawyer for the same misconduct. *See, e.g., In re Friedman,* 23 P.3d 620, 631 (Alaska 2001) (in finding that presumptive sanction was disbarment under Standards 5.11(a) and 5.11(b) for lawyer who drew on trust funds to pay himself fees before they were due, court observed that subsection (a) applied because lawyer engaged in serious criminal conduct that would have been a felony in Alaska and subsection (b) also applied because conduct involved "dishonesty, fraud, deceit, or misrepresentation"; court imposed three-year suspension instead of disbarment, though, because of other precedent and mitigating factors); *People v. Evanson,* 223 P.3d 735, 738 (Colo. O.P.D.J. 2009) (citing both Standards 5.11(a) and (b), court disbarred lawyer convicted of several federal offenses, including conspiracy to commit tax fraud, for his role in creating and promoting illegal tax schemes resulting in the fraudulent concealment of more than $60 million of clients' income from the IRS; court finding that lawyer "engaged in serious criminal conduct involving a dishonest motive") *In re White,* 996 So.2d 266 (La. 2008) (lawyer's conduct, conviction relating to his conspiracy with a judge to violate the civil rights of a litigant in a case pending before the judge, entailed fraud and deceit, falling under Standards 5.11(a) and (b) warranting disbarment).

- **Serious Adverse Reflection on Fitness to Practice**

Courts have concluded that many kinds of intentional conduct involving dishonesty, fraud, deceit, or misrepresentation seriously, adversely reflect on a lawyer's fitness to practice law and thus warrant disbarment under 5.11(b). Among the kinds of misconduct for which courts have disbarred under Standard 5.11(b) are lies and misrepresentations. *See, e.g., In re Redeker*, 868 P.2d 318, 323 (Ariz. 1994) (lawyer's participation in preparing a forged trust document and sending it to an insurance company to rely upon as well as repeated lies to disciplinary authorities evidenced a breach of his duty to maintain personal honesty and integrity as addressed in Standard 5.11(b), warranting disbarment; "duty to avoid conduct involving dishonesty, fraud, deceit, or misrepresentation is perhaps the most fundamental ethical duty of a lawyer and is correspondingly supremely important") (citation omitted); *People v. Thompson*, 142 P.3d 261 (Colo. O.P.D.J. 2006) (disbarment warranted for lawyer who used forged document to misrepresent status of case to minor client and abandoned matter without refunding retainer); *People v. Kolbjornsen*, 35 P.3d 181, 184 (Colo. O.P.D.J. 1999) (disbarment warranted for submitting false information to bankruptcy court, conduct that met all the criteria under Standard 5.11(b), inter alia; "misconduct caused significant financial harm to [respondent's former employer], it deceived and misled a court charged with the responsibility of rendering a just and fair decision, it necessitated further unnecessary judicial proceedings and it reflected adversely upon the profession"); *In re Hertach*, 109 P.3d 1218, 1226 (Kan. 2005) (lawyer's purposeful omission and criminal conduct in concealing secret partnership with sheriff in order to obtain a contract for county services reflected upon his honesty and fitness, warranting disbarment under Standard 5.11(b); court noting that respondent violated "a public duty—the public's right to have an attorney act in a trustworthy fashion"); *Ky. Bar Ass'n v. Reynolds*, 378 S.W.3d 310, 312 (Ky. 2012) (lawyer who extorted money from clients facing felony charges to pay sheriff in exchange for favorable consideration of clients' cases "circumvented the system that he is sworn to uphold and betrayed the trust of the public in the fair administration of justice"; disbarment warranted under Standard 5.11); *In re Bradley*, 62 So.3d 52, 54 (La. 2011) (lawyer's conviction for conspiracy to bribe state official to secure tax credits for client's film production company demonstrated clear lack of moral fitness warranting disbarment; court noting lawyer "significantly harmed a program designed to provide economic benefits to the state and also caused serious harm to the reputation of the legal profession"); *In re Petal*, 30 So.3d 728, 732 (La. 2010) (lawyer's conviction of a serious crime with elements of dishonesty and conspiracy to commit bribery "reflects adversely on his moral fitness to practice law," warranting disbarment under Standard 5.11(b)); *Att'y Grievance Comm'n v. Sheinbein*, 812 A.2d 981, 996 (Md. 2002) (disbarment imposed on lawyer who committed the crimes of obstructing or hindering a police officer when he took intentional steps to assist his son in fleeing the country after learning his son was the main suspect in a murder investigation; court stating that although lawyer's "appalling" actions did not directly affect his practice or his clients, his acts were "criminal in nature and directly harmful to the legal profession," demonstrating that he was not fit to practice law). *But see People v. Rudman*, 948 P.2d 1022 (Colo. 1997) (acknowledging disbarment as presumptive sanction under Standard 5.11(b) for intentional pattern of lies by lawyer, as personal representative of estate, to sole beneficiary of estate; but three-year suspension imposed given mitigating factors); *Grievance Adm'r v. Rostash,* 577 N.W.2d 452 (Mich. 1998) (Standard 5.11(b) cited, but 180-day suspension, not disbarment, imposed for lawyer who aided and assisted an elected prosecutor in violating his office and public trust and then misrepresented his involvement with prosecutor during disciplinary investigation; unblemished record after thirty-six years of practice weighed heavily).

Similarly, various kinds of fraud, including tax fraud, fall within the purview of Standard 5.11(b) as conduct that seriously, adversely reflects on a lawyer's fitness to practice. *See, e.g., In re Grossman,* 2000 WL 1673417, at *2 (T.C. Nov. 6, 2000) (court, imposing suspension instead of disbarment due to mitigating evidence, stated that "consistent with ABA Standard 5.11(b), we should consider sanctions up to and including disbarment to a tax attorney who has committed civil tax fraud because that conduct involves dishonesty, fraud, deceit, or misrepresentation that seriously adversely reflects on a tax lawyer's fitness to practice before the United States Tax Court"); *In re Bruno,* 833 P.2d 698 (Ariz. 1992) (disbarment warranted for lawyer under Standard 5.11(b) for scheme to defraud his employer, resulting in actual losses of more than $1.6 million); *People v. Cohen,* 369 P.3d 289 (Colo. 2016) (attorney disbarred for pleading guilty to thirteen counts of theft, where all the victims of theft were the lawyer's clients or individuals who paid on behalf of her clients); *In re DeRose,* 55 P.3d 126 (Colo. 2002) (disbarment warranted under Standard 5.11(b) for felony conviction of structuring transactions to evade federal financial institution reporting requirements and aiding and abetting); *Att'y Grievance Comm'n v. Bereano,* 744 A.2d 35 (Md. 2000) (disbarment warranted for mail fraud conviction arising from lawyer's legislative lobbying activities when lawyer devised scheme to defraud his lobbying clients of money by false pretenses); *Bd. of Prof'l Responsibility v. Cowan,* 388 S.W.3d 264 (Tenn. 2012) (finding Standard 5.11(b) applicable to willful tax evasion conviction, intentional conduct involving dishonesty that seriously, adversely reflects on a lawyer's fitness and warranting disbarment).

Disbarment under Standard 5.11(b) is also warranted for deceitful conduct that seriously, adversely reflects on a lawyer's fitness to practice. *See, e.g., In re Smith,* 794 P.2d 601 (Ariz. 1990) (disbarment under Standards 5.11(a) and (b) warranted upon federal felony convictions for aiding and abetting a mail fraud and aiding and abetting sale of an unlicensed security arising from lawyer's preparation of two securities opinion letters and one tax opinion letter); *People v. Mascarenas,* 275 P.3d 1287, 1290 (Colo. O.P.D.J. 2011) (in imposing disbarment under Standard 5.11(b) for lawyer's elaborate and unconscionable scheme to defraud purchasers of store owned by his wife, court stated it had "little trouble concluding that Respondent's conduct renders him wholly unfit to practice law"); *People v. Katz,* 58 P.3d 1176, 1195 (Colo.

O.P.D.J. 2002) (disbarment presumptive sanction under Standard 5.11(b), inter alia, for deceit in surreptitious withdrawal of funds from partnership's joint account; court stating that use of funds belonging to third party or another lawyer "strikes at the heart of the fiduciary duties the attorney must hold paramount"; disbarment imposed); *People v. Essay*, 35 P.3d 590 (Colo. O.P.D.J. 2001) (citing Standard 5.11(b), inter alia, court imposed disbarment on lawyer who neglected clients' matters, engaged in dishonesty and misrepresentations, and disposed of 100 boxes of client files requested for review by Office of Attorney Regulation Counsel, resulting in virtually all of lawyer's clients suffering serious legal consequences); *Iowa Supreme Court Att'y. Disciplinary Bd. v. Guthrie*, 901 N.W.2d 493 (Iowa 2017) (court disbarred lawyer for fraudulently billing multiple clients for work not completed and pleading guilty to domestic abuse assault; Sanctions Standards not cited); *In re Schwehm*, 860 So.2d 1108, 1111 (La. 2003) (disbarment warranted under Standard 5.11(b) for lawyer/justice of the peace convicted of two felony counts of malfeasance in office for knowingly and intentionally failing to remit litter fines collected through his office and charging and collecting unauthorized fees for filing peace bonds; court noted board's finding that lawyer's "illegal acts clearly show a failure to maintain the personal honesty and integrity required by the legal profession and the legal system"); *In re Albrecht*, 42 P.3d 887 (Or. 2002) (lawyer who participated in money-laundering scheme engaged in conduct involving dishonesty, deceit, and misrepresentation warranting disbarment under Standard 5.11(b)); *In re Disciplinary Proceeding Against Cramer*, 225 P.3d 881, 887 (Wash. 2010) (disbarment warranted for lawyer who removed from his law office door a posted order revoking his business license and changed name of law business in effort to avoid state tax obligations, all "acts involving dishonesty, deceit, and misrepresentation").

Courts often have disbarred lawyers under Standard 5.11(b) for dishonesty in handling client funds that seriously, adversely reflects on his or her fitness to practice law. *See People v. Hotle*, 35 P.3d 185, 191 (Colo. O.P.D.J. 1999) (finding lawyer's conduct met all the criteria of Standard 5.11(b), inter alia, court imposed disbarment for knowing misappropriation of client funds, among other misconduct; misconduct "caused serious harm to his client and it seriously adversely reflects on his fitness to practice law"); *In re Quist*, 483 S.E.2d 569, 570 (Ga. 1997) (disbarment warranted for intentional dishonesty involving conversion of client property, conduct under Standard 5.11 that "seriously reflects on the lawyer's fitness to practice"). In *Gex v. Miss. Bar*, 656 So.2d 1124 (Miss. 1995), the court found that among the multiple instances of misconduct warranting disbarment under Standard 5.11(b), inter alia, the lawyer had misused clients' money and misrepresented the status of deed of trust and loan information to client and bank. The court said:

> Not only are lawyers expected by their clients to act as professionals but they affirm this duty to the courts of this state when they take

> their oaths on becoming attorneys. The dignity and reputation of the legal profession takes another hit when society learns of the irresponsible and unscrupulous conduct suffered at the hands of attorneys like [respondent].

656 So.2d at 1132.

### *Multiple Acts of Misconduct*

Cases involving multiple acts of misconduct falling under Standard 5.0 quite often cite both Standards 5.11(a) and 5.11(b) in evaluating the appropriate sanction. *See also* discussion of multiple acts of misconduct in the section addressing Standard 5.11(a) above. *See, e.g., People v. Frye*, 935 P.2d 10 (Colo. 1997) (disbarment warranted under Standards 5.11(a) and (b) following three felony convictions for securities fraud, all involving dishonesty and fraudulent practices); *People v. Gerdes*, 891 P.2d 995 (Colo. 1995) (disbarment warranted under Standards 5.11(a) and (b), inter alia, for lawyer who, among other misconduct, executed insurance agent's signature on indemnity agreement without agent's permission, drove while ability impaired, and possessed marijuana); *In re Gustafson*, 41 P.3d 1063 (Or. 2002) (disbarment warranted for deputy district attorney under Standards 5.11(a) and 5.11(b), inter alia, for multiple acts of misconduct including undermining juvenile court's expunction order by releasing juvenile's records in lawyer's disciplinary matter and testifying falsely that she had complied with subpoena); *In re Garvey*, 932 P.2d 549 (Or. 1997) (disbarment warranted under Standards 5.11(a) and 5.11(b), inter alia, for multiple charges of perjury and false swearing regarding participation in client's escape from jail); *In re Leonhardt*, 930 P.2d 844 (Or. 1997) (citing both subsections of Standard 5.11, inter alia, court found disbarment warranted for district attorney convicted of felonies and misdemeanors, making misrepresentations to court and others, and abuse of grand jury process); *In re Disciplinary Proceeding Against Placide*, 414 P.3d 1124 (Wash. 2018) (disbarment warranted where lawyer committed numerous acts of misconduct including unlawfully appropriating funds belonging to two different law firms where she was employed, intentionally deceiving the firms about the extent of her representation of outside clients and the fees she had received from those clients, and failing to return unearned fees; court cited Standards 5.11(a) and 5.11(b) to justify disbarment); *Bd. of Prof'l Responsibility v. Meenan*, 85 P.3d 409 (Wyo. 2004) (citing both subsections of Standard 5.11, court disbarred former elected judicial district attorney who pleaded guilty to charges of forgery, unauthorized use of personal identifying information, and official misconduct with intent to obtain pecuniary benefit; lawyer's children, victims of the misconduct, sought leniency); *Bd. of Prof'l Responsibility v. Vidakovich*, 816 P.2d 885 (Wyo. 1991) (disbarment warranted under both subsections of Standard 5.11 for lawyer with three felony convictions involving misapplication of funds, false entry in bank records, and obstruction of justice).

## *Difficulty in Applying Standard*

Some courts have noted that certain fact patterns do not easily fit into the rubric under Standard 5.11(a) or 5.11(b). For example, in *In re Flannery*, 47 P.3d 891, 895 (Or. 2002), the court, looking to the Sanctions Standards for guidance in determining the appropriate sanction, noted that "the ABA Standards are not a perfect fit." In that case, a deputy district attorney, who had moved from Oregon to Washington, renewed his expired driver's license intentionally using a false address in order to expedite the process so he would have a current driver's license to rent a car for an upcoming trip. The lawyer was later charged and convicted of making a false application for a driver's license and subsequently terminated from his job. The court determined that the lawyer's misconduct fell under Standard 5.1 because he violated "his duty to the public to maintain standards of personal integrity when he committed a crime that reflected adversely on his honesty." *Id.* at 893. The court considered both Standard 5.11 and Standard 5.12, noting that although the lawyer's conduct was "intentional, criminal and dishonest," it did not pose an immediate threat to the public and did not reflect "seriously" on the lawyer's fitness to practice law. *Id.* at 895. Rejecting both standards as not applicable to the specific facts of the case, the court concluded that Standard 5.13 was the "closest fit," noting that the mitigating factors outweighed aggravating factors, and precedent supported the imposition of public reprimand. *Id.* at 896. *See also In re Scholl*, 25 P.3d 710 (Ariz. 2001) (court acknowledged that former judge's felony convictions for filing false tax returns and structuring currency transactions involved acts of dishonesty with elements of specific intent and knowledge under Standards 5.11(a) and (b) but relied on Standard 5.12 in imposing six-month suspension, citing substantial mitigating factors); *In re Discipline of Walton*, 287 P.3d 1098, 1103 (Or. 2012) (sanction for lawyer's unauthorized use of Westlaw account password issued to him while serving as former special prosecutor fell under Standard 5.11 since conduct was intentional, but finding standards "are not a perfect fit in this case," court imposed public reprimand under Standard 5.13 after noting other elements such as "serious criminal conduct" and "conduct that adversely reflects on lawyer's fitness" were not established); *Bd. of Prof'l Responsibility v. Daniel*, 549 S.W.3d 90, 101 (Tenn. 2018) (where lawyer intentionally concealed transactions from his partners and misappropriated partnership, not client, funds, court affirmed Hearing Panel's consideration of Standard 5.12 in addition to Standard 5.11; because the Standards can be used as "flexible guideposts," court determined that three-year suspension to include one-year of active suspension followed by probation under Standard 5.12 was more appropriate than disbarment under Standard 5.11); *Bd. of Prof'l Responsibility v. Cowan*, 388 S.W.3d 264, 269 (Tenn. 2012) (rejecting lawyer's suggestion that Standard 5.11(b) specifically excluded criminal conduct and that criminal conduct must be "pigeonholed" into Standard 5.11(a) to warrant a disbarment sanction, court imposed disbarment, finding Standard 5.11(b) applicable to tax evasion conviction); *Talley v. Bd. of Prof'l Responsibility*, 358 S.W.3d 185 (Tenn. 2011) (court noting ambiguity whether lawyer's conviction of misdemeanor in facilitating securities fraud fell under Standard 5.11(a), a serious crime, or 5.11(b), dishonest conduct, was not controlling since the willful fraud and deceit involved in the offense and considerable aggravating circumstances and no mitigating factors supported the presumptive sanction of disbarment).

## *Downward Adjustment in Sanction*

In some instances, courts have found disbarment recommended under Standard 5.11 too severe, even for serious criminal conduct, especially when presented with significant mitigating evidence such as substance abuse and rehabilitation or other compelling factors. *See, e.g., In re Schuler*, 818 P.2d 138 (Alaska 1991) (lawyer's misdemeanor theft conviction for shoplifting constituted serious criminal conduct under Standard 5.11(a) and dishonest conduct under Standard 5.11(b) warranting disbarment, but two-year suspension imposed in light of mitigating factors, including emotional and personal problems and rehabilitation); *In re Dean*, 129 P.3d 943 (Ariz. 2006) (noting Standard 5.11(b) provided presumptive sanction for prosecutor's false statements in denying secret romantic relationship with judge who presided over felony case misrepresentation but imposing six-month suspension in light of circumstances that allowed judge to escape a disciplinary sanction); *People v. Ritland*, 327 P.3d 914 (Colo. O.P.D.J. 2014) (lawyer was seeking to adopt her second cousin's baby and falsely listed her own husband on the birth certificate and counseled her husband to lie in a related filing in order to facilitate the adoption; although the presumptive sanction under Standard 5.11(b) for such intentional dishonest conduct is disbarment, significant mitigating factors, including cooperation in the disciplinary process and excellent character testimony reduced the sanction to a three-year suspension); *In re Cardwell*, 50 P.3d 897 (Colo. 2002) (concluding disbarment presumptive sanction under Standards 5.11(a) and 5.11(b) for multiple misconduct including assisting client to engage in criminal conduct and lawyer's convictions for perjury and attempting to influence public servant but imposing three-year suspension, with eighteen months stayed, upon consideration of numerous mitigating factors); *People v. Hanks*, 967 P.2d 141 (Colo. 1998) (while disbarment presumptive sanction under Standard 5.11(b) for operating an investment company in a way that involved violations of federal securities laws, court accepted recommendation of inquiry panel for two-year suspension given mitigating factors); *In re Washburn*, 464 S.E.2d 192 (Ga. 1995) (public reprimand too lenient for conviction of fraudulent levy, a crime involving moral turpitude, but court rejected disbarment holding that, under Standard 5.11, is generally appropriate when a lawyer engages in serious criminal misconduct; three-year suspension imposed); *In re Summer*, 105 P.3d 848 (Or. 2005) (citing Standards 5.1 and 5.11(a), disbarment is presumptive sanction for attempted theft by deception, but due to mitigating factors, 180-day suspension imposed for lawyer who attempted to collect twice from different insurers for same client injury); *In re Huffman*, 13 P.3d 994, 1004 (Or. 2000) (court said lawyer's misrepresentations in motions to waive or defer appellate filing fee and costs implicated Standard 5.11(b), inter alia, but found no clear indication that disbarment was appropriate sanction; noting misconduct merited "significant suspension," court imposed two-year suspension); *In re Koliha*, 9 P.3d 102 (Or. 2000) (Standard 5.11(b), inter alia, implicated for misconduct that included engaging in the unauthorized practice of law during suspension and failing to cooperate with state bar's investigation, but one-year suspension imposed after consideration of aggravating and mitigating factors and state case law); *In re Neisner*, 16 A.3d 587 (Vt. 2010) (two-year suspension ordered after lawyer's felony convictions for, inter alia, giving false information to police authorities arising from lawyer's involvement in an automobile accident and initially persuading his wife to falsely claim she had been driving, court noting disbarment was presumptive sanction under Standard 5.11 but nonetheless held suspension warranted in light of mitigating factors, including acknowledgment of alcoholism and subsequent rehabilitation); *In re Wysolmerski*, 702 A.2d 73 (Vt. 1997) (repeated dishonesty with clients, other lawyers, and court generally merits disbarment under Standard 5.11(b), inter alia, but imposing three-year suspension for this and other misconduct given mitigating factors); *In re Disciplinary Proceeding Against Christopher*, 105 P.3d 976 (Wash. 2005) (mitigating factors along with consideration of unanimity and proportionality justified departure from presumptive sanction under Standard 5.11(b) and imposition of eighteen-month suspension on lawyer who falsified court documents and forged secretary's signature to hide lawyer's mishandling of client matter); *In re Disciplinary Proceedings Against George*, 746 N.W.2d 236 (Wis. 2008) (suspension of four years and three months imposed, instead of presumptive sanction of disbarment under Standard 5.11, inter alia, on former state senator convicted of felony misuse of federal program funds in light of lack of prior disciplinary record, long record of public service, and real prospects for rehabilitation).

## *Mental Disability Mitigating Factor*

Whether a mental disability mitigates a Standard 5.11 disbarment is dependent upon the facts in each case. *Compare People v. Lujan*, 890 P.2d 109, 110 (Colo. 1995) (one-year suspension rather than disbarment under 5.11(b) for lawyer who stole from her law firm but "does not deserve to be disbarred because of certain extraordinary and tragic factors in mitigation, including the sudden emergence of a mental disorder that caused the misconduct"), *with People v. Goldstein*, 887

P.2d 634, 638 (Colo. 1994) (disbarment warranted for lawyer with felony conviction for forging federal bankruptcy court judge's signature and other misconduct, including numerous misrepresentations; rejecting mental disability, in this case "success neurosis," as mitigating factor, causal connection not established), *and In re Staar,* 924 P.2d 308, 312 (Or. 1996) (two-year suspension warranted for lawyer who falsely alleged under oath in petition for restraining order that she had been abused by an individual and falsely alleged that she was living with him; court found that "[i]n this case, it is only the mitigating factor that the accused was suffering from a mental disability or impairment at the time of her misconduct that leads us to select a sanction less than disbarment" under Standards 5.11(a) and 5.11(b), inter alia). For a discussion of when a mental disability or chemical dependency may mitigate a sanction, see Annotation to Standard 9.3(i).

### *Disagreement as to Appropriate Sanction*

Judges on the same court sometimes disagree as to whether disbarment or a lesser sanction is necessary given the facts presented in certain cases. *Compare In re Fioramonti,* 859 P.2d 1315, 1322 (Ariz. 1993) (three-year suspension due to mitigating factors rather than disbarment under Standard 5.11(b), inter alia, for lawyer who manufactured evidence, lied under oath at his deposition, and suborned perjury by means of false affidavits; one dissenting justice argued for disbarment under Standard 5.11(b), inter alia, given "the egregiousness of respondent's misconduct" coupled with prior court decision), *with Fla. Bar v. Liberman,* 43 So.3d 36 (Fla. 2010) (dissent opposed majority's disbarment of lawyer convicted of felony count of trafficking in the drug Ecstasy, urging suspension when crime had occurred six years before, was product of lawyer's addiction, did not arise in connection with the practice of law, and lawyer had led a drug-free and otherwise exemplary existence since the time of the offense). *See also In re Freeman,* 506 S.E.2d 872 (Ga. 1998) (court imposed ninety-day suspension for guardian of estate who wrote checks on estate funds and loaned the money to his brother, finding no evidence in aggravation and voluminous evidence in mitigation; dissenting, Justice Carol Hunstein joined by Justice Hugh Thompson urged disbarment under Standard 5.11); *In re Acree,* 495 S.E.2d 293, 294 (Ga. 1998) (in dissent, Justice Hunstein, joined by Justice Robert Benham and Justice Thompson, urged disbarment under Standard 5.11 rather than two-year suspension imposed by majority for misdemeanor of bank larceny because crime involved fraudulent mishandling of funds; "[b]ecause the record clearly establishes that [respondent] engaged in felonious conduct involving dishonesty, fraud, deceit and misrepresentation and that he engaged in deceptive practices during the disciplinary process, a factor not considered by the majority, I would disbar [him] from the practice of law in this State"); *In re Burchett,* 630 N.E.2d 205 (Ind. 1994) (disbarment presumptive standard under Standard 5.11(a) for converting funds through forgery in order to support drug habit yet, given mitigating factors, six-month suspension imposed; Justice Brent Dickson, dissenting, finding sanction inadequate); *In re Watkins*, 656 So.2d 984 (La. 1995) (imposing two-year suspension for federal misdemeanors, including making false statements to obtain Social Security Income benefits for client, though noting disciplinary board member's conclusion that fraudulent conduct warranted disbarment under Standard 5.11, inter alia; Justice Harry Lemmon, dissenting, suggesting mitigating factors do not reduce baseline sanction of disbarment below a three-year suspension and Justice Bernette Johnson dissenting, asserting that lawyer's multiple offenses, coupled with pattern of misconduct, warranted more severe sanction and noting irony that lawyer would be reinstated to practice while still serving probationary sentence).

## *State Precedent Supporting Lesser Sanctions*

Some courts have held that while the presumptive sanction under Standard 5.11 would be disbarment for certain misconduct, comparison with their own precedent persuades them to impose lesser sanctions. *See, e.g., Iowa Supreme Ct. Att'y Disciplinary Bd. v. Bieber*, 824 N.W.2d 514 (Iowa 2012) (upon consideration of the facts, mitigating factors, and court's precedent, as well as cases from other jurisdictions, court imposed six-month suspension on lawyer convicted of misprision of a felony for helping his clients facilitate a fraudulent real estate transaction); *Asher v. Miss. Bar*, 661 So.2d 722 (Miss. 1995) (eighteen-month suspension for lawyer who misled client, including lying about filing complaint, fraudulently used clerk's stamp, and forged client's signature to falsify complaint because precedent could support eighteen-month suspension, including one case that cited Standard 5.11 but ultimately resulted in a suspension); *In re Davenport*, 49 P.3d 91 (Or. 2002) (disbarment under Standard 5.11(a) was presumptive sanction for false testimony under oath in bankruptcy proceeding, but two-year suspension imposed after considering aggravating and mitigating factors and case law favoring a lengthy suspension); *In re Eadie*, 36 P.3d 468 (Or. 2001) (intentional misrepresentation by omission in settlement agreement and intentional misrepresentation regarding scheduling of case seriously, adversely reflected on lawyer's fitness to practice under Standard 5.11(b), but three-year suspension imposed upon consideration of case law); *In re Disciplinary Proceeding Against Christopher*, 105 P.3d 976 (Wash. 2005) (rejecting presumptive disbarment under Standard 5.11(b) and instead imposing eighteen-month suspension on lawyer who falsified court documents and forged secretary's signature to hide mishandling of case, court followed precedent of similar case in which lawyer who falsified sworn admissions to court received a six-month suspension).

**5.12 Suspension is generally appropriate when a lawyer knowingly engages in criminal conduct which does not contain the elements listed in Standard 5.11 and that seriously adversely reflects on the lawyer's fitness to practice.**

## Annotation

Lawyers who knowingly engage in criminal conduct other than that described in Standard 5.11 should be suspended in cases in which their conduct seriously, adversely reflects on their fitness to practice. As with disbarment, suspension can be imposed even when no criminal charges have been filed against the lawyer. *See, e.g., In re Depew*, 237 P.3d 24, 35 (Kan. 2010) (lawyer engaged in illegal conduct when he exposed himself to court administrative assistant, warranting one-year suspension; court noting that Sanctions Standards "do not require that a respondent be charged or convicted by law enforcement before conduct may be considered illegal"); *Att'y. Grievance Comm'n v. Giannetti*, 175 A.3d 119 (Md. 2017) (lawyer willfully failed to file state and federal income taxes for seven years; indefinite suspension imposed); *Att'y Grievance Comm'n v. Atkinson*, 745 A.2d 1086, 1091 (Md. 2000) ("A conviction for tax evasion not a necessary predicate to support a finding of dishonesty" for willful failure to file and pay state and federal income taxes for ten years; indefinite suspension imposed); *State ex rel. Okla. Bar Ass'n v. Dobbs*, 94 P.3d 31, 47 (Okla. 2004) (notwithstanding lack of criminal conviction, one-year-and-one-day suspension imposed for multiple acts of misconduct, including lawyer's false civil deposition testimony amounting to perjury; finding that "witness immunity doctrine does not preclude imposition of professional discipline").

### *Conduct Warranting Suspension*

Standard 5.12 has been applied to a wide variety of misconduct. *See, e.g., People v. Pierson*, 917 P.2d 275, 277 (Colo. 1996) (while determining the appropriate sanction is a close question given lawyer's total disregard of the disciplinary proceedings, court concluded that a three-year suspension was appropriate for lawyer who misrepresented to purchasers that his personal residence was free and clear of encumbrances, failed to give purchasers title commitment by date of closing, failed to file documents as promised, and left state with no forwarding address; court stated, "The seriousness of the respondent's dishonest conduct in conjunction with his default could easily warrant disbarment"); *In re Melvin*, 807 A.2d 550, 554 (Del. 2002) (eighteen-month suspension for experienced public defender's misdemeanor convictions arising from his refusal to comply with order of protection and destruction of wife's journals to hinder police investigation; court noting lawyer "held a unique position of public trust and knew or should have known that his criminal conduct would seriously adversely reflect on his own fitness to practice law and on the integrity of the profession"); *Att'y. Grievance Comm'n v. Reno*, 103 A.3d 565 (Md. 2014) (despite no conviction for the offense, lawyer suspended after buying a handgun for someone who could not legally possess a firearm); *In re Sargent*, BD-2013-061 (Mass. 2013), *available at* http://www.mass.gov/obcbbo/bd13-061.pdf (accepting parties' joint recommendation, former law school dean suspended from practice for three years for his misconduct in knowing that LSAT scores and grades for incoming students in some law school classes were inflated because he directed that certain low-scoring students be excluded from the computation and then distributed that data to the ABA and *U.S. News & World Report*, among others); *In re Disciplinary Action Against Dvorak*, 611 N.W.2d 147, 150 (N.D. 2000) (lawyer who sent letter to witness requesting that witness "correct" her statements or face defamation action engaged in an unlawful attempt to dissuade witness from providing information to the court and letter to witness's employer stating that witness admitted making untrue statements served no substantial purpose other than to embarrass witness; one-year suspension under North Dakota Standard 5.12, inter alia); *In re Smith*, 236 P.3d 137 (Or. 2010) (ninety-day suspension under Standard 5.12, inter alia, for lawyer whose misconduct included the crime of criminal trespass, when he and his client entered client's former place of employment before business hours, knowing that client was not authorized to use her key to enter the facility or to grant him entry); *In re Leisure*, 113 P.3d 412, 418 (Or. 2005) (applying Standard 5.12, inter alia, court imposed an eighteen-month suspension for lawyer who knowingly wrote more than 200 nonsufficient-funds checks over a lengthy period of time, finding that such "conduct suggests a disrespect for the law and for the duties of the legal professional"); *In re Ervin*, 694 S.E.2d 6 (S.C. 2010) (lawyer arrested following road-rage incident where he pointed a firearm at a female driver and male passenger who extended their middle fingers and shouted at him as he tried to pass their vehicle; six-month suspension imposed); *cf. In re Goff*, 837 So.2d 1201, 1206 (La. 2003) (noting baseline sanction of suspension under Standard 5.12, inter alia, for misconduct including aiding nonlawyer in the unauthorized practice of law and failing to ensure that nonlawyer employees' conduct complied with lawyer's professional obligations, court imposed nine-month suspension, and in face of significant mitigating factors, court noted that, "[u]nquestionably, engaging in runner-based solicitation is one of the most serious professional violations an attorney may commit"; "[w]e have not hesitated to disbar attorneys who have engaged in such practices").

- **Possession of Illegal Drugs**

Possession of illegal drugs is among the most often cited criminal conduct in cases involving Standard 5.12. *See, e.g., People v. Madrid*, 967 P.2d 627 (Colo. 1998) (three-year suspension for misconduct including conviction for possession of one ounce of cocaine; court noting that lawyer accepted cocaine in lieu of legal fees, thus misconduct had direct connection with the practice of law); *People v. Stevens*, 866 P.2d 1378 (Colo. 1994) (suspension for one year and one day for judicial officer who purchased $25 worth of crack cocaine); *People v. Robinson*, 839 P.2d 4, 6 (Colo. 1992) (convicted deputy district attorney suspended for one year under Standard 5.12 for use and possession of cocaine; although Standard 5.22 not cited, court distinguished six-month suspension imposed in another disciplinary cocaine-use case, noting that while all lawyers must abstain from criminal conduct, the deputy district attorney here "undertook an even higher responsibility to the public with respect to this obligation by virtue of his public office as an attorney engaged in law enforcement"); *In re Nixon*, 49 A.3d 1193 (Del. 2012) (two-year suspension for lawyer with large quantities of marijuana and Ecstasy in his home who pleaded guilty to two misdemeanor counts of possession of controlled substance and one count possession of drug paraphernalia; court citied Standard 5.12, inter alia, noting that drafters of the Sanctions Standards specifically distinguished criminal conduct such as possession of narcotics from the types of conduct that fall within Standard 5.11); *Fla. Bar v. De La Torre*, 994 So.2d 1032 (Fla. 2008) (relying on Standard 5.12 as well as case law, court imposed eighteen-month suspension on lawyer who pleaded nolo contendere to five criminal charges, including two felonies—possession of cocaine and battery on a law-enforcement officer—and failed to report the criminal matters for seven years); *Iowa Supreme Ct. Att'y Disciplinary Bd. v. Cannon*, 821 N.W.2d 873, 883 (Iowa 2012) (separate convictions for possession of cocaine, operating a boat while intoxicated, and operating motor vehicle while intoxicated evidenced a pattern of criminal conduct involving alcohol and drugs that "undermines the reputation of the bar as a whole and reflects negatively on [lawyer's] fitness to practice law," warranting thirty-day suspension); *In re Betts*, 359 P.3d 70 (Kan. 2015) (relying on Standard 5.12, inter alia, lawyer convicted of possessing marijuana and drug paraphernalia and driving under the influence suspended indefinitely); *In re Meek*, 289 P.3d 95 (Kan. 2012) (forty-month suspension, stayed by probation after one year, under Standard 5.12, inter alia, for unlawful receipt of prescription pain medication from client resulting in conviction); *In re Ramsay*, 799 N.W.2d 604 (Minn. 2011) (ninety-day suspension after conviction for third-degree possession of cocaine; Sanctions Standards not cited); *In re Allen*, 949 P.2d 710 (Or. 1997) (one-year suspension was appropriate under Standard 5.12 for engaging in criminal acts that reflected adversely on lawyer's fitness to practice after lawyer befriended drug-addicted homeless man and in misguided effort to provide assistance furnished transportation and money for man to purchase heroin, resulting in man's death from a lethal overdose); *In re Disciplinary Proceedings Against Compton*, 787 N.W.2d 831, 833 (Wis. 2010) (two-year suspension warranted under Standard 5.12 for convictions including possession of heroin; court noting lawyer's criminal conduct "seriously adversely" reflected on his fitness to practice); *Bd. of Prof'l Responsibility v. Cundy*, 201 P.3d 419 (Wyo. 2008) (lawyer's arrest for possession of marijuana, along with other misconduct, warranted one-year suspension under Standard 5.12, inter alia).

- **Sexual Misconduct**

Other crimes falling under Standard 5.12 involve various sexual misconduct. *See, e.g., People v. Benight*, 2016 WL 7856476 (Colo. O.P.D.J. 2016) (lawyer convicted of unlawful sexual conduct suspended for two years; finding that Standard 5.12 established presumptive sanction); *In re Egbune*, 971 P.2d 1065 (Colo. 1999) (third-degree sexual assault against client warranted suspension for one year and one day; court rejected lawyer's contention that before he could be found to have committed a criminal act he had a right to be tried by jury or proof of the crime beyond a reasonable doubt); *In re Tenenbaum*, 880 A.2d 1025 (Del. 2005) (approving stipulation to three-year suspension under Standard 5.12, inter alia, for a pattern of illegal activity involving verbal and physical sexual harassment of female clients and employees); *In re Snyder*, 913 N.E.2d 1243 (Ind. 2009) (approving agreement for discipline and imposing suspension for at least twenty-four months without automatic reinstatement for lawyer convicted of felony child solicitation); *Iowa Supreme Court Att'y. Disciplinary Bd. v. Moothart*, 860 N.W.2d 598 (Iowa 2015) (indefinite suspension with no possibility of reinstatement for thirty months for lawyer guilty of five cases of sexual harassment in the practice of law; lawyer made sexually suggestive comments and propositions of sex and discussed sexual favors in exchange for legal services with five different women); *Iowa Supreme Ct. Att'y Disciplinary Bd. v. Templeton*, 784 N.W.2d 761, 767, 768 (Iowa 2010) (in imposing indefinite suspension with no reinstatement for three months on lawyer with a long history of compulsive and deviant sexual behavior who pleaded guilty to six counts of invasion of privacy-nudity, court noted that "[t]here must be some rational connection other than the criminality of the act between the conduct and the actor's fitness to practice law" (citation omitted); finding lawyer's "criminal acts of invading [his victims'] privacy reflects adversely on his fitness to practice"); *In re Cranmer*, 196 P.3d 932 (Kan. 2008) (six-month suspension warranted for conviction on seven counts of lewd and lascivious behavior involving lawyer's public exposure of his sex organ); *cf. Columbus Bar Ass'n v. Linnen*, 857 N.E.2d 539 (Ohio 2006) (lawyer suspended indefinitely with reinstatement conditioned upon independent mental-health exam after convictions of numerous misdemeanor offenses involving him appearing naked in front of women and photographing their reactions).

- **Possible Exception for Sexual Assault of Minor**

An exception to the presumptive sanction of suspension for misconduct involving sexual assault has emerged in the area of sexual assault on minors. Some courts are holding that disbarment is the presumptive sanction under these circumstances, consistent with increasingly severe criminal penalties for such offenses. *See, e.g., In re Grant*, 317 P.3d 612 (Cal. 2014) (lawyer disbarred after pleading guilty to one felony count of knowing possession of child pornography); *In re Lesansky*, 17 P.3d 764 (Cal. 2001) (lawyer disbarred for conviction of attempt to commit a lewd or lascivious act on a minor); *People v. Rogers*, No. 10PDJ024, 2010 WL 5401443 (Colo. O.P.D.J. Oct. 13, 2010) (disbarment warranted for lawyer who failed to appear at criminal trial on felony charges of sexually assaulting minor stepdaughter; as a matter of law disbarment is presumed sanction for lawyer who engages in a sex act with a child); *In re Bewig*, 791 A.2d 908 (D.C. 2002) (lawyer disbarred for conviction of misdemeanor sexual contact with a minor, a crime of moral turpitude); *In re Hudgins*, 540 N.E.2d 1200 (Ind. 1989) (lawyer disbarred for conviction of child molestation); *In re O'Shaughnessy*, 78 A.D.3d 36 (N.Y. App. Div. 2010) (in reciprocal proceedings, court imposed disbarment for lawyer's four felony convictions relating to his sexual conversations with minors in Internet chat rooms and sending pornographic images over the Internet instead of suspension coextensive with his fifteen-year term of criminal probation imposed by originating disciplinary jurisdiction; Sanctions Standards not cited); *In re Disciplinary Action Against Hoffman*, 820 N.W.2d 704 (N.D. 2012) (disbarment imposed on lawyer who, while on suspension, was convicted of continuous sexual abuse of a child, corruption of a minor, and attempted gross sexual imposition); *In re Disciplinary Proceeding Against Day*, 173 P.3d 915, 922 (Wash. 2007) (while acknowledging that suspension was presumptive sanction based under Standard 5.12 for lawyer's conviction for felony child molestation, court imposed disbarment finding that the Sanctions Standards were not applicable in determining sanctions for acts involving moral turpitude and noting that the court can fashion its own presumptive sanction if the Sanctions Standards do not provide direct guidance for such violations; court stated that "[g]reater societal awareness of sexual crimes against children and the resulting abuse of trust are arguably justifiable reasons for increasing presumptive sanctions for attorneys who engage in such misconduct").

Still, in some cases courts have strictly adhered to Standard 5.12 and imposed suspension rather than disbarment for sexual misconduct involving minors. *See, e.g., People v. Graham*, 933 P.2d 1321 (Colo. 1997) (under Standard 5.12, six-month suspension imposed, instead of three months recommended by grievance committee, for serving alcohol to a seventeen-year-old minor and sexually assaulting her; favorable treatment reports and victim's unwillingness to cooperate in the disciplinary proceedings were factors considered by the court); *In re Conn*, 715 N.E.2d 379 (Ind. 1999) (imposing two-year suspension for conviction of exploitation of minor arising from lawyer downloading child pornography from the Internet while in law school and for failing to disclose information about federal criminal investigation on bar application); *In re Kern*, 551 N.E.2d 454, 456–57 (Ind. 1990) (imposing two-year suspension for misdemeanor conviction of child molestation after considering that misconduct was an isolated incident and that lawyer did not know the age of the victim but knew that she was a mother of a child over one year old; court noting that "offense of child molesting, however is not only a serious crime abhorred by our society and strictly proscribed by our criminal laws, but, by its very nature, it renders the perpetrator unfit to be an officer of the Court and warrants the strictest sanction"; Sanctions Standards not cited); *In re Baca*, 253 P.3d 348 (Kan. 2011) (indefinite suspension, under Standard 5.12, warranted for lawyer convicted of indecent exposure for sending photographs of his genitals over the Internet to police officer posing as a minor); *In re Fierro*, 869 P.2d 728 (Kan. 1994) (imposing indefinite suspension for lawyer who pleaded guilty to six counts of attempted indecent liberties with a child involving lewd fondling or touching of six young girls; Sanctions Standards cited generally); *Att'y Grievance Comm'n v. Mitchell*, 521 A.2d 746 (Md. 1987) (court imposed indefinite suspension for second-degree sexual conviction arising from lawyer's performance of sexual acts on thirteen-year-old boy; dissent urged disbarment); *In re Richardson*, 492 S.E.2d 788 (S.C. 1997) (imposing indefinite suspension for convictions of assault and battery of a minor arising out of an incident in which a thirteen-year-old girl reported that lawyer grabbed her buttock and exposed himself to her; Sanctions Standards not cited); *In re Wolf*, 826 P.2d 628 (Or. 1992) (eighteen-month suspension warranted under Standard 5.12, inter alia, for criminal conduct involving lawyer's sexual intercourse with and serving wine to sixteen-year-old personal injury client).

Significant mitigation or the lack of physical contact between the lawyer and the minor victim are among the factors considered by the courts in cases resulting in the imposition of suspension rather than disbarment for sexual misconduct cases involving minors. *See, e.g., In re Christie*, 574 A.2d 845 (Del. 1990) (three-year suspension imposed for convictions of sexual harassment, indecent exposure, endangering the welfare of a child, and unlawfully dealing with a child after considering significant mitigating factors including lawyer's participation in residential treatment program and remorse); *Att'y Grievance Comm'n v. Thompson*, 786 A.2d 763, 772 (Md. 2001) (lawyer's agreement to continue treatment for his disorder and limit his contact with children were among the factors considered in mitigation by the court in imposing indefinite suspension rather than disbarment for lawyer's conviction of stalking a boy; court noting that "it makes no difference that Respondent merely stalked a thirteen year old boy, without consummating an act of sexual abuse or other misdeed . . . such act violates the implicit trust the public and we expect from adults interacting with children"; dissenting justices urged disbarment); *Att'y Grievance Comm'n v. Childress*, 770 A.2d 685, 696 (Md. 2001) (imposing indefinite suspension for using the Internet to solicit sex with young teenage girls; citing cases from other jurisdictions and noting that "[u]nlike the cited cases, [respondent] did not sexually touch the victims involved in this case"; dissent urged disbarment); *In re Lever*, 60 A.D.3d 37, 51 (N.Y. App. Div. 2008) (in imposing suspension for the longer of three years or the term of his criminal probation, upon lawyer's conviction of a misdemeanor attempted criminal sex act with a minor following lawyer's sexually explicit Internet conversations with an undercover police officer posing as a thirteen-year-old girl, court relied on substantial mitigation while rejecting disbarment cases since the conduct in those cases involved actual sexual contact with the minor; but in a strong dissent, Justice James Catterson, urging disbarment and calling for a bright-line rule, stated, "I believe that a convicted and registered sex offender merits disbarment, even when the crime, as in the instant case, is inchoate"); *Disciplinary Counsel v. Goldblatt*, 888 N.E.2d 1091 (Ohio 2008) (mitigating factors considered, included lawyer's successful treatment to control sexual deviance and his cooperation, in determining that indefinite suspension was appropriate for conviction of compelling prostitution and possessing criminal tools in attempt to arrange a sexual encounter with an underage girl as young as nine years old and downloading images of nude children after conviction). *But see State ex rel. Okla. Bar Ass'n v. Foster*, 995 P.2d 1138 (Okla. 2000) (imposing public reprimand for lawyer who viewed a minor's breasts and made inappropriate comments to the minor following the incident; mitigation included lawyer's almost 50 years of practice without prior discipline, his service to the judiciary, his conduct following his plea and in response to the disciplinary complaint, and the fact that he no longer practiced law; Sanctions Standards not cited); *Disciplinary Counsel v. Grossman*, 37 N.E.3d 155 (Ohio 2015) (lawyer pled guilty to one count of receipt of child pornography and admitted to communicating online with an undercover police officer posing as the father of an eleven-year old girl and discussing various sexual acts involving the fictitious minor before the lawyer went to a prearranged location expecting to meet her; lawyer was suspended indefinitely and may only reapply for reinstatement when he has completed his probation for the criminal offense).

- **Tax Violations**

Violations of tax laws are often analyzed under Standard 5.12 with courts finding that such illegal conduct reflects directly on a lawyer's fitness to practice law. *See, e.g., In re Scholl*, 25 P.3d 710 (Ariz. 2001) (imposing six-month suspension upon former judge for seven felony convictions for filing false tax returns and structuring currency transactions to avoid treasury reporting requirements); *People v. Woodford*, 81 P.3d 370 (Colo. O.P.D.J. 2003) (fifteen-month suspension for multiple violations, including failure to file tax returns for three years, conduct that seriously, adversely reflected on lawyer's fitness to practice); *In re Lovelace*, 182 P.3d 1244 (Kan. 2008) (indefinite suspension due to mental-health issues, instead of six-month suspension recommended by hearing panel, after finding that lawyer's criminal acts in failing to pay federal income taxes reflected directly on his fitness); *In re Thomas*, 700 So.2d 490 (La. 1997) (imposing fifteen-month suspension, with nine months deferred and two years of probation following misdemeanor failure to file federal income tax return conviction); *In re Shealy*, 700 So.2d 488 (La. 1997) (imposing one-year suspension for conviction of misdemeanor failure to file income tax return); *Lockett v. Bd. of Prof'l Responsibility*, 380 S.W.3d 19, 27 (Tenn. 2012) (four-year suspension imposed on lawyer whose "willful failure to file income tax returns" met the requirements of Standard 5.12); *cf. In re Spencer*, 58 P.3d 228, 237 (Or. 2002) (sixty-day suspension warranted for misconduct that deprived State of California and San Diego County of more than $20,000 in taxes and fees where lawyer intentionally prepared fraudulent DMV record and registered future clients' motor home in Oregon when they had no domicile there; court finding that the "continuing nature of the registration violation seriously adversely reflects on the accused's fitness to practice law").

- **Domestic Violence**

Lawyers who commit acts of domestic violence generally face suspension under Standard 5.12, with most courts focusing on the conduct versus whether the lawyer's violent acts resulted in a criminal conviction or, if convicted, whether for a misdemeanor or a felony. *See, e.g., People v. Musick*, 960 P.2d 89 (Colo. 1998) (noting that the actual nature of the lawyer's conduct is more important for disciplinary purposes than the statutory label put on it, court imposed one-year-and-one-day suspension for commission of three assaults on girlfriend, although no criminal charges were filed; rejecting respondent's contention that minor assault outside the context of a law practice not resulting in a criminal conviction should not result in disciplinary sanctions); *People v. Falco*, 2016 WL 4442171 (Colo. O.P.D.J. 2016) (lawyer suspended for nine months after physically striking his twenty-weeks' pregnant wife while their three young children were in the house; court cited Standard 5.12 to determine the level of sanction). *See also People v. Groland*, 908 P.2d 75 (Colo. 1995) (suspension for one year and one day under Standard 5.12 warranted for lawyer who violated conditions of probation imposed for domestic violence offenses, including repeatedly contacting former wife in violation of restraining orders, threatening to kill others, refusing to be deposed, and failing to comply with child support); *People v. Scott*, 121 P.3d 366 (Colo. O.P.D.J. 2005) (one-year-and-one-day suspension warranted under Standard 5.12 for lawyer who engaged in a pattern of criminal conduct, including assault, false imprisonment, and harassment of his ex-wife; court determined criminal conduct seriously adversely reflected on lawyer's fitness to practice law); *Fla. Bar v. Scheiber*, 631 So.2d 1081, 1082 (Fla. 1994) (suspension of 120 days under Florida Standard 5.12, with condition that lawyer complete program for batterers of women, following criminal battery charge for beating up girlfriend; court noted that "[p]leading nolo contendere to a misdemeanor is relevant to an attorney's fitness to practice law"); *In re Walker*, 597 N.E.2d 1271, 1272 (Ind. 1992) (sixty-day suspension imposed on chief deputy prosecutor for engaging in acts of domestic violence, although no conviction at issue; court stressed that because prosecutor had certainly encountered domestic assaults, "this incident calls into question his ability to zealously prosecute or to effectively work with the victims of such crimes" and, as a practitioner, his "effectiveness with his own clients or with adversaries in situations involving issues of domestic violence is compromised by his own contribution to this escalating societal problem"; "[i]n both his capacities, we believe the perception of his fitness is tainted"); *Iowa Supreme Court Atty. Disciplinary Bd. v. Deremiah*, 875 N.W.2d 728 (Iowa 2016) (three-month suspension for domestic abuse after lawyer, while intoxicated, assaulted his girlfriend in her bedroom); *Iowa Supreme Ct. Att'y Disciplinary Bd. v. Schmidt*, 796 N.W.2d 33 (Iowa 2011) (thirty-day suspension for misconduct including conviction for domestic abuse after lawyer assaulted his wife, causing her physical injuries and traumatizing their children; court found lawyer's actions especially egregious since he attempted to prevent law enforcement authorities from getting involved and would have imposed at least six-month suspension but for mitigating circumstances); *In re Cardenas*, 60 So.3d 609 ((La. 2011) (one-year suspension for lawyer convicted of misdemeanor domestic abuse battery in the presence of a child); *In re Grella*, 777 N.E.2d 167, 171 (Mass. 2002) (in imposing a two-month suspension for misdemeanor assault and battery, court found support in Standard 5.12 that lawyer's sustained and violent attack on his estranged wife adversely reflected on his fitness as a lawyer, stating that "[e]ngaging in violent conduct is antithetical to the privilege of practicing law, and such conduct generally will warrant suspension from the practice of law"); *In re Margrabia*, 695 A.2d 1378 (N.J. 1997) (lawyer convicted of simple assault after striking his wife and child during an argument suspended three months); *In re Zulandt*, 93 A.D.3d 77, 81 (N.Y. App. Div. 2012) (three-year suspension imposed for misdemeanor assault conviction arising from lawyer's violent argument with his former girlfriend resulting in him throwing her to the ground, repeatedly striking her on the face, and destroying her personal property; court noting lawyer engaged in a "calculated pattern of cruelty"); *In re Hunter*, 980 A.2d 755 (R.I. 2009) (one-year suspension imposed on lawyer charged with, inter alia, three misdemeanor counts of domestic assault).

On the other hand, some courts have imposed a sanction less than suspension on lawyers who engaged in acts of domestic violence. *See People v. Senn*, 824 P.2d 822, 825 (Colo. 1992) (concluding conduct sufficiently serious to warrant public censure on lawyer who, while intoxicated, committed the offense of prohibited use of weapon when he discharged a gun aimed above his wife's head during an argument; no risk of actual injury to wife, lawyer's treatment for alcoholism, and reconciliation with wife among mitigating factors considered; court noting, notwithstanding dismissal of criminal charges, "disciplinary proceedings supplement the work of the criminal courts to maintain respect for the rule of law and protect the public" even when misconduct not related to practice of law); *In re Principato*, 655 A.2d 920 (N.J. 1995), and *In re Magid*, 655 A.2d 916 (N.J. 1995) (in cases decided on same day, court imposed public reprimand on two lawyers who had committed simple assaults in a domestic context, one of whom was a first assistant county prosecutor; but court explained that its more lenient sanction was due, in part, to fact that issue was a matter of first impression in New Jersey, cautioning that in the future it ordinarily would suspend a lawyer convicted of an act of domestic violence).

- **Driving Under the Influence of Alcohol or Drugs**

Courts have found that driving while intoxicated reflects adversely on one's fitness to practice law and thus warrants suspension under Standard 5.12. *See, e.g.*, *People v. Van Buskirk*, 962 P.2d 975 (Colo. 1998) (six-month suspension for lawyer's misconduct resulting in convictions for careless driving, hit and run, disorderly conduct, and driving under the influence (DUI)); *In re Steiner*, 817 A.2d 793 (Del. 2003) (three-year suspension under Standard 5.12 warranted following convictions for misdemeanor second-degree vehicular assault and misdemeanor DUI); *Iowa Supreme Ct. Bd. of Prof'l Ethics & Conduct v. Ruth*, 636 N.W.2d 86 (Iowa 2001) (indefinite suspension with no possibility of reinstatement for six months for conviction of operating while intoxicated, among other misconduct, citing Standard 5.12); *In re Frahm*, 241 P.3d 1010, 1018 (Kan. 2010) (citing Standard 5.12, inter alia, and suspending lawyer for three years following conviction for DUI and two counts of aggravated battery; rejecting lawyer's argument that misconduct did not seriously, adversely reflect fitness to practice law and finding that lawyer's criminal conduct was neither "trivial nor technical" and that it "seriously adversely reflects on his fitness to practice law"); *In re O'Neill*, 172 P.3d 1179 (Kan. 2007) (suspending respondent indefinitely for a felony DUI conviction and failing to disclose numerous arrests and convictions on bar application, including multiple convictions for DUI); *In re Stewart*, 342 S.W.3d 307, 313 (Mo. 2011) (In suspending lawyer indefinitely after four DUI convictions, the last resulting in a felony conviction, the court stated: "The damage wrought in our state every year by drunken drivers is well-documented and need not be repeated here, save to recognize that its tragic impact reaches into nearly every community. This Court must insist that attorneys be keenly aware of the parameters the law places on their conduct, and [respondent's] repeated disregard for those boundaries simply cannot be excused."); *In re McDonough*, 77 P.3d 306 (Or. 2003) (holding eighteen-month suspension warranted for class A misdemeanors including DUI, driving on suspended license, reckless driving, and recklessly endangering another person); *cf. In re Kimball*, 805 So.2d 1167, 1170 (La. 2002) (citing Standard 5.12, suspension is baseline sanction for lawyer's felony possession of crack cocaine conviction, which the court found "clearly reflects on his moral fitness to practice law"; but disbarment imposed for abandonment of six clients' cases).

When offenses are substance abuse related, however, some courts will consider whether the impairment impacts the lawyer's ability to practice law in addition to relying on evidence of sobriety and rehabilitation before downwardly adjusting the sanction. *See, e.g., State ex rel. Okla. Bar Ass'n v. McBride*, 175 P.3d 379, 389 (Okla. 2007) (rejecting disciplinary authority's request for severe sanction of disbarment, court imposed reprimand plus deferred suspension for lawyer for various alcohol-related offenses, including four DUI convictions; distinguishing cases in which respondents' alcohol-related offenses affected client representation and suspensions were Imposed).

- **Misdemeanors**

Misdemeanor convictions also can implicate Standard 5.12 when the misconduct raises a question about fitness to practice. *See, e.g., People v. Hill*, 71 P.3d 1023, 1025 (Colo. O.P.D.J. 2003) (lawyer suspended for six months, under Standard 5.12, stayed entirely by two years' probation for misdemeanor assault conviction arising from physical altercation with his stepson; court noting that infliction of bodily harm on another by lawyer is "sufficiently serious to warrant suspension") (citation omitted); *In re Howard*, 765 A.2d 39, 45 (Del. 2000) (rejecting recommended two-year suspension and imposing three-year suspension under Standard 5.12 on lawyer with two misdemeanor drug convictions who admitted that his conduct reflected adversely on his fitness to practice); *In re Greenburg*, 9 So.3d 802, 808 (La. 2009) (a sixty-day suspension, under Standard 5.12, inter alia, with thirty days deferred subject to completion of anger management counseling imposed on one lawyer and a public reprimand imposed on another lawyer for engaging in a "stunning lack of decorum and civility" when the two lawyers exchanged profanities and had a physical altercation leading to one of the lawyer's being convicted of simple battery); *In re Soileau*, 737 So.2d 23 (La. 1999) (under Standard 5.12, inter alia, misdemeanor hunting violations of the Migratory Bird Treaty Act and intentionally misleading court about four prior convictions during sentencing hearing warranted two-year suspension, with one year deferred); *In re Disciplinary Proceeding Against Perez-Pena*, 168 P.3d 408, 414 (Wash. 2007) (sixty-day suspension for lawyer convicted of misdemeanor assault on client; citing Standard 5.12, court stated that "[a]ssaulting one's client during a fee dispute 'seriously' adversely reflects on one's fitness to practice").

## *No Serious Adverse Reflection on Fitness to Practice*

The black letter of Standard 5.12 provides that the lawyer's criminal conduct must "seriously adversely" reflect on fitness to practice law in order for the standard's baseline suspension to apply. The question of when misconduct rises to the level of having a serious adverse effect on fitness to practice was explored in *Grievance Adm'r v. Fink,* 612 N.W.2d 397 (Mich. 2000). In that case the lawyer pleaded guilty to misdemeanor assault and battery following a physical altercation with his former law partner during an acrimonious deposition involving a lawsuit the former partner had filed against the lawyer. In remanding the case to the disciplinary board for determination of the appropriate sanction in light of its recent adoption of the ABA Sanctions Standards, the court drew the board's attention to Standard 5.12, noting its application to offenses involving violence. On remand, in *Grievance Adm'r v. Fink,* No. 96-181-JC (Mich. A.D.B. 2001), *available at* http://www.adbmich.org/coveo/opinions/2001-04-25-96o-181a.pdf, the board found that Standard 5.12 required an assessment of the conduct itself, and not simply whether the crime fit within the definition of "violent," before determining whether the conduct seriously, adversely reflected on the lawyer's "fitness," which is the focus of Standard 5.12. Concluding that suspension was not appropriate and imposing a reprimand instead, the board determined that this particular shoving incident did not reflect on the respondent's fitness to practice due to several factors, including that it was "provoked, abbreviated, did not involve clients, did not produce injuries and was the product of a momentary loss of control in an unusual case." *Id.* at p. 7. The board did, however, reaffirm a warning to lawyers that they "may generally expect a suspension if they engage in assaultive conduct in the course of their duties." *Id.* at p. 19. *See also People v. Saxon,* 2016 WL 8540133 at *22 (Colo. O.P.D.J. 2016) (after emotionally and physically abusing a romantic partner for months, lawyer was suspended for three years; the court stated that "the profession cannot tolerate such behavior"); *In re Hickox,* 57 P.3d 403, 405 (Colo. 2002) (in imposing six-month suspension for domestic violence conviction that seriously adversely reflected on lawyer's fitness to practice, court reiterated that "[w]e have traditionally taken a serious view of misconduct by an attorney involving the infliction of bodily harm on another"); *Iowa Supreme Ct. Att'y Disciplinary Bd. v. Wheeler,* 824 N.W.2d 505 (Iowa 2012) (although the commission of a crime alone does not establish lack of fitness, here, lawyer's federal conviction for making a false statement to a bank when he acted as a straw man to assist a client in purchasing a home were criminal acts connected to his fitness to practice law); *In re Disciplinary Proceeding Against Perez-Pena,* 168 P.3d 408, 414 (Wash. 2007) (conviction for misdemeanor assault for lawyer who pushed his client during a dispute was conduct that "seriously" reflected on his fitness to practice "because the assault was on a client and took place during the course of representation").

If the criminal misconduct is deemed to only "adversely" reflect on fitness to practice law and not "seriously adversely" reflect on fitness, courts may apply a different standard—often Standard 5.13. *See, e.g., People v. Miller,* 409 P.3d 667, 675 (Colo. O.P.D.J. 2017) (court utilized Standard 5.13 instead of Standard 5.12 because "DUI offenses have not been deemed in Colorado to 'seriously' adversely reflect on a lawyer's fitness to practice law"); *People v. Graham*, No. 07PDJ064, 2008 WL 4328190 (Colo. O.P.D.J. July 31, 2008) (ninety-day suspension, stayed entirely by one-year probation, warranted for two separate misdemeanor convictions, one for driving while ability impaired, the other for failing to register as a sex offender and failing to report both convictions; hearing board found that individually the two misdemeanors adversely, rather than seriously, adversely, reflected on lawyer's fitness, warranting presumptive sanction under Standard 5.13 rather than Standard 5.12, but that lawyer's failure to report the driving while ability impaired was sufficiently aggravating factor to make public censure inappropriate). *But see Iowa Supreme Ct. Att'y Disciplinary Bd. v. Keele*, 795 N.W.2d 507 (Iowa 2011) (since disciplinary board failed to establish a sufficient nexus between lawyer's illegal possession of a firearm resulting in a federal conviction and his ability to function as a lawyer, court dismissed the discipline complaint, finding the conduct did not adversely reflect on his fitness to practice law); *In re Flannery*, 47 P.3d 891, 895 (Or. 2002) (noting that the principal difference between Standard 5.12 and Standard 5.13 "lies in the degree to which the conduct in question adversely reflects on the lawyer's fitness," court concluded that although lawyer's intentional misrepresentation of his address on a driver's license application "does reflect adversely on his fitness to practice law, it does not do so 'seriously'"; public reprimand imposed under Standard 5.13).

## *Multiple Offenses*

Disciplinary cases falling under Standard 5.12 may include multiple acts of misconduct resulting in the application of additional Sanctions Standards. *See, e.g., People v. Woodford*, 81 P.3d 370 (Colo. O.P.D.J. 2003) (fifteen-month suspension warranted under Standards 5.12, 4.52, and 4.42(a), inter alia, for lawyer who failed to file tax returns for three years, prepared unenforceable trust documents for client, and created trust documents that did not address or accomplish purposes client paid lawyer to achieve); *People v. Jaramillo*, 35 P.3d 136 (Colo. O.P.D.J. 1999) (one-year-and-one-day suspension warranted under Standard 5.12 for lawyer convicted of reckless driving, driving without insurance, driving while license was under restraint, and leaving scene of accident, in addition to Standard 6.22 for lawyer's failure to comply with order imposing child-support obligation); *In re O'Neill*, 172 P.3d 1179 (Kan. 2007) (indefinite suspension warranted for pattern of misconduct including a felony DUI conviction under Standard 5.12 and for making false statement of material facts by failing to disclose numerous arrests and convictions on bar application under Standards 6.12 and 7.2); *In re Smith*, 236 P.3d 137 (Or. 2010) (ninety-day suspension imposed, concluding suspension is presumptive sanction under Standards 5.12 and 6.22 for advising client to take frivolous action and committing the crime of criminal trespass when lawyer and his client entered client's former place of employment before business hours knowing that client was not authorized to use her key to enter the facility or to grant lawyer entry); *Bd. of Prof'l Responsibility v. Cundy*, 201 P.3d 419 (Wyo. 2008) (one-year suspension warranted under Standard 5.12 for possession of marijuana as well as under Standards 4.42 and 4.52 for neglect of clients' criminal matters).

## *Departure from Suspension*

In some circumstances, courts analyzing cases under Standard 5.12 find suspension too harsh given the particular mitigating facts. *See, e.g., People v. Gould*, 912 P.2d 556 (Colo. 1996) (use or possession of illegal drug offenses normally warrant suspension under Standard 5.12, but public censure imposed given mitigating factors, including absence of a selfish motive, disclosure to the disciplinary counsel, imposition of other penalties, demonstrated remorse, and no evidence of cocaine addiction); *People v. Rotenberg*, 911 P.2d 642 (Colo. 1996) (ordinarily suspension would be warranted for driving while intoxicated resulting in injury to client and lawyer's previous discipline but significant mitigating factors, including his voluntary participation in alcohol antabuse program and evidence that he would recover from dependency made public censure sufficient to protect the public); *In re Schaeffer*, 45 A.3d 149 (Table) at *6 (Del. 2012) (lawyer's misconduct in calling 911 and falsely reporting a nonexistent hostage situation during dispute with former employee was a "knowing and intentional exaggeration" falling under Standard 5.12, but public reprimand imposed due to mitigating factors); *In re Gooding*, 917 P.2d 414 (Kan. 1996) (imposition of discipline stayed and two years' probation imposed on lawyer first convicted and then acquitted of possession of narcotic drugs after federal court granted his petition for writ of habeas corpus; court considered multiple mitigating factors, including no felony conviction and sustained period of successful rehabilitation).

The converse is also true; courts may analyze facts seemingly fitting under Standard 5.12 but then impose disbarment given the severity of the misconduct involved. For example, in *In re Brown*, 674 So.2d 243, 246 (La. 1996), the Louisiana Supreme Court disbarred a lawyer convicted of negligent homicide after she shot her lover during an emotional verbal exchange. The lawyer expressing remorse claimed the gun just "went off" and that she did not intend to kill her girlfriend. In affirming the disciplinary board's recommendation of disbarment and rejecting the hearing panel's recommendation of an eighteen-month suspension under Standard 5.12, the court agreed with the board that precedent supported disbarment when a lawyer caused the death of another person through the use of a deadly weapon. The court further said:

> The gravity of the crime reflects heavily on respondent's fitness to practice law. We cannot overlook the fact that respondent's actions resulted in the senseless destruction of a life and will obviously forever change

> the lives of the victim's family. . . . The actual resulting injury could not have been more severe. Moreover, respondent demonstrated a violent reaction to an admittedly non-threatening situation. Her response to this apparently stressful situation creates concern regarding her continued ability to represent clients given the pressures associated with the practice of law. The sanction imposed must, of necessity, reasonably correspond with the gravity of the misconduct.

*Id.* at 249; *see also People v. Rogers,* No. 10PDJ024, 2010 WL 5401443 (Colo. O.P.D.J. Oct. 13, 2010) (in default proceedings, court disbarred lawyer who sexually assaulted stepdaughter and failed to appear at criminal trial on those charges, noting that Standard 5.12, inter alia, applied, but the Sanctions Standards and applicable case law, taken together, supported disbarment when misconduct was sexual assault of a minor); *Att'y Grievance Comm'n v. Painter,* 739 A.2d 24 (Md. 1999) (in imposing disbarment on lawyer indicted for repeated acts of domestic violence against his wife and children, court recognized suspension precedent was consistent with Standard 5.12 for domestic violence by lawyers but noted that facts presented extreme domestic violence and aggravating factors included prior assault and battery convictions while serving as judge); *In re Disciplinary Proceeding Against Day,* 173 P.3d 915 (Wash. 2007) (court disbarred lawyer for sexual molestation of client, a minor, noting that while suspension was the appropriate presumptive sanction under Standard 5.12, here case law and not Standard 5.12 was applicable in determining presumptive sanction for violations involving acts of moral turpitude). *But see People v. McCaffrey,* 925 P.2d 269, 270 (Colo. 1996) (finding it a "close question" whether three-year suspension under Standard 5.12, inter alia, rather than disbarment, was adequate following guilty pleas to felony criminal trespass and unlawful use of controlled substance, and serious neglect of three client matters; suspension imposed); *In re Martin,* 888 So.2d 178, 182 n.8 (La. 2004) (concluding disbarment was baseline sanction but imposing three-year suspension given compelling mitigating factors, including lawyer's depression following felony convictions of aggravated assault on a peace officer in standoff with police after lawyer wielded loaded revolver in front of ex-wife's house while intoxicated; court stated that "the ABA Standards are not intended to be applied in a rigid, inflexible manner [but] are helpful guidelines that supplement the rules and decisions of this court").

**5.13 Reprimand is generally appropriate when a lawyer knowingly engages in any other conduct that involves dishonesty, fraud, deceit, or misrepresentation and that adversely reflects on the lawyer's fitness to practice law.**

## Annotation

Reprimands under Standard 5.13 are imposed for knowing engagement in conduct involving dishonesty, fraud, deceit, or misrepresentation that adversely reflects on the lawyer's fitness to practice law. One distinction between facts triggering a reprimand under Standard 5.13 and those resulting in suspension under Standard 5.12 is that conduct under the former has an adverse reflection on fitness that does not rise to the level of being "seriously" adverse. *See, e.g., In re Bria*, 86 A.3d 1118 at *8 (Table) (Del. 2014) (in deciding between imposing sanctions under Standards 5.12 and 5.13, the court determined that lawyer's knowing failure to fulfill state and federal tax obligations for tax years 2007 through 2012 met "the test of 'seriously adversely' reflecting on his ability to practice" making suspension the presumptive sanction); *In re Betts*, 217 P.3d 30, 33 (Kan. 2009) (public censure imposed under Standard 5.13, rather than suspension under Standard 5.12, on lawyer who falsified auto insurance card for his wife, with court accepting hearing panel finding that respondent's intent was not to deceive law enforcement but to appease wife; court noting that misconduct adversely reflected on his fitness to practice law, but did not "seriously adversely" reflect on fitness); *In re Flannery*, 47 P.3d 891 (Or. 2002) (public reprimand under Standard 5.13 issued to deputy district attorney for misrepresentation of address on application for driver's license; distinguishing between Standards 5.12 and 5.13 based on how seriously the conduct adversely reflected on fitness to practice, court noted misrepresentation was trivial and lawyer had no financial personal gain).

Some courts draw a distinction between Standards 5.12 and 5.13 by interpreting the term "other conduct" in Standard 5.13 to mean noncriminal conduct. *See, e.g., In re Rosen*, 198 P.3d 116, 120 (Colo. 2008) (relying on Standard 5.13, court stated that reprimand was warranted for "conduct involving dishonesty, fraud, deceit, or misrepresentation, as long as it falls short of actual criminality or comparable intentional conduct seriously adversely reflecting on one's fitness to practice law," and suspension, under Standard 5.1, generally is reserved for criminal conduct that is "knowingly dishonest conduct directed toward someone other than a client or tribunal"; six-month suspension, stayed entirely, imposed on lawyer who knowingly made deceitful statements about deceased client and who misinformed insurer about actual timing of client's death); *People v. Ra'shadd*, 110 P.3d 388, 393 (Colo. O.P.D.J. 2005) ("[r]eprimand is generally appropriate when a lawyer knowingly engages in non-criminal conduct 'that involves dishonesty, fraud, deceit, or misrepresentation and that adversely reflects on the lawyer's fitness to practice law'"; here, disbarment imposed for misconduct including knowing conversion of client funds and misrepresentation of lawyer's child support obligations to the court); *In re Schaeffer*, 45 A.3d 149 at *9 (Table) (Del. 2012) ("The main distinction between Standard 5.12 and Standard 5.13 appears to be the seriousness of the conduct, with Standard 5.12 focused on 'criminal conduct' that 'seriously adversely reflects on the lawyer's fitness to practice' and Standard 5.13 focused on 'other [presumably noncriminal] conduct.'"); *In re Convisser*, 242 P.3d 299, 313 (N.M. 2010) (public reprimand warranted under Standard 5.13 when "a lawyer knowingly engages in non-criminal conduct involving dishonesty, fraud, deceit, or misrepresentation that adversely reflects on his or her fitness to practice law"; however, "totality of Respondent's misconduct," including the unauthorized practice of law, warranted one-year suspension, deferred, in addition to the public reprimand).

### *Knowing Versus Intentional*

As in Standard 5.12, the mens rea involved under Standard 5.13 is "knowing," not "intentional." *See, e.g., In re Disciplinary Action Against Edison*, 724 N.W.2d, 579, 584 (N.D. 2006) (under North Dakota Standards Imposing Lawyer Sanctions 5.13, inter alia, lawyer hired by insurance company to represent insured defendant in personal injury lawsuit reprimanded for filing "on behalf of Defendant" an amended answer known to be false since lawyer had actual knowledge that the defendant had died; court noting that "a knowing act does not require an evil intent or a bad purpose; rather, the term means the act was done in the exercise of the performer's free will and was not done under coercion"); *In re Kumley*, 75 P.3d 432, 436, 438 (Or. 2003) (citing Standard 5.13, reprimand imposed on inactive lawyer running for state legislator who falsely stated in three government election forms that he was an "attorney," creating a "false impression" that he was actively practicing law; court concluded that lawyer committed violations "knowingly, that is, with the 'conscious awareness of the nature or attendant circumstances of the conduct but without the conscious objective or purpose to accomplish a particular result'") (citation omitted); *In re Warren*, 704 A.2d 789, 792 (Vt. 1997) (rejecting private admonition and imposing public reprimand under Standard 5.13 because lawyer "knew" he violated ethics rules when he sent improper letter to wife of man living with lawyer's estranged wife, offering to represent the woman in a divorce).

In some instances, courts have imposed a public reprimand under Standard 5.13, even when the lawyer's mental state was found to be intentional. *See In re Carpenter*, 95 P.3d 203, 211 (Or. 2004) (public reprimand of lawyer who posted message on Internet falsely representing himself to be a local high school teacher, implying that teacher had had improper relationships with students; while finding Standard 5.13 to most closely fit the misconduct, the court agreed with bar that Sanctions Standards "may not be a perfect fit in this case" because lawyer acted intentionally, conduct was not criminal, did not arise from practice of law, did not benefit the lawyer personally, and did not seriously, adversely reflect on fitness to practice as under other sections of Standard 5.0); *see also In re Gatti*, 8 P.3d 966, 977 (Or. 2000) (public reprimand of lawyer who intentionally misrepresented his identity in order to obtain damaging information for lawsuit; court declined to recognize an "investigatory exception" to disciplinary rules that prohibit dishonesty, fraud, and misrepresentation).

## *Criminal Conduct Warranting Reprimand*

Courts commonly apply Standard 5.13 and its presumptive sanction of reprimand to noncriminal conduct, but some courts have considered Standard 5.13 also applicable to criminal conduct. *See, e.g., In re Charles*, 847 P.2d 592 (Ariz. 1993) (censure warranted under Standard 5.13 for lawyer who did not have criminal intent but nevertheless engaged in dishonesty when he signed the name of a very ill and lifelong friend/client to a power of attorney and later used the document to withdraw funds from client's bank account without disclosing to the bank that the client had died); *People v. Buckley*, 848 P.2d 353 (Colo. 1993) (public censure of district attorney under Standard 5.13 for shoplifting $17.99 hair dryer; citing cases in which court imposed public censure for convictions of misdemeanor offenses when misconduct was not directly related to practice of law); *In re Ellis*, 204 P.3d 1161 (Kan. 2009) (public censure upon finding that lawyer had violated disciplinary rule barring a criminal act involving deceit by taking food from an office cafeteria without paying for it, although he was not prosecuted for offense); *In re Conwell*, 20 P.3d 1260 (Kan. 2001) (criminal diversion agreement for possession of cocaine, marijuana, and drug paraphernalia warranted public censure under Standard 5.13); *State ex rel. Okla. Bar Ass'n v. Garrett*, 127 P.3d 600, 609 (Okla. 2005) (alcohol-addicted lawyer arrested on two counts of felonious sexual battery for groping two women while intoxicated received public censure and one-year probation; court acknowledging that the misconduct was result of alcohol abuse rather than sexual deviancy; Justice Steven Taylor dissenting, urged a lengthy suspension noting the case presented "issues that strongly affect public confidence in our legal system"); *In re Flannery*, 47 P.3d 891, 896 (Or. 2002) (court determined that Standard 5.13 was "the closest fit" and imposed public reprimand on lawyer who pleaded guilty to a misdemeanor for intentionally misrepresenting his address on a driver's license renewal application).

Some misdemeanor tax offenses have garnered a reprimand under Standard 5.13. *See, e.g., People v. Perkell*, 969 P.2d 703 (Colo. 1998) (in reciprocal disciplinary proceeding, public censure appropriate for lawyer convicted of misdemeanor failing to file federal income tax return); *People v. Tauger*, 893 P.2d 121 (Colo. 1995) (guilty plea to federal misdemeanor charge for failure to file federal income tax return warranted public censure when lawyer had no prior discipline in twenty-three years of practice and was experiencing significant personal problems due to hospitalization of son); *Iowa Supreme Ct. Att'y Disciplinary Bd. v. Lustgraaf*, 792 N.W.2d 295 (Iowa 2010) (lawyer's negligent failure to file income tax returns for four years constituted a criminal act warranting public reprimand notwithstanding lack of criminal charges or conviction). *But see In re Brunton*, 144 P.3d 606 (Kan. 2006) (notwithstanding hearing panel's recommendation of censure, under Standard 5.13, court suspended the imposition of a disciplinary sanction provided that lawyer who had been convicted of willful failure to file federal income tax returns, among other misconduct, complied with stated conditions for a two-year period).

## *Dishonest Conduct Warranting Reprimand*

Courts have invoked Standard 5.13 in ordering reprimands for various forms of noncriminal conduct involving dishonesty. In *Bd. of Prof'l Responsibility v. Curry*, 266 S.W.3d 379 (Tenn. 2008), the court imposed a public censure under Standard 5.13, inter alia, on a lawyer who affixed an unauthorized endorsement of an insurance company that had no legal claim to proceeds on the back of a settlement check in order to deposit it. The court found that while the misconduct did not rise to a criminal act of forgery, as the lawyer did not intend to defraud anyone, he misrepresented to the depository bank that he had authority to do so as an "agent" of the insurance company. *See also In re Sutton*, 394 P.3d 836 (Kan. 2017) (citing Standard 5.13 as appropriate for a lawyer's dishonest conduct, court imposed public censure on lawyer who gave dishonest legal advice via letter to ignore a valid court order; lawyer was involved in a divorce proceeding wherein the parents disagreed as to which school system to send their kids to; the court order stated that the children would continue going to school at their current school, but the respondent advised his client that the court order did not declare it so and also sent a letter asserting this falsehood to the opposing parent and the school's principal); *In re Discipline of Walton*, 287 P.3d 1098, 1104 (Or. 2012) (in rejecting recommended six-month suspension and imposing reprimand, court noted Standard 5.13 "most closely fits" lawyer's misconduct involving his intentional misuse of a Westlaw password for Internet research).

Courts may look to reprimand as a sanction under Standard 5.13 to discipline lawyers for dishonest acts not directly related to the practice of law but reflecting character issues. In *In re Lamberis*, 443 N.E.2d 549, 551 (Ill. 1982), the court imposed a public censure on a lawyer who knowingly plagiarized two published works in a thesis submitted in satisfaction of the requirements for a master's degree. The court noted that although the academic forum may appear to be "fairly distant from the practice of law," sanctions were "appropriate and required because both the extent of the appropriated material and the purpose for which it was used evidence the respondent's complete disregard for values that are most fundamental in the legal profession." *See also In re Tatham*, 829 P.2d 1215, 1216 (Ariz. 1992) (lawyer who was also a licensed optometrist submitted inaccurate documents to optometry board to satisfy professional education requirements publicly censured; court stating that "dishonesty and negligence exhibited here, albeit outside of his legal practice, are contrary to values that are fundamental to the legal profession"); *In re Hinden*, 654 A.2d 864 (D.C. 1995) (in reciprocal proceedings, public censures imposed on lawyer who plagiarized twenty-three pages of a fifty-six-page chapter in legal treatise he authored); *In re Hawthorne*, 309 A.D.2d 285 (N.Y. App. Div. 2003) (public censure warranted for lawyer whose misconduct included false statements during hearing regarding his awareness of the court's prior child support order entered against him). In a 2013 proceeding before the Disciplinary Board of the Washington State Bar Association, *In re Pless*, No. 12#00117 (Wash. 2013) *available at* http://mcle.mywsba.org/DisciplineFiles/1748/0081.pdf, a former assistant law school dean for admissions and financial aid was publicly reprimanded, under Standard 5.13, inter alia, for inflating LSAT scores and grade point averages for several law school classes and reporting those inaccuracies to the ABA and *U.S. News & World Report*, among others, as well as for altering and misreporting other numbers, including overstating the number of total applications and understating the number of admission offers.

More often, courts apply Standard 5.13 to noncriminal conduct occurring in connection with or related to the practice of law. *See, e.g., In re Hohn*, 832 P.2d 192 (Ariz. 1992) (public censure warranted under Standard 5.13, inter alia, for wrongful filing of *lis pendens* and sending claim letter to title company in attempt to freeze assets of mobile park manager, against whom lawyer had dispute arising from personal business dealings); *In re Mulhall*, 768 P.2d 1173, 1174 (Ariz. 1989) (public censure under Standard 5.13 warranted for failure to inform client that statute of limitations had run on case and the "settlement came from [lawyer's] own funds"); *People v. Newman*, 925 P.2d 783, 785 (Colo. 1996) (public censure under Standard 5.13 warranted for misrepresentations by corporation's counsel, on inactive status, in letter to customer of corporation falsely stating that he engaged in multistate practice and implying that customer would be liable for attorney's fees paid to him by corporation; court also registered concern for "the offensive style of the respondent's letters" but imposed public censure based upon mitigating factors); *People v. Fitzgibbons*, 909 P.2d 1098 (Colo. 1996) (public censure under Standard 5.13 warranted for lawyer who requested that holder of promissory note falsify credit report and filed frivolous libel suit against note holder present); *Fla. Bar v. Cocalis*, 959 So.2d 163, 167 (Fla. 2007) (finding lawyer's failure to advise opposing counsel that he inadvertently received adversary party's medical records containing notes of a phone conversation between opposing counsel and adversary's treating physician that was damaging to plaintiff's case more than minor misconduct, making diversion inappropriate, and warranting reprimand under Florida Standard 5.13, inter alia; court noting lawyer's "conduct offends our well-recognized policy that cases should be decided on the merits and not by a lawyer's stooping to sneaky or underhanded trial tactics"); *In re Cassity*, 875 P.2d 548, 552 (Utah 1994) (imposing public reprimand under Standard 5.13 and six months' probation for failure to remit to client rightful portion of settlement proceeds after a fee dispute arose between lawyer and client; "reluctantly" concurring, Chief Justice Michael Zimmerman stated he would heartily endorse more serious discipline had the disciplinary prosecution focused on the more serious misconduct by respondent, "his deliberate misrepresentation to the California bankruptcy court that the full settlement amount was to go to [lawyer] as a fee, a representation made with the sole purpose of defrauding the National Labor Relations Board out of its lien"). *But see In re Wilks*, 99 A.3d 228 (Table) (Del. 2014) (court imposed discipline under Standard 4.22, instead of Standard 5.13, because the lawyer's actions violated his duties to his client rather than his duties to the general public; court imposed reprimand because lawyer's actions affected only one client; lawyer believed that his client's personal injury claim was not viable and believed that the only valid claim was for reimbursement of out-of-pocket expenses; he never advised his client of this and proceeded to ignore many requests by client to file a lawsuit on their behalf, including fifty emails from January 25, 2009, to August 30, 2010); *In re Gershater*, 886 P.2d 343, 345 (Kan. 1994) (rejecting reprimand as an appropriate sanction under Standard 5.13 for dishonest conduct directly involved in the practice of law, noting former commentary to the section generally included "conduct related to, but not directly involved in, the practice of law"; court imposed one-year suspension for various misconduct, including making false statements to the court and lying to opposing counsel).

In other instances, the connection to law practice is somewhat more attenuated. *Compare Romero-Barcelo v. Acevedo-Vila*, 275 F. Supp. 2d 177, 214 (D.P.R. 2003) (public reprimand under Standard 5.13 warranted for submitting false statements in complaint lawyer filed against challenger with Federal Elections Commission during political campaign and failing to notify the commission of falsity after the statements were retracted; court noting that "mere fact that some may consider the behavior here as par for the course in both the legal and political process when it is in actuality unethical suggests that we have been too lax in enforcing the clearly articulated duties of the bar"), *and In re Kumley*, 75 P.3d 432 (Or. 2003) (public reprimand warranted for inactive lawyer who falsely used "attorney" designation in forms that he submitted to two state agencies in connection with his candidacy for state legislator), *with In re Royer*, 78 P.3d 449, 457 (Kan. 2003) (rejecting recommendation of public reprimand under Standard 5.13, inter alia, and imposing three-month suspension on lawyer who arranged sale of client's storm-damaged building, which had a negative value, to homeless man for $1 in order to avoid demolition costs; court distinguished this action, directly related to the practice of law, from cases that generally include "conduct related to, but not directly involved in, the practice of law"). *See also People v. Miller*, 409 P.3d 667 (Colo. 2017) (court imposed sanctions under ABA Standard 5.13 for a misdemeanor DUI offense even though "DUI offenses have not been deemed in Colorado to 'seriously' adversely reflect on a lawyer's fitness to practice law"); *People v. Fahselt*, 807 P.2d 586, 588 (Colo. 1991) (convictions of felony vehicular assault, misdemeanor of DUI, failing to maintain liability insurance, and reckless driving warranted public censure in conjunction with mitigating factors; court agreeing with hearing board that although misconduct serious and reflected upon lawyer's fitness to practice, it did not "*seriously* adversely reflect on that fitness").

## *Departure from Baseline Sanction of Reprimand*

Courts have rejected a reprimand for conduct falling under Standard 5.13 as too lenient after considering aggravating factors. *See, e.g., People v. Alster*, 221 P.3d 1088 (Colo. O.P.D.J. 2009) (in default proceedings, lawyer's misuse of client fund account by placing personal funds into account to hide personal assets from his creditors generally warranted public censure under Standard 5.13, but aggravating factors and case law from other jurisdictions supported ninety-day suspension); *In re Rosen*, 198 P.3d 116 (Colo. 2008) (six-month suspension, stayed entirely by probation, warranted for lawyer who engaged in a pattern of dishonest behavior when he knowingly deceived insurer and negotiated settlement after client's death, notwithstanding that reprimand was presumptive sanction for noncriminal conduct involving dishonesty, fraud, deceit, or misrepresentation); *In re Gershater*, 886 P.2d 343 (Kan. 1994) (rejecting reprimand under Standard 5.13, inter alia, as inappropriate, court imposed one-year suspension on lawyer who, among other misconduct, lied to the court and opposing counsel about her reasons for not appearing for trial and in a letter to her clients attempted to blame the trial judge and opposing lawyer for the default judgment entered against them; court finding misconduct intentional); *Bd. of Prof'l Responsibility v. Maddux*, 148 S.W.3d 37 (Tenn. 2004) (reprimand under Standard 5.13 was baseline sanction for law partner who converted funds from law firm but aggravating factors including multiple offenses, pattern of misconduct, and dishonest motive justified increase to thirty-day suspension); *In re Disciplinary Proceeding Against Juarez*, 24 P.3d 1040 (Wash. 2001) (reprimand under Standard 5.13 was presumptive sanction for misrepresenting ability to pay restitution ordered in prior disciplinary case but eighteen-month suspension followed by one-year probation conditioned upon supervision by another lawyer warranted because of prior disciplinary offenses, pattern of misconduct, and multiple offenses).

Standard 5.13 also may apply to certain misconduct in cases involving additional, more serious offenses warranting more severe discipline. In such cases the final sanction imposed should be consistent with the most serious violations. *See, e.g., In re Holmes*, 416 P.3d 143, 159 (Kan. 2018) (citing Standards 5.11 and 5.13, inter alia, court found that the respondent's conduct "fits in standards which indicate reprimand, suspension, and disbarment" and suspended the lawyer for one year; suspension due to failure to timely pay attorney registration fee and failure to pay late fees; lawyer continued to represent clients multiple times in court and failed to notify clients of suspended law license during this period; lawyer also provided false information in letter to disciplinary administrator about the reason behind the law license suspension and omitted instances that occurred from October 17 through October 23, 2015); *In re Disciplinary Proceeding Against Dynan*, 98 P.3d 444 (Wash. 2004) (finding Standard 5.13 applicable only for submitting false billings to opposing counsel and disbarment under Standard 5.11 presumptive sanction because of other serious criminal conduct including false swearing under oath, but lack of intent to deceive court and no direct or indirect benefit among the mitigating factors considered in imposing six-months' suspension).

**5.14 Admonition is generally appropriate when a lawyer engages in any other conduct that reflects adversely on the lawyer's fitness to practice law.**

## Annotation

Courts will impose minimal discipline—that is, a private admonition—in cases involving a minimal infraction. *See, e.g., In re PRB Docket No. 2007-046,* 989 A.2d 523, 529 (Vt. 2009) (court imposed private admonition on two criminal defense lawyers who had misled a potential witness about whether they were recording telephone conversation with the witness, noting that "the panel found that respondents violated the rules out of a 'determination to defend their client against serious criminal charges,' and nothing else"). *But see People v. Miller,* 409 P.3d 667 (Colo. 2017) (court imposed public censure under Standard 5.13 versus admonition under Standard 5.14, because Standard 5.14 "speaks to conduct that is not necessarily knowing or criminal in nature"; lawyer was sanctioned for pleading guilty to a misdemeanor charge of driving under the influence with a blood alcohol content of 0.254); *Toth v. Disciplinary Bd.,* 562 N.W.2d 744, 748 (N.D. 1997) (court cautioned that under North Dakota Standard 5.14, "an admonition is only appropriate for conduct other than dishonesty, fraud, deceit, or misrepresentation 'that reflects adversely on the lawyer's fitness to practice law'"; noting disparity between disciplinary board's finding of misrepresentation, serious misconduct, and issuance of an admonition, a mild sanction, court found charges not proven and dismissed complaint).

In some cases, courts find that Standard 5.14 applies but impose a more severe sanction due to aggravating factors or because additional offenses are involved. *See, e.g., People v. Barnthouse,* 941 P.2d 916 (Colo. 1997) (presumptive private censure under Standard 5.14, inter alia, for fighting in public place and failing to report guilty plea and deferred judgment on disorderly conduct charge, but public censure imposed in light of aggravating factors, including prior discipline history); *In re Meyer,* 970 P.2d 652 (Or. 1999) (appearing on behalf of client at DMV hearing while under the influence of intoxicants violated duty to avoid conduct that reflects adversely on the lawyer's fitness to practice law under Standard 5.14; conduct also interfered with legal proceeding, warranting ninety-day suspension); *In re Disciplinary Proceeding Against Juarez,* 24 P.3d 1040 (Wash. 2001) (failure to timely notify appellate court of lawyer's suspension demonstrated lack of personal integrity adversely reflecting on fitness to practice law, warranting presumptive admonition under Standard 5.14, but eighteen-month suspension with twelve-month supervised probation imposed because of multiple instances of misconduct).

Notwithstanding the opinion in *In re PRB Docket No. 2007-046,* 989 A.2d 523 (Vt. 2009), which was published but omitted the respondents-lawyers' names and other identifying information, private admonitions under Standard 5.14 generally are not published. Thus, the contours of the application of Standard 5.14 may best be understood by examining cases holding Standard 5.14 not applicable. *See, e.g., In re Hickox*, 57 P.3d 403 (Colo. 2002) (in imposing six-month suspension, court found private letter of admonition insufficient for lawyer who pleaded guilty to disturbing the peace, assault, and domestic violence, holding that misconduct should be analyzed as criminal conduct under Standard 5.12); *In re Blase*, 920 P.2d 931, 938 (Kan. 1996) (rejecting panel recommendation of "formal admonition," purportedly based on Standard 5.14, for lawyer's dishonesty involving a check-kiting scheme and imposing published censure instead); *Att'y Grievance Comm'n v. Spery*, 810 A.2d 487 (Md. 2002) (distinguishing conversion of real estate partners' funds from misconduct that would fall under Standards 5.13 and 5.14; noting little difference between stealing from clients and stealing from real estate partners in disbarring lawyer under Standard 5.11).

## 5.2 Failure to Maintain the Public Trust

**Absent aggravating or mitigating circumstances, upon application of the factors set out in Standard 3.0, the following sanctions are generally appropriate in cases involving public officials who engage in conduct that is prejudicial to the administration of justice or who state or imply an ability to influence improperly a government agency or official:**

**5.21 Disbarment is generally appropriate when a lawyer in an official or governmental position knowingly misuses the position with the intent to obtain a significant benefit or advantage for himself or another, or with the intent to cause serious or potentially serious injury to a party or to the integrity of the legal process.**

## Annotation

Standard 5.2 applies specifically to government lawyers and others who hold official positions, such as prosecutors and judges. Because of their official status, such lawyers have a heightened responsibility as guardians of the public trust and must exercise care in maintaining the integrity of the legal process. *See, e.g., In re Swindall*, 468 S.E.2d 372, 373 (Ga. 1996) (in imposing disbarment on a U.S. Congressman convicted of nine counts of perjury before the grand jury, court stated lawyer's "violations warrant a severe level of discipline in light of the fact that he occupied a public office in which he discharged public responsibility"); *In re Williams*, 218 So.3d 1009, 1014 (La. 2016) (court considered Sanctions Standards in determining that permanent disbarment appropriate for assistant district attorney who pled guilty to conspiracy to commit bribery in accepting and agreeing to accept payments with the intention of being influenced and rewarded in connection with a DWI scheme; court found that the "conduct clearly amounts to intentional corruption of the judicial process"); *In re Boylan*, 744 A.2d 158, 161 (N.J. 2000) (disbarment for lawyer who, while serving as municipal court judge, engaged in scheme to defraud the city of money by reducing traffic fines for female defendants in exchange for sexual favors, coached defendants to lie in open court, and used the false statements as a factual basis to justify reductions; court found "it is appropriate to discipline an attorney for conduct as a judge if the conduct itself corrupts the judicial process or evidences a lack of the character and integrity that are necessary in an attorney"; "[s]o deep and so profound is the impugnment of the integrity of the legal system that disbarment is the only appropriate penalty"; Sanctions Standards not cited); *Disciplinary Counsel v. Hoskins*, 891 N.E.2d 324, 341 (Ohio 2008) (permanent disbarment imposed for a pattern of serious misconduct as a judge and lawyer, including attempting to conceal a possible conflict of interest arising from his ownership of a building in which the parole authority leased space, and to benefit secretly from illegally acquired funds of a known felon by negotiating the sale of his building to the felon, as well as his mishandling of two probate estates while in private practice; court noted that the "persistent, serious, and varied nature of respondent's malfeasance establish that only the full measure of our disciplinary authority can protect the public and restore the integrity of the judiciary and the bar, particularly given the principle that judges must be held to the highest standards of integrity and ethical conduct"; Sanctions Standards not cited); *Lawyer Disciplinary Board v. Clifton*, 780 S.E.2d 628 (W. Va. 2015) (court disbarred assistant prosecuting attorney who engaged in sexual relations with a victim, a defendant, and a person seeking help for a defendant, citing Sanctions Standards and noting the destruction of trust in lawyers and the legal system created by attorney's actions).

Public officials subject to disbarment often have engaged in conduct involving fraud and deceit or are found to have violated criminal laws. For example, in *In re Riddle*, 700 N.E.2d 788 (Ind. 1998), disbarment under Standard 5.2, inter alia, was warranted for an elected prosecutor whose misconduct constituted the criminal act of ghost employment as well as perpetuating a fraudulent scheme when he knowingly, intentionally, and secretly hired a chief deputy prosecuting attorney, assigned him no prosecutorial duties but had him run the day-to-day operations of the prosecutor's private law office for the prosecutor's own profit. *See also People v. Brown*, 840 P.2d 348, 351 (Colo. 1992) (disbarment warranted for deputy public defender whose numerous offenses included conviction of embezzlement of public property by soliciting and converting funds from his indigent clients, using cocaine, and submitting false information and fabricated evidence; court noted that "[a]s a public official, the respondent undertook a very high responsibility and obligation to the public to abstain from criminal conduct"); *In re Bean*, 60 N.E.3d 1021 (Ind. 2016) (disbarment of lawyer, who, while serving as clerk-treasurer of town, stole over $20,000 from town by writing checks to himself; Sanctions Standards not cited); *In re Edwards*, 694 N.E.2d 701 (Ind. 1998) (disbarring judge who used his law license as a means to barter for sex, created a fraudulent court decree, lied to other judges, and engaged in the private practice of law while serving as full-time judge; Sanctions Standards not cited); *In re Jackson*, 27 So.3d 273, 277 (La. 2010) (assistant city attorney convicted of malfeasance in office for dismissing DWI charge against a private client was disbarred under Standard 5.21; court found that lawyer intentionally corrupted the judicial process, "interfered with the administration of justice and misused his governmental position to obtain a significant benefit for his client"); *Disciplinary Counsel v. Terry*, 63 N.E.3d 88 (Ohio 2016) (judge permanently disbarred for conduct and resulting criminal convictions on mail fraud charges related to actions taken in official capacity as judge; Sanctions Standards not cited); *Dis-*

*ciplinary Counsel v. Phillips*, 843 N.E.2d 775 (Ohio 2006) (disbarment warranted for assistant county prosecutor following convictions for bribery, theft in office, possession of drugs, possession of criminal tools, and attempted tampering with evidence; Sanctions Standards not cited); *Disciplinary Counsel v. Gallagher*, 693 N.E.2d 1078, 1079 (Ohio 1998) (former judge disbarred permanently following felony conviction for distribution of cocaine; court rejected addiction to cocaine as mitigating factor, noting "[m]itigating factors relevant to this individual attorney pale when he is viewed in his institutional role as a judge"; Sanctions Standards not cited); *Office of Disciplinary Counsel v. Pozonsky*, 177 A.3d 830, 846 (Pa. 2018) (judge disbarred for theft and use of illegal drugs being held in evidence in criminal and delinquency proceedings, acts that "seriously undermine the public's confidence and trust in the integrity of their judicial system"; Sanctions Standards not cited); *Office of Disciplinary Counsel v. Preski*, 134 A.3d 1027, 1033 (Pa. 2016) (court disbarred lawyer who served as chief of staff to member of state house of representatives and misappropriated millions of dollars in public resources, stating that "transgressions of a lawyer who is also a public servant are even more injurious to the reputation of the bar because they bring dishonor both to the profession and to our democratic institutions"; Sanctions Standards not cited).

## *Intent to Obtain Significant Benefit for Self*

Disbarment under Standard 5.21 is recommended when lawyer serving as a public official knowingly misuses a public position with the intent to obtain a significant benefit for himself or herself. *See, e.g., People v. Brown*, 726 P.2d 638, 641 (Colo. 1986) (in imposing disbarment under Standard 5.21 on district attorney convicted of forgery and altering public records by deleting two traffic tickets in order to obtain a more favorable insurance rate, court noted that lawyer used "the power and prestige of his position to attain his objective, and thus implicated the office of district attorney in his unlawful activity"); *In re Howes*, 52 A.3d 1, 17, 22 (D.C. 2012) (citing Standard 5.21 and noting that "benefits need not be financial to be significant," court imposed disbarment on prosecutor who intentionally misused federal witness vouchers, stating "failure to sanction respondent with our most extreme sanction would endorse respondent's reasoning that honorable ends justify unlawful means, failing to deter others from adopting similar attitudes"); *In re King*, 33 So.3d 873, 878 (La. 2010) (former district judge disbarred after guilty plea on one felony count of conspiracy to commit public payroll fraud in connection with coercion of staff to conduct campaign fundraising activities on his behalf to retire his judicial campaign debt; court reviewed Standards 5.11(a) and (b) but concluded that "[e]ven more fitting is Standard 5.21" for judge knowingly and intentionally misusing his office with intent to obtain a significant benefit for himself).

Courts not citing the Sanctions Standards also have looked to the issue of intentional personal gain in evaluating misconduct by public officials, although disbarment has not been imposed consistently across jurisdictions. *Compare In re Skandalakis*, 621 S.E.2d 750, 752 (Ga. 2005) (disbarring county commissioner upon felony conviction for false statement to FBI agent; court found that lawyer "appears to have breached the public trust not only by voting on the contract when he harbored a conflict of interest, but also by making a false statement about his vote"); *In re Hampton*, 533 N.E.2d 122, 128 (Ind. 1989) (in imposing disbarment on lawyer who served as county license branch manager for ghost employment arising from payment of salaries to his three children and private legal secretary from public funds, and misappropriation of public funds to pay personal and family expenses, court noted that "[i]t would be a travesty to tolerate the entrustment of private legal interests to a person who has so grossly breached the public trust"); *and In re Cammarano*, 98 A.3d 1184 (N.J. 2014) (judge disbarred for promising expedited zoning approvals for unspecified construction projects in return for money from government witness disguised as developer); *with In re Brooks*, 449 S.E.2d 87 (Ga. 1994) (disbarment presumptive sanction for former superior court judge for sexual battery against several women, including county employees, but three-year suspension imposed because of mitigating factors including state bar membership for more than forty years and judge for 16, no prior judicial or state bar disciplinary actions, and providing restitution to victims in the form of counseling costs); *La. State Bar Ass'n v. Babovich*, 515 So.2d 1070 (La. 1987) (twenty-four-month suspension rather than disbarment for misuse of position as city councilman resulting in federal conviction for mail fraud conspiracy due to mitigating circumstances); *and In re Vasquez*, 1 A.D.3d 16 (N.Y. App. Div. 2003) (imposing six-month suspension rather than disbarment on director and general counsel for city agency convicted of misdemeanor official misconduct for forging memorandum authorizing salary increase for himself; court viewed serious misconduct in light of substantial mitigation).

Courts may impose a sanction less than disbarment despite it being the presumptive sanction under Standard 5.21. This occurs when significant mitigating factors are present. For example, in *In re Disciplinary Proceedings Against George*, 746 N.W.2d 236 (Wis. 2008), the court suspended for four years and three months a lawyer who had served as state senator and pleaded guilty to federal conspiracy charges to commit offenses against federal program funds, having used his influence to receive illegal kickbacks. The referee had recommended disbarment under Standard 5.21, inter alia, but the court favored suspension over disbarment in light of mitigating factors. The court said it was influenced by the fact that this was the only disciplinary complaint filed against the lawyer since he was admitted to practice nearly thirty years earlier, that he had been in public service, and that his prospects for rehabilitation were real. *See also People v. Larsen*, 808

P.2d 1265, 1269–70 (Colo. 1991) (court noted that conduct of former district attorney who pleaded guilty to possession of less than one ounce of marijuana and official misconduct arising out of his failure to prosecute his wife and employee for drug-related offenses "seriously injured the integrity of the legal profession, warranting disbarment under ABA Standard 5.21 for misuse of position, rather than suspension under ABA Standard 5.22 for failure to follow proper procedures or rules"; however, three-year suspension imposed because lawyer demonstrated substantial mitigation and his crimes were less serious than those committed in disbarment cases involving district attorneys; three justices dissented, urging disbarment); *Ohio State Bar Ass'n v. Mason*, 94 N.E.3d 556, 561 (Ohio 2017) (court imposed an indefinite suspension, instead of disbarment, on a judge convicted of a single, unpremeditated, violent assault, with reinstatement conditioned upon clear and convincing evidence that the judge is "now a proper person to be readmitted to the practice of law"; Sanctions Standards not cited).

Mitigating factors similarly persuaded the North Dakota Supreme Court to depart from the baseline sanction of disbarment and impose a one-year suspension in a case involving a lawyer convicted of making false and fictitious statements in response to two letters he received from a senator and during an FBI interview regarding prohibited campaign activities while serving as chair of a federal housing finance agency. In *In re Disciplinary Action Against Korsmo*, 718 N.W.2d 6 (N.D. 2006), although the hearing panel referred to North Dakota Standard 5.21, inter alia, it concluded, and the court agreed, that disbarment was inappropriate in light of significant mitigating factors, including that lawyer's statements were not under oath and there was no evidence that he received a substantial benefit for himself. He was suspended instead.

## *Intent to Obtain Significant Benefit for Another*

Disbarment under Standard 5.21 is also recommended when a public official knowingly misuses a public position with the intention of obtaining a significant benefit for another person, such as a client or someone with whom the official has a close personal relationship. In *In re Rosenthal*, 382 N.E.2d 257 (Ill. 1978), two lawyers were disbarred after they participated in and facilitated an extortion scheme perpetrated by a public official against their client to benefit client's zoning request. Emphasizing that one of the lawyers being an assistant attorney general was significant in imposing disbarment, the court concluded:

> Corruption within government could not, in most instances, thrive but for those few attorneys, who, like respondents, are willing to tolerate such illegal activity if it will benefit their client. The practice of law is a privilege and demands a greater acceptance of responsibility and adherence to ethical standards than respondents have demonstrated.

> Their conduct, in facilitating and participating in the paying of money to [building and zoning committee secretary], was clearly a breach of required professional conduct.

*Id.* at 261. In *In re Williams,* 218 So.3d 1009 (La. 2016), the court disbarred an assistant district attorney for accepting a series of gifts and a cash payment to aid in providing favorable dispositions of DWI cases; *see also In re Jackson,* 27 So.3d 273 (La. 2010) (court disbarred an assistant city attorney responsible for prosecuting DWI violations after he accepted $500 from a private client and dismissed a DWI charge against that client; his conduct led to a felony conviction for malfeasance in office and the court determined that Standard 5.21, inter alia, applied, thus making disbarment the baseline sanction and finding a downward departure from the baseline sanction unwarranted); *Attorney Grievance Comm'n v. McDonald,* 85 A.3d 117, 144 (Md. 2014) (court disbarred deputy state's attorney who had improperly interfered with investigations and prosecutions of former employee of the state's attorney's office, citing Sanctions Standards "in order to protect the public, maintain the public's confidence in the legal profession, and deter similar misconduct by public officials in the future"); *State ex rel. Okla. Bar Ass'n v. Lile,* 194 P.3d 1275 (Okla. 2008) (rejecting joint stipulation for public censure and tribunal's recommendation of suspension of two years and one day, court imposed disbarment on judge who abused his position by, inter alia, attempting to influence the criminal prosecution of the mother of his son on drug charges and filing false travel reimbursement claims; Sanctions Standards not cited); *In re Leonhardt,* 930 P.2d 844, 849 (Or. 1997) (citing Standard 5.21, inter alia, court concluded disbarment warranted for district attorney's misconduct, including conviction for falsifying official records and action taken to secure baseless grand jury indictments of two law enforcement officers in an attempt to influence criminal investigation of lawyer's fiancé, a felon; court stated that "[t]he injury to the accused police officers, to the criminal justice system, and to the public's confidence in the legal process and its public officials was actual and substantial"). *But see In re Gribble,* 933 P.2d 672, 675 (Kan. 1997) (objecting to the indefinite suspension imposed by the majority one justice urged disbarment, noting that respondent "mocked" the rules of professional conduct when he falsified hearing dockets and dismissed eight of his clients' driver's license suspension cases while serving as a hearing officer for the Kansas Department of Revenue).

### *Intent to Cause Serious Injury*

Similarly, disbarment is appropriate when the public official acts with the intent to cause serious or potentially serious injury to a party, the public, or to the integrity of the legal process itself. *See, e.g., In re Howes,* 52 A.3d 1, 25 (D.C. 2012) (in imposing disbarment, court stated that prosecutor's intentional misuse of government vouchers and subsequent fraudulent acts to conceal the misuse resulted in the reduction of criminal sentences for nine convicted felons, and "affected the liberty interests of many and the safety of our larger community"); *Fla. Bar v. Mogil,* 763 So.2d 303 (Fla. 2000) (reciprocal disbarment was warranted under Standard 5.21 for misconduct that caused "serious or potentially serious injury to . . . the integrity of the legal process"; former judge sent criminal defense attorney anonymous harassing communications, distributed a statement on judicial stationery disparaging criminal defense lawyers and threatened retaliation for unfounded complaints against judges, and engaged in dishonesty during judicial removal proceedings); *In re Jackson,* 27 So.3d 273 (La. 2010) (city attorney convicted of malfeasance in office after he dismissed DWI charges against his private client while acting in his official capacity, causing actual harm to the legal system and legal profession and potentially serious harm to the public; permanent disbarment imposed under Standard 5.21, inter alia); *Disciplinary Counsel v. Phillips,* 843 N.E.2d 775, 778 (Ohio 2006) (in imposing disbarment, court stated that prosecutor's abuse of public office and willingness to accept bribes to affect the outcome of pending criminal cases "lessened confidence in the legal profession and compromised its integrity by conveying the impression that favorable outcomes could be purchased in Cuyahoga County"; Sanctions Standards not cited).

**5.22 Suspension is generally appropriate when a lawyer in an official or governmental position knowingly fails to follow proper procedures or rules, and causes injury or potential injury to a party or to the integrity of the legal process.**

## Annotation

Suspension is an appropriate sanction when lawyers serving in official or governmental positions knowingly act improperly and their conduct adversely affects a party or the integrity of the legal profession. *See In re Abrams,* 257 P.3d 167, 173 (Ariz. 2011) (court imposed two-year suspension under Standard 5.22 on lawyer who, while serving as judge, maintained an intimate relationship with one lawyer while she was appearing in cases before him and abused his power against another lawyer who repeatedly rebuffed his sexual propositions by retaliating against her from the bench; court noted that proposal of a reprimand failed to acknowledge the seriousness of his misconduct and the harm it inflicted on the legal system, stressing that judge "placed his own sexual desires above his obligation to 'exhibit the highest standards of honesty and integrity'") (citation omitted). In *People v. Biddle,* 180 P.3d 461 (Colo. O.P.D.J. 2007), a three-year suspension under Standard 5.22 was warranted for a lawyer who, while serving as magistrate for a judicial district and later as judge for county court, had an affair with a deputy district attorney who practiced in his courtroom. The court said:

> The actual injury and serious potential injury caused to the integrity of the legal process is the most disturbing factor in this case. An independent and honorable judicial system is crucial to our system of justice. Indeed, the integrity of our judicial system is at the core of our democratic system of government. When a public official flagrantly abandons his ethical duties, he necessarily damages the public's confidence in the rule of law and the integrity of our judicial system.

*Id.* at 465; *see also People v. Pautler,* 35 P.3d 571, 585 (Colo. O.P.D.J. 2001) (three-month suspension under Standard 5.22, inter alia, for deception when deputy district attorney posed as public defender in order to encourage surrender of murder suspect; finding respondent's misconduct "meets or exceeds every requirement set forth in §5.22"); *In re Gelof,* 142 A.3d 506 (Del. 2016) (citing Standard 5.2, court suspended deputy attorney general thirty days for convincing court's chief of security to draw and point his gun at another lawyer as a practical joke, which not only created a potentially dangerous situation, but also caused actual harm by diverting court resources to investigate and address the conduct and by necessitating that other lawyers in the department take on the deputy's caseload during his suspension); *In re Mears*, 723 N.E.2d 873, 875 (Ind. 2000) (ninety-day suspension warranted for lawyer who, while serving as county judge, violated the public trust "when she placed her personal interests above her professional obligations by regularly requiring her staff to run personal errands for her during working hours or while they were earning compensatory time"; Sanctions Standards not cited); *In re Gribble*, 933 P.2d 672 (Kan. 1997) (indefinite suspension warranted for lawyer who, while serving as part-time hearing officer for department of revenue, dismissed driver's license suspension cases of eight clients who had retained him to represent them on DUI charges, falsified hearing dockets, and gave false statements to an investigator when questioned about one case); *In re Griffing*, 236 So.3d 1213, 1221 (La. 2017) (in a case of first impression, court suspended Assistant United States Attorney six months for maintaining an intimate, secret relationship with an FBI agent who was called as a witness in cases handled by the AUSA, stating that public officials are held to a higher standard than ordinary attorneys; Sanctions Standards not cited); *Disciplinary Counsel v. Kramer*, 75 N.E.3d 1174 (Ohio 2016) (lawyer serving as hearing officer at county's board of revision suspended for one year for knowingly falsifying his public-employee time records; Sanctions Standards not cited); *Disciplinary Counsel v. Dann*, 979 N.E.2d 1263, 1269 (Ohio 2012) (finding that lawyer's status as state's attorney general weighed in favor of greater sanction—actual six-month suspension with no part stayed; "Like judges, the attorney general has a heightened duty to the public by virtue of his elected office . . . [and his] criminal and ethical violations reflect poorly on his fitness to practice law and the legal profession as a whole, but also cause incalculable harm to the public perception of the attorney general's office and those government agencies, departments, and institutions that the attorney general advises and represents"; Sanctions Standards not cited); *In re Gustafson*, 968 P.2d 367 (Or. 1998) (six-month suspension under Standard 5.2, inter alia, for deputy district attorney who violated her duty to maintain the public's trust by engaging in conduct prejudicial to the administration of justice when she made unjustified threats of prosecution against defense counsel to secure his favorable testimony).

Suspension also may be imposed if the public official acts improperly but not for his or her own benefit. *See Disciplinary Counsel v. Weithman*, 34 N.E.3d 865 (Ohio 2015) (magistrate committed no quantifiable harm but harmed the judiciary as a whole with his comments, demeanor, and threats to litigants; suspended for two years, stayed on the condition that he commit no further misconduct and comply with lawyer assistance program contract; Sanctions Standards not cited); *In re Illuzzi*, 683 A.2d 1008, 1009 (Vt. 1996) (eighteen-month suspension warranted, under Standard 5.22 for lawyer who served on state senate judiciary committee and filed complaints on senate letterhead against a judge whose wife was disciplinary counsel and prosecuted lawyer in prior disciplinary proceeding that resulted in lawyer's suspension; in rejecting board's disbarment recommendation, court stated that "[w]e discern no serious injury, potential or actual . . . nor do we discern any direct benefit to respondent from filing the complaints").

A court also may apply Standard 5.22 when disciplining official misconduct reflecting an egregious lapse of judgment causing harm to others. In *In re Campbell*, 199 P.3d 776, 780 (Kan. 2009), a county attorney was suspended for six months in connection with his decision to allow parents of minors who attended a party to view altered photos from the party depicting underage drinking and a partially clothed female minor engaging in sexual activity, notwithstanding the girl's claim of sexual assault and her parent's request that the county attorney seal the photographs from public view. Unmoved by the respondent's contention that he shared the photos in order to deter underage drinking in the community, the court determined the ninety-day suspension recommended by the hearing panel inadequate, citing respondent's "continued inability or unwillingness to come to grips with the devastation his conduct has wrought . . . " The court found the lawyer's actions had done actual damage to at least one minor depicted in the photos and had the potential to chill reports from victims of future sex crimes.

## *Criminal Conduct*

When a public official, sworn to uphold the law, engages in criminal conduct, courts find the breach of public trust particularly troubling. *See, e.g., In re Serstock*, 432 N.W.2d 179, 185 (Minn. 1988) (citing Standard 5.22 in imposing indefinite suspension on chief deputy city attorney who failed to file income tax returns and improperly dismissed traffic tickets of friends; in discussing cases imposing severe discipline on public officials for violations of public trust, the court stated that "[r]espondent's actions, widely publicized, can only serve to reduce the public's trust and belief . . . [and] stern disciplinary sanctions will help to restore the public's trust in the legal system"); *Ohio State Bar Ass'n v. McCafferrty*, 17 N.E.3d 521 (Ohio 2014) (court indefinitely suspended judge convicted of making false statements to federal law enforcement officers regarding corruption investigation; court noted that judges are held to the highest possible standard of ethical conduct and that the conviction arose from dishonest conduct; Sanctions Standards not cited); *Disciplinary Counsel v. Dann*, 979 N.E.2d 1263, 1267 (Ohio 2012) (noting that "the unique harm to the legal profession and to public confidence in our government when the attorney general—the chief law-enforcement officer for the state of Ohio—engages in misconduct," court imposed six months' suspension on lawyer convicted of filing false financial disclosure statements and soliciting improper compensation; Sanctions Standards not cited); *In re Disciplinary Proceedings Against Chvala*, 730 N.W.2d 648, 650 (Wis. 2007) (state senator's conviction for directing state employees to manage senate campaigns during state time and making an unlawful contribution to a political action committee "involved breaches of the public trust," warranting two-year suspension); *cf. In re Ryan*, 824 N.E.2d 687, 689

(Ind. 2005) (in imposing nine-month suspension on prosecutor who operated a business with his wife to obtain international driver's licenses directed primarily at defendants charged with driving without a license, court stated, "As a public officer charged with the administration of justice, respondent's behavior had the capacity to bolster or damage the public's perception of the criminal justice system"; Sanctions Standards not cited); *State ex rel. Okla. Bar Ass'n v. Maddox*, 152 P.3d 204, 209 (Okla. 2006) (finding lawyer "betrayed his trust as a public official," court imposed two-year suspension for elected district attorney who pleaded guilty to embezzlement following charges that he unlawfully submitted reimbursement claims for mileage while driving a state-owned automobile; extraordinary delay in disciplinary process a factor in mitigation; Sanctions Standards not cited).

## *Public Official's Failure to Follow Procedures or Rules*

The timeliness of a prosecutor's disclosure of exculpatory evidence may lead to suspension. *See In re Larsen*, 379 P.3d 1209, 1215 (Utah 2016) (six-month suspension for failure to disclose, prior to trial, that prosecutor "had shown the defendant's photograph (and no other photographs) to the eyewitnesses of the two robberies" in order to allow "the defendant to adequately prepare his defense"; Sanctions Standards cited regarding effect of multiple charges).

Potential injury to the integrity of the legal process is sufficient to lead to suspension. *See In re Estelle*, 336 P.3d 692 (Alaska 2014) (citing Standard 5.22, among others, court suspended judge for forty-five days for failure to decide three matters in a timely manner, within six months, and signing pay affidavits for self that stated that no matters were pending for over six months).

## *Public Official Status as Aggravating Factor*

In some instances, courts deciding cases under Standard 5.22 have found a lawyer's status as a public official to be an aggravating factor, or have observed that public officials are held to a higher standard of conduct than other lawyers. *See, e.g., In re Holste*, 358 P.3d 850, 858 (Kan. 2015) (imposing two-year suspension on lawyer who misused position as county attorney by threatening criminal prosecution in attempt to elect settlement of a civil litigation; "public's trust in the appropriate, good-faith exercise of [prosecutorial] discretion is seriously challenged by respondent's bullying of his opposing counsel"); *In re Swarts*, 30 P.3d 1011, 1031 (Kan. 2001) (ordering supervised probation for approximately three months followed by agreed retirement from office and the practice of law for elected county attorney who committed numerous acts of misconduct, including creating evidence for criminal defendant's plea hearing, obtaining incriminating statements from criminal defendant without advising defendant of *Miranda* rights, flippantly advising father to chain his child to bed, and arranging for public corporal punishment of children at courthouse; court stressed that "'prosecutor is a servant of the law and a representative of the people of Kansas.' When one undertakes the responsibility of prosecution we must view his or her conduct by an enhanced standard") (citation omitted); *In re Richmond*, 996 So.2d 282, 289 (La. 2008) (reiterating that "an attorney occupying a position of public trust is held to a higher standard of conduct than an ordinary attorney," court imposed six-month suspension, all but sixty days deferred followed by probation, for state representative's false statement on election form regarding his domicile address; Sanctions Standards cited generally); *Lawyer Disciplinary Bd. v. Amos*, 760 S.E.2d 424 (W. Va. 2014) (imposing seventy-five day suspension on assistant prosecutor for inappropriate conduct with a represented respondent in an abuse and neglect matter to which he was assigned, citing the tremendous potential for injury to the public and the administration of justice). *But see Lockett v. Bd. of Prof'l Responsibility*, 380 S.W.3d 19 (Tenn. 2012) (finding hearing panel abused its discretion in considering Standard 5.2 applicable since misconduct by lawyer who became Knox County law director, an elected position, was unrelated to his service in public office and occurred before he assumed office and, therefore, not a breach of public trust).

Even in cases in which a court does not base its sanction on Standard 5.22, the fact that the lawyer is in a government position is often used as a basis for increasing the period of a suspension. *See, e.g., In re Philpot*, 31 N.E.3d 468 (Ind. 2015) (court suspended, for a minimum of four years, county clerk who had been convicted of mail fraud and theft from a federally funded program, finding his position as an elected official who had betrayed the public trust and violated his oath of office was an aggravating factor); *Disciplinary Counsel v. Norris*, 666 N.E.2d 1087, 1089 (Ohio 1996) (two-year suspension of prosecutor for misdemeanor cocaine possession; recognizing that prosecutor "committed this misdemeanor while serving as an elected public official whose sworn duty was to prosecute the very crime he was committing"; not citing Sanctions Standards); (*Lawyer Disciplinary Bd. v. Scott*, 579 S.E.2d 550 (W. Va. 2003) (while annulment of license was recommended, court imposed three-year suspension on elected county prosecutor who committed twenty-two violations of the Rules of Professional Conduct, including lying and falsifying court documents; finding status as public official an aggravating factor, court noting decision consistent with prior cases involving misconduct by public officials, where the ultimate penalty of annulment was imposed in only two cases).

**5.23 Reprimand is generally appropriate when a lawyer in an official or governmental position negligently fails to follow proper procedures or rules, and causes injury or potential injury to a party or to the integrity of the legal process.**

## Annotation

Officials whose failure to follow procedures is not intentional or purposeful, but rather negligent, are subject to reprimand or public censure under Standard 5.23 when that failure results in injury or potential injury to a party or the legal process. *See, e.g., Bd. of Prof'l Responsibility v. Murray,* 143 P.3d 353, 356 (Wyo. 2006) (public censure ordered under Standard 5.23, inter alia, when specially appointed deputy county attorney made extrajudicial statements related to the character of the defendant and expressed his opinion as to defendant's guilt; while respondent did not act intentionally—either knowingly or purposefully—to violate ethical rules, his conduct "was wrong").

A court may find misconduct that is deemed "willful" as a matter of law is nonetheless "inadvertent" or the result of inexperience and thus warrants no greater sanction than a public reprimand. *See, e.g., In re Discipline of Russell,* 797 N.W.2d 77, 91 (S.D. 2011) (in imposing public censure on lawyer for using his office as elected county state's attorney to advance and defend his political career and publicizing grand jury transcripts, court found that the misconduct was the "product of a relatively inexperienced prosecutor"; court acknowledged that it has not adopted Sanctions Standards but does consult them); *In re Disciplinary Proceedings Against Ziegler,* 750 N.W.2d 710 (Wis. 2008) (trial court judge who, over the course of several years, had presided over eleven cases involving a bank for which the judge's husband served as director was publicly reprimanded; court found that while the judge had "inadvertently" failed to disclose the conflict and disqualify herself, her conduct was nonetheless "willful" because she had known that her husband served on the bank board and should have known the judicial code barred her participation in those cases; Sanctions Standards not cited).

A lawyer whose misconduct arises out of a desire to carry out official duties is still subject to public reprimand. See *In re Krull,* 860 N.W.2d 38 (Iowa 2015) (public reprimand of part-time magistrate who signed a warrant for search of his own client's home, despite respondent's argument that nearest alternative magistrate was thirty miles away, given that this was the second such occurrence and respondent had not learned that recusal was necessary after prior private admonition; Sanctions Standards not cited).

## *Inappropriate Comments*

Inappropriate comments by judicial officers and prosecutors also have resulted in reprimand under Standard 5.23. *See, e.g., In re Dooley,* 376 P.3d 1249 (Alaska 2016) (while finding no actual injury or bias, court found judge to have negligently made inappropriate comments that reflected on the integrity of the judiciary in five separate cases; court applied the Sanctions Standards as an analogy to the extent possible, while acknowledging the difficulty in applying them to judges); *People v. Sharpe,* 781 P.2d 659, 661 (Colo. 1989) (public censure warranted under Standard 5.23 for district attorney who used racial epithet in conversation with defense lawyer in hallway outside courtroom; court noted racial epithet was intolerable and cast doubt on integrity of legal process, and that lawyers, especially public officials, "must scrupulously avoid statements as well as deeds that could be perceived as indicating that their actions are motivated to any extent by racial prejudice"); *People v. Gilbert,* 173 P.3d 1113 (Colo. O.P.D.J. 2007) (public censure warranted under Standard 5.23, inter alia, for magistrate who made an ex parte phone call to litigant, referring to litigant and himself by their first names in a recorded voicemail, and later refused to recuse himself when same litigant asked him in court to do so; court found that respondent violated duties as an attorney as well as judicial official to the justice system); *see also Lawyer Disciplinary Bd. v. Sims,* 574 S.E.2d 795 (W. Va. 2002) (prosecutor's extrajudicial statements to newspapers about assessor in connection with grand jury proceeding warranted public reprimand, especially after circuit court previously cautioned prosecutor against making such statements; Sanctions Standards not cited).

## *Prosecutors' Failure to Follow Procedures or Rules*

Courts may invoke Standard 5.23 when, for example, a prosecutor violates a duty of disclosure to defense counsel in a criminal case, thereby interfering with the administration of justice. In *In re Jordan,* 91 P.3d 1168, 1174 (Kan. 2004), the court publicly censured a lawyer for misconduct in the prosecution of two criminal cases, finding that the prosecutor "recklessly violated her duty to the legal system to refrain from interfering with the administration of justice" when her failure to comply with discovery requests resulted in declaration of two mistrials and dismissal of cases. The court cited Standard 5.23, inter alia, to support reprimand as the presumptive sanction for negligent, rather than intentional, misconduct, notwithstanding the court's conclusion that some of the prosecutor's conduct was intentional. *Compare State ex rel. Oklahoma Bar Ass'n v. Miller,* 360 P.3d 508 (Okla. 2015) (court ordered public censure for two prosecutors in murder trial for intentionally misleading defense regarding witness's contradictory statements; court's decision was 5–4, with the dissent supporting suspension as the sanction; Sanctions Standards not cited). Determining when a reprimand may be the appropriate sanction for a prosecutor's failure to follow proper procedures can result in conflicting opinions when the parameters of a prosecutor's ethical duty to disclose exculpatory material to the defense is a case of first impression. *Compare In re Att'y C.*, 47 P.3d 1167 (Colo. 2002) (court acknowledged that prosecutor failed to disclose evidence in timely manner but reversed hearing board's imposition of public censure and dismissed the charges, finding that the professional conduct rule governing disclosure of evidence is violated only if the prosecutor acts intentionally) *and In re Kline*, 113 A.3d 202 (D.C. Ct. App. 2015) (court found that prosecutor intentionally withheld statement he thought was not exculpatory under the belief that ethics rule was coextensive with Brady obligation but did not impose a sanction as prosecutor had not received any training regarding the application of the rule, no allegations of dishonesty were made, and his understanding, though wrong, was reasonable; Sanctions Standards not cited) *with In re Disciplinary Action Against Feland*, 820 N.W.2d 672, 680 (N.D. 2012) (in imposing admonition notwithstanding matter of first impression, court held that disclosure rule was "not ambiguous," "creates an affirmative duty upon a prosecutor" and "does not create an exception for unintentional violations," noting that applying rule only to intentional withholding of evidence would result in no discipline for "recurring pattern of negligent but unintentional violations").

## *Mitigating Circumstances*

Even when the conduct is intentional, the court may find sufficient mitigating circumstances to reduce the sanction to a public reprimand. *See, e.g., In re Chavez*, 390 P.3d 965 (N.M. 2017) (finding that a district attorney and deputy district attorney had violated rules of professional conduct by issuing subpoenas that were not ordered by a judge or grand jury and not connected to any case before the court; court cited Standard 5.22, but, based on respondents' lack of bad faith or intent to deceive, issued formal reprimand instead of suspension).

**5.24 Admonition is generally appropriate when a lawyer in an official or governmental position engages in an isolated instance of negligence in not following proper procedures or rules, and causes little or no actual or potential injury to a party or to the integrity of the legal process.**

## Annotation

As in other cases, lawyers in official or governmental positions may be privately admonished for an isolated instance of negligent failure to follow procedures or rules without formal charges being brought or a public record made. *See, e.g., In re Disciplinary Action Against Feland*, 820 N.W.2d 672, 686–87 (N.D. 2012) (rejecting recommendation of sixty-day suspension, court ordered an admonition for prosecutor whose failure to disclose exculpatory evidence was an isolated instance of negligence; citing Standard 5.24, inter alia, and acknowledging that admonition was intended to be a nonpublic form of discipline; "[a]lthough there may be little or no distinction between the practical effect of a reprimand or an admonition when the 'private' admonition is announced in a published opinion of this Court, the distinction is important to the extent that the sanction defines the severity of the offense on the lawyer's disciplinary record").

Discussions of Standard 5.24 are rare. Comparable judicial disciplinary cases imposing private reprimand on judges who engage in misconduct offer some insight. *See, e.g., In re Inquiry Concerning a Judge*, 788 P.2d 716, 723, 723 n.11 (Alaska 1990) (to ensure consistency, Sanctions Standards "provide a 'theoretical framework within which to organize and analyze the relevant factors to be considered in discipline sanction cases'" (citation omitted); when sanctioning judges, court said it would analogize to the Standards while recognizing that they are "limited in analogical scope because judges are held to a higher level of scrutiny than are ordinary lawyers"; citing Standard 5.24, inter alia, court noted negligent conduct with little injury usually warranted admonition).

A private reprimand may be imposed when the respondent judge's conduct was found to be not willful, was isolated, and did little or no harm. *See, e.g., In re McCormick*, 639 N.W.2d 12 (Iowa 2002) (judge's violation of ethics code in allowing campaign poster for local sheriff candidate to be placed in family's yard was a single isolated event that occurred outside the courtroom; was negligent and caused little known injury; private reprimand warranted but public reprimand imposed for other more serious misconduct of submitting false information during the investigation; Sanctions Standards not cited); *Miss. Comm'n on Judicial Performance v. Blakeney*, 905 So.2d 521, 530 (Miss. 2004) (private reprimand of judge who allowed newspaper photographer to take photograph of defendants in court proceeding, in violation of Code of Judicial Conduct; rejecting recommendation of public reprimand, court stated "[b]y comparison with other offenses committed by judges which have resulted in sanctions, we are hard pressed to find the judge's offense to be of any significant magnitude"; Sanctions Standards not cited). (Note that typically respondent judges' names and other identifying information are omitted from published opinions resulting in private reprimand; in this case the court acknowledged judge's identity no longer confidential due to publicity generated by local media and reference by the court to the judge's prior public reprimand case).

A private reprimand may be appropriate even when there is a pattern of misconduct, provided the misconduct is sufficiently minor and respondent's actions were not willful. *See, e.g., Miss. Comm'n on Judicial Performance v. Justice Ct. Judge T.T.*, 922 So.2d 781, 785 (Miss. 2006) (private reprimand of judge who accepted plea agreement that did not comply with statute imposing minimum mandatory penalty for criminal offense due to failure to read and be familiar with applicable statutes: "The actions of the court were not due to intentional, malicious, or gross misconduct. Therefore, [respondent] is not guilty of egregious legal error, nor of bad faith. Nevertheless, the neglect should be labeled misconduct because of the continuing pattern of legal error." Sanctions Standards not cited); *Miss. Comm'n on Judicial Performance v. Former Judge U.U.*, 875 So.2d 1083 (Miss. 2004) (private reprimand for judge who exhibited pattern of delays in rendering opinions and orders; pattern was not willful misconduct but was prejudicial to administration of justice and violated judicial canon requiring judge to dispose promptly of court business; Sanctions Standards not cited); *cf. Miss. Comm'n on Judicial Performance v. Agin*, 17 So.3d 578, 581 (Miss. 2009) (even when judge's misconduct found to be not "*willful* misconduct in office or *willful* and persistent failure to perform his duties," (emphasis in original) public rather than private reprimand warranted when judge failed to rule on motion for summary judgment for nearly a year, thus repeating same dilatory behavior that resulted in two prior disciplinary sanctions, a public reprimand and an admonishment; aggravating factors considered, including a pattern of misconduct with litigants suffering harm; Sanctions Standards not cited). *But see In re Cannizzaro*, 901 So.2d 1035, 1037 (La. 2005) (public reprimand warranted for judge who accepted campaign contributions without using a campaign committee; even though judge's actions were not product of any dishonest or improper motive and he corrected practice as soon as violation was brought to his attention, judge engaged in a pattern of improper conduct in violation of the judicial code, and his failure to abide by the code "had the potential to seriously undermine the public's confidence in the integrity of the judiciary").

# 6.0 Violations of Duties Owed to the Legal System

## Annotation

The public expects lawyers, as officers of the court, to abide by the substantive and procedural rules and laws. Lawyers must operate within the bounds of the law and cannot create or use false evidence or make a false statement of fact or law to a tribunal, MODEL RULES OF PROF'L CONDUCT R. 3.3 and R. 3.4. Ethical standards require that a lawyer refrain from filing frivolous lawsuits, MODEL RULES OF PROF'L CONDUCT R. 3.1, from improperly delaying a trial; MODEL RULES OF PROF'L CONDUCT R. 3.2, from improperly communicating with a party, juror, witness, or judge; MODEL RULES OF PROF'L CONDUCT R. 3.5, R. 4.2, and R. 4.3; and from threatening criminal prosecution or otherwise interfering with the legal process, MODEL RULES OF PROF'L CONDUCT R. 3.4, R. 3.6, R. 4.1, and R. 4.4.

Lawyers offering false testimony violate the bedrock principle of honesty underlying the legal system, and courts have found that such serious breaches merit serious consequences. *See, e.g., In re Fioramonti*, 859 P.2d 1315 (Ariz. 1993) (three-year suspension for perjury, suborning perjury, and manufacturing evidence during a disciplinary proceeding); *Att'y Grievance Comm'n v. Zodrow*, 19 A.3d 381, 392 (Md. 2011) (disbarment warranted for failing to make pertinent disclosures and acting with intentional dishonesty when offering false testimony in personal bankruptcy proceeding; "[r]espondent's misconduct . . . is 'one infected with fraud, deceit and dishonesty'") (citation omitted); *In re Disciplinary Action Against Kaiser*, 484 N.W.2d 102, 109 (N.D. 1992) (rejecting public reprimand, court found two-year suspension appropriate for two instances of testifying falsely under oath; lawyer's first materially false statement under oath violated duty to the legal system under Standard 6.0 and also Standards 6.11 and 6.12, and second false statement eight years later aggravated seriousness of lawyer's misconduct); *cf. In re Disciplinary Action Against Korsmo*, 718 N.W.2d 6 (N.D. 2006) (two-year suspension for making false statements rejected and lesser suspension imposed where court, distinguishing *In re Kaiser*, found that purpose of discipline is not to punish but to protect the public, and Korsmo's lie was not under oath and did not result in substantial benefit to him).

Courts also impose discipline when lawyers abuse the legal system by violating ethics rules crafted to discourage them from pursuing actions not based in good faith, and from improperly gaining an unfair advantage in litigation or thwarting the ends of justice. Courts routinely impose sanctions against lawyers who file frivolous lawsuits in violation of Model Rule 3.1. *See In re Levine*, 847 P.2d 1093 (Ariz. 1993) (six-month suspension followed by two years of probation imposed on lawyer who pursued frivolous claims; nature of duty violated was respondent's abuse of the legal process under Standard 6.2); *In re Alexander*, 300

P.3d 536 (Ariz. 2013) (when deciding whether a filing is frivolous, an objective standard is applied, but a subjective standard is used to determine if a lawyer acted in good faith; six-month suspension for lawyer who continued to pursue federal racketeering lawsuit despite knowing it lacked legal and factual merit); *Brunswick v. Statewide Grievance Comm'n*, No. HHDCV05010799, 2006 WL 895007 (Conn. Super. Ct. Mar. 22, 2006) (reprimand for lawyer who made frivolous allegations in motion to vacate); *In re Obert*, 282 P.3d 825, 840 (Or. 2012) (six-month suspension imposed for misconduct including knowingly filing frivolous appeal); *In re Yelverton*, 105 A.3d 413 (D.C. 2014) (attorney who filed frivolous postconviction motions in a criminal matter suspended for thirty days); *Dodrill v. Exec. Dir.*, 824 S.W.2d 383 (Ark. 1992) (one-year suspension imposed on lawyer who was continually insulting and abusive and who made unfounded allegations in lawsuit); *In re McGraw*, 414 P.3d 841, 850 (Or. 2018) ("[A] lawyer takes a 'frivolous' position when there is no basis in law or in fact for that legal position"); *Weatherbee v. Va. State Bar*, 689 S.E.2d 753 (Va. 2010) (a finding that attorney did not violate RPC 1.1 does not preclude a finding that he violated RPC 3.3, because those rules impose different professional responsibilities and are not duplicative, repetitive, or synonymous); *In re Disciplinary Proceedings Against Bach*, 887 N.W.2d 335 (Wis. 2016) (to prove a violation, evidence must show that the attorney in fact knew the claim or factual position she was advancing was unwarranted); *In re Disciplinary Proceedings Against Katerinos*, 782 N.W.2d 398 (Wis. 2010) (public reprimand appropriate sanction for lawyer who, among other misconduct, continued to pursue frivolous small claims litigation to clients' detriment and advanced claim or defense that was unwarranted under existing law).

Unreasonably delaying a court proceeding, conduct prohibited by Rule 3.2 of the ABA Model Rules of Professional Conduct, is a disciplinable offense. *See, e.g.*, *People v. Maynard*, 238 P.3d 672, 688 (Colo. O.P.D.J. 2009) (suspending lawyer who "established a pattern and practice of filing matters at the last possible minute as a tactic to delay proceedings"); *In re Smith*, 659 N.E.2d 896 (Ill. 1995) (seventeen-month suspension, with twelve months stayed subject to successful completion of probation conditions, warranted for lawyer who failed to assist court in expeditious disposal of dissolution of marriage cases, including failing for more than one year to file transcript of prove-up hearing that was necessary predicate to circuit court's entry of final judgment); *Iowa Supreme Ct. Att'y Disciplinary Bd. v. Knopf*, 793 N.W.2d 525, 531 (Iowa 2011) (lawyer's neglect in curing default resulting in dismissal constituted conduct "prejudicial to the administration of justice" and warranted three-month suspension); *In re Albrecht*, 779 N.W.2d 530, 542 (Minn. 2010) (neglect of client matters "undermines public confidence in the legal system which harms the public, the legal profession and the justice system"); *Lawyer Disciplinary Bd. v. Hardin*, 619 S.E.2d 172 (W. Va. 2005) (two-year suspension for lawyer who, among other misconduct, failed to make reasonable efforts to expedite litigation).

Sanctions are also imposed for various types of improper courtroom communication, including improper contact with a party to the litigation, a juror, a witness, or a judge. *See, e.g., In re Howes*, 940 P.2d 159 (N.M. 1997) (public censure imposed on assistant U.S. attorney who improperly communicated with a represented defendant); *In re Disciplinary Proceeding Against Ferguson*, 246 P.3d 1236, 1239 (Wash. 2011) (ninety-day suspension for lawyer who "appeared ex parte before a superior court judge in a contested matter without notice to opposing counsel, failed to disclose all relevant facts at ex parte hearing, and obtained relief through misrepresentation and deceit").

Courts may impose sanctions on lawyers who threaten criminal prosecution or otherwise interfere with a legal process in violation of Rules 3.4, 3.6, 4.1, and 4.4 of the ABA Model Rules of Professional Conduct. *See also In re Brizzi*, 962 N.E.2d 1240 (Ind. 2012) (public reprimand warranted for prosecutor who made public statements that had substantial likelihood of materially prejudicing adjudicative proceedings and substantial likelihood of heightening public condemnation of criminal defendants); *In re Ulanowski*, 800 N.W.2d 785 (Minn. 2011) (indefinite suspension for lawyer who, among other misconduct, made misrepresentations to district court, submitted frivolous claims for purposes of forcing property owner to sign over deed, violated court rules, harassed opposing counsel, and improperly threatened client with criminal prosecution in order to recover attorney's fees for unrelated civil matter); *Disciplinary Counsel v. King*, 617 N.E.2d 676 (Ohio 1993) (public reprimand for lawyer who wrote letter threatening criminal prosecution in order to obtain advantage in civil matter); *Flowers v. Bd. of Prof'l Responsibility*, 314 S.W.3d 882 (Tenn. 2010) (eighteen frivolous appeals in clients' immigration cases; one-year suspension imposed).

### 6.1 False Statements, Fraud, and Misrepresentation

**Absent aggravating or mitigating circumstances, upon application of the factors set out in Standard 3.0, the following sanctions are generally appropriate in cases involving conduct that is prejudicial to the administration of justice or that involves dishonesty, fraud, deceit, or misrepresentation to a court:**

**6.11 Disbarment is generally appropriate when a lawyer, with the intent to deceive the court, makes a false statement, submits a false document, or improperly withholds material information, and causes serious or potentially serious injury to a party, or causes a significant or potentially significant adverse effect on the legal proceeding.**

## Annotation

### *Truth as Duty of Officer of Court*

A lawyer who engages in deceptive conduct in legal proceedings violates the most fundamental duty of an officer of the court. *See People v. Costa,* 56 P.3d 130, 135 (Colo. O.P.D.J. 2002) (in reciprocal disciplinary matter, disbarment warranted under Standard 6.11, inter alia, for lawyer who made material misrepresentation to court about discovery in personal injury matter, misconduct that "invariably bears a potentially significant adverse effect on the legal proceeding, places the client at significant risk, demeans the profession and diminishes the public trust in the administration of justice"); *In re Vanderslice,* 116 A.3d 1244 (Del. 2015) (disbarment is appropriate where attorney misappropriated client funds and failed to disclose additional misappropriation of funds during the course of prior disciplinary proceedings); *In re Rawls,* 936 N.E.2d 812 (Ind. 2010) (disbarment under Standard 6.11, inter alia, for lawyer whose misconduct included making a series of intentional misrepresentations to disciplinary commission during its investigations, creating fraudulent receipt, criminally forging client's name on it, and submitting it to the commission with intent to deceive); *In re Quaid,* 646 So.2d 343, 350 (La. 1994) (Disbarment was warranted under Standard 6.11, inter alia, for lawyer who, among other misconduct, made false statements in documents and testimony submitted before the Social Security Administration in attempt to receive inflated fees: "Respondent presumably engaged in such deception in order to protect his own situation as an attorney and to safeguard for himself the fees he had improperly collected from his client. Such conduct violates the most fundamental duty of an officer to the court."). In *In re Caranchini,* 956 S.W.2d 910 (Mo. 1997), a lawyer was disbarred under Standard 6.11 for misconduct that included intentionally submitting false documents, intentionally making false statements, and intentionally withholding material information. The court said:

> This misconduct is an affront to the fundamental and indispensable principle that a lawyer must proceed with absolute candor towards the tribunal. In the absence of that candor, the legal system cannot properly function. . . . Under these circumstances, the protection of the public and the maintenance of the integrity of the legal profession require the most severe sanction available.

*Id.* at 919–20; *see also In re Morse,* 7 A.3d 1259, 1267 (N.H. 2010) (Disbarment was warranted under Standard 6.11 for lawyer's misconduct relating to mishandling of estate and deliberate lies to court: "As officers of the court, attorneys are prohibited from making false statements of material fact to a tribunal. 'The confidence of judges to rely with certainty upon the word of attorneys forms the very bedrock of our judicial system.'") (citation omitted).

In *In re Gabell,* 858 P.2d 404 (N.M. 1993), the New Mexico Supreme Court cited Standard 6.11 in disbarring a lawyer who underreported his income to the IRS and to the state by approximately $60,000 and then, in subsequent formal discovery in a lawsuit concerning the funds, lied under oath and fraudulently manufactured documents to comport with his income tax forms. Imposing disbarment, the court explained the crucial requirement of honesty in a lawyer's role as officer of the court:

> When false evidence is presented during the course of litigation, the adversarial system is compromised. The effectiveness of our system of justice depends upon a full and truthful disclosure of facts at all stages of a legal proceeding. Only in this way can justice be attained and public confidence in the legal system be preserved.

*Id.* at 405; *see also In re Paulson,* 216 P.3d 859 (Or. 2009) (disbarment under Standard 6.11, inter alia, for lawyer whose misconduct included intentionally making false statements in motions to postpone and abate in effort to deceive courts about his suspended status; in one client's child custody matter, in particular, client was seriously injured); *In re Garvey,* 932 P.2d 549 (Or. 1997) (by committing perjury before the grand jury and facilitating the escape of his inmate client from jail, lawyer engaged in a violation of his duty to the legal system under Standard 6.1 and was disbarred).

### *Adverse Effect on a Legal Proceeding*

Courts use strong language to describe harm to the legal system by lawyers who intentionally make false statements or withhold material information when involved in a legal proceeding. *See, e.g., In re Peasley*, 90 P.3d 764, 773 (Ariz. 2004) (disbarment warranted under Standard 6.11 for prosecutor who intentionally elicited false testimony from detective in two capital murder trials to secure convictions and death penalty against defendants; noting that harm was "particularly egregious," court said it "cannot conceive of a more serious injury, not just to the defendants but to the criminal justice system, than a prosecutor's presentation of false testimony in a capital murder case"); *In re Vanderslice*, 116 A.3d 1244 (Del. 2015) (applying Standard 6.11, inter alia, attorney disbarred for failing to disclose additional instances of misappropriation during the course of the disciplinary proceedings); *Fla. Bar v. Rightmyer*, 616 So.2d 953, 955 (Fla. 1993) (disbarment was warranted for lawyer based on perjury convictions: "No breach of professional ethics, or of the law, is more harmful to the administration of justice or more hurtful to the public appraisal of the legal profession than the knowledgeable use by an attorney of false testimony in the judicial process. When it is done it deserves the harshest penalty."); *In re Sniadecki*, 924 N.E.2d 109, 119 (Ind. 2010) (disbarment warranted under Standard 6.11, inter alia, for lawyer's misconduct involving serious acts of misrepresentation, including filing false compliance affidavit with Indiana Supreme Court, forging documents to be filed in court, and engaging in criminal acts of dishonesty; harm to the standing of lawyers and the profession by his misconduct "is tremendous"); *In re Mintz*, 317 P.3d 756 (Kan. 2014) (attorney indefinitely suspended where he initially provided false information to law enforcement officers investigating the death of attorney's friend); *In re Arabia*, 156 P.3d 652, 659 (Kan. 2007) (disbarment appropriate under Standard 6.11, inter alia, for lawyer who, among other misconduct, drafted misleading pleadings to change name of his legal assistant, omitting material information that assistant had outstanding fugitive warrant in another state; court concluded that respondent's multiple violations and "established lack of integrity constitute a disgrace to the legal profession"); *In re Clark's Case*, 37 A.3d 327 (N.H. 2012) (disbarment warranted under Standard 6.11 for lawyer who, in filling out bankruptcy form, knowingly made false statement to bankruptcy court; respondent's misconduct both caused injury to his client and had the potential to adversely affect her interests and the integrity of the bankruptcy proceedings); *In re Barber*, 904 P.2d 620 (Or. 1995) (disbarment under Standard 6.11, inter alia, for intentionally altering fee agreement by deleting another lawyer's name and misrepresenting time and expenses on statement for fees; lawyer's misconduct caused potential for serious injury to legal system and legal profession, creating potential to mislead court, undermine the judicial process, and interfere with litigation outcome); *In re Weidner*, 883 P.2d 1293 (Or. 1994) (disbarment warranted under Standard 6.11, inter alia, for numerous violations of criminal statutes and disciplinary rules, including making misleading statements and performing notary services after expiration of notarization commission; documents intended to be relied on, as sworn statements, by courts, judicial system and potential supporters of lawyer's client were false, court noted, creating potential for harm to his client's interest by undermining credibility of affidavits favorable to her position).

### *False Statements to Tribunal*

Courts generally find disbarment the appropriate sanction under Standard 6.11 for false statements, fraud, and misrepresentation to a tribunal because such conduct violates the most fundamental obligation of truth that a lawyer owes the legal system. *See, e.g., People v. Goodman,* 334 P.3d 241 (Colo. O.P.D.J. 2014) (applying Standard 6.11, inter alia, attorney disbarred after he altered documents produced in a civil case and lied to disciplinary authorities to conceal his underlying misconduct); *People v. Calvert,* 280 P.3d 1269 (Colo. O.P.D.J. 2011) (lawyer intentionally recorded false deed of trust, which seriously injured one client and threatened another couple who were clients with grave potential injury; disbarment under Standard 6.11, inter alia); *People v. Ra'shadd,* 110 P.3d 388 (Colo. O.P.D.J. 2005) (disbarment warranted under Standard 6.11 for making, certifying, and submitting false statements to court with intent to deceive regarding status of lawyer's child support obligation); *In re Stover,* 104 P.3d 394 (Kan. 2005) (disbarment warranted under Standard 6.11, inter alia, for respondent's misconduct that included testifying falsely before judge that she had complied with court order); *Att'y Grievance Comm'n v. Kent,* 653 A.2d 909 (Md. 1995) (lawyer disbarred under Standard 6.11, inter alia, for misconduct that included making false statements to trial judge regarding his alleged lack of knowledge of other lawyer's prior representation of state's chief witness, his client's accomplice, in murder prosecution against his client); *In re Morse,* 7 A.3d 1259 (N.H. 2010) (court concluded suspension insufficient to protect public and preserve integrity of legal profession and disbarred lawyer under Standard 6.11 for misconduct including deliberate lies to court regarding filing of income tax returns on behalf of estate); *In re Leonhardt,* 930 P.2d 844 (Or. 1997) (disbarment warranted under Standard 6.11, inter alia, for district attorney who falsified public records and lied about it to court and others); *In re Disciplinary Proceedings Against Kamb,* 305 P.3d 1091 (Wash. 2013) (disbarment appropriate where attorney misrepresented to tribunal that a suppression order had been entered when it had not and then altered a court order to conceal his deception; court held Standard 5.11 applicable but not Standard 6.11, which would also seem to apply).

Courts find accord with disbarment under Standard 6.11 for misconduct involving false statements, false documents or withholding material information even without specifically relying on the Sanctions Standards. *See, e.g., In re McCarthy,* 173 A.3d 536 (Table) (Del. 2017) (court upheld hearing panel recommendation and disbarred a Pennsylvania lawyer admitted pro hac vice in Delaware under Standard 6.11 for intentionally failing to disclose altered medical records and his client's fraudulent conduct); *In re Baber*, 106 A.3d 1072 (D.C. 2015) (attorney who submitted false information to the court in his motion to withdraw disbarred; Sanctions Standards not cited); *In re Slattery*, 767 A.2d 203 (D.C. 2001) (disbarment warranted for president of local chapter of fraternal organization who converted $10,000 of organization's funds for personal use and made false statements about the fund during sworn deposition); *In re Randolph*, 554 S.E.2d 485 (Ga. 2001) (disbarment warranted for lawyer's misconduct including material misrepresentations in clients' bankruptcy petition and installment application; rejecting recommended sanction of two-year suspension and finding significant sanction necessary in light of aggravating factors); *In re Ingersoll*, 710 N.E.2d 390 (Ill. 1999) (disbarment warranted for, among other misconduct, falsely representing on pauper's application that client owned no real estate and filing false motions for discovery sanctions); *Att'y Grievance Comm'n v. Lane*, 790 A.2d 621 (Md. 2002) (disbarment warranted for lawyer who engaged in pattern of material misrepresentations amounting to intentional dishonesty to clients whose matters lawyer failed to diligently pursue); *In re Boylan*, 744 A.2d 158, 160 (N.J. 2000) (disbarment appropriate for lawyer who, while municipal court judge, coached female defendants to lie in open court to gain reductions in traffic fines and also solicited defendants for sexual favors; "There are certain acts by attorneys that so impugn the integrity of the legal system that disbarment is the only appropriate remedy."); *In re Munroe*, 89 A.D.3d 1, 8 (N.Y. App. Div. 2011) (reciprocal disbarment instead of two-and-a-half-year suspension imposed by originating jurisdiction warranted for lawyer's egregious pattern of misconduct, including fabricating stock certificates to support false claim to courts, disciplinary counsel, and others of ownership in deceased client's company; court found that "the only conceivable purpose for such fabrication is personal gain"); *In re Robb*, 287 A.D.2d 1, 5 (N.Y. App. Div. 2001) (disbarment warranted for misconduct that included creating or preserving evidence that lawyer knew or should have known was false and submitting unsupportable and frivolous invoices for $2.5 million in legal fees against former corporate client who had terminated lawyer's services; court noted that lawyer's "aggravating pattern of dilatory and obstructive conduct throughout the proceeding . . . demonstrate his disregard for the rule of law as well as the ethical standards of the legal profession"); *Dayton Bar Ass'n v. Buren*, 703 N.E.2d 767 (Ohio 1998) (in default proceeding disbarment warranted for ongoing course of deceit including failure to disclose full amount of attorney's fees to bankruptcy court and assisting client to establish new company and divert revenue); *In re Curlin*, 562 S.E.2d 652 (S.C. 2002) (disbarment for conduct including forgery of signature on deed, routinely signing as witness and notarizing legal documents in absence of signatory, and preparing false and fraudulent documentation to cover conversion scheme).

## *Material Information*

A court's inquiry may turn on whether the false statements of fact are material. *See People v. Albright*, 91 P.3d 1063 (Colo. O.P.D.J. 2003) (disbarment warranted under Standard 6.11, inter alia, for intentionally dishonest conduct in bankruptcy proceedings, including hiding material information and attempting to suborn perjury); *People v. Poll*, 65 P.3d 483 (Colo. O.P.D.J. 2003) (disbarment warranted for misconduct including falsely implying to trial court that clients caused delay in responding to discovery when lawyer effectively had abandoned case and, as a result, clients suffered serious harm; citing Colorado cases imposing disbarment as appropriate sanction for material misrepresentations to tribunal); *People v. Costa*, 56 P.3d 130 (Colo. O.P.D.J. 2002) (court cited Standard 6.11, inter alia, and imposed disbarment for misconduct that included blatant material misrepresentation to court that discovery was ready for production); *In re Oberhellmann*, 873 S.W.2d 851, 854 (Mo. 1994) (disbarment warranted under Standard 6.11 for lawyer who knowingly made false statements to court in seeking to retain federal diversity jurisdiction, used his mother's address in interrogatory answers filed with court to claim that client was Illinois resident, and advised client to give false deposition testimony about her place of residence; court rejected lawyer's contention that "where" a case is tried is immaterial, stating that "[a] fact that invokes the jurisdiction of a court is a material fact"). *But see In re Krigel*, 480 S.W.3d 294, 301 (Mo. 2016) (attorney who made misrepresentations to the court in an adoption proceeding suspended for six months and placed on probation for two years under Standard 6.12 instead of disbarment under Standard 6.11; lawyer knew material information being withheld from court, but disbarment, which is reserved for "clear cases of gross misconduct," was not appropriate given lack of prior discipline in more than thirty years of practice).

## *Multiple Instances*

Multiple dishonest acts also result in disbarment under Standard 6.11, which refers in the singular to an instance of intentional dishonesty that causes serious or potentially serious injury to a party or causes a significant or potentially significant adverse effect on a legal proceeding. *See People v. Goodman*, 334 P.3d 241 (Colo. O.P.D.J. 2014) (lawyer who engaged in multiple instances of falsifying documents over an extended period of time disbarred under Standard 6.11, inter alia); *Statewide Grievance Comm'n v. McGee*, No. CV02009371S, 2003 WL 22333085, at *2, *5 (Conn. Super. Ct. Oct. 2, 2003) (disbarment warranted under Standard 6.11, inter alia, for lawyer's numerous acts of misconduct, including filing an accounting that the probate court found "to be 'deliberately misleading and manufactured for the purpose of hiding [lawyer's] deliberate wrongdoing'"; "[t]he duties violated by the respondent in this case are repeated and serious, involving lack of competence, diligence, fidelity to the client, and candor and honesty both toward the client and the court, most probably, in many instances, rising to the level of criminality"); *In re Nathanson*, 112 P.3d 162 (Kan. 2005) (citing Standard 6.11, court imposed disbarment against lawyer who repeatedly prepared, fraudulently signed, and filed pleadings and correspondence using another lawyer's name); *In re Placer*, 216 So.3d 787 (La. 2016) (lawyer who fabricated evidence before domestic relations tribunal in her divorce, among other misconduct, disbarred under Standard 6.11); *In re Pinkston*, 852 So.2d 966 (La. 2003) (permanent disbarment warranted under Standard 6.11 for suspended lawyer's egregious misconduct, including making intentional false statements to court and concealing evidence); *Harrison v. Miss. Bar*, 637 So.2d 204 (Miss. 1994) (disbarment warranted under Standard 6.11, inter alia, for lawyer who engaged in pattern of dishonesty in child custody matters, including helping mothers hide children from fathers and failing to disclose whereabouts of children to fathers or to court); *In re Garvey*, 932 P.2d 549 (Or. 1997) (disbarment warranted under Standard 6.11 for multiple convictions of perjury and false swearing regarding lawyer's participation in client's escape from jail); *In re Leonhardt*, 930 P.2d 844 (Or. 1997) (disbarment warranted under Standard 6.11, inter alia, for district attorney who intentionally fabricated charges against police officers, presented charges to grand jury, and lied to court); *In re Palmisano*, 683 A.2d 1348 (Vt. 1996) (disbarment warranted under Standard 6.11, inter alia, for multiple acts of dishonestly withholding information from bankruptcy court and for affirmative misrepresentations to that court regarding $10,000 payment by client); *In re Disciplinary Proceedings Against Michael*, 805 N.W.2d 110 (Wis. 2011) (lawyer's license revoked for misconduct including use of aliases in dealing with employees and local law enforcement to evade payment of legal obligations, giving employees false information regarding their entitlement to payment, making false statements in court filings, altering a temporary restraining order, and violating numerous professional rules related to candor before a tribunal).

## *Lack of Fitness to Practice*

Courts often specifically find that lawyers who engage in repeated instances of making false statements or submitting false information in legal proceedings have demonstrated a "lack of fitness to practice" necessitating disbarment. *See, e.g.*, *In re Ivy*, 374 P.3d 374 (Alaska 2016) (lawyer who testified falsely in civil and disciplinary proceeding disbarred; court applied Standard 6.11, inter alia, in finding that the lawyer's dishonest behavior exceeded that in typical cases); *In re Frank*, 942 So.2d 1050, 1071 (La. 2006) (citing Standard 6.11, inter alia, court imposed permanent disbarment for lawyer's submission of false affidavit and false petition with intent to deceive the court into believing that decedent's children were sole heirs, resulting in surviving spouse being placed at risk of losing any rights she may have had to decedent's estate; court found that lawyer's misconduct began several years after readmission, leading to belief "beyond any doubt whatsoever that respondent lacks the good moral character and fitness to practice law in Louisiana"); *In re Gabell*, 858 P.2d 404 (N.M. 1993) (disbarment warranted under Standard 6.11 for lawyer who purposely lied under oath and manufactured documents to gain advantage in litigation, showing complete lack of fitness to practice law); *Disciplinary Counsel v. Lawson*, 956 N.E.2d 839, 847 (Ohio 2011) (permanent disbarment warranted for lawyer's repeated acts, including conspiring with a physician to unlawfully obtain prescription drugs by deception, engaging others in that conspiracy, and making false statements to clients, court officers, disciplinary investigators, and courts to cover up misconduct; rejecting board recommendation of suspension, court found that "[t]he discipline for a repeated offense may be much greater than would have been imposed were it a first offense . . . such greater discipline . . . is a determination of the attorney's fitness to practice") (citation omitted).

## *Deceit in the Disciplinary Process*

Disbarment also is considered the appropriate sanction when the dishonest acts occur in the context of disciplinary proceedings. *See People v. Goodman*, 334 P.3d 241 (Colo. 2014) (applying Standard 6.11, inter alia, attorney who submitted false evidence during the course of his disciplinary trial disbarred); *People v. Hellewell*, 827 P.2d 527 (Colo. 1992) (misconduct including attempting to mislead court regarding conversion of client funds during proceedings for immediate suspension warranted disbarment under Standard 6.11, inter alia); *Fla. Bar v. Orta*, 689 So.2d 270 (Fla. 1997) (lawyer originally suspended for three years for tax evasion disbarred under Florida Standard 6.11 for making intentional false statements about assets in reinstatement petition); *Fla. Bar v. Newhouse*, 520 So.2d 25 (Fla. 1988) (disbarment warranted under Florida Standard 6.11, inter alia, for lawyer whose misconduct included asking court in previous disciplinary case to consider late petition by falsely claiming that his counsel failed to abide by filing deadline); *In re Mays*, 495 S.E.2d 30 (Ga. 1998) (disbarment warranted under Standard 6.11, inter alia, for lawyer who let limitations period expire, misrepresented to client that case had settled, paid personal funds for purported settlement, and testified falsely at disciplinary hearing on the matter); *In re Rawls*, 936 N.E.2d 812 (Ind. 2010) (citing Standard 6.11, inter alia, in disbarring lawyer for misconduct that included making a series of intentional misrepresentations to the disciplinary commission during its investigations and intentionally forging a fraudulent receipt and submitting it to the commission); *In re Williams*, 362 P.3d 816 (Kan. 2015) (citing Standard 6.11, lawyer disbarred for misconduct including lying to disciplinary authority and fabricating evidence in disciplinary proceeding relating to abandonment of client in a tax matter); *In re Gustafson*, 41 P.3d 1063 (Or. 2002) (disbarment warranted under Standard 6.11, inter alia, for false testimony under oath regarding lawyer's possession of juvenile records, which were subject to expunction order but which lawyer released as exhibits in her defense in bar disciplinary matter); *But see In re Meyers*, 808 S.E.2d 650 (Ga. 2016) (attorney who submitted false billing statements to corporate client suspended for two years instead of disbarred, where it was determined that his failure to admit to violations alleged in the disciplinary proceedings was not an aggravating factor; Sanctions Standards not cited).

Some courts that do not cite to the Sanctions Standards nonetheless agree that deceit during the disciplinary process warrants disbarment. *See, e.g., In re Lee*, 95 A.3d 66, 68 (D.C. 2014) (attorney disbarred following misappropriation of funds and for his "flagrant dishonesty and false testimony" during the disciplinary proceedings); *In re Cleaver-Bascombe*, 986 A.2d 1191 (D.C. 2010) (disbarment warranted for lawyer who submitted falsified timekeeping vouchers for purpose of seeking unearned compensation from public funds and committed perjury by falsely testifying before disciplinary hearing committee that such work had been performed); *In re McClain-Sewer*, 77 A.D.3d 204 (N.Y. App. Div. 2010) (disbarment of lawyer for misconduct including false statements and testimony before disciplinary committee regarding his knowledge of suspension and his continued practice of law); *Weiss v. Comm'n for Lawyer Discipline*, 981 S.W.2d 8 (Tex. App. 1998) (disbarment appropriate for lawyer who made misrepresentations to grievance committee).

## *Reciprocal Disciplinary Proceedings*

Generally, when a lawyer is disbarred in one jurisdiction for deceiving a tribunal, another jurisdiction in which the lawyer is also licensed imposes the same discipline. *See, e.g., People v. Distel*, 76 P.3d 473 (Colo. O.P.D.J. 2003) (court bound to impose disbarment in default reciprocal proceeding upon lawyer's disbarment in Arizona for misconduct that included making knowing material misstatements to tribunal); *In re Light*, 769 N.W.2d 768 (Minn. 2009) (lawyer disbarred following imposition of disbarment by North Dakota court for multiple instances of misconduct including false statements during disciplinary process).

That a lawyer received a lesser sanction in one jurisdiction for engaging in acts intended to deceive a tribunal, however, does not preclude another jurisdiction from reciprocally disbarring the lawyer. *See, e.g., People v. Costa*, 56 P.3d 130 (Colo. O.P.D.J. 2002) (while New Mexico court had imposed formal reprimand, in reciprocal proceeding, Colorado court found disbarment warranted for misconduct that included blatant material misrepresentation to court that discovery was ready for production; court cited Colorado precedent and Standard 6.11, inter alia, to justify imposing harsher discipline of disbarment for misrepresentation, noting that imposing the same discipline that was imposed in New Mexico would result in grave injustice); *Att'y Grievance Comm'n v. Zodrow*,

19 A.3d 381 (Md. 2011) (disbarment warranted as reciprocal discipline for lawyer suspended in Colorado for misconduct in own personal bankruptcy proceeding, including failure to make pertinent disclosures about his interest in property and monthly obligation under a promissory note, and giving false testimony to tribunal regarding his law firm's receipt of funds; court said suspension would be inconsistent with Maryland case law); *In re Storment*, 873 S.W.2d 227 (Mo. 1994) (in reciprocal disciplinary proceeding, lawyer suspended in Illinois for counseling client to lie on witness stand but was disbarred in Missouri under Standard 6.11); *In re Lowell*, 14 A.D.3d 41 (N.Y. App. Div. 2004) (declining to reciprocate three-year suspension imposed in New Jersey, court disbarred lawyer for submitting false documents to court, counseling client to lie, and eliciting false testimony, among other misconduct; collecting New York cases imposing disbarment for fraud, dishonesty, and misrepresentation); *cf. Att'y Grievance Comm'n v. McHale*, 2018 N.Y. Slip Op. 3770 (N.Y. App. Div. 2018) (court declines to impose reciprocal discipline on attorney suspended for five years by the bankruptcy court, instead imposing a three-month suspension).

## *Adjustment for Mitigating Factors*

The Sanctions Standards provide that recommended sanctions may be adjusted downward after consideration of mitigating circumstances. *See* Standards for Imposing Lawyer Sanctions pt. II, Theoretical Framework (ABA 1992); Standard 9. Thus, in some cases, courts acknowledge that while disbarment is the presumed sanction under Standard 6.11, a lesser sanction is warranted based on an analysis of mitigating circumstances. *See, e.g., In re Cardwell*, 50 P.3d 897 (Colo. 2002) (while disbarment under Standard 6.11, inter alia, is presumed sanction for defense lawyer's knowing false statement to court that client had no prior alcohol-related driving offenses, which led court to accept client's plea and to impose suspended sentence, three-year suspension with eighteen months stayed actually imposed after analysis of eight mitigating factors); *In re Lutz*, 897 P.2d 807 (Colo. 1995) (one-year-and-one-day suspension, rather than disbarment under Standard 6.11, inter alia, for forging waiver of service forms and misrepresenting to court that no testamentary instrument relating to decedent's estate existed when lawyer already had received a holographic will; mitigating factors leading to reduced sanction included lawyer's forty-seven years in practice and stated plans to retire that year); *People v. Maynard*, 219 P.3d 430 (Colo. O.P.D.J. 2008) (one-year-and-one-day suspension for failing to diligently complete a brief and making false statements to the court in an effort to secure more time to complete it; while court found that Standard 6.11 applied, it determined suspension appropriate sanction because lawyer self-reported and timely attempted remediation); *Fla. Bar v. Cox*, 794 So.2d 1278, 1286 (Fla. 2001) (one-year suspension for prosecuting attorney who improperly withheld material information by concealing identity of confidential informant even though disbarment was presumptive sanction under Florida Standard 6.11, inter alia, because of prosecutor's "previously unsullied reputation," and an "apparently isolated lack of judgment" and reputational testimony offered).

In *Fla. Bar v. Cibula*, 725 So.2d 360, 364 (Fla. 1999), the court imposed a ninety-one-day suspension on a lawyer who twice lied under oath about personal income in an effort to avoid alimony obligations, noting that "[n]o breach of professional ethics, or of the law, is more harmful to the administration of justice or more hurtful to the public appraisal of the legal profession than the knowledgeable use by an attorney of false testimony in the judicial process." In determining the appropriate discipline, the court examined the range of sanctions from disbarment to public reprimand imposed for misrepresentations in cases involving personal matters. The court said:

> While we recognize that dissolution of marriage proceedings present an emotional time for both parties, when lawyers are litigants they do not cast aside the oath they take as an attorney or their professional responsibilities. Lawyers have an ethical responsibility as officers of the court to rise above the tactics that all too often permeate a dissolution proceeding. Not only does the law demand truthfulness under oath, but the obligations of our profession demand it. As former Justice Ehrlich has stated, "our profession can operate properly only if its individual members conform to the highest standard of integrity in all dealings within the legal system." (citation omitted).

*Id.* at 365. The court, noting that the referee found no mitigating factors, took into account the sanctions recommendations of the referee and the disciplinary authority, as well as the fact that the misconduct occurred seven years earlier during the lawyer's dissolution of marriage proceeding. *See also In re Bilbe*, 841 So.2d 729 (La. 2003) (lawyer, among other misconduct, made knowing false statements to immigration judge, including misrepresentation that motion was unopposed and that client's Immigrant Visa Petition had been approved by the Immigration and Naturalization Service; court imposed three-year suspension instead of disbarment under Standard 6.11, inter alia, after considering mitigating factors, including lawyer's suspension from practice before Executive Office for Immigration Review and the Immigration and Naturalization Service); *In re Donaho*, 98 S.W.3d 871 (Mo. 2003) (lawyer suspended indefinitely for faxing to disciplinary committee copies of money orders ostensibly paid to client in restitution but never actually mailed to client; although intentional deceit would justify disbarment under Standard 6.11, suspension imposed because of mitigating factors including lack of prior discipline, possible drinking problem, and expression of remorse); *In re Carey*, 89 S.W.3d 477, 503 (Mo. 2002) (indefinite suspensions imposed on two lawyers who, among other misconduct, knowingly and intentionally withheld and denied existence of certain documents and information from discovery in lawsuit filed against them by former client; suspension rather than disbarment under Standard 6.11 warranted after consideration of lawyers' lack of prior discipline, charitable involvement, and satisfaction of $850,000 civil judgment for misrepresentations); *In re Discipline of Bloomfield*, 2016 WL 1223218 (Nev. March 25, 2016) (lawyer suspended for five years instead of being disbarred pursuant to Standard 6.11 due to mitigating factors including cooperation in disciplinary proceeding, remorse, strong character witnesses, and lack of prior discipline); *In re Wysolmerski*, 702 A.2d 73, 75 (Vt. 1997) (noting that Standard 6.11, inter alia, and cases from various jurisdictions indicated that respondent's "grave misconduct," including repeated dishonesty with clients, other lawyers, and courts, generally merits disbarment but lawyer avoided disbarment only because of mitigating factors; three-year suspension imposed).

## *Comparison with Similar Cases*

Courts' analyses of facts that appear to call for disbarment under Standard 6.11 often will include a review of state case law for comparison with sanctions imposed in similar circumstances. When courts in the jurisdiction have imposed a lesser sanction for similar misconduct, that rationale seems to take precedence over the recommendation for disbarment under the Sanctions Standards. *See, e.g., People v. Maynard*, 219 P.3d 430, 439 (Colo. O.P.D.J. 2008) (disbarment under Standard 6.11 would have been presumed sanction for lawyer who lied to court in effort to buy more time to complete client's brief, but lawyer's "admirable action" in self-reporting misconduct and other mitigating factors merited one-year-and-one-day suspension in light of discipline imposed in similar cases); *In re Neitlich*, 597 N.E.2d 425, 428 (Mass. 1992) (lawyer's conduct in post-divorce proceeding involved perpetrating fraud on court and opposing counsel by active misrepresentation of terms of client's pending real estate transaction; court acknowledged recommendation for disbarment under Standard 6.1 but imposed one-year suspension because it was consistent with previous cases); *In re Disciplinary Action Against Kaiser*, 484 N.W.2d 102 (N.D. 1992) (while disbarment under Standard 6.11 ordinarily appropriate for false testimony under oath, court imposed two-year suspension after comparison of application of Sanctions Standards to similar facts by other courts); *In re Kluge*, 66 P.3d 492 (Or. 2003) (although disbarment appropriate under Standard 6.11, inter alia, for misconduct that included bringing ex parte motion to disqualify judge and failing to notify opposing counsel or judge, court imposed two-year suspension after analyzing sanctions for analogous misconduct in other Oregon cases); *In re*

*Eadie*, 36 P.3d 468 (Or. 2001) (intentional failure to disclose material fact that costs would be sought from settlement agreement and knowing misrepresentation of judge's intent regarding scheduling of case warranted disbarment, but three-year suspension imposed instead following analysis of state case law regarding reduced sanctions for similar conduct).

**6.12 Suspension is generally appropriate when a lawyer knows that false statements or documents are being submitted to the court or that material information is improperly being withheld, and takes no remedial action, and causes injury or potential injury to a party to the legal proceeding, or causes an adverse or potentially adverse effect on the legal proceeding.**

## Annotation

### *No Intent to Deceive*

Suspension is appropriate when a lawyer has not acted with intent to deceive the tribunal, but knows that false information is being submitted or that material information is being improperly withheld and takes no remedial action, with resulting injury or potential injury to a party or an adverse or potentially adverse effect on the legal proceeding. *See In re Ziman*, 847 P.2d 106 (Ariz. 1993) (ninety-day suspension under Standard 6.12 for lawyer who, while not acting with intent to deceive court, entered into and filed stipulation regarding custody and child support without client's knowledge or consent and without disclosing lack of client consent to court; terms also imposed upon lawyer requiring, inter alia, practice monitor for one year); *People v. Trogani*, 203 P.3d 643 (Colo. O.P.D.J. 2008) (suspension of one year and one day with all but ninety days stayed warranted under Standard 6.12, inter alia, for lawyer who committed misconduct by urging judge to accept plea agreement for client even though lawyer knew other judge opposed disposing client's probation revocation matters as part of plea agreement; mere fact that lawyer believed she was following normal, customary practice to achieve a result in best interests of her client and judicial system did not justify or excuse her failure to fully disclose judge's position to other judge in regard to plea agreement, but did demonstrate it was not her specific intent to deceive the court); *In re Morris*, 953 P.2d 387 (Or. 1998) (not necessary that accused lawyer acted with intent to defraud court when altering final accounting and filing it with court, only that she knew that alteration and filing were unauthorized, thus creating need for ancillary proceedings with respect to information contained in accounting; suspension of 120 days, decreased on appeal from nine months, warranted under Standard 6.12, inter alia); *In re Disciplinary Proceeding Against Dynan*, 98 P.3d 444 (Wash. 2004) (decreasing hearing board's nine-month suspension to six months for lawyer who did not intend to deceive the court but submitted declarations for attorney's fees that attached invoices on which actual hourly rate of $100–$120 had been removed and replaced with rate of $150 per hour; suspension under Standard 6.12 presumptive sanction for such misrepresentation to court and opposing counsel).

- **Affirmative False Statements**

Even though Standard 6.12 applies when a lawyer has not acted with specific intent to deceive, many cases referencing Standard 6.12 involve lawyers who affirmatively make false statements to tribunals, either orally or in writing. *See In re Hanlon*, 110 P.3d 937 (Alaska 2005) (three-year suspension under Standard 6.12 appropriate for misconduct that included knowingly providing misleading information to a client and bar investigators and failing to diligently pursue client matters by fabricating a settlement agreement in attempt to avoid malpractice liability); *In re Roose*, 69 P.3d 43 (Colo. 2003) (citing Standard 6.12, inter alia, court overturned disbarment for suspension of one year and one day for lawyer who knowingly mischaracterized factual events in notice of appeal; noting that distinction between knowledge and intent is critical in imposing sanctions, court said that intent may not be presumed from proof of knowledge, but must be separately proved by clear and convincing evidence; finding that appropriate sanction for knowingly submitting materially false statements, as long as it caused at least some injury to a party or adverse effect on the legal proceeding, was suspension); *People v. Reed*, 955 P.2d 65 (Colo. 1998) (six-month suspension warranted under Standard 6.12, inter alia, for lawyer whose misconduct included disguising handwriting and signing substitute counsel's name to pleading submitted on behalf of both parties without any indication by lawyer that he was signing in representative capacity); *People v. Wotan*, 944 P.2d 1257, 1263 (Colo. 1997) (one-year-and-one-day suspension warranted for violations that included filing a false certificate, which "by itself would justify a period of suspension" under Standard 6.12); *People v. Baca*, 363 P.3d 211, 222 (Colo. O.P.D.J. 2015) (citing Standard 6.12, inter alia, court suspended lawyer for one year and one day, staying all of it and imposing three years of probation, for misrepresenting client's immigration status to court; court noted that "Lawyers' honesty forms the backbone of the legal system."); *People v. Ritland*, 327 P.3d 914, 929 (Colo. O.P.D.J. 2014) (while disbarment presumptive sanction under Standard 6.1, three-year suspension appropriate where lawyer made false statements to tribunal and submitted false evidence because ". . . misconduct occurred as she was wrestling with painful personal circumstances rather than in the course of representing a client"); *In re Lankenau*, 138 A.3d 1151 (Del. 2016) (attorney suspended for eighteen months for making false statements to mortgage company and misappropriating client funds); *In re Amberly*, 996 A.2d 793 (Table) (Del. 2010) (citing Standard 6.12 in reciprocal discipline case, court imposed six-month suspension for misconduct involving knowing false statements to a tribunal and misleading statements to disciplinary counsel); *In re Shearin*, 721 A.2d 157 (Del. 1998) (one-year suspension warranted under Standard 6.12, inter alia, for lawyer who, among other misconduct, misrepresented identity of her client and filed a brief containing scandalous remarks concerning the trial judge); *In re Brown*, 672 A.2d 577 (D.C. 1996) (sixty-day reciprocal suspension based upon discipline imposed by Maryland Court of Appeals for misconduct that included repeated written misrepresentations of fact to tribunal); *In re Loiseau*, 957 N.E.2d 609, 610 (Ind. 2011) (ninety-day suspension for misconduct that included knowingly making false representations to immigration judge that petitioner's wife had a pending asylum case in which lawyer was counsel; statements were "made with the intent to withhold the very information he admits the immigration judge would want to know for purpose of maintaining consistent rulings" on asylum petitions); *Iowa Supreme Ct. Att'y Disciplinary Bd. v. Crotty*, 891 N.W.2d 455 (Iowa 2017) (court suspended lawyer who submitted forgeries to the probate court for sixty days; Sanctions Standards not cited); *In re Warren*, 888 S.W.2d 334 (Mo. 1994) (six-month suspension under Standard 6.12 for misconduct that included making material false statement on bar application); *N.C. State Bar v. Erickson*, 702 S.E.2d 555 (Table) (N.C. Ct. App. 2010) (five-year suspension warranted for lawyer's extensive pattern of knowing misconduct in advising and assisting clients in two different schemes to avoid payment of legitimate debts, including drafting and filing documents that were frivolous and fraudulent); *In re Page*, 955 P.2d 239 (Or. 1998) (thirty-day suspension warranted under Standard 6.12 and Oregon case law in reciprocal discipline case where lawyer purposely falsified documents in marriage dissolution proceeding without notice to or approval of opposing counsel and presented false statements to court as agreed terms); *In re Claussen*, 909 P.2d 862 (Or. 1996) (one-year suspension warranted under Standard 6.12, inter alia, for pattern of misconduct that included filing false documents to prevent bankruptcy court from discovering multiple conflicts of interest and repeatedly failing to disclose material information to the court that lawyer had a duty to disclose); *In re Disciplinary Proceeding Against Conteh*, 284 P.3d 724 (Wash. 2012) (citing Standard 6.12, inter alia, court imposed six-month suspension on lawyer for knowing false statements on his asylum application); *In re Disciplinary Proceeding Against Carmick*, 48 P.3d 311 (Wash. 2002) (sixty-day suspension warranted under Standard 6.12 for lawyer who, among other misconduct, made misrepresentations to obtain ex parte order from superior court); *Bd. of Prof'l Responsibility v. Davidson*, 205 P.3d 1008 (Wyo. 2009) (lawyer suspended for two months for knowingly making false accusation in court filing that judge engaged in unethical conduct; Standard 6.12 not specifically cited); *cf. People v. North*, 964 P.2d 510, 513 (Colo. 1998) (due to mitigating factors, public censure under Standard 6.13 rather than suspension under Standard 6.12 was appropriate discipline for lawyer who recklessly and falsely answered "no" to question on his application for admission to state bar regarding whether he had ever been investigated, arrested, charged, convicted, imprisoned, placed on probation or parole, or forfeited collateral for any offense against the law; court found respondent's conduct reckless, not merely negligent, so without any mitigating factors, "at least a short period of suspension would be appropriate").

## *Omission or Nondisclosure*

Conduct disciplinable under Standard 6.12 is not limited to affirmative false statements made by a lawyer, but also may arise from a lawyer's knowing failure to act, whether or not the lawyer intends the omission to deceive the tribunal. *See In re Moak,* 71 P.3d 343 (Ariz. 2003) (six-month-and-one-day suspension warranted under Standard 6.12 for lawyer who, in a civil action based upon his client's first accident, knowingly failed to disclose injuries his client received in a second accident and knowingly failed to distinguish injuries his client sustained in the first accident from those he sustained in the second resulting in the judge, jury, and opposing parties being misled in the trial involving the first accident); *People v. Casey,* 948 P.2d 1014 (Colo. 1997) (forty-five-day suspension warranted under Standard 6.12 for failure to inform court that client in trespass case was using another's identity); *People v. Mason,* 938 P.2d 133 (Colo. 1997) (six-month suspension warranted under Standard 6.12 for nondisclosure of material fact in dispute with bank concerning ownership of cabin; specifically lawyer failed to disclose that client had transferred to lawyer ownership interest in cabin); *In re Lagrone,* 843 So.2d 1057 (La. 2003) (six-month suspension warranted under Standard 6.12 for various misconduct including failure to disclose insurance proceeds in client's bankruptcy matter); *In re Griffith,* 800 N.E.2d 259 (Mass. 2003) (one-year suspension warranted under Standard 6.12 for failure to make important disclosures during discovery and trial in federal wrongful death action against city alleging police misconduct; court held that not disclosing that decedent had tested positive for HIV was an intentional material omission; collecting Massachusetts disciplinary cases on false representation and material omissions); *Miss. Bar v. Robb,* 684 So.2d 615 (Miss. 1996) (six-month suspension for lawyer's deceitful conduct in failing to provide information to opposing counsel about ex parte contempt order secured against client's former husband and luring him into state under false pretenses and arranging for his arrest); *Miss. Bar v. Land,* 653 So.2d 899, 910 (Miss. 1994) (one-year suspension warranted under Standard 6.12 for deliberate concealment of evidence of BB gun shooting relevant and material to issue of causation of eye injury and another theory of liability; court found that lawyer's handling of case "went far beyond what could be considered a discovery dispute"); *In re Eisenstein,* 485 S.W.3d 759 (Mo. 2016) (lawyer suspended indefinitely under Standard 6.12, inter alia, for misconduct that included concealing until second day of trial in divorce proceeding his possession of opposing party's payroll information that was improperly obtained by his client as well as improperly obtained direct examination questions of opposing counsel); *In re Lawrence,* 98 P.3d 366, 376 (Or. 2004) (ninety-day suspension warranted under Standard 6.12, inter alia, for misrepresentation by nondisclosure to judge and disciplinary authorities about details of her contact with alleged victim/spouse; court noted that "[a] person must be able to trust a lawyer's word as the lawyer should expect [the lawyer's] word to be understood, without having to search for equivocation, hidden meanings, deliberate half-truths or camouflaged escape hatches") (citation omitted); *In re Huffman*, 13 P.3d 994, 998 (Or. 2000) (citing Standard 6.12, inter alia, and imposing two-year suspension on lawyer with net worth of more than $1 million who filed motions to waive or defer $100 appellate filing fee and cost of trial transcript preparation; court specified that "'Misrepresentation' may include an affirmative misstatement, an intentional failure to disclose material facts that may or may not have been intended to deceive, or a combination of both"); *In re Gustafson*, 968 P.2d 367 (Or. 1998) (six-month suspension warranted under Standard 6.12 for deputy district attorney who, among other misconduct, knowingly failed to disclose to judge material fact concerning alleged impeachment information about juvenile's defense lawyer that could affect case and for failure to correct judge's false impression regarding significance of information).

### *False Statements or Improper Withholding by Others*

False statements to the court or the improper withholding of material information merits a sanction regardless of who engages in the misconduct when the lawyer knows of the activity and fails to take remedial action. *See, e.g., Idaho State Bar v. Warrick*, 44 P.3d 1141 (Idaho 2002) (30-day suspension warranted for lawyer who failed to take reasonable remedial measures in connection with prosecution witness's false testimony regarding plea agreement with state); *In re Wahlder*, 728 So.2d 837 (La. 1999) (six-month suspension deferred subject to one-year supervised probation for lawyer who witnessed client affixing signature of client's wife on settlement documents without her knowledge and then attempted to hide misconduct from client's wife and from court).

### *Injury to Parties and Adverse Effect on Legal Proceeding*

Harm to parties and the legal system resulting from false statements or improper withholding by others can be calculated in various ways, including loss of legal rights, time, and money. *See, e.g., In re Alcorn*, 41 P.3d 600 (Ariz. 2002) (six-month suspension instead of recommended thirty days warranted under Standard 6.12 for two lawyers who, while representing uninsured physician as defendant in medical malpractice action, failed to disclose to trial court and to defendant hospital secret agreement that produced a sham ten-day trial, thus working a fraud on the court; court found that the misconduct caused very serious injury to the system, wasting time and scarce resources, and damage to jurors and witnesses who had their lives disrupted in furtherance of a farce); *In re Bowen*, 872 P.2d 1235 (Ariz. 1994) (one-year suspension warranted under Standard 6.12 for lawyer who, among other misconduct, knowingly submitted false statement in answer to complaint specifically denying his clients' indebtedness while knowing they were liable for the debt—or at least part of it—when he filed the answer, harming opposing party pursuing the debt); *In re Porter*, 980 P.2d 536 (Colo. 1999) (forty-five-day suspension warranted under Standard 6.12, inter alia, for lawyer who submitted false statements in certificate of review that resulted in loss of client's cause of action); *In re Novi*, 422 P.3d 707 (Table) (Nev. 2018) (in unpublished decision, one-year suspension under Standard 6.12 for lawyer who, inter alia, on at least five occasions omitted relevant information or misrepresented information to court; court noted that one client was harmed because lawyer failed to file petition to seal client's criminal record and lawyer did not refund unearned fees); *N.C. State Bar v. Erickson*, 702 S.E.2d 555 (Table) (N.C. Ct. App. 2010) (five-year suspension for lawyer involved in two different schemes to avoid payment of legitimate debts, who drafted and filed documents that were frivolous and, in some instances, fraudulent, and whose conduct caused significant harm to clients, lenders and their counsel, and the court system).

## *Suspension Versus Disbarment (Standards 6.12 Versus 6.11)*

On occasion, judges on the same court have a difference of opinion on whether a certain set of facts establishing dishonest conduct by a lawyer warrants disbarment under Standard 6.11 or suspension under Standard 6.12. For example, in *Fla. Bar v. Dove*, 985 So.2d 1001 (Fla. 2008), the court, rejecting the hearing referee's recommendation for a public reprimand and disciplinary counsel's request for a one-year suspension, imposed a three-year suspension on a lawyer who "made knowing material misrepresentations to the termination of parental rights and adoption courts, did not deal with those tribunals with candor, and withheld material information from the courts, which potentially could cause and did cause a significant adverse effect on the legal proceedings and the interested parties." *Id.* at 1009. While recognizing the severity of the misconduct and applicability of Standard 6.11, inter alia, the majority refused to follow the presumption of disbarment due to the mitigating factors, including evidence of rehabilitation. In a detailed and critical dissenting opinion, Justice R. Fred Lewis urged disbarment. *See also In re O'Neill*, 172 P.3d 1179 (Kan. 2007) (court, acknowledging lack of unanimity as to discipline and that dissent would disbar the lawyer, imposed indefinite suspension, citing Standard 6.12, inter alia); *In re Watkins*, 656 So.2d 984 (La. 1995) (adopting disciplinary board's recommendation, court imposed two-year suspension followed by a one-year probationary period upon reinstatement on lawyer who pleaded guilty to making false statements to receive Social Security income and collecting excessive fees in representing Social Security claimants; in dissent, Justice Bernette Johnson said baseline sanction should be disbarment under Standard 6.11, inter alia, especially considering five other instances of similar misconduct by lawyer and noting with irony that under the majority ruling respondent would be reinstated in Louisiana while still serving out her federal probationary sentence). In *Miss. Bar v. Mathis*, 620 So.2d 1213 (Miss. 1993), a lawyer was suspended for one year for deceiving the court and opposing counsel in concealing the existence of an autopsy covertly performed at lawyer's request while challenging defendants' request for exhumation of body and false discovery responses. Justice Michael Sullivan, joined by Justice James Smith, dissented, finding disbarment justified and noting that suspension under Standard 6.12 is recommended when a lawyer merely *has knowledge* that false statements are submitted to a court *or knows* that material information is improperly being withheld and takes no remedial action. The lawyer in this case, they said, "went far beyond this type of nonfeasance. His intentional conduct evinced dishonesty, deceit, and misrepresentations that seriously adversely reflect on his fitness to practice law. [His] false statements and improper withholding of material information caused injury to his client by subjecting her to monetary sanctions and seriously impeded the legal proceedings in which he was involved." *Id.* at 1225.

In some instances, courts will impose disbarment rather than the period of suspension that has been recommended when the lawyer has repeated similar misconduct. *See, e.g., People v. Bottinelli,* 926 P.2d 553, 558 (Colo. 1996) (disbarment for misconduct including false accusations of conspiracy against judges and lawyers; departure from recommendation of suspension for false statements under Standard 6.12 warranted because of aggravating circumstances including prior discipline for similar misconduct "with no apparent effect on his subsequent behavior").

## *Mens Rea*

In some cases, courts refer to Standard 6.12 because the requisite mental state is the same as set forth in the applicable rule of professional conduct, "knowingly" or "knowing." *See, e.g., In re Amberly,* 996 A.2d 793 (Table) (Del. 2010) (six-month suspension imposed under Standard 6.12, inter alia, in reciprocal discipline action for findings that lawyer *knowingly* made false statements to the Virginia court and made misleading statement to counsel for the Virginia bar; lawyer had been publicly admonished by the Virginia bar and suspended for thirty days in the District of Columbia); *In re Jones,* 951 P.2d 149 (Or. 1997) (because lawyer did not challenge trial panel's conclusion that he violated disciplinary rule prohibiting lawyers from engaging in misrepresentation, he would be deemed, for purposes of sanction, to have acted with knowledge when he had his client sign blank documents that contained perjury clauses and when he filed those documents with court; forty-five-day suspension imposed under Standard 6.12, inter alia); *Bd. of Prof'l Responsibility v. Parrish,* 2018 WL 3853472 (Tenn. August 14, 2018) (lawyer suspended under Standard 6.12 instead of censured, inter alia, for knowingly making false and pejorative statements about judges in motions to recuse).

In other instances courts seem to use the mental states of "intentionally" and "knowingly" interchangeably when describing misconduct resulting in suspension under Standard 6.12. *See, e.g., Iowa Supreme Ct. Att'y Disciplinary Bd. v. Dunahoo*, 799 N.W.2d 524, 533 (Iowa 2011) (indefinite suspension for, among other misconduct, lawyer's false certification that bankruptcy client had been domiciled in district for 180 days when, at time of filing bankruptcy petition, which he knowingly filed in the wrong district, he knew client resided in another district; court stated, "[o]n our de novo review, we find [respondent's] venue error was intentionally made for his own convenience"); *Miss. Bar v. Land*, 653 So.2d 899, 909 (Miss. 1994) (imposing one-year suspension under Standard 6.12, court said lawyer knowingly concealed potentially significant facts and evidence "intended to deceive opposing counsel and client from pursuing their claim, as well as the court in learning all the facts of this case"); *cf. In re Egbune*, 971 P.2d 1065, 1073 (Colo. 1999) (lawyer's false accusations against opposing lawyer and judge of having improper ex parte communication "were done recklessly, not merely negligently, which for our purposes is equivalent to knowingly"; while short period of suspension under Standard 6.12 appropriate for such misconduct, court imposed one-year-and-one-day suspension for additional misconduct including sexual assault). *But see In re Worth*, 82 P.3d 605, 615 (Or. 2003) (reversing trial panel's conclusion that bar did not prove lawyer made willful misrepresentation to disciplinary authorities, court found incorrect mental state was applied; "[b]y applying that mental state, the trial panel required the Bar to prove a more egregious mental state than is required, because this court has recognized that 'willful' is synonymous with 'intentional'").

## *Disciplinary Context*

Suspension for making false statements also can be occasioned by a lawyer's behavior during a disciplinary proceeding. *See, e.g., People v. Hassan*, 45 P.3d 1283 (Colo. O.P.D.J. 2002) (eighteen-month suspension for misconduct including submitting false billing statements to disciplinary authorities); *In re Hatcher*, 2016 WL 3309678 (Nev. June 14, 2016) (lawyer suspended for one year under Standard 6.12 for making false statements to disciplinary counsel about whether she had employed process server suspected of filing false affidavits, including in cases filed by lawyer, and for making false statements relating to exempt status for trust account requirements; lawyer also made similar false statements about process server to judge and police department); *Cleveland Metro. Bar Ass'n. v. Kealy*, 927 N.E.2d 591 (Ohio 2010) (18-month suspension for, among other misconduct, knowingly making false statements to bar association investigator that lawyer had never received notices of pretrial or trial dates); *Bd. of Prof'l Responsibility v. Mears*, 418 P.3d 829 (Wyo. 2018) (lawyer suspended for nine months under Standard 6.12 for knowingly deceiving disciplinary counsel and board, including falsification of emails and making misrepresentations about whether she had repaid money borrowed from client). *Cf. In re Worth*, 82 P.3d 605 (Or. 2003) (ninety-day suspension for, among other misconduct, knowingly making false statement to the bar; facts analyzed under Standard 7.2).

## *Comparison with Similar Cases*

As discussed above with regard to Standard 6.11, some courts cite to the Sanctions Standards, but then instead impose the sanction based on a comparison of existing case law in the jurisdiction. *See, e.g., In re Rosenzweig*, 838 P.2d 1272 (Ariz. 1992) (lawyer altered installment note and submitted it with intent to deceive court and cause hardship to defendant, then lied under oath to disciplinary authorities about matter; three-year suspension imposed instead of disbarment or censure, in part because of fact that similar misconduct in another case was more egregious); *Iowa Supreme Ct. Bd. of Prof'l Ethics & Conduct v. Daggett*, 653 N.W.2d 377 (Iowa 2002) (sixty-day suspension for misconduct that included false statement to judge that lawyer had filed application to reinstate certiorari proceedings when lawyer had prepared application but not filed it; court compared to other cases where neglect was accompanied by misrepresentation); *In re Holliday*, 15 So.3d 82, 95 (La. 2009) (court imposed three-year suspension rather than disbarment for lawyer's serious pattern of misconduct, including prompting lawyer's stepmother to offer false testimony in order to deflect responsibility, noting lack of prior case law directly on point); *Asher v. Miss. Bar*, 661 So.2d 722 (Miss. 1995) (imposing eighteen-month suspension for lawyer who actively lied to client and fraudulently covered up misconduct by using clerk's stamp and forging clerk's signature, court compared conduct with that of other lawyers and compared sanctions imposed in those cases); *In re Dugger*, 54 P.3d 595 (Or. 2002) (nine-month suspension for testifying falsely under oath and making material misrepresentations of fact at hearing; although sole mitigating factor was cooperation with disciplinary authorities and aggravating factors included prior disciplinary record, multiple offenses and failure to appreciate wrongfulness of conduct, court nonetheless found misconduct not as egregious as similar misconduct deserving longer suspensions under Oregon case law).

**6.13 Reprimand is generally appropriate when a lawyer is negligent either in determining whether statements or documents are false or in taking remedial action when material information is being withheld, and causes injury or potential injury to a party to the legal proceeding, or causes an adverse or potentially adverse effect on the legal proceeding.**

## Annotation

### *When Reprimand Is Appropriate*

Reprimand or censure is generally appropriate when a lawyer is negligent in allowing false or misleading information to be submitted to a tribunal in a legal proceeding. *See, e.g., In re Liotti*, 667 F.3d 419 (4th Cir. 2011) (public admonition for, among other misconduct, lawyer misrepresenting certain matters to court, failing to correct prior misrepresentation of material fact, and false accusation that district judge suppressed informant's letter); *see also In re Boettcher*, 861 P.2d 599, 603 (Ariz. 1993) (censure warranted under Standard 6.13, inter alia, because lawyer "clearly negligent" in isolated instance of relying on incorrect information provided by unreliable process server in moving for extension of time and conduct caused both potential and actual injury to client by allowing client's case to be dismissed); *In re Garnice*, 833 P.2d 700 (Ariz. 1992) (failure to adequately research out-of-state law and to make reasonable inquiry into factual allegations in case involving child support arrearage resulted in ambiguous statements in pleadings and warranted reprimand (censure in Arizona) under Standard 6.13, inter alia); *People v. Dalton*, 840 P.2d 351 (Colo. 1992) (censure appropriate under Standard 6.13, inter alia, for lawyer's undignified, discourteous, and disruptive statements about judge, prosecutor, and court reporter in criminal proceedings; while actual harm inflicted may have been slight, respondent's conduct had potential for causing harm to a party or an adverse effect on the proceedings); *People v. Peters*, 82 P.3d 389 (Colo. O.P.D.J. 2003) (public censure appropriate sanction under Standard 6.13, inter alia, for lawyers who acted negligently in failing to ensure that their methods to expedite execution of affidavits of service by having process server's signature notarized when the signatory was not present, would not impact the veracity of the documents; lawyers believed that a faulty jurat would not impact validity of information contained in affidavits, they did not make false statement to court, did not intend to deceive court, and undertook substantial remedial action); *In re Dillon*, 176 A.3d 716 (Table) (Del. 2017) (lawyer reprimanded and ordered to complete two-year period of probation under Standard 6.13, inter alia, for misconduct including negligent failure to ensure correctness of information submitted to court in certificate of compliance); *In re Stull*, 985 A.2d 391

(Del. 2009) (citing Standard 6.13, inter alia, court ordered public reprimand and probation for lawyer who failed to maintain proper financial books and records and filed inaccurate certificates of compliance for four years); *Iowa Supreme Ct. Att'y Disciplinary Bd. v. Buchanan*, 757 N.W.2d 251 (Iowa 2008) (lawyer's conduct in offering to withhold evidence in potential criminal prosecution violated ethics rules and public reprimand, not private admonishment as imposed by grievance commission, warranted); *In re Jordan*, 91 P.3d 1168 (Kan. 2004) (public censure of county prosecutor under Standard 6.13, inter alia, for making false statement to court regarding warrant issued for arrest of defense witness and actions leading to declaration of two mistrials and dismissal of cases that amounted to conduct prejudicial to administration of justice); *In re Senecal*, 974 P.2d 517 (Kan. 1999) (in rejecting hearing panel's private admonition recommendation and imposing public censure on lawyer who misled county attorney regarding purported correction of client's sentence, resulting in premature release of felon, court noted dissenting hearing member's conclusion that lawyer should be sanctioned under Standard 6.13, inter alia; public censure imposed notwithstanding finding that lawyer knew he actually was proposing an untimely modification of felony sentence that had been correctly entered to run consecutively rather than concurrently); *Disciplinary Counsel v. Cuckler*, 804 N.E.2d 966 (Ohio 2004) (public reprimand warranted for misrepresenting professional status by using title "deputy chief legal counsel" without any disclaimer that lawyer had not yet passed bar examination and was not licensed to practice law; court, which did not cite Sanctions Standards, found no evidence of detrimental reliance on respondent's misrepresentation and considered that lawyer generally performed nonlawyer work as legislative aide); *In re Robinson*, 639 A.2d 1384, 1387 (Vt. 1994) (court imposed public reprimand on lawyer for misconduct including advising client to disobey court order in contested child custody matter; "Respondent's misconduct was apparently the result of a negligent misunderstanding of his duty to obey the court order in light of changed circumstances [and] did not willfully seek to undermine the court"); *Bd. of Prof'l Responsibility v. Custis*, 348 P.3d 823 (Wyo. 2015) (lawyer reprimanded under Standard 6.13, inter alia, for negligently making material misrepresentations in appellate brief in criminal matter).

## *More Than Mere Negligence*

Lawyers have been censured for misconduct that clearly exceeds the negligence benchmark contemplated by Standard 6.13, but which does not rise to the knowledge requirement in Standard 6.12. *See, e.g., People v. Bertagnolli*, 861 P.2d 717, 721 (Colo. 1993) (public censure warranted even though none of Standards 6.12, 6.13, or 6.14 "precisely fit[s] the facts and ethical violation in this case"; lawyer making false statement of fact in closing argument by referring to witness's testimony without disclosing witness's desire to correct error in testimony "went beyond mere negligence and, although it caused no actual harm . . . it cannot be said that the potential for harm was negligible"); *In re Scahill*, 767 N.E.2d 976, 981 (Ind. 2002) (reprimand and admonishment for lawyer whose failure to disclose client's constructive fraud allowed trial court to be misled into entering award that could not be enforced and wife not receiving share funds; court tied sanction to lawyer's belief that duty of confidentiality precluded duty to disclose while cautioning that certain circumstances may require a lawyer's resignation from the case and noting that "proceeding to facilitate a client's misleading of the court is not an acceptable option"); *In re Reciprocal Iowa Supreme Ct. Att'y Disciplinary Bd. v. Cannon*, 789 N.W.2d 756 (Iowa 2010) (public reprimand warranted for lawyer who plagiarized seventeen pages of a published writing in a brief filed in federal bankruptcy court; respondent had candidly admitted before the court that his activity represented dishonesty and not negligence or incompetence and conduct constituted misrepresentation); *In re Bridge*, 724 A.2d 462 (Vt. 1998) (public reprimand warranted for assistant attorney general who knowingly made false statement to court in making appearance in friend's case, implying that attorney general had given him permission to represent private client; due to many mitigating circumstances, no greater sanction than reprimand was required); *In re Disciplinary Proceedings Against Bowe*, 800 N.W.2d 367 (Wis. 2011) (public reprimand for lawyer who made repeated misrepresentations before circuit court, including failing to inform it of known jurisdictional defect and falsely representing that opposing party had been served; while rejecting suspension based on respondent's lack of dishonest motive and apologetic and cooperative nature during disciplinary process, court admonished lawyer that public reprimand sanction should not be interpreted as indicating that it was untroubled by her conduct).

**6.14 Admonition is generally appropriate when a lawyer engages in an isolated instance of neglect in determining whether submitted statements or documents are false or in failing to disclose material information upon learning of its falsity, and causes little or no actual or potential injury to a party, or causes little or no adverse or potentially adverse effect on the legal proceeding.**

## Annotation

Private discipline should be reserved for instances of lesser or isolated misconduct "when there is little or no injury to a client, the public, the legal system, or the profession, and when there is little likelihood of repetition by the lawyer." MODEL RULES FOR LAWYER DISCIPLINARY ENFORCEMENT R. 10(A)(5) (2007). Conduct should not be considered lesser misconduct if it involves dishonesty, fraud, deceit, or misrepresentation by a lawyer. *See, e.g.*, MODEL RULES FOR LAWYER DISCIPLINARY ENFORCEMENT R. 9(B)(5) (2007). Courts and disciplinary boards should consider whether the lawyer made a misrepresentation or false statement, or whether the lawyer was negligent in determining that false information was submitted by an individual other than the lawyer or failed to disclose the existence of material information after learning of its falsity. *In re Girardi*, 611 F.3d 1027, 1039 (9th Cir. 2010) (junior associate privately reprimanded for role in drafting and submitting briefs to court containing false statements; citing significant mitigating factors as supportive of private reprimand, including associate's inexperience in practice of law and "his earnest, albeit unsuccessful, effort to persuade his more-experienced colleagues not to continue their frivolous appeal"); *Fla. Bar v. Kleppin*, No. SC09-784, 2010 WL 6983305, at *14 (Fla. Feb. 22, 2010) (disciplinary referee recommended admonishment for lawyer who, among other misconduct, failed to properly investigate affidavit client filed with court containing several false statements that had been procured by client; citing Florida Standard 6.14, inter alia, the court noted that "[p]ublic reprimand is very similar actually to the admonishment, the only difference being the injury that it would cause"). *But see In re Reines*, 771 F.3d 1326, 1328 (Fed. Cir. 2014) (attorney publicly reprimanded for disseminating a complimentary email he received from a judge who referred to himself as the attorney's "friend for life"; the attorney improperly implied an ability to influence the court; in referring matter to California disciplinary authorities, court imposed protective order sealing the record and leaving it to California authorities to determine when disclosure appropriate).

**6.2 Abuse of the Legal Process**
**Absent aggravating or mitigating circumstances, upon application of the factors set out in Standard 3.0, the following sanctions are generally appropriate in cases involving failure to expedite litigation or bring a meritorious claim, or failure to obey any obligation under the rules of a tribunal except for an open refusal based on an assertion that no valid obligation exists:**

**6.21 Disbarment is generally appropriate when a lawyer knowingly violates a court order or rule with the intent to obtain a benefit for the lawyer or another, and causes serious injury or potentially serious injury to a party or causes serious or potentially serious interference with a legal proceeding.**

## Annotation

### *Failure to Follow Court Orders*

A lawyer will likely be disbarred for knowingly violating a court order with the intent to benefit himself, herself, or another and when the conduct causes injury or potentially serious injury to a party, or causes serious or potentially serious interference with a legal proceeding. *See In re Lincoln*, 823 P.2d 1275, 1278 (Ariz. 1992) (disbarring lawyer with prior disciplinary history, under Standard 6.21, inter alia, for neglecting estate and failing to cooperate on three separate occasions with state bar requests for information regarding misconduct; respondent violated "ethical duties owed both to the Estate, which in fact injured the Estate, and to the legal system"); *People v. Ward*, 2017 WL 1046462 (Colo. O.P.D.J. February 9, 2017) (citing Standard 6.21, inter alia, court disbarred lawyer who, in addition to undertaking representation of two clients after stipulating to a suspension, refused to refund retainers and comply with court order directing their disgorgement); *People v. Albright*, 91 P.3d 1063 (Colo. O.P.D.J. 2003) (disbarring lawyer under Standard 6.21, inter alia, for misconduct including failing to comply with court order and pursuing numerous frivolous actions in response to lawsuit by prospective buyers of lawyer's property; noting respondent acted with intent and knowledge of the consequences of her actions, court found that she violated a succession of court orders, she was aware of her conduct, and she acted with conscious object to avoid paying sanctions she was ordered to pay); *Statewide Grievance Comm'n v. McGee*, No. CV02009371S, 2003 WL 22333085 (Conn. Super. Ct. Oct. 2, 2003) (lawyer disbarred under Standard 6.21, inter alia, for failure to comply with probate court order to reimburse $12,000 in wrongfully withheld funds when lawyer had been engaged in systematic bilking of estates, which he tried to conceal by claiming exaggerated service fees); *Fla. Bar v. Bailey,* 803 So.2d 683 (Fla. 2001) (lawyer who used client's assets for personal purposes disbarred under Florida Standard 6.21, inter alia, for failure to segregate or safeguard client's stock proceeds in contravention of two federal court orders; court noted that lawyer's claimed entitlement to stock did not permit violation of court orders); *Fla. Bar v. Newhouse,* 520 So.2d 25 (Fla. 1988) (disbarring lawyer who intentionally disbursed settlement proceeds to himself and another party in violation of court order, and assisted clients in violating that court order).

## *Intentionally Misusing Judicial Process*

Lawyers also are disbarred under Standard 6.21 for intentionally misusing the judicial process and causing serious injury or potentially serious injury to a party, or serious or potentially serious interference with a legal proceeding. *See People v. Kolbjornsen,* 35 P.3d 181 (Colo. O.P.D.J. 1999) (disbarment warranted under Standard 6.21, inter alia, for lawyer's submission of false information to bankruptcy court relating to facts material to court's determination); *Fla. Bar v. Flinn,* 575 So.2d 634 (Fla. 1991) (court disbarred lawyer under Florida Standard 6.21, inter alia, for misconduct including falsely accusing judges of accepting bribes and consistently failing to abide by court rules, causing judges and commissioners to recuse themselves from workers' compensation cases in which the lawyer represented a party); *In re Romious,* 240 P.3d 945 (Kan. 2010) (finding Standard 6.21, inter alia, court disbarred lawyer who engaged in a consistent pattern of rude, disruptive, and at times criminal misconduct before local, state, and federal courts, resulting in disorderly conduct conviction and a contempt adjudication that led to jail time); *In re Sanai,* 383 P.3d 821, 845 (Or. 2016) (in reciprocal disciplinary proceeding, court disbarred lawyer under Standard 6.21, inter alia, for, in context of parent's dissolution of marriage in another state, knowingly and repeatedly filing frivolous actions in state and federal court, disregarding court orders, and engaging in harassing conduct; "pervasive and ongoing, his misconduct stretched out over multiple years and involved multiple incidents, all despite repeated admonitions from the bench to cease such actions").

## *Multiple Acts of Misconduct*

Lawyers who engage in multiple acts of misconduct in addition to disregarding a court order, may find their sanctions elevated from suspension to disbarment. *See People v. Cozier,* 74 P.3d 531 (Colo. O.P.D.J. 2003) (two instances of knowing violation of court order and rule would warrant suspension under Standard 6.22, but disbarment under Standard 6.21 necessary because of additional instances of misconduct). In *People v. Scruggs,* 52 P.3d 237, 240 (Colo. O.P.D.J. 2002), the court acknowledged the recommended sanction of suspension under Standard 6.22 for violation of a court order, but imposed disbarment for the lawyer's additional knowing misappropriation and client abandonment. The court stated that the other misconduct coupled with the lawyer's disregard of court orders "lend additional support to the conclusion that disbarment is warranted." *See also In re Munroe*, 89 A.D.3d 1 (N.Y. App. Div. 2011) (disbarment, rather than suspension, for lawyer's egregious pattern of misconduct, including refusal to obey court orders, evidenced pattern of disdain for the courts).

## *Adjustment for Mitigating Factors*

Courts will analyze the facts of a case under Standard 6.21 but select suspension as a sanction after consideration of mitigating factors (discussion of mitigation and aggravation generally under Standard 9.0). *See, e.g., In re DuBarry*, 814 So.2d 1273 (La. 2002) (court departed from the baseline sanction of disbarment under Standard 6.21, inter alia, for lawyer's dilatory and vindictive practices over ten-year period during fee dispute with former client and imposed one-year suspension because of mitigating factors that included lawyer's personal and emotional problems, cooperative attitude, and imposition of other penalties and sanctions in connection with the civil litigation). Discussion of the impact of mitigating factors is addressed in further detail in Annotation to Standard 9.3.

## *Comparison with Similar Cases*

In some instances, courts will look to precedent involving similar conduct when imposing less than disbarment, the presumptive sanction under Standard 6.21. *See, e.g., In re Rice*, 260 P.3d 1020 (Alaska 2011) (based on court's analysis of relevant case law, four-year suspension, rather than disbarment under Standard 6.21, warranted for lawyer's misconduct that included failure to comply with bar counsel's subpoena for production of documents); *In re Eadie*, 36 P.3d 468 (Or. 2001) (presumptive disbarment under Standard 6.21, inter alia, reduced to three-year suspension following analysis of jurisdictional precedent addressing similar conduct, which included abuse of legal process by improperly attempting to interject fact of defendant's insurance in personal injury case and assuring jury it could award damages without harming defendant); *In re Huffman*, 983 P.2d 534, 549 (Or. 1999) (though several aggravating factors present, court found disbarment under Standard 6.21, inter alia, not appropriate in light of jurisdictional precedent for similar conduct and lack of prior disciplinary record; two-year suspension imposed for disclosing client confidences and threatening to press criminal charges in an effort to collect fees owed by client).

**6.22 Suspension is generally appropriate when a lawyer knows that he or she is violating a court order or rule, and causes injury or potential injury to a client or a party, or causes interference or potential interference with a legal proceeding.**

# Annotation

## *Knowing Violation of Court Order*

The mens rea under Standard 6.22, like that under Standard 6.21, is "knowing." Under Standard 6.21, however, there must be an intent to benefit the lawyer or another. Such intent is not included in Standard 6.22. *See, e.g., In re Arrick,* 775 P.2d 1080, 1086 (Ariz. 1989) (six-month suspension warranted under Standard 6.22, inter alia, for misconduct including inexcusable delay in complying with court order to repay client funds; lawyer's "conduct injured his client and constituted a knowing violation of a court order directly applicable to him"; "[t]his was not a case of negligence, oversight, or neglect in which a reprimand would be the proper form of discipline"); *In re Roose,* 69 P.3d 43 (Colo. 2003) (absent finding of intent to obtain a benefit by disobeying district court's order or to deceive court of appeals, appropriate sanction for both knowingly submitting materially false statements and knowingly violating court order, as long as those acts caused at least some injury to a party or adverse effect on the legal proceeding, was suspension of a year and a day under Standard 6.22, inter alia); *People v. Harding,* 967 P.2d 153 (Colo. 1998) (one-year-and-one-day suspension, with conditions, under Standard 6.22 for lawyer who violated court order requiring placement of disputed attorney's fees in trust account and who failed to disclose to other co-counsel lawyer a professional relationship with that lawyer's client; respondent had prior disciplinary record); *In re Shearin,* 721 A.2d 157, 166 (Del. 1998) (referring to relevant Delaware precedent for similar behavior, court imposed a one-year suspension under Standard 6.22, inter alia, for knowing violations of court orders and rules, causing interference with legal proceedings, and violating bankruptcy rules; court noted that lawyer engaged in a pattern of misconduct demonstrating "complete disregard for her responsibilities as an officer of this Court imbued with public trust in the proper administration of justice"); *Disciplinary Counsel v. Stafford,* 946 N.E.2d 193, 201 (Ohio 2011) (eighteen-month suspension for knowing failure to comply with discovery requests, court orders compelling production, and lawyer's use of delay tactics to that end; in holding suspension appropriate, court accepted findings of the board that, in aggravation, lawyer's pattern of delaying the discovery process in multiple cases "was done to gain a tactical advantage, which suggests a selfish motive"); *In re Crist,* 965 P.2d 1023 (Or. 1998) (five-year suspension of arbitrator for, among other misconduct, disregarding court's directives and violating his duty to the legal system under Standard 6.22); *Hyman v. Bd. of Prof'l Responsibility*, 437 S.W.3d 435 (Tenn. 2014) (presumed sanction of suspension—in this case six months—for knowing violation of court order is proper in light of previous disciplinary history for similar violations); *Bd. of Prof'l Responsibility v. Cannon*, 189 P.3d 857 (Wyo. 2008) (citing Standard 6.22, inter alia, court suspended lawyer for two months for multiple acts of misconduct, including failure to appear at Order to Show Cause hearing issued because of lawyer's failure to provide discovery). *But see In re Koyste*, 111 A.3d 581 (Del. 2015) (lawyer who knowingly violated protective order regarding photographs in client's sexual abuse prosecution received public reprimand instead of suspension due to mitigating factors and precedent).

### *Violation of Orders When Lawyer Is a Party*

Knowing violations can occur when a lawyer fails to comply with a court order in a matter in which the lawyer is a party. *See e.g., People v. Myers*, 969 P.2d 701 (Colo. 1998) (suspension for one year and one day warranted under Standard 6.22 for lawyer charged with DUI who failed to appear in court to proceed with case; court held that failure to appear exacerbated misconduct of DUI, thus sanction greater than public censure was necessary); *People v. Blunt*, 952 P.2d 356 (Colo. 1998) (one-year-and-a-day suspension warranted under Standard 6.22 for repeated violation of court orders in partnership dispute by filing *lis pendens* action against property and interference with liquidator's attempt to sell property, resulting in finding of criminal contempt); *People v. Duggan*, 282 P.3d 534 (Colo. O.P.D.J. 2012) (eighteen-month suspension under Standard 6.22, inter alia, for lawyer who refused to comply with rules governing suspension and failed to attend disciplinary hearing); *Iowa Supreme Ct. Att'y Disciplinary Bd. v. Axt*, 791 N.W.2d 98, 101–02 (Iowa 2010) (two-year suspension for second domestic abuse conviction and repeated violations of court order prohibiting contact with abuse victim); *In re Robinson*, 819 So.2d 280 (La. 2002) (noting that lawyer's actions did not occur in the context of the practice of law and did not adversely affect clients, court imposed one-year suspension, with eleven months deferred, for violating court's preliminary injunction against further contact with surgeon who received numerous inappropriate personal communications from lawyer); *Stark Cnty. Bar Ass'n v. Ake*, 855 N.E.2d 1206, 1210 (Ohio 2006) (six-month suspension, stayed in its entirety, imposed on lawyer who, while representing himself in own divorce case, deliberately violated numerous court orders; court observed that "[t]hese violations represent abuses of the legal process and disserve the lawyer's professional duty to honor and protect the legal system"; "[f]rustration with judicial rulings never excuses a lawyer, while acting on his own behalf or on behalf of a client, from abiding by a court order"); *In re Disciplinary Proceeding Against Cottingham*, 423 P.3d 818 (Wash. 2018) (lawyer in boundary dispute with neighbor was suspended for eighteen months pursuant to Standard 6.22 for repeatedly filing motions and appeals of the matter after it had been resolved by trial and appellate courts and after finding by courts that his filings were frivolous).

- **Failure to Pay Child Support, Maintenance, or Alimony**

Courts often impose suspension when lawyers knowingly fail to comply with a divorce decree ordering payment of spousal maintenance or child support. *See People v. Quigley*, 359 P.3d 1045 (Colo. O.P.D.J 2015) (citing Standard 6.22 court suspended lawyer for one year and one day for failure to pay court-ordered child support, rejecting defense that lawyer did not have the ability to comply with the order); *People v. McNamara*, 275 P.3d 792 (Colo. O.P.D.J. 2011) (case law supported suspension of one year and one day under Standard 6.22, inter alia, for lawyer's knowing failure to pay court-ordered child support, among other misconduct); *Fla. Bar. v. Langston*, 540 So.2d 118 (Fla. 1989) (suspension for ninety-one days was appropriate sanction for contempt of court during divorce proceedings between lawyer and spouse for failure to pay temporary alimony and child support as ordered by the court). In *In re Vanderbilt*, 253 P.3d 774 (Kan. 2011), the court ruled that an indefinite suspension was warranted for misconduct that included lawyer repeatedly failing to pay court-ordered child support and continuing to be noncompliant following a contempt of court order and three-week period of incarceration. The court, citing Standard 6.22, inter alia, found suspension appropriate, noted reinstatement was conditioned upon respondent purging himself of the contempt of court that was the subject of the proceedings. *See also In re Anderson*, 795 P.2d 64, 65 (Kan. 1990) (willful defiance of child-support order from another state and resigning from employment solely to avoid wage garnishment for child-support obligations warranted indefinite suspension; hearing panel finding lawyer's "pattern of behavior is clear and convincing evidence of his contempt for judicial process and indifference to legal obligation"; in rejecting lawyer's assertion that Sanctions Standards have "no weight in the law," court cited its specific prior reliance on them); *In re Ring*, 692 N.E.2d 35 (Mass. 1998) (three-month suspension under Standard 6.22 for repeated violation of court orders to pay spousal support and other expenses in lawyer's divorce; depression caused by breakup of marriage reduced length of suspension but did not mitigate sanction to public reprimand). *But see People v. Primavera*, 904 P.2d 883 (Colo. 1995) (recognizing presumption of a short period of suspension for failure to pay child support, but finding public censure appropriate when attorney failed to pay child support over only a four-month period and paid support in full by court-ordered contempt deadline); *People v. Cantrell*, 900 P.2d 126, 128 (Colo. 1995) (though suspension appropriate under Standard 6.22 for willful failure to pay court-ordered child support, public censure imposed; court reasoned that lesser sanction warranted in light of "predominant mental state" of negligence with respect to lawyer's handling of client property, his cooperative attitude, and dismissal of contempt citations related to child support obligations).

### *Violation of Disciplinary Orders*

Failure to obey disciplinary orders or cooperate with a disciplinary investigation is also grounds for suspension under Standard 6.22. *See In re Albertsen*, 420 P.3d 1218 (Alaska 2018) (citing Standard 6.22, court imposed two-year-and-one-day suspension for, inter alia,failure to respond to disciplinary charges and participate in fee arbitration); *People v. Duggan*, 282 P.3d 534 (Colo. O.P.D.J. 2012) (eighteen-month suspension under Standard 6.22, inter alia, for lawyer who refused to comply with rules governing suspension and failed to attend disciplinary hearing); *People v. Swarts*, 239 P.3d 441, 443 (Colo. O.P.D.J. 2010) (three-month suspension with condition of reinstatement for lawyer who appeared in criminal case on behalf of his wife while under administrative suspension, and for failing to comply with CLE requirements and pay registration fees; distinguishing this case from other cases imposing disbarment on lawyers who violate court order by practicing law while under disciplinary suspension the court stated that "[a]lthough this is not a particularly egregious case in terms of harm, lawyers are officers of the court, and the public expects them to abide its orders"); *In re Nelson*, 102 P.3d 1140 (Kan. 2004) (indefinite suspension imposed under Standard 6.22, inter alia, for multiple ethical violations, including failure to forward written response to disciplinary complaint and failure to comply with orders of bankruptcy court); *In re Mathews*, 827 So.2d 1129, 1132 (La. 2002) (eighteen-month suspension under Standard 6.22, inter alia, for misconduct including bad faith obstruction of disciplinary process; court held: "[R]espondent's failure to cooperate with the [Office of Disciplinary Counsel] caused harm to the legal system by requiring [it] to expend additional time and resources to investigate this matter. The baseline sanction for this misconduct is a suspension."); *In re Rhodes*, 13 P.3d 512 (Or. 2000) (two-year suspension warranted under Standard 6.22 for failure to comply with legal obligations and failure to respond to letters from state bar and local disciplinary committee; court found that conduct caused substantial actual injury to the legal system, including to the bar by increasing the costs of its investigation).

### *Interference with Legal Proceeding*

Suspension is also appropriate when a lawyer interferes directly with the legal process. *See, e.g., In re Brady*, 387 P.3d 1 (Alaska 2016) (six-month suspension for neglecting litigation matter and failing to expedite litigation); *In re Member of the State Bar of Arizona*, 2018 Ariz. Lexis 145 (ninety-day suspension for threatening to jeopardize client's immigration and criminal proceedings in collection of fee; court found collection of fee owed is not a dishonest motive under aggravating factors); *People v. Bontrager*, 407 P.3d 1235 (Colo. O.P.D.J 2017) (nine-month suspension under Standard 6.22 for, inter alia, advancing claims that lacked substantial justification and caused harm or potential harm); *People v. Sigley*, 951 P.2d 481 (Colo. 1998) (thirty-day suspension with requirement of reinstatement proceedings for, among other misconduct, threatening criminal charges against associate lawyer in fee dispute to obtain an advantage in a civil matter, an offense that by itself would warrant at least a short suspension under Standard 6.22); *Fla. Bar v. Berthiaume*, 78 So.3d 503, 510 (Fla. 2011) (suspension of ninety-one days warranted under Florida Standard 6.22 for lawyer who knowingly served fraudulent subpoena containing language threatening incarceration or contempt of court for noncompliance in effort to obtain records relating to dishonored checks issued to lawyer by client; calling lawyer's dishonest conduct disrespectful to the court and destructive to the legal system as a whole, court said, "[r]espondent abused the subpoena power for her personal investigation into someone's private finances [and] sought to deceive the bank so it would provide her with the financial records of her client, when she had no authority to seek this confidential information"); *In re Feld's Case*, 815 A.2d 383, 391 (N.H. 2002) (upon respondent's petition for reconsideration, court vacated public reprimand and imposed one-year suspension under Standard 6.22 for, among other misconduct, assisting clients in promulgation of false discovery answers and causing potential if not actual injury to opposing party's lawful pursuit of information during discovery process; rejecting hearing referee's finding that lawyer did not have dishonest motive, court stated "[i]ntentionally assisting in the promulgation of false answers is . . . inherently dishonest"); *In re McGraw*, 414 P.3d 841 (Or. 2018) (eighteen-month suspension under Standard 6.22 for overcharging fees in conservatorship matter; judge had to conduct line-by-line review of fees); *In re Meyer*, 970 P.2d 652 (Or. 1999) (ninety-day suspension under Standard 6.22, inter alia, for appearing at hearing while intoxicated; conduct forced hearing officer to reschedule hearing and required state's witness to make himself available a second time, creating interference with legal proceeding); *In re Stauffer*, 956 P.2d 967, 977 (Or. 1998) (two-year suspension for, among other actions, dilatory conduct causing "a staggering amount of unnecessary litigation and the multi-year probate of an essentially no-asset estate, which should have been closed promptly"); *In re Jeffery*, 898 P.2d 752 (Or. 1995) (nine-month suspension under Standard 6.22, inter alia, for lawyer who, among other misconduct, threatened to refuse to present a defense for client in criminal case in order to create reversible error; lawyer's threatened refusal to cooperate deprived court of orderly process and necessitated continuance in case and appointment of new counsel for defendant); *In re White*, 815 P.2d 1257 (Or. 1991) (three-year suspension warranted under Standard 6.22, inter alia, for lawyer's abuse of the legal process by filing a multitude of vexatious actions on behalf of client, intentionally using legal system as a tool to harass, rather than to resolve client's legitimate disputes); *In re Disciplinary Proceedings Against Lopez*, 106 P.3d

221 (Wash. 2005) (sixty-day suspension for, among other misconduct, failing to timely and adequately respond to Ninth Circuit's order to show cause regarding failure to prosecute appeal).

## *Disruptive Conduct*

Disruptive behavior can merit suspension when it interferes with the orderly conduct of court business. *See People v. Clough*, 74 P.3d 552 (Colo. O.P.D.J. 2003) (suspension under Standard 6.22 appropriate for lawyer's disorderly conduct in client's misdemeanor assault case, including yelling, using profanity and accusing witness of being drunk; disbarment imposed for additional misconduct under Standard 4.11); *Office of Disciplinary Counsel v. Breiner*, 969 P.2d 1285, 1293 (Haw. 1999) (imposing six-month suspension for lawyer's argumentative, disruptive and contemptuous conduct in court, court stated that "[w]e have no doubt that [respondent's] behavior during the . . . trial interfered with the proceedings. [He] could simply have preserved issues regarding the conduct of the trial by voicing his objections on the record and moving on. Instead, he elected to argue with the trial court and comment on and defy its rulings . . .); *Att'y Grievance Comm'n v. Usiak*, 18 A.3d 1, 15 (Md. 2011) (sixty-day suspension for lawyer who walked out of courtroom during criminal proceeding following an unfavorable ruling by court, contrary to trial court's instructions; court held: "His decision to disrupt the legal proceedings and to disrespect the trial judge in the manner in which he did was a calculated response to the judge's anticipated ruling. In Respondent's zeal to manipulate the outcome of the court proceedings, [he] subordinated his responsibility to his client to his own desire to advance his own agenda."). *But see In re Coe*, 903 S.W.2d 916 (Mo. 1995) (public reprimand rather than suspension for lawyer's disruptive behavior during federal criminal trial resulting in lawyer being held in contempt four times; court considered, among other mitigating factors, that lawyer's conduct did not harm client or any other member of the public).

## *Adjustment for Aggravating or Mitigating Factors*

In many cases, courts will find that a suspension is warranted under Standard 6.22, but ultimately impose a lesser or more serious sanction based on the specific facts of the matter. *See, e.g., People v. Foster*, 276 P.3d 583 (Colo. O.P.D.J. 2011) (while suspension presumptive sanction, public censure imposed for lawyer's deliberate and frivolous relitigation in sixth appeal reasserting judicial bias issue in his own post-dissolution proceedings; mitigating circumstances of unblemished record, more than twenty years of practice and cooperative attitude noted); *In re Brown*, 103 A.3d. 515 (Del. 2014) (lawyer knowingly violated court order by filing action against insurer and causing harm, but mitigating factors and the fact that the client was extremely difficult reduced discipline from suspension to censure); *In re Kirschner*, 793 N.W.2d 196, 202 (N.D. 2011) (while suspension was presumptive sanction under Standard 6.22 for lawyer who "knew he was violating a court order and that his absence would tend to disrupt proceedings before the tribunal," court imposed public reprimand because conduct was an isolated instance of failing to appear for a scheduled trial); *In re Sione*, 330 P.3d. 588 (Or. 2014) (reciprocal disciplinary case in which Standards 6.22 and 7.0 apply; however, the mitigating factors outweighed the aggravating factors and a public censure was issued); *In re Jaffee*, 15 P.3d 533 (Or. 2000) (Standard 6.22 relevant for determining sanction for failure to respond to orders of United States District Court; however, disbarment imposed in light of a number of aggravating factors and other violations).

**6.23 Reprimand is generally appropriate when a lawyer negligently fails to comply with a court order or rule, and causes injury or potential injury to a client or other party, or causes interference or potential interference with a legal proceeding.**

## Annotation

### *Negligent Violation of Court Order*

Most courts impose a reprimand or public censure on lawyers who engage in misconduct at trial or who violate a court order or rule that causes injury or potential injury to a client or other party, or who cause interference or potential interference with a legal proceeding, and whose mental state at the commission of the offense is that of negligence. *See, e.g., People v. Davis*, 950 P.2d 598, 601 (Colo. 1998) (public reprimand for failing to verify that co-counsel had filed bankruptcy documents as required by federal statutes and bankruptcy rules; court found that misconduct "largely attributable to his unlucky choice and unwise reliance on co-counsel," who was subsequently suspended for neglect of other bankruptcy matters); *People v. Cabral*, 888 P.2d 245 (Colo. 1995) (relying on inquiry panel's approval of parties' stipulation, court imposed public censure under Standard 6.23 for failure to attend clients' court hearings due to a scheduling conflict); *In re Chavez*, 251 P.3d 628 (Kan. 2011) (public censure imposed under Standard 6.23 for lawyer who, among other misconduct, failed to appear as ordered on behalf of a client before the Immigration Court; court found respondent negligently violated his duty); *In re Miller*, 112 P.3d 169 (Kan. 2005) (public censure under Standard 6.23, inter alia, for lawyer's misconduct that included repeated disregard of orders of court with respect to failing to handle his client's estate in a timely manner); *Bd. of Prof'l Responsibility v. Bustos*, 224 P.3d 873 (Wyo. 2010) (public reprimand warranted for isolated instance of neglecting to respond to a disciplinary show cause order filed as a result of lawyer's failure to timely file brief on behalf of client; court accepted board's recommendation and cited Standard 6.23 in finding public reprimand appropriate).

### *Interference or Potential Interference with a Legal Proceeding*

Courts often impose public censures under Standard 6.23 when a lawyer interferes or potentially interferes with a legal proceeding, and such conduct is not limited to an isolated instance. *See, e.g., In re Brown*, 392 P.3d 474, 479 (Alaska 2017) (court accepted parties' stipulation and issued reprimand under Standard 6.23 for failure to comply with appellate rules and orders in criminal appeal despite fact that lawyer's conduct was knowing; court agreed that the "degree of injury to her client and the degree of disruption to appellate procedures does not warrant a suspension"); *People v. Carey*, 938 P.2d 1166, 1168 (Colo. 1997) (public censure under Standard 6.23 appropriate instead of private censure because lawyer, on two occasions, requested that arresting officers in DUI case not appear at client's DMV hearing); *People v. Casias*, 279 P.3d 667 (Colo. O. P.D.J 2011) (in case of factual first impression, lawyer publicly censured for misleading criminal defendant client that hiring him on private basis would be superior; court looked to Standard 6 generally and discussed analogous precedent in other jurisdictions); *In re Coe*, 903 S.W.2d 916 (Mo. 1995) (public reprimand for lawyer's disruptive behavior during federal criminal trial); *In re Disciplinary Proceeding Against Kagele*, 72 P.3d 1067, 1078 (Wash. 2003) (reprimand imposed for lawyer who "acted negligently" under Standard 6.23 in failing to expedite litigation for three separate clients, therefore not an isolated violation; suspension also imposed for other misconduct); *Bd. of Prof'l Responsibility v. Moriarity*, 345 P.3d 51 (Wyo. 2015) (in reciprocal discipline case, lawyer who was voluntarily disbarred in originating jurisdiction for filing frivolous civil complaints on behalf of client was publicly censured; court agreed originating jurisdiction overcharged and concluded public censure under Standard 6.23 appropriate); *Bd. of Prof'l Responsibility v. Chapman*, 150 P.3d 182 (Wyo. 2007) (public censure under Standard 6.23 for lawyer's failure to reveal existence of an audiotape or to timely provide it to defendant during formal written discovery, although contents of tape were timely revealed).

### *Failure to Cooperate in Disciplinary Process*

Courts also impose public reprimands when lawyers fail to cooperate in disciplinary investigations or neglect to comply with orders from disciplinary authorities. *See, e.g., People v. Stauffer*, 745 P.2d 240 (Colo. 1987) (in default proceeding public censure warranted under Standard 6.23 for lawyer who did not cooperate with grievance committee and file answer to complaint made by doctor expert witness who complained that lawyer failed to pay his fee); *Akron Bar Ass'n v. Fink*, 959 N.E.2d 1045 (Ohio 2011) (public reprimand warranted for lawyer's misconduct during disciplinary investigation, failing to respond to letters of inquiry regarding complaints from former clients, and failing to comply with two subpoenas ordering him to appear and be deposed; lawyer's misconduct violated court rule prohibiting lawyers from neglecting or refusing to assist or testify in an investigation or hearing; Sanctions Standards not cited); *In re Blais*, 696 A.2d 1231, 1234 (Vt. 1997) (public reprimand warranted under Standard 6.23, inter alia, for failure to cooperate with bar counsel in investigation over a twelve-month period; and failing to comply with duty to account to his client for fees paid).

### *Adjustment for Aggravating or Mitigating Factors*

Sometimes a court will impose a reprimand under Standard 6.23 not because the conduct was the result of negligence, but rather because, in the court's opinion, aggravating or mitigating factors render a suspension too harsh or an admonition too lenient. *See, e.g., People v. Dover,* 944 P.2d 80 (Colo. 1997) (modifying disciplinary panel's recommendation of private censure to public censure for lawyer who appeared as counsel while suspended; public censure rather than more serious suspension because no actual harm to clients resulted from his current actions, he did not represent clients in court proceedings but instead informed court of his suspension at an early stage and he represented that he was retiring from practice); *People v. Janiszewski,* 901 P.2d 476 (Colo. 1995) (public censure warranted for lawyer's knowing attempts to introduce testimony during jury trial that had been ruled inadmissible and reference to inadmissible evidence during closing argument; court imposed public censure instead of short period of suspension because lawyer had practiced ten years without discipline and his actions appeared to be an aberration from his normal conduct); *In re Kirschner,* 793 N.W.2d 196 (N.D. 2011) (while suspension was presumptive sanction, under Standard 6.22 of North Dakota Standards for Imposing Lawyer Sanctions, for lawyer who knowingly failed to appear for scheduled trial, court imposed public reprimand, concluding there were several relevant mitigating factors not cited by the hearing panel, primarily relying on lawyer's many years of experience with no history of misconduct, his remorse, and lack of a selfish motive).

**6.24 Admonition is generally appropriate when a lawyer engages in an isolated instance of negligence in complying with a court order or rule, and causes little or no actual or potential injury to a party, or causes little or no actual or potential interference with a legal proceeding.**

## Annotation

Unless aggravating factors exist, courts likely will impose an admonition or private reprimand upon a lawyer who, in an isolated instance, negligently fails to comply with a court rule. *See, e.g., In re PRB File No. 2007-003,* 987 A.2d 273, 276 (Vt. 2009) (admonishment warranted under Standard 6.24, inter alia, for isolated instance of failing to promptly and fully comply with discovery orders; lawyer's "violations were not intentional; his omissions resulted from disorganization, over reliance on his client, and his lack of experience in complex litigation—but not from an intent to conceal these documents"). *But see People v. Barnthouse,* 941 P.2d 916 (Colo. 1997) (private censure under Standard 6.24 would have been appropriate for lawyer who negligently failed to report guilty plea and deferred judgment to disciplinary agency as required but for aggravating factors, including prior discipline; public censure imposed).

Conversely, more severe discipline is imposed when an incident is not isolated. *See, e.g., In re Mundie,* 453 F. App'x 9, 20 (2nd Cir. 2011) (public rather than private reprimand warranted for misconduct by immigration lawyer that included repeated failure to comply with court's scheduling orders that resulted in dismissal of thirty-eight cases in which lawyer appeared based on his default; court cited lawyer's "long-running pattern of failures to comply with scheduling orders" in rejecting private reprimand); *In re Disciplinary Proceeding Against Kagele,* 72 P.3d 1067 (Wash. 2003) (rejecting argument for admonition under Standard 6.24 in favor of reprimand under Standard 6.23 as presumptive sanction, because failure to expedite litigation for three clients was not an isolated incident).

In some cases, when conduct straddles the border between that warranting a reprimand and that calling for an admonition, courts look to mitigating factors to justify imposition of an admonition. In *United States v. Koubriti,* 305 F. Supp.2d 723 (E.D. Mich. 2003), for example, the court found that statements by U.S. Attorney General John Ashcroft warranted a sanction of formal judicial admonishment for violating, on two occasions, a court order prohibiting public comments on pending prosecution of three defendants arrested on terrorism-related charges just six days after September 11, 2001. Because the attorney general did not willfully violate the order, according to the court, more severe forms of discipline such as disbarment or suspension were not warranted. Rather, the court said the sanction should be either a reprimand or an admonition because the attorney general's public statements, including an erroneous pretrial statement that the defendants were suspected of having knowledge of the September 11th attacks, were inadvertent. Even though his comments created real potential for prejudice and interference with proceedings, the court found admonishment appropriate because there had been eighteen months between violations, he arguably lacked notice of the order at the time of the first violation, he made statements in service of his legitimate and vital obligation to keep the nation informed about the Justice Department's efforts in the war on terror, no actual prejudice resulted from his remarks, and he issued a personal apology. Recognizing that admonitions generally are a private form of discipline, the court said that its resolution in this case necessarily and unavoidably was and should be available for public scrutiny because the position of attorney general is such a highly visible and public office. *See also In re Anonymous*, 896 N.E.2d 916, 918 (Ind. 2008) (private reprimand for lawyer who improperly used subpoenas before the commencement of litigation to give impression that orders were issued by court and noncompliance could result in contempt; court stated that "[a]n offense of this gravity would usually have warranted discipline more severe than a private reprimand, but in light of the lack of adverse consequences and Respondent's cooperation with the Commission, the Court approves the agreed discipline").

**6.3 Improper Communications with Individuals in the Legal System**
**Absent aggravating or mitigating circumstances, upon application of the factors set out in Standard 3.0, the following sanctions are generally appropriate in cases involving attempts to influence a judge, juror, prospective juror or other official by means prohibited by law:**

**6.31 Disbarment is generally appropriate when a lawyer:**

**(a) intentionally tampers with a witness and causes serious or potentially serious injury to a party, or causes significant or potentially significant interference with the outcome of the legal proceeding; or**

**(b) makes an ex parte communication with a judge or juror with intent to affect the outcome of the proceeding, and causes serious or potentially serious injury to a party, or causes significant or potentially significant interference with the outcome of the legal proceeding; or**

**(c) improperly communicates with someone in the legal system other than a witness, judge, or juror with the intent to influence or affect the outcome of the proceeding, and causes significant or potentially significant interference with the outcome of the legal proceeding.**

## Annotation

Disbarment is warranted in cases where a lawyer engages in misconduct that significantly interferes with the outcome of a legal proceeding and that causes serious injury to a party. Such prohibited conduct includes ex parte or improper communications with a judge, juror, or someone in the legal system, or intentionally tampering with a witness, with the intent of affecting the outcome of a legal proceeding.

### *Witness Tampering*

Intentional witness tampering is serious misconduct deserving of the harshest sanction. *See In re Blair,* 40 A.3d 883 (D.C. 2012) (automatic disbarment warranted for lawyer's conviction of one felony count of witness tampering); *Fla. Bar v. de la Puente,* 658 So.2d 65 (Fla. 1995) (disbarment warranted under Florida Standard 6.31, inter alia, for lawyer who, among other misconduct, attempted to suborn perjury by telling a witness to lie regarding forged signature on insurance check); *In re Sniadecki,* 924 N.E.2d 109 (Ind. 2010) (lawyer disbarred under Standard 6.31(a), inter alia, for deceitful and fraudulent misconduct, including attempting to bribe a witness in disciplinary proceedings); *In re Tolen,* 265 P.3d 546 (Kan. 2011) (disbarment warranted under Standard 6.31(a), inter alia, for misconduct stemming from conviction on one count of victim tampering, evidencing a dishonest motive and that caused actual injury to the public and the profession); *In re Laudumiey*, 849 So.2d 515 (La. 2003) (permanent disbarment of two lawyers in consolidated disciplinary proceeding based on criminal convictions for obstruction of justice; lawyers had attempted to persuade subpoenaed witnesses to testify before federal grand jury that lawyers did not know that witnesses were paying runners to solicit clients); *In re Fabacher*, 646 So.2d 915 (La. 1994) (when coupled with misdemeanor criminal conviction for witness tampering, failure to reply to three subpoenas issued by disciplinary counsel and other incidents of noncooperation with Office of Disciplinary Counsel warranted disbarment rather than a suspension under Standard 6.22).

In *Att'y Grievance Comm'n v. Kent*, 653 A.2d 909 (Md. 1995), a defense lawyer was disbarred under Standard 6.31 for repeated tampering with the prosecution's chief witness in a murder case against the lawyer's client. The court noted that the lawyer's unauthorized meetings with the witness, aimed at preventing the witness from testifying, violated not only court orders but also ethical obligations. The court emphasized the seriousness of the misconduct, stating:

> As a result of this tampering, [the lawyer] deprived the State of the testimony of the material witness and virtually ensured that the two individuals whom [the witness] has previously identified as murderers, robbers, and rapists would be acquitted. [The witness] himself was convicted of these crimes and two life sentences were imposed upon him. It is difficult to imagine a more serious interference with the outcome of legal proceedings.

*Id.* at 921; *see also In re Disciplinary Proceedings Against Simmons*, 757 P.2d 519 (Wash. 1988) (disbarment under Standard 6.31(a) for giving adverse witness, known by the lawyer to have a drinking problem, two one-half gallon bottles of whiskey the day before witness testified at trial). *But see In re Smith*, 848 P.2d 612, 614 (Or. 1993) (disbarment called for under Standard 6.31 for lawyer who violated his duty to the legal system by communicating improperly with a witness in a judicial proceeding, but mitigating circumstances reduced sanction to thirty-five-day suspension).

Other jurisdictions that do not rely on the Sanctions Standards have reached comparable results for witness tampering. *See, e.g., In re Yaccarino*, 564 A.2d 1184, 1196 (N.J. 1989) (disbarment of former judge who, among other misconduct, conspired with others to corrupt witnesses and destroy evidence; court reiterated that tampering with witnesses is among certain acts that "so impugn the integrity of the legal system that disbarment is the only appropriate remedy"); *In re Simels*, 94 A.D.3d 108 (N.Y. App. Div. 2012) (disbarment appropriate following lawyer's federal felony conviction for arranging to pay a witness $5,000 in a criminal case if the witness signed an affidavit containing false testimony and agreed to testify falsely at trial); *In re Patrick*, 702 S.E.2d 566 (S.C. 2010) (accepting lawyer's consent to disbarment for misconduct stemming from out-of-state convictions for tampering with witnesses, assault with deadly weapon, domestic assault, and criminal intimidation).

## *Ex Parte Communication with Judge*

Disbarment is also appropriate for ex parte communication with a judge with the intent to influence the outcome of a case. *See, e.g., People v. Bannister*, 814 P.2d 801 (Colo. 1991) (disbarment warranted under Standard 6.31(b) for multiple instances of misconduct including lawyer's ex parte offer to withdraw motion to recuse judge and grievance lawyer filed against judge in exchange for favorable ruling on motion filed in dissolution of marriage proceeding); *Fla. Bar v. Bailey*, 803 So.2d 683, 694 (Fla. 2001) (criminal defense lawyer disbarred under Florida Standard 6.31, inter alia, for multiple counts of egregious misconduct including sending ex parte letter to the judge scheduled to sentence client and a second letter with copy to prosecutor, making disparaging statements about client in attempt to further lawyer's own interests; court found that lawyer's self-dealing and willingness to compromise client confidences "especially disturbing"); *In re McCool*, 172 So.3d 1058 (La. 2015) (disbarment appropriate for lawyer who used social media containing false and inflammatory information to encourage members of the public to communicate directly with judges regarding his pending cases; lawyer caused actual harm by attempting to influence the judges' future rulings, thereby threatening the independence of the judiciary; case includes extensive discussion of Standard 6.3 in main and concurring opinions); *In re Disciplinary Proceedings Against Michael*, 805 N.W.2d 110 (Wis. 2011) (revoking lawyer's law license for extensive misconduct, including improper ex parte communications with a circuit judge in the form of a fax that included prejudicial accusations against the victim in a criminal matter and the opposing party in a related civil matter). *But see People v. Tatum*, 814 P.2d 388 (Colo. 1991) (imposing public reprimand for threatening to file disciplinary complaint against judge in attempt to obtain favorable ruling on motion for continuance; three dissenting justices would have imposed more severe sanction in keeping with Standards 6.31 or 6.32).

## *Improper Communication with Others in Legal System*

A lawyer's improper communication with other individuals who play a role in the legal system is sanctionable under Standard 6.31(c). Where such conduct occurs with the intent to influence or affect the outcome of the proceeding, it warrants disbarment. *See, e.g., In re Alexander*, 2014 WL 1778656 (Review Dept., Cal. State Bar Ct. April 30, 2014) (disbarment for lawyer who, while serving as district attorney, had ex parte conversation with criminal defendant he knew to be represented and lied about the conversation when asked about it; lawyer's conduct was aggravated by three instances of prior discipline, including period of probation following suspension that was in effect when ex parte communication occurred); *People v. Viar*, 848 P.2d 934 (Colo. 1993) (disbarment warranted under Standard 6.31(c), inter alia, following lawyer's criminal conviction for arranging bribe and facilitating destruction of client's records in county court system and district of attorney's office in effort to "fix" client's DUI ticket); *People v. Bannister*, 814 P.2d 801, 804 (Colo. 1991) (disbarment appropriate under 6.31(c), inter alia, for pattern of "gross misconduct" including lawyer's threat to pursue obstruction of justice criminal charges against opposing counsel if he opposed motion); *Fla. Bar v. Adams and Filthaut*, 198 So.3d 593 (Fla. 2016) (permanent disbarment for two lawyers who conspired with other firm members and a police officer to have opposing counsel arrested for DUI in the middle of a contentious civil trial); *In re O'Dwyer*, 221 So.3d 1 (La. 2017) (permanent disbarment for, inter alia, disrupting proceedings in federal court through abusive and racially offensive communications and pleadings, making unsubstantiated allegations that certain attorneys were corrupt, and filing frivolous sanctions motions to retaliate against parties and lawyers); *In re Robinson*, 46 So.3d 662 (La. 2010) (disbarment and order of restitution warranted for lawyer who, among other misconduct, threatened former client with civil defamation suit and criminal prosecution for filing a disciplinary complaint against him; court found disbarment appropriate under the Sanctions Standards, especially in light of numerous aggravating factors including existence of a dishonest or selfish motive); *In re Zappin*, 160 A.D. 3d 1 (N.Y. App. Div. 2018) (disbarment for lawyer who, while representing himself in divorce, ignored court orders, created fake website about child's lawyer in custody action, filed disciplinary complaint against court-appointed psychiatric expert, sent text messages to wife threatening to ruin her legal career, and filed police report falsely accusing wife of domestic violence); *In re Linietsky*, 263 A.D.2d 102 (N.Y. App. Div. 1999) (disbarment for misconduct including threat to implicate repair shop's lawyers in murder if lawyer's automobile was not released promptly from repair shop); *cf. In re Bilbe*, 841 So.2d 729 (La. 2003) (disciplinary board recommended disbarment under Standard 6.31, inter alia, for lawyer's persistent and repeated communications with executives of represented party in attempt to effectuate favorable settlement after party's counsel instructed lawyer on seven occasions not to contact client; court, however, imposed three-year suspension based on mitigating factors).

**6.32 Suspension is generally appropriate when a lawyer engages in communication with an individual in the legal system when the lawyer knows that such communication is improper, and causes injury or potential injury to a party or causes interference or potential interference with the outcome of the legal proceeding.**

## Annotation

Courts have imposed suspensions under Standard 6.32 when a lawyer knowingly engages in improper communications with judges. In *Grievance Adm'r v. Lopatin*, 612 N.W.2d 120 (Mich. 2000), the Michigan Supreme Court, for the first time, adopted the Sanctions Standards on an interim basis and remanded the case for reconsideration directing the hearing panel to reconsider the sanction in light of the standards. The lawyer in *Lopatin* engaged in an improper ex parte communication by providing a court of appeals judge with a supplemental legal memorandum analyzing two recent court cases the lawyer cited during oral argument without serving a copy of the memorandum on opposing counsel, the other appellate panel judges or filing it with the court clerk. Although finding that "[e]very unlawful ex parte communication on the merits is injurious to the integrity of the legal system and must be taken seriously," the court recognized that "the *Standards* do provide for gradations." *Id.* at 132. The court found that the facts of this case were more appropriately resolved under Standard 6.32, and not Standard 6.31(b).

On remand, the Michigan Attorney Discipline Board applied the analysis set forth in the Sanctions Standards, confirmed that Standard 6.32 applied to the ex parte contact and imposed a 180-day suspension. *Grievance Adm'r v. Lopatin*, No. 92-224-GA (Mich Att'y Discipline Bd. Aug. 15, 2001), *available at* http://www.adbmich.org/download/92o-224.pdf. (For more on the application of the Sanctions Standards in *Lopatin* and Michigan cases following it, see generally Jennifer Sabourin, *Annual Survey of Michigan Law June 1, 2000–May 31, 2001*, 48 WAYNE L. REV. 785 (2002)). *See also In re Bolton*, 820 So.2d 548 (La. 2002) (lawyer with case pending approached the judge in courthouse parking lot, asked about procedure for giving a "gift" to a judge, referenced pending personal injury case, inquired when case could be set on the docket, and then asked about making a $5,000 contribution to the judge; lawyer said his intentions were misinterpreted, and in suspending lawyer under Standard 6.32 court deferred to hearing committee's finding regarding subjective intent in finding incident to be an inappropriate ex parte communication and not bribery attempt); *In re Kluge*, 66 P.3d 492 (Or. 2003) (two-year suspension for, among other misconduct, improper ex parte communication in bringing motion to disqualify judge in violation of Standard 6.3; conduct involved dishonesty and misrepresentation and potentially harmed client and prejudiced administration of justice); *In re Thompson*, 940 P.2d 512 (Or. 1997) (sixty-three-day suspension for lawyer who also was party to the lawsuit, and upon receiving appellate opinion ruling in favor of opposing party drove to the courthouse and verbally confronted one of the appellate judges while shaking opinion in outstretched hand; in suspending lawyer court held that ex parte contact occurred because case was still within court's jurisdiction and subject to modification by court); *Bd. of Prof'l Responsibility v. Parrish*, 2018 WL 3853472 (Tenn. August 14, 2018) (six-month suspension under Standard 6.32, inter alia, with one month active and the remainder probated for lawyer who filed recusal motions containing pejorative statements about judges); *In re Disciplinary Proceeding Against Ferguson*, 246 P.3d 1236 (Wash. 2011) (ninety-day suspension warranted under Standard 6.32 for lawyer's ex parte appearance to obtain contempt order and writ of restitution on behalf of her clients without providing prior notice to opposing counsel, in violation of notice and hearing requirements applicable to obtain such orders; lawyer also received a reprimand for other misconduct).

### *Improper Communication with Jurors, Witnesses, or Opposing Parties*

Courts also impose suspensions pursuant to Standard 6.32 for improper communications with jurors, witnesses, and opposing parties. *See People v. Olson*, 2016 WL 5076078 (Colo. O.P.D.J. July 25, 2016) (thirty-month suspension under Standard 6.32 for lawyer facing disciplinary charges following conviction for domestic battery who tried to persuade his wife not to testify truthfully at disciplinary hearing); *In re Favata*, 119 A.3d 1283 (Del. 2015) (six-month-and-one-day suspension for prosecutor's attempt to intimidate unrepresented defendant and for misleading court about statements at issue); *Fla. Bar v. Committe*, 136 So.3d 1111 (Fla. 2014) (three-year suspension under Florida Standard 6.32 for lawyer who filed frivolous lawsuit and, when ordered to pay the defendant's attorney's fees and costs, refused to do so; when defendant tried to collect fees and costs lawyer reported him to federal authorities for alleged extortion); *Fla. Bar v. Abramson*, 3 So.3d 963 (Fla. 2009) (lawyer's improper comments suggesting that judge behaved unprofessionally and treated lawyer disrespectfully to prospective jurors in court potentially interfered with the outcome of the legal proceedings; misconduct fell under Florida Standard 6.32; ninety-one-day suspension imposed); *In re Gamble*, 338 P.3d 576 (Kan. 2014) (citing Standard 6.32, inter alia, court imposed sixty-day suspension on lawyer who in course of representing biological father in adoption proceeding sent unrepresented eighteen-year-old birth mother message containing legal advice and false statements regarding adoptive parents; lawyer tried to induce birth mother to revoke consent to adoption and court concluded the communication was emotional blackmail); *In re Griffing*, 236 So.3d 1213, 1216 (La. 2017) (under Standard 6.32, suspension of one year and one day with portion deferred to probation for Assistant U.S. Attorney in secret relationship with FBI agent who threatened defendant with arrest at his workplace unless he "stopped spreading such rumors" about the relationship); *In re Ruffin*, 54 So.3d 645 (La. 2011) (six-month suspension with all but thirty days deferred for assistant district attorney's admitted misconduct in threatening criminal charges against an individual to obtain an advantage in civil matter, and knowing abusing of position in order to collect payment owed to a friend); *In re Ulanowski*, 800 N.W.2d 785, 795 (Minn. 2011) (indefinite suspension for misconduct that included harassing opposing counsel in one matter and threatening former client with criminal prosecution in another; while not citing Sanctions Standards, court found suspension appropriate based in part on lawyer's intent "to embarrass, delay, or burden opposing counsel" and to improperly recover attorney's fees from former client); *In re Discipline of Callister*, 401 P.3d 211 (Table) (Nev. 2017) (thirty-five-day suspension and mandatory ethics CLE under Standard 6.32 for lawyer who offered witnesses $7,000 to testify they never saw decedent sign will that was the subject of litigation; lawyer's conduct complicated legal proceedings, added expense, imposed systemic costs, and fostered public cynicism of the legal process); *In re Disciplinary Action Against Dvorak*, 611 N.W.2d 147 (N.D. 2000) (one-year suspension for lawyer's misconduct including intentional bullying of witness by threatening defamation action if witness did not correct privileged statements made on guardian *ad litem* questionnaire); *In re Yarborough*, 559 S.E.2d 836 (S.C. 2002) (indefinite suspension for misconduct including attempt to intimidate prosecution's witness in ongoing criminal case against lawyer by threatening civil action seeking $50 million in damages); *Hyman v. Bd. of Prof'l Responsibility*, 437 S.W.3d 435 (Tenn. 2014) (six-month suspension under Standard 6.32, inter alia, for lawyer who, among other misconduct, engaged in ex parte communication with represented party and threatened deponent with incarceration); *Ciardi v. Office of Prof'l Conduct*, 379 P.3d 1287 (Utah 2016) (two-year suspension for lawyer who was disruptive in trial court, clerk's office, and before ethics committee by making disparaging statements about a judge, a bailiff, and the disciplinary process; Sanctions Standards not cited).

**6.33 Reprimand is generally appropriate when a lawyer is negligent in determining whether it is proper to engage in communication with an individual in the legal system, and causes injury or potential injury to a party or interference or potential interference with the outcome of the legal proceeding.**

## Annotation

### *Negligent Improper Communications*

Courts impose public reprimands or censures upon lawyers who negligently engage in improper communications with judges, jurors, witnesses, or opposing parties and whose contact either causes injury, or potential injury, to a party or interferes with a legal proceeding. *See, e.g., In re Bemis*, 938 P.2d 1120 (Ariz. 1997) (censure and one-year supervised probation for negligent attempt at ex parte communications with two judges regarding pending litigation); *People v. McCray*, 926 P.2d 578 (Colo. 1996) (public censure for arranging to have client's represented wife come to lawyer's office to execute motions to dismiss criminal charges and civil case seeking restraining order against husband, without notice to wife's counsel); *In re Hurley*, 183 A.3d 703 (Table) (Del. 2018) (public reprimand under Standard 6.33, inter alia, for sending antagonistic, inflammatory, and demeaning emails to opposing counsel when lawyer should have known his unprofessional correspondence violated the rules); *Fla. Bar v. Von Zamft*, 814 So.2d 385 (Fla. 2002) (public reprimand under Florida Standard 6.33 warranted for lawyer in state's attorney's office who engaged in ex parte communication with judge presiding over capital murder case, who was a friend of the lawyer, even though lawyer did not represent any of the parties in the case, in order to advise judge that granting prosecutor's pretrial motion for continuance was in everyone's best interest); *Office of Disciplinary Counsel v. Kaiama*, 2017 WL 1629365 (Haw. May 1, 2017) (public censure for lawyer who, with reckless disregard for the truth or falsity of the allegation, accused a judge of committing war crimes under international conventions; court held that but for mitigating factors lawyer's conduct would have warranted suspension under Standard 6.32); *In re Klemp*, 418 P.3d 733 (Or. 2018) (public reprimand under Standard 6.33 for engaging in improper communication with an unrepresented person; lawyer should have known the unrepresented individual misunderstood the lawyer's role and this caused potential injury because the individual was unable to make a fully informed decision about seeking representation of her own); *In re Griffin*, 711 S.E.2d 890 (S.C. 2011) (public reprimand for lawyer who improperly threatened to report an alleged disciplinary matter involving opposing counsel in order to obtain an advantage in settlement negotiations of a civil case); *In re Barton*, 554 S.E.2d 680 (S.C. 2001) (public reprimand for city solicitor who sent prospective jurors questionnaires with cover letter on municipal court's stationery asking jurors to return questionnaires to city solicitor's office); *In re Disciplinary Proceedings Against Hudec*, 848 N.W.2d 287 (Wis. 2014) (public reprimand and payment of costs for filing a brief containing salacious and irrelevant facts calculated to prejudice a party and for failure to serve opposing counsel with reply brief; Sanctions Standards not cited). *Cf. In re Mullins*, 649 N.E.2d 1024, 1026 (Ind. 1995) (although not relying on Sanctions Standards, court imposed public reprimand on lawyer who sought ex parte emergency guardianship of client in persistent vegetative state without informing court of parallel proceedings by client's parents to withdraw nutrition and hydration; court indicated that it might have imposed more stringent sanction had lawyer not acted out of "misguided pursuit of ideological objectives," among other factors); *In re Howes*, 940 P.2d 159 (N.M. 1997) (public censure of assistant U.S. attorney for improper communication with represented criminal defendant by accepting calls from jailed defendant, listening to what defendant had to say, and not informing public defender even though court found that lawyer's actions were intentional rather than the result of negligence or ignorance).

## *Additional Misconduct*

When a case involves other misconduct in addition to improper communications, courts may impose a reprimand under Standard 6.33 and include additional sanctions. *See, e.g., In re Eadie*, 36 P.3d 468 (Or. 2001) (standing alone, filing ex parte disqualification motion would have warranted reprimand under Standard 6.33 because of negligent mental state in failing to understand legal obligation to serve opposing counsel; court increased sanction to three-year suspension because of additional misconduct); *In re Smith*, 739 A.2d 1191 (Vt. 1999) (public reprimand and six-month probation appropriate under Standard 6.33 for repeated direct contact with represented adverse party); *In re Disciplinary Proceeding Against Carmick*, 48 P.3d 311, 321 (Wash. 2002) (reprimand for negligently contacting represented party included with more severe sixty-day suspension for knowing misrepresentations to court in ex parte proceeding; court cites then existing commentary to Standards 6.1 and 6.3, stating that "[t]he ethical duties violated by improper ex parte contact and by misrepresentations to a tribunal are violations of duties owed to the legal system"); *cf. In re Higgins*, 884 P.2d 1094 (Ariz. 1994) (probation continued for additional two-year term for lawyer who, among other violations, unintentionally misrepresented to court that opposing counsel had approved ex parte motion).

For a difference of opinion on the application of Standard 6.33, compare the majority and dissenting opinions in *In re Illuzzi*, 632 A.2d 346 (Vt. 1993). In that case, the majority imposed a six-month suspension for the lawyer's repeated pattern of unauthorized direct contact with an insurer, noting that public reprimand would have sufficed if it was the first violation. The court also found that the lawyer's prior disciplinary history weighed heavily as an aggravating factor. In dissent, Chief Justice Frederic Allen emphasized that the application of Standard 6.33 focuses on improper communications with individuals in the legal system and requires a showing that the lawyer knows the communication is improper coupled with injury or interference with the legal proceeding. He asserted that the facts should have been analyzed under Standard 7.4 for violation of duty owed to profession, and would have imposed public reprimand.

**6.34 Admonition is generally appropriate when a lawyer engages in an isolated instance of negligence in improperly communicating with an individual in the legal system, and causes little or no actual or potential injury to a party, or causes little or no actual or potential interference with the outcome of the legal proceeding.**

## Annotation

Unless aggravating factors exist, courts are likely to impose an admonition or private reprimand upon a lawyer who, in an isolated instance, negligently engages in an improper communication with an individual in the legal system and causes little or no injury or interference with the outcome of the legal proceeding. *See, e.g., Kaufman v. Am. Family Mut. Ins. Co.*, 601 F.3d 1088 (2010) (admonishment for defense lawyer who communicated ex parte with judge's law clerk concerning how best to preserve the court's jurisdiction over pending sanctions motions against opposing counsel following a dismissal of underlying case; court found admonishment appropriate due to lack of any resulting prejudice to the plaintiff or any other interested party, and opposing counsel had been apprised of the communication and its purpose); *In re Anonymous*, 43 N.E.3d 568 (Ind. 2015) (private reprimand for lawyer who engaged in ex parte communication with a judge while seeking an emergency petition for guardianship over a child by failing to provide advance notice to mother or putative father before obtaining temporary restraining order; good intentions regarding welfare of the child did not justify disregarding basic statutory safeguards designed to protect the rights of other parties; Sanctions Standards not cited); *Att'y Disciplinary Bd. v. Att'y Doe*, No. 792, 878 N.W.2d 189 (Iowa 2016) (private admonition for lawyer who sent a single unprofessional ex parte email to a judge, had no disciplinary history, took responsibility for his actions, and harmed no clients; Sanctions Standards not cited). *Cf. In re Evans*, 782 P.2d 315, 323 (Ariz. 1989) (although lawyer violated rule prohibiting ex parte communication, no sanction imposed; court held that "[b]y providing for a record of the communication and enabling its immediate refutation by opposing counsel, respondent prevented any of [the] dangers [associated with ex parte communications] from occurring"; while citing Standard 6.34, court noted that its rules did not provide for admonition and that its opinion would serve that purpose).

Even the relatively less culpable mental state of negligence must be proven to impose an admonition. *See, e.g., In re Att'y C.*, 47 P.3d 1167 (Colo. 2002) (reversing public censure against prosecutor for failure to disclose exculpatory evidence to defense until after preliminary hearing; although disclosure was not timely, prosecutor lacked intent necessary for sanction because rule was unclear as to prosecutor's obligation to disclose prior to any critical stage of proceeding); *In re*

*Anonymous*, 786 N.E.2d 1185 (Ind. 2003) (private reprimand warranted for lawyer's ex parte communication with judge in divorce proceedings, during which lawyer sought temporary restraining order (TRO) against client's husband without notice to husband; court emphasized that failure to provide notice was based on lawyer's "reasonable" misinterpretation of the local rules, but private reprimand still appropriate given lawyer's ex parte communication with judge). Conversely, more severe discipline is imposed when other misconduct or aggravating factors are present. *See, e.g., In re Wool*, 733 A.2d 747 (Vt. 1999) (public reprimand with eighteen-month probation for lawyer's negligent misconduct, including sending motions directly to opposing party who was represented by counsel; finding Standard 6.34 most applicable, the court instead imposed public reprimand in light of aggravating factors and lawyer's additional misconduct in failing to perform fiduciary duties owed to vulnerable clients); *In re Free*, 640 A.2d 22 (Vt. 1994) (public reprimand for knowingly instituting a lawsuit partially in name of nonclient without permission and improperly contacting nonclient who lawyer knew to be represented by counsel; while no actual injury occurred and lawyer lacked dishonest or selfish motive, prior disciplinary record was serious aggravating factor; rejecting bar counsel's recommendation of a private admonition under Standard 6.34, inter alia, which refers to negligent conduct and is recommended absent aggravating or mitigating factors).

## 7.0 Violations of Duties Owed as a Professional

**Absent aggravating or mitigating circumstances, upon application of the factors set out in Standard 3.0, the following sanctions are generally appropriate in cases involving false or misleading communication about the lawyer or the lawyer's services, improper communication of fields of practice, improper solicitation of professional employment from a prospective client, unreasonable or improper fees, unauthorized practice of law, improper withdrawal from representation, or failure to report professional misconduct.**

## Annotation

The ABA Model Rules of Professional Conduct include many rules that define certain standards of conduct relating to a lawyer's role as a professional. What were Model Rules of Prof'l Conduct R. 7.1, 7.2, 7.4, and 7.5 and are now Model Rules of Prof'l Conduct R. 7.1 and 7.2, after the ABA House of Delegates amended the Rules in August 2018, address lawyer advertising and marketing. They also address the solicitation of clients, Model Rules of Prof'l Conduct R. 7.3, and the unauthorized practice of law, Model Rules of Prof'l Conduct 5.5. Other rules cover bar admission and disciplinary matters, Model Rules of Prof'l Conduct R. 8.1; reporting professional misconduct, Model Rules of Prof'l Conduct R. 8.3; and committing a criminal act reflecting adversely on the lawyer's fitness, Model Rules of Prof'l Conduct R. 8.4(b).

Restrictions on lawyer advertising have undergone major transformation since the U.S. Supreme Court, more than thirty-five years ago in *Bates v. State Bar of Arizona*, 433 U.S. 350 (1977), struck down an Arizona Supreme Court rule prohibiting lawyers from advertising in newspapers or other media. The court in *Bates* held that such activity is protected by the First Amendment, stressing that while the First Amendment permits regulation of and reasonable restrictions on lawyer advertising that is false, deceptive, misleading, or illegal in nature, a newspaper advertisement publicizing lawyers' "legal clinic" and claiming lawyers offered "very reasonable" prices on certain services was not misleading and fell within the scope of protected speech. Following its seminal decision in *Bates*, the Supreme Court continued to strike down certain ethical prohibitions on legal advertising, so that courts and disciplinary bodies seldom impose disbarment or even suspension under Standard 7.0 for violations of lawyer advertising rules. *See, e.g.*, *Shapero v. Ky. Bar Ass'n*, 486 U.S. 466 (1988) (Kentucky could not, consistent with First Amendment, inter alia, categorically prohibit lawyers from soliciting legal business for pecuniary gain by sending truthful and nondeceptive letters to potential clients known to face particular legal problems; such advertising constitutionally protected commercial speech that state could regulate through less restrictive and more precise means); *Zauderer v. Office of Disciplinary Counsel of the Supreme Ct. of Ohio*, 471 U.S. 626 (1985) (reversal of Ohio Supreme Court holding that violations of certain Ohio professional conduct rules warranted public reprimand; lawyer may not be disciplined for soliciting legal business through printed advertising containing truthful and nondeceptive information and advice regarding legal rights of potential clients); *In re R.M.J.*, 455 U.S. 191 (1982) (Missouri Supreme Court rule regulating lawyer advertising and prohibiting deviation from limited list of areas of practice in addendum to rule banning lawyer from identifying jurisdictions in which he or she is licensed, and prohibiting lawyer from mailings announcing opening of an office to persons other than "lawyers, clients, former clients, personal friends and relatives," violates First Amendment absent showing that advertising was misleading or that mailings and handbills would be more difficult to supervise).

Reprimands or admonitions for negligent conduct appear to be the most common sanctions imposed when a lawyer violates professional duties relating to advertising. Similar sanctions are often imposed for charging an excessive or improper fee, improperly withdrawing from representation or failing to report professional misconduct. Such sanctions help to ensure that the public is protected and the bar is educated about the type of conduct that warrants discipline. Disbarment and suspension—particularly suspensions of six months or longer—are less common, but not unheard of when a lawyer's misconduct meets the criteria under Standards 7.1 and 7.2. The standards and cases set out below identify those circumstances.

**7.1 Disbarment is generally appropriate when a lawyer knowingly engages in conduct that is a violation of a duty owed as a professional with the intent to obtain a benefit for the lawyer or another, and causes serious or potentially serious injury to a client, the public, or the legal system.**

## Annotation

Disbarment should be imposed when a lawyer knowingly engages in conduct that violates a duty owed as a professional with the intent to benefit the lawyer or another, and the lawyer causes serious injury or potentially serious injury to a client, the public, or the legal system.

### *Mens Rea*

The mental state necessary for disbarment under Standard 7.1 is "knowingly . . . with the intent to obtain a benefit for the lawyer or another. . . ." *See, e.g., Fla. Bar v. Behm,* 41 So.3d 136, 140 (Fla. 2010) (permanent disbarment instead of six-month suspension under Florida Standard 7.1, inter alia, for lawyer who deliberately and knowingly refused to file income tax returns and pay federal income taxes since admission to the bar because such conduct is "fundamentally inconsistent with the basic obligations of a lawyer, who is sworn to uphold the law"); *In re Disciplinary Action Against Nassif,* 547 N.W.2d 541 (N.D. 1996) (disbarment warranted under Standard 7.1, inter alia, for lawyer who assisted office staff in the unauthorized practice of law and shared fees generated from their work with intent to gain personally, thus violating a duty owed to the profession); *In re Paulson,* 216 P.3d 859, 887 (Or. 2009) (relying on Standards' analytical framework, court disbarred lawyer under Standard 7.1, inter alia, for intentional conduct including non-responsiveness to disciplinary authorities' requests for information, ignoring statutory obligation to seek court approval before collecting fee for services as a personal representative, deliberately disregarding duties applicable to suspended lawyers, and intentionally practicing law while suspended; court found lawyer's current and past misconduct demonstrated "a persistent disregard for the rules of professional conduct and the duties that the accused owes to his clients, the public, the legal profession, and the legal system"); *In re Disciplinary Proceeding Against Van Camp,* 257 P.3d 599 (Wash. 2011) (lawyer who deceived client with ambiguous fee agreement purposely drafted to lawyer's advantage acted with the requisite mental state under Standard 7.1 to warrant disbarment).

### *Advertisement and Solicitation*

As noted above, disbarment under Standard 7.0 for violations of lawyer advertising rules is rare. Conduct involving direct in-person, live telephone, or real-time electronic solicitation of professional employment, however, does not enjoy the same First Amendment protection afforded to advertising. *See generally* Model Rules of Prof'l Conduct R. 7.3 (2013). *Compare Ohralik v. Ohio State Bar Ass'n*, 436 U.S. 447 (1978) (holding constitutional prophylactic ban on in-person solicitation by lawyers for pecuniary gain likely to pose dangers that state has right to prevent), *and Fla. Bar v. Went For It, Inc.*, 515 U.S. 618, 631 (1995) (in upholding the constitutionality of professional conduct rules prohibiting lawyers from sending targeted direct mail solicitations to victims and their relatives for thirty days following an accident or disaster, the court stated that "[t]he purpose of the thirty-day targeted direct-mail ban is to forestall the outrage and irritation with the state-licensed legal profession that the practice of direct solicitation only days after accidents has engendered"), *with Bates v. State Bar of Ariz.*, 433 U.S. 350 (1977) (concluding that lawyer advertising may not be subject to blanket ban, although false, deceptive, or misleading advertising may be subject to restraint).

Lawyers engaged in improper solicitation of clients, therefore, have been subject to disbarment under Standard 7.1. In these cases courts also may look to other simultaneous and serious misconduct, aggravating and mitigating circumstances, and often whether the solicitation targets are particularly vulnerable. *See, e.g., Fla. Bar v. Weinstein*, 624 So.2d 261, 262 (Fla. 1993) (disbarment for, inter alia, in-person solicitation of brain-damaged patient in hospital room; "[w]e . . . view [the lawyer's] in-person solicitation of a brain-injured patient in a hospital room, accompanied by lying to health-care personnel, as one of the more odious infractions that a lawyer can commit; his conduct brings his profession into disrepute and reduces it to a caricature"); *In re Weaver*, 281 P.3d 502 (Kan. 2012) (disbarment appropriate for lawyer's pattern of misconduct, including solicitation of loan modification clients by falsely advertising firm as specializing in consumer financial legal services and guaranteeing clients they would receive money back if loans were not modified, taking money from clients and turning over their matters to nonlawyers, and providing no legal services for clients; court found lawyer engaged in predatory conduct on vulnerable clients, many of whom were in dire financial straits); *In re Naquin*, 775 So.2d 1060 (La. 2000) (disbarment for lawyer who improperly solicited an accident victim's widow as a client when he knew she already was represented by counsel).

## *Use of Nonlawyers to Solicit Business*

Whether a lawyer directly contacts a prospective client personally or hires another to do so does not matter. In particular, the use of "runners"—nonlawyers who recruit, recommend, or direct people to the services of a given lawyer in return for a fee or other compensation from the lawyer—has given rise to numerous disciplinary cases. *See, e.g., Fla. Bar v. Barrett*, 897 So.2d 1269, 1276 (Fla. 2005) (disbarment for egregious use by lawyer of employee, an ordained minister, to improperly solicit twenty-two clients; lawyer paid employee to complete hospital chaplain's course and sent "him under the guise of providing spiritual comfort to people in their most needy time"); *In re Sinowski*, 720 S.E.2d 597, 599 (Ga. 2011) (disbarment for two lawyers who compensated at least forty-six nonlawyer runners to recommend and secure employment and shared legal fees with them; court held: "Although [lawyers] were not disciplined previously, their conduct was egregious—they cast a wide net covering more than 1,300 cases. Their scheme was highly organized and very lucrative; and it was not short lived. They were motivated by greed and they are not remorseful.").

Louisiana, in particular, has spawned a number of cases dealing with runner-based solicitation schemes, mostly resulting in disbarment. *See, e.g., In re Coney*, 891 So.2d 658 (La. 2005) (permanently disbarring lawyer who, during a seventeen-year scheme, used runners to solicit personal injury clients and then, to conceal his cash payments to them, purposely structured his check-cashing activity so as not to trigger federal currency transaction requirements); *In re O'Keefe*, 877 So.2d 79, 88 (La. 2004) (permanent disbarment for lawyer "at the epicenter of one of the largest runner-based solicitation schemes in Louisiana"; "respondent may not have originated the scheme, it is clear that it could not have existed without his funding and cooperation"; lawyer's activities caused harm to countless clients who were unknowingly drawn into his solicitation scheme and caused grave harm to the entire legal profession in Louisiana); *In re Kirchberg*, 856 So.2d 1162 (La. 2003) (permanent disbarment for lawyer who paid runners between $200 and $500 cash per personal injury client solicited for his law practice); *In re Cuccia*, 752 So.2d 796 (La. 1999) (disbarment under Standard 7.1 for paying two dozen runners $500 each to solicit personal injury clients, typically at accident scenes, resulting in up to 100 new clients each month). *But see In re Goff*, 837 So.2d 1201 (La. 2003) (nine-month suspension, rather than disbarment, with court distinguishing from cases of more egregious participation in runner-based solicitation schemes; lawyer facilitated solicitation scheme but was neither originator nor active participant, and cooperated in disciplinary counsel's investigation and prosecution of runner-based solicitation).

The New Jersey Supreme Court, in *In re Pajerowski*, 721 A.2d 992 (N.J. 1998), took the opportunity to review its decisions involving runner-based solicitations, starting with its seminal case on the issue, *In re Frankel*, 120 A.2d 603 (1956). In *Pajerowski*, the court reiterated its strong disapproval of such unethical misconduct by disbarring a lawyer who employed a runner to contact and solicit business from accident victims at their homes or in hospital emergency rooms on the same day or shortly after they were injured. The court said the lawyer acted out of economic greed and took advantage of persons who were vulnerable, and his actions harmed the public and cast the profession in a negative light. *See also In re Saghir*, 86 A.D.3d 121 (N.Y. App. Div. 2011) (disbarment for, inter alia, using a nonlawyer, a federal prison inmate, to solicit clients in federal prison on lawyer's behalf, compensating and sharing fees with the nonlawyer for such services, and aiding nonlawyer in preparing motions for lawyer's clients; decision does not cite Sanctions Standards); *Disciplinary Counsel v. Furth*, 754 N.E.2d 219 (Ohio 2001) (permanent disbarment for numerous serious violations, including lawyer's responsibility for acts of his nonlawyer employee in improperly soliciting father of juvenile involved in a middle school shooting; Sanctions Standards not cited).

## *Excessive or Improper Fees or Expenses*

Courts have relied on Standard 7.1 to disbar lawyers for charging their clients unreasonable, improper, or excessive fees or expenses, in violation of their duty to act as a professional. *See, e.g., In re Mincey*, 477 S.E.2d 116 (Ga. 1996) (disbarment under Standard 7.11 [sic], inter alia, for charging improper fee by taking in excess of thirty-five grams of cocaine as fee for legal services and knowingly engaging in conduct that violated a duty owed to the profession to obtain a benefit for himself, causing potentially serious injury to the public and the legal system); *In re Harrington*, 385 P.3d 905 (Kan. 2016) (disbarment under Standard 7.1, inter alia, for lawyer's misuse of durable power of attorney to convert client funds and pay himself improper attorney's fees from client's accounts); *In re Romious*, 240 P.3d 945 (Kan. 2010) (disbarment warranted under Standard 7.1, inter alia, for lawyer who charged client a flat fee of $3,500 and later changed the agreement to an hourly fee of $3,500, for knowingly engaging in conduct that violated duty owed as a professional with the intent to obtain a benefit for himself, causing serious or potentially serious injury to a client, the public, or the legal system); *In re Mitchell*, 145 So.3d 305 (La. 2014) (disbarment of lawyer who submitted hundreds of unsubstantiated expenses, for which client then paid, and after which firm refunded client; Standard 7.1 not specifically cited); *In re Quaid*, 646 So.2d 343 (La. 1994) (disbarment under Standard 7.1, inter alia, for lawyer who deceived disabled client in order to obtain a pecuniary benefit for himself at the expense of client; lawyer charged and retained fees several thousands of dollars in excess of those authorized by Social Security Administration for services in connection with claims for disability benefits and advised the client of his right to do so); *In re Disciplinary Proceeding Against Van Camp*, 257 P.3d 599 (Wash. 2011) (disbarment under Standard 7.1 for lawyer who, inter alia, knowingly and intentionally charged an excessive and unreasonable flat fee of $25,000 based on a confusing fee agreement that he knew was ambiguous, especially since prior discipline put him on notice that his such agreement was problematic; client was seriously injured by lawyer's actions, as fee of $25,000 was a substantial amount of money to client, and lawyer failed to make any restitution).

A lawyer's mishandling of fees, or failure to perform promised work or return unearned fees, also may fall within the category of cases warranting disbarment.

*See, e.g., In re Hamer,* 808 S.E.2d 647 (Ga. 2017) (disbarment under Standard 7.1, inter alia, for lawyer who knowingly deceived and failed to provide services to client and engaged in pattern of neglect of client matters); *In re Jones-Joseph,* 181 So.3d 651 (La. 2015) (sanction against lawyer already disbarred, with five-year minimum period for readmission, for similar failure to perform services, was to extend that period by an additional five years); *In re Zak,* 73 N.E.3d 262 (Mass. 2017) (disbarment for lawyer who repeatedly charged advance fees for mortgage assistance relief services and did not deposit the fees in a client trust account, in violation of state and federal statutes prohibiting such conduct; Sanctions Standards not cited).

## *Unauthorized Practice of Law*

A lawyer who is suspended, disbarred, or on inactive status is ineligible to practice law. By engaging in the unauthorized practice of law while suspended, disbarred, or on inactive status a lawyer violates a duty owed as a professional, and such misconduct is subject to disbarment under Standard 7.1 when the lawyer has done so with the intent to obtain a benefit for himself or another person, and has caused serious injury or potentially serious injury. *See, e.g., People v. Kanwal,* 357 P.3d 1236 (Colo. O.P.D.J. 2015) (disbarment under Standard 7.1, inter alia, for lawyer who knowingly disobeyed rules of tribunal and continued to practice law while suspended); *Fla. Bar v. Norkin,* 183 So.3d 1018 (Fla. 2015) (suspended lawyer disbarred for continuing to practice law and failing to comply with rule requiring notice of suspension to clients, opposing and co-counsel, and courts; Sanctions Standards not cited); *In re McDaneld,* 389 P.3d 976 (Kan. 2017) (lawyer disbarred for continuing to appear on behalf of multiple clients after having license suspended and failing to cooperate with disciplinary investigation); *In re Rost,* 211 P.3d 145 (Kan. 2009) (disbarment warranted under Standard 7.1, inter alia, for retired lawyer's conduct in continuing to practice law without an active-status license, in violation not only of rule prohibiting unauthorized practice of law but also of prior disciplinary settlement agreement allowing him to retire so as not to face sanctions for other rule violations); *In re O'Dwyer,* 221 So.3d 1 (La. 2017) (lawyer, who was disbarred in federal court and interimly suspended from state practice, disbarred by state for filing pleadings in federal court using cousin's name, among other violations, which undermined public confidence in the legal system and caused substantial expenditures by the court); *In re Petal,* 30 So.3d 728 (La. 2010) (permanent disbarment under Standard 7.1, inter alia, for lawyer who engaged in unauthorized practice of law by appearing in court on behalf of a limited liability company after he was suspended from practice); *In re Richard,* 826 So.2d 542 (La. 2002) (lawyer knowingly and intentionally engaged in practice of law while ineligible to do so, misconduct that occurred within same general time frame as unrelated misconduct in original disciplinary case against him, in which he had been disbarred; following Louisiana case law, court found him guilty of additional violations that warranted disbarment and that were added to his record for consideration in the event he applied for readmission after becoming eligible to do so); *Att'y Grievance Comm'n v. James*, 735 A.2d 1027, 1036 (Md. 1999) (court disbarred lawyer who practiced law during period of suspension, stating that the lawyer's "disregard for this Court's order suspending him from the practice of law threatens the integrity of the legal profession and of the judicial system, and constitutes the sort of conduct that must be deterred for the protection of the public"); *In re Overboe*, 844 N.W.2d 851 (N.D. 2014) (disbarment under North Dakota Standard 7.1 for initiating garnishment action while suspended, among other conduct also supporting disbarment under other Standards).

### *Assisting in the Unauthorized Practice of Law*

A lawyer who allows a suspended or disbarred lawyer to perform legal services under his or her auspices is assisting in the unauthorized practice of law and violates duties owed to the profession. *See In re Goel*, 46 A.D.3d 26 (N.Y. App. Div. 2007) (suspension of one year and until further order of court for lawyer who aided her husband, a disbarred lawyer, in the unauthorized practice of law by allowing him access to her law practice and allowing him to assist her in representing a client, despite receipt of prior letter of caution issued to lawyer addressing similar concerns). A lawyer also assists in the unauthorized practice of law when he or she allows support staff such as paralegals to perform unsupervised legal tasks or to hold themselves out to the public as lawyers. *See, e.g., People v. Calvert*, 280 P.3d 1269, 1290 (Colo. O.P.D.J. 2011) (respondent seriously injured clients by knowingly disregarding his duty to supervise his paralegal, a nonlawyer—even while he armed her with his log-in and password to file pleadings in bankruptcy cases; Standard 7.1 applicable sanction for respondent's misconduct, whose "self-dealing and assistance of a nonlawyer in her unauthorized practice of law have no place in the legal profession, the great strength of which lies in the honor and integrity of its practitioners"); *People v. Milner*, 35 P.3d 670 (Colo. O.P.D.J. 2001) (citing Standard 7.1, inter alia, in disbarring lawyer for multiple instances of misconduct, including aiding in unauthorized practice of law; lawyer's paralegal met with client for initial interview without lawyer's oversight and accepted legal representation of client, advised client against seeking temporary custody of client's children, and advised client against discussing the children's welfare with social services, all constituting unauthorized practice of law); *In re Guirard*, 11 So.3d 1017, 1030 (La. 2009) (disbarment appropriate sanction for two partners' systematic delegation of handling of their clients' cases to their nonlawyer staff, failure to supervise their nonlawyer staff, facilitation of the unauthorized practice of law by nonlawyer staff, and impermissible fee sharing with their nonlawyer staff: "This was a systematic practice as part of the 'business first' model knowingly employed by respondents. By structuring their law firm in the manner in which they did, respondents harmed their clients."); *In re Woods,* 841 So.2d 713 (La. 2003) (disbarment on consent for multiple serious violations, including lawyer's failure to supervise staff, thereby enabling her nonlawyer husband to engage in unauthorized practice of law; citing Standard 7.1, inter alia); *In re Saghir,* 86 A.D.3d 121 (N.Y. App. Div. 2011) (disbarment for, inter alia, aiding a nonlawyer in the unauthorized practice of law by directing or assisting a federal prison inmate in preparing motions for lawyer's clients; decision does not cite Sanctions Standards); *In re Hancock,* 55 A.D.3d 216 (N.Y. App. Div. 2008) (disbarment for lawyer who, inter alia, allowed a disbarred felon to use his name freely on court papers and to advertise himself as a paralegal; decision does not cite Sanctions Standards); *Sneed v. Bd. of Prof'l Responsibility,* 301 S.W.3d 603 (Tenn. 2010) (permanent disbarment under Standard 7.1, inter alia, for several acts of knowing misconduct, including aiding nonlawyer and her business in unauthorized practice of law; lawyer appeared in advertisement for business, paid nonlawyer money, and gave no outward indication that his practice was distinct from the business; testimony from client that nonlawyer had given her advice regarding her immigration case and that nonlawyer prepared papers for her immigration hearing that lawyer then attended).

### *Omissions and Misrepresentations in Bar Admission Applications*

An omission of material fact or a misrepresentation on a bar admission application also constitutes a breach of duty owed as a professional under Standard 7.0. Lawyers who have been admitted after making such misstatements or omissions often are subsequently disbarred (with some courts specifically citing Standard 7.1 and others not referencing it) for engaging in such misconduct. *See, e.g., In re Demos,* 875 A.2d 636 (D.C. 2005) (reciprocal but not identical discipline by disbarring lawyer for intentional misrepresentations on bar application to Arizona federal bar in which lawyer sought to avoid state bar membership requirement by stating he resided in New Mexico and his law firm was located in District of Columbia; D.C. address was merely mail drop); *In re Verma,* 691 N.E.2d 1211 (Ind. 1998) (disbarment for purposeful false statements on Maryland and Pennsylvania bar applications regarding lawyer's length of practice in Indiana that were calculated to take advantage of bar admission reciprocity agreements); *In re Stamps,* 874 So.2d 113 (La. 2004) (disbarment for husband and wife lawyers who failed to disclose in bar examination applications that they had been employed by and engaged in unauthorized practice of law for lawyer in another state before admission to bar; Sanctions Standards not cited); *Att'y Grievance Comm'n v. Joseph,* 31 A.3d 137 (Md. 2011) (disbarment for lawyer who traveled to California with intent to reside there and attempted to practice law by intentionally misrepresenting his residency status in applications for pro hac vice admissions in California state and federal courts); *Att'y Grievance Comm'n v. Joehl*, 642 A.2d 194 (Md. 1994) (disbarment under Standard 7.1 appropriate for omitting from bar application material information about battery arrest and driving record and testifying falsely before inquiry panel about knowledge of license suspensions; court noted that Illinois, New Jersey, New York, and other jurisdictions also disbar for such misconduct); *In re Scavone*, 524 A.2d 813, 820 (N.J. 1987) (failure to disclose past disciplinary actions on bar application warranted revocation of license to practice law: "Candor and honesty are a lawyer's stock and trade. Truth is not a matter of convenience. Sometimes lawyers may find it inconvenient, embarrassing, or even painful to tell the truth. Nowhere is this more important than when an applicant applies for admission to the bar."); *In re DeMaria*, 154 A.D.3d 1161 (N.Y. App. Div. 2017) (revoking admission of lawyer who omitted the fact on application that he had been suspended by Saskatchewan admission authorities for a serious breach of integrity); *In re Osredkar*, 25 A.D.3d 199 (N.Y. App. Div. 2005) (disbarment for lawyer who failed to disclose requested legal employment information on bar application, and following admission fabricated letters of recommendation and falsified law school transcript); *In re Application of Callam*, 81 N.E.3d 448 (Ohio 2017) (revoking lawyer's license, but allowing reapplication after two years, for failure to disclose on application, or update before admission, information regarding charges against him, and ultimate guilty plea, for dishonest conduct related to insurance license).

## *Omitting Past Convictions*

A frequent omission on bar applications for which courts disbar lawyers under Standard 7.1 is past convictions. *See, e.g., In re Spinner*, 19 A.D.3d 803 (N.Y. App. Div. 2005) (revocation of admission proper sanction for material false statements on bar admission application when applicant failed to fully disclose that he had been arrested in New Jersey for possession of marijuana, had pleaded guilty to disorderly conduct, and had twice been arrested in New York, resulting in dismissal of the charges on one occasion and a plea of guilty to disorderly conduct); *In re Updegraff*, 242 A.D.2d 119 (N.Y. App. Div. 1998) (disbarment for, inter alia, failure to file a record of conviction for petit larceny with the court, failure to reveal two prior arrests on his application for admission to the New York State Bar, and failure to disclose suspension for failure to pay child support); *In re Dabney*, 836 N.E.2d 573 (Ohio 2005) (revoking license for failure to disclose on bar application lawyer's conviction on five separate prostitution-related offenses); *cf. Stewart v. Miss. Bar*, 84 So.3d 9, 16 (Miss. 2011) (citing its exclusive authority over admissions and reinstatements to practice law, the court denied disbarred lawyer's second petition for reinstatement primarily for answering falsely when asked whether he had any expunged criminal convictions; "practice of law is a revocable privilege, not a right . . . [and] [b]y seeking readmission to practice law, [respondent] opened his past to inspection and could not refuse to disclose expunged criminal records").

## *Failure to Report Professional Misconduct*

Sanctions for failure to report misconduct by another lawyer occur infrequently, but when they do, suspension or public reprimand is often imposed. Disbarment, however, has been found appropriate in at least one case that involved such misconduct. *See In re Steinmeyer*, 718 S.E.2d 426 (S.C. 2011) (accepting lawyer's consent agreement and disbarring her for, among other things, failing to timely report violations of ethics rules of her former employer; lawyer admitted that former employer's misconduct occurred up to three years before she reported it).

## *Improper Withdrawal from Representation*

Conduct involving a lawyer's improper withdrawal from representation is included among the violations of duties owed as a professional that can result in disbarment under Standard 7.1. *See, e.g., Read v. State Bar*, 807 P.2d 1047 (Cal. 1991) (respondent's pattern of misconduct involving wide range of improper behavior, including withdrawal from representation of numerous clients without informing them or providing for their representation, warranted disbarment); *In re Phillips*, No. 05-O-03782, 2011 WL 9375622 (Cal. Bar Ct. Mar. 4, 2011) (disbarment warranted for misconduct including improper withdrawal as counsel less than two weeks prior to trial and before his clients could retain new counsel); *In re Rochon*, 776 So.2d 432 (La. 2001) (disbarment warranted for misconduct including nine instances of failing to properly withdraw as counsel by abandoning law practice; finding lawyer violated duties owed to his clients, the public, the legal system, and the profession); *In re Wooden*, 562 S.E.2d 649 (S.C. 2002) (disbarment appropriate for neglect and failure to withdraw from representation in eleven client matters).

## *Failure to Cooperate with Disciplinary Authorities*

Failure to cooperate with disciplinary authorities during the course of a disciplinary investigation against a lawyer may result in disbarment. In disbarring a lawyer for such misconduct, courts often will cite Standard 7.1. *See, e.g., People v. Goodman*, 334 P.3d 241 (Colo. O.P.D.J. 2014) (disbarment for lawyer who presented fabricated documents and false statements in civil suit and again to disciplinary authorities); *In re Bourcier*, 939 P.2d 604, 606 (Or. 1997) (disbarment for lawyer who, among other misconduct, repeatedly failed to respond to inquiries from the bar after court had previously suspended him for the same misconduct; "[t]his court considers the failure to cooperate with a disciplinary investigation to be a serious ethical violation"); *In re Dickerson*, 905 P.2d 1140 (Or. 1995) (disbarment under Standard 7.1, inter alia, for lawyer who violated rule governing duty to cooperate by failing to respond to inquiries from disciplinary counsel after being notified personally by the bar that he was the subject of investigation; lawyer's cumulative misconduct, including lying to clients, converting clients' funds to his own use, failing to account for clients' funds, failing to return clients' property or files, and neglecting legal matters entrusted to him by clients, mandated disbarment); *In re Disciplinary Proceeding Against Simmerly*, 285 P.3d 838, 851–52 (Wash. 2012) (applying Standard 7.1, court disbarred lawyer who, inter alia, made intentional misrepresentations in context of bar disciplinary investigation; board correctly recharacterized the injury as serious, relying on earlier decision in which court "stated unequivocally that '[f]alsifying information during an attorney discipline proceeding' itself harms the public and the legal system") (citation omitted); *In re Disciplinary Proceeding Against Scannell*, 239 P.3d 332, 342 (Wash. 2010) (presumptive sanction is disbarment for lawyer who, inter alia, intentionally failed to cooperate in disciplinary proceedings with intent to frustrate and delay those proceedings: "If every lawyer subject to a disciplinary investigation were as intransigent as [he] has been, disciplinary proceedings would be expensive, long, and hard-fought procedural wars that might or might not be effective at uncovering wrongdoing and protecting the public. In short, [lawyer's] behavior poses a serious threat to lawyer self-regulation and is rightfully redressed under ABA Standards 7.1.").

## *Other Misconduct*

The duty a lawyer owes as a professional encompasses many of the acts that also may fall under other chapters of the Sanctions Standards, but courts sometimes single out Standard 7.1. *See, e.g., People v. Ward*, 2017 WL 1046462 (Colo. O.P.D.J. 2017) (disbarment under Standard 7.1, inter alia, for lawyer who took on bankruptcy matters knowing that he could not complete the work because of impending suspension); *Fla. Bar v. Blackburn*, 244 So.3d 168, 171 (Fla. 2018) (disbarment for lawyer who initiated sexual relations with two clients while they were in prison, exploiting their circumstances, and thereby breeding "contempt and distrust of lawyers" and demonstrating "severe moral turpitude" "wholly inconsistent with professional standards").

**7.2 Suspension is generally appropriate when a lawyer knowingly engages in conduct that is a violation of a duty owed as a professional and causes injury or potential injury to a client, the public, or the legal system.**

## Annotation

### *Mens Rea*

Knowledge is the requisite mental state for application of Standard 7.2. Unlike Standard 7.1, this Standard does not require that the lawyer intentionally seek to benefit himself or another. Thus, when a lawyer knowingly violates a duty as a professional and causes actual or potential injury, courts generally impose suspensions under Standard 7.2. *See, e.g., In re Shumate*, 626 N.E.2d 459, 461 (Ind. 1993) (thirty-day suspension for making false statement in connection with disciplinary matter; citing Standard 7.2, court said, "A suspension for a definite period of time comports with that suggested by the American Bar Association where an attorney 'knowingly engages in conduct that is a violation of a duty owed to the legal profession.'"); *In re Ganley*, 549 N.W.2d 368 (Minn. 1996) (citing Standard 7.2 in suspending lawyer for six months for knowingly falsely notarizing client's affidavit and submitting altered document to court).

Suspension is appropriate when a lawyer knowingly violates a duty owed to the profession and causes injury or potential injury to a client, the public, or the legal system, even when he or she does not intentionally abuse the professional relationship by engaging in deceptive conduct. *See, e.g., People v. Alster*, 221 P.3d 1088, 1092 n.6, (Colo. O.P.D.J. 2009) (in imposing ninety-day suspension under Standard 7.2, for lawyer who knowingly misused trust account to hide personal assets from his creditors, court stated lawyer violated a rule "defining a certain standard of conduct rather than a rule fundamental to his professional relationship with a client"); *In re Pelletier*, 84 A.3d 960 (Del. 2014) (lawyer not licensed in Delaware opened office, claiming it was for purpose of facilitating referrals to Delaware attorneys, but performed legal services on behalf of clients and held himself out as intending to provide legal representation in the state; citing Standard 7.2 and discussing the definition of "knowledge" in the Standards, the court found the respondent knowingly engaged in the unauthorized practice of law, suspended him for one year, and barred him from practicing pro hac vice in the state for that period); *In re Crews*, 159 S.W.3d 355, 361 (Mo. 2005) (lawyer's conduct need not be intentional when it comes to deceiving a client in order to warrant discipline; imposing indefinite suspension, court noted that "[w]hile Respondent may not have intentionally set out to abuse the professional relationship between himself and his clients, [he] committed misconduct when attempting to shroud his substandard actions with the varying explanations that he proffered"); *In re Snyder*, 35 S.W.3d 380 (Mo. 2000) (citing Standard 7.2, inter alia, in imposing indefinite suspension on lawyer who may not have intentionally, or deceptively, set out to abuse the professional relationship between himself and his clients but engaged in obvious violations of the conflict of interest rules and inflicted pecuniary harm upon his clients). *But see In re Discipline of Sione*, 330 P.3d 588 (Or. 2014) (court reprimanded lawyer in reciprocal discipline case while also acknowledging applicability of Standard 7.2 to lawyer's knowing failure to cooperate with California disciplinary authorities and appear for a client's trial; court cited extensive mitigation factors).

Some courts interchangeably use the terms "knowingly" and "intentionally" when evaluating the mental state under Standard 7.2. For example, in *In re Royer*, 78 P.3d 449, 457 (Kan. 2003), the court recites that under Standard 7.2 a suspension is warranted when lawyer "knowingly engages in conduct" but then, in applying the facts, the court finds that the lawyer's violations of duties owed as a professional were "intentional." *Id.* at 457. In imposing a three-month suspension on the lawyer who arranged the sale of his client's unsafe storm-damaged building, which had negative value, to a homeless man for one dollar in order to avoid demolition costs, the court determined that the lawyer's conduct harmed the purchaser and the city, which was required to expend taxpayer funds to demolish the building as a result of the transfer. At least one court clarified the confusion between knowledge and intent. In *In re Disciplinary Proceeding Against Preszler*, 232 P.3d 1118, 1127 (Wash. 2010), the court imposed a three-year suspension on a lawyer who, inter alia, charged an unreasonable fee for representing a bankruptcy client in a personal injury claim. The lawyer argued he did not act knowingly in that he believed in good faith his fee was reasonable, a claim the court called "irrelevant." Stressing Standard 7.2 only requires proof that the lawyer acted "knowingly" rather than with intent, the court said, to act with knowledge the lawyer did not need to act with "the conscious objective or purpose to accomplish a particular result." (See Definitions in the black letter Standards). "[He] simply needed to be consciously aware of the circumstances that made his fee unreasonable." *Id.*

## *Injury*

Suspension under Standard 7.2 is warranted when a lawyer's misconduct causes injury or potential injury to a client, the public, or the legal system. *See, e.g., Maddux v. Bd. of Prof'l Responsibilty*, 409 S.W.3d 613, 624 (Tenn. 2013) (lawyer representing son and his mother in law suit disputed that tendering funds collected directly to the son, instead of to the court registry, caused potential injury to the mother; citing Standard 7.2, inter alia, and discussing definition of "potential injury," the court held that substantial evidence supported finding of potential injury to the mother because direct payment to her son failed to protect her separate interests in those funds); *In re Disciplinary Proceeding Against Hicks,* 214 P.3d 897 (Wash. 2009) (presumptive sanction for lawyer's misconduct in submitting letter in response to inquiry from bar disciplinary board that contained falsehoods about handling of trust account was suspension under Standard 7.2, rather than disbarment under Standard 7.1, absent finding that lawyer's conduct caused serious or potentially serious injury to client, public, or legal system; two-year suspension imposed). The level of injury was particularly relevant in *In re Disciplinary Proceeding Against Lynch,* 789 P.2d 752 (Wash. 1990), where the court found the recommended six-month suspension insufficient, suspended a deputy prosecuting attorney for two years under Standard 7.2 after he admitted to violating his oath of duties as a lawyer and engaging in conduct prejudicial to the administration of justice. The lawyer had allowed a photograph of undercover police officers to come into the possession of a drug dealer. The extent of potential injury in the case was great, the court said, pointing out that the lawyer's misconduct led to mistrust between the drug enforcement unit and the prosecuting attorney's office, placed drug enforcement unit members at risk of extreme danger because the photograph showed undercover officers in their working clothes, jeopardizing the effectiveness of their investigations, and causing all drug enforcement unit personnel to be rotated out of the unit eight months after the photograph was discovered even though they normally served staggered two-year terms.

## *Solicitation of Legal Employment*

Although most cases involving improper solicitation of legal employment by a lawyer, or by a nonlawyer at the direction of the lawyer, include the element of intentionality and are analyzed under Standard 7.1, suspension under Standard 7.2 is sometimes imposed for such conduct. *See, e.g., People v. Jones,* 422 P.3d 1093 (Colo. O.P.D.J. 2018) (one-year-and-one-day suspension for lawyer who purchased foreclosure information and improperly sent solicitation letters to homeowners that lacked designation as "advertising material," misled recipients about the actual identity of the sender by placing in envelope's return address space "Re: Mesa County Public Trustee Auction" and not his name, and misled recipients to believe immediate action was required at risk of fine or imprisonment; the court found Standard 7.2 applied because, following Standards Theoretical Framework, the "ultimate sanction imposed should at least be consistent with the sanction for the most serious instance of misconduct among a number of violations . . ."); *Fla. Bar v. Dopazo,* 232 So.3d 258 (Fla. 2017) (one-year suspension citing Florida Standard 7.2 warranted for lawyer who improperly solicited, at the hospital, mother of a child with brain injuries after 2004 reprimand for similar improper contacts); *Fla. Bar v. Letwin,* 70 So.3d 578 (Fla. 2011) (citing Florida Standard 7.2, court imposed one-year suspension for lawyer's unethical solicitation of more than 900 prospective clients via a solicitation letter that was knowingly misleading); *In re Trauffer*, 532 S.E.2d 96 (Ga. 2000) (six-month suspension and public reprimand for lawyer who directed nonlawyer staff to call nonlawyers and solicit professional employment); *Matter of Wray*, 91 N.E.3d 578 (Ind. 2018) (while not citing Standards, court suspended lawyer for nine months and required petition for reinstatement for improper solicitation of homeowners to sue installers, builders, or manufacturers via lawyer's agent, the home inspector); *In re Broome*, 815 So.2d 1 (La. 2002) (suspension for one year and one day under Standard 7.2 was proper sanction for lawyer's direct solicitation of prospective clients who already were being represented by the Department of Justice in class-action lawsuit, and for making statements designed to mislead prospective clients into believing he was working with the Department of Justice; misconduct was knowing and intentional but caused no serious harm to a client, the public, or legal profession, and so disbarment not warranted); *Miss. Bar v. Turnage*, 919 So.2d 36 (Miss. 2005) (lawyer's solicitation of more than 100 prospective clients in insurance litigation warranted four-month suspension); *Cincinnati Bar Ass'n v. Rinderknecht*, 679 N.E.2d 669 (Ohio 1997) (court suspended lawyer indefinitely for organizing a program in conjunction with a business consultant and a doctor to monitor police scanners and call recent accident victims at home to secure legal and medical services; employees listening to scanners often arrived at the accident scene before police and other emergency personnel).

## *Excessive or Improper Fees*

Suspension can be appropriate when a lawyer charges an unreasonable, improper, or excessive fee. *See, e.g.*, *People v. Egbune*, 58 P.3d 1168, 1175 (Colo. O.P.D.J. 1999) (six-month suspension under Standard 7.2, inter alia, for lawyer whose misconduct included charging his client an unreasonable fee after taking over client's personal injury case from prior lawyer, mishandling funds claimed by the prior lawyer and failing to disclose information he was under a duty to disclose in order to conceal his misconduct; court held that the "misconduct in this case involves violations of duties to the profession and duties to a client and, consistent with precedent and the ABA *Standards*, requires a moderate period of suspension"); *In re Tun*, 26 A.3d 313 (D.C. 2011) (eighteen-month suspension for misconduct including lawyer's admitted "double billing," a practice in which he sought payment for the same time period from two or more clients on 162 occasions; does not cite Sanctions Standards); *Fla. Bar v. Parrish*, 241 So.3d 66 (Fla. 2018) (in addition to transactions constituting conflict of interest, lawyer took "prohibited fee" when he had client sign agreement giving lawyer's firm a security interest in client's Lamborghini to pay for current and future legal fees and giving firm right to sell car to pay those fees if client could not do so in ninety days for at least $30,000; citing Florida Standard 7.2, court suspended lawyer for three years); *In re Obert*, 282 P.3d 825, 844 (Or. 2012) (six-month suspension warranted under Standard 7.2, inter alia, for lawyer whose misconduct included knowingly collecting excessive fee, wrongfully depositing it into his business account, and failing to promptly refund the monies to client; "accused caused actual injury to his clients, the Bar, the legal system, and the legal profession"); *Sallee v. Bd. of Prof'l Responsibility*, 469 S.W.3d 18 (Tenn. 2015) (court found that lawyer charged excessive fee in wrongful death matter and improperly withheld items from clients after her services were terminated, including slides of deceased daughter's brain tissue, requiring clients to sue to get it back; citing Standards 7.0 and 7.2, court suspended lawyer for one year); *In re Disciplinary Proceeding Against Brothers*, 70 P.3d 940 (Wash. 2003) (one-year suspension under Standard 7.2 for consciously charging grossly unreasonable fee, i.e., one-third value of property lawyer transferred to trust, or $36,663, for preparing quitclaim deed, work for which lawyer normally charged $50, and lawyer had committed prior fee-related misconduct); *Bd. of Prof'l Responsibility v. Fulton*, 133 P.3d 514 (Wyo. 2006) (three-year suspension under Standard 7.2, inter alia, for lawyer who included billed paralegal time for legal services that should have been generally covered by the contingency percentage).

A lawyer's failure to perform promised work or to return unearned fees also falls within the category of cases warranting suspension under Standard 7.2. *See, e.g.*, *Fla. Bar v. Adorno*, 60 So.3d 1016, 1036 (Fla. 2011) (three-year suspension, instead of recommended public reprimand, for lawyer who misused class-action mechanism to leverage the City of Miami into a $7 million settlement on behalf of seven named plaintiffs while abandoning thousands of putative class members; lawyer also claimed $2 million fee for his law firm from the settlement, and obtained nondisclosure agreement with named plaintiffs for which the "only logical reason" was keeping settlement secret from other putative class members); *In re McPherson*, 196 P.3d 921 (Kan. 2008) (six-month suspension was appropriate sanction for lawyer whose misconduct included delaying for ten months the refund of unearned portion of a client's retainer); *In re Ramsey*, 951 So.2d 1077 (La. 2007) (lawyer suspended for one year and one day for six counts of misconduct involving failing to provide accountings and refund unearned fees to clients, failing to communicate with clients, and failing to refund an excessive fee, inter alia); *In re Slaughter*, 778 So.2d 1138 (La. 2001) (accepting consent petition for deferred six-month suspension for failure to account for and refund unearned fee to one client; relying upon Standard 7.2, inter alia); *In re Disciplinary Proceeding Against Preszler*, 232 P.3d 1118 (Wash. 2010) (three-year suspension under Standard 7.2 for lawyer who, inter alia, charged unreasonable fee for representing bankruptcy client in personal injury claim; lawyer did little work in case, charged one-third contingency fee even though case had already settled, and client suffered injury in that client was on tight budget and was in bankruptcy).

In some instances the fee itself might be reasonable, but the lawyer's billing or collection method was found to be objectionable. *See, e.g., People v. Mascarenas,* 103 P.3d 339 (Colo. O.P.D.J. 2003) (ninety-day suspension under Standard 7.2, inter alia, for lawyer who charged monthly compounded interest knowing he had not provided accounting and knowing client was unaware of either amount owed or interest accruing); *People v. Hassan,* 45 P.3d 1283 (Colo. O.P.D.J. 2002) (among other misconduct, respondent failed to issue written final disbursement statement; citing former commentary to Standard 7.2, court noted suspension is appropriate when the lawyer does not mislead a client but engages in a pattern of charging excessive or improper fees; eighteen-month suspension warranted); *In re Kraushaar,* 997 P.2d 81, 89–90 (Kan. 2000) (one-year suspension for county attorney who obtained reimbursement of personal expenses from public funds: "By asking the county to pay for personal expenses and pretending they were professional expenses, [respondent] violated a duty he owed as a professional. The duty is to be honest and maintain the integrity of his profession and public office. He caused injury to the public by misusing public money."); *In re Disciplinary Action Against Delorme,* 795 N.W.2d 293 (N.D. 2011) (citing North Dakota Standard 7.2 in finding thirty-day suspension appropriate for knowingly charging client an hourly rate of $175 after having agreed to $125 per hour, overbilling for mileage, and billing for more than twenty-four hours on a given day, for unnecessary tasks and for time in which no legal services were provided).

## *Unauthorized Practice of Law*

Continuing to represent clients while suspended is the unauthorized practice of law and under certain circumstances has been held to warrant suspension under Standard 7.2. *See, e.g., People v. Swarts,* 239 P.3d 441 (Colo. O.P.D.J. 2010) (three-month suspension under Standard 7.2, inter alia, for lawyer's unauthorized practice of law in representing his wife in criminal matter while administratively suspended for failing to comply with continuing legal education and lawyer registration requirements; disbarment may have been appropriate if lawyer had been practicing while suspended for disciplinary, as opposed to administrative, reasons); *In re Williams,* 842 So.2d 353 (La. 2003) (citing Standard 7.2, court imposed two-year suspension on already suspended lawyer for engaging in the unauthorized practice of law by twice appearing at and actively participating in depositions and failing to inform opposing counsel of his suspension); *In re Barker,* 351 P.3d 1256 (Kan. 2015) (citing hearing panel's thorough consideration of Standard 7.2, court indefinitely suspended lawyer for, among other misconduct, engaging in unauthorized practice of law and failing to respond to disciplinary authorities); *In re Koliha,* 9 P.3d 102 (Or. 2000) (one-year suspension under Standard 7.2, inter alia, for violating duty as a professional by representing a client in a circuit court proceeding during period of administrative suspension for failure to pay bar dues and failing to respond to inquiries from disciplinary authorities; lawyer did not have a disciplinary record). *But see In re Devers*, 974 P.2d 191 (Or. 1999) (lawyer under disciplinary suspension who negotiated terms of settlement and drafted settlement agreement engaged in unauthorized practice of law; misconduct implicated several Standards, including Standard 7.2, but court held disbarment under Standard 8.1 for continuing to practice law after suspension dispositive because of disciplinary record).

In some cases suspended lawyers are disciplined for engaging in the unauthorized practice of law by continuing to give the impression they are in good standing. *See, e.g., People v. Davies*, 883 P.2d 16 (Colo. 1994) (ninety-day suspension under Standard 7.2 for misrepresentation to judge regarding lawyer's suspension for non-payment of registration fees; lawyer's registration fee was not received until two days after lawyer responded affirmatively to judge's question about lawyer's licensure status); *Flowers v. Bd. of Prof'l Responsibility*, 314 S.W.3d 882 (Tenn. 2010) (citing Standard 7.2, court imposed one-year suspension for, inter alia, practicing law while suspended for failing to pay registration fee and comply with continuing education requirements, and not notifying clients and tribunals of administrative suspension).

Representing clients while not admitted to the bar of a given jurisdiction also may constitute the unauthorized practice of law and can lead to suspension. *See, e.g., In re Convisser*, 242 P.3d 299, 313 (N.M. 2010) (one-year deferred suspension and public reprimand for unauthorized practice of law by lawyer who, while on inactive status in Virginia, solicited client in New Mexico prior to licensure; citing Standards 7.2 and 7.3, the court rejected lawyer's argument that his newly reactivated Virginia license coupled with the expectation that he soon would be admitted in New Mexico created an exception, stating: "Moving from inactive to active status to practice law is not simply an empty formality, nor is the initial admission to practice law. If those formalities are to have any meaning, a lawyer must refrain from practicing law until he or she is clearly authorized to do so.").

## *Assisting in the Unauthorized Practice of Law*

Assisting nonlawyers or ineligible lawyers in the unauthorized practice of law is also a violation of a duty owed as a professional for which courts have imposed suspension under Standard 7.2. *See, e.g., People v. Reynolds*, 933 P.2d 1295 (Colo. 1997) (three-year suspension for numerous violations, including assisting nonlawyer in unauthorized practice of law); *People v. Stewart*, 892 P.2d 875 (Colo. 1995) (three-year suspension for, inter alia, aiding a nonlawyer in the unauthorized practice of law; client usually met first with lawyer's nonlawyer assistant and paid retainer to nonlawyer; suspension rather than disbarment due to mitigating factors, including that during the relevant time the respondent was suffering from depression and other physical and emotional problems); *In re Gaff*, 524 S.E.2d 728 (Ga. 2000) (one-year suspension appropriate for lawyer who employed disbarred lawyer as paralegal to work in lawyer's second law office without sufficient supervision, allowing disbarred lawyer to engage in the unauthorized practice of law, theft, and forgery); *In re Discipio*, 645 N.E.2d 906, 911 (Ill. 1994) (two-year suspension warranted for lawyer who divided legal fees with disbarred lawyer and allowed disbarred lawyer to meet with clients, gather information, and prepare pertinent documents in workers' compensation cases referred by the disbarred lawyer; the court reiterated that "[f]or a disbarred attorney to be seen performing what the public may perceive as legal functions can only lessen the public's regard for the effectiveness of our attempt to discipline errant attorneys, and would foment the belief that the public was not being protected from unethical attorneys") (citation omitted); *In re Roswold*, 249 P.3d 1199 (Kan. 2011) (one-year suspension under Standard 7.2, inter alia, for facilitating unauthorized practice by lawyer's former law partner; lawyer knew former partner was not admitted pro hac vice in case and allowed former partner to meet, advise, and represent client in lawsuit); *In re Goff*, 837 So.2d 1201 (La. 2003) (nine-month suspension for misconduct including failing to supervise nonlawyers, aiding in unauthorized practice of law, and facilitating runner-based solicitation scheme, though lawyer was neither originator nor active participant).

Some suspension cases falling under Standard 7.2 have involved lawyers' misconduct in connection with living trust schemes. *See People v. Cassidy*, 884 P.2d 309 (Colo. 1994) (six-month suspension for lawyer who allowed nonlawyer preparers and marketers of living trust packages to use his name and thereby aided in the unauthorized practice of law; lawyer also found to have engaged in unauthorized practice of law by preparing opinion letters while on inactive status attesting to validity of the living trusts sold by insurance company); *Disciplinary Counsel v. Kramer*, 866 N.E.2d 498 (Ohio 2007) (six-month suspension stayed on condition that lawyer commit no further misconduct found appropriate for lawyer who, in context of company's sale of insurance and living trusts, provided form letters and retainer agreements so company's agents could recommend his services to its customers and for aiding company's nonlawyer agents in unauthorized practice of law); *Cincinnati Bar Ass'n v. Heisler*, 866 N.E.2d 490 (Ohio 2007) (six-month suspension stayed on condition that lawyer commit no further misconduct held appropriate for aiding in unauthorized practice of law while affiliated with company selling estate-planning services including living trusts, and for sharing legal fees with nonlawyers); *In re Disciplinary Proceeding Against Shepard*, 239 P.3d 1066 (Wash. 2010) (two-year suspension for, inter alia, assisting a nonlawyer in the unauthorized practice of law; lawyer affiliated himself with nonlawyer who gave legal advice in connection with a living trust scam targeting senior citizens causing serious or potentially serious injury to his clients; while disbarment was presumptive sanction under Standard 7.1, suspension was imposed given lawyer's attempt to remediate the harm caused).

## *Failure to Supervise*

Lawyers also can be suspended under Standard 7.2 for failing to supervise nonlawyer as well as lawyer employees within a practice. *See, e.g.,; In re Phillips*, 244 P.3d 549 (Ariz. 2010) (citing Standard 7.2, court imposed six-month suspension for managing partner who knowingly failed to supervise firm employees, resulting in employees committing ethical breaches and violations of firm's policies and ethical rules); *In re Faucheux*, 818 So.2d 734 (La. 2002) (six-month suspension deferred and respondent placed on one-year of probation for inadequate supervision of nonlawyer employee resulting in forgery of client's name on settlement documents); *In re Wilkinson*, 805 So.2d 142, 146 (La. 2002) (sixty-day suspension for failure to supervise nonlawyer employee who mishandled succession matter, resulting in nearly $10,000 cost to client to redeem foreclosed property); *Att'y Grievance Comm'n v. Kimmel*, 955 A.2d 269 (Md. 2008) (violations of ethical rules requiring adequate supervision warranted ninety-day suspension when out-of-state partners in law firm had no disciplinary record; lawyers failed to supervise firm associate practicing in another state); *In re Discipline of Anderson*, 2016 WL 315270 (Nev. January 22, 2016) (because lawyer improperly supervised nonlawyer employee in loan modification matters, that individual was able to misappropriate funds; citing Standards 7.2 and 4.12 and taking into account lawyer's gambling addiction, court imposed eighteen-month stayed suspension with probation); *Mahoning Cty. Bar Ass'n v. Lavelle*, 836 N.E.2d 1214 (Ohio 2005) (lawyer's misconduct, including failure to supervise nonlawyers in his law office, warranted eighteen-month suspension with twelve months of suspension conditionally stayed if lawyer complied with terms imposed by monitor appointed by county bar association).

## *Failure to Report Professional Misconduct*

Standard 7.0 includes sanctions for failure to report professional misconduct as a violation of a lawyer's duty owed as a professional. Although courts have imposed suspensions on lawyers for such failures, Standard 7.2 is rarely cited. In *In re Brigandi*, 843 So.2d 1083, 1988–89 (La. 2003), the court imposed a two-year suspension with all but six months deferred on a contract lawyer who, inter alia, failed to report his employer's operation of runner-based solicitation scheme at the law office. The court said:

> Attorneys are often in the best position to witness the systemic harm to the legal profession from organized schemes of misconduct, such as

> solicitation, which might not be readily apparent to the general public. As a result, our professional rules impose an obligation on all members of the bar to report any misconduct they become aware of in the course of their practice. An attorney's failure to do so must be viewed as a serious offense.

*Id.* at 1088–89. *See also In re Dowd*, 160 A.D.2d 78 (N.Y. App. Div. 1990) (five-year suspension for lawyers, shareholders in a collection agency, for paying kickbacks and failing to report kickback demands made by city official); *Lisi v. Several Att'ys*, 596 A.2d 313 (R.I. 1991) (in consolidated case, court imposed a sanction of suspension on four lawyers (others were publicly censured) for, inter alia, making loans to judge and failing to report judge's misconduct in soliciting the loans); *cf. In re Tomar, Simonoff, Adourian, O'Brien, Kaplan, Jacoby & Graziano*, PC, 953 A.2d 1201 (N.J. 2008) (suspensions ranging from six months to one year for significant pattern of misconduct committed by several lawyers in a defunct firm, including failure to report another's professional misconduct; but suspensions suspended in favor of probation due to delays in disciplinary proceedings and mitigating factors).

### *Failure to Self-Report*

Ethics opinions from the American Bar Association and other issuing entities generally agree that self-reporting of misconduct may not be required for various reasons, including the privilege against self-incrimination. *See generally* Model Rules of Prof'l Conduct Ann. R. 8.3 (2011), Reporting Professional Misconduct. Yet courts occasionally will cite the Sanctions Standards in imposing discipline for failure to report one's own professional misconduct. *See, e.g., People v. Goode*, 423 P.3d 407 (Colo. O.P.D.J. 2018) (lawyer who failed to self-report twenty-eight felony convictions for torturing dogs and cats suspended for two years with court citing Standards 5.12 and 7.2); *In re Gaudet*, 922 So.2d 477 (La. 2006) (failure to report lawyer's own misconduct listed as violation of duties as a professional; citing Sanctions Standards, generally, in suspending lawyer for six months, with three months deferred, for this and other violations); *In re Yeager*, 863 So.2d 495 (La. 2003) (finding lawyer violated duties as professional, court accepted consent discipline for three-year suspension for, inter alia, failure to self-report professional misconduct arising from criminal charges; Sanctions Standards not cited); *cf. In re Stewart*, 342 S.W.3d 307 (Mo. 2011) (indefinite suspension warranted for lawyer's four separate convictions for DUI; considering in aggravation lawyer's failure to self-report said conduct when he was admonished in an earlier disciplinary action; decision cites the Sanctions Standards, but not Standards 7.0 or 7.2 specifically).

## *Improper Withdrawal from Representation*

Suspension under Standard 7.2 can be imposed for improper withdrawal from representation. *See, e.g., People v. Spurlock,* 2017 WL 3587547 (Colo. O.P.D.J. June 22, 2017) (lawyer who abandoned client and ignored multiple requests from successor counsel and court order directing him to return client files suspended for one year and one day; court cited to Standard 7.0 instead of 7.2 in finding a suspension the presumptive sanction); *In re Herrington,* 222 P.3d 492 (Kan. 2010) (indefinite suspension under Standard 7.2, inter alia, for abandoning client without notice); *In re Rumsey,* 71 P.3d 1150 (Kan. 2003) (one-year suspension under Standard 7.2, inter alia, for failing to inform client in writing that she did not have a case and failing to withdraw from representation so that client could seek other counsel before statute of limitations expired, and also for filing a petition against another client knowing that he had not withdrawn from representing her in a divorce).

Some courts imposing suspension for improper withdrawal have relied upon the Sanctions Standards generally, without citing Standard 7.2, or do not cite the Standards at all. *See, e.g., In re Kehoe,* 678 N.E.2d 394 (Ind. 1997) (ninety-day suspension for failing to surrender estate papers and refund unearned fees; citing Sanctions Standards, but not Standard 7.2 specifically); *In re Pitschke,* 627 N.E.2d 440 (Ind. 1994) (sixty-day suspension for failing to withdraw from divorce case after being discharged and attempting to appear at hearing after client wrote letter stating lawyer should withdraw; citing Sanctions Standards, but not Standard 7.2 specifically); *In re Gaston,* 65 So.3d 1239, 1246 (La. 2011) (six-month deferred suspension for, inter alia, lawyer's knowing misconduct in failing to complete agreed-upon work in client's divorce and failing to return unearned fee upon termination of representation: "Respondent knowingly violated duties owed to her clients and the legal profession, and her conduct caused harm to her clients. Under the ABA's *Standards for Imposing Lawyer Sanctions,* suspension is the baseline sanction for this type of knowing misconduct."); *In re Disciplinary Proceeding Against Lopez,* 106 P.3d 221 (Wash. 2005) (sixty-day suspension for misconduct including failure to take reasonably practicable steps to protect client's interests upon termination of representation). *But see People v. Roberts,* 241 P.3d 555, 559 (Colo. O.P.D.J. 2010) (lawyer's failure to return clients' file or arbitration fee when lawyer's noncommunication and neglect of their case had effectively terminated the client-lawyer relationship fell under Standard 7.2, but disbarment warranted given totality of the misconduct, including conversion of client funds).

## *Failure to Cooperate with Disciplinary Authorities*

The failure to cooperate with disciplinary authorities can subject a lawyer to suspension under Standard 7.2. As is the case generally, such suspensions may be imposed in conjunction with underlying infractions involving other ethics rules and their relevant Sanctions Standards. Courts often factor in aggravating and mitigating circumstances in imposing suspensions under Standard 7.2 that run from fully deferred or stayed suspensions to indefinite suspensions. *See, e.g.*, *In re Riddle*, 857 P.2d 1233, 1235–36 (Ariz. 1993) (eighteen-month suspension under Standard 7.2, inter alia, for lawyer who violated duty to maintain integrity of the profession; "[r]espondent's failure to cooperate with the self-regulating disciplinary system of the legal profession violated one of his most fundamental duties as a professional"); *People v. Swarts*, 239 P.3d 441 (Colo. O.P.D.J. 2010) (three-month suspension under Standard 7.2, inter alia, for misconduct that included lawyer's failure to answer disciplinary complaint or otherwise participate in disciplinary proceedings); *People v. Hassan*, 45 P.3d 1283, 1293 (Colo. O.P.D.J. 2002) (eighteen-month suspension under Standard 7.2, inter alia, for submitting false documents to regulation counsel and technical conversion of client funds; "[r]espondent's submission of an agreement and settlement statements to the Office of Attorney Regulation Counsel created for the purpose of attempting to explain his negligent misappropriation of client funds is serious misconduct, justifying a suspension"); *In re Gentry*, 227 P.3d 956 (Kan. 2010) (indefinite suspension pursuant to Standard 7.2 for lawyer whose knowing misconduct included failing to provide written responses to both initial and formal complaints in disciplinary investigation); *In re Corrin*, 184 P.3d 923 (Kan. 2008) (lawyer's lack of cooperation and communication with the disciplinary administrator's audit of client trust account, performed following investigation into failure to distribute client's settlement proceeds, warranted indefinite suspension under Standard 7.2, inter alia; court found evidence existed to conclude that respondent "knowingly" violated ethics rule in connection with his continued lack of cooperation with the disciplinary administrator's audit of respondent's client trust account); *In re Whitehead*, 816 So.2d 284, 288 (La. 2002) (one-year suspension with six months deferred under Standard 7.2, inter alia, for lawyer's failure to cooperate in two disciplinary investigations as well as failure to pursue three client matters, communicate with clients, and refund unearned fees; "disciplinary system was harmed by respondent's consistent failure to cooperate, requiring the [disciplinary counsel] to undergo the extra expense and time of issuing subpoenas to compel a response"); *In re Montez*, 812 N.W.2d 58 (Minn. 2012) (two-year suspension for lawyer's misconduct including making false statements to Director of the Office of Lawyers Professional Responsibility and failing to cooperate in disciplinary investigation); *In re Edinger*, 700 N.W.2d 462, 468 (Minn. 2005) (indefinite suspension for misconduct including concealing misuse of client trust account: "It is imperative that a lawyer fully cooperate with the Director's inquiries on trust account overdrafts and timely and truthfully respond to any ensuing disciplinary investigation. Failure to cooperate with the disciplinary process is a serious violation and itself warrants discipline, including suspension."); *In re Wyllie*, 952 P.2d 550 (Or. 1998) (one-year suspension under

Standard 7.2, inter alia, for alcoholic lawyer who failed to cooperate with lawyer's assistance committee and thus violated duty as a professional); *In re Schaffner*, 918 P.2d 803, 807 n.6 (Or. 1996) (suspension of 120 days under Standard 7.2, inter alia, for failure to cooperate with bar's investigation; "duty to respond to investigatory inquiries from the Bar is owed to the profession"); *In re McCoy-Jacien*, 186 A.3d 626 (Vt. 2018) (lawyer violated terms of probation by failing to file taxes and failing to respond to numerous requests from disciplinary counsel, the probation monitor, seeking to determine if taxes had been filed; finding that failure to respond to regulator's inquiries constituted a violation of duty to the legal profession, the court, citing Standard 7.2, suspended lawyer for nine months); *In re Disciplinary Proceedings Against Boyle*, 813 N.W.2d 215 (Wis. 2012) (sixty-day suspension for, inter alia, lack of diligence in client matter and failure to cooperate during disciplinary investigation; Sanctions Standards not cited).

### *False Statements and Dishonesty*

Courts have imposed suspensions under Standard 7.2 for lawyers making false statements and engaging in dishonest conduct during the course of a representation or court proceedings. *See, e.g., In re Lyons*, 2016 WL 7048434 (Ariz. O.P.D.J April 6, 2016) (lawyer who knowingly made false statements to courts and disciplinary authorities claiming she suffered from a variety of illnesses and injuries, including cervical cancer, suspended for three years; court, referring to Standard 7.2 and lawyer's refusal to provide disciplinary authorities with requested documentation about the cervical cancer, found that the lawyer "was using this horrific, and apparently fraudulent, diagnosis to garner sympathy and inappropriate delays . . ."); *Fla. Bar v. Berthiaume*, 78 So.3d 503, 510 (Fla. 2011) (ninety-one-day suspension under Florida Standard 7.2 for lawyer's abuse of court's subpoena power in signing and serving without legal authority a fraudulent subpoena directing bank to produce client's financial records; court noted: "Respondent has engaged in serious misconduct—she abused the subpoena power, which is a power of the court, for her personal investigation. Such dishonest conduct demonstrates the utmost disrespect for the court and is destructive to the legal system as a whole."); *In re Lund*, 19 P.3d 110 (Kan. 2001) (suspension for one year under Standard 7.2, inter alia, for depositing personal funds into client trust account, using the account to pay personal expenses, and misrepresenting to court trustee that account held only client trust funds so that lawyer could avoid garnishment of account); *In re Bordelon*, 894 So.2d 315 (La. 2005) (baseline sanction is suspension under Standard 7.2 when lawyer intentionally concealed status of promissory note during disciplinary process; sixty-day suspension given lawyer's otherwise spotless disciplinary record).

Lawyers also have been disciplined under Standard 7.2 for deceitful conduct toward their law firms. *See, e.g., Fla. Bar v. Winters*, 104 So.3d 299 (Fla. 2012) (citing Florida Standard 7.2, inter alia, court imposed sixty-day suspension for one associate and ninety-one days for another for deceitful conduct in copying and maintaining possession of client files for their personal use without firm's permission); *Fla. Bar v. Kossow*, 912 So.2d 544, 548 (Fla. 2005) (consistent with Florida Standard 7.2, thirty-day suspension for lawyer who continued representing clients outside of the law firm where he was employed and accepting new clients for benefit of his private law practice, despite knowledge of his law firm's policy against outside employment: "Without question, [respondent] intentionally violated his professional duty to the firm, and his misappropriation of firm time and resources harmed the firm. We caution that in the future, the discipline imposed may be harsher for attorneys who represent outside clients in violation of firm policy, misuse their firms' resources to represent those clients, and act dishonestly by failing to disclose those clients to their firms."); *In re Cupples*, 979 S.W.2d 932 (Mo. 1998) (imposing an indefinite suspension under Standard 7.2 for secretly maintaining a separate law practice while engaged in full-time practice with law firm, and using firm assets to represent private clients, court found lawyer's dealings with his employer-law firm dishonest and deceitful); *In re Busby*, 855 P.2d 156 (Or. 1993) (four-month suspension under Standard 7.2, inter alia, for lawyer in "of counsel" capacity making misrepresentations to office administrator of law firm relating to income that was being withheld from firm, resulting in the respondent receiving more fees than he was entitled to receive).

### *Omissions and Misrepresentations in Bar Admission Applications*

Courts will suspend lawyers who have knowingly omitted, misrepresented, or otherwise been dishonest in providing required information on their bar applications. *See, e.g.*, *In re Scott*, 19 A.3d 774 (D.C. 2011) (three-year suspension with reinstatement conditioned on demonstration of fitness to practice for lawyer found to have made false statements in connection with her application for admission to the District of Columbia Bar and who was disciplined in another state for professional misconduct; sanction reflected appropriate discipline for lawyer's misconduct involving dishonesty with aggravating factors, with an enhancement for misconduct committed in other state); *In re Rodriguez*, 753 N.E.2d 1289 (Ind. 2001) (ninety-day suspension for failure to disclose on bar application attendance at two colleges, academic dismissal from both, and a semester suspension from one); *In re Conn*, 715 N.E.2d 379 (Ind. 1999) (two-year suspension for failure to amend bar application to reflect federal investigation regarding child pornography and post-bar admission conviction of sexual exploitation of minors based upon the results of that investigation); *In re O'Neill*, 172 P.3d 1179 (Kan. 2007) (indefinite suspension under Standard 7.2, inter alia, for lawyer's failure to disclose five arrests or convictions on application for admission to the Kansas bar); *Att'y Grievance Comm'n v.*

*Thomas-Bellamy*, 149 A.3d 601 (Md. 2016) (indefinite suspension imposed in reciprocal disciplinary case where lawyer was suspended by the D.C. Court of Appeals for one year with reinstatement conditioned on showing of fitness after lawyer found to have made purposeful misrepresentation in supplemental submission as part of D.C. bar application; Sanctions Standards not cited); *In re Moore*, 812 N.E.2d 1197 (Mass. 2004) (two-year suspension for omitting on bar application information that might reveal lawyer's resignation from Connecticut bar and charges of sexual harassment against lawyer); *In re Finn*, 742 N.E.2d 1075 (Mass. 2001) (three-month suspension for misrepresentations on Georgia bar application regarding student loans and default judgment); *In re Fauci*, 28 A.D.3d 192 (N.Y. App. Div. 2006) (finding that the character of two lawyers, brothers, was called into serious question, the court suspended one lawyer for three years for, among other violations, falsely notarizing his own bar application by signing his brother's name and suspended the other lawyer for eighteen months for, among other misconduct, offering false testimony regarding his brother's bar application).

### *Other Misconduct*

Courts impose suspensions under Standard 7.2 for various other kinds of misconduct that violates a lawyer's duty owed as a professional. These violations are as divergent as the mishandling of cases to false notarization of documents. *See*, e.g., *In re Leblanc*, 972 So.2d 315 (La. 2007) (one-year-and-one-day suspension under Standard 7.2 for lawyer who knowingly assisted a judge in violating judicial conduct rules and campaign finance laws when he gave judge $800 cash as contribution to legislative campaign of judge's niece solicited by the judge several months after he had entered a $1.5 million judgment in favor of lawyer's client); *In re Young*, 849 So.2d 25 (La. 2003) (six-month suspension under Standard 7.2, inter alia, for mishandling two criminal matters; in one matter, lawyer refused to proceed with trial because he believed defendant was guilty, and in the other representation, he filed motions as delay tactic; court found lawyer's conduct caused actual harm to administration of justice and created potential harm to clients' interests); *In re Ganley*, 549 N.W.2d 368 (Minn. 1996) (six-month suspension for misconduct that included violating duty to profession by falsely notarizing client's affidavit and altering affidavit, without sending copy of changes to client, and submitting altered document to court).

Abuse of the professional relationship, such as when a lawyer engages in sexual relations with a client during the course of representation, is also a violation for which lawyers have been suspended under Standard 7.2. *See, e.g., People v. Easley*, 956 P.2d 1257, 1259 (Colo. 1998) (sixty-day suspension for lawyer who, inter alia, engaged in sexual relationship with client who was plaintiff in sexual harassment lawsuit; court reiterated "that a sexual relationship between lawyer and client during the course of the professional relationship is inherently and insidiously harmful") (citation omitted); *People v. Riddle*, 35 P.3d 146 (Colo. O.P.D.J. 1999) (thirty-day suspension, under Standard 7.2, for engaging in consensual sexual relationship with client during course of representing her in divorce proceedings; client was also an experienced lawyer, affair occurred when case was on appeal, and respondent incorrectly believed representation was at an end and behavior was not predatory); *In re Depew*, 237 P.3d 24 (Kan. 2010) (one-year suspension for lawyer who engaged in a pattern of inappropriate sexual conduct with five court administrative assistants, including while serving as a pro tem judge; court cited Standard 7.2 in finding suspension appropriate for his knowing and intentional misconduct and the actual injury caused to both the administrative assistants and the administration of justice in the district court).

Standard 7.2 also is mentioned when courts cite to other Standards in cases involving multiple acts of misconduct. *See, e.g., In re Lopez*, 252 P.3d 312 (Or. 2011) (nine-month suspension in reciprocal discipline action related to acts of misconduct in seven client matters, including engaging in misleading advertising, mishandling client property and legal matters, failing to communicate with clients, and improperly handling client settlements and collection of fees; citing Standard 7.2, inter alia, in finding suspension appropriate given that majority of lawyer's misconduct was committed knowingly); *In re Disciplinary Proceeding Against Poole*, 193 P.3d 1064 (Wash. 2008) (one-year suspension and probation for lawyer who failed to provide bar association with requested billing records; court noted Standard 7.2, inter alia, was properly applied by hearing officer); *In re Disciplinary Proceeding Against DeRuiz*, 99 P.3d 881 (Wash. 2004) (two consecutive six-month suspensions along with law practice management counseling proper under Standard 7.2 for conduct including neglect of cases, failure to communicate with clients, failure to refund fees, and failure to cooperate with disciplinary investigation).

**7.3 Reprimand is generally appropriate when a lawyer negligently engages in conduct that is a violation of a duty owed as a professional, and causes injury or potential injury to a client, the public, or the legal system.**

## Annotation

Reprimand or censure is the appropriate sanction in cases where a lawyer negligently violates her duties owed as a professional and the misconduct causes little or no injury to a client, the public, or the legal system. In these cases, courts have found that the imposition of this lesser, but public sanction best serves to protect the public. A public sanction also informs both the public and other members of the profession that certain acts are improper under the professional conduct rules. *See, e.g., In re Comfort*, 159 P.3d 1011 (Kan. 2007) (public censure appropriate for lawyer who published to various members of the community an indignant letter he wrote to another lawyer who had made an open records request to his client; court adopted hearing panel's conclusion that, by *publishing* the letter, lawyer served no substantial purpose other than to embarrass the lawyer who had made the request); *In re Disciplinary Action Against Mertz*, 712 N.W.2d 849 (N.D.2006) (rejecting recommended one-month suspension, court imposed public reprimand under Standard 7.3, for lawyer's inappropriate statements in letter sent to individual who filed a vicious-animal-at-large complaint against lawyer's daughter after being bitten by daughter's dog); *In re Dickey*, 722 S.E.2d 522 (S.C. 2012) (reprimand warranted for lawyer's Internet websites and profiles containing material misrepresentations and statements creating unjustified expectations); *Bd. of Prof'l Responsibility v. Curry*, 266 S.W.3d 379 (Tenn. 2008) (public censure warranted under Standard 7.3, inter alia, for unauthorized endorsement on settlement check of third payee who had no legal interest in the proceeds); *In re Pless*, No. 12#00117 (Wash. 2013) *available at* http://mcle.mywsba.org/DisciplineFiles/1748/0081.pdf (reprimand under Standard 7.13, inter alia, warranted for former assistant law school dean who failed to have proper procedures in place to ensure accuracy of reporting student LSAT and grade point average scores).

## *Mens Rea*

A reprimand is appropriate under Standard 7.3 when a lawyer's mental state at the time of the misconduct is negligent, as opposed to intentional or knowing. *See, e.g., People v. Peters*, 82 P.3d 389 (Colo. O.P.D.J. 2003) (public censure under Standard 7.3 for two lawyers who were negligent in execution of pre-signed affidavits when process server was not present); *In re Elgart*, 999 A.2d 853 (Del. 2010) (Standard 7.3, inter alia, and case law support sanction of public reprimand for lawyer who served as successor attorney representing personal injury client and negligently failed to distribute insurance proceeds to client for approximately seven years after proceeds were received by law firm and failed to make disclosures to disciplinary counsel); *Fla. Bar v. Williams-Yulee*, 138 So.3d 379 (Fla. 2014) (public reprimand for personal solicitation of campaign contributions in judicial election based upon misinterpretation of Code of Judicial Conduct, rendering conduct negligent, not intentional); *Fla. Bar v. Silver*, 788 So.2d 958 (Fla. 2001) (public reprimand under Florida Standard 7.3 for unintentional failure to notify health-care providers of receipt of funds and final settlement after instituting personal injury lawsuit on behalf of client and violating rule requiring safekeeping of property). *But see Matter of Member of Bar Hurley*, 183 A.3d 703 (Table) (Del. 2018) (in unpublished decision court accepted board's recommendation of public reprimand with conditions even though it disagreed with board's finding that misconduct was negligent, not knowing, in regard to demeaning correspondence to opposing lawyers; court suggested that it would have considered a more severe sanction had the board recommended one); *In re Roth*, 7 P.3d 241 (Kan. 2000) (Kansas Supreme Court imposed public censure under Standard 7.3 even though finding that lawyer intentionally obtained and recorded frivolous mortgages in favor of his law firm on property devised to heirs, and intentionally provided false information to hearing panel); *In re Warren*, 704 A.2d 789, 790 (Vt. 1997), is a case in which a lawyer received a public reprimand even though the court found knowing conduct on his part. The lawyer's wife had filed for divorce and was living with another man. The lawyer sent an initial letter to that man's wife informing her that their spouses were living together and offering to help her "at no cost to you but at great expense to him." He wrote her a second letter and a third, in which he then identified himself as a lawyer who could help because he specialized in domestic relations law. Rather than respond to the lawyer, the woman filed a disciplinary complaint. The court ruled that the lawyer knew when he sent the letters that his offer to represent the woman violated ethics rules, especially because he had specifically attempted to conceal his conduct; injury was avoided only because the woman decided to file a complaint instead of following up on the lawyer's advice, the court noted in imposing a public reprimand based on his misconduct, his prior disciplinary record, and his refusal to acknowledge the wrongful nature of his actions.

## *Injury*

A Standard 7.3 analysis includes the component of an injury to a client, the public or the legal system, whether actual and potential in nature. Misconduct can result in significant actual or potential injury even when a lawyer's mental state is merely negligent. Standard 7.3 does not specify whether the potential or actual injury must be significant or of lesser impact. *See In re Augenstein*, 870 P.2d 399 (Ariz. 1994) (citing Standard 7.3 and imposing public censure, court stated that lawyer's failure to respond to numerous letters from the state bar was a breach of his duty to maintain the integrity of the profession, causing injury or potential injury to a client, the public, or the legal system); *People v. Eamick*, 168 P.3d 519, 524 (Colo. O.P.D.J. 2007) (public reprimand under Standard 7.3 warranted for lawyer who refused to pay for deposition transcript he ordered on client's behalf; court finding that misconduct caused financial harm to the client and "potential injury to the good standing of lawyers who rely on the services provided by court reporters"); *In re Doughty*, 832 A.2d 724 (Del. 2003) (disagreeing with the disciplinary board's conclusion that the potential for harm was minimal, the court determined that, under Standard 7.3 a public reprimand and two-year period of probation was warranted for lawyer who failed to maintain books and records, falsely certified to court that books and records were being maintained in compliance with Delaware law, and that all tax obligations were being met); *In re Comfort*, 159 P.3d 1011 (Kan. 2007) (court found that lawyer caused actual harm to another lawyer when a client terminated him after the respondent published to various members of the community an indignant letter he had sent to the lawyer); *In re Fink*, 22 A.3d 461, 487 (Vt. 2011) (lawyer's failure to put contingent fee in writing and charging an unreasonable fee caused potential injury to the client had lawyer been able to collect the fee and not dismissed from the case, as well as actual injury to the public and the legal profession "because lack of written contingent agreements and excessive fees feed public distrust of lawyers and decrease public confidence in the profession").

## *Solicitation of Legal Employment*

Solicitation of legal employment usually involves an intentional or knowing mental state and thus falls under Standards 7.1 or 7.2. However, a public reprimand or censure can result from conduct involving the solicitation of legal employment if the lawyer behaves negligently. *See, e.g., In re Schmidt*, 976 So.2d 1267 (La. 2008) (reciprocal discipline of public reprimand appropriate for lawyer who opened law office in South Carolina following train derailment and solicited clients with advertisements and letters containing misleading statements); *In re Anis*, 599 A.2d 1265 (N.J. 1992) (public reprimand warranted for lawyer who sent solicitation letter containing incorrect statements, including that attorney's fees would be one-third of recovery contrary to statutory graduated fee provisions); *In re Singleton*, 719 S.E.2d 667 (S.C. 2011) (public reprimand for, inter alia, lawyer's admitted misconduct in failing to file a copy of a direct solicitation letter sent to a prospective client facing criminal drug charges and with whom lawyer had no prior relationship; decision does not cite Sanctions Standards).

## *Excessive, Improper, or Uncommunicated Fees*

Courts typically impose reprimands or censures when lawyers engage in a single instance of charging an excessive or improper fee. For example, in *In re Green*, 11

P.3d 1078 (Colo. 2000), the Colorado Supreme Court found that public censure was warranted under Standard 7.3 for a single instance of a lawyer charging $69,000 for successfully handling the appeal of a $7,400 judgment. Although the lawyer's hourly rate of $165 was found to be reasonable, the court determined that charging a lawyer's hourly rate for "clerical services," such as faxing documents, making telephone calls to clerk's office, and delivering documents to opposing counsel is "unreasonable as a matter of law." *Id.* at 1088. Further, the court found the unreasonable fees included charging excessive time for some legal work, such as six hours billed ($990) for reviewing and faxing the court of appeals' twelve-page opinion. *See also People v. Dalton*, 367 P.3d 126 (Colo. O.P.D.J. 2016) (public censure under Standard 7.3 for failure to put fee agreement in writing as required by Colorado Rules of Professional Conduct); *People v. Feather*, 180 P.3d 437 (Colo. O.P.D.J. 2007) (public censure under Standard 7.3 warranted for lawyer who acted negligently in charging an unreasonable contingent fee when he claimed a perpetual one-third interest in monthly payments made to client from oil and gas royalties as a result of judgment obtained by lawyer against client's ex-husband for child support); *Fla. Bar v. Kavanaugh*, 915 So.2d 89, 94 (Fla. 2005) (referee's recommended sanction of public reprimand for lawyer's action in charging clearly excessive fee in violation of disciplinary rule had reasonable basis in existing case law and in Florida Standard 7.3; court noted that "[w]hile we have declined the Bar's invitation to invoke a greater sanction, we nevertheless caution that lawyers who charge excessive fees are guilty of serious ethical breaches that diminish public confidence in the legal profession"); *In re Hellerud*, 714 N.W.2d 38 (N.D. 2006) (citing Standard 7.3, inter alia, the court imposed a public reprimand for lawyer who negligently charged an excessive fee, including charging legal assistant's time without client approval and no mention of such charge in retainer agreement); *In re Paulson*, 71 P.3d 60, 61 (Or. 2003) (public reprimand for billing a client $67.50 for time spent responding to client's complaint to the bar against the lawyer; "In other words, the accused billed [client] for a fee that she had no obligation to pay. Without such an obligation, the fee is clearly excessive"; court referencing Standard 7.0 generally and that lawyer's conduct was negligent); *In re Light*, 615 N.W.2d 164 (S.D. 2000) (public censure under Standard 7.3, inter alia, for failing to advise client of change in terms of contingency fee agreement from percentage of net recovery to gross recovery, such that lawyer received additional $8,900); *In re Fink*, 22 A.3d 461 (Vt. 2011) (public reprimand under Standard 7.3 for lawyer's unreasonable yet isolated instance of attempting to charge a 12 percent contingent fee for facilitating communication with client's out-of-state counsel); *In re Sinnott*, 845 A.2d 373, 378 (Vt. 2004) (public reprimand under Standard 7.3 for negligently engaging in single violation of professional duty consisting of performing an estimated three to four hours of automated or routine tasks that did nothing to advance client's goals, yet charged unreasonable fee of $1,200 to client based on boilerplate agreement; the court found that "clear and convincing evidence in the record supports the panel's conclusion that the fee calculation had nothing to do with work performed and that the work performed was of no value to the client"); *In re Disciplinary Proceedings Against Phillips*, 825 N.W.2d 470 (Wis. 2012) (public reprimand warranted for lawyer who charged an unreasonable fee when he failed to return unearned fees advanced by client's parents); *Board of Prof'l Responsibility v. Allred*, 378 P.3d 594 (Wyo. 2016) (public censure for failing to exercise professional judgment in regard to billing; lawyer should have written off unproductive, excessive, and redundant hours charged to client); *Bd. of Prof'l Responsibility v. Asay*, 374 P.3d 295 (Wyo. 2016) (public censure under Standard 7.3, inter alia, for failure to disclose hourly fee or how costs were to be paid, failure to communicate with client regarding fees or to take into consideration client's financial condition, and failure to produce written contingency fee agreement). *But see In re Proceeding Against Egger*, 98 P.3d 477, 487 (Wash. 2004) (in imposing six-month suspension, court reiterated that "Standard 7.2, rather than Standard 7.3 [applies] in cases involving single instances of excessive billing when the attorney acted knowingly").

A single instance of a lawyer failing to return unearned fees also may warrant a public reprimand under Standard 7.3. *See, e.g., In re Thurston*, 371 P.3d 879 (Kan. 2016) (after withdrawing from matter and failing to provide client with accounting of advance fee paid, lawyer who did not return unearned portion of fee publicly censured); Bd. of Prof'l Responsibility v. Hiatt, 382. P.3d 778 (Wyo. 2016) (public censure for failure to return unearned portion of fee to client and failing to cooperate regarding transfer of file to replacement counsel).

## *Unauthorized Practice of Law*

A lawyer who negligently engages in the unauthorized practice of law may be sanctioned under Standard 7.3. *See, e.g., In re Lee*, 198 P.3d 140 (Kan. 2008) (citing Standard 7.3, inter alia, court imposed public censure for lawyer who practiced law while his license was suspended for failure to comply with annual registration requirements); *In re Convisser*, 242 P.3d 299 (N.M. 2010) (public reprimand and one-year deferred suspension for lawyer's isolated instance of engaging in the unauthorized practice of law; finding both Standards 7.2 and 7.3 appropriate in determining sanction for lawyer who, while on inactive status in another state, had passed the New Mexico bar exam, had not been formally admitted when the representation in New Mexico began and had not secured local counsel); *Bd. of Prof'l Responsibility v. Brimley*, 344 P.3d 259 (Wyo. 2015) (public censure for lawyer licensed in Utah but not Wyoming who filed appearances in Wyoming Circuit Court on behalf of four defendants charged with motor vehicle violations).

## *Assisting in the Unauthorized Practice of Law*

Courts have found that lawyers aid in the unauthorized practice of law, warranting reprimand or censure under Standard 7.3, when they negligently fail to supervise nonlawyers who engage in activities constituting the practice of law. *See In re Juhnke*, 41 P.3d 855 (Kan. 2002) (public censure, under Standard 7.3, rather than recommended unpublished censure, warranted for lawyer who failed to properly supervise disbarred lawyer employed as law clerk, allowing disbarred lawyer to engage in the unauthorized practice of law); *In re Davis*, 123 A.D.3d 155, 156 (N.Y. App. Div. 2014) (reciprocal discipline of public censure for unknowingly "permitting . . . nonattorney to use . . . username and/or password to electronically file involuntary bankruptcy petitions"; Sanctions Standards not cited); *In re Grossman*, 91 A.D.3d 156 (N.Y. App. Div. 2011) (public censure for lawyer who assisted in unauthorized practice of law when, after becoming aware that nonlawyer had mailed out letters on his letterhead and bearing his purported signature in matters in which lawyer had been retained, did not advise the court or the other parties that he was unaware of, and had not authorized these letters; Sanctions Standards not cited); *Disciplinary Counsel v. Willis*, 772 N.E.2d 625 (Ohio 2002) (public reprimand warranted for lawyer who permitted employee, a disbarred lawyer, to act as if he were licensed during depositions, at a pretrial conference, and with clients); *In re Boyce*, 613 S.E.2d 538, 540 (S.C. 2005) (lawyer who did not prepare closing documents or perform title exam and participated in "witness only" real estate closing when no other state licensed lawyer was involved "has the effect of assisting in the unauthorized practice of law," warranting public reprimand; Sanction Standards not cited).

Another scenario in which courts have imposed public reprimands under Standard 7.3 involves lawyers who associate with out-of-state lawyers performing in-state legal services without obtaining the requisite authorization. *See, e.g., People v. Robinson*, 803 P.2d 474, 478 (Colo. 1990) (public censure for lawyer whose misconduct included assisting in unauthorized practice by failing to request that out-of-state lawyer appearing for firm on behalf of clients be specially admitted; court noting that "[i]ndeed, if any of the respondent's clients had suffered demonstrable injury by reason of his misconduct, we would impose an even more severe sanction than the recommended public censure"); *In re Lerner*, 197 P.3d 1067, 1078 (Nev. 2008) (public reprimand under Standard 7.3 for lawyer's assistance in unauthorized practice by out-of-state lawyer who performed legal activities constituting a regular or repetitive course of business and were not incidental to out-of-state lawyer's representation of out-of-state clients; court observed: "Here, [respondent] violated a duty to the public and to the profession to refrain from assisting in the unauthorized practice of law, and he did so knowingly. But the record does not indicate that any harm was suffered by the firm's clients, and evidence of potential harm is at most speculative."); *Disciplinary Counsel v. Pavlik*, 732 N.E.2d 985 (Ohio 2000) (public reprimand appropriate sanction for Ohio lawyer who, through neglect or omission, aided in unauthorized practice of law by an out-of-state lawyer not admitted in Ohio who was hired by law firm to act as business broker and financial consultant for corporate clients; lawyer failed to disclose to clients out-of-state lawyer's limited authority and failed to take steps to assure that out-of-state lawyer did not exceed that authority).

Disciplinary cases involving lawyers who work with companies to market living trusts have resulted in public censure rather than suspension because of mitigating factors. *See, e.g.*, *People v. Laden*, 893 P.2d 771 (Colo. 1995) (approving conditional admission and recommendation of public censure for aiding in the unauthorized practice of law by agreeing to accept referrals from nonlawyers selling living trust document packages; suspension under Standard 7.2 mitigated by fact that lawyer ceased accepting referrals when he realized ethical impropriety and by his cooperation with disciplinary proceedings); *People v. Volk*, 805 P.2d 1116 (Colo. 1991) (public censure for aiding in unauthorized practice of law when nonlawyer insurance sales representatives sold living trusts and lawyer received payments for review of trust documents; baseline suspension under Standard 7.2 mitigated by several factors including cooperative attitude in disciplinary proceeding and voluntary imposition of interim suspension); *Comm'n on Prof'l Ethics & Conduct v. Baker*, 492 N.W.2d 695 (Iowa 1992) (lawyer's participation in living trust marketing schemes resulted in, inter alia, aiding in the unauthorized practice of law, conflicts of interest, and improper referrals warranting public reprimand, after consideration of mitigating factors, including that no client complained); *Columbus Bar Ass'n v. Moreland*, 780 N.E.2d 579 (Ohio 2002) (substantial mitigating factors, including lawyer's lack of experience and absence of dishonest motive, considered in imposing public reprimand for lawyer who, inter alia, assisted in the unauthorized practice of law when he entered into a business relationship with a company that marketed living trusts).

### *Failure to Supervise*

Lawyers also may be publicly reprimanded under Standard 7.3 for failing to supervise nonlawyers, as well as lawyer employees within a practice. *See, e.g.*, *In re Ehrlich*, 351 P.3d 1268 (Kan. 2015) (public censure for lawyer who knew, before statute of limitations ran, that suspended lawyer acting as law clerk had not obtained service in personal injury case, and who did not ensure that said lawyer, while practicing as respondent's associate attorney after regaining license, competently and diligently handled the matter); *Bd. of Prof'l Responsibility v. Custis*, 348 P.3d 823 (Wyo. 2015) (public censure for lawyer who signed and submitted to court a brief prepared by paralegal that contained misrepresentations).

### *Omissions and Misrepresentations in Bar Admission Applications*

While most cases of omission or misrepresentation by bar applicants—a breach of duty owed as a professional under Standard 7.0—are analyzed under Standards 7.1 or 7.2, some courts impose public reprimand when the requisite mental state for those Standards is absent. *See, e.g., In re Lucas*, 672 N.E.2d 934, 936 (Ind. 1996) (public reprimand when lawyer harbored no intent to deceive admission authorities by omitting on Indiana bar application three civil lawsuits in which he was a defendant, had a speeding ticket, and had an arrest for public intoxication, and also failing to disclose on Florida bar application outstanding debts, the civil lawsuits, and the speeding ticket; lawyer's "nondisclosure on his bar applications was the product of something less than a conscious, premeditated plan to keep certain information from the admissions authorities"); *In re Garbarini*, 76 A.D.3d 379 (N.Y. App. Div. 2010) (public censure, rather than suspension, for lawyer's misconduct, including failure to disclose on bar application misdemeanor arrest for driving under the influence of alcohol and conviction of the traffic violation of driving while impaired; mitigating factors considered, including misconduct resulted from a serious substance abuse problem, which the lawyer addressed, and there was no injury to clients); *In re Harper*, 223 A.D.2d 200 (N.Y. App. Div. 1996) (public censure for omitting in bar application dismissal from L.L.M. program for plagiarism; in imposing sanction, court considered remorse, isolated nature of misconduct, and high regard in which respondent was held by teachers, colleagues, and clients); *Bd. of Prof'l Responsibility v. Jolley*, 805 P.2d 862 (Wyo. 1991) (public censure under Standard 7.3 for lawyer who, while stating on application for admission to bar that he had been arrested for assault and battery, omitted that he had been arrested for assault with the intent to commit rape).

## *Failure to Report Professional Misconduct*

When failure to report another lawyer's professional misconduct is the product of mere negligence, the appropriate baseline sanction is a reprimand under Standard 7.3. *See, e.g., In re Pyle*, 91 P.3d 1222 (Kan. 2004) (published censure under Standard 7.3, inter alia, for lawyer whose misconduct included failing to report alleged frivolous filings by another lawyer); *In re Riehlmann*, 891 So.2d 1239, 1249 (La. 2005) (former prosecutor learned during a barroom conversation with his terminally ill friend, another former prosecutor, that the latter had intentionally suppressed exculpatory blood evidence in a criminal case prosecuted a decade earlier; nearly five years after friend's death, lawyer attested to the disclosure in an affidavit on behalf of defendant who was set to be executed by lethal injection; imposing public reprimand under Standard 7.3, the court stated that "[w]hile we adhere to our observation . . . that an attorney's failure to comply with the reporting requirement is a 'serious offense,' in the instant case, we find that respondent's conduct was merely negligent"); *In re Toups*, 773 So.2d 709 (La. 2000) (public reprimand under Standard 7.3, inter alia, for assistant district attorney who failed to report to disciplinary counsel or other appropriate authority attempt by another assistant district attorney to have criminal battery charges continued against a husband who that assistant district attorney represented in divorce matter;

while court concluded that the baseline sanction for respondent's conduct was suspension, it found public reprimand appropriate considering existence of only one aggravating factor and several mitigating factors, including absence of a dishonest or selfish motive and cooperative attitude toward proceedings). *But see Att'y U. v. Miss. Bar*, 678 So.2d 963, 971 (Miss. 1996) (in reversing public reprimand imposed on lawyer and findings by the Complaint Tribunal that lawyer violated duty to report another lawyer's misconduct, court held that there was no obligation to report since information lawyer received from client about an improper fee splitting arrangement another lawyer had with the client did not "dictate a firm opinion on the part of a reasonable lawyer that the conduct in fact occurred"; Sanctions Standards not cited).

### *Improper Withdrawal from Representation*

Standard 7.3 provides that the presumptive sanction is public reprimand for negligence when a lawyer improperly withdraws from representation. Even when improper withdrawal has involved greater culpability than mere negligence, courts have imposed public reprimands. *See In re Disciplinary Action Against Anseth*, 562 N.W.2d 385, 390 (N.D. 1997) (overturning Disciplinary Board's dismissal of charges and imposing public reprimand, under Standard 7.3, rather than suspension that "would ordinarily be appropriate for [respondent's] knowing failure to fulfill his obligations" to his client, by failing to surrender to client original documents following client's discharge of lawyer, failing to either timely complete work undertaken prior to his discharge or to inform client of incomplete status of work; aggravating factor "largely balanced" by mitigating factors); *cf. In re Disciplinary Proceedings Against Smead*, 806 N.W.2d 631 (Wis. 2011) (public reprimand for lawyer's improper termination of representation in failing to notify client of suspension and inability to further participate in client's defense and failing to account for and refund unearned fees; although lawyer previously had been disciplined, present misconduct arose when lawyer took on pro bono the heavy caseload of another suspended lawyer; Sanctions Standards not cited).

### *Failure to Keep Proper Books*

Public reprimands have been used to address failures to maintain proper financial records and inaccurate reports about the same, when there has been an additional factor that the court sees as requiring more than a private reprimand. *See, e.g., In re Malik*, 167 A.3d 1189 (Del. 2017) (public reprimand for lawyer who failed to provide clients with information regarding fee agreements, failed to supervise employee's work in reconciling firm's books and records, and misrepresented the maintenance of the books and records in Certificate of Compliance of financial recordkeeping procedures filed with Supreme Court); *In re Castro*, 160 A.3d 1134 (Del. 2017) (public reprimand for lawyer who failed to properly maintain her firm's books and records for three consecutive years, filed inaccurate Certificates of Compliance, and failed to give her flat-fee clients proper notice that the fee was refundable if not earned by her); *In re Woods*, 143 A.3d 1223 (Del. 2016) (private reprimand converted to public reprimand for lawyer who violated condition of probation by misrepresenting the accuracy of his Certificates of Compliance).

## *Upward and Downward Deviation*

As with other Sanctions Standards, a baseline reprimand under Standard 7.3 may be affected by aggravating or mitigating factors. *See People v. Beasley*, 241 P.3d 548 (Colo. O.P.D.J. 2010) (while public reprimand was appropriate under Standard 7.3 for lawyer's failure to supervise nonlawyer assistants, one-year-and-one-day suspension imposed based on lawyer's additional violations, including mishandling client funds and failure to act with diligence in client matter and to keep clients informed). The variability may be as wide as suspension to no sanction at all. *Compare In re Mopsik*, 902 So.2d 991, 995 (La. 2005) (sixty-day suspension, rather than reprimand under Standard 7.3, for experienced lawyer who negligently "failed to exercise any meaningful supervisory oversight" over his paralegal to whom he had delegated responsibility for domestic dispute matter, failed to accept responsibility for misconduct, and whose actions created clear potential for harm to vulnerable victim, although intervening factors had prevented actual harm; paralegal presented to judge a pleading styled "Temporary Petition for Joint Custody" and failed to inform judge of temporary restraining order against petitioning parent, resulting in judge granting visitation for petitioning parent, only to vacate order when he learned about restraining order), *with In re Cabibi*, 922 So.2d 490 (La. 2006) (rejecting disciplinary board's recommendation of suspension and finding no formal discipline warranted for lawyer who failed to supervise his daughter, a nonlawyer and only employee of law firm, in preparing language for codicil giving lawyer substantial gift from client; finding no harm or intent, and mitigating factors including unblemished disciplinary record, absence of dishonest or selfish motive, and lawyer's good character and reputation).

**7.4 Admonition is generally appropriate when a lawyer engages in an isolated instance of negligence in determining whether the lawyer's conduct violates a duty owed as a professional, and causes little or no actual or potential injury to a client, the public, or the legal system.**

## Annotation

An admonition under Standard 7.4 is the presumptive sanction when a lawyer's violation of a duty as a professional involves just one incident, the lawyer's mental state is negligent rather than intentional or knowing, and the misconduct results in little demonstrable or potential injury. *See, e.g., In re Van Dox*, 152 P.3d 1183 (Ariz. 2007) (informal reprimand under Standard 7.4 for out-of-state lawyer's unauthorized practice of law in a mediation conducted in Arizona resulting in little or no actual injury; lawyer's confusion on issue of whether conduct permitted was reasonable); *In re Anonymous*, 932 N.E.2d 671 (Ind. 2010) (private reprimand for local counsel who failed to ensure that Kentucky lawyer was properly admitted to practice in state before signing an appearance with him and allowing him to appear in court and take depositions in state, conduct constituting assisting in the unauthorized practice of law; court cautioned Indiana lawyers serving as local counsel for out-of-state lawyers who neglect their duty may be subject to more stringent discipline in future cases and out-of-state lawyers who fail to comply with the rules may be sanctioned for the unauthorized practice of law in the state; decision does not cite Sanctions Standards); *In re Anonymous*, 787 N.E.2d 883 (Ind. 2003) (court approved agreed discipline of a private reprimand for lawyer who hired suspended lawyer to work in law office, first as a bookkeeper, and then as a paralegal); *Ky. Bar Ass'n v. Unnamed Attorney*, 191 S.W.3d 640, 641 (Ky. 2006) (employment of suspended lawyer who participated in meeting with prospective clients and answered questions concerning legal issues warranted private reprimand; court published private reprimand "so that the public and members of the bar may learn from Respondent's mistakes"); *In re Gerber*, 868 N.W.2d 861, 870 (N.D. 2015) (Minnesota lawyer not licensed in North Dakota admonished for improperly holding himself out as a lawyer while working as lobbyist in North Dakota branch of Minnesota firm; court cited Standard 7.4 and also stated that "although this Court has recognized an admonition is intended to be a nonpublic form of discipline . . . we have acknowledged that any sanction this court imposes will be de facto public") (citation omitted); *In re PRB Docket No. 2002.093*, 868 A.2d 709, 712 (Vt. 2005) (private reprimand for placing a misleading advertisement claiming that lawyer's firm employed "injury experts," as such claim could not be verified or factually substantiated and probably created an unjustified expectation in the minds of consumers concerning the firm's results; concluding misconduct was "an isolated instance of negligence with little or no resulting harm," warranting private reprimand under Standard 7.4); *In re PRB Docket No. 2015.002*, 125 A.3d 152, 155 (Vt. 2015) (lawyer who inadvertently did not reduce contingent fee agreement to writing due to lengthy pre-existing lawyer-client relationship based on hourly billing admonished under Standard 7.4); *cf. In re Atanga*, 636 N.E.2d 1253, 1259–60 (Ind. 1994) (Justice Frank Sullivan, Jr., dissenting from imposition of thirty-day suspension for "reckless" published statement critical of a judge, arguing that Standard 7.4 applies because incident was no more than an isolated instance that caused little or no actual or potential injury: "The statements made by [respondent] that are the subject of this proceeding appear at the very end of a long story covering parts of three pages in an obscure newsletter. . . . Publication of these statements in such an obscure place cannot possibly cause injury.").

## *Upward Deviation*

Although private admonition was the presumptive sanction, state precedent has compelled a more severe sanction for certain misconduct. *See People v. Gray*, 35 P.3d 611 (Colo. O.P.D.J. 2001) (presumptive sanction of private admonition under Standard 7.4 suggested for failure to use appropriate letterhead identifying status of suspended lawyer and failure to supervise suspended lawyer regarding handling of funds resulting in technical conversion; private reprimand was appropriate under Sanctions Standards as lawyer's misconduct was negligent, involved only one client, and caused little or no actual harm to the client, the profession, or the legal system; nonetheless, deviating upward to public censure because technical conversion, even if negligent, warrants more severe discipline under Colorado law; listing Colorado cases in accord).

## 8.0 Prior Discipline Orders

**Absent aggravating or mitigating circumstances, upon application of the factors set out in Standard 3.0, the following sanctions are generally appropriate in cases involving prior discipline.**

## Annotation

Recidivist lawyers are addressed in Standard 8.0. While such lawyers may also be found to have demonstrated a pattern of misconduct through repeated misdeeds, and that may also serve as an aggravating factor under Standard 9.22, these violations are so serious as to warrant special discussion. *See People v. Swarts*, 414 P.3d 1168, 1171 (Colo. O.P.D.J. 2018) (recognizing the uniqueness of Standard 8.0 because it "serves as an overlay to other presumptive sanctions"). In some cases, the repeated misconduct may also result in the lawyer being found to have violated the prior disciplinary order.

Courts impose enhanced sanctions for continued misconduct after prior discipline as a means of safeguarding both the public and the legal system from lawyers who create an unacceptable risk of harm. *See People v. Mason*, 212 P.3d 141, 147 n.16 (Colo. O.P.D.J. 2009) ("ABA *Standard* 8.0 implicates duties owed to a client, the public, the legal system, and/or the profession."). Under Standard 8.0, some courts will impose graduated sanctions in matters involving prior discipline. *See In re McCoy-Jacien*, 186 A.3d 626 (Vt. 2018) (in case where lawyer knowingly violated terms of prior disciplinary order, court cited supportively the principle of "gradual gradation" as being "appropriate depending on the severity of the subsequent conduct"; opinion cites to *In re Davis*, 889 P.2d 621 (Ariz. 1995)). *See also* Annotation to Standard 8.2.

The need for special consideration in such cases is explored in *In re Steiner*, 817 A.2d 793 (Del. 2003), where the Delaware Supreme Court noted that, under Standard 8.0, an enhanced sanction is necessary when a lawyer subject to prior discipline engages in further misconduct, because that lawyer presents "such a serious risk." *Id.* at 797. In *Steiner*, the lawyer was initially placed on interim suspension after being indicted on two counts of first-degree vehicular assault and one count of DUI. After pleading guilty to three misdemeanor criminal charges, the criminal judge sentenced him to three years of probation with conditions that included participation in a substance abuse program and a "zero tolerance" provision for drug and alcohol use. The lawyer violated probation by consuming alcohol on two separate occasions, resulting in the termination of probation and eighteen months of home confinement.

In the disciplinary case, the Delaware Supreme Court found that the lawyer's original misconduct that led to the interim suspension, driving a car while intoxicated, was aggravated by "further acts of knowing misconduct," the criminal probation violations, "similar to acts for which [he] was already under suspension." *Id.* at 798. The court concluded that a three-year suspension "is fair and is consistent with our goals of protecting the public and the administration of justice, preserving confidence in the legal profession, and deterring other lawyers from similar misconduct." *Id.* at 799.

*Steiner* is different from the majority of cases under Standard 8.0 in that it involved a lawyer's continued criminal conduct, rather than conduct involving the practice of law. In fact, the most common circumstances for which lawyers are disbarred or suspended under Standard 8.0 involve lawyers who have been disbarred or suspended from the practice of law but nevertheless continue to practice. Under that and other instances in which a suspended lawyer knowingly engages in further similar acts of misconduct, absent other aggravating or mitigating circumstances, disbarment is generally warranted under Standard 8.1, the *Steiner* court said.

## *Relationship of Standard 8.0 to Standard 9.22 (Aggravating Factors)*

As noted above, in addition to Standard 8.0, courts often consider prior discipline as an aggravating factor under Standard 9.22, if the lawyer engages in misconduct that is similar to previously sanctioned misconduct. In many cases, courts examine Standards 8.0 and 9.22 concurrently in determining the appropriate sanction. When they do so, the aggravating factors under Standard 9.22 of prior disciplinary offenses, a pattern of misconduct, and multiple offenses are most often at issue. For example, in *People v. Mason*, 212 P.3d 141, 149 (Colo. O.P.D.J. 2009), the court found that the lawyer's disbarment was warranted under Standard 8.1, inter alia, for violating a court order and agreement not to practice law during his suspension. Noting that the facts before it included substantial evidence in aggravation under Standard 9.22, including the lawyer's lengthy history of disciplinary offenses and pattern of misconduct, demonstrated in his insistence on practicing law while under suspension, the court concluded: "Any further effort to rehabilitate Respondent given his prior disciplinary history and defiance of court orders, would only endanger the public and diminish the integrity of the of the [sic] disciplinary system." Aggravating factors also were established in *In re Bock*, 265 P.3d 552 (Kan. 2011), a case in which a lawyer's extensive disciplinary record for the same misconduct supported suspension under Standard 8.2. The court found that the lawyer's suspension also was warranted under Standard 9.22, identifying eight of eleven aggravating factors, including prior disciplinary offenses, a pattern of misconduct, multiple offenses, and intentionally failing to comply with rules or orders of the disciplinary process. (More cases involving aggravating factors are discussed in the Annotation to Standards 8.1 and 8.2).

In some cases, the question of whether a previous suspension for failing to register (typically considered administrative in nature) constitutes prior discipline has arisen in some cases. While not citing to the Sanctions Standards, the Supreme Court of Ohio answered that question in the affirmative. In *Toledo Bar Ass'n. v. Crosser*, 67 N.E.3d 789 (Ohio 2016), a lawyer received a one-year stayed suspension for misconduct that included neglect and attempts to conceal that neglect through misrepresentations to the impacted clients. While the trier of fact found no aggravating factors, the Court held the lawyer's prior suspension for failing to register was prior discipline and therefore an aggravating factor. *Id.* at 790. *See also Disciplinary Counsel v. Denslow*, 77 N.E.3d 964 (Ohio 2017) (Ohio Supreme Court disagreed with stipulation stating that respondent had no prior discipline due to lawyer's previous suspension for failure to comply with annual registration requirements). *See also* Annotation to Standard 8.1.

### *Prior Discipline and Unfair Influence on Trier of Fact*

Concern about a lawyer's prior discipline unfairly influencing a trier of fact in a disciplinary proceeding is addressed in MRLDE Rule 11(D)(5). That Rule provides that prior discipline shall not be divulged to a hearing committee or other disciplinary trier of fact until after it has made a finding of misconduct, unless the information is probative of issues in the current disciplinary hearing. The reason for this restriction is because rarely will prior discipline be relevant in determining whether the misconduct alleged in the current disciplinary complaint has occurred. MODEL RULES FOR LAWYER DISCIPLINARY ENFORCEMENT R. 11(D)(5) (2007).

Some states use bifurcated hearings so that triers of fact do not consider evidence of prior discipline until after a hearing on the current charges of misconduct. *See e.g.*, MICH. SUP. CT. R. 9.115(J) (2014) (proceedings bifurcated into a misconduct phase and a separate sanctions phase following a finding of misconduct); WASH. E.L.C. 10.15 (hearing officer or panel can grant written motion requested by either party that disciplinary proceeding be bifurcated with a violation hearing followed by sanction hearing).

**8.1 Disbarment is generally appropriate when a lawyer:**

**(a) intentionally or knowingly violates the terms of a prior disciplinary order and such violation causes injury or potential injury to a client, the public, the legal system, or the profession; or**

**(b) has been suspended for the same or similar misconduct, and intentionally or knowingly engages in further similar acts of misconduct that cause injury or potential injury to a client, the public, the legal system, or the profession.**

## Annotation

Disbarment is warranted when a previously disciplined lawyer intentionally or knowingly violates the terms of the previous disciplinary order or repeats the same or similar misconduct for which the lawyer was suspended and, as a result, causes injury or potential injury to a client, the public, the legal system, or the profession. In *In re Chavez*, 1 P.3d 417 (N.M. 2000), the New Mexico Supreme Court stated the rationale for disbarment under Standard 8.1:

> A more severe sanction is necessary to protect the public when a lesser sanction has proven insufficient to stop a suspended lawyer from repeating the same type of misconduct with another client and to vindicate the Court's authority when a lawyer has disregarded the directions issued by the Court in a prior order imposing a term of suspension.

1 P.3d at 423.

### *Mens Rea*

Disbarment under both Standards 8.1(a) and 8.1(b) requires a showing that the lawyer acted either "intentionally or knowingly." (See Definitions in the black letter Standards.) "'Intent' is the conscious objective or purpose to accomplish a particular result. 'Knowledge' is the conscious awareness of the nature or attendant circumstances of the conduct but without the conscious objective or purpose to accomplish a particular result." By including both "intentional" and "knowing" in the black letter, Standard 8.1 differs slightly from the paradigm of other Sanctions Standards, which distinguish between intentional misconduct warranting disbarment and knowing misconduct warranting suspension.

The North Dakota Supreme Court discussed the Standard 8.1 mens rea requirement in *In re Disciplinary Action Against Larson*, 512 N.W.2d 454 (N.D. 1994), the lawyer's third disciplinary case. In her first disciplinary case, the lawyer was suspended for ninety days for mishandling client funds and, in a second disciplinary proceeding for two years, again, for mishandling funds and, concurrently, for seven months for practicing law while under the first suspension. Disciplinary counsel then brought the third action seeking the lawyer's disbarment for practicing law in violation of the second suspension order. The lawyer maintained, among other arguments, that she could not be disbarred under Standard 8.1(a) because it required proof that she "knowingly" or "intentionally" violated the latest suspension order and, "because those terms are not defined, they must be given an ordinary meaning of willful, in the sense of having been done with an 'evil intent or bad purpose.'" *Id.* at 457. Rejecting that argument and finding that both North Dakota Standards 8.1(a) and 8.1(b) applied, the court noted that "the term 'willfully' in a professional disciplinary proceeding means acts that were done in the exercise of the performer's free will and were not done under coercion." *Id.* The court disbarred her, concluding the lawyer knowingly and intentionally continued to practice law after the effective date of her suspension.

Courts disbarring lawyers under Standard 8.1 often make particular note of the lawyer's state of mind. *See, e.g., People v. Corbin*, 82 P.3d 373 (Colo. O.P.D.J. 2003) (finding disbarment warranted under Standard 8.1, inter alia, for lawyer who knowingly practiced law while suspended by filing at least twelve trademark applications for others in which he listed himself as attorney of record, and who ignored the suspension order and misrepresented to clients that he was still authorized to practice law); *In re Feuerhake*, 89 A.3d 1058 (Del. 2014) (respondent disbarred for knowingly violating suspension order and for practicing law while employed as a paralegal, appearing in court and at depositions, and accepting fees for work performed post-suspension; court stressed that the respondent acted with a knowing state of mind, citing to his conscious awareness of the suspension order and its requirements); *Fla. Bar v. Poe*, 786 So.2d 1164 (Fla. 2001) (disbarring a suspended lawyer under Florida Standard 8.1(b), inter alia, for numerous instances of intentional neglect and practicing while ineligible when current suspension stemmed from similar complaints); *In re Jackson*, 1 So.3d 454, 456 (La. 2009) (disbarment warranted under Standard 8.1(b) as lawyer, inter alia, knowingly and intentionally engaged in unauthorized practice of law while suspended when he was suspended for that same misconduct; rejecting argument that the lawyer believed he provided "law clerk-like services"); *In re Grady*, 782 So.2d 570 (La. 2001) (disbarment warranted under Standard 8.1(b), inter alia, for lawyer who had been suspended for engaging in similar acts of knowing and intentional misconduct, including failing to terminate representation after becoming ineligible and failing to communicate).

Absent a finding of intent, the misconduct does not fall under the Standard 8.1 rubric. *See, e.g., In re Gershater*, 946 P.2d 993 (Kan. 1997) (imposing published censure for failure to withdraw from client's divorce case and not notifying client of lawyer's one-year suspension; finding lawyer's conduct was a result of oversight and concluding lawyer lacked dishonest intent to violate notification rule thus blunting impact of Standard 8.1(b) requiring disbarment for same or similar misconduct); *cf. Fla. Bar v. Lobasz*, 64 So.3d 1167 (Fla. 2011) (disbarment, not three-year suspension, warranted for violating order of suspension by representing former client at immigration hearing and continuing to advise new counsel on client matters; noting that lawyer's lack of conscious intent to violate suspension order by appearing at hearing did not overcome the presumption of disbarment in such cases, especially as misconduct extended to rendering legal advice).

## *Violation of Prior Disciplinary Order*

Disbarment under Standard 8.1(a) for flaunting a previous court order serves the fundamental goals of maintaining the integrity of the court as well as protecting the public, the primary purpose of disciplinary sanctions. *See generally* Annotation to Standard 1.1. *See, e.g., People v. Mason*, 212 P.3d 141, 149 (Colo. O.P.D.J. 2009) (disbarment warranted under Standard 8.1, inter alia, for lawyer's violation of a court order to not practice law while under suspension, misconduct for which he had been disciplined, in representing a mortgagor in a foreclosure action and in preparing and filing a liquor license application; "[a]ny further effort to rehabilitate Respondent given his prior disciplinary history and defiance of court orders, would only endanger the public and diminish the integrity of the of the [sic] disciplinary system"); *Att'y Grievance Comm'n v. James,* 735 A.2d 1027, 1036 (Md. 1999) (disbarment warranted under Standard 8.1(a) for deliberate violation of suspension order by continuing to practice law; rejecting lawyer's argument that he posed no threat to the public because his ability to represent clients was adequate, concluding that "[respondent's] disregard for this Court's order suspending him from the practice of law threatens the integrity of the legal profession and of the judicial system, and constitutes the sort of conduct that must be deterred for the protection of the public").

One state supreme court dealt with an unusual set of facts when disbarring a lawyer who engaged in the unauthorized practice in violation of the court's prior order. In *In re Tonwe*, 929 A.2d 774 (Del. 2007), the Delaware Supreme Court considered the case of a Pennsylvania lawyer never admitted in Delaware. That lawyer violated a 1991 cease-and-desist order from the Delaware Supreme Court prohibiting her from practice in Delaware when, from 2003 to 2006, she represented more than 100 Delaware residents in Delaware matters. In 1991, the respondent was convicted of bribing a federal immigration official and served thirty-seven months in prison, resulting in her disbarment in Pennsylvania, Ohio, and the District of Columbia in addition to the Delaware cease-and-desist order. After being reinstated in Pennsylvania and resuming her legal practice there, the lawyer also resumed her unauthorized practice of law in Delaware. Since Delaware's rules did not address the disbarment of a lawyer who was not licensed there or otherwise authorized to practice law there, the Delaware court looked to and adopted a definition of disbarment in Maryland's Rules of Professional Conduct, which specified that disbarment "when applied to an attorney not admitted . . . to practice law, means the unconditional exclusion from the admission to or the exercise of any privilege to practice law in this State" (citation omitted). *Id.* at 781. In rejecting the lawyer's challenge to its jurisdiction, the Delaware Supreme Court noted that the lawyer's physical presence in the state was not required to establish that she was providing legal services there because she accepted Delaware residents as clients, who were involved in Delaware automobile accidents seeking recovery under Delaware insurance policies.

### *Practicing Law During Disbarment*

Lawyers who originally were disbarred by courts for ethical violations have been disbarred again when they are found to have continued to practice law after their disbarment, sometimes permanently. In *Fla. Bar v. Neely*, 675 So.2d 592 (Fla. 1996), for example, the court permanently disbarred an already disbarred lawyer for meeting with a would-be client, accepting $1,000 to prepare a legal malpractice suit against another lawyer and for filing a complaint in circuit court on behalf of a corporation and representing that corporation in a legal capacity for nearly two months. *See also In re Lewis*, 856 So.2d 1191, 1197 (La. 2003) (previously disbarred lawyer permanently disbarred for misconduct including practicing law while disbarred: "Respondent engaged in conduct that was actively intended to frustrate the administration of justice. This court cannot and will not tolerate such conduct by an attorney. Respondent's actions convincingly demonstrate he does not possess the requisite moral fitness to practice law in this state.").

### *Practicing Law During Disciplinary Suspension*

Disbarment under Standard 8.1(a) is more frequently imposed when a lawyer who is suspended from the practice of law continues to practice. Courts generally impose disbarment in such cases, with many emphasizing that lawyers who violate prior disciplinary orders exhibit a disrespect for the court and its authority. *See, e.g., In re Tarletz*, 798 P.2d 381, 383 (Ariz. 1990) (practicing law while under suspension for failure to pay dues, together with prior misconduct, warranted disbarment: "[W]hen the record establishes a lawyer's willingness to violate the terms of his suspension order, disbarment is appropriate 'as a prophylactic measure to prevent further misconduct by the offending individual.'") (citation omitted); *People v. Heupel*, 2017 WL 3585235 (Colo. O.P.D.J. July 11, 2017) (disbarment appropriate for lawyer who practiced law while suspended and committed other misconduct including conversion of client funds; holding disbarment was presumptive sanction under Standard 8.1(a) and Standard 4.11); *In re Smith*, 989 P.2d 165 (Colo. 1999) (citing Standard 8.1(a), court found disbarment appropriate reciprocal discipline when U.S. Court of Appeals for the Tenth Circuit disbarred lawyer for practicing law before it in violation of prior suspension order; lawyer provided no evidence or legitimate reason why disbarment would result in an injustice and court previously ruled disbarment was appropriate for a lawyer who continued to practice law after being suspended); *Disciplinary Counsel v. Evans*, 2018 WL 793993 (Conn. January 10, 2018) (in unpublished decision citing to Standard 8.1, court held that practicing law while suspended, coupled with long history of discipline, demonstrated respondent's "deep disrespect for judicial authority" and imposed disbarment); *Fla. Bar v. D'Ambrosio*, 25 So.3d 1209, 1220 n.6 (Fla. 2009) (disbarment warranted for lawyer's misconduct constituting the practice of law while suspended and in contempt of court's prior suspension order; court reiterated: "Thus, by the previous case and the case herein, [respondent] has repeatedly demonstrated disrespect of the Court's orders of suspension. This repeated misconduct, as well as his other disciplinary history, demonstrates that [he] has engaged in cumulative misconduct."); *Fla. Bar v. Forrester*, 916 So.2d 647 (Fla. 2005) (while respondent was suspended for sixty days, she continued operating her law practice by hiring and directing a young, inexperienced recent law school graduate; citing Florida Standard 8.1, court found disbarment warranted); *In re McDaneld*, 389 P.3d 976 (Kan. 2017) (lawyer practiced law during suspension by appearing in court in at least eight cases and not cooperating with disciplinary counsel investigating his unauthorized practice of law; citing Standard 8.1, the court disbarred him, disagreeing with disciplinary counsel's recommendation of indefinite suspension); *In re Jackson*, 1 So.3d 454, 458–59 (La. 2009) (permanent disbarment warranted for engaging in the unauthorized practice of law while under suspension when lawyer previously was suspended for same misconduct; court held lawyer's "failure to respect the authority of this court clearly demonstrates that he lacks the fitness to engage in the practice of law in this State"); *In re Cohen*, 769 So.2d 531, 535 (La. 2000) (disbarment warranted under Standard 8.1, inter alia, for lawyer who neglected numerous client matters, many taken on while ineligible to practice, and when lawyer had been suspended for misconduct stemming from more than ten similar complaints; court stated that the "sheer number of complaints against respondent demonstrates in a convincing fashion that he has a complete lack of regard for the welfare of his clients and his professional obligations as a member of the bar of this state"); *In re Devers*, 974 P.2d 191 (Or. 1999) (finding Standard 8.1 dispositive, court disbarred lawyer whose activities during suspension included negotiating terms of settlement and drafting settlement agreement, which constituted practice of law); *In re Jones*, 825 P.2d 1365, 1368 (Or. 1992) (holding that misconduct included intentionally continuing to practice law after suspension by communicating with counsel representing opponent of respondent's "former" client in ongoing legal action; disbarment warranted under Standard 8.1, inter alia, with court reasoning that "[b]y failing to refrain from the practice of law in compliance with this court's 1989 discipline order, the accused disobeyed this court's order and breached his duty to the legal system"); *In re Meeder*, 488 S.E.2d 875 (S.C. 1997) (disbarment of lawyer who, inter alia, continued representing client during suspension). *But see In re Discipline of Crowley*, 406 P.3d 958 (Table) (Nev. 2017) (in unpublished disposition lawyer suspended for eighteen months instead of disbarment for practicing law while suspended by handling estate matter; court cited to Standard 8.1(a) as calling for presumptive sanction of disbarment but imposed suspension instead because disbarment in Nevada is permanent, and this matter involved an isolated instance of unauthorized practice of law).

### *Practicing Law During Administrative Suspension*

In disciplining lawyers for the unauthorized practice of law while suspended, a number of courts make no distinction regarding the reason for the prior suspension. Thus, courts disbar lawyers under Standard 8.1 for practicing while under "administrative suspension"—that is, suspension for failure to pay bar membership dues, disciplinary assessments, and/or failure to comply with continuing legal education requirements. *See, e.g., In re Tarletz*, 798 P.2d 381, 382 (Ariz. 1990) (court imposed a second disbarment on lawyer for holding herself out as a lawyer and practicing law on several occasions, including making court appearances on behalf of clients while under suspension for failure to pay dues, noting that court had disbarred lawyer in a prior disciplinary proceeding, but making a new finding of disbarment "so that the record is complete should respondent apply for readmission in this or any other jurisdiction"); *People v. Redman*, 902 P.2d 839 (Colo. 1995) (disbarment warranted under Standard 8.1 for lawyer who had been disciplined for unauthorized practice of law while under administrative suspension); *In re Bonnette*, 840 So.2d 512 (La. 2003) (disbarring lawyer for, inter alia, handling two cases in city court when lawyer had been certified ineligible to practice law for nonpayment of bar membership dues); *In re Devers*, 974 P.2d 191 (Or. 1999) (disbarment following practice during reciprocal disciplinary suspension in addition to administrative suspension for failure to pay Professional Liability Fund assessment and bar dues; finding Standard 8.1 dispositive and citing former commentary with approval); *In re Disciplinary Proceedings Against Trudgeon*, 787 N.W.2d 795 (Wis. 2010) (revoking suspended lawyer's license to practice for several acts of misconduct, including continuing to practice during suspension for noncompliance with mandatory continuing legal education requirements); *In re Disbarment of Rogers*, 60 V.I. 293 (V.I. 2013) (lawyer who was suspended for failing to comply with continuing legal education requirements continued practicing law and ignored disciplinary office's request for response to complaints by judges; court cited to Standard 8.1 and respondent's knowing and flagrant disregard of the suspension order). *But see Office of Disciplinary Counsel v. Lau*, 900 P.2d 777 (Haw. 1995) (in case of first impression, holding that practicing law ten days after suspension warranted additional suspension for 120 days; canvassing other jurisdictions imposing sanctions for similar misconduct and noting that, although issue of sanctions for practice while under administrative suspension for failure to pay registration fees was not before the court, states have imposed sanctions in such situations); *In re Koliha*, 9 P.3d 102 (Or. 2000) (one-year suspension—not under Standard 8.1—for failing to cooperate with disciplinary investigation and for representing client in an Oregon circuit court for more than two years after suspension for failure to pay bar dues; distinguishing unauthorized practice while suspended for failure to pay bar dues from more egregious cases involving unauthorized practice while suspended for previous disciplinary violations).

## *Injury or Potential Injury*

Courts nearly always opt for disbarment under Standard 8.1(a) when the lawyer's intentional or knowing violation of a prior disciplinary order injurs or potentially injurs a client, the public, the legal system, or the profession. See, *e.g.*, *People v. Zimmermann*, 960 P.2d 85, 88 (Colo. 1998) (disbarment under Standard 8.1(a) for, inter alia, accepting advance fees after order of suspension entered; court stressed that "[h]is clients sustained actual harm because they received little or no benefit from the fees they paid to him and then they had to turn around and pay other lawyers additional fees for the legal services they had paid the respondent to perform"); *People v. Zodrow*, 276 P.3d 113 (Colo. O.P.D.J. 2011) (disbarment warranted under Standard 8.1, inter alia, for lawyer whose unauthorized practice during suspension, failing to inform clients of suspension, and allowing clients to believe he was licensed caused actual harm; injury involved filing complaint outside applicable statute of limitations period, leading to dismissal of case, and causing client emotional and potential financial harm, stress, and eroding her trust in the profession); *In re Miller*, 238 P.3d 227 (Kan. 2010) (lawyer engaged in unauthorized practice of law during disciplinary suspension by hiring independent contractor to do legal work that he was precluded from doing because of his suspension resulting in potential injury to the legal profession, and disbarment warranted under Standard 8.1, inter alia); *In re Paulson*, 216 P.3d 859 (Or. 2009) (disbarment warranted under Standard 8.1, inter alia, for respondent who did not withdraw from representing several clients, took few or no steps to aid them in transferring their cases to other lawyers in advance of his suspension, and who practiced law while suspended, thus causing actual and potential injury to clients and, in one child custody case, actual injury was serious); *cf. In re Rost*, 211 P.3d 145 (Kan. 2009) (disbarment under Standard 8.1(a) appropriate for retired lawyer who continued to practice law in violation of a prior disciplinary agreement allowing him to retire and avoid further sanctions and who caused potential harm to an ill and feeble elderly man to whom he provided legal advice). *But see People v. Swarts*, 414

P.3d 1168, 1191 (Colo. O.P.D.J. 2018) (while finding the elements of both Standards 8.1(a) and 8.1(b) had been met regarding lawyers continuing to practice law while suspended and knowingly engaging in similar misconduct resulting in prior discipline, disciplinary judge found these Standards should not form basis for presumptive sanction because "the degree of injury appears to be quite small, the magnitude of the misconduct very modest, and the pattern of misconduct only an incipient one"; three-year suspension imposed in this "close case").

## *Failure to Notify Others of Suspension*

Another common scenario where courts disbar lawyers under Standard 8.1(a) occurs when a lawyer violates the suspension order or rule requiring the suspended lawyers to notify clients, opposing counsel, or the court of the suspension. *See, e.g., People v. Swan*, 938 P.2d 1164 (Colo. 1997) (disbarring suspended lawyer for failure to notify client, opposing counsel or court of suspension, and effectively abandoning client during suspension by neglecting case). In *People v. Dolan*, 873 P.2d 766 (Colo. 1994), a lawyer was given thirty days to wind up pending matters after the court imposed a ninety-day suspension but failed to wind up his practice and notify arbitrators and clients. The court applied Standard 8.1(a), inter alia, and disbarred the lawyer, stating there was

> no evidence in this proceeding that the respondent continued to practice law after his suspension became effective. However, we find it equally serious that the respondent first took no steps to protect the legal interests of [his clients] as he was required to do . . . and then asserted before the district court and the grievance committee that he could take no action on the [clients'] behalf because of the order of suspension.

*Id.* at 769. *See also In re McCann*, 894 A.2d 1087 (Del. 2005) (finding disbarment appropriate under Standard 8.1 for lawyer who knowingly disobeyed prior suspension by failing to turn over files to active member of bar, failing to notify parties of his suspension, and paying himself fees from estates during his suspension); *In re Sniadecki*, 924 N.E.2d 109 (Ind. 2010) (disbarment warranted under Standard 8.1(a), inter alia, for misconduct including lawyer's failure to notify all active clients of his suspension); *In re Jones*, 241 P.3d 90 (Kan. 2010) (disbarment under Standard 8.1(a), inter alia, warranted for continuing to practice law during indefinite suspension and failing to inform clients of and protect their interests during suspension); *In re Harris*, 257 P.3d 1231 (Kan. 2011) (citing Standard 8.1, inter alia, in finding disbarment warranted for lawyer's misconduct including failure to notify clients in writing of suspension); *In re Israel*, 230 A.D.2d 293 (N.Y. App. Div. 1997) (immediate disbarment warranted for practice while under suspension; lawyer also failed to notify clients of his suspension in violation of court rules; decision does not cite Sanctions Standards).

### *Contempt of Court in Lieu of or in Addition to Further Discipline*

Courts have also dealt with violations of previous suspension orders by finding the lawyer in contempt of court and imposing a fine, imprisonment, or other sanctions instead of imposing further discipline. *See, e.g., In re Haigh,* 7 N.E.3d 980, 985 (Ind. 2014) (egregious violations of suspension order led to court finding lawyer in contempt, fining and disbarring him from practicing law while suspended; respondent's post-suspension unauthorized practice of law included accepting employment as general counsel to a company, holding himself out on his website as being "the best deal in town for an inventor to obtain all legal work for securing patents from the USPTO," and providing legal advice to others); *In re Wolfe,* 961 N.E.2d 994 (Ind. 2011) (holding lawyer in contempt for appearing at a hearing on behalf of friend while under suspension for nonpayment of annual registration fees and fining him $500); *In re Moore,* 866 N.E.2d 897, 899 (Mass. 2007) (court found lawyer in contempt for violating prior suspension order and barred him from applying for reinstatement for four years from the date of the judgment and further held "[n]or is there merit to the respondent's assertion that neither this court nor a single justice may exert disciplinary authority over him because any legal advice he rendered involved a Federal immigration law matter rather than a State law issue"); *In re Sneed,* 302 S.W.3d 825, 827 (Tenn. 2010) (convicting lawyer on fifty counts of contempt for, inter alia, willful violations of suspension order and imposing a ten-day imprisonment on each count to run partially concurrent and partially consecutive as well as a fine of $2,500, court concluded that a finding of criminal contempt "should be imposed in appropriate cases 'when necessary to prevent actual, direct obstruction of, or interference with, the administration of justice'") (citation omitted). *See also Board of Overseers of the Bar v. Murphy,* 607 A.2d 530 (Me. 1992) (preparing deed and wills on forms designating lawyer as "Attorney-at-Law" and failure to remove designation "Attorney-at-Law" under lawyer's name in his office directory constituted violation of order disbarring him from practice of law and warranted finding of contempt); *In re Abbott,* 175 A.D.2d 396 (N.Y. App. Div. 1991) (finding lawyer in contempt of court and imposing $500 fine for willful violation of suspension orders by maintaining legal office, using letterhead identifying himself as "Attorney and Counselor at Law," failing to promptly notify of suspension in writing, and representing clients); *Office of Disciplinary Counsel v. Marcone,* 855 A.2d 654 (Pa. 2004) (maintaining law office in state constituted contempt of prior suspension order, despite fact that office was limited to practice before federal district court; collecting sister state cases revealing consistent hostility to state bar member maintaining law office for purpose of limited federal practice).

Nor are contempt citations and lawyer disciplinary sanctions mutually exclusive remedies for a court addressing additional misconduct by suspended or disbarred lawyers. *See In re Boyer,* 988 P.2d 625 (Colo. 1999) (finding lawyer in contempt for negotiating settlements in auto accident cases in violation of previous order immediately suspending him); *Fla. Bar v. Lobasz,* 64 So.3d 1167 (Fla. 2011) (disbarment warranted for lawyer held in indirect contempt for violating order of suspension by representing former client at immigration hearing and continuing to advise new counsel on client matters; court concluded disbarment is presumptive sanction in contempt cases involving a clear violation of a suspension order absent strong extenuating circumstances); *Fla. Bar v. Ross,* 732 So.2d 1037 (Fla. 1998) (disbarring under Florida Standard 8.1(a), inter alia, and finding in contempt a suspended lawyer whose misconduct included repeatedly ignoring duty to withdraw from case, requesting payment for his own testimony, attempting to obtain fee in exchange for avoiding giving testimony, and avoiding service of subpoena through false representation; opinion discusses court's inherent contempt power, noting that if a lawyer subject to a disciplinary order violates that order, he or she stands in contempt of court, and that both suspended and disbarred lawyers remain subject to the court's contempt powers); *In re Kersey's Case,* 842 A.2d 121 (N.H. 2004) (disbarment warranted under Standard 8.1(a) for lawyer, originally suspended for three months as a result of a contempt citation in Vermont and suspension order in Massachusetts, and then held in contempt in New Hampshire for twice refusing to comply with court orders to turn over client files and trust accounts and for practicing law after being suspended); *In re Herkenhoff,* 931 P.2d 1382 (N.M. 1997) (two findings of direct criminal contempt against lawyer based on his continued practice of law in face of disbarment order, misrepresentation of his status as "retired," and failure to appear before court as ordered warranted sentence of five months' incarceration); *In re Herkenhoff,* 889 P.2d 840 (N.M. 1995) (disbarring suspended lawyer and also imposing fine for contemptuous refusal to abide by conditions of court's orders).

### *Same or Similar Misconduct*

When past and present offenses are identical or strikingly similar, courts are more likely to find baseline disbarment is warranted under Standard 8.1(b). As the Florida Supreme Court stated, in applying Florida Standard 8.1(b), in *Fla. Bar v. Vining,* 761 So.2d 1044, 1049 (Fla. 2000), to determine appropriate discipline, the court considers prior and cumulative misconduct, treating cumulative more severely than isolated misconduct. The court added that cumulative misconduct of a similar nature warranted more severe discipline than dissimilar conduct might. The lawyer's "latest transgression is the proverbial 'straw that broke the camel's back,'" the court concluded, imposing disbarment in light of disciplinary history and pattern of similar misconduct. *See also Fla. Bar v. Ratiner,* 238 So.3d 117, 126 (Fla.

2018) (lawyer who was suspended for disparaging conduct arising out of his representation of plaintiffs against the same defendant should be disbarred under Standard 8.1(b); continued similar misconduct was "intentional and egregious" and showed a progression of improper behavior indicative of an unwillingness to follow professional conduct rules). *See also In re Feeley*, 859 P.2d 1329 (Ariz. 1993) (disbarment, under Standard 8.1(b), inter alia, for failure to handle client matters with diligence and candor when lawyer was under suspension for matters arising out of similar circumstances); People v. Ward, 2017 WL 1046462 (Colo. O.P.D.J. February 9, 2017) (disbarment appropriate under Standard 8.1(b) when lawyer suspended for violating the same ethics rule similarly neglects and disregards court orders in two bankruptcy matters she undertook to complete knowing that disciplinary stipulation for new suspension was pending); *People v. Bottinelli*, 926 P.2d 553 (Colo. 1996) (disbarment warranted under Standard 8.1(b), inter alia, when, among other misconduct, lawyer made false accusations of conspiracy against judges and lawyers less than three months after lawyer's reinstatement following six-month suspension for similar misconduct); *In re Lober*, 241 P.3d 81 (Kan. 2010) (disbarment of lawyer whose previous one-year suspension for failure to keep client reasonably informed and to cooperate with disciplinary investigation triggered application of Standard 8.1(b) to lawyer's same misconduct in the instant proceeding); *In re Lyons*, 722 So.2d 998 (La. 1998) (disbarment warranted under Standard 8.1(b), inter alia, when misconduct giving rise to instant proceeding for neglect, failure to communicate with clients, conversion, and failure to cooperate with disciplinary counsel began five years after lawyer's readmission following a two-year suspension for like misconduct); *In re Linietsky*, 263 A.D.2d 102 (N.Y. App. Div. 1999) (disbarment warranted for, inter alia, a pattern of threatening, harassing, and extortionate behavior following three admonitions predicated on excessive fees and threats against judges, lawyers, and clients; Sanctions Standards not cited); *In re Bourcier*, 939 P.2d 604 (Or. 1997) (disbarment under Standard 8.1(b), inter alia, for misconduct including repeated failure to cooperate with disciplinary investigation after a three-year suspension for same conduct). *But see Fla. Bar v. Morgan*, 938 So.2d 496, 500 (Fla. 2006) (noting that while Florida Standard 8.1 supports disbarment when lawyer was disciplined twice before for similar misconduct—first a public reprimand and then suspension for ten days for inappropriate courtroom behavior—lawyer's third time before the court for the same misconduct warranted next level of available discipline, a rehabilitative ninety-one-day suspension, not disbarment; court warned that if lawyer appeared again for similar misconduct, "we may find it necessary to apply standard 8.1 and disbar him").

The public protection rationale for disbarment is particularly compelling when a lawyer has a long record of the same misconduct. *See, e.g., People v. Rozan*, 277 P.3d 942, 954 (Colo. O.P.D.J. 2011) (while lawyer's misappropriation of client funds warranted mandatory disbarment, disbarment was also appropriate under Standard 8.1(b) for failure to return unearned fees in light of lawyer's lengthy disciplinary history; court noted that "[g]iven the serious nature of Respondent's misconduct, his lengthy disciplinary record in Texas for similar misconduct, and the substantial risk he presents to the public, we find that disbarment is warranted"); *In re Caver,* 841 So.2d 770 (La. 2003) (permanent disbarment warranted when lawyer engaged in two acts of unauthorized practice of law while disbarred, and had been admonished or reprimanded on thirteen occasions prior to his disbarment); *In re Disciplinary Action Against Swanson,* 638 N.W.2d 240 (N.D. 2002) (disbarment warranted under Standard 8.1(b), inter alia, for lawyer whose prior similar misconduct had resulted in two reprimands and two suspensions); *In re Disciplinary Action Against Leier,* 562 N.W.2d 741, 744 (N.D. 1997) (in representing clients between 1985 and 1993, respondent exhibited reprehensible conduct resulting in eleven separate disciplinary files with misconduct including failing to diligently represent his clients' interests, mishandling client funds, and lying to clients; the court noted, "[e]specially where there is a pattern of repeated conduct violations, as in this case, disbarment is justified and necessary").

The recent disbarment of a Tennessee lawyer is of interest. In *In re Homer L. Cody,* BOPR No. 2017-2770-9-WM (Tenn., August 28, 2018) the court disbarred the respondent, who had been publicly censured in 2002 and suspended three times through 2017, for engaging in a conflict of interest with the same clients in the same matter and engaging in the unauthorized practice of law. *See also Cody v. Bd. of Prof'l Responsibility,* 471 S.W.3d 420 (Tenn. 2015). Cody did not dispute the facts underlying these suspensions but claimed the court's and disciplinary board's actions were illegitimate so he need not obey those directives.

Repeated misconduct need not be identical to that resulting in earlier discipline to warrant disbarment under Standard 8.1(b), but sufficiently similar instead. *See, e.g., In re Davis,* 43 A.3d 856 (Del. 2012) (disbarment warranted for lawyer who, inter alia, engaged in unauthorized practice of law while suspended for false notarizations and misrepresentation and who, during suspension, made misrepresentations about facts and circumstances of criminal violation arising from an auto accident in reinstatement questionnaire; court noted that underlying conduct resulting in his prior suspension was sufficiently similar to instant misconduct to trigger disbarment under Standard 8.1(b)); *In re Matney,* 811 P.2d 885 (Kan. 1991) (holding disbarment under Standard 8.1(b) proper because suspended lawyer's misdemeanor theft conviction was sufficiently similar to misconduct giving rise to indefinite suspension for use of money belonging to others for lawyer's own benefit); *In re Disciplinary Proceeding Against VanDerbeek,* 101 P.3d 88 (Wash. 2004) (rejecting respondent's argument that 1987 reprimand was too dissimilar to be considered an aggravating prior offense in padded billing case, court found that past and present misconduct pertained to violations of rule prohibiting conduct involving dishonesty, fraud, deceit, or misrepresentation).

## *When Lesser Sanctions Have Failed*

Under Standard 8.1(b), courts have held disbarment may be necessary to protect the public from further misdeeds when lesser sanctions have proved inadequate to dissuade similar misconduct. *See, e.g., In re C de Baca,* 11 P.3d 426 (Colo. 2000) (most important factor in this case is respondent's prior discipline, which included admonishments, public censure, and two suspensions; despite frequent opportunities for rehabilitation, he continued to engage in misconduct so disbarment was merited this time); *People v. Dolan,* 873 P.2d 766, 769 (Colo. 1994) (disbarment warranted for neglect of legal matters when lawyer had extensive history of discipline for similar misconduct; citing Standard 8.1(b), inter alia, the court wrote that "respondent's continuing pattern of professional misconduct following two prior orders of suspension and multiple private discipline demonstrates the futility of imposing still another period of suspension"); *In re Jones,* 241 P.3d 90, 103–04 (Kan. 2010) (in imposing disbarment under Standard 8.1(b), inter alia, on lawyer previously disciplined three times, the court stated: "[I]t is clear that the respondent does not appreciate the seriousness of his misconduct. . . . Despite his prior disciplinary experience, he brushed aside his obligation to follow this court's rules, to protect the public from potential injury, or to hold the legal profession in high regard. Apparently, the respondent learned little from his prior disciplinary experiences."); *In re Dennis,* 188 P.3d 1, 23 (Kan. 2008) (court imposed disbarment instead of another indefinite suspension under Standard 8.1(b), inter alia, for lawyer's repeated violations of court orders and failure to comply with known deadlines, noting that "[w]e are convinced that the respondent has not learned from his previous indefinite suspension, as he shows no remorse for his actions in this case and no recognition of the wrongfulness of or possible consequences for those actions."); *State ex rel. Counsel for Discipline v. Bouda,* 806 N.W.2d 879, 883 (Neb. 2011) (in addition to theft from employer, pattern of neglect, and deception, court found lawyer's "recalcitrance and recidivism," inter alia, "demonstrate beyond any reasonable dispute that he is unfit to practice law" warranting disbarment); *In re Kramer,* 800 A.2d 111, 132 (N.J. 2002) (in imposing disbarment for multiple acts of misconduct, including practicing law during suspension, court considered that lawyer "willfully and repeatedly engaged in improprieties resulting in thirty-eight instances in which he has been sanctioned, criticized or disciplined" and concluded that lawyer was "obviously incapable of or unwilling to conform to the requirements of the legal profession").

Courts not relying on Standard 8.1(b) also cite public protection as the rationale for imposing disbarment for repeated similar misconduct. *See, e.g., Iowa Supreme Ct. Att'y Disciplinary Bd. v. D'Angelo,* 710 N.W.2d 226, 236 (Iowa 2006) (lawyer's license revoked with court stressing: "This will be the last time we consider [respondent's] ethical violations. He has misappropriated client funds, practiced law after his license was suspended, neglected his clients, made misrepresentations to the court, and repeatedly failed to cooperate with the Attorney Disciplinary Board. These numerous violations are unacceptable, and we conclude the public will not be protected if [he] is allowed to practice law again."); *Iowa Supreme Ct. Bd. of Prof'l Ethics & Conduct v. Sullins,* 648 N.W.2d 127 (Iowa 2002) (revoking license of lawyer with long record of prior disciplinary actions who continued to engage in pattern of serious ethical violations); *In re Smith,* 75 So.3d 902, 906 (La. 2011) (knowing and intentional unauthorized practice of law, settlement of client's claim without consent, and conversion of settlement funds warranted disbarment; court held that lawyer's 2009 disbarment for similar misconduct occurred after the current violations but was relevant to assessing lawyer's fitness to practice in the future, noting that lawyer "has victimized both clients and third parties in the past, and it is highly likely he will continue to do so in the future if given an opportunity"; citing Sanctions Standards, but not Standard 8.1(b) specifically); *Att'y Grievance Comm'n v. Dunietz,* 795 A.2d 706, 713 (Md. 2002) (disbarring lawyer for neglect and disregard of grievance process coupled with prior disciplinary record for same or similar misconduct indicating persistent pattern of behavior; court stated, "We recognize by our action here the need to protect the public from further victimization by a recalcitrant attorney and to motivate other attorneys 'to adopt appropriate practices in the future.'") (citation omitted); *In re Hogan,* 56 A.D.3d 887, 888 (N.Y. App. Div. 2008) (disbarring lawyer who, though repeatedly disciplined for similar misconduct, "persistently demonstrated an apathetic and neglectful attitude towards representation of his clients in serious matters").

## *Timing of Prior Misconduct*

The time between a prior and subsequent offense is an issue that arises both in the context of finding a baseline sanction under Standard 8.1 and in the context of assessing prior misconduct as an aggravating factor under Standard 9.22(a) or as a mitigating factor under Standard 9.32(m).

### • Remoteness in Time

Remoteness of a prior offense can be a mitigating factor. *See generally* Annotation to Standard 9.32(m) (Remoteness of Prior Offenses). Some courts, however, have held that offenses committed several years in the past are still sufficiently proximate for consideration under Standard 8.1 and therefore warrant disbarment. *In re Wenger,* 112 P.3d 199, 210 (Kan. 2005) provides an example. In *Wenger,* a lawyer had been suspended twice in Iowa, first in 1991 and then in 1998 prior to his 2003 suspension in Kansas for failing to pay the annual registration and the CLE fees. He remained administratively suspended when new disciplinary proceedings were initiated for conduct occurring in matters he was handling for two different clients prior to his suspension in Kansas. The lawyer argued that his Iowa suspension was remote in time and should not be considered in calculating discipline in the Kansas proceeding. The Kansas Supreme Court disagreed, finding the Iowa discipline not remote in time and calling the connections between his acts in Iowa and his conduct in Kansas "striking[ly] similar." In Iowa, the court noted, the lawyer failed to diligently pursue a matter entrusted to him, did not cooperate with an investigation of a disciplinary complaint, fabricated evidence, and gave false testimony at the disciplinary hearing. In Kansas, he lied to his clients and neglected matters entrusted to him, failed to cooperate with the investigations of his disciplinary complaints, failed to file an answer to the complaints, and failed to participate in the panel hearing although he had been notified of the time and place. Since his conduct in Iowa led to a suspension, the Kansas court applied Standard 8.1(b) and disbarred the lawyer. *See also State ex rel. Counsel for Discipline v. Ellis*, 808 N.W.2d 634 (Neb. 2012) (prior discipline in 2003 resulting in one-year suspension was not too remote in time to be considered an aggravating factor in instant case where prior misconduct was similar to current charges and sufficient to establish cumulative acts of misconduct warranting disbarment); *In re Disciplinary Action Against Swanson*, 638 N.W.2d 240 (N.D. 2002) (disbarment warranted for failure to close estate for more than thirteen years, inter alia, because lawyer engaged in similar misconduct resulting in two private reprimands and two prior suspensions, the last of which was seven years ago); *cf. In re Disciplinary Proceeding Against VanDerbeek*, 101 P.3d 88 (Wash. 2004) (disbarring lawyer for bill-padding practices that continued even after settlement of lawsuit brought by twenty-eight clients for excessive billing; noting other cases in which courts had considered as aggravating prior misconduct dating back nine to thirty years, court found that lawyer's prior reprimand for misconduct involving dishonesty that occurred more than fifteen years earlier was not too remote to serve as an aggravating factor when it was imposed for similar misconduct and held that hearing officer and board erred in finding remoteness of 1987 reprimand to be mitigating factor); *see also In re Disciplinary Proceeding Against Cohen*, 67 P.3d 1086 (Wash. 2003) (considering thirty- and ten-year-old admonitions and reprimands for similar misconduct as aggravating factor and expressly declining to find that remoteness of prior similar disciplinary offenses were mitigating).

- **In the Same General Time Frame**

At the other end of the temporal spectrum is the issue of prior and present misconduct being too close in time to be considered separate offenses applicable for the "same or similar" misconduct analysis of Standard 8.0. Courts have found that, in such cases, the notion of fairness precludes severability, querying whether the prior discipline served as a fair warning to the lawyer or whether the misdeeds are too contemporaneous for that purpose. In *In re Jones*, 747 So.2d 1081, 1084 (La. 1999), for example, a lawyer represented clients and made four court appearances after becoming ineligible to do so due to his failure to comply with mandatory continuing legal education requirements and failure to pay bar membership dues. The lawyer's disciplinary history included two admonitions and a suspension. The court found that since the misconduct in the present case occurred before its earlier order suspending the lawyer, he could not be found to have engaged in similar misconduct after being warned not to do so by the court. Nonetheless, in concluding that disbarment was warranted, the court noted that disciplinary proceedings in the suspension case were initiated at the time of the latest misconduct and the lawyer "should have been aware at the time of the instant misconduct that the disciplinary authorities found his unauthorized practice of law to be sanctionable conduct."

When acts of misconduct occur in the same general time frame, a court might weigh the former misconduct in aggravation as evidence establishing a pattern of misconduct rather than falling under the "same or similar misconduct" rubric of Standard 8.1(b). *See, e.g., In re Van Buskirk*, 981 P.2d 607 (Colo. 1999) (rejecting disbarment under Standard 8.1(b) in favor of three-year suspension for lawyer who pleaded guilty to second-degree felony burglary and third-degree misdemeanor assault when lawyer had been suspended for conduct in 1998 that the court found "very similar," namely convictions for hit and run, careless driving, disorderly conduct, and DUI; stating that if 1998 suspension were treated as previous discipline, disbarment would be appropriate under Standard 8.1(b), but all acts in instant case occurred prior to imposition of 1998 discipline and were more properly viewed as a pattern of misconduct under Standard 9.32(c)); *People v. Regan*, 871 P.2d 1184 (Colo. 1994) (one-year suspension for neglect by lawyer previously suspended for similar misconduct when present misconduct was found to have occurred during same time period as past violation; court treated current and previous misconduct as evidence of pattern of misconduct under Standard 9.22(c), noting that had respondent engaged in the instant misconduct after his suspension, there would be no question but that disbarment would be appropriate under Standard 8.1(b); *cf. In re Davis*, 43 A.3d 856, 900 (Del. 2012) (disbarment imposed under Standard 8.1(b), inter alia, where record "reflects a continuing pattern of misrepresentation for a personal benefit"). *But cf. Att'y Grievance Comm'n v. Manning*, 569 A.2d 1250, 1254 (Md. 1990) (disbarment warranted for failure to diligently pursue clients' interests, failure to communicate with clients, and repeated failure to respond to bar counsel's information requests when lawyer was under suspension for acts of neglect that occurred in same time period; "[a]lthough the suspension he is presently serving could not have had a deterrent effect on the previously committed violations, the large number of similar complaints over a more than two-year span demonstrates a disturbing pattern"; Sanctions Standards not cited).

The Louisiana Supreme Court developed a line of cases following *La. State Bar Ass'n v. Chatelain*, 573 So.2d 470 (La. 1991), directing that, under most circumstances, when the underlying conduct at issue occurs before or within the same time period as the misconduct that formed the basis for a previous sanction, the subsequent discipline should be determined as if both proceedings had been before the court simultaneously. In *Chatelain*, the court said disbarment was appropriate in the third disciplinary action against the lawyer because the misconduct in the third disciplinary proceeding occurred before the violations in the two previous disciplinary cases, which also resulted in disbarment. All three cases involved the same pattern of misconduct. For that reason, the court determined that it would not impose disbarment again or extend the period of time in which the lawyer could apply for readmission. Instead, the court found the lawyer guilty of additional violations warranting disbarment that would be added to his record for consideration if he applied for readmission after becoming eligible to do so. *Accord In re Barrios*, 54 So.3d 649 (La. 2011) (finding disbarment baseline sanction under Sanctions Standards for disbarred lawyer's knowing pattern of failing to diligently pursue client matters, to return unearned fees, and to cooperate with disciplinary investigations; concluding that the *Chatelain* approach applied as misconduct at issue occurred during same time period as that resulting in lawyer's earlier disbarment for same violations; but the court also found that the lawyer's failures to cooperate with the disciplinary investigation occurred outside the time period subject to *Chatelain* and thus warranted a two-year extension in the time period lawyer must wait before applying for readmission); *In re Szuba*, 896 So.2d 976 (La. 2005) (presenting variation of *Chatelain* in which the court considered, in a consolidated matter, two sets of formal charges against the suspended lawyer; court applied *Chatelain* to the first case because the misconduct occurred in the same relevant time frame and was nearly identical to the misconduct in the prior proceeding; court found lawyer guilty of additional violations that would be added to his record for consideration in the event he applied for readmission, but since the unauthorized practice of law occurred after the order of suspension, additional discipline of one-year-and-one-day suspension was warranted); *In re Boudreau*, 860 So.2d 1119 (La. 2003) (variation of *Chatelain* pattern in which substantive misconduct occurred in same time frame as misconduct underlying previous sanction, but failure to cooperate with disciplinary investigation occurred after rendering of previous opinion; failure to cooperate was treated separately and resulted in six-month suspension to run consecutively with suspension imposed for abandonment of client matter); *In re Richard*, 826 So.2d 542 (La. 2002) (declining to again disbar lawyer who engaged in the practice of law while ineligible, when misconduct occurred within same general time as misconduct forming basis of prior disbarment; judging as if both sets of charges had been before court at the same time and finding lawyer guilty of additional misconduct warranting disbarment to be considered if the lawyer seeks readmission). *But see In re Wyche*,

849 So.2d 508 (La. 2003) (in imposing permanent disbarment court declined to follow *Chatelain* approach although lawyer's misconduct occurred in same time frame as prior misconduct because lawyer's refusal to cooperate in investigation of instant complaint hindered investigation of facts necessary to bring simultaneous formal charges).

### *Aggravating and Mitigating Factors*

In keeping with the Theoretical Framework, STANDARDS FOR IMPOSING LAWYER SANCTIONS pt. II (ABA 1992), disbarment under Standard 8.1 should be imposed only after consideration of pertinent aggravating or mitigating factors. Under Standard 9.21, aggravating circumstances are any considerations or factors that may justify an increase in the degree of discipline to be imposed. There are many instances in which facts establishing baseline disbarment under Standard 8.1 overlap with aggravating factors under Standard 9.22 that involve consideration of past misconduct. Many courts bolster findings that disbarment is warranted under Standard 8.1(b) by looking at the balance of aggravating and mitigating circumstances. *See, e.g., People v. Mason*, 212 P.3d 141 (Colo. O.P.D.J. 2009) (lawyer's violation of a court order not to practice law while under suspension warranted disbarment under Standards 8.1(a) and 8.1(b); similarly holding lawyer's prior suspension for unauthorized practice of law supported the aggravating factors of prior discipline, pattern of misconduct, and multiple offenses); *In re Grady*, 782 So.2d 570 (La. 2001) (in light of lawyer's prior suspension for similar offenses, disbarment warranted under Standard 8.1(b), inter alia, for conversion, neglect, mishandling of client funds and failure to communicate, return unearned fees, and cooperate in disciplinary process; aggravating factors included prior misconduct, failure to cooperate, and vulnerability of the victims); *In re Reynolds*, 737 So.2d 1272 (La. 1999) (disbarment under Standard 8.1 appropriate given lawyer's extensive disciplinary history—including suspension, subsequent revocation of probation, and four admonitions—for same or similar misconduct involving conversion, improper fee collection, neglect, and failure to cooperate with disciplinary authorities; no mitigating factors, but nine aggravating factors including prior disciplinary offenses, dishonest or selfish motive, a pattern of misconduct, and multiple offenses). For further discussion and cases, *see* Annotation to Standard 9.0.

There are also cases in which courts have declined to impose disbarment under Standard 8.1 due to mitigating factors under Standard 9.3. *See, e.g., Fla. Bar v. Temmer*, 753 So.2d 555, 558 (Fla. 1999) (lawyer charged with possession of marijuana, cocaine, valium, and drug paraphernalia while completing three years of disciplinary probation following ninety-day suspension for drug-related misconduct; court noted that "but for the substantial mitigation presented, disbarment [under Florida Standard 8.1(b)] might have been in order here," court imposed ninety-one-day suspension, this time requiring lawyer to prove rehabilitation before reinstatement, followed by three years of probation); *In re Vanderbilt*, 253 P.3d 774 (Kan. 2011) (while disbarment was baseline under Standard 8.1(b) for misconduct arising in lawyer's post-divorce matter, including failure to pay child support and contempt of court finding, court imposed indefinite suspension based on mitigating factors of lack of dishonest or selfish motive, cooperation in discipline process, expression of remorse, and remoteness of prior offenses); *In re Johnson*, 335 P.3d 634, 643 (Kan. 2014) (suspended lawyer who did not notify clients, courts, and opposing counsel of his suspension and who received four prior disciplinary sanctions and five administrative suspensions was suspended indefinitely instead of disbarred; minority of the court would have disbarred, but majority deferred to mitigation found by hearing panel that "the respondent has begun a personal transformation from an attorney with a bad attitude and disregard for the rules to an attorney with respect for the rules which govern our profession").

## *Cases Under Both Standards 8.1(a) and 8.1(b)*

A lawyer's misconduct sometimes falls under both paragraphs (a) and (b) of Standard 8.1. *In re Benge*, 783 A.2d 1279 (Del. 2001), a case in which a lawyer had been repeatedly disciplined for neglecting clients' matters, provides such an example. In *Benge*, the lawyer had been given a private admonition and placed on a two-year private probation for failing to protect the interests of an elderly client with a personal injury claim. While on probation, he was subject to four other disciplinary proceedings resulting in a public reprimand and another two years of probation. The lawyer was then suspended for one year for numerous violations regarding a creditor in a bankruptcy matter. Still, the lawyer continued to neglect client matters. The court noted that in addition to repeating the same type of misconduct, the lawyer failed to adhere to previous disciplinary orders, including failing to make monthly payments to the client protection fund during his suspension. The court analyzed the misconduct under Standards 8.1(a) and (b), inter alia, finding disbarment was warranted. *See also People v. Kanwal*, 357 P.3d 1236, 1246 (Colo. O.P.D.J. 2015) (Standards 8.1(a) and (b) applied to conduct of lawyer who knowingly violated suspension order by preparing immigration documents for client while suspended and who knowingly engaged in conduct similar to that for which he was suspended; disciplinary judge ordered disbarment, stating that given "the purposeful nature of Respondent's actions, we cannot trust that he will adhere to the Rules of Professional Conduct in the future . . ."); *Fla. Bar v. Bitterman*, 33 So.3d 686 (Fla. 2010) (disbarment for suspended lawyer under Florida Standards 8.1(a) and (b), inter alia, for misrepresenting her status as a member in good standing of The Florida Bar; fact that lawyer did not engage in the unauthorized practice of law was irrelevant given that lawyer's misrepresentation was a violation of suspension order and constituted misconduct similar to that underlying the suspension); *V.I. Bar Ass'n v. Boyd-Richards*, No. 88/1994, 1999 WL 970781 (V.I. Oct. 14, 1999) (disbarment under Standards 8.1(a) and (b), inter alia, for lawyer who intentionally violated disciplinary order by refusing to maintain escrow account for client funds, failing to return client funds, and failing to keep appropriate records, and when same misconduct precipitated prior suspension).

**8.2 Suspension is generally appropriate when a lawyer has been reprimanded for the same or similar misconduct and engages in further similar acts of misconduct that cause injury or potential injury to a client, the public, the legal system, or theprofession.**

## Annotation

Lawyers often are suspended when they engage in the same or similar misconduct for which they were previously reprimanded or censured, and when that misconduct causes injury or potential injury to a client, the public, the legal system, or the profession. As the Florida Supreme Court noted in *Fla. Bar v. Walkden*, 950 So.2d 407, 410 (Fla. 2007): "In determining the appropriate discipline, we consider prior misconduct and cumulative misconduct, and treat cumulative misconduct more severely than isolated misconduct."

As with disbarment under Standard 8.1, the rationale behind suspension under Standard 8.2 is protection of the public from further misdeeds by a lawyer whose repeated misconduct demonstrates a lack of trustworthiness. This concern for public protection is often reflected prominently in courts' reasoning when imposing suspensions under this Standard. *See, e.g., In re Johanning*, 254 P.3d 545, 555 (Kan. 2011) (indefinite suspension for mishandling of client property warranted under Standard 8.2, inter alia, as lawyer previously received censures and probation for same misconduct, following "repeated attempts by the disciplinary system to educate and supervise the respondent," including more than seven years of counseling about the need for trust accounting; court noted that "[c]learly, past attempts to educate and encourage a modification of behavior have failed"); *In re Lober*, 78 P.3d 442, 448 (Kan. 2003) (one-year suspension under Standard 8.2 for already disciplined lawyer who on five prior occasions failed to communicate with clients and failed to cooperate with disciplinary authorities; "[p]rior admonitions and probation have apparently been ineffective in bringing an end to this behavior which harms clients and the legal system"); *In re Tapia*, 777 P.2d 378, 380 (N.M. 1989) (indefinite suspension for a minimum of two years with one year deferred for misconduct because, previous formal reprimand "does not appear to have persuaded him to conform his conduct to acceptable standards"; "[o]ur concern is with injury or potential injury to clients, the legal system, or the public, and when a lawyer has been reprimanded but continues to engage in the same or similar misconduct, suspension is the appropriate sanction"); *Bd. of Prof'l Responsibility v. Hiatt*, 422 P.3d 940, 955 (Wyo. 2018) (court rejected board-recommended censure and imposed thirty-day suspension for neglect of custody matter, repeated failure to respond to client emails and telephone calls, and charging an unreasonable nonrefundable retainer; applying Standard 8.2 analysis, the court stated that "when an attorney continues to engage in professional and ethical misconduct in spite of previous sanctions, our concern weighs more heavily towards deterrence, maintaining the integrity of the legal system, and protecting the public") (citation omitted).

Standard 8.2 also provides a means to ensure efficacy of the disciplinary process when a lawyer has shown repeated disrespect for it. *See, e.g., In re Davis*, 889 P.2d 621, 624 (Ariz. 1995) (sixty-day suspension followed by two-year probation under Standard 8.2, inter alia, for violating terms of probation and failing to cooperate with disciplinary authorities when lawyer was previously reprimanded for repeatedly failing to respond to inquiries and orders from the state bar; court found that "[m]erely extending the probation or adding additional terms would not provide her or other lawyers with a meaningful indication of the seriousness of violating probationary terms and ignoring the State Bar's information requests"; "anything less than suspension would make a mockery of the disciplinary process"); *In re Disciplinary Action Against Lucas*, 789 N.W.2d 73, 78 (N.D. 2010) (citing North Dakota Standard 8.2 in ordering thirty-day suspension for improper communications with a represented party and noting, "This court's disciplinary orders are not intended to be 'empty noise'"; court rejected public reprimand because prior reprimand for similar misconduct failed to deter respondent from repeating the conduct) (citation omitted).

## *Mens Rea*

Unlike Standard 8.1, which requires a mental state of "intentionally or knowingly," Standard 8.2 does not articulate a requisite mental state, but rather suggests suspension is appropriate when a lawyer repeats the same or similar misconduct for which he or she has been previously reprimanded and which causes injury or potential injury. An evaluation of case law indicates that cases under Standard 8.2 frequently involve neglect or negligent misconduct. *See, e.g., People v. Frank*, 752 P.2d 539 (Colo. 1988) (thirty-day suspension under Standard 8.2, inter alia, when lawyer continued to neglect duties to his client even after he had been privately censured for neglect); *In re Disciplinary Action Against Jones*, 487 N.W.2d 599, 601 (N.D. 1992) (thirty-day suspension under Standard 8.2, inter alia, for lack of communication and neglect when lawyer had been privately reprimanded for similar misconduct on two prior occasions; "[s]uch a pattern of neglect should not be overlooked"); *Flowers v. Bd. of Prof'l Responsibility*, 314 S.W.3d 882 (Tenn. 2010) (one-year suspension for several instances of misconduct stemming from lawyer's negligent and dilatory representation of immigration clients; citing Standard 8.2, inter alia, in finding suspension appropriate in light of lawyer's prior private reprimand for multiple instances of neglect and failure to move with reasonable promptness in his immigration cases).

Some cases relying on Standard 8.2, however, have involved knowing and intentional misconduct. *See, e.g., In re Miranda*, 823 P.2d 1278 (Ariz. 1992) (suspending for three months with two years of probation under Standard 8.2, inter alia, for various violations including intentional failure to comply with terms of previously imposed probation); *Fla. Bar v. Letwin*, 70 So.3d 578 (Fla. 2011) (one-year rehabilitative suspension for knowingly and intentionally sending 900 prospective clients a letter containing materially false statements and improperly soliciting employment; suspension warranted in light of lawyer's previous sanctions for misrepresentation); *In re Hasty*, 335 P.3d 110 (Kan. 2014) (indefinite suspension under Standard 8.2, inter alia, for previously censured lawyer who, in representing school bus owner and bus driver in negligence action, knowingly failed to respond to discovery requests and appear for hearings and knowingly failed to inform clients of assessment of attorney's fees against them; court also considered as prior discipline in this matter two instances where the lawyer had been placed on diversion, one for similar misconduct as that resulting in the indefinite suspension); *In re Polsley*, 85 P.3d 693 (Kan. 2004) (indefinite suspension under Standard 8.2 for lawyer's knowing conversion of deceased mother-in-law's Social Security direct deposit benefit checks, resulting in conviction of theft of government property; lawyer disciplined on two occasions, an informal admonishment and a censure, and then suspended for failing to pay annual bar registration fee and continuing education requirement fee, and for failing to comply with annual continuing legal education requirements).

## *Same or Similar Misconduct*

Cases under Standard 8.2 turn on the similarity between prior and subsequent misconduct. Courts have imposed suspensions when prior misconduct and current misconduct are identical or nearly so. *See, e.g., In re Ockrassa*, 799 P.2d 1350, 1354 (Ariz. 1990) (suspending for ninety days public defender-turned-prosecutor who again violated conflicts rules; in deciding between informal reprimand and suspension, court considered lawyer's disciplinary history, noting that under Standard 8.2 the lawyer "has demonstrated an insensitivity to conflicts of interest evidenced by a pattern of misconduct" for which he had been censured and informally reprimanded); *People v. Al-Haqq*, 2016 WL 6835526 at *12 (Colo. O.P.D.J. 2016) (lawyer previously disciplined five times suspended for twenty-four months for same and similar misconduct including neglect and failure to adequately communicate with clients; Office of the Presiding Disciplinary Judge rejected regulation counsel's argument that presumptive sanction of disbarment under Standard 8.1 was proper due to prior suspension, holding instead that Standard 8.2 applied because misconduct underlying that suspension was not sufficiently similar to conduct charged in current matter); *In re Beauregard*, 2018 WL 2694235 (Del. 2018) (imposing six-month suspension court found lawyer "previously disciplined for substantially the same books and records violations" should have been in "hyper-vigilant state when he assumed the same supervisory responsibilities at his new law firm"; presumptive suspension under Standard 8.2 particularly appropriate in this matter); *In re Johanning*, 254 P.3d 545 (Kan. 2011) (indefinite suspension under Standard 8.2, inter alia, for intentional mishandling of client funds, misconduct for which lawyer had previously been sanctioned); *In re Disciplinary Action Against Lucas*, 789 N.W.2d 73 (N.D. 2010) (thirty-day suspension for lawyer's improper communications with a represented party, when lawyer had been reprimanded for similar conduct and that sanction failed to deter him from repeating the conduct); *cf. In re Rivera*, 813 P.2d 1015 (N.M. 1991) (failure to respond to client inquiries and to return unearned fees warranted six-month suspension under Standard 8.2 when lawyer had been formally reprimanded for nearly identical violations; court deferred suspension for one year, placing lawyer on probation because he did not act dishonestly, client was reimbursed and suffered no harm, and lawyer presented mitigating factors including six-months of sobriety); *Hyman v. Bd. of Prof'l Responsibility*, 437 S.W.3d 435 (Tenn. 2014) (application of Standard 8.2 supported by significant evidence; lawyer had been disciplined five prior times for the same or similar misconduct including making threats and alleged assault against others).

Suspensions are also appropriate for conduct that, while not identical or nearly identical, is similar to prior misconduct. *See, e.g., In re Brady*, 387 P.3d 1 (Alaska 2016) (after lawyer had been censured for similarly neglecting an ERISA appeal, court, citing Standard 8.2, approved six-month stipulated suspension for lawyer who failed to diligently pursue a claim and appeal on behalf of a client, including not timely responding to motions and missing deadlines); *In re Kellogg*, 50 P.3d 57 (Kan. 2002) (adopting panel's conclusions upon consideration of Standard 8.2, inter alia, and imposing indefinite suspension when lawyer had been twice previously disciplined and then placed on two-year probation, but continued to engage in similar misconduct, including padding bills); *In re Grady*, 731 So.2d 878 (La. 1999) (imposing one-year-and-one-day suspension under Standard 8.2, inter alia, for failure to terminate representation when lawyer was ineligible to practice law for failure to comply with mandatory continuing legal education requirements, failure to so notify client of status of case, and failure to appear or respond to disciplinary proceeding, when lawyer had prior disciplinary offenses including private reprimand for similar acts).

Standard 8.2, unlike Standard 8.1, does not include a subsection (a) addressing violations of a prior disciplinary order. *See Walwyn v. Bd. of Prof'l Responsibility*, 481 S.W.3d 151, 168 (Tenn. 2015) (court rejected lawyer's argument that Standard 8.2 was inapplicable to his case because that Standard only applies to misconduct "that is a direct result of the violation of a prior disciplinary order," holding that to be an incorrect interpretation of the Standard). At least one court has found such a violation to be a "further act of misconduct" under Standard 8.2. *See Office of Disciplinary Counsel v. Lau*, 900 P.2d 777 (Haw. 1995) (suspension of 120 days for appearing at a hearing on behalf of prison inmate while under disciplinary suspension order; canvassing cases from various jurisdictions imposing suspension or disbarment for practicing while suspended, court stated:

> For purposes of ABA Standard 8.2, practicing law while suspended is a "further act[ ] of misconduct." At a bare minimum, such violations and acts of misconduct harm the legal system, the profession, and the public by encouraging disrespect for the law and the courts and reinforce a perception of privilege and arrogance. Thus, we hold that practicing law while suspended or disbarred warrants the severe sanctions of suspension or disbarment.

900 P.2d at 783. *See also In re Disciplinary Action Against Stensland*, 799 N.W.2d 341, 347 (N.D. 2011) (one-year suspension warranted under Standard 8.2, inter alia, for lawyer's "ongoing pattern of misconduct" for which he received two prior consent probations, an admonition, and two suspensions for similar misconduct; misconduct including at least two instances of fraudulently affixing a client's name to a document and filing it with a court, failure to properly notify clients of a prior suspension, falsely certifying to court compliance with notification requirements, repeated and flagrant failure to communicate with clients, and mishandling and refusing to return unearned client funds suggests "a pattern of dishonesty to the courts and flagrant disregard of his clients' welfare").

## *Timing of Prior Sanction*

As with consideration of a disciplinary history under Standard 8.1(b), the timing of a previous sanction is important to the analysis under Standard 8.2, along with Standard 9.32(m).

### • Remoteness in Time

Courts generally look to the temporal relationship between repeated similar violations. They tend to place less weight on remote violations and greater weight on violations when the subsequent misconduct occurs in close proximity to the imposition or completion of a prior sanction. *See, e.g., Fla. Bar v. Dopazo*, 232 So.3d 258 (Fla. 2017) (one-year suspension under Florida Standards for Imposing Lawyer Sanctions warranted for lawyer who improperly solicited, at the hospital, mother of a child with brain injuries after 2004 reprimand for similar improper contacts; rejecting lawyer's claim of remoteness in time of prior offense, the court stated that because the second inappropriate solicitation occurred in 2007, three years after first sanction, "his public reprimand should have been fresh in his mind, especially because he committed the same rule violation of solicitation a second time"); *In re Beauregard,* 2018 WL 2694235 at*14 (Del. 2018) (cited above regarding "Same or Similar Misconduct"; disagreeing with disciplinary board, the court placed less emphasis on remoteness of prior discipline because only four years elapsed between completion of first sanction and current misconduct; "It is hard to imagine remoteness in time to be a factor in repetitive books and records violations.").

Remoteness in time becomes determinative if a prior sanction is too far removed from the current misconduct. *See* Annotation to Standard 9.32(m) (Remoteness of Prior Offenses as Mitigating Factor). *See, e.g., In re Allred,* 27 P.3d 977, 981 (N.M. 2001) (discipline imposed more than ten years previously could be considered as aggravating factor, even though parties had stipulated to remoteness as a mitigating factor: "There is a difference . . . between not having a prior disciplinary record and having one, albeit remote in time. . . . Where, as here, the prior discipline was imposed more than 10 years previously, its relevance as an aggravating factor will likely depend on the similarity between the prior violations and the current ones. . . . In this case, the similarity is striking"; three-year suspension, deferred after first year in favor of supervised probation upon satisfaction of various conditions, was warranted sanction); *In re Disciplinary Action Against Howe,* 626 N.W.2d 650 (N.D. 2001) (lawyer who had been disciplined five times asserted that sanctions in 1977 and 1988 should not be relevant because they were far apart and relatively remote in time; in imposing 120-day suspension under North Dakota Standard 8.2, the court concluded that those disciplinary actions were relevant in establishing a pattern of misconduct and found that the hearing panel did not err in considering lawyer's entire record of prior sanctions as aggravating circumstances). *But see In re Vanderbilt,* 253 P.3d 774 (Kan. 2011) (despite finding disbarment appropriate under Standard 8.1(b) for previously suspended lawyer's misconduct involving his child support obligations, imposing indefinite suspension based on several mitigating factors including the remoteness in time of the prior offenses and the general remoteness in character of those offenses).

- **Close Proximity in Time to Prior Conduct**

When a lawyer's repeated misconduct occurs before the prior sanction is imposed, some courts have held that Standard 8.2 does not apply. *See, e.g., In re Kraushaar,* 997 P.2d 81 (Kan. 2000) (finding Standard 8.2 not on point when lawyer's subsequent misconduct occurred before decision in prior disciplinary case; imposing one-year suspension based on other factors).

Courts, instead, may view repeated misconduct as a reason to extend the discipline imposed in the prior proceeding rather than suspend under Standard 8.2. In *In re Gold,* 734 So.2d 1210, 1212 (La. 1999), for example, the Louisiana Supreme Court considered the lawyer's disciplinary history that included suspension on two occasions and fourteen formal private reprimands and admonitions, most involving failure to cooperate and failure to appear under a subpoena. The court noted that, in its 1997 opinion sanctioning the lawyer, it warned the lawyer that any *future* misconduct would be treated harshly. In the instant case the court imposed another public reprimand and extended the lawyer's probation instead of imposing a suspension, stating, "If the misconduct at issue had occurred after that warning in our 1997 opinion, we would be inclined to impose a very lengthy suspension. However, the instant misconduct occurred prior to that opinion and could have been considered and dealt with in that opinion." *Cf. In re Reul*, 74 A.D.3d 1630 (N.Y. App. Div. 2010) (failure to timely disclose existence of new escrow account and inadvertent overdraft on that account warranted one-year extension of lawyer's stayed suspension involving similar misconduct, i.e., mishandling escrow accounts and client funds; while such conduct fell under the reporting requirement condition of the stay of suspension, imposition of suspension was inappropriate; Sanctions Standards not cited).

## *Gradual Gradation*

The severity of prior discipline also bears on the appropriate sanction for repeated similar misconduct. *See, e.g., In re Davis*, 889 P.2d 621, 624 (Ariz. 1995) ("Regarding the discipline of a lawyer previously sanctioned, we have determined that 'a graded response from reprimand, to suspension, to disbarment is sometimes appropriate, depending on the severity of the subsequent conduct.'") (citation omitted). This "gradual gradation" in sanctioning was initially described by the Arizona Supreme Court in *In re Redondo*, 861 P.2d 619, 623 (Ariz. 1993). There, the court imposed a two-year suspension under Standard 8.2, inter alia, for the lawyer's neglect of legal matters in dealing with a number of clients, among other violations. The lawyer had two prior informal reprimands for similar misconduct in the past. The court noted that the pattern of carelessness showed "wholesale negligence rather than malice." Deciding between suspension and disbarment, the court said:

> We think that the spirit of the ABA Standards is better met by gradual and graded sanctions. If we thought the public could only be protected by disbarment, we would do so promptly. But we can protect the public just as well by a carefully crafted disposition which includes a lengthy term of suspension followed by a lengthy term of *supervised* probation. This will clearly protect the public from [respondent] and at the same time give him an opportunity to cure his significant problems before he is ever allowed to practice on an unsupervised basis again.

The dissent found this case is one in which gradual and graded sanctions were both ineffective and inappropriate. Arguing for disbarment, the dissent wrote:

> For too many years, respondent has been an irresponsible, unguided missile. As a result, he has injured at least 10 different clients . . . Considering the number and variety of ethical violations committed by respondent, along with the Disciplinary Commission's determination that his 'level of carelessness is so great as to make him a hazard to the profession,' . . . the only appropriate sanction in this case is disbarment. By affording respondent the opportunity to practice law in the future, this court does a disservice both to the public and to the legal profession.

*Id.* at 625; *see also In re Brown*, 910 P.2d 631 (Ariz. 1996) (lawyer, whose misconduct included failure to cooperate with disciplinary authorities, is suspended for nine months upon court's determination that a more severe sanction was warranted since lawyer was previously censured, and informally reprimanded on four occasions for failure to cooperate); *Fla. Bar v. Letwin*, 70 So.3d 578, 584 (Fla. 2011) (one-year rehabilitative suspension for improper solicitation of employment containing false statements of material fact; noting that suspension under Florida Standard 8.0 was warranted given lawyer's prior public reprimand for misrepresentation and ninety-day suspension with three years of probation for contempt, neglect, and misrepresentation; rejecting disciplinary referee's recommendation of a ninety-day suspension in light of the "seriousness" of lawyer's prior disciplinary misconduct and continuing pattern of misconduct).

### *Cumulative Discipline*

One result of rigidly applying the gradation concept is that courts sometimes impose suspension under Standard 8.2 rather than disbarment, notwithstanding numerous instances of similar past misconduct and repeated admonitions, reprimands, or low-level suspensions. *See, e.g., In re Brown*, 910 P.2d 631, 634 (Ariz. 1996) (imposing nine-month suspension when lawyer was censured or informally reprimanded on four prior occasions for failure to cooperate with bar; coupled with lawyer's failure to obey the prior disciplinary order, court expressed "great concern" over his "apparent indifference to the disciplinary process" and felt compelled to find suspension was appropriate sanction); *Iowa Supreme Ct. Att'y Disciplinary Bd. v. McCarthy*, 814 N.W.2d 596, 600 (Iowa 2012) (noting that lawyer was "no stranger to the disciplinary process," court imposed indefinite suspension in light of lawyer's pattern of neglect, his lack of respect for the disciplinary process, and his disciplinary history involving similar neglect in some instances resulting in four admonishments, four public reprimands, four temporary suspensions, and a six-month suspension); *In re Potter*, 112 P.3d 216, 224 (Kan. 2005) (imposing indefinite suspension under Standard 8.2, inter alia, for lawyer's numerous disciplinary violations, including being subject to eight prior proceedings, and the recurring pattern of those violations; warning that "[t]he level of discipline should impress upon the respondent the necessity of changing his behavior"); *In re Brooks,* 696 N.W.2d 84 (Minn. 2005) (court reiterating that more severe sanctions are imposed when the current misconduct is similar to misconduct for which the attorney has already been disciplined; indefinite suspension warranted since lawyer's previous discipline involved similar misconduct resulting in prior public reprimand and three admonitions; Sanctions Standards not cited); *In re Latimore,* 252 A.D.2d 217, 220 (N.Y. App. Div. 1999) (lawyer's "continuing neglect in the face of two prior admonitions" warranted one-year suspension; court stated that a lawyer who has "neglected legal matters and has a prior disciplinary history is subject to suspension"); *In re Disciplinary Action Against Stensland,* 799 N.W.2d 341, 347 (N.D. 2011) (noting concern with lawyer's "ongoing pattern of misconduct" and lengthy disciplinary history that included two consent probations, an admonition, and two suspensions, one involving similar misconduct, court held one-year suspension appropriate under Standard 8.2); *In re Porter,* 890 P.2d 1377, 1386 (Or. 1995) (sixty-three-day suspension under Standard 8.2, inter alia, for misrepresentation in letter to opposing counsel; lawyer had been subject to "numerous prior disciplinary reprimands" and two prior admonitions, including an admonition for engaging in conduct involving misrepresentation to a court occurring less than three months before conduct in the present case); *In re Disciplinary Proceeding Against Ray,* 678 N.W.2d 246, 250 (Wis. 2004) (noting that "Prior disciplinary cases have frequently followed a progressive discipline scheme," court imposed a six-month suspension on lawyer for, inter alia, improper termination of representation and failure to cooperate in disciplinary proceedings in light of sixty-day suspension two years earlier).

The State of Washington has addressed the issue of discipline for cumulative admonitions in its Rules for Enforcement of Lawyer Conduct. WASH. STATE CT. RULES FOR ENFORCEMENT OF LAWYER CONDUCT R. 13.6 (2014). Rule 13.6 provides that a lawyer may be subject to sanctions if he or she receives three admonitions within a five-year period. Upon evidence that a respondent lawyer has had such discipline, a review committee may authorize the filing of a formal complaint and a proceeding will be conducted in the same manner as any disciplinary proceeding. The issues in the proceeding are whether the lawyer has received three admonitions within the five-year period and, if so, what sanction or other remedy should be recommended.

## *Aggravating Factors*

The mechanism of applying aggravating factors also allows for adjustments beyond a single step up from the prior sanction when a lawyer repeats misconduct after accumulating multiple prior sanctions. *See generally* Annotation to Standard 9.2 (Aggravating Factors). Thus, when a lawyer continues the misconduct for which he or she has been admonished repeatedly, reprimanded, suspended, or placed on probation, protection of the public and the integrity of the disciplinary process may require disbarment instead of suspension under Standard 8.2. In some cases factors in aggravation have served to increase the severity of a sanction from suspension under Standard 8.2 to disbarment. *See, e.g., In re Rathbun*, 169 P.3d 329, 335 (Kan. 2007) (disbarment for lawyer's repetition of similar misconduct while under disciplinary probation; court held: "While every such violation does not result in an escalation of the severity of punishment, in this case the violation reflects a pattern of misconduct that spans a decade, involves 21 separate cases, and occurs while the respondent is already on probation. Repeated attempts at probation and rehabilitation have failed."); *In re Decker*, 916 So.2d 1023 (La. 2005) (baseline suspension for repetition of nearly identical misconduct increased to disbarment because of numerous aggravating factors and no mitigating factors, prior suspension, and $5,500 unearned fee that had not been refunded); *In re Hilburn*, 737 So.2d 27 (La. 1999) (disbarment for knowing and intentional neglect of legal matters and conversion of funds; citing Standard 8.2 because prior disciplinary record consisted of suspension for one year and one day for misappropriation of funds from local bar association while acting as treasurer, in addition to two admonitions; finding other standards pertinent as well as many aggravating factors).

As in Standard 8.1, the facts establishing support for a Standard 8.2 suspension will often include aggravating factors under Standard 9.2. *See In re Jarvis*, 349 P.3d 445 (Kan. 2015) (lawyer suspended indefinitely for helping client with dementia obtain loan to pay lawyer's outstanding legal fees; court cited to Standards 8.2 and aggravating factors including four prior disciplinary sanctions, refusal to acknowledge wrongfulness of conduct, vulnerability of the victim, and multiple offenses); *In re Bock*, 265 P.3d 552 (Kan. 2011) (indefinite suspension for failure to properly communicate with clients, to handle client matters with diligence and competence, and to fully cooperate with disciplinary process; aggravating factors including prior disciplinary offenses and pattern of misconduct supported suspension under Standard 8.2).

### *Mitigating Factors*

Conversely, mitigating factors can serve to decrease the severity of a sanction imposed under Standard 8.2. *See generally* Annotation to Standard 9.3 (Mitigating Factors). *See also In re Quinn*, 184 P.3d 235 (Kan. 2008) (one-year suspension warranted for misconduct involving mishandling of trust accounts under Standard 8.2, inter alia, given lawyer's two prior informal admonitions for similar misconduct; conditionally suspending imposition of suspension for three years based on several mitigating factors including twenty-six years of practice, often representing underserved clients, lawyer's immediate response to disciplinary complaint, and prior misconduct did not implicate quality of her representation); *In re Ketter*, 992 P.2d 205, 214 (Kan. 1999) (lawyer with misdemeanor conviction for lewd and lascivious behavior had twice received informal admonitions based on repeated instances of indecent exposure fit under Standard 8.2 because "he is being reprimanded for conduct similar to that for which he has already been reprimanded"; nonetheless, majority stayed suspension in favor of three-year probation period, with conditions, based upon assurances by the lawyer's treating psychologist; dissenting justices argued that indefinite suspension was warranted under Standard 8.2, noting that significant opportunities had been presented to the lawyer to alter his behavior or at least confront the behavior that gave rise to the charges, and that any further opportunities served only to encourage respondent's unwillingness to identify and confront his problems); *In re Nicholson*, 419 P.3d 701 (Table) (Nev. 2018) (because of mitigating circumstances, six-month instead of one-year suspension appropriate under Standard 8.2 for lawyer who failed to repay to client a debt he was directed to repay under a prior disciplinary reprimand); *In re Cohen*, 8 P.3d 953 (Or. 2000) (court acknowledged that under Standard 8.2 suspension is appropriate when a lawyer has been reprimanded for similar misconduct, but imposed public reprimand instead given significant mitigating factors including complete candor and cooperation and lawyer's mental disability, to which court gave great weight as being principally responsible for lawyer's misconduct). *Cf. In the Matter of Johnson*, 815 S.E.2d 55 (Ga. 2018) (court did not decrease Special Master's recommended suspension of at least 100 days plus reprimand for neglecting copyright matters and failing to communicate with client in personal injury matter, when lawyer had been disciplined for the same and similar misconduct; however, in imposing six-month suspension, court highlighted mitigating factors of lawyer's completion of "In-Office Consultation and Assessment with the Law Practice Management Program of the State Bar" and relevant CLE, as well as counseling for emotional problems while disciplinary matter was pending).

**8.3 Reprimand is generally appropriate when a lawyer:**

**(a) negligently violates the terms of a prior disciplinary order and such violation causes injury or potential injury to a client, the public, the legal system, or the profession; or**

**(b) has received an admonition for the same or similar misconduct and engages in further similar acts of misconduct that cause injury or potential injury to a client, the public, the legal system, or the profession.**

## Annotation

### *Prior Disciplinary Order*

Under Standard 8.3 a reprimand is appropriate when the lawyer's mental state is one of negligence in violating a prior disciplinary order or when the lawyer engages in further misconduct after receiving an admonition for similar misconduct and under both scenarios the violation causes injury or potential injury to a client, the public, the legal system, or the profession. In *People v. Dieters*, 883 P.2d 1050 (Colo. 1994), for example, the lawyer engaged in the practice of law while his license was suspended. Noting that under Standard 8.1(a) disbarment generally is warranted when a lawyer continues to practice law while suspended, the court was receptive to and explored public censure under Standard 8.3(a) because some evidence established that the lawyer mistakenly believed he had been reinstated. Therefore, his conduct was negligent rather than intentional. Further, disciplinary counsel had stipulated that there was no evidence of actual harm caused. Nonetheless, the court ultimately ruled that, due to aggravating factors in the case, the lawyer should be suspended for ninety days. *See also In re Martin*, 35 A.3d 419 (Table) (Del. 2011) (unpublished disposition in which court ordered public reprimand and probation for one year for negligently violating conditions of prior private admonition requiring lawyer to, inter alia, provide pre-certification by a certified public accountant of compliance with recordkeeping obligations; public reprimand based on lack of injury to clients, lawyer self-reported his violation, and other offenses were committed out of negligence); *In re Q.F.C.*, 728 N.W.2d 72 (Minn. 2007) (disciplinary board's recommendation of public reprimand and two-year probation was appropriate sanction for lawyer who, inter alia, failed to comply with terms of private disciplinary probation to submit trust account books and records to the Office of Lawyers Professional Responsibility; reinstating private probation, however, based on disciplinary board's procedural error; decision does not cite Sanctions Standards); *In re Crowley*, 2016 WL 2742371 (Table) (Nev. 2016) (unpublished disposition where, citing

Standard 8.3(a), court publicly reprimanded respondent instead of holding him in contempt for continuing to practice law after suspension, failing to follow post-suspension notice requirements, and failing to pay costs of prior disciplinary proceeding); *cf. In re Quinn*, 184 P.3d 235, 246 (Kan. 2008) (rejecting hearing panel's recommendation of public censure under Standards 8.3(a) and (b), inter alia, for mishandling trust accounts, misconduct for which respondent previously received two informal admonitions including an admonition to seek counsel in learning how to appropriately maintain an attorney trust account; one-year suspension "necessary to impress upon Respondent the seriousness of her disregard for proper trust accounting and recordkeeping," but suspension stayed due to several mitigating factors).

### *Same or Similar Misconduct*

Reprimands commonly are imposed on lawyers who have been admonished and then engage in the same or similar acts of misconduct. This approach is set forth in subsection (b) of Standard 8.3, which suggests a public reprimand be imposed after a lawyer has been given an admonition for misconduct but then engages in the same or similar misconduct. *See In re O'Brien-Reyes*, 868 P.2d 945 (Ariz. 1994) (finding censure warranted under Standard 8.3, with one-year probation, for failing to file timely notice of appeal, failing to communicate with clients, and failing to cooperate with state bar investigators when lawyer had previously received informal reprimand for similar misconduct); *In re Evans*, 857 P.2d 1258 (Ariz. 1993) (public censure and two-year probation under Standard 8.3(b), inter alia, warranted for failure to cooperate with state bar investigation when lawyer had been informally reprimanded, equivalent to admonition in Arizona, for same misconduct); *In re Finestrauss*, 32 A.3d 978 (Del. 2011) (lawyer's failure to timely pay his law practice's payroll tax obligations to federal, state, and local tax authorities following an earlier admonition for the same offense required a public reprimand and eighteen-month probation; court expressing concern that lawyer took no steps to assure tax delinquencies would not recur); *In re Lerner*, 197 P.3d 1067, 1078 (Nev. 2008) (public reprimand under Standard 8.3(b), inter alia, for lawyer's assistance in unauthorized practice by out-of-state lawyer, when lawyer previously received three private reprimands for similar or identical misconduct; while private reprimand may have been sufficient due to apparent lack of any harm to firm's clients, public reprimand warranted because "a private reprimand has not had any effect on his conduct and in light of the aggravating factors"); *Clark's Case*, 619 A.2d 220 (N.H. 1992) (imposing public censure for failure to cooperate with disciplinary committee when lawyer had received letter of private reprimand six months previously for identical misconduct).

## *Aggravating and Mitigating Factors*

In the context of Standard 8.3, repeated misconduct is also an issue in calculating aggravating factors under Standard 9.22, including 9.22 (a) prior disciplinary offenses, (c) a pattern of misconduct, and (d) multiple offenses. *See* Annotation to Standard 9.2; *In re McIntee*, 833 N.W.2d 431 (N.D. 2013) (after receiving an admonition for representing a client against a former client in a substantially related matter, lawyer received a public reprimand under Standards 8.3(b) and 9.22(a) for jointly representing co-executors with opposing interests and then representing one of the co-executors in a suit against the other). When aggravating factors are present in a Standard 8.3 case, a sanction of reprimand may properly be adjusted upward. This occurred in *In re Frank*, 885 S.W.2d 328 (Mo. 1994), where a lawyer was issued two written admonitions within a six-week period, first for unreasonable delay and failure to keep clients informed and then for similar infractions, as well as failure to respond to requests for information from disciplinary authorities. Thereafter, the lawyer continued to neglect his duties to eleven other clients, failed to diligently pursue their cases, failed to communicate with them, and failed to respond to disciplinary authorities. The Missouri Supreme Court cited Standard 8.3(b) for the base sanction of reprimand. The court found no mitigating factors and several aggravating factors, including prior disciplinary offenses, multiple offenses, a pattern of misconduct, and refusal to acknowledge the wrongfulness of the misconduct. Thus, the court stated:

> Reprimand is not the proper sanction for respondent . . . [T]wo previous written admonitions from the bar committee have done nothing to curb respondent's misconduct. Respondent's thirty-nine ethical violations in the representation of eleven clients demonstrate a disturbing, continuing disregard for the rights and interests of his clients. A sanction stronger than a reprimand is clearly necessary to protect the public and the legal profession.

*Id.* at 334. Noting that the volume and repeated nature of respondent's ethical violations made the question of whether to disbar or suspend a close question, the court chose to suspend the lawyer for two years. *See also In re Wiechman*, 222 P.3d 485 (Kan. 2010) (one-year suspension for, inter alia, engaging in improper physical contact with a client, misconduct for which lawyer previously received a private admonition; rejecting disciplinary panel's recommendation of public censure under Standard 8.3(b), instead imposing suspension based on several aggravating factors, inter alia, a pattern of misconduct); *In re Disciplinary Action Against Askew*, 776 N.W.2d 816 (N.D. 2010) (sixty-day suspension for failure to act with reasonable diligence and to properly communicate with client; finding public reprimand appropriate baseline sanction under Standard 8.3(b) as one of lawyer's four prior admonitions involved similar misconduct, but imposing suspension because all four prior admonitions constituted the aggravating factor of prior disciplinary offenses under Standard 9.22(a)).

An upward adjustment in the severity of the sanction is also proper when more serious violations are present. *See* Standards for Imposing Lawyer Sanctions pt. II, Theoretical Framework (ABA 1992) ("The ultimate sanction imposed should at least be consistent with the sanction for the most serious instance of misconduct among a number of violations; it might well be and generally should be greater than the sanction for the most serious misconduct."). *See also In re Riddle*, 857 P.2d 1233 (Ariz. 1993) (holding public censure under Standard 8.3 to be baseline sanction for lack of diligence when lawyer was previously informally reprimanded for, inter alia, neglecting a legal matter; imposing eighteen-month suspension due to violation of several Sanctions Standards, including numerous aggravating factors under Standards 9.22); *In re Roswold*, 249 P.3d 1199 (Kan. 2011) (rejecting hearing panel's recommendation of published censure under Standard 8.3(b), inter alia, for lawyer's failure to have former partner admitted pro hac vice in several client matters, misconduct that previously led to lawyer's required participation in a diversion program; imposing one-year suspension given the severity of these offenses, the injury caused, and lawyer's knowing violation of the rules).

Conversely, mitigating circumstances can be the deciding factor in a court's decision whether to impose a reprimand under Standard 8.3(b). Mitigating factors were important in *In re Coe*, 903 S.W.2d 916, 916 (Mo. 1995), when the Missouri Supreme Court imposed a public reprimand under Standard 8.3(b), rather than a suspension as recommended by disciplinary counsel, for four instances of disrupting a trial. The disruption involved, among other things, the lawyer continuing to challenge the judge after he sustained objections, making statements such as, "Can you in the name of Jesus be fair" and "I wish Jesus would touch you so you would stop being so bias [sic] every time I get up." The lawyer also gestured with her arms, legs, and body, while facing the jury and audience, in order to express displeasure with a ruling. The court noted that the lawyer had received a prior admonition for walking out of a trial in protest of the court's ruling, taking the file with her, and returning only after receiving a subpoena. In imposing the public reprimand under Standard 8.3(b) for repeated similar misconduct, the court in *Coe* distinguished the facts from *In re Vincenti*, 458 A.2d 1268 (N.J. 1983), a case in which a lawyer was involved in twenty-two counts of misconduct in two separate trials. In *Vincenti*, the lawyer received a one-year suspension for, inter alia, accusing the judge of extortion, collusion, cronyism, racism, and prejudging; making a frivolous judicial disqualification motion; physically threatening and cursing at opposing counsel; and showing disrespect to the judge, court officers, witnesses, and parties. The court in *Coe* found that the lawyer's misconduct was far less serious by comparison and did not harm her client or the public. In addition, the court looked at mitigating factors, noting that the lawyer had already been sanctioned for the charged misconduct by a contempt order, had offered a profuse public apology, and promised not to commit similar misconduct in the future.

**8.4 An admonition is generally not an appropriate sanction when a lawyer violates the terms of a prior disciplinary order or when a lawyer has engaged in the same or similar misconduct in the past.**

## Annotation

An admonition is a sanction that should only be imposed in cases of minor misconduct, when a lawyer's acts cause little or no injury to a client, the public, the legal system, or the profession, and when the lawyer is unlikely to engage in further misconduct. Courts conclude that lawyers who later engage in additional similar acts of misconduct, or who violate the terms of a prior disciplinary order, have not been deterred, rejecting private admonition as a sanction and instead imposing a more severe sanction. For example, in *In re Lerner,* 197 P.3d 1067, 1078 (Nev. 2008), the Nevada Supreme Court considered Standard 8.4 and the issue of deterrence. In *Lerner,* the lawyer was found to have continually allowed an associate lawyer not licensed in Nevada to conduct activities constituting the practice of law notwithstanding that he had received private reprimands on three separate occasions for similar activities. In deciding to impose a public rather than a private reprimand, the court noted that the Sanctions Standards recommend a public reprimand when a lawyer negligently engages in a violation that causes injury or potential injury to a client or the public while a private reprimand generally is appropriate when the lawyer has engaged in an isolated instance of nonwillful misconduct that causes little or no actual or potential injury. When a lawyer already received a private reprimand for similar misconduct, the court continued, the Sanctions Standards indicate that another private reprimand is not appropriate. In *Lerner,* the lawyer knowingly violated a duty to the public and to the profession and the court ordered him to refrain from assisting in the unauthorized practice of law, concluding that "[d]espite the lack of apparent harm, which could possibly indicate that a private reprimand would be sufficient . . . [respondent] did not engage in an isolated instance of misconduct." Similarly, in *In re McDonald,* 755 A.2d 389 at *1 (Table) (Del. 2000), an unpublished disposition, the Delaware Supreme Court imposed a public reprimand on a lawyer for failing to timely file an affidavit under mandatory continuing legal education requirements and failing to respond to several requests from the Office of Disciplinary Counsel. In determining whether to impose a public reprimand or a private admonition, the court noted that the lawyer had been sanctioned for the same misconduct and received private admonitions for late filings in two prior reporting years. Despite characterizing the lawyer's violation as "a discreet one," the court relied on Standard 8.4 in rejecting private admonition as an appropriate sanction in light of the lawyer's disciplinary history. *See also In re Grandell,* 2018 WL 3213784 (Del. June 29, 2018) (unpublished disposition in which Delaware

Supreme Court affirmed Board of Professional Responsibility Report citing Standard 8.4 in support of its conclusion that second private reprimand "unlikely to have any real effect" on respondent; court imposed public reprimand and two years of probation for knowing violation of multiple conditions of prior private disciplinary order).

## 9.0 Aggravation and Mitigation

### 9.1 Generally

**After misconduct has been established, aggravating and mitigating circumstances may be considered in deciding what sanction to impose.**

## Annotation

Each disciplinary case involves unique facts and circumstances. In striving for fair and consistent disciplinary sanctions, consideration must be given to the facts pertaining to the professional misconduct and to any aggravating or mitigating factors. *See* Standard 3.0, which calls for a court imposing discipline after finding lawyer misconduct to consider the duty violated, the lawyer's mental state, the actual or potential injury, and the existence of aggravating or mitigating factors. *See also In re Lehtinen*, 332 B.R. 404, 417 (B.A.P. 9th Cir. 2005) (bankruptcy court's apparent failure to weigh appropriate aggravating and mitigating factors in imposing sanction warranted vacation of suspension order and remand for consideration of such factors; court stated that "[t]his was technically an abuse of discretion"); *In re Triem*, 929 P.2d 634 (Alaska 1996) (Sanctions Standards contemplate that aggravating factors be considered after a finding of misconduct); *In re Beauregard*, 189 A.3d 1236, 1251 (Del. 2018) ("Mitigating and aggravating factors are considered to determine whether we should depart from the presumptive sanction."); *Att'y Grievance Comm'n v. Mixter*, 109 A.3d 1, 68 (Md. 2015) ("[W]e consider the nature of the ethical duties violated in light of any aggravating or mitigating circumstances."); *In re Tigue*, 900 N.W.2d 424 (Minn. 2017) (although similar cases are considered to ensure discipline is consistent, discipline is imposed on a case-by-case basis after considering both aggravating and mitigating circumstances); *In re Farris*, 472 S.W.3d 549, 563 (Mo. 2015) ("Though disbarment is the presumptive discipline, the Court must consider mitigating and aggravating circumstances before determining whether to depart from this discipline in a particular case.") (citing *In re Belz*, 258 S.W.3d 38, 42 (Mo. 2008) (in imposing indefinite suspension on lawyer with bipolar disorder who misappropriated client funds, court refuted disciplinary counsel's argument that Missouri adheres to an automatic disbarment rule in misappropriation cases "without regard to any of the mitigating circumstances," reiterating that, consistent with its approach in prior cases and the Sanctions Standards, mitigating factors are always considered in determining correct sanction and that, even in misappropriation cases, exceptional mitigating factors may warrant a sanction other than disbarment); *State ex rel. Counsel for Discipline v. Thew*, 794 N.W.2d 412 (Neb. 2011) (determining the appropriate sanction for lawyer in disciplinary proceeding requires consideration of any aggravating or mitigating factors, but lawyer failed to establish that depression was mitigating factor in his pattern of misconduct involving numerous instances of neglect and deceit, and therefore disbarment warranted); *Disciplinary Counsel v. Brown*, 720 N.E.2d 525, 529 (Ohio 1999) ("Standard 9.0 collects the aggravating and mitigating factors into helpful lists that organize and focus what is an inherently factual determination. We note that this strategy—collecting aggravated and mitigating circumstances into manageable lists—resembles the board's recently proposed Guidelines for Imposing Lawyer Sanctions ('Ohio Sanctions'), which recite the ABA Standards' lists of aggravating and mitigating circumstances nearly verbatim."); *In re Disciplinary Proceeding Against Pfefer*, 344 P.3d 1200 (Wash. 2015) (Board looks to Sanctions Standards to determine appropriate sanction, including weighing aggravating and mitigating factors); *In re Disciplinary Proceeding Against Abele*, 358 P.3d 371, 383 (Wash. 2015) ("Aggravating and mitigating factors in the Sanction Standards can alter the presumptive sanction, but only if they are sufficiently compelling to justify a deviation."); *In re Meisel*, 893 N.W.2d 558, 570 (Wis. 2017) ("Both aggravating and mitigating factors may be taken into consideration in determining the appropriate sanction for attorney misconduct."). *But see In re Nguyen*, 447 B.R. 268, 277 (B.A.P. 9th Cir. 2011) (disciplinary sanctions imposed by bankruptcy court against debtor's lawyer for incompetence and shoddy office practices upheld; court stated that "[w]hile the ABA Standards remain a helpful guide in the imposition of sanctions," the Sanction Standards are "ill-adapted" to federal bankruptcy proceedings and the court's failure to apply each criterion of the Standards, such as mitigating and aggravating factors, was not an abuse of discretion); *cf. In re Henry*, 2017 Bankr. LEXIS 1877 (Bankr. D. Alaska 2017) (existence of aggravating or mitigating factors may impact sanctions under the ABA Standards).

While aggravating and mitigating circumstances generally relate to the offense at issue, matters independent of the specific offense but relevant to a lawyer's fitness to practice or matters arising incident to the disciplinary proceeding also may be considered.

## *Weighing the Factors—A Factual and Flexible Approach*

Determining the weight of aggravating and mitigating circumstances is, essentially and necessarily, a process that depends on the specific facts of each case. *See, e.g., In re Stepovich*, 386 P.3d 1205, 1211 (Alaska 2016) (reiterating that "there is no 'magic formula' for determining how aggravating and mitigating circumstances affect an otherwise appropriate sanction" and "[e]ach case presents different circumstances which must be weighed against the nature and gravity of the lawyer's misconduct") (citations omitted); *In re Olsen*, 326 P.3d 1004 (Colo. 2014) (ABA Annotated Standards call for a flexible two-step inquiry that includes consideration of aggravating and mitigating factors); *Fla. Bar v. Ticktin*, 14 So.3d 928, 937 (Fla. 2009) (rejecting argument that hearing referee should have found additional aggravating factors, court stated that "[m]erely because there is some evidence pertaining to an aggravating factor does not mean that that evidence rises to the level necessary to support a finding of that aggravator"); *In re Hall*, 377 P.3d 1149, 1160 (Kan. 2016) (while clear and convincing evidence is not required to support aggravating and mitigating circumstances, "some evidence" of those factors must be presented for weighing); *In re Discipline of Mines*, 612 N.W.2d 619, 626–27 (S.D. 2000) (court must "decide each case 'upon its own particular set of facts,' properly balancing the aggravating and mitigating circumstances") (citations omitted); *In re Neisner*, 16 A.3d 587, 596 (Vt. 2010) (citing former commentary to Standard 9.1, court also emphasized that each disciplinary case involves "a unique combination of mitigating and aggravating factors for the adjudicating body to consider when determining whether the sanction recommended by the ABA Standards is appropriate"); *In re Disciplinary Proceeding Against Romero*, 94 P.3d 939, 944–45 (Wash. 2004) (citing former commentary to Standard 9.1 that fair disciplinary sanctions require consideration of both aggravating and mitigating factors, court noted: "Accordingly, we do not consider aggravating and mitigating factors in a vacuum. Rather, we view the factors to consider the totality of the circumstances and fashion an appropriate sanction for the unique facts and circumstances of each case.").

### *When Both Aggravating and Mitigating Factors Are Present*

Courts typically weigh the strength of aggravating and mitigating factors against each other when both are present in a case. *See, e.g., In re Abrams*, 257 P.3d 167 (Ariz. 2011) (mitigating factors did not outweigh aggravating factors to overcome presumptive sanction of two-year suspension for former judge who had engaged in a sexual relationship with a lawyer who appeared in his courtroom, sexually harassed a newly admitted lawyer, and chastised her in court when she declined his sexual advances); *In re Peasley*, 90 P.3d 764, 779 (Ariz. 2004) (in weighing the aggravating and mitigating circumstances, court found prosecutor's "multiple offenses and dishonest motive are exceptionally serious aggravators" that "outweigh the mitigating factors of significant delay, cooperative attitude toward the disciplinary proceeding, and good character and reputation," warranting the presumptive sanction of disbarment); *People v. Beecher*, 350 P.3d 310 (Colo. O.P.D.J. 2014) (lawyer's misconduct stemmed from concern for client's safety and harm was minimal; however, this was not enough to overcome aggravating factors and lawyer suspended for six months); *Atty. Griev. Comm'n v. Framm*, 144 A.3d 827 (Md. 2016) (although cooperation with disciplinary counsel found to be a mitigating factor, it was not enough to overcome substantial aggravating factors in case where lawyer failed to advise client with diminished capacity adequately about the costs of litigation, failed to conduct minimal research, and was excluded from putting on testimony during client's divorce case due to abuses of discovery; disbarment warranted); *In re Eskola,* 891 N.W.2d 294 (Minn. 2017) (court weighed three aggravating and four mitigating factors and determined aggravating factors trumped mitigation, resulting in indefinite suspension for lawyer who misappropriated client funds); *In re Zamora,* 21 P.3d 30 (N.M. 2001) (court weighs mitigating against aggravating factors to determine discipline necessary to guard public while at same time to provide lawyer with as much encouragement and opportunity for rehabilitation as warranted by circumstances of case; court ordered disbarment of lawyer who abused crack cocaine and self-reported misappropriations from client trust account while in residential recovery program); *In re Cozzolino,* 811 A.2d 638 (R.I. 2002) (once misconduct established, court weighs mitigating and aggravating factors in each case to fashion appropriate sanction; in ordering disbarment for misconduct including failure to initiate proceedings on clients' behalf, and failure to keep clients reasonably informed, court considered several aggravating factors, including extensive disciplinary history, long history of neglecting client matters, chronic inability to communicate properly with clients, and persistent failure to cooperate in a timely manner with the disciplinary process); *In re Wehde,* 517 N.W.2d 132 (S.D. 1994) (in determining appropriate discipline for conduct in question, court reiterated that each disciplinary case is decided upon its own particular set of facts, properly balancing aggravating and mitigating circumstances; in imposing two-year suspension, court considered lawyer's breach of numerous legal tenets, including failure to act competently and failure to preserve identity of clients' funds and property, involved common thread of extremely poor case management, exemplary professional career for more than 30 years, deaths, and personal tragedies); *In re Discipline of Crawley,* 164 P.3d 1232, 1237 (Utah 2007) (reiterating that "[t]he standards 'permit[] flexibility and creativity in assigning sanctions,'" the court stated that "[i]t is a delicate and often difficult task to craft sanctions appropriate for individual attorneys, no two of which have engaged in the same misconduct under the same aggravating and mitigating circumstances"); *In re Discipline of Tanner,* 960 P.2d 399 (Utah 1998) (finding multiple aggravating factors, court disagreed with trial court's assessment of mitigating factors and found most severe sanction of disbarment warranted for lawyer's grievous misconduct, including felony conviction for creating and using a forged document and lying to FBI agent; with regard to mitigating factors, courts must consider them in light of particular misconduct, not in isolation). *See also* Leslie C. Levin, *The Emperor's Clothes and Other Tales About the Standards for Imposing Lawyer Discipline Sanctions,* 48 Am. U. L. Rev. 1 (1998) (noting lack of guidance in ABA Sanctions Standards for difficult task of weighing aggravating and mitigating factors).

A baseline sanction under any given Sanctions Standard can be adjusted upward or downward depending on the weight courts assign to the mitigating or aggravating factors in a given case. Thus, when aggravating factors outweigh mitigating factors, a sanction can be increased. *See, e.g., In re Ivy,* 374 P.3d 374 (Alaska

2016) (five aggravating factors compared to one mitigating factor would not reduce presumptive sanction of disbarment for lawyer who falsely testified in private civil litigation and in subsequent disciplinary proceedings); *People v. Heaphy*, 2015 WL 11081955 (Colo. O.P.D.J. September 9, 2015) (disbarment the presumptive sanction for knowing misappropriation of client funds; mitigating factors such as no prior discipline were insufficient to warrant lesser sanction); *People v. Clough*, 74 P.3d 552 (Colo. O.P.D.J. 2003) (lack of prior discipline did not rise to level necessary to reduce presumed sanction of disbarment for misconduct that included knowing conversion of client funds when aggravating factors included dishonest motive, multiple offenses, client vulnerability, and indifference to restitution); *In re Saint-Louis*, 147 A.3d 1135 (D.C. 2016) (usual mitigating factors, such as lack of prior discipline, did not lead to a lesser sanction for lawyer who intentionally or recklessly engaged in misappropriation); *Maddux v. Bd. of Prof'l Responsibility*, 288 S.W.3d 340 (Tenn. 2009) (affirming imposition of five-month suspension for commingling and other misconduct when lawyer's expression of regret, a mitigating factor, was insufficient to merit reduction in sanction when weighed against multiple aggravating factors including prior disciplinary offenses, pattern of misconduct, multiple offenses, vulnerability of the victim, and substantial experience in practice of law); *In re Maynard*, 2018 68 V.I. 32 (V.I. 2018) (seven aggravating factors and two mitigating factors warranted an upward adjustment in period of suspension, to eighteen months, for lawyer who failed to properly administer an estate); *In re Disciplinary Proceeding Against Conteh*, 389 P.3d 591 (Wash. 2017) (no basis to depart from presumptive sanction of suspension when there were five aggravating factors and zero mitigating factors for lawyer who failed to take action in lawsuits for two clients); *In re Disciplinary Proceeding Against Hall*, 329 P.3d 870 (Wash. 2014) (seven aggravating factors and no mitigating factors warranted suspension of two years for lawyer who mismanaged an elderly client's estate). *But see In re McCoy-Jacien*, 186 A.3d 626 (Vt. 2018) (aggravating factors outweighed mitigating circumstances and so no basis to impose less severe sanction; however, there was also no justification to increase discipline against lawyer for failing to file tax returns in violation of probation).

Conversely, when factors in mitigation outweigh factors in aggravation, the sanction may be decreased. *See, e.g., In re Hislop*, 2016 Ariz. LEXIS 342 (Ariz. 2016) (lawyer's mitigating factors outnumbered and outweighed aggravating factors resulting in probation instead of presumptive sanction of suspension for lawyer who failed to properly maintain operating and trust accounts); *Neal v. Matthews*, 30 S.W.3d 92, 96 (Ark. 2000) (lawyer's federal conviction of bribery warranted five-year suspension, not disbarment, after court's application of three aggravating factors—dishonest or selfish motive, multiple offenses, and substantial experience in the law—not considered in isolation but weighed against mitigating factors including no prior disciplinary record, timely good faith effort to make restitution, remorse, and cooperative attitude, which "far outweigh" aggravating factors); *Statewide Grievance Comm'n v. Glass*, 699 A.2d 1058 (Conn. App. Ct. 1997) (in affirming reprimand sanction, court determined that trial court did not abuse its discretion in finding that, although lawyer was involved in pattern of misconduct involving fraudulent real estate transactions, this aggravating factor was offset by mitigating ones, including no prior disciplinary history, lack of motive for personal gain or intention to commit crime, inexperience in law, presence of a learning disability, and cooperation with authorities); *In re Hewett*, 11 A.3d 279 (D.C. 2011) (presumption of disbarment for intentional misappropriation overcome by extraordinary circumstances and mitigating factors of admission of wrongdoing, full cooperation with disciplinary authorities, prompt return of disputed funds, and unblemished record of personal conduct; six-month stayed suspension imposed); *Fla. Bar v. Tauler*, 775 So.2d 944 (Fla. 2000) (misconduct including misappropriation warranted three-year suspension rather than disbarment in light of mitigating factors including lawyer's severe financial hardship brought on by husband's health problems and bankruptcy, a clear commitment to providing legal assistance to those in need, an isolated incident of misconduct, and timely and good faith restitution to clients); *In re Ortman*, 709 S.E.2d 784, 785 (Ga. 2011) (one-year suspension rather than disbarment imposed where circumstances and mitigating factors sufficient to justify a lesser penalty such as no prior disciplinary history, evidence of good character and reputation, isolated incident, and lawyer who pleaded guilty to one felony count of aggravated battery had various physical conditions that led him to be particularly sensitive to his physical safety); *In re Bilbe*, 841 So.2d 729 (La. 2003) (three-year suspension rather than disbarment warranted for lawyer who made false statements to immigration judge and displayed disrespectful and disruptive behavior in court since mitigating factors, including no prior disciplinary record in more than twenty years as well as suspension from practice in immigration courts, outweighed aggravating factors); *Appeal of Salomon*, 127 N.H. LEXIS 124 (N.H. 2017) (after considering aggravating and mitigating factors, downward deviation from the baseline sanction of a suspension appropriate, especially considering lawyer's cooperation with the disciplinary process); *In re Grew's Case*, 934 A.2d 537 (N.H. 2007) (based upon mitigating factors including lack of prior disciplinary record, efforts to make restitution prior to being indicted, cooperation with disciplinary process, sincere remorse, and personal and financial problems, and criminal penalties, two-year suspension rather than baseline sanction of disbarment appropriate for lawyer who engaged in misdemeanor-level insurance fraud); *Disciplinary Counsel v. Smith*, 93 N.E.3d 955 (Ohio 2017) (suspension of eighteen months with the final twelve months conditionally stayed appropriate for lawyer whose misconduct included making false representations to the court and to his client when seeking postconviction relief); *State ex rel. Okla. Bar Ass'n v. Conrady*, 275 P.3d 133 (Okla. 2012) (in imposing suspension for two years and one day, court weighed substantial mitigating factors, including no prior disciplinary history in thirty-six years of practice, against the baseline sanction of disbarment for lawyer's criminal conviction arising from a shooting incident at his ex-girlfriend's apartment); *In re Cope*, 549 S.W.3d 71 (Tenn. 2018) (mitigating factors including no prior discipline, full and free disclosure to Board, cooperative attitude in proceedings, character and reputation, and remorse outweighed aggravating factors of dishonest motive and substantial practice experience; discipline reduced from disbarment to twenty-five-month suspension); *In re Disciplinary Proceeding Against Shepard*, 239 P.3d 1066 (Wash. 2010) (two-year suspension rather than presumptive sanction of disbarment given lawyer's efforts to remediate the harm caused by his misconduct of affiliating himself with a living trust scam targeted at seniors).

## 9.2 Aggravation

**9.21 Definition. Aggravation or aggravating circumstances are any considerations or factors that may justify an increase in the degree of discipline to be imposed.**

**9.22 Factors which may be considered in aggravation.**
**Aggravating factors include:**

- **(a) prior disciplinary offenses;**
- **(b) dishonest or selfish motive;**
- **(c) a pattern of misconduct;**
- **(d) multiple offenses;**
- **(e) bad faith obstruction of the disciplinary proceeding by intentionally failing to comply with rules or orders of the disciplinary agency;**
- **(f) submission of false evidence, false statements, or other deceptive practices during the disciplinary process;**
- **(g) refusal to acknowledge wrongful nature of conduct;**
- **(h) vulnerability of victim;**
- **(i) substantial experience in the practice of law;**
- **(j) indifference to making restitution;**
- **(k) illegal conduct, including that involving the use of controlled substances.**

## Annotation

### *Prior Disciplinary Offenses Generally*

Not all "prior disciplinary offenses" are judged by courts to be aggravating. In evaluating whether prior offenses constitute an aggravating factor, courts generally look to the timing of the current offense in relation to the prior offense, similarities in the misconduct, the number of prior offenses, the seriousness of the prior misconduct and the resulting sanction, and the relative recency of the prior offense. *See, e.g., In re Ford*, 128 P.3d 178 (Alaska 2006) (aggravating factor of prior disciplinary offenses found when lawyer had record of three disciplinary matters within ten-year period, as well as previous admonishment for court order violation); *Ligon v. Tapp*, 519 S.W.3d 315, 323 (Ark. 2017) (fourteen sanctions between 1984 and 2013, five of which occurred in the nine years prior to current case, found aggravating: "it indicated that prior disciplinary actions were insufficient to curtail his conduct"); *Statewide Grievance Comm'n v. Schaffer*, No. CV030196758, 2004 WL 303654 (Conn. Super. Ct. Feb. 2, 2004) (lengthy disciplinary history dating back to 1995 found aggravating when violations were significant and involved similar mishandling of client funds); *In re Rumsey*, 343 P.3d 93 (Kan. 2015) (six prior disciplinary offenses between 1977 and 2003 found to be aggravating); *In re Harrington*, 710 So.2d 243 (La. 1998) (disbarment upon federal court convictions aggravated by extensive disciplinary history, including fifteen prior sanctions ranging from private reprimand to twelve-month suspension); *McIntyre v. Miss. Bar*, 38 So.3d 617, 627 (Miss. 2010) (in imposing disbarment for commingling client funds and advancing funds to clients, court found lawyer's prior disciplinary offenses an aggravating factor that outweighed the mitigating factors, rejecting lawyer's assertion that "six ethical violations over a forty-year career—five of which were deemed 'minor'—do not warrant aggravation"); *In re Jones*, 951 P.2d 149, 152 (Or. 1997) (in analyzing lawyer's prior disciplinary record, the court stated that "[t]hose considerations are important, because they can serve to heighten or diminish the significance of earlier misconduct"; forty-five-day suspension appropriate, rather than thirty-day suspension if lawyer had absence of prior discipline). Prior, nonpublic disciplinary sanctions may also be considered in aggravation, as can misconduct dealt with through diversion/alternative to discipline programs. *See, e.g., In re Brown*, 392 P.3d 474 (Alaska 2017) (2014 private admonition found aggravating); *In re Hasty*, 335 P.3d 110, 116 (Kan. 2014) (noting that lawyer had been previously disciplined on three occasions, including instances in 2002 and 2007 where he "participated in the Attorney Diversion Program").

As discussed above regarding Standard 8.0, courts not only consider prior discipline as an aggravating factor under Standard 9.22(a), but as a reason in and of itself for discipline. In many cases, courts examine Standards 8.0 and 9.22 concurrently.

## • Timing of Prior Disciplinary Offenses

Some courts have declined to find prior disciplinary offenses aggravating when that misconduct occurred within the same time frame as the current misconduct. *See, e.g., People v. Braham*, 409 P.3d 655, 663 (Colo. O.P.D.J. 2017) (because "the conduct addressed in the instant disciplinary proceeding occurred before Respondent was suspended in the [prior] consolidated cases, the Court considers that misconduct as a pattern of misconduct rather than as a prior disciplinary offense"); *People v. Lindemann*, 93 P.3d 1125 (Colo. O.P.D.J. 2004) (although hearing board did not consider prior discipline of year-and-a-day suspension as aggravating factor because current misconduct occurred as part of the same episode and during same time frame as prior disciplinary charges, other aggravating factors and no mitigation warranted imposition of disbarment for multiple offenses and pattern of misconduct, including misappropriation of client funds); *In re Vaughan*, 801 So.2d 1058 (La. 2001) (prior discipline not treated as aggravating factor, but instead court considered prior misconduct case and actions forming basis of immediate matter as if they were before court simultaneously when conduct forming basis of immediate disciplinary proceeding occurred within same time frame as misconduct at issue in prior matter; three-year suspension to run concurrently with suspension of one year and one day imposed in prior case; cited with approval in *In re Blanson,* 930 So.2d 943 (La. 2006)). *See also In re Kluge,* 66 P.3d 492, 509 (Or. 2003) (court placed "only some weight" on lawyer's prior disciplinary record as aggravating factor because he was not sanctioned for those prior violations until after he had committed violations at issue in present case); *cf. In re Disciplinary Proceeding Against Lopez,* 106 P.3d 221, 232 (Wash. 2005) (hearing officer erred in focusing on timing of prior sanction by concluding that lawyer's prior reprimand could not be considered as aggravating factor in present case; citing Standard 9.22(a), the court said that "[o]ur reading of this standard is that the *prior misconduct,* not the sanction for such conduct, must precede the subsequent misconduct, but the attorney must be under investigation for the earlier misconduct at the time of the subsequent misconduct").

In evaluating the timing of prior disciplinary offenses, the Washington Supreme Court considers whether the lawyer knew he or she was under investigation for the older offense when committing the more recent one. *See, e.g., In re Disciplinary Proceeding Against Haley,* 138 P.3d 1044, 1050–51 (Wash. 2006) (in prior disciplinary case lawyer committed offense in 1993 but was not charged with violations until 2004, and more recent offenses occurred before 2004 so lawyer was correct in asserting that court should not consider the other disciplinary proceedings because he was not under investigation for the offense when committing subsequent ones; court determined that other aggravating factors, however, supported imposition of one-year suspension recommended by disciplinary board); *In re Disciplinary Proceeding Against Brothers,* 70 P.3d 940, 945 (Wash. 2003) (lawyer's prior offense, withdrawing large sum of money from estate account without establishing basis for fee, "should be given great weight in determining the proper sanction" even though lawyer had not yet been formally disciplined for the first offense, since he was aware that he was under investigation and he already had returned the money when he charged client in present case a grossly unreasonable fee).

Courts also have found that a prior offense can be too remote in time to be considered aggravating, leading instead to application of the mitigating factor "remoteness of prior offenses" under Standard 9.32(m). *See, e.g., People v. Dalton,* 367 P.3d 126 (Colo. O.P.D.J. 2016) (prior public censure in 1992 and private admonition in 1981 deemed mitigating factor impacting weight given to prior discipline aggravating factor); *People v. Eaton,* 240 P.3d 1282 (Colo. O.P.D.J. 2010) (lawyer's prior disciplinary offense, which took place eighteen years earlier, qualified as remote in time, itself a mitigating factor; because these two considerations offset one another, court accorded neither any weight in determining two-year suspension was appropriate sanction for neglect of two clients' matters); *In re Ketter*, 992 P.2d 205 (Kan. 1999) (informal admonition based on three convictions for indecent exposure some eleven years before present disciplinary complaint was too remote to be considered in aggravation; but 1996 informal admonition based on charge of lewd and lascivious conduct was not too remote in disciplinary proceeding arising from respondent's 1998 misdemeanor conviction for same misconduct); *cf. People v. Morris*, 2016 WL 8290616 (Colo. O.P.D.J. December 2, 2016) (rejecting argument that discipline for prior offenses within five years were remote in time and noting that lawyer was on disciplinary probation at time of commission of current offenses); *Fla. Bar v. Varner*, 992 So.2d 224 (Fla. 2008) (in finding that remoteness of prior disciplinary history did not mitigate lawyer's misconduct, court noted that under Florida Standard 9.22(a) remote instances of minor misconduct shall not be considered as an aggravating factor but here lawyer's prior disciplinary offense was strikingly similar to the current offenses of neglect and misrepresentation, warranting one-year suspension).

In other instances, courts will still find a prior offense to be an aggravating factor, but lessen its weight due to remoteness in time. *See, e.g., People v. Ginsberg*, 967 P.2d 151 (Colo. 1998) (importance of letter of admonition in 1972 and private censure in 1997 was lessened by fact that prior offenses occurred during thirty-three-year legal career); *In re Spears*, 72 So.3d 819 (La. 2011) (while an aggravating factor, lawyer's past disciplinary history given little weight because of remoteness and dissimilarity to instant misconduct involving negligent commingling and conversion; court imposed suspension of one-year-and-one-day, fully deferred by probation); *In re Dugger*, 54 P.3d 595, 610 (Or. 2002) ("Remoteness in time diminishes the significance of a prior offense as an aggravating factor, but does not function as a mitigating factor" for disciplinary purpose); *In re PRB Docket No. 2013.153*, 96 A.3d 468, 472 (Vt. 2014) (three prior disciplinary actions in 1987, 1994, and 2003 were insufficient aggravating factors because "[t]hese cases are both remote in time to the present case and the violations are unrelated to the present charges, and we do not give them much weight as aggravating factors"; lawyer admonished); *In re Disciplinary Proceedings Against DeMaio*, 773 N.W.2d 439 (Wis. 2009) (prior reprimand eleven years earlier given little weight since it was fairly remote in time and did not involve similar misconduct); *cf. In re Alex*, 205 So.3d 895 (La. 2016) (although past disciplinary history was remote, it was similar enough to current misconduct to justify aggravation; court imposed suspension of one year and one day, with thirty days deferred).

The ongoing impact of prior discipline may also influence a court's assessment of whether it should be considered in aggravation. *See, e.g., Disciplinary Counsel v. Bunstine*, 41 N.E.3d 384 (Ohio 2015) (noting that prior suspension would have been aggravating but for fact that pending charges prevented respondent from seeking reinstatement from the prior suspension).

- **Similarity of Misconduct**

Courts seem more likely to find prior disciplinary offenses an aggravating factor when they involve the same or similar misconduct, even if remote in time. *See, e.g., People v. Swarts,* 414 P.3d 1168 (Colo. O.P.D.J. 2018) (imposing three-year suspension on lawyer who defied an order suspending his license to practice law; misconduct mirrored earlier unauthorized practice of law and flouted authority of the court); *People v. Beale,* 2017 WL 1046461 (Colo. O.P.D.J. February 9, 2017) (disbarment warranted when respondent had been suspended before for similar misconduct but knowingly engaged in further similar felonious acts); *People v. Mason,* 212 P.3d 141, 148 (Colo. O.P.D.J. 2009) (disbarring lawyer for unauthorized practice of law when disciplinary history included three-year suspension for substantially similar misconduct, court noted that "[i]n both cases, Respondent represented others and when caught explained that he thought his conduct was authorized, that he was not acting as a lawyer, even though he assisted others in defending their legal positions and filed legal documents for them"); *In re Spiller,* 788 A.2d 114, 118 (Del. 2001) (with reference to prior public reprimand and two-year probation for similar misconduct, court observed, "[i]t is significant and disturbing that [respondent's] present acts of misconduct occurred while he was on probation"); *In re Douglass,* 859 A.2d 1069 (D.C. 2004) (in imposing ninety-day suspension for lawyer's neglect of client's matter and conflict of interest when he demanded the client release him from liability, court considered that lawyer's prior discipline for neglect of client matters aggravated the incompetence and neglect misconduct in the instant case but did not aggravate the conflict of interest violation); *In re Brost,* 850 N.W.2d 699 (Minn. 2014) (explaining that more severe sanctions are imposed when current misconduct is similar to previously sanctioned misconduct; aggravating factor established when lawyer's prior misconduct was similar and also serious, involving theft and deceit of clients, which warranted disbarment); *State ex rel. Counsel for Discipline v. Ellis,* 808 N.W.2d 634 (Neb. 2012) (rejecting lawyer's argument that prior offense was too remote, court imposed disbarment, relying in part on previous disciplinary offense for similar conduct involving neglect and dishonesty and concluding that cumulative misconduct warranted more severe sanction); *In re Jackson,* 223 P.3d 387 (Or. 2009) (lawyer's history of neglectful conduct that triggered gradually escalating responses (admonition, reprimand, and thirty-day suspension) found aggravating; suspension of 120 days imposed); *In re LaBahn,* 67 P.3d 381, 385 (Or. 2003) (lawyer had received letter of admonition for misconduct similar to that involved in present case, where he knowingly neglected to file proof of service resulting in dismissal of client's tort claim; court found that letter constituted evidence of misconduct "that heightens, at least to a moderate degree, the significance of the accused's neglect of [client's] case" and was an aggravating factor; sixty-day suspension imposed); *In re Disciplinary Proceeding Against Wickersham,* 310 P.3d 1237,

1245 (Wash. 2013) (rejecting claim that 2006 reprimand was too remote, observing that "the passage of time is less important to determining whether previous misconduct is remote than the similarities between the episodes of misconduct"); *In re Disciplinary Proceeding Against Van Camp*, 257 P.3d 599, 614 (Wash. 2011) (lawyer disciplined three times in last twenty-five years for violations similar to those in present case, including misconduct involving charging an excessive fee; "[w]e routinely consider misconduct dating back many years as an aggravating factor where the misconduct is similar"); *cf. Iowa Supreme Ct. Bd. of Prof'l Ethics & Conduct v. Ries*, 812 N.W.2d 594, 598 (Iowa 2012) (prior reprimand for neglect of two clients' appeals and ignoring numerous client inquiries about status of another matter appropriately considered aggravating in the current case charging lawyer with failure to return client's inadvertent overpayment of fees since "common thread between those matters and the present case is a pattern of ignoring responsibilities as an attorney and letting events simply run their course"; thirty-day suspension).

When the prior offenses are unrelated or only tangentially related to the current offense, however, courts may be reluctant to find aggravation. *See In re Knappenberger*, 186 P.3d 272 (Or. 2008) (two-year suspension rather than disbarment appropriate sanction for lawyer's new misconduct in charging an illegal fee to one client and charging an excessive fee to second client; only moderate weight given to lawyer's prior disciplinary record because current violations involved a different disciplinary rule and occurred before earlier disciplinary decisions); *In re Cohen*, 8 P.3d 953, 959 (Or. 2000) (prior admonition is considered in determining sanction in subsequent disciplinary proceeding if the misconduct that gave rise to prior admonition was of same or similar type as that at issue; court stated that "However, if a letter of admonition involved misconduct wholly different in nature from the misconduct at issue in the case at bar, then we ordinarily shall not consider that letter" under Standard 9.22(a)). *But see In re Hickox*, 57 P.3d 403 (Colo. 2002) (finding hearing board erred in not weighing lawyer's prior disciplinary offenses more heavily in determining appropriate sanction even though that misconduct was different than the assault at issue and stating that court frequently has considered prior disciplinary conduct of a dissimilar nature an aggravating factor). Courts evaluating the severity of the prior misconduct often note multiple prior offenses or a history of bad behavior, even though a pattern of misconduct is itself a separate aggravating factor.

## *Dishonest or Selfish Motive*

A lawyer's dishonest or selfish motive for engaging in misconduct can be considered an aggravating factor. For example, courts have found dishonest or selfish motive in cases involving lawyers who acted with motivation to secure a financial or personal advantage or were dishonest in misusing client funds. Courts also consider dishonest motive when a lawyer has tried to deceive the court, clients, or his or her law firm. At the opposite extreme of a dishonest or selfish motive as an aggravating factor is the "absence of a dishonest or selfish motive" as a mitigating factor under Standard 9.32(b).

- **Financial or Personal Gain**

A court is likely to find a dishonest and selfish motive when a lawyer financially or personally benefits from the misconduct. *See, e.g., People v. Braham,* 409 P.3d 655, 663 (Colo. O.P.D.J. 2017) (in ordering disbarment, court weighed this aggravating factor heavily, concluding the lawyer "acted selfishly in retaining client funds that he did not earn in full . . . [and] acted dishonestly by filing [client's] bankruptcy documents with her electronic signature without her review or approval"); *People v. Calvert,* 280 P.3d 1269 (Colo. O.P.D.J. 2011) (recording a false deed of trust to secure his own financial interest in loans lawyer made to one client supported finding of dishonest motive and retraction of earlier fee agreement and demanding additional money from another client supported finding of selfish motive); *People v. Gustafson,* 128 P.3d 788 (Colo. O.P.D.J. 2005) (knowing conversion of client funds over two years by failing to transfer to client approximately $80,000 in settlement funds belonging to estate and instead using funds for his own purposes demonstrated dishonest and selfish motive); *Office of Disciplinary Counsel v. Au,* 113 P.3d 203 (Haw. 2005) (lawyer was motivated by monetary gain by his use of a runner and depositing unearned fees into his office account; finding aggravating factor under Standard 9.22(b) and imposing five-year suspension); *In re Shriver,* 278 P.3d 964 (Kan. 2012) (in imposing six-month suspension, court noted that lawyer's misconduct in dealing with his mother's estate was motivated by dishonesty and selfishness by putting himself in a position to receive a greater distribution than his mother intended); *In re Belz,* 258 S.W.3d 38 (Mo. 2008) (lawyer acted with dishonest and selfish motive in taking his clients' funds on multiple occasions; indefinite suspension warranted); *In re Kimmell,* 31 P.3d 414 (Or. 2001) (lawyer acted with dishonest and selfish motive when he stole a jacket from a department store; six-month suspension imposed); *In re Disciplinary Proceeding Against Holcomb,* 173 P.3d 898 (Wash. 2007) (court looked to whether lawyer intended to benefit financially or deceive court and applied aggravating factor in holding that lawyer should be suspended for six months for using client as source of funds for own personal purposes by taking loans and delaying repayment of last loan for more than a year). *But see In re Walton,* 287 P.3d 1098 (Or. 2012) (no evidence that lawyer acted with dishonest or selfish motive to obtain a personal benefit when he used a Westlaw password without authorization to do Internet research on behalf of indigent clients; finding one aggravating factor outweighed by mitigating factors warranted public reprimand).

- **Lying Under Oath or Deceiving the Court**

Courts have also held that lying under oath clearly establishes a dishonest and selfish motive. *See, e.g., People v. Maynard,* 219 P.3d 430 (Colo. O.P.D.J. 2008) (aggravating factor of dishonest motive under Standard 9.22 applied to lawyer who mailed a brief to Colorado Supreme Court and intentionally backdated it to make it appear to be timely filed); *People v. Small,* 962 P.2d 258 (Colo. 1998) (lawyer had dishonest or selfish motive under Standard 9.22(b) when he falsely testified under oath that he had insurance at time of car accident; public censure imposed); *In re Swindall,* 468 S.E.2d 372 (Ga. 1996) (disbarment warranted by lawyer's six felony convictions for perjury; aggravating factor in dishonest motive); *In re Disciplinary Action Against Kaiser,* 484 N.W.2d 102 (N.D. 1992) (two episodes of testifying falsely under oath warranted two-year suspension; although lawyer argued that inappropriate family loyalties induced him to lie under oath, court found that possible profit potential was equally motivating factor); *cf. In re Davenport,* 49 P.3d 91, 105 (Or. 2002) (dishonest but not selfish motive, in that lawyer did not engage in misconduct for any personal gain; aggravating factor under Standard 9.22(b) established for lawyer who knowingly gave false testimony under oath during bankruptcy examination and two-year suspension imposed); *In re Disciplinary Proceeding Against Ferguson,* 246 P.3d 1236, 1250 (Wash. 2011) (lawyer's "multiple false and misleading statements to the court" supported hearing officer's finding of dishonest or selfish motive as an aggravating factor under Standard 9.22(b); ninety-day suspension imposed).

- **False Statements to Clients and Others**

False statements to a client, opposing counsel, or other individuals can result in a finding of dishonest or selfish motive under Standard 9.22(b). *See, e.g., In re Arrick,* 882 P.2d 943, 950 (Ariz. 1994) (lawyer's deliberate misrepresentations to his client "designed to cover his negligence" supported dishonesty or selfish motive, as an aggravating factor); *In re Wilks,* 99 A.3d 228 (Table) (Del. 2014) (Standard 9.22(b) applied to lawyer who lied to client about having an agreement with defense counsel that would toll the statute of limitations; conduct found to be inherently dishonest and intended to selfishly conceal lawyer's neglect of claims); *In re Fountain,* 913 A.2d 1180 (Del. 2006) (lawyer was dishonest and had a selfish motive under Standard 9.22(b) when he led client into believing that he would pay the state in reimbursement of client's Medicaid fraud if client made the check payable to the lawyer; disbarment imposed); *In re Shores,* 279 P.3d 710 (Kan. 2012) (lawyer's false statements to client that he had filed her divorce petition was motivated by dishonesty; disbarment for multiple acts of misconduct); *In re Wolterbeek's Case,* 886 A.2d 990, 995 (N.H. 2005) (court considered aggravating factors, including dishonest or selfish motive, and imposed disbarment on lawyer who "engaged in a course of misconduct motivated by his self-interest" by using deception to acquire an interest in client's foreclosed property); *In re Summer*, 105 P.3d 848 (Or. 2005) (lawyer acted with dishonest motive under Standard 9.22(b) when he made knowing and material misrepresentations to a self-insured entity in an effort to recover twice for client's injuries).

- **Billing and Fee-Related Practices**

A dishonest or selfish motive under Standard 9.22(b) has been found when a lawyer seeks financial or personal gain through billing or fee-related practices. *See, e.g., In re Rumsey*, 71 P.3d 1150 (Kan. 2003) (selfish motive was established when lawyer filed client's divorce action in another county in order to increase his legal fees); *In re Guste*, 118 So.3d 1023 (La. 2012) (dishonest motive found in charging excessive fees when lawyer billed nursing home resident for nonlegal services such as chauffeuring, at lawyer's hourly rate; two-year suspension imposed); *Att'y Grievance Comm'n v. Stinson*, 50 A.3d 1222 (Md. 2012) (several aggravating factors, including dishonest motive in retaining unearned fees, double billing time spent on document preparation, and inflating hours in client billings, warranted disbarment); *In re O'Brien*, 29 P.3d 1044 (N.M. 2001) (lawyer displayed selfish motive in deceitful billing practices and charging excessive fees warranting suspension for minimum of two years); *Disciplinary Counsel v. Smith*, 96 N.E.3d 234 (Ohio 2017) (lawyer used unethical billing practices and charged excessive fees in five cases involving three clients who operated nursing homes in Ohio; aggravating factor of dishonest or selfish motive applied because the lawyer received financial benefit, justifying two-year suspension); *In re Paulson*, 216 P.3d 859 (Or. 2009) (lawyer acted with selfish motive, churning file to increase his fees, among other misconduct that warranted disbarment). *But see In re Katz*, 981 A.2d 1133, 1145 (Del. 2009) (lawyer who represented both lender and borrowers in real estate transaction, without necessary disclosures, was paid legal fee from loan settlement proceeds; board reasoned "that while this does not alone prove a selfish motive, the fact that the Respondent benefitted financially from each of these unlawful loans cannot be ignored").

- **Dishonest Motive by Prosecutors**

Courts also have held that conduct less obvious than that involving misappropriation of client funds or dishonest fee and billing practices constitutes an aggravating factor under Standard 9.22(b). For example, dishonest or selfish motives have been attributed to prosecutors. *See, e.g., In re Peasley*, 90 P.3d 764, 779 (Ariz. 2004) (dishonest motive was "exceptionally serious" aggravating factor in determining proper sanction for prosecutor who, in capital murder trial, intentionally and repeatedly presented false testimony in effort to bolster witnesses' credibility solely for purpose of obtaining convictions and death penalty sentence for two defendants; obtaining conviction at any cost demonstrated dishonest motive and warranted disbarment); *People v. Pautler*, 35 P.3d 571 (Colo. O.P.D.J. 2001) (finding that prosecutor who misrepresented himself to suspect as public defender was motivated in part by gaining advantage in subsequent legal proceedings, which supported existence of aggravating factor of dishonest or selfish motive); *Cleveland Metro. Bar Ass'n v. Hurley*, 34 N.E.3d 116, 119 (Ohio 2015) (dishonest motive applied when lawyer "used his position as assistant prosecutor to illegally access a secure criminal-justice database for purely personal and selfish reasons"; Sanctions Standards not cited).

- **Personal Gratification and Self-Protection**

Some courts have interpreted a dishonest or selfish motive under Standard 9.22(b) to encompass personal gratification, including that involving sexual misconduct. *See, e.g., In re Wolf*, 826 P.2d 628 (Or. 1992) (engaging in sexual intercourse with and serving wine to sixteen-year-old client warranted eighteen-month suspension, with aggravating factor including lawyer who acted from a selfish motive under Standard 9.22(b), in this instance, the motive of sexual gratification); *In re Disciplinary Proceeding Against Day*, 173 P.3d 915 (Wash. 2007) (in imposing disbarment, court agreed with disciplinary board that conviction for a crime that involved touching of minor for purpose of sexual gratification demonstrated selfish motive and hearing officer erred in not finding it an aggravating factor); *In re Disciplinary Proceedings Against Voss*, 795 N.W.2d 415, 422 (Wis. 2011) (suspension for four years and eight months warranted for lawyer who "repeatedly took advantage of his position of power and victimized a very vulnerable person for his own selfish motives" when he engaged in sexual intercourse with his client numerous times and then undertook a series of actions to intimidate, embarrass, and harass the client in retribution for making a complaint against him); *cf. Fla. Bar v. Helinger*, 620 So.2d 993, 996 (Fla. 1993) (court noted that "[s]elfish motivation is not limited to motivation for financial gain"; lawyer's obscene phone calls for personal gratification clearly a selfish motive and so not mitigating under Standard 9.32(b); two-year suspension imposed).

Other less obvious conduct that has been considered to establish a selfish motive includes lawyers acting for the purposes of revenge or vindictiveness, to protect themselves or their law firms. *See, e.g., In re Wolff*, 810 N.W.2d 312, 315 n.4 (Minn. 2012) (in reciprocal proceedings, affirming finding by hearing officer in originating jurisdiction "that respondent's 'conduct in abandoning clients and misleading the court and clients evidence[d] a selfish motive (the intent to protect oneself)'"); *In re Lackey*, 37 P.3d 172 (Or. 2002) (lawyer's conduct was undertaken with a selfish motive, that is, to exact revenge on his superiors at the Oregon National Guard and so was an aggravating factor under Standard 9.22(b)); *In re Disciplinary Proceeding Against Kamb*, 305 P.3d 1091 (Wash. 2013) (lawyer's motive in altering signed order was dishonest and selfish in that he sought to hide the fact that he had failed to request the order on time); *In re Disciplinary Proceeding Against Simmerly*, 285 P.3d 838, 847 (Wash. 2012) (lawyer "'acted with both a dishonest and a selfish' motive" when he submitted false information about his trust account and fabricated client ledgers during the disciplinary process; disbarment for this and other misconduct); *In re Disciplinary Proceeding Against Schafer*, 66 P.3d 1036 (Wash. 2003) (lawyer who violated client confidences and was partly motivated by vindictiveness found to have met standard for having selfish motive under Standard 9.22(b)). *But see In re Carpenter*, 95 P.3d 203, 212 (Or. 2004) (court found no selfish motive under Standard 9.22(b) when proof that lawyer acted out of personal animosity was equivocal and evidence was "insufficient to prove that the accused's motive was directed at achieving personal or financial gain or to 'exact revenge'" (citations omitted); lawyer had testified that online message he posted accusing a teacher of engaging in sexual conduct with students was prompted because lawyer heard and believed community rumors that teacher had engaged in affairs with school-age girls and post was made on a whim and as a practical joke because lawyer and teacher had attended that same high school).

When a selfish motive is an element of the underlying finding of misconduct, a court may rule that it cannot also be an aggravating factor in determining the appropriate sanction. In *In re Discipline of Tanner*, 960 P.2d 399, 402, at n.1 (Utah 1998), for example, a lawyer was disbarred under Standard 4.2 for settling a case without contacting his client, forging his client's signature to a settlement check, keeping settlement proceeds, and lying to an FBI agent about the conduct. The court held that "because a selfish motive is an element of Rule 4.2(a), we do not give selfish motive additional weight as an aggravating factor."

### *Pattern of Misconduct*

When evidence demonstrates repeated instances of similar misconduct, courts have held that the aggravating factor of "a pattern of misconduct" may be established under Standard 9.22(c). Courts sometimes apply this as an aggravator together with "multiple offenses" under Standard 9.22(d) or use one or the other without fully distinguishing between the two. *See, e.g., People v. Braham*, 409 P.3d 655, 663 (Colo. O.P.D.J. 2017) (lawyer engaged in pattern of misconduct by abandoning three clients and converting the funds of two clients; noting that the court "is troubled that Respondent has repeatedly breached his ethical duties to numerous clients from 2014 to 2016" and considers this a significant factor in aggravation); *People v. Sugar*, 360 P.3d 1041, 1046 (Colo. O.P.D.J. 2015) (assisting more than 150 clients to unlawfully avoid tax liabilities over the course of a decade shows a significantly aggravating pattern of misconduct); *People v. D'Acquisto*, 146 P.3d 1041 (Colo. O.P.D.J. 2006) (lawyer engaged in pattern of misconduct by failing to professionally represent clients and by failing to appear in court on six separate client matters); *In re Brown*, 714 N.E.2d 630 (Ind. 1999) (pattern of misconduct by lawyer who mishandled partnership fees, charged excess fees, and failed to abide by CLE requirements found aggravating factor); *In re Holmes*, 416 P.3d 143, 157 (Kan. 2018) (pattern of misconduct in unauthorized practice of law found because lawyer "repeatedly provided false and misleading information to the disciplinary administrator's office regarding his knowledge of the suspension and the extent of his unauthorized practice of law"; one-year suspension imposed); *In re Cranmer*, 196 P.3d 932 (Kan. 2008) (municipal court convicted respondent of seven counts of lewd and lascivious behavior for activity occurring on separate occasions; accordingly, misconduct coupled with aggravating factors that included pattern of misconduct warranted six-month suspension); *In re Keithley*, 850 P.2d 227 (Kan. 1993) (rejecting lawyer's argument that pattern of misconduct was not established since only one victim was involved; jury's conviction of lawyer for aggravated incest with stepdaughter involving more than twenty-five admitted instances of sexual intercourse indicated pattern sufficient to be considered as aggravating factor, warranting disbarment); *In re Gines*, 869 So.2d 778, 782 (La. 2004) (pattern of misconduct among the numerous aggravating factors demonstrated by lawyer's "consistent pattern of disregard for her obligations under the Rules of Professional Conduct" as well as a pattern of neglect of client matters, failure to communicate, and failure to account for fees, warranting disbarment); *Att'y Grievance Comm'n v. Coppola*, 19 A.3d 431, 456 (Md. 2011) (disbarment for misconduct in lawyer's provision of estate planning services to children of incompetent person; lawyer engaged in series of acts that formed a pattern of misconduct, albeit with one goal in mind; in dissent, two justices found no "pattern of misconduct" under Standard 9.22(c) "[b]ecause a series of acts undertaken to accomplish a particular result in a single case does not constitute a pattern of misconduct"); *McIntyre v. Miss. Bar*, 38 So.3d 617 (Miss. 2010) (finding that six prior disciplinary sanctions indicated a pattern of misconduct and served as an aggravating circumstance; disbarment warranted for commingling funds and lending money to clients); *In re Chase*, 121 P.3d 1160 (Or. 2005) (thirty-day suspension in light of aggravators including pattern of misconduct by lawyer who repeatedly failed to pay court-ordered support); *In re Disciplinary Proceeding Against Cohen*, 82 P.3d 224, 233 (Wash. 2004) (similarity between lawyer's past misconduct and the current matter involving neglect and failure to communicate with his client "makes these previous matters highly relevant" and is evidence of a pattern of misconduct, an aggravating factor; one-year suspension with restitution imposed); *In re Disciplinary Proceeding Against Schafer*, 66 P.3d 1046 (Wash. 2003) (six-month suspension appropriate for multiple disclosures of client's secrets and confidences to expose corrupt judge evidencing aggravating factor of pattern of misconduct). *But see In re Alexander*, 300 P.3d 536 (Ariz. 2013) (no pattern where lawyer had no prior disciplinary record and misconduct arose from lawyer's actions in a single matter, involved the same people, and spanned approximately ninety days); *In re Levine*,

847 P.2d 1093 (Ariz. 1993) (no pattern as contemplated by Standard 9.22(c) because lawyer had no prior disciplinary record, nor did court find existence of multiple counts of misconduct necessarily constituted a "pattern"); *In re Reardon*, 759 A.2d 568, 577, 578 (Del. 2000) (pattern of misconduct "may be discerned from two or more recognizably consistent acts that serve as predictor of future misconduct"; in this case, although the lawyer owed the same duty of diligence to his two clients, court disagreed with board's conclusion that the two cases, standing alone, presented "pattern of neglect," noting that the "two acts of misconduct viewed in isolation are [not] recognizably consistent acts sufficient to constitute the separate aggravating factor of 'a pattern of misconduct' beyond 'the commission of multiple offenses' factor already found by the Board").

As with other factors, the timing of the instances of misconduct is significant in determining whether a pattern of misconduct exists. *See, e.g., In re O'Brien-Reyes*, 868 P.2d 945 (Ariz. 1994) (while respondent's previous informal reprimand for similar conduct, viewed in conjunction with conduct presently at issue, may create appearance of a pattern of misconduct, no aggravating factor found because both previous and present misconduct occurred during same time period and significant mitigation existed during that period; court imposed censure with one-year probation); *Idaho State Bar v. Malmin*, 78 P.3d 371 (Idaho 2003) (private reprimand issued nine years earlier is sufficiently remote in time as to not indicate a continuing pattern of behavior); *In re Redden*, 153 P.3d 113 (Or. 2007) (court stated that even though lawyer engaged in serious neglect as to single client's legal matter, there was no pattern of misconduct as aggravator under Standard 9.22(c) because lawyer had no prior disciplinary history and record was devoid of any evidence that lawyer engaged in similar misconduct in the past; based on lack of aggravating factor, sixty-day suspension imposed instead of 120-day suspension); *cf. In re Disciplinary Proceeding Against Burtch*, 175 P.3d 1070 (Wash. 2008) (in imposing disbarment, court stated that evidence of pattern of misconduct admissible for consideration as aggravating factor even if not charged in formal complaint).

Courts have held that aggravation under Standard 9.22(c) can be based on misconduct other than the charged violations of the Rules of Professional Conduct, which helps to distinguish this Standard from the aggravating factor multiple offenses under Standard 9.22(d). *See In re Disciplinary Proceeding Against Starczewski*, 306 P.3d 905, 915 (Wash. 2013) (applying pattern of misconduct aggravating factor based on history of dishonesty, frivolous claims, and disregard for judicial and disciplinary warnings; "The ABA Standards are clear that the pattern-of-misconduct factor applies to mere misconduct not violations of the RPCs.").

## *Multiple Offenses*

Multiple offenses committed in the context of a single disciplinary proceeding may be an aggravating factor, and, as noted above, courts may also apply both and the aggravating factor of a pattern of misconduct under Standard 9.22(c). *See, e.g., Ala. State Bar v. Hallett*, 26 So.3d 1127 (Ala. 2009) (lawyer's multiple violations of professional conduct rules arising from his representation of divorce client, including excessive fees and conflicts of interest, supported finding of multiple offenses as aggravating factor under Standards 9.22(d) and 9.22(c) of the Alabama Standards for Imposing Lawyer Discipline); *In re Moak*, 71 P.3d 343 (Ariz. 2003) (among other misconduct, multiple serious offenses committed by respondent including dishonesty and misrepresentations while representing two clients, and deception to the court and opposing parties served as substantial aggravators under Standard 9.22(d) as well as pattern of misconduct under Standard 9.22(c), warranting six-month-and-one-day suspension); *In re Sisk*, 54 A.3d 257 (Table) (Del. 2012) (delay in dealing with client matters and unresponsiveness to client inquiries supported finding of multiple offenses as aggravating factor; public reprimand and two-year probation imposed in light of mitigating factors outweighing aggravating factors); *Fla. Bar v. Irish*, 48 So.3d 767 (Fla. 2010) (lawyer's conviction of six felonies for trafficking, possession, sale, and delivery of illegal drugs, and his misuse of client funds to support his drug habit was sufficient to establish multiple offenses aggravator; disbarment imposed); *Office of Disciplinary Counsel v. Au*, 113 P.3d 203 (Haw. 2005) (multiple, unrelated instances of unethical conduct in three separate disciplinary matters supported application of, inter alia, Standard 9.22(d), as aggravating factor; five-year suspension imposed); *In re Holmes*, 416 P.3d 143 (Kan. 2018) (lawyer committed six rule violations in the course of missing a deadline to pay bar fees, failing to pay late fee, and consequently engaging in unauthorized practicing law due to administratively suspended license; one-year suspension imposed); *In re Rumsey*, 71 P.3d 1150 (Kan. 2003) (multiple offenses a factor in aggravation when lawyer suspended for one year for fourteen ethics violations); *Ky. Bar Ass'n v. Bierbauer*, 282 S.W.3d 318 (Ky. 2009) (permanent disbarment warranted for lawyer whose multiple instances of misconduct included five bar disciplinary files, four different clients, eighteen different violations, and conversion of $3,850 of unearned fees); *In re McNeely*, 98 So.3d 275 (La. 2012) (in imposing three-year suspension, court found that multiple counts of neglect, failure to communicate, and failure to return unearned fees supported consideration of multiple offenses as aggravator); *Att'y Grievance Com'n v. Barton*, 110 A.3d 668, 700 (Md. 2015) (aggravating factor applied to lawyer who committed sixteen rule violations against nine clients; citing Standard 9.22(d) court explained that "an attorney commits multiple offenses when he or she committed numerous violations of the Rules, particularly against different clients"); *In re Disciplinary Action Against Britton*, 484 N.W.2d 110 (N.D. 1992) (aggravating factors including multiple offenses under Standard 9.22(d) and pattern of misconduct under Standard 9.22(c) for, inter alia, negligent representation of clients warranted two years' suspension); *In re Leisure*, 113 P.3d 412 (Or. 2005) (eighteen-month suspension imposed for lawyer's repeated willingness to issue checks that she knew she could not cover resulting in "multiple offenses" as aggravating factor under Standard 9.22(d)); *In re Disciplinary Proceeding Against Simmerly*, 285 P.3d 838 (Wash. 2012) (twenty-six counts of proven misconduct supported the hearing officer's finding of five aggravating factors, including multiple offenses; disbarment imposed for misuse of client funds and intentional misrepresentations during the disciplinary process). *But see In re Ketter*, 992 P.2d 205 (Kan. 1999) (aggravating factor of "multiple offenses" should not apply unless multiple violations of disciplinary rules found in current proceeding; otherwise, there would be no distinction between aggravating factors of "multiple offenses" and "prior disciplinary offenses"; court finding that lawyer's conviction for indecent exposure eleven years earlier was too remote in time to be considered an aggravating factor to the current charge for conviction of lewd and lascivious behavior; imposition of discipline suspended and lawyer placed on three years' probation).

Some courts have declined to apply this aggravating factor when the number of offenses is de minimis or when only one event or offense violates multiple rules. *See, e.g., People v. Kanwal*, 357 P.3d 1236, 1243 (Colo. O.P.D.J. 2015) (little aggravating weight given to multiple offenses when lawyer "did not engage in more than two distinct types of misconduct"; disbarment ordered based on other factors); *In re Disciplinary Proceeding Against Longacre*, 122 P.3d 710, 726 (Wash. 2005) (multiple counts are commonly charged simply because most discrete behaviors violate more than one rule of professional conduct; "Surely, the ABA Standards and this court never intended that all attorneys charged with multiple counts of misconduct be subject to the 'multiple offenses' aggravating factor. The test for 'multiple offenses' must require something more."); *Bd. of Prof'l Responsibility v. Custis*, 348 P.3d 823, 835 (Wyo. 2015) (lawyer filed brief containing material misrepresentations and court found "while this conduct violated more than one rule of professional conduct, it does not constitute 'multiple offenses'").

## *Bad Faith Obstruction of Disciplinary Proceedings*

Courts have found that a lawyer's bad faith obstruction of a disciplinary proceeding by intentionally failing to comply with disciplinary rules or orders constitutes an aggravating factor under Standard 9.22(e). This Standard contains a bad faith requirement coupled with a mens rea requirement of intent. The type of behavior that qualifies under this aggravating factor ranges from failure to cooperate with a disciplinary investigation by refusing to respond to requests for information, to engaging in delay tactics, to displaying a contemptuous attitude toward the disciplinary proceedings. *See, e.g., People v. McNamara*, 275 P.3d 792 (Colo. O.P.D.J. 2011) (lawyer's failure to abide by disciplinary judge's orders and his recalcitrance during pretrial discovery militated in favor of giving great weight to Standard 9.22(e) as aggravator; suspension for one year and one day for lawyer who failed to pay court-ordered child support and negligently converted client's retainer); *People v. Barbieri*, 61 P.3d 488, 495 (Colo. O.P.D.J. 2000) (disbarment warranted for lawyer who failed to comply with orders entered in case, refused to provide information properly requested during preparation of case and, by so doing, sought in bad faith to obstruct disciplinary proceeding; court found: "In disciplinary matters involving an attorney's conduct, compliance with unchallenged orders issued by the disciplinary body is not elective; it is mandatory. Failure to do so, almost invariably, will insure substantially enhanced discipline."); *Iowa Supreme Ct. Bd. of Prof'l Ethics & Conduct v. Ramey*, 639 N.W.2d 243 (Iowa 2002) (in default proceeding, lawyer's failure to respond to disciplinary proceeding was aggravating factor suggesting overall attitude of disrespect and disregard for legal profession and therefore properly considered in imposing three-year suspension for failure to carry out contract of employment); *In re Graham*, 807 So.2d 829 (La. 2002) (citing Standard 9.22(e), the court held that the lawyer's intentional failure to cooperate in disciplinary investigations prejudiced lawyer's own position when complaints against her were relatively minor and could have been quickly resolved if she had complied with her professional obligation to cooperate; bad faith obstruction of disciplinary proceeding among aggravating factors considered in imposing one-year-and-one-day suspension); *In re Schenck*, 194 P.3d 804, 811 (Or. 2008) (lawyer's refusal to cooperate in disciplinary investigation out of what he called his "Dutch stubbornness" and after two written requests was strong aggravating factor under Standard 9.22(e) that supported one-year suspension from practice of law); *In re Skagen*, 149 P.3d 1171, 1193 (Or. 2006) (lawyer's long delay in producing trust account statement and deposit slip that tended to prove allegations against him constituted "bad faith obstruction of the disciplinary proceeding" under Standard 9.22(e), particularly when lawyer falsely represented he did not have certain records and later offered them as evidence; in imposing one-year suspension, court found that the "accused's repeated refusal to cooperate with the Bar in other aspects of its investigation and formal proceedings further supports our finding of this aggravating factor"); *V.I. Bar Ass'n. v. Brusch*, S.Ct. BA Nos. 2007/64, 2007/65, 2008 WL 901533 (V.I. Mar. 3, 2008) (lawyer exhibited bad faith under Standard 9.22(e) by intentionally failing to comply with rules and bar notices; multiple offenses warranted disbarment); *In re Disciplinary Proceeding Against Jones*, 338 P.3d 842 (Wash. 2014) (factor applied when lawyer served frivolous lawsuit on prosecution witness three weeks before hearing in an attempt to intimidate or chill testimony and refused to answer questions about attempts to pay judgment or sanctions and about extent of assets even after the hearing officer ordered him to answer); *In re Disciplinary Proceeding Against Sanai*, 302 P.3d 864 (Wash. 2013) (court held that application of this factor based on behavior during hearing did not violate due process because it was not a new charge); *In re Disciplinary Proceeding Against Greenlee*, 143 P.3d 807, 815 n.4 (Wash. 2006) (upholding hearing officer's finding that lawyer showed repeated disregard for discipline process by failing to respond to bar requests for information absent threat of deposition, repeatedly avoiding service of process and "playing games" by using back or private entrances to his office; aggravating factor considered in imposing six-month suspension for failing to advise client to seek independent legal advice before instructing client to sign release of malpractice claim). *But see People v. Taggart*, 2017 WL 3097676 (Colo. O.P.D.J. 2017 June 13, 2017) (declining to apply Standard 9.22(e) because lawyer's failure to participate in proceeding was addressed by Colo. RPC 8.1(b) charge and there was no evidence of other intentional bad faith); *People v. Goodman*, 334 P.3d 241, 249 (Colo. O.P.D.J 2014) (declining to consider bad faith obstruction as aggravating factor based on respondent's failure to participate after filing of answer, noting that disciplinary counsel cited no rule or order that would mandate participation in the disciplinary proceeding nor any authority that suggests failure to participate qualifies as bad faith obstruction); *People v. Calvert*, 280 P.3d 1269 (Colo. O.P.D.J. 2011) (disciplinary counsel argued that lawyer engaged in bad faith obstruction of proceeding by denying a number of allegations in his answer, which he later admitted during the disciplinary proceedings while lawyer maintained he was cooperative in all aspects of disciplinary process; court applied neither Standard 9.22(e) as aggravator nor Standard 9.32(e) as mitigator because hearing board heard no evidence substantiating either position; other aggravating factors considered in imposing disbarment sanction); *In re Becker*, 947 A.2d 1120 (Table) (Del. 2008) (lawyer's failure to fulfill probationary requirements of psychiatric evaluation and care did not constitute bad faith obstruction when lawyer was unable to comply due to significant cost involved but lawyer could have done much more to rectify his books and records during probationary period); *Fla. Bar v. Senton*, 882 So.2d 997 (Fla. 2004) (court agreed with lawyer's argument that referee improperly found lawyer's failure to comply with and challenge to unprecedented order for blood sample to be an aggravating factor under Florida Standard 9.22(e); lawyer's good faith challenge of a disciplinary order cannot be held to be bad faith obstruction, and lawyer complied after court directed sample be given).

### *Deceptive Practices During the Disciplinary Process*

A lawyer's submission of false evidence, false statements, or other deceptive practices during the disciplinary process, whether it be before the hearing committee, disciplinary board, or court, and whether by omission or commission, may be an aggravating factor under Standard 9.22(f). *See, e.g., Ala. State Bar v. Quinn*, 926 So.2d 1018 (Ala. 2005) (citing Standard 9.22(f) of Alabama Standards for Imposing Lawyer Discipline, court said that lawyer's testimony at hearing was totally lacking in credibility and false; disbarment for lawyer who at minimum was accomplice to distribution of marijuana, due to aggravating circumstances surrounding his conviction, even if offense alone did not warrant it); *In re Egbune*, 971 P.2d 1065 (Colo. 1999) (lawyer's submission of false statements to disciplinary hearing board in response to allegations that he sexually assaulted his client was most serious of several aggravators; one-year suspension imposed); *Fla. Bar v. Batista*, 846 So.2d 479 (Fla. 2003) (lawyer's attempt to have clients sign affidavits repudiating their disciplinary complaints constituted a deceptive practice and was properly considered in aggravation under Florida Sanctions Standard 9.22(f)); *Idaho State Bar v. Malmin*, 78 P.3d 371 (Idaho 2003) (evidence supported findings that lawyer knowingly made false statement in connection with disciplinary proceeding when she provided state bar with three varying accounts over the course of the investigation to account for delay in filing money judgment papers on behalf of divorce client); *Iowa Supreme Ct. Bd. of Prof'l Ethics & Conduct v. Bernard*, 653 N.W.2d 373, 375 (Iowa 2002) (lawyer's false statement to disciplinary board concerning substance abuse problem found aggravating; while lawyer claimed false statement was product of his addiction and he was in state of denial at time statement was made, "[n]evertheless, his drug and alcohol addiction does not excuse his conduct"); *In re Holmes*, 416 P.3d 143 (Kan. 2018) (aggravating factor found when lawyer misrepresented and omitted facts necessary to prevent misapprehension in written correspondence to disciplinary administrator during investigation and throughout disciplinary proceedings; one-year suspension imposed); *In re Warner*, 851 So.2d 1029 (La. 2003) (lawyer's submission during disciplinary investigation of an altered release he had counseled his client to forge was properly considered in aggravation under Standard 9.22(f); one-year-and-one-day suspension imposed); *Att'y Grievance Comm'n v. Dominguez*, 47 A.3d 975, 985 (Md. 2012) (lawyer's false statements to disciplinary counsel that she was never assigned to handle a homeless person's expungement case as a volunteer pro bono attorney despite entering into a pro bono retainer agreement with the client "clearly implicates factor (f)" of Standard 9.22; disbarment for neglect of several clients' matters); *In re Solny*, 96 A.D.3d 76 (N.Y. App. Div. 2012) (in imposing two years' suspension, court considered in aggravation lawyer's false testimony in disciplinary proceeding that he had permission to transfer $600,000 of his uncle's money just weeks before his uncle's death; this factor not outweighed by lawyer's testimony of the pressures he was under in caring for his uncle, raising four children, attending to his law practice while his wife stayed in Canada for extended periods to take care of her ill mother); *In re Huffman*, 13 P.3d 994 (Or. 2000) (lawyer engaged in deceptive practices during disciplinary process by failing to respond fully and truthfully to inquiries from state bar regarding extent of personal assets was factor in aggravation under 9.22(f)); *In re Disciplinary Proceeding Against Whitt*, 72 P.3d 173, 180 (Wash. 2003) (aggravating factor of providing falsified information during disciplinary proceeding not mitigated because wrongdoer made admission after being accused of deception; court held that lawyer "not only did not cooperate, she acted most egregiously by intentionally falsifying multiple documents and lying during the investigatory proceedings to avoid discipline" and that whether her falsification was looked at as separate count or as aggravating factor to two other counts, her "misconduct relating to her veracity weighs heavily in favor of disbarment"); *In re Winkel*, 866 N.W.2d 642, 652 (Wis. 2015) (citing ABA Standard 9.22(f) in determining that lawyer's hearing testimony was "plagued with 'non-responsive' answers, 'circumlocution and prevarication,' 'layers of obfuscation,' and conflicts with deposition testimony"). *But see In re Carpenter*, 95 P.3d 203 (Or. 2004) (court concluded aggravating factor under Standard 9.22(f) was not supported by evidence that lawyer submitted false statements to trial panel when he testified there were rumors in the community about a teacher having had sexual relations with students in light of the teacher's testimony that such vague rumors did exist); *In re Disciplinary Proceeding Against Placide*, 414 P.3d 1124, 1140 (Wash. 2018) (rejecting hearing officer's application of Standard 9.22(f) to pro se lawyer's cross-examination of witnesses that included false or misleading assertions; "As part of her presentation of a defense, an attorney is entitled to challenge witnesses. . . . To conclude otherwise might chill the right of an attorney accused of misconduct to put the [prosecution] to a vigorous proof[.]").

When a false statement or other deceptive practice during the disciplinary process forms the basis for a separate charge of misconduct against the lawyer, courts generally will not also treat that conduct as an aggravating factor under Standard 9.22(f). *See People v. Olson*, 2016 WL 5076078 (Colo. O.P.D.J. July 25, 2016) (thirty-month suspension for lawyer who engaged in domestic violence while attempting to persuade spouse not to testify truthfully or to avoid service of a subpoena; court explained that aggravating factor would not be applied because the act of witness tampering formed the basis of the disciplinary charges); *In re Gallagher*, 26 P.3d 131, 139 (Or. 2001) (since the court already had found that lawyer's repeated lies during the disciplinary process constituted misconduct under ethics rules it would be "'double-counting' to conclude that that same conduct also supports application of ABA Standard 9.22(f)."; two-year suspension warranted for numerous misrepresentations to the bar and dishonesty during settlement negotiations in client's matter).

## *Refusal to Acknowledge Wrongful Nature of Conduct*

Courts may find an aggravating factor under Standard 9.22(g) when a lawyer refuses to acknowledge the wrongful nature of his or her conduct. Circumstances where courts will find that the evidence establishes this factor in aggravation vary. *See, e.g., People v. Pautler*, 35 P.3d 571 (Colo. O.P.D.J. 2001) (assertion of prosecutor, who posed as public defender to secure murder suspect's surrender, that he would make same decisions and engage in same deceitful misconduct given same circumstances was an aggravating factor of significant consequence; under

Standard 9.22(g), by giving such testimony, respondent evidenced failure to recognize or even acknowledge the improper conduct in which he engaged); *In re Melvin*, 807 A.2d 550, 554 (Del. 2002) (finding sufficient evidence of aggravation under Standard 9.22(g), the court was "deeply concerned" by lawyer's disingenuous attempt before hearing board to minimize severity of misconduct by arguing that his wife's destroyed journals had no evidentiary value or, alternatively, that he did not know they had evidentiary value at time he had them destroyed; eighteen-month suspension); *Att'y Grievance Comm'n v. Mininsohn*, 846 A.2d 353, 376 (Md. 2004) (finding aggravating factor under Standard 9.22(g), court agreed with lower tribunal that lawyer exhibited "a certain callousness toward his situation" and a "reluctance to accept responsibility for his actions"; disbarment imposed for failing to comply with his tax obligations, failing to promptly deliver client funds, and failing to prepare and submit draft order as indicated by judge); *In re Stein*, 177 P.3d 513, 529 (N.M. 2008) (disbarment warranted with aggravating factor under Standard 9.22(g) for lawyer who maintained he did nothing wrong but evidence established repeated knowing and intentional misconduct relating to conflicts of interest and misrepresentations; court noted that "[i]n light of what Respondent knew and what he intentionally did, it is, to say the least, troubling that he has steadfastly maintained that he has acted ethically."); *In re Quintana*, 29 P.3d 527, 531 (N.M. 2001) (refusal to acknowledge deliberate and wrongful nature of misconduct "particularly pertinent in light of the egregious nature of respondent's conduct" of misappropriating client funds from trust account to pay personal expenses, and making misrepresentations to client and to court to hide misappropriations; disbarment ordered); *In re Disciplinary Action Against Crary*, 638 N.W.2d 23 (N.D. 2002) (refusal to acknowledge wrongfulness of conduct included lawyer's belated suggestion, after he had failed to repay loan from client, that he was entitled to keep $3,500 for his expenses in providing personal services to client; lawyer disbarred); *In re McGraw*, 414 P.3d 841 (Or. 2018) (although lawyer in nearly all material respects acknowledged factual accuracy of disciplinary allegations, he claimed that his conduct was not blameworthy and would not acknowledge conduct was detrimental in any respect; court held that under those circumstances, lawyer had failed to acknowledge wrongful nature of the conduct); *In re Disciplinary Proceeding Against Ferguson*, 246 P.3d 1236, 1251 (Wash. 2011) (factor applied when lawyer expressed no remorse, remained unrepentant in the face of abundant evidence and even her own testimony, and rationalized conduct by characterizing her violations as "unfortunate labelling").

- **Exercising Right to Defend Distinguishable**

A lawyer's refusal to acknowledge the wrongful nature of his or her conduct, however, is not automatically found to be an aggravating factor. Courts have held that a lawyer's exercise of his or her right to defend against disciplinary charges by denying the alleged misconduct or expressing a reasonable belief that he or she is innocent should not be held against the lawyer for purposes of aggravation under Standard 9.22(g). *See, e.g., Fla. Bar v. Corbin,* 701 So.2d 334, 337 n.2 (Fla. 1997) (improper for referee to consider in aggravation fact that lawyer refused to acknowledge wrongful nature of his conduct because "[respondent's] claim of innocence cannot be used against him"; ninety-day suspension for making false statements to tribunal and in disciplinary proceeding); *In re West,* 804 S.E.2d 340, 342 (Ga. 2017) ("even an assertion of innocence ultimately adjudicated to the contrary is not necessarily an aggravating factor"); *In re Suttle,* 701 S.E.2d 154 (Ga. 2010) (lawyer's refusal to acknowledge wrongful nature of his or her behavior should not automatically be considered factor in aggravation, particularly when lawyer has honest and objectively reasonable belief in innocence); *In re McCool,* 172 So.3d 1058, 1082 (La. 2015) (in disbarment case involving lawyer who engaged in campaign of unethical efforts to influence judicial proceeding, aggravating factor applied because lawyer was "[c]ompletely unapologetic for her misconduct, [] made it abundantly clear she would continue to use social media and blogs to effect her agenda to bring about the changes she sought in the underlying cases . . . [and] will not admit to any wrong doing whatsoever"); *Att'y Grievance Comm'n v. Monfried,* 794 A.2d 92, 105 (Md. 2002) (mere filing of exceptions in exercise of lawyer's right to defend against allegations of wrongdoing does not equate to finding lack of remorse or that lawyer does not acknowledge the wrongfulness of conduct, and so not considered aggravator in imposing sanction; "[w]e will not consider the fact that an attorney exercised his or her right to file exceptions . . . as an aggravating factor in imposing a sanction"); *In re Smith,* 236 P.3d 137, 149 (Or. 2010) (declining to apply Standard 9.22(g) as aggravating factor when lawyer defended charges by consistently asserting he had provided sound legal advice to his client; "accused's reliance on those arguments—although unavailing—cannot be used to enhance the penalty that would otherwise be imposed for his violations"); *In re Davenport,* 49 P.3d 91, 105 (Or. 2002) (bar must point to some evidence other than lawyer's refusal to concede bar's factual allegations to support finding of aggravation under Standard 9.22(g)); "Put differently: Every lawyer should have the opportunity to defend against accusations respecting his or her personal character and professional responsibility without reprisal for doing so"; two-year suspension for false testimony); *Bd. of Prof'l Responsibility v. Daniel,* 549 S.W.3d 90, 104 (Tenn. 2018) ("the mounting of a defense, without more, should not be applied as an aggravating factor"); *In re Disciplinary Proceeding Against Marshall,* 217 P.3d 291, 307 (Wash. 2009) (although lawyer showed no remorse for his conduct, court declined to "penalize him for making arguments in his defense" and, therefore, did not consider his refusal to acknowledge the wrongful nature of his conduct in aggravation; but more than enough aggravating factors to warrant disbarment for attempting to pressure clients for additional fees and trying to bully clients into settling claims). *But see People v. Musick*, 960 P.2d 89 (Colo. 1998) (while aggravating factor not applied in face of legitimate defense to charges of misconduct, court declined to regard lawyer's failure to take any steps toward rehabilitation or even recognize that he had a problem as legitimate exercise of a defense to charges of misconduct).

The Florida Supreme Court, in determining whether Standard 9.22(g) is deemed an aggravating factor, has also drawn a distinction between a lawyer's defense that rests on factual questions from a defense based on questions of law. When a lawyer's continued claims of innocence rest on a question of law, the court says, the aggravating factor of failing to acknowledge the wrongfulness of the conduct applies. *Compare Fla. Bar v. Germain*, 957 So.2d 613, 622 (Fla. 2007) (court approved application of aggravating factor under Standard 9.22(g) when lawyer stipulated to most of the facts, did not dispute that he engaged in misconduct including lying under oath, yet continued to assert that his actions did not constitute unethical conduct; court stated, "[t]hese are legal issues. With a minimum of legal research, [respondent] could have discovered that his conduct did constitute unethical conduct and either curtailed his activities or avoided them altogether.") *with Fla. Bar v. Karten*, 829 So.2d 883 (Fla. 2002) (since lawyer disputed factual finding that he had engaged in misconduct giving rise to rule violations, referee erred in finding as an aggravating factor lawyer's refusal to acknowledge wrongful nature of misconduct; but disbarment still appropriate for lawyer who improperly profited from selling client's property).

- **Lack of Remorse**

Although there is not a specific aggravating factor for lack of remorse, under Standard 9.22(g), courts often equate a lawyer's lack of regret or remorse with failing to acknowledge the wrongful nature of the misconduct. *See, e.g., People v. Katz*, 58 P.3d 1176 (Colo. O.P.D.J. 2002) (in disbarring lawyer for, inter alia, conversion of funds and commingling of property, court found lack of remorse an aggravating factor under Standard 9.22(g) when lawyer only expressed regret that his conduct resulted in disciplinary proceeding against him); *Att'y Grievance Comm'n v. Mixter*, 109 A.3d 1, 70 (Md. 2015) (in applying Standard 9.22(g), court found lawyer had not once acknowledged committing any improper act, lawyer had asserted that victims' feelings of harassment were "subjective" and irrelevant, and in 106 pages of exceptions, lawyer only asserted, in one sentence, that he was "sincerely remorseful" without elaboration; disbarment ordered); *Matter of Zappin*, 160 A.D.3d 1, 5 (N.Y. App. Div. 2018) (in disbarment case with numerous instances of "extensive and unbridled" litigation misconduct, lawyer's lack of remorse and evident lack of respect for the judicial process deemed serious aggravating factors); *In re Fitzhenry*, 162 P.3d 260, 275 (Or. 2007) (while not citing Standard 9.22(g) as an aggravating factor, court gave weight to trial panel's assessment that lawyer's only real remorse was "more for his predicament, than for committing any violation of the rules which govern his profession"); *In re Disciplinary Proceeding Against Miller,* 66 P.3d 1069, 1078 (Wash. 2003) (disbarment warranted for misconduct, including preparing client's will that named lawyer as beneficiary; upholding hearing officer's finding that lawyer was "not genuinely remorseful about his misconduct," believing that he did nothing wrong established aggravating factor under Standard 9.22(g), court noted that it previously found that "lack of remorse is a powerful aggravating factor").

Some jurisdictions have held that evidence demonstrating a pattern of misconduct can support the application of Standard 9.22(g). *See, e.g., In re Lemmons,* 545 S.E.2d 885 (Ga. 2001) (aggravating factor under Standard 9.22(g) evidenced by repetition of similar misconduct); *In re Devers,* 974 P.2d 191 (Or. 1999) (lawyer's practicing law while suspended and by disputing that his conduct was the practice of law evidenced refusal to acknowledge wrongful nature of his conduct under Standard 9.22(g).

### *Vulnerability of Victim*

In determining whether the vulnerability of the victim of a lawyer's misconduct constitutes an aggravating factor under Standard 9.22(h), courts look to a variety of characteristics, including the age of the victim, the victim's level of education or sophistication, and whether the victim of lawyer misconduct suffers from disabilities or impairments.

- **The Elderly**

Courts often have found that Standard 9.22(h) applies to cases where the victims of lawyer misconduct are elderly. The advanced age of the victim also may be considered in combination with other factors demonstrating vulnerability. *See, e.g., People v. Taggart,* 2017 WL 3097676 at *1 (Colo. O.P.D.J. June 13, 2017) (sixty-six-year-old client whose finances were in "dire straits" found vulnerable; two-year suspension ordered); *People v. McGarry,* 175 P.3d 107 (Colo. O.P.D.J. 2007) (seventy-four-year-old and disabled client was vulnerable victim; two year suspension imposed for neglect of client's matter and subsequent dishonesty); *People v. Haines,* 179 P.3d 1021 (Colo. O.P.D.J. 2006) (elderly personal representative of estate particularly vulnerable because of age, living out of state, and investing complete trust in lawyer to assist in carrying out fiduciary duties owed to estate; disbarment warranted for lawyer who took advantage of her position of trust when she misappropriated estate funds); *In re Coggs,* 14 P.3d 1123 (Kan. 2000) (ninety-year-old client who placed trust in lawyer handling her estate matters was vulnerable victim of misconduct that included self-dealing and conflicts of interest warranting indefinite suspension from the practice of law); *In re Letellier,* 742 So.2d 544, 548 (La. 1999) (lawyer disbarred for commingling and converting funds of vulnerable elderly client with psychiatric problems, among other misconduct; most egregious aggravating factor in instant case "is the fact that Respondent took advantage of an obviously vulnerable victim"; "[client's] age, history of psychological problems, slovenly demeanor and living conditions, and the news video footage of his home to be consistent with reports that [he] was unable to care for either himself or his financial affairs"); *In re Coffey's Case,* 880 A.2d 403 (N.H. 2005) (lawyer's misconduct of charging excessive fees and entering into business transaction with client was particularly egregious in light of elderly client's vulnerability due to declining mental health); *In re Disciplinary Action Against Crary,* 638 N.W.2d 23 (N.D. 2002) (eighty-five-year-old woman who had recent stroke and was dependent upon lawyer for her personal needs was particularly vulnerable victim of misconduct that included conflicts of interest arising from loan lawyer took from his client and commissions he earned on annuities he obtained for client; disbarment ordered); *Utah State Bar v. Jardine,* 289 P.3d 516, 534 (Utah 2012) (in imposing eighteen-month suspension, several aggravating factors considered, including vulnerability of victim, an eighty-seven-year-old woman in poor health, but evidence did not support application of that factor to two other clients, who court determined were no "more vulnerable than any other consumer of legal service"); *In re Disciplinary Proceedings Against Felli,* 718 N.W.2d 70, 89 (Wis. 2006) (three years' suspension warranted for lawyer rather than the eighteen-month suspension recommended for egregious misconduct targeting "vulnerable elderly women and either directly or indirectly through financial planners solicit[ing] his services in various fiduciary capacities").

- **Children**

Courts generally have considered children especially vulnerable and in need of greater protection. Lawyers who engage in misconduct involving children are subject to even closer scrutiny by courts and Standard 9.22(h) is often found to be an aggravating factor in such cases. *See, e.g., People v. Spalsbury,* 111 P.3d 1052 (Colo. O.P.D.J. 2005) (one-year-and-one-day suspension imposed on lawyer for failure to pay child support; court stressed vulnerability of his affected children and lawyer's failure to contribute to the family also placed additional burdens on former wife); *People v. Hohertz,* 102 P.3d 1019 (Colo. O.P.D.J. 2004) (divorce client and her children were especially vulnerable due to lawyer's failure to obtain restraining order against client's physically abusive husband resulting in client and her children being forced to leave the state; disbarment imposed for, inter alia, numerous instances of neglect); *In re Fierro,* 869 P.2d 728 (Kan. 1994) (vulnerability of victims considered aggravating factor in imposing indefinite suspension on lawyer involved in lewd fondling or touching of six young girls); *Att'y Grievance Comm'n v. Greenleaf,* 91 A.3d 1066 (Md. 2014) (minority of victim deemed aggravating factor when lawyer deliberately preyed on, and intended to violate, a person whom he believed to be under the age of consent; disbarment ordered); *Att'y Grievance Comm'n v. Thompson*, 786 A.2d 763, 773 (Md. 2001) (in imposing indefinite suspension, court noted thirteen-year-old boy stalked by lawyer was, due to his age alone, vulnerable to harm; "childhood 'is a time and condition of life when a person may be most susceptible to influence and to psychological damage.'") (citation omitted); *In re Rhodes*, 13 P.3d 512 (Or. 2000) (failure to pay child support harmed children, who were vulnerable victims; two-year suspension imposed for lawyer's failure to comply with his legal obligations); *In re Disciplinary Proceeding Against Day*, 173 P.3d 915 (Wash. 2007) (lawyer's victim, an eleven-year-old, was highly vulnerable, and lawyer abused trust he had established with the victim and his mother). *Cf. People v. Falco*, 2016 WL 4442171 (Colo. O.P.D.J. July 7, 2016) (victim vulnerability found when lawyer assaulted spouse in the marital home, a place where it was unlikely that anyone would come to her aid; in addition, victim was pregnant mother of three young children, making her particularly vulnerable, which merited considerable weight in aggravation; nine-month suspension ordered).

This aggravating factor has also been applied in cases of a lawyer's failure to pay child support. *See People v. Quigley*, 359 P.3d 1045, 1051 (Colo. O.P.D.J. 2015) ("the law charges parents with providing for their children precisely because they are not yet capable of doing so themselves"); *In re Disciplinary Counsel v. Curry*, 858 N.E.2d 392 (Ohio 2006) (failure to pay child support or respond to default order to pay harmed vulnerable victims).

- **Unequal Power Relationship**

Courts also may find a client vulnerable when an unequal power relationship exists between the lawyer and victim. Cases in which such unequal power relationships exist include, but are not limited to, those involving lawyers who make inappropriate sexual comments or enter into a sexual relationship with a client. *See, e.g., In re Brion*, 212 P.3d 748, 751 (Alaska 2009) (in imposing three-year suspension with two years stayed for, inter alia, neglect of six matters court considered clients victimized by lawyer "especially vulnerable to neglect and lack of diligence because most of them resided out-of-state"); *In re Abrams*, 257 P.3d 167, 174 (Ariz. 2011) (newly admitted lawyer who was sexually harassed and chastised in court when she declined former judge's sexual advances was a particularly vulnerable victim; the court stressed that "[n]othing threatens public confidence in the courts and the legal system more than a judge who abuses his power and exploits the prestige of his office for personal benefit"; two-year suspension for this and other misconduct); *People v. Good*, 893 P.2d 101, 103 (Colo. 1995) (client found vulnerable and aggravating factor established under Standard 9.22(h) where lawyer engaged in sexual relationship with her; in imposing one-year-and-one-day suspension, court noted, "[o]ften the lawyer-client relationship is characterized by the dependence of the client on the lawyer's professional judgment, and a sexual relationship may well result from the lawyer's exploitation of the lawyer's dominant position."); *In re Tenenbaum*, 880 A.2d 1025 (Del. 2005) (victims of lawyer's sexual harassment and offensive touching were vulnerable due to their status as his clients in domestic relations matters or employees of his law firm and/or due to other personal circumstances); *In re Hodge*, 407 P.3d 613, 645 (Kan. 2017) (client deemed vulnerable because while she was an experienced businesswoman, she "was not experienced in legal matters and relied to her detriment on the respondent"); *In re Bishop*, 179 P.3d 1096, 1104 (Kan. 2008) (personal acquaintance with lawyer made clients particularly vulnerable to accepting numerous false explanations for inordinate delays, resulting in a "long period of deception" warranting an indefinite suspension); *In re Vogel*, 482 S.W.3d 520, 540 (Tenn. 2016) (with respect to court-appointed lawyer and client, noting that "[t]heir difference in age, education and position made [lawyer] an authority figure with all the power in their relationship"); *In re Discipline of Tanner*, 960 P.2d 399, 402 (Utah 1998) (in imposing disbarment, court considered multiple aggravating factors, including client's vulnerability due to his adversarial relationship with police and recurring absences from home, which may have led lawyer to believe client would avoid reporting lawyer's suspected misconduct; "Professional ethics require that an attorney not take advantage of a vulnerable client simply because he can."). *See also* ABA Comm'n on Ethics and Prof'l Responsibility, Formal Op. 92–364 (1992) (sexual relationship between lawyer and client may involve unfair exploitation of the lawyer's fiduciary position and/or significantly impair a lawyer's ability to represent the client competently, and therefore may violate both the ABA Model Rules of Professional Conduct and the ABA Model Code of Professional Responsibility).

- **Physical or Mental Disability or Impairment**

Courts find an aggravating factor established under Standard 9.22(h) when the victim of the lawyer's misconduct suffers from a physical or mental disability or impairment. *See, e.g., In re Stepovich*, 386 P.3d 1205, 1212 (Alaska 2016) (when lawyer hired to draft will, court found client who was gravely ill with cancer to be vulnerable because "while the [lawyer] may not have known how ill he was, lawyer was aware [client] was ill"); *People v. Rosenfeld*, 180 P.3d 448 (Colo. O.P.D.J. 2007) (client who suffered from post-traumatic stress syndrome admired lawyer and failed to appreciate harm caused by lawyer's lack of diligence is vulnerable under Standard 9.22(h)); *In re Rumsey*, 71 P.3d 1150 (Kan. 2003) (vulnerability of victims found a factor in aggravation when one client suffered head injury and mental breakdown before she sought lawyer's representation and, in fact, was so emotionally distraught at hearing that she could not testify); *V.I. Bar Ass'n. v. Brusch*, S.Ct. BA Nos. 2007/64, 2007/65, 2008 WL 901533 (V.I. 2008) (victim of lawyer's misconduct vulnerable in that he was vision impaired); *In re Disciplinary Proceeding Against Greenlee,* 143 P.3d 807, 815 n.5 (Wash. 2006) ("This court has listed physical or mental disability as one form of vulnerability"; here aggravating factor under Standard 9.22(h) because of lawyer's former client, who was partially disabled and poorly educated).

- **Sophistication of Victim**

Courts sometimes discuss the victim's general degree of sophistication or relative socioeconomic status in evaluating vulnerability. For example, the Colorado Disciplinary Judge in *People v. Fischer,* 237 P.3d 645 (Colo. O.P.D.J. 2010), looked at the client's level of sophistication in determining whether vulnerability existed for purposes of Standard 9.22(h). In *Fischer,* the judge found that a client facing severe financial difficulties and possibility of losing her home at time she entered into loans with her lawyer was vulnerable. The judge pointed out that the lawyer represented the client in a matter in which she placed her trust in him, noting that under these circumstances, unsophisticated as well as sophisticated clients are always vulnerable. *See also Fla. Bar v. Brutus,* 216 So.3d 1286, 1290 (Fla. 2017) (aggravating factor applied when lawyer "testified before the referee that his client needed help, that she could not afford to pay much money to secure a divorce, and that she was homeless"); *In re Woodring,* 210 P.3d 120 (Kan. 2009) (having previously recognized that a client's financial condition can make client particularly vulnerable to lawyer's misconduct, court found low-income clients referred through Kansas Legal Services, both who paid $308 for representation, were vulnerable to respondent's misconduct); *In re Trahant,* 108 So.3d 67, 73 (La. 2012) (innocent clients were vulnerable victims of lawyer with high volume real estate practice who facilitated a pattern of fraudulent real estate closings when he abdicated his professional responsibilities without the appropriate supervision or oversight of other employees who "did not act in an ethical manner"); *Att'y Grievance Comm'n v. Dominguez,* 47 A.3d 975, 986 (Md. 2012) (lawyer's homeless clients clearly were victims "because the homeless lack the resources and the capability to safeguard their own interests"; Standard 9.22(h) among the aggravating factors implicated for, inter alia, neglect of clients' matters warranting disbarment); *Lorain Cnty. Bar Ass'n v. Godles,* 943 N.E.2d 988 (Ohio 2010) (client vulnerable due to his lack of sophistication regarding legal matters); *In re Ramirez,* 408 P.3d 1065, 1069 (Or. 2018) (victim deemed vulnerable because lawyer knew that the client "was not legally sophisticated, had limited resources, [and] was impaired by alcoholism"); *Flowers v. Bd. of Prof'l Responsibility,* 314 S.W.3d 882 (Tenn. 2010) (no error in hearing panel's conclusion that lawyer's immigration clients were vulnerable victims under Standard 9.22(h) in light of their inability to speak and write English, the difficult circumstances confronted by many of his clients, their limited resources, and a lack of a solid understanding of the broader culture; various misconduct, including neglect and lack of responsiveness in clients' immigration matters, warranted one-year suspension); *In re Disciplinary Proceeding Against Gillingham*, 896 P.2d 656, 662 (Wash. 1995) ("the phrase 'unsophisticated' does not automatically equate with the term 'vulnerable'"; here, vulnerability of the victim was aggravator under Standard 9.22(h), but that factor still was questionable because while record was clear that victim was difficult client, it was equivocal on subject of sophistication; sixty-day suspension for obtaining loan from client without proper safeguards, and drafting will in which lawyer is named as beneficiary). *But see In re Becker*, 947 A.2d 1120 *16 (Table) (Del. 2008) (client bank was not a "vulnerable victim" because of its sophistication); *Matter of Disbarment of Taylor*, 60 V.I. 356, 380 (V.I. 2014) (rejecting argument that involuntarily detained individual in criminal, immigration, and similar matters is vulnerable for purposes of ABA Standard 9.22(h); client must suffer from a physical or mental disability or some comparable trait that renders the client "particularly vulnerable to an unethical lawyer"); *In re Welcome*, 2013 WL 3316234 (V.I. June 28, 2013) (although client had an elementary-school-level education and needed assistance filing the grievance, court held that lack of a formal education, language or cultural barriers, and similar traits do not render a client vulnerable for purposes of aggravation); *In re Disciplinary Proceeding Against Stansfield*, 187 P.3d 254, 264 (Wash. 2008) (even though client "was poor and living in Guatemala, had seven children, had little schooling, was illiterate in Spanish, and was unable to speak English," court held the record did not establish that respondent was aware of many of these characteristics or that he took advantage of them).

- **Court Overrules Trier of Fact About Client Vulnerability**

There are cases, however, where the trier of fact finds that the lawyer's client is vulnerable but the courts decide otherwise, failing to find client vulnerability as an aggravating factor. *See, e.g., In re Barker*, 321 P.3d 767 (Kan. 2014) (hearing panel erred finding client vulnerable based solely on inexperience with legal matters because nearly every client fits into this category); *In re Wall*, 38 P.3d 640, 648 (Kan. 2002) (panel erred in finding that seriously and permanently injured personal injury client who relied on lawyer to protect her claim from being barred by statute of limitations was vulnerable victim under Standard 9.22(h); in rejecting this aggravating factor the court noted "every personal injury plaintiff relies on counsel to protect his or her claim from being barred by the statute of limitations" and since client did not appear before the panel, a traditional element of fact-finding, listening, and observing the witness testify was missing); *In re Disciplinary Proceeding Against Kagele*, 72 P.3d 1067, 1079 (Wash. 2003) (hearing officer erroneously determined that clients' vulnerability rose to the level to be an aggravating factor: "People hire attorneys because they are in situations serious enough to require legal expertise and advice. A client's need for an attorney does not render him or her vulnerable and neither does hiring an attorney for the first time."); *In re Disciplinary Proceeding Against Anschell*, 69 P.3d 844, 858 (Wash. 2003) (court acknowledging that immigration clients generally can be vulnerable "due to unfamiliarity with the system and cultural and language differences" but here no evidence to support hearing officer's finding that particular immigration client was "under any physical or mental disability or was otherwise particularly vulnerable" other than that she was trusting and completely dependent on respondent for legal advice, which did not amount to a showing of vulnerability); *In re Disciplinary Proceeding Against Carmick*, 48 P.3d 311 (Wash. 2002) (rejecting vulnerability of victim as aggravating factor when record did not establish a physical or mental disability or other vulnerability, although bar counsel characterized victim as unsophisticated and trusting but did not provide support for this assertion; reprimand and sixty days' suspension for dishonesty in securing ex-parte court order and negotiating client's child support arrearage with represented opposing party).

- **Third Parties**

Courts have also applied Standard 9.22(h) in cases where the misconduct impacts third parties. *See, e.g., People v. Gilbert*, 173 P.3d 1113, 1120 (Colo. O.P.D.J. 2007) (in determining the appropriate sanction for violations of the judicial code, court applied the ABA Standards for Imposing Lawyer Sanctions and found, in aggravation, that litigant was "particularly vulnerable" in that she was placed in a "difficult predicament" when magistrate assigned to determine merits of her case made four improper ex parte phone calls to her); *In re Crossen*, 880 N.E.2d 352, 387 (Mass. 2008) (finding judge, law clerk, and their families were victims of lawyer's dupery, court stressed special hearing officer's finding that law clerk was a "young, innocent and vulnerable victim" who lawyer "targeted and exploited," bringing him "to the brink of desperation"); *In re Knappenberger*, 108 P.3d 1161 (Or. 2005) (lawyer's prohibited communication with represented parties involved vulnerable victims because individuals were lawyer's employees who had sued him in federal court on employment-related claims); *In re Gustafson*, 968 P.2d 367, 378 (Or. 1998) (defense lawyer was vulnerable victim of deputy district attorney's unjustified threats of criminal or ethical prosecutions; "[t]his court does not view threats of a possible criminal investigation originating from a deputy district attorney as empty gestures, because a deputy district attorney is in a unique position to initiate and pursue a criminal investigation"); *Bd. of Prof'l Responsibility v. Daniel*, 594 S.W.3d 90 (Tenn. 2018) (in case involving lawyer's misappropriation of law partnership funds, law firm partners were vulnerable victims when the lawyer, apart from being a partner in his firm, also solely managed the partnership's finances and account books); *Bd. of Prof'l Responsibility v. Maddux*, 148 S.W.3d 37 (Tenn. 2004) (fiduciary duty of loyalty that exists between partners and the trust that law firms must place in their lawyer to act as representatives of the firm caused the law firm to be vulnerable with respect to respondent's misconduct in converting funds; law firm's vulnerability should be treated as an aggravating factor). *But see In re Disciplinary Proceeding Against Christopher,* 105 P.3d 976, 982 (Wash. 2005) (arbitrator and opposing counsel were not vulnerable victims of lawyer's falsification of court documents; while they had every reason to believe the lawyer, there was no basis for characterizing them as particularly vulnerable, especially in light of their legal expertise; "trust relationship alone does not create a vulnerable victim").

## *Substantial Experience in the Practice of Law*

Substantial years of practice can be considered an aggravating factor under Standard 9.22(i) because a lawyer with a great deal of experience should know better than to engage in misconduct. *See, e.g., In re Stepovich,* 386 P.3d 1205, 1212 (Alaska 2016) (in ordering twelve-month suspension, court found aggravating factor of substantial experience, noting "although he had limited experience in probate matters, an attorney with his thirty-two years of practice should nonetheless have recognized the conflict at issue here"); *In re Zawada,* 92 P.3d 862 (Ariz. 2004) (lawyer's substantial experience as a prosecutor was aggravating factor since he knew how his improper cross-examination would affect defense experts' credibility; six-month-and-one-day suspension appropriate for depriving defendants of fair trials in two cases); *In re Peasley,* 90 P.3d 764 (Ariz. 2004) (prosecutor's substantial experience carries weight as aggravating factor under Standard 9.22(i) because his experience allowed him to try murder cases and understand advantages of eliciting false testimony at trial; disbarment imposed); *People v. Mason,* 212 P.3d 141, 148 (Colo. O.P.D.J. 2009) (in imposing disbarment, court noted that more than twenty years of law practice experience should have given lawyer who engaged in unauthorized practice "a better perspective on the activities he could and could not perform as a result of his suspension"); *People v. Donaldson,* 166 P.3d 317 (Colo. O.P.D.J. 2007) (lawyer's experience in practicing law since 1978 and past experience with lawyer regulation process was aggravating and evidenced his awareness of duty to refrain from violating any disciplinary rules, including practicing law prior to reinstatement from administrative suspension); *In re Vickers,* 729 S.E.2d 355 (Ga. 2012) (several aggravating factors including lawyer's six years of law practice experience warranted disbarment sanction for mail fraud conviction involving real estate fraud); *In re Holmes,* 416 P.3d 143 (Kan. 2018) (substantial experience deemed aggravating when attorney had been practicing for twenty-five years, nine of which took place in the jurisdiction where the misconduct was committed); *In re Southall,* 165 So.3d 894 (La. 2015) (noting substantial experience present when lawyer was admitted in 1988); *In re Strickland,* 124 P.3d 1225, 1232 (Or. 2005) (holding responsible legal positions such as hearings officer and mediator for many years constituted substantial experience in law, even though lawyer lacked substantial experience representing clients; but court disagreed with trial panel's reliance on fact that respondent was admitted to practice in four states as tending to prove substantial experience; "[t]hat fact adds nothing to the evidence as to the accused's actual experience working on legal matters"); *In re Disciplinary Proceedings Against Theobald,* 786 N.W.2d 834 (Wis. 2010) (practicing law for fourteen years when lawyer committed misconduct found aggravating factor in determining sanction for her for failing to act with reasonable diligence and promptness in representing bankruptcy client and failing to communicate with client after dismissal of bankruptcy petition; sixty-day suspension imposed).

Courts differ as to the number of years a lawyer needs to have practiced law in order to apply "substantial experience" as aggravating factor. *Compare In re Disciplinary Proceeding Against Ferguson,* 246 P.3d 1236, 1250 (Wash. 2011) ("substantial experience" as aggravating factor under Standard 9.22(i) warranted" when a lawyer has practiced for ten years or more at time of misconduct; here respondent's practice of law for eleven years supported hearing officer's finding), *with Att'y Grievance Comm'n v. Childress,* 770 A.2d 685 (Md. 2001) (considering ten years of experience and the instant case the first disciplinary proceeding initiated against him as mitigating and suspending lawyer who engaged in sexual Internet chat room conversations with minors followed by in-person meetings).

Other cases where courts discuss the length of time that will lead to the establishment of an aggravating factor under Standard 9.22(i) include *In re Grossman,* 2000 WL 1673417 (U.S. Tax Ct. Nov. 6, 2000) (thirty years of experience as tax lawyer and prior positions of responsibility at IRS viewed as aggravating factor for lawyer who committed civil tax fraud); *People v. Haines,* 179 P.3d 1021 (Colo. O.P.D.J. 2006) (lawyer's recognized expertise in the field of elder law plus nearly twenty-two years of practice found as aggravating factor in case where lawyer misappropriated funds from estate); *In re Melvin,* 807 A.2d 550 (Del. 2002) (aggravating factor established in disciplinary action against lawyer with twenty-one years of experience who knowingly violated court order and destroyed documents with potential evidentiary value); *In re O'Neill,* 172 P.3d 1179 (Kan. 2007) (twenty years in practice constituted substantial experience as aggravating factor for lawyer who was indefinitely suspended for failing to disclose five arrests and/or convictions in his bar application and misconduct that resulted in felony conviction for DUI); *In re Rumsey,* 71 P.3d 1150 (Kan. 2003) (finding in aggravation fact that lawyer had practiced for twenty-five years at time of misconduct that included violating ethics rules governing competence, diligence, communication, fees, safekeeping property, termination of representation, candor toward tribunal, and interference of lawyer's judgment by person paying legal fees); *In re Grevemberg,* 838 So.2d 1283 (La. 2003) (more than fifty-six years of experience constituted aggravating circumstance in discipline for lawyer who drafted will naming himself as residual legatee).

Even within the same jurisdiction, courts have reached different conclusions as to what constitutes "substantial experience." *Compare People v. Townshend,* 933 P.2d 1327 (Colo. 1997) (lawyer with six years of practice found to have substantial experience), *with People v. Hensley-Martin,* 795 P.2d 262, 265 (Colo. 1990) (lawyer with six to eight years of law practice found by hearing board to be "inexperienced and naive"). *Cf. People v. Goodman,* 334 P.3d 241 (Colo. O.P.D.J. 2014) (in matter involving lawyer who had been practicing law for seven to eight years, court observed that case law suggests ten years of practice generally qualifies as substantial experience but also cited precedent holding that lawyer practicing for six to eight years merited mitigation for inexperience under ABA Standard 9.32(f); court applied neither an aggravating factor of substantial experience nor a mitigating factor of inexperience, but noted that lawyer's experience would carry no weight in mitigation because a lawyer needs no experience to understand that intentionally presenting false documents to a tribunal is inherently dishonest). *See generally* Leslie C. Levin, *The Emperor's Clothes and Other Tales About the Standards for Imposing Lawyer Discipline Sanctions,* 48 AM. U. L. REV. 1, 50 (1998) (collecting cases applying weight of factor inconsistently and resulting in disparity in sanctions imposed).

## *Indifference to Making Restitution*

Under Standard 9.22(j) a lawyer's indifference to making restitution has been found an aggravating factor whether that indifference is overt or implicit. *See, e.g., In re Augenstein,* 871 P.2d 254, 258 (Ariz. 1994) (indifference to making restitution found as additional aggravating factor in imposing two-year suspension when lawyer whose misconduct included neglect of client matters and failure to communicate with client expressed desire to make restitution to injured clients but then made no effort to compensate them; court stated that, "[f]urthermore, although respondent claims that financial inability rather than indifference was the reason for his inaction, we find that his credibility is undermined by his failure to contact his clients and offer to them even a mere apology for his neglect."); *In re Wimmershoff,* 3 P.3d 417 (Colo. 2000) (private sanction too lenient for single instance of charging improper fee when lawyer refused to refund any part of $1,000 unreasonably charged; imposing public censure and ordering refund); *People v. Haines,* 179 P.3d 1021 (Colo. O.P.D.J. 2006) (finding this factor to the lack of good faith effort to replace money lawyer took even after personal representative and litigation counsel asked her to do so and even though lawyer met other financial obligations at time she was asked to return money); *People v. Gustafson,* 128 P.3d 788 (Colo. O.P.D.J. 2005) (making full restitution nearly two years after lawyer converted settlement funds and only days before disciplinary hearing represented indifference to making restitution); *In re Barker,* 321 P.3d 767 (Kan. 2014) (indifference to making restitution applied in aggravation when lawyer acknowledged amount of damages incurred by client but at no time prior to hearing made any offer to make payments); *In re Woodring,* 210 P.3d 120 (Kan. 2009) (finding of indifference to making restitution for unearned legal fees supported by ample evidence, when lawyer failed to make restitution by time of hearing or oral argument and provided no evidence of inability to reimburse clients); *In re Parker,* 815 So.2d 794, 796 (La. 2002) ("indifference to making restitution" one of nine aggravating factors in Sanctions Standards established when disbarred lawyer failed to refund unearned fees after acknowledging in writing that he owed them); *In re Ward,* 726 N.W.2d 497 (Minn. 2007) (rejecting stipulated one-year suspension in favor of indefinite suspension when lawyer's failure to make restitution to former client after entering into unfair business transaction was aggravating factor; also imposing requirement that reinstatement petition include proof of satisfaction of judgment entered against lawyer by former client); *In re Disciplinary Proceeding Against Jones,* 338 P.3d 842 (Wash. 2014) (applying this factor to lawyer's failure to pay more than $138,000 in court-ordered sanctions imposed for frivolous litigation). *But cf. In re Disciplinary Proceeding Against Kagele,* 72 P.3d 1067 (Wash. 2003) (fact that respondent indifferent to paying restitution to nine clients not aggravating factor because record did not support that he retained unearned fees or that fees received in each case were not reasonable for actual work he performed; lawyer cannot be penalized for belief that he is under no obligation to return fees but court did find his conduct hindered clients' right to terminate representation and aggravated circumstances of his misconduct warranting no reduction of the recommended one-year suspension).

## *Illegal Conduct, Including That Involving Use of Controlled Substances*

On February 4, 1992, the ABA House of Delegates adopted amendments to the Sanctions Standards to permit a court to take drug or alcohol use into consideration either as aggravating or mitigating factors. At that time the House adopted Standard 9.22(k), providing that "illegal conduct, including that involving the use of controlled substances," should be considered an aggravating factor. At the same time, Standard 9.32(i) was amended to permit a court to take into consideration in mitigation a lawyer's dependency on drugs or alcohol when (1) there is medical evidence that the respondent is affected by a chemical dependency; (2) the chemical dependency caused the misconduct; (3) recovery from the dependency has been demonstrated by a meaningful and sustained period of successful rehabilitation; and (4) the recovery arrested the misconduct and recurrence of that misconduct is unlikely. See the discussion in Annotation to Standard 9.32(i).

An analysis of cases demonstrates that, in situations where controlled-substance use fails to qualify for mitigation under Standard 9.32(i), the sanction for a lawyer who engages in illegal use of a controlled substance may still include consideration of the use-of-controlled-substances aggravating factor under Standard 9.22(k). For cases finding an aggravating factor where a lawyer engages in illegal conduct that involves the use of controlled substances, see, for example, *People v. Madrid*, 967 P.2d 627 (Colo. 1998) (lawyer's acceptance of one ounce of cocaine as payment for legal services from client facing drug charges was aggravating factor with three-year suspension imposed), *People v. Tuthill*, 158 P.3d 275 (Colo. O.P.D.J. 2007) (finding aggravating factor under Standard 9.22(k) for lawyer's felony possession of a controlled substance—methamphetamine—and driving under the influence of drugs); *In re Howard*, 765 A.2d 39, 45 (Del. 2000) (lawyer's guilty pleas to two drug-related misdemeanors was aggravating factor; noting significance of ethical violation, court stated that "[e]ven though the injury caused by [the lawyer's] misconduct is not quantifiable, it is beyond question that public confidence in the integrity of the legal profession, which is the foundation of our entire system of justice, is undermined when any lawyer engages in illegal conduct, with accompanying publicity, as occurred in [this] case"); *Iowa Supreme Ct. Bd. of Prof'l Ethics & Conduct v. Bernard*, 653 N.W.2d 373 (Iowa 2002) (lawyer's guilty plea to misdemeanor for methamphetamine possession was aggravating factor); *In re Harrington*, 293 P.3d 686 (Kan. 2013) (lawyer's guilty plea to battery, driving under the influence of alcohol and obstruction of official duty, in addition to testifying that she ingested cocaine, was aggravating; two-year suspension imposed); *In re McGraw*, 217 P.3d 25 (Kan. 2009) (lawyer's conviction for possession of methamphetamine, a class C felony, was aggravating factor); *Ky. Bar Ass'n v. Bierbauer*, 282 S.W.3d 318 (Ky. 2009) (increase in sanction justified due to seven aggravating factors, including Standard 9.22 (k), for felony drug conviction based on attempt to manufacture crystal methamphetamine in lawyer's home); *In re Kimball*, 805 So.2d 1167 (La. 2002) (conviction of felony drug offense—possession of crack cocaine—found aggravating factor under Standard 9.22(k)); *In re Hasbrouck*, 705 A.2d 350 (N.J. 1998) (illegal conduct was aggravating factor for painkiller-addicted lawyer convicted of theft and of burglarizing doctors' homes to get office keys to obtain samples of prescription drugs; lawyer's addiction was not considered as mitigation in view of her grievous misconduct to support that addiction); *In re Penn*, 548 N.W.2d 526 (Wis. 1996) (conviction for using marijuana and cocaine while serving as county district attorney was taken into account in aggravation).

Illegal conduct found aggravating under Standard 9.22(k) is not limited to the use of controlled substances. *See, e.g., In re McCann*, 894 A.2d 1087 (Del. 2005) (respondent's failure to timely file and pay federal and state income tax obligations constituted illegal conduct under Standard 9.22(k)); *In re* Ellis, 204 P.3d 1161 (Kan. 2009) (lawyer who stole food from café at his workplace engaged in illegal conduct, an aggravating factor under Standard 9.22(k)); *In re Islas*, 112 P.3d 210 (Kan. 2005) (convictions of three felonies and one misdemeanor constituted illegal conduct under Standard 9.22(k); indefinite suspension imposed); *Att'y Grievance*

*Comm'n v. Thompson*, 786 A.2d 763 (Md. 2001) (conviction for stalking thirteen-year-old boy was aggravating factor).

Courts are reluctant to rely on Standard 9.22(k) as a significant aggravating factor when the illegal conduct at issue formed the basis for the disciplinary charges. *See In re Vance*, 421 P.3d 53 (Alaska 2018) (court declined to apply Standard 9.22(k) because criminal conduct was the basis for the Rule 8.4(b) violation that lawyer admitted); *People v. Olson*, 2016 WL 5076078 (Colo. O.P.D.J. July 25, 2016) (lawyer's domestic violence and efforts to suppress victim from testifying at disciplinary hearing were illegal, but because the criminal conduct formed the basis of the disciplinary charges, court gave little weight to this factor in aggravation); *In re Nixon*, 49 A.3d 1193 (Table) (Del. 2012) (finding no aggravating factors since illegal conduct, conviction of two counts possession of controlled substances and one count drug paraphernalia, as an aggravating factor under Standard 9.22(k), overlapped with the misconduct itself; two-year suspension imposed); *In re Disciplinary Proceeding Against Kamb*, 305 P.3d 1091 (Wash. 2013) (court held that this aggravating factor cannot apply to a count where the illegal conduct formed the basis of charge, but noted that it could apply to different count even though no criminal charges filed).

## *Other Aggravating Factors*

Some courts consider aggravating factors other than those specified in Standard 9.22 in determining whether to increase the presumptive sanction for a lawyer's misconduct. In *In re Howes*, 52 A.3d 1 (D.C. 2012), for example, the court found "the gravity" of the lawyer's fraudulent misconduct over a two-year period an aggravating factor that outweighed the impact of mitigation. In that case, a former Assistant U.S. Attorney was disbarred for misusing witness vouchers, misconduct that was compounded by his failing to make mandatory disclosure of the voucher use to the court or opposing counsel.

The *Howes* court, as have others, may also consider a lawyer's misconduct aggravated by his status as a prosecutor or public official because of his or her additional duties to the public. *See, e.g., People v. Groland*, 908 P.2d 75, 77 (Colo. 1995) (respondent's role as deputy district attorney at time some of the misconduct occurred constituted aggravating factor "because public officials engaged in law enforcement have assumed an even greater responsibility to the public than have other lawyers"); *Fla. Bar v. Cox*, 794 So.2d 1278, 1285 (Fla. 2001) (while declining to formally characterize respondent's prosecutorial role as aggravating factor, court discusses its importance at length, finding that respondent's "failure to abide by a prosecutor's duty to ensure the fairness of a criminal proceeding is essential to evaluating the gravity of the duty violated in this case"); *In re Sutton*, 959 P.2d 904 (Kan. 1998) (aggravating factor found because respondent held position of trust as assistant county attorney); *Lawyer Disciplinary Bd. v. Busch*, 754 S.E. 729 (W. Va. 2014) (position as elected prosecuting attorney at the time of misconduct, a position of public trust, is aggravating factor); *Lawyer Disciplinary Bd. v. Sims*, 574 S.E.2d 795, 796 (W. Va. 2002) (prosecutor's statements to newspapers about assessor in connection with grand jury proceeding warranted public reprimand after removal from elected office with the court finding that prosecutor's deliberate practice and pattern of repeatedly making extrajudicial statements that had a substantial likelihood of materially prejudicing adjudicative proceedings was aggravating factor; court noted that "[e]thical violations by a lawyer holding a public office are viewed as more egregious because of the betrayal of the public trust attached to the office") (citation omitted); *In re Penn*, 548 N.W.2d 526 (Wis. 1996) (respondent's position as chief county law enforcement official considered aggravating factor in discipline for illegal drug use and fact that it occurred in the company of individuals subject to prosecution by his office for non-drug criminal offenses). *Cf. Bd. of Prof'l Responsibility v. Argeris*, 341 P.3d 1030, 1038 (Wyo. 2014) (in matter where lawyer served as county and prosecuting attorney, court cited lawyer's behavior that led to deterioration in relationships with county commissioners as aggravating factor). *But see Lockett v. Bd. of Prof'l Responsibility*, 380 S.W.3d 19 (Tenn. 2012) (finding hearing panel abused its discretion in considering lawyer's pursuit of elected public office an aggravating factor when misconduct was unrelated to his service in public office and error in considering lawyer's previous service on disciplinary hearing panel as an independent aggravating factor; four years' suspension imposed for failure to file income tax returns and theft conviction arising from failure to remit fees to law firm).

## 9.3 Mitigation

**9.31 Definition. Mitigation or mitigating circumstances are any considerations or factors that may justify a reduction in the degree of discipline to be imposed.**

**9.32 Factors which may be considered in mitigation.**
**Mitigating factors include:**
**(a) absence of a prior disciplinary record;**
**(b) absence of a dishonest or selfish motive;**
**(c) personal or emotional problems;**
**(d) timely good faith effort to make restitution or to rectify consequences of misconduct;**
**(e) full and free disclosure to disciplinary board or cooperative attitude toward proceedings;**
**(f) inexperience in the practice of law;**
**(g) character or reputation;**
**(h) physical disability;**
**(i) mental disability or chemical dependency including alcoholism or drug abuse when:**
**(1) there is medical evidence that the respondent is affected by a chemical dependency or mental disability;**
**(2) the chemical dependency or mental disability caused the misconduct;**
**(3) the respondent's recovery from the chemical dependency or mental disability is demonstrated by a meaningful and sustained period of successful rehabilitation; and**
**(4) the recovery arrested the misconduct and recurrence of that misconduct is unlikely;**
**(j) delay in disciplinary proceedings;**
**(k) imposition of other penalties or sanctions;**
**(l) remorse;**
**(m) remoteness of prior offenses.**

# Annotation

### *Absence of a Prior Disciplinary Record*

In most jurisdictions, courts acknowledge the absence of a prior disciplinary record as a mitigating factor when imposing discipline. *See, e.g., People v. Muhr,* 370 P.3d 677 (Colo. O.P.D.J. 2016) (lawyer who engaged in misconduct that violated most basic of client-centered duties had no prior discipline in nearly twenty-five years of practice, a meritorious mitigating factor considered; suspension of one year and one day warranted); *In re McCarthy*, 173 A.3d 536 (Table) (Del. 2017) (absence of prior disciplinary record as mitigating factor under Standard 9.32(a) established); *Att'y Grievance Comm'n v. Stillwell*, 73 A.3d 243 (Md. 2013) (in reciprocal disciplinary case, absence of prior disciplinary record as mitigating in originating jurisdiction noted lawyer's misconduct of misrepresenting his status as to the law firm where he was employed, improperly charging personal expenses, and asserting positions on behalf of clients without informed consent warranted six-month suspension); *In re Sinnott*, 845 A.2d 373 (Vt. 2004) (lack of prior disciplinary record mitigating under Standard 9.32(a) for lawyer who charged unreasonable fee). *But see In re Peasley*, 90 P.3d 764, 776 (Ariz. 2004) (while court recognized that, on occasion, it had given great weight to an unblemished disciplinary record, in this case respondent's prior record not given great weight because at least two reported decisions discussed instances of lawyer's prosecutorial misconduct; although those cases did not result in formal discipline nor did lawyer's misconduct cause convictions to be reversed, they "demonstrate that his misconduct in this matter was not entirely out of character"). Some courts have held that the absence of prior discipline is not a mitigating factor. *See, e.g.*, *In re Torgerson*, 870 N.W.2d 602 (Minn. 2015) (concluding that the referee improperly considered lack of disciplinary history as a mitigating factor).

The absence of a prior disciplinary record may be the only mitigating factor in a disciplinary case, and one that will be noted by a court generally when a respondent fails to appear in the disciplinary proceeding. *See, e.g.*, *People v. Stern*, 201 P.3d 559 (Colo. O.P.D.J. 2009) (despite lawyer's failure to participate in proceedings or present evidence in mitigation, court found mitigating under Standard 9.32(a) the lawyer's lack of prior disciplinary record); *People v. Albright*, 91 P.3d 1063 (Colo. O.P.D.J. 2003) (lawyer did not appear and only factor court found in mitigation was absence of prior disciplinary record under Standard 9.32(a)); *In re Brown-Manning*, 185 So.3d 728 (La. 2016) (absence of prior disciplinary record was sole mitigating factor found in default proceeding; court ordered one year and one day suspension for lawyer who neglected her clients' legal matters, failed to communicate with her clients, and failed to refund unearned fees); *Disciplinary Counsel v. Zaccagnini*, 955 N.E.2d 977 (Ohio 2011) (appropriate to consider lawyer's lack of prior disciplinary record, inter alia, as a mitigating factor in determining permanent disbarment appropriate for lawyer incarcerated following federal conviction for conspiracy to unlawfully obtain lucrative contracts to provide appraisals of commercial real estate for county auditor's office and unable to participate in disciplinary proceedings).

When "absence of a prior disciplinary record" is the sole mitigating factor presented, some courts give it little weight, concluding that it was not sufficiently compelling to justify a departure from the presumptive sanction. *See, e.g.*, *In re Ivy*, 374 P.3d 374 (Alaska 2016) (only mitigating factor was lack of prior disciplinary offenses and did not reduce the presumptive sanction of disbarment); *In re Elowitz*, 866 P.2d 1326 (Ariz. 1994) (lawyer's failure to diligently and competently handle legal matters, communicate adequately with clients, safeguard clients' property, among other misconduct, warranted disbarment, notwithstanding absence of prior disciplinary record); *People v. Hindman*, 958 P.2d 463, 464 (Colo. 1998) (only mitigator was absence of prior discipline, a factor that "by itself does not convince us that anything but disbarment is warranted" for misconduct including neglect of client's legal matters and misappropriation of client funds); *People v. Sugar*, 360 P.3d 1041, 1046 (Colo. O.P.D.J. 2015) (lawyer who engaged in pattern of misconduct by assisting clients in evading their tax obligations had no prior discipline in nearly twenty-five years of practice, a mitigating factor entitled to "average weight"; disbarment warranted); *People v. Adkins*, 57 P.3d 750 (Colo. O.P.D.J. 2001) (lack of prior disciplinary action sole factor in mitigation and alone does not call for sanction less than disbarment for lawyer's failing to hold client's property in her possession separate from her own property and knowing conversion of funds belonging to estate); *Atty. Griev. Comm'n v. Greenleaf*, 91 A.3d 1066 (Md. 2014) (lack of prior disciplinary action sole factor in mitigation and alone does not call for sanction less than disbarment for lawyer's egregious misconduct of solicitation of minors); *Atty. Griev. Comm'n v. Zhang*, 100 A.3d 112 (Md. 2014) (lack of prior attorney discipline only mitigating factor present, and was not enough to overcome an order of disbarment for an attorney who engaged in a pattern of deception that was motivated by desire to help a family member); *In re Brandt*, 10 P.3d 906 (Or. 2000) (single mitigator of lack of prior disciplinary record under Standard 9.32(a) insufficient to alter presumptive sanction of suspension for respondent's intentional failure to avoid conflicts of interest, lack of candor in dealings with client, and misrepresentations to client and state bar); *In re Disciplinary Proceeding Against Jones*, 338 P.3d 842 (Wash. 2014) (absence of prior disciplinary record, the one mitigating circumstance applicable in proceeding against lawyer for misconduct arising out of lawyer's litigation practices involving his mother's estate, where lawyer failed to comply with discovery requests, engaged in frivolous litigation, and dishonestly and intentionally manipulated value of estate assets and caused actual injury to his brothers, did not justify departure from presumptive sanction of disbarment); *In re Disciplinary Proceeding Against Stansfield*, 187 P.3d 254 (Wash. 2008) (two reprimands appropriate sanctions for lawyer's actions in representing decedent's estate without authority and representing clients whose interests were materially adverse, where reprimands were presumptive sanctions; aggravating circumstances of multiple offenses and substantial experience in the practice of law were balanced by mitigating factor of absence of prior disciplinary record); *Lawyer Disciplinary Bd. v. Scotchel*, 768 S.E.2d 730 (W. Va. 2014) (annulment of law license for misconduct that included knowingly and intentionally charging unreasonable fees despite performing little if any substantive work and failing to turn over sale proceeds; only mitigating factor was lack of prior disciplinary record).

Courts will accord more weight to the absence of a prior disciplinary record as a mitigating factor when it is accompanied by other mitigating circumstances. *See, e.g., In re Zaleon*, 504 S.E.2d 702 (Ga. 1998) (absence of prior disciplinary record, as well as full and free disclosure to disciplinary authorities, lawyer's good reputation, and her remorse mitigated sanction warranted in lawyer's mishandling of funds; six-month suspension rather than disbarment); *In re Thomson*, 464 S.E.2d 818 (Ga. 1996) (six-month suspension appropriate for lawyer who impaired his escrow account given mitigating factors including lack of prior disciplinary offenses, cooperation in disciplinary process, no attempt to conceal his conduct, and lack of training in operating law practice); *In re Pelsinger*, 190 A.D.2d 158 (N.Y. App. Div. 1993) (lawyer with pervasive pattern of commingling escrow funds suspended for three years rather than disbarred due to significant mitigating circumstances including previously unblemished disciplinary record, rendering of pro bono services, absence of lawyer's venality, lack of injury to client, and prehearing admission of commingling). *But see In re Melvin*, 807 A.2d 550 (Del. 2002) (lawyer with no prior disciplinary record and involved in highly emotional family situation at time of misconduct sanctioned with eighteen-month rather than recommended twelve-month suspension after pleading guilty to misdemeanor criminal contempt of a protection order and hindering prosecution).

- **Relation to Length of Practice**

Often the absence of a disciplinary record is weighed against the number of years a lawyer has practiced law; courts find more compelling the situation where a lawyer has a longer history of practice absent prior discipline. *See, e.g., In re Wimmershoff*, 3 P.3d 417 (Colo. 2000) (lawyer publicly censured when lack of prior disciplinary record in more than twenty years of practice was mitigating factor in case involving one instance of charging improper fee); *People v. Carrigan*, 358 P.3d 650 (Colo. O.P.D.J 2015) (absence of a prior disciplinary record given minimal weight because lawyer had been practicing for just two years and thus was of lesser consequence than if he had possessed substantial experience in the practice of law); *People v. Beecher*, 224 P.3d 442 (Colo. O.P.D.J. 2009) (lack of prior discipline of any sort in more than twenty years of practice in a firm, as solo practitioner and as city attorney, a weighty mitigator for lawyer who engaged in intimate relationship with client he was representing in divorce; suspension of year and a day appropriate); *In re Krigel*, 480 S.W.3d 294 (Mo. 2016) (disbarment inappropriate sanction for lawyer who had practiced for more than thirty years without complaint; stayed six-month suspension subject to completion of two years of probation imposed);

*In re Sheehan*, 27 P.3d 972 (N.M. 2001) (almost thirty years with no prior discipline appropriate factor to consider in mitigation for lawyer whose misconduct included failing to disburse trust funds in accordance with trust instrument, paying his own legal fees from trust, and billing client for nonlegal services at his customary rate; deferred three-year suspension warranted); *Bd. of Prof'l Responsibility v. Mulligan*, 162 P.3d 468 (Wyo. 2007) (absence of prior disciplinary record under Standard 9.32(a) factor in mitigation of billing misrepresentation when lawyer had been licensed since 1968 and had never had any other complaints filed against him).

- **Seriousness of Offense**

Courts also consider the seriousness of the present offense and weigh it against the absence of a prior disciplinary record. Thus, even when a lawyer has had a long and unblemished career, the lack of a disciplinary record will not usually mitigate the sanction when the offense is very serious, such as, for example, conversion of client funds. *See, e.g., People v. Brown*, 161 P.3d 1286 (Colo. O.P.D.J. 2007) (while lawyer presented no mitigating evidence, hearing board considered absence of prior disciplinary record over thirty-five years of law practice, but ultimately disbarred lawyer for conversion of client funds); *People v. Haines*, 179 P.3d 1021 (Colo. O.P.D.J. 2006) (disbarment warranted for lawyer who misappropriated $70,000 even though it was lawyer's first and only breach of ethics rules in nearly twenty-two years of practice); *Fla. Bar v. Hall*, 49 So.3d 1254 (Fla. 2010) (disbarment imposed instead of recommended ninety-day suspension on lawyer who engaged in serious felonious and fraudulent conduct in her personal affairs notwithstanding her membership in the bar since 1986 with no prior disciplinary history); *In re Mayne*, 783 N.W.2d 153 (Minn. 2010) (lawyer's conviction for felony financial exploitation of a vulnerable adult was serious misconduct; mitigating factors, including lack of prior discipline, fell short of what is required to deviate from disbarment sanction); *In re Melograne*, 888 A.2d 753, 757 (Pa. 2005) (lack of prior discipline among the factors the court found "insufficient to warrant imposition of anything less than disbarment" for serious misconduct based on lawyer's conviction for conspiracy to violate civil rights when he, while serving as district judge, conspired with two court employees to cause two defendants to be found guilty in statutory appeals cases); *V.I. Bar v. Brusch*, S.Ct. BA Nos. 2007/64, 2007/65, 2008 WL 901533, at *8 (V.I. Mar. 3, 2008) (absence of disciplinary record found among mitigating factors but did not alter disbarment for respondent's misconduct; "[i]ndeed, the circumstances in these cases present a picture of a highly experienced, reputable attorney who inexplicably engaged in a pattern of misconduct that included a total failure to communicate with clients, knowingly converting client funds, and violating several rules and Court orders associated with the ensuing disciplinary proceedings"); *In re Disciplinary Proceeding Against Whitt*, 72 P.3d 173, 181 (Wash. 2003) (court held that lack of prior discipline history by itself "is not per se protection against disbarment"; here, lawyer's lack of prior discipline insufficient to overcome egregious acts of multiple, intentional fabrications and false representations).

When the underlying violation is less serious and lack of prior disciplinary record is established as a mitigating factor, courts tend to be more lenient with the sanction ultimately imposed. *See, e.g., In re Koliha*, 9 P.3d 102 (Or. 2000) (lawyer's lack of prior disciplinary record mitigating in proceedings for misconduct that included unauthorized practice while suspended for failure to pay bar dues; distinguished from cases of unauthorized law practice while suspended due to previous disciplinary violation; one-year suspension).

## *Absence of Dishonest or Selfish Motive*

The presence or absence of a dishonest or selfish motive may be considered a mitigating factor under Standard 9.32(b), and as with other aggravating and mitigating factors, whether it is found to exist is a question of fact. For example, in *In re Van Dox*, 152 P.3d 1183, 1190 (Ariz. 2007), the court ruled that the hearing officer did not err in finding that, based on the facts presented, the lawyer lacked a dishonest or selfish motive and had established such as a mitigating factor. The lawyer was licensed in Florida and Virginia and had accepted a fee of $1,000 to conduct mediation services in Arizona. In affirming the hearing officer's finding that the lawyer negligently rather than knowingly engaged in the unauthorized practice of law, the court held that the question was one of fact and that the hearing officer's findings should not be disturbed unless clearly erroneous, noting, "In no case have we found a dishonest or selfish motive solely from the receipt of reasonable compensation." *See also In re Hislop*, 2016 Ariz. LEXIS 342 (Ariz. 2016) (absence of dishonest or selfish motive found as mitigating factor; lawyer reprimanded for failing to properly maintain his trust account); *Fla. Bar v. Ticktin*, 14 So.3d 928, 938 (Fla. 2009) (court rejected bar's challenge and affirmed hearing referee's finding in mitigation of the absence of dishonest motive, stating that "referee's findings as to mitigation . . . carry a presumption of correctness and will not be disturbed unless clearly erroneous or without support in the record") (citation omitted); *Atty. Grievance Comm'n v. Olszewski*, 107 A.3d 1159, 1168 (Md. 2015) (lawyer's misconduct was considered to be the product of "representational paralysis in the face of a difficult case" rather than dishonesty; therefore absence of dishonest or selfish motive was considered a mitigating factor); *In re Shepperson*, 674 A.2d 1273 (Vt. 1996) (no indication that lawyer's filing of incomprehensible legal briefs over seven years was intentional or based on corrupt motives, and lawyer suspended for not less than six months and until lawyer can demonstrate fitness to practice law). *But see In re Cleland*, 2 P.3d 700, 705 (Colo. 2000) (disapproving hearing board's finding that lawyer did not have dishonest motive when he misappropriated client funds, charged unauthorized interest, and misrepresented status of a case, court said that "[t]he fact that [lawyer] may not have had a dishonest motive in every single instance of misconduct does not demonstrate that the mitigating factor exists"; disbarment imposed rather than recommended three years' suspension); *People v. Carter*, 364 P.3d 1164, 1176 (Colo. O.P.D.J. 2015) (court explained that while "we do not find that Respondent intended to act dishonestly or selfishly, we also believe she recklessly failed to ensure she understood and followed the rules governing client funds. We cannot reward this laxity by giving her credit in mitigation."); *Cincinnati Bar Ass'n v. Hackett*, 950 N.E.2d 969 (Ohio 2011) (court rejected parties' stipulation and hearing officer's finding, as a mitigating factor, the absence of a dishonest or selfish motive and instead found lawyer possessed a selfish motive in entering into an employment agreement with his associate stating he would receive 95 percent of the fees generated if a client followed the associate when the associate left the firm, deemed an aggravating factor).

- **Meant to Do Good for Client**

In some instances, an absence of dishonest or selfish motive can be inferred from a lawyer's intention to do good for his or her client. *See, e.g., Disciplinary Counsel v. Tomasky*, No. MMXCV054001846S, 2006 WL 3409101 (Conn. Super. Ct. Aug. 28, 2006) (allowing mitigating factor of absence of dishonest or selfish motive and disagreeing with complainants who accused lawyer of dishonesty and selfish attempt to avoid repaying retainer agreement for foreign adoptions; even though lawyer's return of retainers was delayed, evidence suggested that the reason was an attempt, albeit misguided, to salvage deteriorating situation concerning the adoptions and lack of resources); *In re Discipline of Reade*, 405 P.3d 105 (Nev. 2017) (while finding absence of dishonest and selfish motive as mitigating factor, court imposed four-year suspension for knowingly making false representations to regulatory agency to prevent client from being prosecuted for money laundering); *In re Convisser*, 242 P.3d 299, 314 (N.M. 2010) (because lawyer's misrepresentations and unauthorized practice of law "centered around his single-minded purpose of righting what he perceived to be a wrong committed," there was no evidence that he "was acting with a selfish motive or desire to secure a private benefit for himself"; one-year deferred suspension imposed); *In re Howser*, 987 P.2d 496 (Or. 1999) (clear and convincing evidence that lawyer acted without selfish or dishonest motive even when he knew he had current client conflict of interest and failed to withdraw promptly because client lacked funds to retain other counsel; although Sanctions Standards provided preliminarily that suspension was appropriate, lawyer was publicly reprimanded when mitigating factors outweighed aggravating factors); *In re Gildea*, 936 P.2d 975, 985 (Or. 1997) (court satisfied that lawyer who cared for client/personal friend by placing client in care facility, safeguarding personal property, and performing legal work "acted throughout in good faith and that he attempted to further [client's] best interests at all times. This amounts to an absence of a dishonest or selfish motive under ABA Standard 9.32(b), and constitutes a significant mitigating circumstance"; nonetheless, fact that lawyer assigned client's trust deed to himself, deposited her personal check in his personal account, failed to inventory her personal possessions, and failed to provide accountings, together with certain aggravating circumstances, warranted 120-day suspension); *cf. Att'y Grievance Comm'n v. Marcalus*, 996 A.2d 350, 364 (Md. 2010) (lawyer's voluntary disclosure to police that he previously had exchanged sex act for a prescription pain pill with alleged rape victim who accused lawyer's client of rape strongly mitigated against harsh punishment for lawyer's illegal conduct in distributing the controlled substance; in imposing sixty-day suspension rather than disbarment, court noted that lawyer's conduct likely never would have come to light had he not volunteered information to police and that "[h]is choice to reveal those actions evinced no selfishness; to the contrary, it demonstrated a willingness to prioritize his client's interests ahead of his own").

Courts also have rejected lawyers' claims that they acted without selfish motive and in the best interest of their clients, thereby refusing to find mitigation under Standard 9.32(b). *See, e.g., Att'y Grievance Comm'n v. Garcia*, 979 A.2d 146, 155 (Md. 2009) ("[Respondent's] argument that an intentional and admitted fraud perpetrated against the immigration authorities is mitigated by the purported protection of the interests of a client, from which he failed to personally profit, is fatuous."); *In re Feld's Case*, 815 A.2d 383, 391 (N.H. 2002) (rejecting as mitigating factor lawyer's claim that he acted in his clients' interests in impeding discovery, court noted that "[i]ntentionally assisting in the promulgation of false answers is . . . inherently dishonest"). *See also In re Disciplinary Proceeding Against Trejo*, 185 P.3d 1160, 1174 (Wash. 2008) (agreeing with disciplinary board's finding that the mitigating factor of absence of dishonest motive did not apply and rejecting lawyer's assertion that his cooperation with the disciplinary office's auditing process evidenced a lack of dishonest motive; court reiterated that respondent "bears the burden of proof as to whether there was an absence of dishonest or selfish motive").

- **Meant No Harm**

In other instances, courts may find a lawyer lacked a dishonest or selfish motive because of a paucity of evidence to demonstrate that the lawyer meant harm. *See, e.g., Disciplinary Counsel v. Driscoll*, No. CV074025804S , 2000 WL 35605723 (Conn. Super. Ct. Nov. 13, 2007) (absence of dishonest or selfish motive constituted relevant mitigating factor in face of no evidence that lawyer intended harm when he failed to communicate with client or answer grievance complaint); *Statewide Grievance Comm'n v. Johnson*, No. CV054012328S, 2006 WL 3359731 (Conn. Super. Ct. Nov. 1, 2006) (citing Standard 9.32(b) as relevant mitigating factor when no evidence that lawyer had dishonest or selfish motive when she failed to pursue employment discrimination claim with the Equal Employment Opportunity Commission or to advise client of her inability to do so); *In re Rooney*, 709 N.W.2d 263, 272 (Minn. 2006) (misappropriation of $27,700 in client trust account mitigated by presence of numerous circumstances, "none of which alone would suffice to avoid disbarment," including lack of dishonest or selfish motive in that court found lawyer did not lie to disciplinary director or to clients or otherwise attempt to conceal his misconduct, he fully cooperated with investigation, his clients suffered no harm, and he "intended only to temporarily borrow his clients' funds, not to permanently defraud his clients"); *In re Smith*, 236 P.3d 137 (Or. 2010) (affirming absence of dishonest or selfish motive under Standard 9.32(b) as mitigating factor for lawyer who believed he was giving sound legal advice to his client when he counseled his client to commit criminal trespass when he and his client entered client's former place of employment before business hours); *cf. In re Farrar*, 949 A.2d 438, 441 (Vt. 2008) (lack of dishonest motive one of several factors mitigating lawyer's misconduct in acknowledged commingling of client funds in his trust account as a result of monthly reconciliations performed by his secretary; imposing public reprimand, court noted that "while recognizing that respondent did not act selfishly, we will not minimize his infraction merely because he was unaware that his acts violated the rules of professional conduct").

## *Personal or Emotional Problems*

A lawyer's personal or emotional problems, although not an excuse for misconduct, may be considered as mitigating and to a reduced sanction. This may arise under a variety of circumstances and often there is overlap between Standard 9.32(c) and Standards 9.32(h), "physical disability," or 9.32(i), "mental disability or chemical dependency including alcoholism or drug abuse."

### • Personal or Emotional Problems Versus Physical or Mental Disability

Whether a mitigating circumstance should be classified under "personal or emotional problems" in Standard 9.32(c), "physical disability" under Standard 9.32(h) or "mental disability" under Standard 9.32(i) is not always clear. *See, e.g., People v. Kotarek*, 941 P.2d 925, 926 (Colo. 1997) (three-month rather than six-month suspension imposed on lawyer who submitted fraudulent mileage reimbursement request and billing time sheets when he offered evidence of significant mitigation, including psychiatric medical evidence that separation and marriage dissolution "were enormously stressful and debilitating during the relevant time period"; noting Standard 9.32(c) and other stipulated mitigating factors, without further analysis); *People v. D'Acquisto*, 146 P.3d 1041, 1047 (Colo. O.P.D.J. 2006) (although respondent failed to prove mitigation for a mental disability or impairment, under Standard 9.32(h), the evidence as a whole established that he "is a young, naïve, and inexperienced lawyer with substantial personal and emotional problems, rather than a lawyer who is fundamentally dishonest or beyond rehabilitation," qualifying as mitigation under Standard 9.32(c)); *Fla. Bar v. Tauler*, 775 So.2d 944, 947 (Fla. 2000) (three-year suspension instead of disbarment for conversion; court finding diminished culpability as a result of lawyer's personal and emotional distress arising from an overbearing husband who was the "prime mover in the wrongdoings committed by" her); *In re Stoller*, 902 So.2d 981 (La. 2005) (analyzing the interplay between "mental disability" and emotional problems, court accepted respondent's medical condition as the latter under Standard 9.32(c) but determined it carried very little weight in mitigation under Standard 9.31(i) as a result of his repeated and deliberate actions over a lengthy period of time); *Hancock v. Bd. of Prof'l Responsibility*, 447 S.W.3d 844 (Tenn. 2014) (mitigating factor of suffering from personal or emotional problems warranted suspension of thirty days after lawyer called a bankruptcy judge a bully and a clown and demanded the judge apologize for denying lawyer's fee application); *Lawyer Disciplinary Bd. v. Sturm*, 785 S.E.2d 821 (W. Va. 2016) (lawyer who repeatedly failed to take action in cases, communicate with her clients, return an unearned fee, and respond to disciplinary investigation suspended for ninety days with mitigation found in the lawyer being under duress due to "significant personal events outside her control" that provided a reasonable explanation for some communication lapses). For further discussion of mental disability as a mitigating factor and the applicable four-part analysis, see Annotation to Standard 9.32(i).

In some instances, a respondent has emotional problems as well as a mental disability. *See, e.g., People v. Wotan*, 944 P.2d 1257, 1264 (Colo. 1997) (lawyer's misconduct of communicating with adverse party known to be represented by counsel, neglecting client matters, bringing frivolous lawsuit, imposing secret surcharge on clients, failing to pay federal withholding taxes, and accusing former employees of conspiring to testify falsely against him mitigated by evidence that at the time of the misconduct respondent was experiencing personal and emotional problems in the form of a major depressive disorder requiring hospitalization; court cited Standard 9.32(c), among other mitigators, but suspension for one year and one day imposed because of lawyer's apparent total inability to appreciate wrongfulness of misconduct and his "predilection for blaming his employees for problems that were of his own making"); *People v. Sweetman*, 218 P.3d 1123, 1131 (Colo. O.P.D.J. 2008) (taking note of respondent's transfer to disability inactive status, court stating that "[w]hile this circumstance falls short of proving Respondent suffered from a mental disability at the time of the events presented in this case, this undisputed fact *may* shed light on Respondent's misconduct"; court cited both Standards 9.32(c) and 9.32(h)); *cf. In re Hull*, 767 A.2d 197, 201–02 (Del. 2001) (court imposed two-year as opposed to one-year suspension recommended by board, on lawyer who failed to communicate with her clients, failed to consult her clients about litigation decisions, and failed to keep her clients reasonably informed; board considered, as a mitigating factor under Standard 9.32(c), psychiatrist's testimony concerning lawyer's numerous personal and emotional problems and court said it weighed too heavily the psychiatrist's view of her prospective chance of recovery and weighed too lightly the ongoing public risk).

- **Proof of Emotional Problems Versus Mental Disability**

The level of proof required to demonstrate a mitigating factor under Standard 9.32(c) differs from that required under Standard 9.32(i). Under Standard 9.32(i), establishing a "mental disability" requires a four-part analysis—medical evidence, causality, rehabilitation, and unlikely recurrence risk, whereas mitigation under Standard 9.32(c) does not. *See In re Thompson*, 911 A.2d 373 (Del. 2006) (record showed that board gave "appropriate weight" to lawyer's condition of major depressive disorder as personal or emotional problem under Standard 9.32(c) and that medical evidence supported board's conclusion that lawyer failed to satisfy mental disability under Standard 9.32(i)); *In re Woodring*, 210 P.3d 120, 130 (Kan. 2009) (lawyer argued that his depression and financial difficulties were emotional and personal problems contributing to his violation of the rules and should have been found as mitigating factors; court noted that under Standard 9.32(i), a finding that a mental disability qualifies as a mitigating factor required showing four factors, and lawyer failed to make a showing as to any of them so no mitigating factor applicable, even under 9.32(c)); *In re Moorman*, 217 So.3d 316 (La. 2017) (mitigating factor of mental disability found when expert testimony and documentary evidence established lawyer was clinically depressed when misconduct occurred resulting in three-year suspension); *In re Stoller*, 902 So.2d 981, 989 (La. 2005) (when considering record as a whole, no causal connection between respondent's misconduct and his medical condition, Parkinson's disease and depression, and medications he was taking for both, therefore lawyer failed to prove that mitigating factor of mental disability under Standard 9.32(i) was applicable; alternatively, respondent suggested that his medical condition may be considered as a personal or emotional problem under Standard 9.32(c); court held: "[I]t would be an exercise in absurdity if we were to hold that a medical condition which does not satisfy the requirements to be considered in mitigation as a mental disability could be entitled to the same weight if simply relabeled as a personal and emotional problem. Thus, while we accept respondent's medical condition as a personal or emotional problem, we determine it carries very little weight in mitigation."); *In re Koch*, 198 P.3d 910, 912 (Or. 2008) (lawyer's neglect, failure to provide accounting, and failure to return fee mitigated by personal or emotional problems under 9.32(c) on strength of her written responses to bar that personal difficulties affected client representations, although record didn't disclose source of problems; lawyer had made short statement at hearing that "she was sorry that her personal life had interfered with her practice" and then had left the room in tears); *In re Disciplinary Proceeding Against Poole*, 193 P.3d 1064, 1074 (Wash. 2008) (court agreed with disciplinary board that lawyer's bipolar disorder and anxiety disorder constituted a mitigating factor as personal and emotional problems, but under circumstances of the case carried little weight because problems merely impacted but did not cause the misconduct; court distinguished mental disability as mitigating factor under Standard 9.32(i), which requires that disability caused the misconduct, from Standard 9.32(c), that "only requires 'a connection between the asserted problem and the misconduct'") (citation omitted). *But see In re Cimino*, 3 P.3d 398, 402 (Colo. 2000) (lawyer who entered into prohibited business transaction with corporate client while simultaneously representing corporation claimed personal and emotional problems in mitigation caused by his new stepchildren and his wife's insistence that he pursue repayment of loan to corporation; court held hearing board erred in refusing to consider lawyer's personal and emotional problems, noting that "[w]e have never held that a lawyer must introduce medical or other expert evidence on the issue of the presence of personal or emotional problems"; nonetheless, error was harmless because court considered issue and found lawyer's problems were not a significant factor in causing or affecting misconduct).

Nonetheless, some courts look for proof that personal or emotional problems actually caused the misconduct; while courts still may find a mitigating factor under Standard 9.32(c) even without such causation, they generally accord the mitigator less weight in reaching the sanction. *See, e.g., People v. Rhodes*, 107 P.3d 1177 (Colo. O.P.D.J. 2005) (while finding mitigating factor under Standard 9.32(c) due to lawyer's emotional condition in which he contemplated suicide as result of financial pressures, sought assistance from Lawyer's Assistance Program, and received medication for depression, court upheld sanction of disbarment, stressing that lawyer presented no evidence that his emotional conduct caused his conversion of client funds); *People v. Hohertz*, 102 P.3d 1019 (Colo. O.P.D.J. 2004) ("physical or emotional problems" under Standard 9.32 found in mitigation when lawyer's disciplinary history showed chronic severe depression; nonetheless no evidence that depression was direct cause of misconduct including neglect, violation of client confidences, and dishonesty; disbarment imposed); *In re Quintana*, 29 P.3d 527 (N.M. 2001) (personal and emotional problems will not mitigate conduct unless meaningful and sustained period of rehabilitation is shown; because lawyer made no such showing, his personal problems were not appropriate mitigation of his misconduct); *In re Disciplinary Proceeding Against Hicks*, 214 P.3d 897, 904 (Wash. 2009) (personal or emotional problems mitigator applied only when demonstrated connection between lawyer's asserted problems and misconduct; lawyer's illness and surgery, which resulted in financial deterioration and closing of personal bank accounts, "arguably demonstrate" connection to trust account violations but other findings did not demonstrate any connection so effect of mitigator, if any, was inconsequential). *But see Iowa Supreme Ct. Atty. Disciplinary Bd. v. Stoller*, 879 N.W.2d 199 (Iowa 2016) (mental health issues not considered a mitigating factor when lawyer who suffered from depressive disorder refused to attribute misconduct to underlying mental health; however, seeking counseling for mental health issues was considered a mitigating factor and lawyer was subsequently suspended for sixty days).

- **Physical Illness or Problem**

While Standard 9.32(c) does not directly reference physical illnesses or problems, some courts have found these to qualify as a mitigating factor under it. Cases rarely clarify how this analysis differs, if at all, from "physical disability" under Standard 9.32(h). *See, e.g., People v. Donaldson*, 166 P.3d 317 (Colo. O.P.D.J. 2007) (three-month suspension warranted for lawyer who practiced law while on administrative suspension for failure to complete CLE requirements; in mitigation citing 9.32(c) to include lawyer's health problems with diabetes and high blood pressure, his wife's cancer, and his financial problems during period of misconduct); *People v. Haines*, 179 P.3d 1021 (Colo. O.P.D.J. 2006) (at about same time as misconduct occurred, respondent suffered from lupus-like infirmity and other health problems and needed to take pain medication, but her condition did not cause her misappropriation of $70,000 and lawyer disbarred; even so, board considered her condition in reaching its conclusions); *People v. Ra'shadd*, 110 P.3d 388 (Colo. O.P.D.J. 2005) (although issue not raised, court noted as mitigating under Standard 9.3 lawyer's personal and emotional problems in that he had difficulty remembering dates and events, was detached at hearing, and testified that he suffered closed-head injury during Operation Desert Storm that was causing him to have seizures; but no evidence to show that any injury caused conversion of client funds, among other misconduct; disbarment warranted); *Fla. Bar v. Shoureas*, 913 So.2d 554 (Fla. 2005) (finding in mitigation under Florida Standard 9.32(c) lawyer's well-documented history of chronic depression; three-year suspension for misconduct relating to competent representation, diligence and promptness, and misconduct toward state bar); *Atty. Grievance Comm'n v. Shuler*, 117 A.3d 38 (Md. 2015) (lawyer's history of physical illness found to be a mitigating factor; lawyer failed to appear on behalf of client for oral argument because she was too ill to travel and to request that oral argument be rescheduled; suspension of thirty days imposed, conditioned on lawyer showing she was physically and mentally competent to resume practice of law).

- **Financial Hardship, Family Problems, and Stress**

Family or financial problems or stress may be considered mitigating factors under Standard 9.32(c). *See, e.g., People v. Culter*, 277 P.3d 954, 963 (Colo. O.P.D.J. 2011) (mitigating factors included personal problems lawyer "faced on several fronts near the time of his disciplinary offenses," including stress due to law partner's abrupt departure from law firm and resulting financial pressures as well as multiple post-decree motions filed by lawyer's ex-wife); *Statewide Grievance Comm'n v. Shluger*, No. CV93 0530972, 1994 WL 9959, at *3 (Conn. Super. Ct. Jan. 5, 1994) ("Although perhaps self-imposed pressure for a more affluent life style ordinarily would not seem to satisfy the standard of 'personal or emotional problems' the court is willing to stretch the standard because of the additional factor of an unsavory work environment created by an employer, since convicted, who was the target of a federal investigation. . . ."); *In re Becker*, 947 A.2d 1120, at *17 (Table) (Del. 2008) (lawyer's financial stress was personal problem that impeded his ability to prepare required corporate tax returns and to seek necessary psychiatric evaluation and thus constituted a mitigating factor under Standard 9.32(c); distinguishing from finding mental disability as mitigating factor, the court reasoned: "Respondent repeatedly indicated all he could do about his problems was put his head in the sand and do nothing about them. While this does not qualify as a mental disability under [Standard 9.32(i)], the Board does believe Respondent truly saw no way out of his dilemma, and therefore could do nothing but put his head in the sand, and ignore his problems."); *In re Huggins*, 727 S.E.2d 500, 500 (Ga. 2012) (mitigating factors included that during the time lawyer neglected five criminal defense matters, he "experienced a number of personal crises, including the sudden death of his mother, the dissolution of his law partnership, a divorce, and the loss of daily contact with his children"); *In re Southall*, 710 So.2d 245 (La. 1998) (lawyer's poor health, that is lupus treated by chemotherapy and steroid medication, resulted in depression and fatigue and was found to be a mitigating factor); *In re Klotz*, 909 N.W.2d 427 (Minn. 2018) (lawyer's stress related to caring for newborn son while his wife worked long hours was among the causes of lawyer's inability to manage law practice and resulting ethical violations and was found to be mitigating factor); *State ex rel. Counsel for Discipline v. Palik*, 820 N.W.2d 862, 867 (Neb. 2012) (in mitigation finding lawyer "beset with personal difficulty during the relevant time," including health problems of his wife, his mother as well as his own, family conflict as a result of his mother being served with divorce papers by his stepfather, for whom lawyer previously had drawn up a prenuptial agreement, fighting with his ex-wife about planning and paying for their children's wedding, and a strained relationship with his sons); *Disciplinary Counsel v. Edwards*, 981 N.E.2d 857 (Ohio 2012) (misappropriation of client funds warranted two years' suspension, all stayed with conditions, after consideration of mitigating factors including lawyer's separation from his wife, his obsession to win her back by loaning her money, his wife's financial difficulties in her business as well as lawyer's own financial problems); *Lockett v. Bd. of Prof'l Responsibility*, 380 S.W.3d 19 (Tenn. 2012) (under Standard 9.32(e), lawyer's personal financial difficulties resulting from his son's illness properly considered as mitigating factor of misconduct including and theft conviction arising from misappropriation of fees owed to law firm and willful failure to file income tax returns); *In re Disciplinary Proceeding Against Dornay*, 161 P.3d 333 (Wash. 2007) (evidence sufficient to establish that lawyer suffered from personal or emotional problems involving her relationship with a county sheriff deputy, with whom she was having an extramarital affair; noting that Washington legislature and its courts have recognized the profound impact of intimate partner violence, court gave substantial weight to it as mitigating factor). *But see In re Abele*, 358 P.3d 371 (Del. 2015) (court rejected lawyer's argument that stress of litigation was mitigating factor, finding lawyer made no attempt to show that stress of trial caused her to misbehave throughout the proceedings).

A number of courts recognize these problems but do not find that they are mitigating. *See People v. Rosenfeld*, 180 P.3d 448 (Colo. O.P.D.J. 2007) (while emotional pain from father's illness and subsequent death may help explain respondent's failure to withdraw from case in which he was admittedly overwhelmed, it did not mitigate his conduct in going forward in complex case without proper preparation when father's death occurred shortly before trial and lack of diligence in case started more than a year before death); *Att'y Grievance Comm'n v. Drew*, 669 A.2d 1344, 1349 (Md. 1996) (court rejecting "workaholism" as a mitigating factor for lawyer's mismanagement of his client escrow account, noting that "[a]cceptance of 'workaholism' as an excuse for lack of diligence would effectively gut RPC 1.3"; one-year suspension imposed); *In re Hyde*, 950 P.2d 806 (N.M. 1997) (pressures of practice of law provide neither excuse nor mitigating factor for deceit and dishonest conduct; indefinite suspension warranted for lawyer who submitted false billing statements for legal work he did not perform, neglected interests of his clients, and misrepresented work he performed); *State ex rel. Okla. Bar Ass'n v. Kinsey*, 212 P.3d 1186, 1197 (Okla. 2009) ("We do . . . agree with the *Hyde* court that the stresses of life are neither an excuse nor a mitigating factor for a lawyer's deceit."); *In re Disciplinary Proceeding Against Curran*, 801 P.2d 962 (Wash. 1990) (court previously had held that personal financial problems, however severe, were not mitigating in disbarment case; respondent and his wife's financial problems, including having to exhaust their savings and sell their home to repay debts relating to accident in which he was driving while intoxicated and two of his passengers were killed, not mitigating factor in considering length of lawyer's suspension).

- **Personal or Emotional Problems Not Enough to Outweigh Imposition of Presumptive Sanction**

As with other mitigating factors, even significant personal or emotional problems may not justify a reduction in sanction when weighed against the severity of the misconduct. Some courts have even increased the sanction imposed, even when personal or emotional problems have been found mitigating. *See, e.g., People* *v. Heaphy*, 2015 WL 11081955 (Colo. O.P.D.J. September 9, 2015) (while mitigating, weight applied to lawyer suffering from personal or emotional problems due to cycle of financial and marital problems was insufficient to overcome sanction of disbarment stemming from knowing conversion and comingling of client funds); *People v. Carwin*, 144 P.3d 1263 (Colo. O.P.D.J. 2006) (lawyer's emotional difficulties alone—including separation from wife of thirty years, death of wife, two children suffering cystic fibrosis, one of them repeatedly hospitalized, and lawyer's own diagnosis of high cholesterol and diabetes—not sufficient mitigation to warrant sanction less than disbarment for conversion of advanced fees paid by clients); *Statewide Grievance Comm'n v. Johnson*, No. CV054012328S, 2006 WL 3359731, at *4 (Conn. Super. Ct. Nov. 1, 2006) (evidence that lawyer was distracted due to personal circumstances of pending grievance proceeding and notice of suspension did not excuse what appeared to be entrenched pattern of inattention to ethical considerations and inability to properly manage her law practice; "[i]t is this entrenched pattern which is deeply disturbing to the court and justifies a period of suspension"); *In re Carey*, 809 A.2d 563 (Del. 2002) (disbarment warranted for intentional misappropriation of client funds despite compelling evidence of personal and emotional problems that led to misconduct); *Fla. Bar v. Korones*, 752 So.2d 586 (Fla. 2000) (mitigating factors, including financial and familial difficulties and health problems, were not sufficient to outweigh the severity of lawyer's offenses, conversion of funds from his uncle's probate estate, filing a false accounting, and paying his son additional funds not to report the misappropriations, warranting disbarment); *In re Rumsey*, 71 P.3d 1150, 1163 (Kan. 2003) (one-year suspension for incompetence and commingling client funds, among other violations; while lawyer's wife began chemotherapy at about same time of misconduct, "[t]his case does not present exceptional circumstances with persuasive mitigating factors [and respondent's] lengthy experience as an attorney and his repeated violations of the same professional rules belie his contention that these violations are a one-time occurrence related to the stress of his wife's illness"); *Conner's Case*, 965 A.2d 1130, 1135 (N.H. 2009) (that respondent was facing a "series of personal problems" at the time of the events, that he had suffered from depression and alcoholism and that he had taken steps toward rehabilitation in dealing with his substance abuse issues did not outweigh deliberate deception of clients over a substantial time; proper sanction was disbarment); *In re Murrow*, 336 P.3d 859 (Kan. 2014) (lawyer's depression directly contributed to his pattern of lack of diligence and communication; however, depression also has rendered him unfit to practice law and one-year suspension imposed); *In re Cozzarelli*, 137 A.3d 412 (N.J. 2016) (testimony from lawyer's doctor regarding severe depression was not mitigating because mitigation from disbarment is not allowed in misappropriation cases); *In re Worth*, 82 P.3d 605 (Or. 2003) (although mitigating factor of personal or emotional problems of illness and death of his mother established, court did not assign it substantial weight; court imposed ninety-day suspension instead of public reprimand imposed by disciplinary board panel); *In re Discipline of Ennenga*, 37 P.3d 1150, 1154 (Utah 2001) (none of the mitigating factors found by trial court, including respondent's personal and emotional problems resulting from his inability to meet his regular financial obligations, rose to level of "truly compelling" or "significant"; personal financial pressures cannot mitigate the offense of misappropriation). *But see In re Rooney*, 709 N.W.2d 263, 272 (Minn. 2006) (lawyer's personal problems included mother's stroke, wife's emergency surgery, and sister-in-law's death from brain cancer; "extraordinary turmoil in [respondent's] personal life at the time of the misconduct, while certainly not an excuse for the misconduct, is a 'circumstance[ ] to be considered in imposing discipline'") (citation omitted).

In June 2018, the Washington Supreme Court found that a lawyer's vicarious traumatization or "compassion fatigue" can qualify as a personal or emotional mitigating factor for disciplinary purposes if such traumatization or fatigue is connected to misconduct. *See In re Disciplinary Proceeding Against Waechter*, No. 201, 645-6, 2018 Wash. LEXIS 418 (June 14, 2018). In Waechter the lawyer was sanctioned for misconduct involving the management of his trust account. During the disciplinary hearing, a doctor testified that the lawyer suffered from vicarious traumatization or compassion fatigue, which should count as an emotional or personal problem and, therefore, a mitigating factor. *Id.* at *15. The doctor stated that compassion fatigue is common for lawyers and happens when they work with traumatized populations. *Id.* Although the court considered this a new type of mitigating factor, it was not enough to overcome the presumption sanction of disbarment for the attorney.

### *Timely Good Faith Effort to Make Restitution or to Rectify Consequences of Misconduct*

Lawyers who make restitution voluntarily or make an effort on their own initiative to rectify the consequences of their misconduct demonstrate that they recognize not only the wrongfulness of their conduct but also their responsibility to the injured client or other party. Courts often find such conduct mitigating under Standard 9.32(d), provided it is made in good faith and in a timely manner.

In *People v. Baca*, 363 P.3d 211 (Colo. O.P.D.J. 2015), the Colorado Supreme Court analyzed under Standard 9.32(d) a lawyer's actions in making restitution and rectifying the consequences of filing a complaint on his client's behalf without asserting any claims for relief, resulting in $91,000 being assessed against the lawyer and his client. The court noted that the lawyer made significant efforts to repay his client so as to rectify the consequences of his misconduct. Although the judgment for $91,000 was awarded against the lawyer and client, the lawyer agreed to assume the entire responsibility for the judgment. The client noted that the lawyer "acted honorably" and was "eternally grateful" to the lawyer for paying the judgment. The court found the lawyer's actions demonstrated a good faith effort to make restitution and thus applied great weight to this factor in mitigation.

- **Good Faith**

The Washington Supreme Court provided a description of good faith in *In re Disciplinary Proceeding Against Preszler,* 232 P.3d 1118 (Wash. 2010). In finding that a lawyer who did not pay restitution on his own initiative, but only when the client demanded it, was not entitled to mitigation under Standard 9.32(d), the court explained:

> [R]estitution is not in good faith when the lawyer's ethical misconduct was knowing and yet the lawyer pays restitution only when a client demands it. In that circumstance, the lawyer is not acting on his or her own initiative, but at the client's behest, and is acting in fear of punishment, not out of an earnest desire to remedy the damage and admit liability. A different notion of good faith would give an incentive to culpable lawyers to withhold restitution until they are caught. Rather than admitting they have done wrong and remedying the harm, they are better off risking that no one notices their misconduct. If they are caught, they would still get full mitigation credit for paying restitution. That cannot be good faith.

*Id.* at 1131. The court noted that the lawyer wrote the check only after obtaining a signed agreement releasing him from liability for any damages, actions showing that he was not yet prepared to assume responsibility for the consequences of his actions and was not entitled to mitigation for restitution because the requisite good faith was absent. *See also In re Otlowski,* 976 A.2d 172 (Del. 2009) (public reprimand for lawyer who, during random audit, discovered that his daughter, an employee, had embezzled funds from his escrow account; lawyer was commended, in particular, for making substantial remedial efforts, including retaining outside accountants and obtaining additional computer software, incurring approximately $42,000 in accounting fees, which court found mitigating under Standard 9.32(d)).

Courts also have considered whether settlement of a civil lawsuit serves as a mitigating factor under Standard 9.32(d). In *In re Disciplinary Proceeding Against VanDerbeek,* 101 P.3d 88 (Wash. 2004), the court found that while the lawyer presumably settled the lawsuit to avoid the expenses of trial and provide some restitution to her clients, she continued to commit misconduct after the plaintiffs and she reached the settlement. As a result, the court found no mitigation under Standard 9.32(d) based on the settlement of the lawsuit.

- **Timeliness**

When courts look to whether a lawyer has made a good faith effort to make restitution or to rectify the consequences of his or her misconduct, much of their focus is on when the lawyer takes such action. Lawyers who make restitution before initiation of disciplinary proceedings present the best case for mitigation. The Washington State Supreme Court, in *In re Disciplinary Proceeding Against Preszler*, 232 P.3d 1118 (Wash. 2010), also provided a definition of timeliness that many other courts have agreed with, providing that "restitution is timely if the lawyer pays [it] before a disciplinary proceeding begins." *Id.* at 1131. Lawyers who make restitution later leave open the possibility that they might earn mitigation, and courts have found mitigation even when restitution is made in response to a complaint filed with the disciplinary agency, but their case is often weaker and sometimes unpersuasive. *See also In re Feld's Case*, 815 A.2d 383, 391 (N.H. 2002) (one-year suspension for lawyer who withheld information during discovery and disclosures made during trial months after initial misconduct did not qualify as mitigating timely good faith efforts to correct any inaccuracy under Standard 9.32(d); lawyer, at the very least, had to bring his misconduct to the attention of opposing party or court "*before* the trial began"; one-year suspension); *In re Lundgren*, 355 P.3d 984 (Utah 2015) (no credit in mitigation for timely restitution when lawyer repaid client only after threat of lawsuit and client made informal complaint); *In re Discipline of Ennenga*, 37 P.3d 1150 (Utah 2001) (reversing trial court's finding that restitution was mitigator where lawyer repaid client only after she threatened suit and complained to disciplinary authority); *In re Hunter*, 769 A.2d 1286 (Vt. 2000) (when misconduct in this case was occurring during proceedings for previous case, lawyer failed to establish restitution was made to clients before disciplinary proceedings were initiated); *In re Disciplinary Proceeding Against Cramer*, 225 P.3d 881 (Wash. 2010) (refusing to apply mitigator under Standard 9.32(d) because lawyer did not start paying off tax warrants until after disciplinary hearing); *In re Disciplinary Proceeding Against Trejo*, 185 P.3d 1160 (Wash. 2008) (lawyer's waiver of fees for client was untimely as it was offered nearly two years after client trust fund checks bounced and state bar association had conducted two audits and had begun disciplinary proceedings and thus mitigating factor under Standard 9.32(d) did not apply).

Decisions in which courts have found a timely good faith effort on the part of lawyers include *In re Wilson*, 982 P.2d 840 (Colo. 1999) (timely good faith effort to rectify consequences of making sexually inappropriate comments to divorce client by calling her the next day to apologize was mitigator under Standard 9.32(d); public censure imposed); *People v. Maynard*, 219 P.3d 430 (Colo. O.P.D.J. 2008) (agreeing with hearing board that substantial weight should be given to lawyer's timely effort to rectify consequences of her misconduct under Standard 9.32(d), court noted that had it not been for lawyer's self-reporting that she failed to complete client's brief and lied to the court in an effort to buy more time to complete it, disbarment would have been presumed sanction; suspension of one year and one day imposed instead); *People v. Peters*, 82 P.3d 389 (O.P.D.J. Colo. 2003) (mitigating factor under Standard 9.32(d) for lawyer who expended great deal of time and his own finances to rectify consequences of negligently filing faulty pre-signed affidavits approximately 349 times in 187 separate lawsuits; public censure imposed); *In re Brown*, 103 A.3d 515 (Del. 2014) (timely effort to rectify consequence of misconduct considered a mitigating factor when the lawyer immediately dismissed a lawsuit that displeased the court and apologized for filing it; public reprimanded warranted); *Fla. Bar. v. Tauler*, 775 So.2d 944, 946 (Fla. 2000) (competent substantial evidence supported referee's finding of good faith and timely restitution by lawyer who testified that knowledge of the arrearage was a "daily struggle" and that she replaced the funds at the earliest possible opportunity by refinancing her family's home; "The factor involving early restitution distinguishes this case from those in which the debt remained outstanding even as the matter was reviewed by this Court"; three-year suspension rather than disbarment imposed for misappropriation and multiple resulting violations); *In re deRosay*, 494 S.E.2d 339 (Ga. 1998) (six-month suspension warranted but court finding mitigation under Standard 9.32 for lawyer who, after commingling client and personal funds resulted in bounced settlement check to client, made complete restitution prior to institution of disciplinary proceeding and sent letter of apology to client); *In re Kehoe*, 678 N.E.2d 394, 397 (Ind. 1997) (ninety-day suspension appropriate for lawyer who neglected and mishandled two estates given mitigating factor of restitution to clients under Standard 9.3; while restitution under threat of disciplinary proceedings carries no mitigating value, court said that "in this instance, the restitution reduces the extent of the injury to the clients caused by the respondent's misconduct, and, in that regard, is a factor we consider"); *In re Eskola*, 891 N.W.2d 294 (Minn. 2017) (repayment of all misappropriated funds considered mitigating factor because no client sustained any financial loss due to lawyer's misconduct); *In re Fairbairn*, 802 N.W.2d 734 (Minn. 2011) (complete restitution of misappropriated funds can constitute a mitigating factor so long as restitution is not prompted by lawyer's fear of getting caught; here referee clearly erred in failing to consider lawyer's complete restitution as mitigating where she reimbursed all misappropriated funds before being notified of disciplinary investigation; eighteen-month suspension imposed); *In re Belz*, 258 S.W.3d 38 (Mo. 2008) (mitigating effort to rectify consequences of misconduct under Standard 9.32(d) when lawyer who misappropriated client funds during four-year period voluntarily restored them to trust account before reporting his misconduct; imposing three-year suspension); *In re Disciplinary Action Against Fisher*, 571 N.W.2d 370 (N.D. 1997) (approving stipulated mitigation under North Dakota Standard 9.3 when lawyer convicted of misdemeanor theft and admitted to charge of shoplifting made timely restitution in good faith; twenty-four-month suspension stayed on condition that he commit no further acts of theft during that time); *In re PRB Docket No. 2014.133,* 136 A.3d 564 (Vt. 2015) (mitigating factor of timely rectifying the consequences found when lawyer improved his recordkeeping that led to misconduct involving his trust account). *But see Fla. Bar v. Maurice,* 955 So.2d 535 (Fla. 2007) (no mitigation when lawyer failed to tie timely good faith effort to make restitution or to rectify consequences of misconduct under Florida Standard 9.3 to fact that complaining parties had no monetary loss for her incompetent representation, she paid bar's costs within two weeks of referee's decision, and she completed required CLE credits; ninety-day suspension); *In re Richmond's Case,* 872 A.2d 1023 (N.H. 2005) (lawyer's withdrawal from conflicting representation in bankruptcy litigation not mitigating factor under Standard 9.32(d) when that action merely satisfied a court rule; six-month suspension imposed for incompetence, misrepresentation of expertise, and conflict of interest).

Even when restitution is timely, other factors, such as a lawyer's desire to avoid detection, can cloud the issue of whether it was made in good faith and should count as a mitigating factor. *See, e.g., People v. Linville,* 114 P.3d 104 (Colo. O.P.D.J. 2005) (giving credit for returning misappropriated $73,000 in charitable trust funds before serious harm occurred and before investigation and formal charges initiated; nonetheless, restitution motivated at least partially by effort to avoid detection, thus not necessarily in good faith; disbarment warranted); *In re Fadeley,* 153 P.3d 682 (Or. 2007) (offers to arbitrate retainer fee conflict and lawyer's tender of $8,000 to the bar to hold in escrow pending outcome of disciplinary matter not mitigating under Standard 9.32(d) when lawyer prefaced offers with statement that he owed client nothing and he never provided client with an accounting).

## *Cooperation in Disciplinary Proceedings*

When a lawyer cooperates during the disciplinary process, courts often find the behavior a basis for mitigation under Standard 9.32(e). However, because most courts have established that lawyers have a duty to cooperate during a disciplinary proceeding, they often do not find mitigation under this Standard unless the lawyer's effort is above and beyond that normally required. In *In re Disciplinary Proceeding Against Trejo,* 185 P.3d 1160, 1176 (Wash. 2008), for example, the Washington Supreme Court held that a lawyer who repeatedly deposited earned fees into trust account and inadequately supervised an employee who conducted a "check-floating" scheme went "above and beyond the compliance required" by volunteering information of possible misconduct outside scope requested by bar. The court found such conduct a mitigating factor under Standard 9.32(e), imposing a three-month suspension followed by two years of probation. *See also In re Abrams,* 257 P.3d 167 (Ariz. 2011) (full and free disclosure to commission and cooperative attitude in judicial disciplinary proceedings was mitigating factor under Standard 9.32(e) for lawyer, a former judge who resigned from the bench after engaging in a sexual relationship with lawyer who appeared in his courtroom and sexually harassing a new lawyer, among other misconduct; lawyer settled case quickly and in doing so avoided subjecting his victims to lengthy, embarrassing disciplinary process; two-year suspension warranted); *In re Gray*, 152 A.3d 581 (Del. 2016) (full disclosure to the disciplinary counsel along with professional and cooperative attitude considered mitigating; lawyer publicly reprimanded for misconduct including failure to safeguard client funds, failure to supervise nonlawyer staff, and failure to timely pay taxes); *In re Fountain*, 878 A.2d 1167, 1172 (Del. 2005) (while lawyer who for many years failed to maintain proper books and records and safeguard client funds cooperated at least in part with disciplinary counsel, on several occasions he did not respond to inquiries; "Accordingly, this factor is not given as much weight as it would have received if there had been full cooperation"; three-year suspension imposed); *In re deRosay*, 494 S.E.2d 339 (Ga. 1998) (cooperative attitude toward proceedings and full and free disclosure with disciplinary board found mitigating under Standard 9.32 for lawyer who wrote checks to himself against client trust account, resulting in bounced settlement check to client; six-month suspension imposed); *In re Belz*, 258 S.W.3d 38, 46 (Mo. 2008) (self-reporting of misconduct under Standard 9.32(e) was "an extremely significant mitigating factor" when lawyer's misappropriation otherwise probably never would have come to light; three-year suspension imposed); *In re Richmond's Case*, 872 A.2d 1023, 1030 (N.H. 2005) (while agreeing that respondent cooperated with committee's inquiries and ensuing hearings, court did not "ascribe significant weight to this factor because a lawyer has a professional duty to cooperate with the committee's investigation"; six-month suspension imposed for lawyer's lack of competence, misrepresentation regarding his expertise, and conflicts of interest); *cf. People v. Rhodes*, 107 P.3d 1177 (Colo. O.P.D.J. 2005) (cooperation in disciplinary proceedings mitigating factor under Standard 9.3 when lawyer openly admitted his misconduct in converting client funds and cooperated in disciplinary proceedings; nonetheless seven mitigating factors not sufficient to take case out of category of those calling for disbarment).

Even when some cooperation is evident, whether a lawyer has revealed facts only after his or her misconduct has come to light can tilt the balance as to whether courts consider disclosure or cooperation a mitigating factor. *See, e.g., In re Hanlon*, 110 P.3d 937 (Alaska 2005) (rejecting mitigation under Standard 9.32(e) when lawyer's admission of wrongdoing, which included providing misleading information to client and bar investigators and failing to diligently pursue client matters, was made only after it became clear that the bar was going to discover his earlier deceitful noncooperation; lawyer's behavior in responding to bar's inquiry, in fact, triggered three aggravating factors that potentially could have led to lawyer's disbarment but three-year suspension imposed instead); *In re Jackson*, 223 P.3d 387 (Or. 2009) (Standard 9.32(e) did not apply when lawyer attempted to explain his neglectful conduct and false statement to tribunal with excuses and explanations that did not fit the facts and it appeared that he was attempting to cover up for his mistakes; suspension of 120 days imposed); *In re Fitzhenry*, 162 P.3d 260, 275 (Or. 2007) (giving no weight to lawyer's "speed in self-reporting to the Bar—that factor is more than offset by [respondent's] deceptive testimony before the trial panel"; suspension of 120 days for knowing misrepresentation with respect to publicly traded corporation's business activities); *cf. In re Mann*, 853 P.2d 1115, 1119 n.12 (Alaska 1993) (imposing only three-year suspension for normally serious violation of misappropriation of client funds, where attorney "voluntarily turned himself in to the Sitka police and the Alaska Bar Association before anyone discovered his misappropriation," where in absence of such self-disclosure, attorney's crime "easily could have gone undetected").

As with other mitigating factors, the severity of the underlying misconduct can outweigh the mitigative value of cooperation or disclosure. *See, e.g., People v. Espe*, 967 P.2d 159 (Colo. 1998) (mitigating factor of cooperation during investigative phase of disciplinary case insufficient to lessen sanction of disbarment for lawyer who pleaded guilty to sexual assault of child); *Atty. Grievance Comm'n v. Framm*, 144 A.3d 827 (Md. 2016) (although cooperation with disciplinary counsel found a mitigating factor, it was not enough to overcome substantial aggravating factors for lawyer who failed to adequately advise her diminished-capacity client about costs of litigation, failed to conduct minimal research, and was excluded from putting on testimony during client's divorce case due to abuses of discovery; disbarment warranted); *Atty. Grievance Comm'n v. Mixter*, 109 A.3d 1 (Md. 2015) (cooperation in disciplinary proceedings mitigating factor under Standard 9.3 when lawyer provided extensive records and documents and did not interfere with bar counsel's investigation; nonetheless the mitigating factors were not sufficient to take case out of category of those calling for disbarment). *But see People v. Miller*, 409 P.3d 667 (Colo. O.P.D.J. 2017) (lawyer publicly censured for driving under the influence was remarkably candid in disciplinary proceedings when arguably not advantageous to do so; mitigating factor was given substantial weight).

## *Inexperience in the Practice of Law*

Inexperience in the practice of law under Standard 9.32(f) often takes into account simply the number of years a lawyer has practiced, with fewer years in practice weighing more heavily toward mitigation. *See, e.g., People v. Gray*, 35 P.3d 611 (Colo. O.P.D.J. 2001) (inexperience in practice most significant factor in arriving at sanction of public censure for lawyer who had virtually no experience at the time of her misconduct in which she allowed experienced but suspended lawyer to spend disputed funds); *In re Hodge*, 407 P.3d 613 (Kan. 2017) (inexperience in practice of law considered mitigating factor for lawyer practicing for nearly five years who violated rules of professional conduct related to entering into a business contract with a client); *In re McGraw,* 217 P.3d 25 (Kan. 2009) (inexperience in practice of law was mitigating for lawyer who had practiced for three years at time he was convicted of possession of methamphetamine and subsequently failed to provide a written response to disciplinary complaint; indefinite suspension imposed); *In re Estrada,* 143 P.3d 731 (N.M. 2006) (mitigating factor for lawyer relatively inexperienced to act as lead counsel in personal injury litigation who was pressured by and vulnerable to influence of more experienced supervising out-of-state counsel; one-year suspension deferred for supervised probation); *In re Redden,* 153 P.3d 113 (Or. 2007) (inexperience in practice was mitigating under Standard 9.32(f) when lawyer who had been admitted to practice in 2002 took no action on client's case from February 2003 to November 2004, resulting in client's lost opportunity to enter into favorable settlement; sixty-day suspension rather than 120-day suspension that had been imposed by disciplinary board trial panel).

Courts also will look at a lawyer's experience in the specific area of law in which he or she was practicing when the disciplinary matter arose, with some courts failing to find mitigation if the lawyer is practicing outside his or her primary substantive area. *See, e.g., In re Stepovich,* 386 P.3d 1205, 1213 (Alaska 2016) ("The ABA Standards list as a mitigating factor 'inexperience in the practice of law' rather than inexperience in the relevant area of practice"—inexperience in probate law not considered a mitigating factor for attorney practicing for thirty-two years); *In re Brown,* 103 A.3d 515 (Del. 2014) (lawyer had significant experience in the practice of law and inexperience in liquidation proceedings was not considered a mitigating factor); *In re Katz,* 981 A.2d 1133 (Del. 2009) (three-month suspension rather than public reprimand recommended by board for lawyer who failed to disclose conflict of interest to clients; lack of experience in real estate law did not constitute mitigating factor); *In re Sylvester,* 144 P.3d 697 (Kan. 2006) (lawyer's primary practice in criminal law was not mitigating factor for misconduct in handling patent case; public reprimand imposed).

Some courts take into account whether a lawyer's lack of experience actually figured into the misconduct, looking for a nexus between the two before finding mitigation under Standard 9.32(f). *See, e.g., People v. Small,* 962 P.2d 258, 261 n.2 (Colo. 1998) (inexperience in practice under Standard 9.32(f) "not particularly relevant" to case where lawyer testified falsely in a civil action and so given little or no weight in court's discipline analysis; public censure warranted); *In re Hunter,* 242 So.3d 1210 (La. 2018) (inexperience has been the basis for some of lawyer's mistakes; lawyer's problems arose from the first two cases she accepted as a solo practitioner); *In re Thomas,* 74 So.3d 695 (La. 2011) (misconduct of lawyer who practiced law while ineligible to do so because she failed to complete required mandatory continuing legal education courses and pay bar dues and disciplinary assessment was largely the result of inexperience in the practice of law along with poor law office management skills; lawyer suspended for two years, with one year deferred); *In re Jensen*, 468 N.W.2d 541 (Minn. 1991) (treating inexperience as a mitigating factor where the lawyer, among other misconduct, had incompetently represented client by neglecting to follow well-established procedural rules); *In re Grew's Case*, 934 A.2d 537 (N.H. 2007) (inexperience in practice of law was not mitigating for lawyer who engaged in misdemeanor insurance fraud in connection with automobile accident when his culpability arose from act performed outside of practice; other mitigators, however, led to two-year suspension rather than baseline sanction of disbarment).

Finally, courts also look to the severity of the underlying misconduct in determining whether inexperience in practice will lead to mitigation under Standard 9.32(f). The more serious the misconduct, the less weight this mitigating factor has. *See, e.g., People v. Bardulis*, 203 P.3d 632, 642 (Colo. O.P.D.J. 2008) (inexperience in practice of law at time of misconduct as mitigating factor under Standard 9.32(f) "has no weight when the substantive violation involves dishonesty," in that lawyer knowingly converted funds belonging to law firm that employed her; disbarment warranted); *In re Hult*, 496 P.3d 879 (Kan. 2018) (inexperience in practice of law was compelling mitigating factor for lawyer practicing for six years but not enough to overcome misconduct that warranted indefinite suspension); *In re Hodge*, 407 P.3d 613 (Kan. 2017) (practicing law for only five years at the time of misconduct not enough to avoid disbarment for engaging in representation of client, without informed consent, whose interests were adverse to lawyer); *In re Williams*, 714 So.2d 699 (La. 1998) (inexperience of lawyer disbarred for converting $27,500 in client funds to his personal use viewed as slight mitigating factor since misconduct not attributable to lack of legal experience but rather to his dishonest character); *In re Grimes* 297 P.3d 564, 570 (Utah 2012) (court gave little weight to practice inexperience as mitigating circumstance when determining whether to depart downward from presumptive sanction of disbarment in misappropriation cases because prohibition on such misappropriation is fundamental to practice of law; "it does not take substantial experience in the practice of law to know that misappropriation is improper"). *See generally* Leslie C. Levin, *The Emperor's Clothes and Other Tales About the Standards for Imposing Lawyer Discipline Sanctions*, 48 Am. U. L. Rev. 1, 53 (1998) (to avoid inconsistent application, factor should be considered in limited circumstances when misconduct is directly attributable to inexperience).

## *Character or Reputation*

Evidence of good character is often presented as a factor in mitigation under Standard 9.32(g) and courts often accept it, particularly when the lawyer has an outstanding reputation or engages in good works. *See, e.g., People v. Rolfe*, 962 P.2d 981, 983 (Colo. 1998) (public censure rather than suspension in light of good character and reputation under Standard 9.32(g), as well as other mitigators, for lawyer whose misconduct included nondisclosures and misrepresentations to trial court; court took into consideration that board had been most impressed by testimony of judge and caseworker as to lawyer's openness, honesty, and competence in numerous direct experiences with him); *People v. Ritland*, 327 P.3d 914 (Colo. O.P.D.J. 2014) (three-year suspension rather than disbarment for lawyer who circumvented proper channels for adopting her second cousin's baby; significant weight given to character evidence that lawyer was well-respected and had an unwavering professional dedication to helping children in need); *Disciplinary Counsel v. Tomasky*, No. MMXCV054001846S, 2006 WL 3409101 (Conn. Super. Ct. Aug. 28, 2006) (evidence of good character and reputation mitigating under Standard 9.32(g) for lawyer who represented clients in their effort to adopt children from Eastern Europe; suspension of 120 days properly balanced injury to clients who suffered from her lack of candor with her otherwise unblemished career); *Fla. Bar v. Brown*, 790 So.2d 1081, 1088 (Fla. 2001) (lawyer's character and reputation may be considered in mitigation under the Florida Standards for Imposing Lawyer Sanctions; here, ninety-day suspension rather than recommended one-year suspension for lawyer involved in campaign contribution reimbursement scheme due to mitigating factors, including finding that lawyer had "enviable" reputation in community and was a "benevolent character" who provided pro bono services and supported charitable causes); *Fla. Bar v. Hmielewski*, 702 So.2d 218, 221 (Fla. 1997) (suspension rather than disbarment for lawyer who made deliberate misrepresentations in medical malpractice action due, in part, to "extremely strong character evidence"); *In re Acree*, 495 S.E.2d 293 (Ga. 1998) (two-year suspension rather than disbarment for lawyer who pleaded guilty to bank larceny; mitigating factor of character or reputation under Standard 9.32(g) found because of lawyer's solid record of supporting and serving his community and outstanding reputation for integrity both in legal community and community at large); *In re Ellis*, 204 P.3d 1161, 1164 (Kan. 2009) (good character and reputation was "evidenced by a number of letters and testimony"); *In re Pryor*, 864 So.2d 157, 165 (La. 2004) (eighteen months of two-year suspension deferred for lawyer who neglected client legal matters in multiple cases and repeatedly failed to cooperate with disciplinary counsel in view of mitigating factors including record "replete with testimony from respected clergy, judges and attorneys who attest to respondent's zealous advocacy in favor of his criminal clients, who are often incarcerated and of limited means"); *In re Wyatt's Case*, 982 A.2d 396 (N.H. 2009) (lawyer's excellent reputation among judges and practicing lawyers considered among mitigating factors in imposing two-year suspension rather than baseline sanction of disbarment for misconduct that included conflicts of interest in representing ward in guardianship proceedings); *Cleveland Bar Ass'n v. Mishler*, 886 N.E.2d 818, 827 (Ohio 2008) (two-year suspension for lawyer whose misconduct included failing to account for client funds, accepting settlement offer without client's knowledge, and obtaining settlement proceeds with forged client endorsements; among other mitigators, letters from lawyers and a former colleague attesting to his honesty and good character; "[t]hat record deserves consideration in the imposition of any sanction"). *But see People v. Sugar*, 360 P.3d 1041 (Colo. O.P.D.J. 2015) (although lawyer testified that she worked hard to develop an excellent reputation in the legal community and volunteered with various legal organizations, disbarment warranted due to the criminal nature and severity of helping clients engage in tax fraud); *Fla. Bar v. Maurice*, 955 So.2d 535 (Fla. 2007) (no clear error in referee's failure to find mitigation based on character as self-starter who put herself through law school while working at a law firm, set up her own practice two years after law school, always took more CLE than necessary, conducted real estate seminar, and chaired bar's real estate committee; ninety-day suspension for incompetent representation and conflict of interest); *In re Chase*, 121 P.3d 1160 (Or. 2005) (thirty-day suspension instead of public reprimand for lawyer who failed to comply with child support order after trial panel incorrectly applied Standard 9.32(g) mitigating factor of character or reputation based on accused's reputation as a parent, not as a lawyer; no evidence in the record supporting the lawyer's good reputation as a lawyer).

Courts accord evidence of character or reputation varying degrees of importance. In *In re Tenenbaum*, 918 A.2d 1109 (Del. 2007), for example, the Delaware Supreme Court noted that a lawyer whose misconduct included sexual assault and indecent exposure nonetheless had a record of substantial public and community service, including significant work with the Community Legal Aid Society, Catholic Charities, and participation in national and state bar associations, that was a mitigating factor. Considering all facts and circumstances before it and aggravating factors, however, the court said that mitigating factors should not reduce the sanction of disbarment. *See also Disciplinary Counsel v. Blaszak*, 819 N.E.2d 689, 694 (Ohio 2004) (two-year suspension with credit for time served under an interim suspension for lawyer convicted of a felony for offering to sell truthful testimony in exchange for $500,000; lawyer had submitted "overwhelming evidence of mitigation," including some ninety letters from at least eight judges and numerous lawyers, public officials, former clients, and friends: "The sheer volume of reference letters is impressive, but we are most moved by the extensive gratitude and appreciation these authors express for respondent's professional assistance in their lives and his achievements in the courts and community. There is little doubt that these authors knew of respondent's conviction, yet their respect for his competence and integrity was undimmed."); *Bd. of Prof'l Responsibility v. Custis*, 295 P.3d 334 (Wyo. 2012) (lawyer presented several witnesses to his good character under Standard 9.32(g), showing he enjoyed reputation as hard-working conscientious lawyer dedicated to his clients and committed to ethical practices, that he had been a mentor to other lawyers, and that he played important and valued role in defending persons accused of criminal conduct; public censure imposed). *But see In re Disciplinary Proceeding Against Marshall*, 157 P.3d 859 (Wash. 2007) (letters attesting to character and reputation submitted during lawyer's interim suspension proceeding not significant as mitigator and do not alter sanction in light of long list of aggravating factors; eighteen-month suspension for misconduct including directing nonlawyer consultant to create false hourly invoice for consulting services).

Even when a good reputation is found mitigating, severe misconduct can and does override that factor in determining the appropriate sanction. *See, e.g., People v. Haines*, 179 P.3d 1021, 1031 (Colo. O.P.D.J. 2006) (lawyer's earned reputation among peers over twenty-two-year career as "a brilliant probate lawyer who has served the bar and public well" insufficient mitigating factor to prevent disbarment when lawyer knowingly misappropriated $70,000 from estate); *In re Vanderslice*, 116 A.3d 1244 (Del. 2015) (lawyer's reputation and character with respect to pro bono and community work insufficient mitigating factor when lawyer repeatedly intentionally deceived, concealed, and perpetuated illegal and dishonest conduct); *Fla. Bar v. Korones*, 752 So.2d 586, 591 (Fla. 2000) (lawyer with "an exemplary career" disbarred for converting funds from his uncle's estate, filing a false accounting, and paying his son to prevent a bar complaint; court noting that "commendable acts cannot exonerate an attorney from the discipline that must be imposed for intentional, egregious ethics violations"); *McIntyre v. Miss. Bar*, 38 So.3d 617 (Miss. 2010) (mitigating factor of good character and reputation applicable for lawyer who commingled and misappropriated clients' funds even though those who testified in support of lawyer may not have been aware of manner in which he handled his business and personal finances; disbarment still warranted); *Disciplinary Counsel v. Schuman*, 92 N.E.3d 850 (Ohio 2017) (despite attorney receiving fifty-five character letters providing persuasive evidence that misconduct was an isolated incident, board determined the misconduct was most serious offense that warranted actual suspension); *Toledo Bar Ass'n. v. Ritson*, 936 N.E.2d 931, 936 (Ohio 2010) (disbarment was appropriate for lawyer who participated in criminal conspiracy to induce real estate agents and appraisers to join professional organizations with false promise of errors-and-omissions insurance coverage; though character testimony and letters "paint the picture of an honest and trustworthy man, they are few in number and come mainly from personal friends"; evidence had some value in mitigation, but carried little weight in light of facts and aggravating factors in this case); *In re Sanai*, 383 P.3d 821 (Or. 2016) (lawyer's favorable character and reputation among lawyers and civic leaders considered a mitigating factor; however, weight of that factor affected by fact that character witnesses knew little or nothing about misconduct giving rise to lawyer's eventual disbarment); *Bd. of Prof'l Responsibility v. Allison*, 284 S.W.3d 316 (Tenn. 2009) (evidence that lawyer had good reputation is mitigating factor, but imposing sixty-day suspension for trust account violations); *In re Discipline of Tanner*, 960 P.2d 399 (Utah 1998) (lawyer's general character and reputation should only mitigate when facts leave the court with questions as to bad faith or intent; here, lawyer in question admitted to flagrantly illegal acts including making and using false power of attorney to settle case without contacting client and keeping settlement amount and provided no valid explanation for these acts; fact that he had managed to conceal his weak character from the public should not weigh in his favor and disbarment imposed); *In re Hunter*, 769 A.2d 1286 (Vt. 2000) (evidence of good character and reputation had little or no effect on discipline imposed on lawyer who misused client funds in light of multiple offenses and continuing and escalating pattern of misconduct; court rejected good character and reputation as mitigating factor and imposed disbarment). *See generally* Leslie C. Levin, *The Emperor's Clothes and Other Tales About the Standards for Imposing Lawyer Discipline Sanctions*, 48 Am. U. L. Rev. 1 (1998) (character and reputation evidence often of little probative value and should be admitted only when witness has substantial direct knowledge of lawyer's practice, is aware of alleged misconduct, and is able to provide testimony about character traits at issue in misconduct).

## *Physical Disability or Impairment*

In 1992, the ABA revised its Sanctions Standards, amending Standard 9.32(h) that had found the existence of a "physical or mental disability or impairment" a mitigating factor. The amendments deleted the reference to "mental disability" and retained only "physical disability" in Standard 9.32(h). At the same time, the ABA added Standard 9.32(i)—"mental disability or chemical dependency including alcoholism or drug abuse"—that imposed more rigorous requirements for a lawyer to establish a mitigating factor for those illnesses. In addition, former Standard 9.32(j), relating to interim rehabilitation as a mitigating factor, was deleted by the 1992 amendments.

Courts will sometimes consider a lawyer's physical disability in mitigation. *See, e.g.*, *People v. Andersen*, 58 P.3d 537 (Colo. O.P.D.J. 2000) (mitigating factor under Standard 9.32(h) for lawyer who suffered from physical disability arising from cocaine and alcohol abuse; although that and other factors in mitigation were substantial, disbarment nonetheless imposed for lawyer who committed theft by forging a check from his law firm's operating account, cashed it, and used the funds for his own benefit); *In re Beauregard*, 886 A.2d 1277 (Del. 2005) (considering in mitigation under Standard 9.32(h) that during period of misconduct, which included failure to maintain records for escrow account and failure to supervise nonlawyer employees, lawyer was disabled and then recuperating from shoulder surgery, followed by onset of symptoms eventually diagnosed as multiple sclerosis; public reprimand imposed); *In re Islas*, 112 P.3d 210 (Kan. 2005) (diabetes and insulin dependency of four daily injections mitigating physical disability under

Standard 9.32(h) for lawyer whose misconduct included failing to inform client of motion to settle, failure to collect payment of back child support from client, and acts giving rise to convictions for making false application for driver's license; indefinite suspension imposed); *In re Southall*, 710 So.2d 245 (La. 1998) (depression and fatigue caused by medical treatment for lupus mitigating factor in sanctioning lawyer who sought to misrepresent and conceal negligent actions from clients; suspension of one year and one day, an upward deviation of board-recommended ninety-day deferred suspension, because of aggravating factors).

Courts often point out that health conditions generally are not mitigating factors in reducing a sanction for misconduct, particularly when no causal connection exists between a disorder and the misconduct or when no evidence of rehabilitation is present. *See, e.g., In re Peasley*, 90 P.3d 764 (Ariz. 2004) (vision problems, pain on left side, periodic vertigo, and difficulty focusing and concentrating during retrial of criminal murder case not mitigating factor; respondent did not establish a causal relationship between his physical problems and his misconduct, as prosecutor, of presenting false testimony in order to secure murder convictions of two defendants; disbarment warranted); *Iowa Supreme Ct. Att'y Disciplinary Bd. v. Knopf*, 793 N.W.2d 525 (Iowa 2011) (refusing to consider personal illness as mitigating factor when it was not shown to have affected lawyer's fitness to practice law; three-month suspension for failing to file and pay state income taxes); *In re Harris*, 745 So.2d 1172 (La. 1999) (lawyer's physical disability from stroke, which made him tire easily and able to work only a few hours a day, found not mitigating since no suggestion that stroke impaired lawyer's mental abilities or prevented him from representing his client; suspension of one year and one day imposed for misconduct including failure to perform work, to respond to clients, and to refund or account for fee); *In re O'Brien*, 29 P.3d 1044, 1049 (N.M. 2001) (lawyer suffered from physical and mental ailments during period she failed to respond to client's request for refund and statement of account; "This Court has repeatedly stated that a medical condition, though met with sympathy and compassion, is not to be considered as a mitigating factor in discipline absent a meaningful and sustained period of successful rehabilitation"; suspension for minimum of two years imposed); *In re Martin*, 980 P.2d 646 (N.M. 1999) (indefinite suspension due to incapacity for lawyer who agreed in consent agreement that his chronic fatigue syndrome materially impaired his ability to represent clients and contributed to misconduct that included failing to maintain trust account records, commingling, and unintentionally misusing client funds; court pointed out that ethics rule requires a lawyer with a physical condition that is chronic and materially impairs the lawyer's ability to represent a client to decline to represent potentially new clients or, where representation has begun, withdraw from representation, otherwise the condition will not be mitigating factor); *In re Disciplinary Proceeding Against Fossedal*, 399 P.3d 1169 (Wash. 2017) (lawyer's pain was not an extraordinary mitigating factor and did not justify departure from presumptive sanction of disbarment for lawyer who misappropriated more than $117,000 in client funds and was convicted of first-degree theft).

### *Mental Disability or Chemical Dependency*

Two conditions courts have struggled with when considering mitigation are mental disability and chemical dependency. These cases often involve lawyers who suffer from debilitating illnesses such as bipolar disorder, depression, senility, alcoholism, and drug abuse. In 1992 the ABA amended Standard 9.32(i) of the Sanctions Standards to include a four-prong test for determining whether a mental disability or chemical dependency should be considered in mitigation. Thus, such a disability can be considered mitigating when:

1. there is medical evidence that the respondent is affected by a chemical dependency or mental disability;
2. the chemical dependency or mental disability caused the misconduct;
3. the respondent's recovery from the chemical dependency or mental disability is demonstrated by a meaningful and sustained period of successful rehabilitation; and
4. the recovery arrested the misconduct and recurrence of that misconduct is unlikely.

In *In re Egbune*, 971 P.2d 1065 (Colo. 1999), the Colorado Supreme Court took note of the new amendment, pointing out that the hearing board had relied on a former provision, Standard 9.32(h), to find the lawyer's diagnosed bipolar disorder as a mitigating factor. Citing the new Standard 9.32(i), the court said mental disability as a mitigating factor now would be confined to "those situations where it is shown by medical evidence that the lawyer is affected by the disability; that the mental disability caused the misconduct; that the lawyer's recovery from the mental disorder is demonstrated by a meaningful period of successful rehabilitation; and that the recovery arrested the misconduct and its recurrence is unlikely." *Id.* at 1073. Because the hearing board did not consider any of those qualifying factors, the court did not consider the lawyer's bipolar disorder to be a mitigating factor. The lawyer was suspended for one year and one day after being accused of making unwanted sexual advances to a client and recklessly accusing a lawyer and a judge of having improper ex parte communication. *See also People v. Bendinelli*, 329 P.3d 300 (Colo. O.P.D.J. 2014) (lawyer presented extensive medical evidence establishing he suffered from mental disability of post-acute withdrawal symptom, the process the brain undergoes when recovering from physical damage caused by substance abuse; lawyer showed sustained period of successful rehabilitation in that it was unlikely misconduct would recur, a factor that weighed heavily in imposing a stayed sixty-day suspension with completion of one-year period of probation).

Other courts, not relying on the Sanctions Standards, similarly require lawyers to meet a standard established by medical evidence of the lawyer's mental disability or psychological impairment, including demonstrating a causal connection between the disability and the misconduct, a meaningful recovery period, and proof that reoccurrence of the misconduct is unlikely before such condition is considered in mitigation. *See, e.g., In re Fairbairn*, 802 N.W.2d 734, 744 (Minn. 2011) (court held lawyer did not meet established standard of proof for her depressive disorder to qualify as a mitigating factor, relying on her psychologist's testimony that lawyer's "disorder would not 'cause someone not to know the difference between wrong and right,' would not 'cause someone to engage in [a] dishonest act,' . . . and would not 'cause . . . [respondent] to misappropriate client funds'"; other significant mitigation considered in imposing eighteen-month suspension instead of disbarment); *Butler Cnty. Bar Ass'n v. Minamyer*, 953 N.E.2d 315, 320 (Ohio 2011) (evidence that lawyer sustained a traumatic brain injury while serving in the Navy Reserve Judge Advocate General's Corps and that he suffered from post-traumatic stress disorder led court to conclude that "respondent's conduct was born of his extensive mental-health problems"; one-year suspension, stayed entirely by probation, imposed for, inter alia, neglect of client's matter); *Office of Disciplinary Counsel v. Christie*, 639 A.2d 782, 785–86 (Pa. 1994) (in imposing five-year suspension on lawyer convicted of thirteen misdemeanor sex offenses involving two minors, court considered evidence presented by lawyer, including expert testimony that lawyer suffered from psychiatric condition "which causes an involuntary attraction to minor and adult males. The testimony further indicated that respondent's criminal conduct was induced by this psychiatric disorder rather than by any willful criminal design"); *Lawyer Disciplinary Bd. v. Santa Barbara*, 729 S.E.2d 179 (W. Va. 2012) (lawyer presented extensive medical evidence establishing he suffered from mental disability of depression, a factor weighed heavily in determining one-year suspension and continued psychological treatment warranted for neglect of client matters). *Cf. Office of Disciplinary Counsel v. Cappuccio*, 48 A.3d 1231, 1240 (2012) (lawyer in similar situation to attorney in Christie disbarred instead of suspended, because lawyer did not present appropriate expert testimony showing causal connection between medical condition and misconduct).

### • Mitigation Versus Seriousness of Offense

Following the enactment of the aforementioned amendment, which gives courts added precision in establishing whether a disability or dependency is mitigating, many courts will not find a lawyer's disability or dependency mitigating unless he or she can establish that it rises to a level that outweighs the seriousness of the underlying misconduct. In *Att'y Grievance Comm'n v. Blair,* 188 A.3d 1009 (Md. 2018), for example, the Maryland Court of Appeals disbarred a lawyer for committing eleven felonies (nine counts of money laundering, one of witness tampering, and one of making a false statement). The court in *Blair* held that the mitigation was insufficient to avoid disbarment under precedent set in *Att'y Grievance Comm'n v. Vanderlinde,* 773 A.2d 463 (Md. 2001). In Vanderlinde, the court announced the principle that "in disciplinary matters, we will not in the future attempt to distinguish between degrees of intentional dishonesty based upon convictions, testimonials or other factors. Unlike matters relating to competency, diligence and the like, intentional dishonest conduct is closely entwined with the most important matters of basic character to such a degree as to make intentional dishonest conduct by a lawyer almost beyond excuse . . . Disbarment ordinarily should be the sanction for intentional dishonest conduct." *Id.* at 488.

The *Vanderlinde* court further explained that:

> [I]n cases of intentional dishonesty, misappropriation cases, fraud, stealing, serious criminal conduct and the like, we will not accept, as "compelling extenuating circumstances," anything less than the most serious and utterly debilitating mental or physical health conditions, arising from any source that is the "root cause" of the misconduct and that also result in an attorney's utter inability to conform his or her conduct in accordance with the law and with the M[L]RPC. Only if the circumstances are that compelling, will we even consider imposing less than the most severe sanction of disbarment in cases of stealing, dishonesty, fraudulent conduct, the intentional misappropriation of funds or other serious criminal conduct, whether occurring in the practice of law, or otherwise.

*Id.* at 385.

*See also People v. Torpy,* 966 P.2d 1040 (Colo. 1998) (court rejected mental disability as a mitigating factor, finding that lawyer's knowing misappropriation of $9,000 in client funds and mismanagement of his operating account warranted disbarment); *People v. Robbins,* 869 P.2d 517 (Colo. 1994) (while not minimizing personal and emotional problems resulting from lawyer's alcoholism and determining that respondent's mental capabilities were impaired by it, court determined lawyer's conversion of client's funds in trust account was primarily result of financial pressures rather than product of alcoholism; disbarment warranted); *In re Poliquin,* 49 A.3d 1115 (Del. 2012) (chemical dependency does not rise to level of mitigating factor under Standard 9.32(i) that would warrant a decrease in potential sanction; lawyer offered no medical evidence, other than his own testimony, to attempt to establish that his addiction to prescription drugs caused his performance issues, so second element of test not satisfied, nor are third and fourth elements satisfied; suspension of six months and one day imposed); *In re Appler*, 669 A.2d 731 (D.C. 1995) (disbarment warranted for lawyer with bipolar disorder who stole more than one million dollars, not because he suffered from bipolar disorder but because that illness caused him to commit serious, damaging crimes in the past and court not convinced that illness would not likely cause commission of similar crimes in the future); *Fla. Bar v. Heptner*, 887 So.2d 1036, 1044 (Fla. 2004) (lawyer who engaged in felony criminal conduct with a client involving the sale and use of cocaine, among other misconduct, failed to establish that his periodic use of cocaine was due to an addiction and that such use rose to a sufficient level to impair his ability to practice law; court held that "his use of cocaine did not 'overshadow the seriousness of his violations[ ] in assessing discipline in this case'") (citation omitted); disbarment warranted); *In re Cozzarelli*, 137 A.3d 412 (N.J. 2016) (in line with New Jersey's bright-line rule that essentially permits no consideration of mitigating factors for misappropriation of clients funds, court rejected evidence lawyer suffered from depression as mitigating factor when lawyer knowingly misappropriated client funds, finding that mental illness did not cause lawyer to suffer a loss of competency, comprehension, or will that excused his misconduct); *In re Thompson*, 539 S.E.2d 396 (S.C. 2000) (lawyer's bipolar disorder did not incapacitate his ability to formulate and carry out elaborate check-kiting scheme using client trust funds and involving more than $1.5 million; lawyer disbarred because his mental illness did not excuse long term pattern and scheme of misconduct in case); *cf. Disciplinary Counsel v. Brown*, 720 N.E.2d 525 (Ohio 1999) (lawyer with history of cocaine abuse did not satisfy any element in Ohio Guidelines three-part threshold test for consideration of chemical dependency as mitigating factor, in that he lacked official diagnosis of chemical dependency, a certificate of completion from treatment program, or a prognosis of future competent practice; disbarment warranted for his history of substance abuse, neglect of clients' interests, failure to attend scheduled court appearances, failure to cooperate in the disciplinary investigation, and failure to complete voluntary drug rehabilitation program).

Other courts have taken a more expansive view in allowing mitigation for mental disability or chemical dependency. *See, e.g., In re Riches*, 877 P.2d 785 (Ariz. 1994) (determining three-year suspension appropriate for mentally impaired lawyer who during five-year period retained sums for himself that belonged to law firm in which he was shareholder; evidence established that misconduct was caused by lawyer's bipolar disorder and but for diagnosis, the appropriate sanction would have been disbarment); *In re Temple*, 596 A.2d 585, 586 (D.C. 1991) (holding for first time "that addiction to prescription drugs lawfully obtained, like alcoholism, can be treated as a mitigating factor in sanctioning" lawyer whose conduct had been substantially affected by chemical dependency; case remanded to determine whether current status of his rehabilitation warranted mitigation); *In re Carlson,* 489 S.E.2d 834 (Ga. 1997) (after considering mitigating factors of lawyer's alcoholism and diagnosed bipolar disorder, court rejected harshest penalty of disbarment and instead imposed twelve-month suspension or until obligation for $43,000 child support arrearage fulfilled, whichever period longer); *Iowa Supreme Ct. Att'y Disciplinary Bd. v. Barry,* 908 N.W.2d 217 (Iowa 2018) (lawyer's mental depression was mitigating factor in imposing indefinite suspension with no possibility of reinstatement for one year; lawyer had established some relationship between his depression and ethical violations, explaining his depression paralyzed him from completing substantive work; that lawyer had forged divorce decree and persisted in lies for fourteen months aggravated the sanction that would have been imposed); *Iowa Supreme Ct. Bd. of Prof'l Ethics & Conduct v. Erbes,* 604 N.W.2d 656 (Iowa 2000) (public reprimand for lawyer whose misconduct of neglecting client matters and failing to cooperate with disciplinary investigation was caused by his clinical depression and lawyer successfully addressed his illness with counseling and drug therapy, completely transformed his office to meet his high standards, learned from his experience, and posed no current threat to the public); *Att'y Grievance Comm'n v. Christopher,* 861 A.2d 692, 701 (Md. 2004) (lawyer's mental condition and impairment arising from alcoholism and severe depression are compelling extenuating factors that affected his ability to function in his normal day-to-day activities between the years 2000 and 2004; record must show "that 'the evidence before the hearing judge was legally sufficient to establish a causal relationship between the misconduct and the alcoholism,' and that the addiction was to a substantial extent responsible for the conduct of the attorney") (citation omitted); *Att'y Grievance Comm'n v. Kenney,* 664 A.2d 854 (Md. 1995) (indefinite suspension rather than disbarment was appropriate sanction where hearing judge found that lawyer's misappropriation of trust and client funds was caused by alcoholism but cautioning that, in the future, absent truly compelling extenuating circumstances, such addiction would not constitute a sufficient mitigator to reduce sanction for misconduct that otherwise would warrant disbarment). While the Vermont Supreme Court found a lawyer's alcoholism and recovery mitigating in *In re Neisner,* 16 A.3d 587, 594 (Vt. 2010), it also said that the evidence indicated that his alcoholism may not have been the primary cause of his misconduct but rather fear, in that he gave the police false information that implicated his wife rather than himself as the driver of a car that hit a motorcycle, injuring the driver. The court also noted that the lawyer first acknowledged his alcoholism and sought treatment the day after the accident, but he let another month pass before confessing his misrepresentations to the authorities. Weighing the alcoholism and recovery equally with other mitigating factors, the court imposed a two-year suspension rather than presumptive sanction of disbarment.

Some courts make a distinction between the use of illegal drugs and the use of alcohol, finding that the latter can be established as a mitigating factor while the former cannot. *See, e.g., In re Marshall,* 762 A.2d 530, 537 (D.C. 2000) (lawyer's cocaine addiction was not a mitigating factor and disbarment was warranted for misappropriation of client funds and submission of fabricated documents to bar counsel; court rejected precedent establishing alcohol addiction as a mitigating factor based primarily on the illegality of cocaine, stating, "[t]o apply a mitigation principle previously used only in connection with lawful conduct to a situation involving criminal behavior distorts that principle beyond recognition."); *Lawyer Disciplinary Bd. v. Brown,* 678 S.E.2d 60, 67 (W. Va. 2009) (reversing board's finding that chemical dependency, like alcoholism, should be considered mitigating factor and annulling lawyer's license for stealing client trust funds and using them to purchase cocaine to support his drug addiction; no compelling extenuating circumstance to justify lesser sanction).

- **Medical Evidence**

The first prong of the four-part test in Standard 9.32(i) requires that a lawyer claiming mental disability or chemical dependency in mitigation establish that fact through medical evidence. *See, e.g., People v. Stewart,* 892 P.2d 875, 878 (Colo. 1995) (three-year suspension rather than disbarment warranted for lawyer who made unauthorized charges to law firm's credit card, aided nonlawyer in unauthorized practice of law, and neglected clients' legal matters in view of mitigating "significant and persuasive" expert evidence that during time of misconduct she suffered from bulimia, severe depression, hypothyroidism, and personality disorder; distinguishing case from others where disbarment considered necessary, court added condition for reinstatement that lawyer show by psychiatric and medical evidence that her physical and mental condition did not interfere with ability to practice law); *In re Cairns,* 132 A.3d 1160 (Del. 2016) (lawyer's chemical dependency [alcoholism] considered mitigating factor after significant evidence was presented; lawyer's commitment to rehabilitation also assisted in finding of mitigation; lawyer suspended for twenty-one-months after pleading no contest to driving under influence and on wrong side of the road when his car collided with oncoming vehicle); *In re Freeman,* 506 S.E.2d 872 (Ga. 1998) (compelling medical evidence of lawyer's clinical depression and that, but for the depression, lawyer would not have written numerous checks on estate of client for whom lawyer was guardian and loaned funds to his brother; ninety-day suspension); *In re Moorman,* 217 So.3d 316 (La. 2017) (mitigating factor of mental disability due to depression found after doctor testified it was reasonable to conclude depression caused misconduct that occurred over three- to four-month period; lawyer suspended for three years); *In re Disciplinary Proceeding Against Fossedal,* 399 P.3d 1169 (Wash. 2017) (lawyer arguing that ABA Standards do not explicitly require medical evidence contravened court's precedent requiring expert testimony to prove medical facts despite all parties agreeing that lawyer was affected by a chemical dependency to opioids; lawyer disbarred); *In re Disciplinary Proceeding Against McLendon,* 845 P.2d 1006 (Wash. 1993) (uncontroverted psychiatric testimony that lawyer who improperly borrowed and converted client funds suffered from bipolar disorder during time misconduct was occurring and abatement of symptoms and misconduct following proper diagnosis and treatment established extraordinary mitigating circumstance warranting two-year suspension rather than disbarment). *But see People v. Katz,* 58 P.3d 1176 (Colo. O.P.D.J. 2002) (disbarment warranted for lawyer who converted funds when he failed to present sufficient evidence to establish that his misconduct was solely caused by his mental condition); *In re Watkins,* 656 So.2d 984 (La. 1995) (despite lawyer's submission of substantial medical documentation, record lacked evidence as to how respondent's mental condition resulted in commission of criminal misconduct of making false statements to receive Social Security income and of collecting excessive fee in representing Social Security claimants; two-year suspension imposed); *Att'y Grievance Comm'n v. Guida,* 891 A.2d 1085 (Md. 2006) (disbarment warranted for lawyer who prepared forged court order and accepted fixed fee from clients without providing any services in return even though lawyer was suffering from major severe depression; mitigation evidence did not rise to level of excusing or mitigating any of lawyer's violations); *In re Complaint as to the Conduct of Webb,* 418 P.3d 2 (Or. 2018) (mitigating factor not found for lawyer who suffered from a mental disorder and could not show it impaired her functioning in a way that contributed to her intentional misconduct warranting disbarment); *In re Wysolmerski,* 702 A.2d 73 (Vt. 1997) (board properly discounted testimony of psychiatrist who based diagnosis of clinical depression on three conversations with respondent after disciplinary proceedings began and years after misconduct, which included acting without clients' approval, binding clients to unauthorized settlements, lying to clients, and making false statements to other lawyers and to courts; three-year suspension imposed); *In re Disciplinary Proceeding Against Petersen,* 846 P.2d 1330 (Wash. 1993) (court held that, even giving full weight to lawyer's expert, lawyer's depression was not extraordinary mitigating circumstance justifying departure from usual sanction of disbarment for conversion of $18,000 in trust funds from 18 different clients; in dicta court declared that diagnosing depression required expert testimony, concluding lawyer's expert was adequately qualified to give expert testimony on depression).

- **Causation**

Under the second prong of 9.32(i), direct causation between a lawyer's mental disability or chemical dependency and the misconduct in question must be established to justify mitigation. Thus, even when medical evidence has established a mental disability or chemical dependency, there must be a causal connection to the misconduct in order for Standard 9.32(i)(2) to be satisfied. Based on former commentary to the Sanctions Standards, courts often analyze causation in degrees, giving the greatest weight in finding mitigation when a lawyer's misconduct is proven to be attributable solely to a disability or dependency. Courts then give "great weight" to a disability or dependency when it is a substantial contributing cause of the offense and, in all other cases in which a disability or dependency is considered as mitigating, the commentary indicates it should be given "little weight." In *People v. Lujan*, 890 P.2d 109, 110 (Colo. 1995), a lawyer who was involved in a serious head-on automobile collision while on vacation in Egypt suffered a closed-head injury and subsequently was sexually assaulted while at the accident site. When she returned to work, she began using her firm's credit card for personal purchases. Medical testimony established that her experience in Egypt brought on major depression and obsessive-compulsive disorder that manifested itself as an overwhelming compulsion to shop. Viewing the "extraordinary and tragic" factors in mitigation, including the lawyer's mental disability established under Standard 9.32(i), the court found suspension, rather than automatic disbarment, warranted. *See also In re Scholl*, 25 P.3d 710 (Ariz. 2001) (lawyer's gambling addiction was not the cause of dishonesty that resulted in felony convictions of filing false tax returns and illegal structuring of currency transactions, committed while he was a judge; six-month suspension imposed); *People v. Braham*, 409 P.3d 655 (Colo. O.P.D.J. 2017) (little weight given to lawyer's claim that alcoholism a mitigating factor when the court did not find clear and convincing evidence of a causal connection between alcoholism and misconduct, which included abandonment and knowing conversion of clients' funds; lawyer disbarred); *People v. Hook*, 91 P.3d 1070 (Colo. O.P.D.J. 2004) (lawyer's alcoholism was principally responsible for misconduct of lawyer who carried concealed weapon and fired it into close bar so panel required to apply "very great weight" to mitigating factor of chemical dependency; three-year stayed suspension appropriate); *In re Enna*, 971 A.2d 110 (Del. 2009) (lawyer failed to establish that his brain injury caused him to commit criminal offenses, including conviction for falsifying physical evidence, or that it constituted a mitigating factor when imposing discipline; disbarment warranted); *Fla. Bar v. Clement*, 662 So.2d 690 (Fla. 1995) (lawyer's misconduct in misappropriating client funds warranted disbarment, even considering his bipolar disorder in mitigation, in light of referee's rejection of psychiatrist's testimony regarding lawyer's ability to distinguish right from wrong; condition did not directly cause misconduct); *In re Abdalla*, 236 So.3d 1223 (La. 2017) (lack of clear and convincing evidence that lawyer's chemical dependency had causal connection to misconduct resulted in lawyer being disbarred for taking law firm money to support his drug habit); *In re Lowell*, 14 AD.3d 41 (N.Y. App. Div. 2004) (declining to follow sanction of three-year suspension in reciprocal discipline proceeding, court imposed disbarment on lawyer who had submitted psychiatric evidence that large doses of medication and a major depressive disorder caused her behavior during hearing but no evidence that her mental condition caused any of the underlying misconduct that included filing forged certifications with the court and assisting a client in transferring assets in violation of a restraining order; Sanctions Standards not cited); *In re Webb*, 418 P.3d 2, 6 (Or. 2018) (while lawyer was grappling with depression and PTSD during time client funds converted, she failed to prove causation; disbarment warranted); *Office of Disciplinary Counsel v. Pozonsky*, 177 A.3d 830 (Pa. 2018) (applying the standard from *Office of Disciplinary Counsel v. Braun*, 553 A.2d 894 [Pa. 1989], court disbarred attorney and former judge who did not establish causal connection by clear and convincing evidence between cocaine addiction and stealing of cocaine from evidence in the cases over which he was presiding); *In re Meisel*, 672 N.W.2d 558 (Wis. 2017) (medical evidence presented by lawyer did not demonstrate that his condition caused him to commit misconduct because lawyer was apparently able to serve other clients free of misconduct; eighteen-month suspension imposed). *See also State ex rel. Okla. Bar Ass'n v. Busch*, 976 P.2d 38, 56 (Okla. 1998) (rejecting lawyer's claim that attention deficit disorder mitigated misconduct that included unauthorized use of client funds, issuing overdrawn checks to client, and failing to communicate with clients because "there is no causal connection between respondent's condition and the ethical violations in contest"; disbarment warranted); *In re Hunter*, 769 A.2d 1286 (Vt. 2000) (no mitigation when lawyer failed to show direct causation between ADD and misconduct that included felony mail fraud based on misuse of client funds and misrepresentations about those funds; disbarment warranted; court adopted the ABA Standard requiring that lawyer show direct causation between the mental disability and the offense before the disability may be considered mitigating); *In re Disciplinary Proceeding Against Brothers*, 70 P.3d 940 (Wash. 2003) (lawyer did not establish connection that his newly diagnosed medical condition affected his mental state at time of misconduct so it cannot be considered mitigating factor; one-year suspension for charging unreasonable fee); *Lawyer Disciplinary Bd. v. Rossi*, 769 S.E.2d 464 (W. Va. 2015) (lawyer failed to present any medical evidence demonstrating he suffered from depression and that depression caused misconduct of failing to communicate with clients, failing to return client files, and engaging in conduct that was prejudicial to the administration of justice; three-year suspension imposed). *But see Ky. Bar Ass'n v. Hill*, 476 S.W.3d 874 (Ky. 2015) (court agreed with board's findings that lawyer's misconduct was causally related to his mental health disorders, and lawyer's efforts to deal with depression and alcoholism were considered mitigating evidence resulting in a suspension of eighteen months); *Lawyer Disciplinary Bd. v. Dues*, 624 S.E.2d 125, 134 (W. Va. 2005) (respondent presented unchallenged medical evidence that his legal deficiencies in thirty-nine ethics violations, including failure to competently represent clients, failure to communicate with clients, and failure to return balance of retainer fees to clients, were directly connected to serious depression; "[i]t is only because of this direct connection that we are compelled to accord the 'greatest weight' to [respondent's] mental disability"; in imposing public reprimand, court adopted Standard 9.32(i) allowing mental disability as mitigator in applying it to instant case).

- **Recovery and Rehabilitation**

The third prong of the four-part test in Standard 9.32(i), rehabilitation, requires the lawyer demonstrate successful recovery or rehabilitation for a meaningful and sustained period of time. *See, e.g.*, *In re Abrams*, 257 P.3d 167 (Ariz. 2011) (respondent claimed mental disability and chemical dependency under Standard 9.32(i); but mitigator requiring evidence of sustained period of successful rehabilitation was not established, diminishing its weight); *In re Merritt-Bagwell*, 122 A.3d 874 (D.C. 2015) (attorney's disbarment stayed and three-year term of probation imposed due to lawyer showing that she had been substantially rehabilitated as a result of psychotherapy to treat persistent depressive disorder that caused her to pay herself without approval from probate court, inter alia); *In re Temple*, 629 A.2d 1203 (D.C. 1993) (lawyer whose misconduct involved guardianship of his nephew and representation of clients established rehabilitation from admitted addiction to legally obtained drugs by clear and convincing evidence; suspended disbarment and three-year probation with strictly monitored conditions imposed); *Ky. Bar Ass'n v. Hill*, 476 S.W.3d 874 (Ky. 2015) (lawyer's ongoing and successful treatment for mental health disorders considered mitigating factor resulting in an eighteen-month suspension from the practice of law instead of recommended five-year suspension); *In re Zamora*, 21 P.3d 30 (N.M. 2001) (proof of significant period of rehabilitation warranted twenty-month retroactive disbarment, when crack cocaine-addicted lawyer who had been subject to an intervention and was in recovery self-reported misappropriation of client trust funds); *cf. In re McClanahan*, 26 So.3d 756 (La. 2010) (mitigation when drug addiction played large role in misconduct and lawyer demonstrated sustained period of successful rehabilitation; court disbarred lawyer nonetheless because of egregious facts and sheer volume of harm to clients and third parties from misconduct that included failure to account for or refund unearned fees, failure to timely remit funds to third-party medical providers, conversion of client funds, and felony theft conviction).

Courts may closely examine evidence of "a meaningful and sustained period of successful rehabilitation." *See, e.g.*, *In re Steiner*, 817 A.2d 793, 798–99 (Del. 2003) (board erred in considering lawyer's alcohol addiction in mitigation after four-month effort at rehabilitation following his convictions for two counts of vehicular assault and one count of driving under the influence; "we cannot concluded (sic) that four months in recovery from a longstanding addiction establishes 'a meaningful and sustained period of successful rehabilitation'" under Standard 9.32(i); three-year suspension warranted); *In re Shelton*, 49 P.3d 10 (Kan. 2002) (doctor established that the lawyer suffered from attention deficit disorder and depression, that those disabilities caused or at least contributed to his misconduct; but lawyer failed to establish that he had successfully completed a meaningful and sustained period of successful rehabilitation, that the misconduct had been arrested, and that recurrence of the misconduct was unlikely; court adopted hearing panel's finding that lawyer's mental disability was not mitigating factor and imposed indefinite suspension); *In re Neal*, 20 P.3d 121 (N.M. 2001) (lawyer's failure to demonstrate prolonged period of rehabilitation under Standard 9.32(i) precluded consideration of depression as mitigating factor; deferred suspension for failure to properly pursue his client's criminal appeal and related misconduct); *In re Chase*, 121 P.3d 1160, 1165 (Or. 2005) (lawyer presented some evidence of mental disability and, at least to some degree, it affected his ability to gain or maintain employment and hampered his ability to pay child support; but disability not mitigating because evidence did not establish that lawyer had recovered from mental disability for a "meaningful and sustained period" or that his recovery, if it existed, had arrested likelihood of future misconduct; thirty-day suspension instead of recommended public reprimand); *In re Disciplinary Proceeding Against Kuvara*, 66 P.3d 1057 (Wash. 2003) (lawyer failed to show "a meaningful and sustained period of successful rehabilitation" as required under Standard 9.32(i)(3) since he had stopped drinking only three days before appearing before the board).

In some cases, treatment for chemical dependency and participation in the Lawyer's Assistance Program are incorporated into the disciplinary sanctions. *See, e.g., In re Freeman*, 506 S.E.2d 872 (Ga. 1998) (court incorporated an order for continued psychotherapy in suspending a lawyer whose misconduct resulted from his clinical depression); *In re Islas*, 972 P.2d 764 (Kan. 1999) (probating indefinite suspension with terms of supervision, abstinence from drugs and alcohol, random drug-screening, and participation in twelve-step program); *Lawyer Disciplinary Bd. v. Santa Barbara*, 729 S.E.2d 179 (W. Va. 2012) (one-year suspension for lawyer who failed to act with reasonable diligence, communicate with clients, keep clients reasonably informed, and properly oversee and manage a client's trust account; lawyer also ordered to undergo psychological and/or psychiatric counseling to deal with his depression and alcohol abuse issues until psychologist or psychiatrist finds that treatment is no longer necessary).

- **Unlikely Recurrence**

Under the fourth prong of the test, a lawyer's recovery under the third prong must have arrested the misconduct such that its recurrence is unlikely. *See, e.g., In re Gooding*, 917 P.2d 414 (Kan. 1996) (recovering alcoholic and cocaine addict free from substance abuse since his arrest and subsequent felony conviction for cocaine possession and who was very active in attending and participating in Alcoholics Anonymous and Cocaine Anonymous had discipline suspended and was placed on probation for two years); *Atty. Grievance Comm'n of Md. v. Donnelly*, 182 A.3d 743 (Md. 2018) (thirty-day suspension warranted when reoccurrence of misconduct was unlikely for a lawyer who was a member of and counsel for a limited liability company and engaged in actions not authorized by that company); *In re Belz*, 258 S.W.3d 38, 46 (Mo. 2008) (bipolar disorder was mitigating factor when court found fourth prong of Standard 9.32(i) present; three-year suspension rather than disbarment warranted for intentional misappropriation in "this rare but appropriate case" where mental illness was shown to have played role in misconduct and other substantial mitigating factors are also present).

*See generally* Richard B. Marx, *Impaired Attorneys and the Disciplinary System*, 73 Fla. B. J. 14 (Dec. 1999) (discussing recovery as mitigation; collecting leading Florida cases dealing with lawyer addiction and imposing sanctions from disbarment to reprimand; noting trend in Florida toward suspension rather than disbarment when misconduct is result of addiction and lawyer has demonstrated participation in recovery program and noting that trend must be tempered against fact that stealing from client is at top of hierarchy of offenses); Stephanie Goldberg, *Drawing the Line: When Is an Ex-Coke Addict Fit to Practice Law?*, 76 A.B.A. J. 48 (1990) (describing struggle within the bar regarding punishment and treatment of addicted lawyers and noting that Sanctions Standards suggest disbarment for sale, distribution, and importation of controlled substances but do not specify sanction for possession and that the ABA Model Rules for Lawyer Disciplinary Enforcement state conditions for readmission after drug and alcohol abuse, including abstinence for at least a year, rehabilitative treatment, and likelihood of future abstention); *see also* Heather Boyd & Brian Turetsky, *Conversion and the Dilemma of Disciplinary Sanctions*, 14 Geo. J. Legal Ethics 1019 (2001) (comparing predictability of sanctioning presumption approach with context-based approach that considers mitigating and aggravating factors); Rhonda Richardson Caviedes, *Remnants of an Attorney Disciplinary Sanction: Which Jurisdictions Impose Automatic Disbarment? What Offenses Warrant the Imposition of an Automatic Disciplinary Sanction?*, 26 J. Legal Prof. 195 (2002) (discussing jurisdictions that retain automatic disbarment as sanction for certain serious misconduct despite updated disciplinary systems encompassing consideration of mitigating circumstances for misconduct in determining sanctions); Melissa E. Nirenberg, *Reconsidering the Wilson Doctrine: Should New Jersey Continue to Automatically and Permanently Disbar Attorneys Who Have Misappropriated Funds?*, 51 Rutgers L. Rev. 713 (1999); Tricia S. Heil, *From Gatekeeping to Disbarment and Back Again: Chemical Dependency and Mental Health Issues in Licensing and Discipline*, 64 Tex. B. J. 158 (2001) (discussing development of law generally on whether alcoholism should be considered mitigating factor).

## *Delay in Disciplinary Proceedings*

Courts often find that a delay in disciplinary proceedings not caused by the respondent qualifies as a mitigating factor under Standard 9.32(j). Still, it is fairly unusual for courts to find that such delay merits a reduction in sanction when it is the sole mitigator in a case. Rather, courts generally find delay as one of several mitigating factors that outweigh aggravating factors and therefore justify a reduced sanction. And, as with all mitigators, courts establish delay by looking at the facts of each case. *See, e.g., In re Schonland,* 21 Vet. App. 428 (Vet. App. 2007) (two-year suspension imposed due to panel's delay in disciplinary proceeding, among other mitigators, for lawyer who failed to prosecute clients' appeals and made misrepresentations to them); *Iowa Supreme Ct. Att'y Disciplinary Bd. v. Wintroub,* 745 N.W.2d 469 (Iowa 2008) (public reprimand rather than recommended concurrent suspension when lengthy delay in proceedings—four and a half years after matters giving rise to charges were filed—was mitigating factor for lawyer whose misconduct included engaging in business transaction with client involving conflicting interests); *In re Bruno,* 227 So.3d 274 (La. 2017) (delay in proceedings found to be mitigating factor when formal charges against lawyer filed over two years after a complaint; ninety-day suspension warranted); *In re Southall,* 165 So.3d 894 (La. 2015) (delay in disciplinary proceedings considered a mitigating factor for lawyer suspended for three years); *La. State Bar Ass'n v. Gold,* 563 So.2d 855, 862–63 (La. 1990) (lawyer's offenses occurred about six years earlier and committee's investigative hearing was not held until four years after offenses; delay in pressing and concluding disciplinary actions "constitutes an ordeal which punishes a respondent over and beyond the discipline imposed by this Court"); *In re Leuenberger,* 93 P.3d 786 (Or. 2004) (public reprimand rather than suspension imposed when significant delay under Standard 9.32(j) found as mitigating factor; lawyer's violation of conflict of interest and disclosure rules occurred in 1998); *In re Unrein,* 917 P.2d 1022 (Or. 1996) (mitigating factor due to four-year delay in proceeding; lawyer suspended for 120 days for applying for and receiving unemployment compensation benefits on four separate occasions while knowing she was ineligible for such benefits); *Bd. of Prof'l Responsibility v. Daniel,* 549 S.W.3d 90 (Tenn. 2018) (delay in disciplinary proceedings against lawyer found to be mitigating factor when disciplinary complaint initiated three years after the misconduct in question was resolved); *Bd. of Prof'l Responsibility v. Maddux,* 148 S.W.3d 37 (Tenn. 2004) (delay in disciplinary proceedings mitigating when disciplinary counsel took more than four years to file discipline petition and nearly eight years had passed since ethical complaint was entered against lawyer for misappropriating funds from his law firm; mitigating factors justified limited period of suspension and thirty-day suspension was appropriate); *cf. In re Disciplinary Proceeding Against VanDerbeek,* 101 P.3d 88 (Wash. 2004) (hearing officer's application of delay mitigator upheld because of substantial delay in prosecuting the majority of grievances against lawyer, mostly six to nine years before the hearing; disbarment nonetheless imposed for lawyer's billing and collection practices).

Some courts look at the circumstances surrounding delay but will not find it as a mitigating factor unless a lawyer is able to show that it resulted in unfair prejudice, or was caused by unjustified prosecutorial delay. *See, e.g., Blair v. State Bar*, 49 Cal.3d 762, 774 (Cal. 1989) (delay in instituting proceedings was not mitigating factor when lawyer failed to show any unnecessary delay by either his clients or the state bar and, even if there were such delay, he failed to demonstrate any specific prejudice; "mere lapse of time is no defense unless *specific* prejudice is shown") (citation omitted); *People v. Albani*, 276 P.3d 64 (Colo. O.P.D.J. 2011) (lawyer unable to establish unfair prejudice as a result of five-year delay in disciplinary proceedings, even though delay made it difficult for all witnesses to precisely recall underlying events and statements, so this mitigating factor not weighed heavily; in 2005, lawyer revealed confidential client information without client's consent during two in camera proceedings; court of appeals' opinion announced in 2009 and complaint filed within a year of the opinion); *In re Saint-Louis*, 147 A.3d 1135 (D.C. 2016) (court refused to consider mitigating factor of delay even though the disciplinary counsel admitted that multiyear delay was inexcusable, because lawyer could not show how the delay prejudiced him; disbarment for misappropriation of funds entrusted to him without authorization and dishonest billing statements); *In re Ponds*, 888 A.2d 234 (D.C. 2005) (five-year delay in disciplinary proceeding, largely attributable to hearing committee taking more than three years to issue its report, did not warrant mitigation of sanction for lawyer's conflict of interest when he did not assert that delay prejudiced him; thirty-day suspension appropriate); *In re Broussard*, 219 So.3d 290 (La. 2017) (rejected finding of delay in the disciplinary proceeding because it was caused by the parties' pursuit of consent discipline); *In re McBride*, 865 N.E.2d 1110, 1119 (Mass. 2007) (lawyer whose misconduct included intentionally misappropriating client funds and neglect argued he was prejudiced by bar counsel's failure to file prompt petition and committee's delays in scheduling hearing dates; court found "numerous legitimate reasons" for delay in disciplinary proceedings against respondent but "[m]ost important . . . we conclude that [respondent] was not prejudiced by the delay"; disbarment warranted); *In re Gross*, 759 N.E.2d 293 (Mass. 2001) (unexplained six-year delay between lawyer's misconduct of soliciting client and alibi witness to engage in impersonation scheme before court and filing discipline petition caused no substantial prejudice or evidence of resulting public embarrassment; eighteen-month suspension warranted); *In re Overboe*, 844 N.W.2d 851 (N.D. 2014) (delay of more than six years between first petition for discipline and hearing and almost four years between filing of last petition and hearing did not destroy the fundamental fairness of disciplinary process resulting in lawyer's disbarment); *In re Disciplinary Proceeding Against Preszler*, 232 P.3d 1118 (Wash. 2010) (delay in disciplinary proceeding as mitigating factor did not apply because lawyer did not meet burden of showing he was unfairly prejudiced or that unjustified prosecutorial delay was the cause); *In re Disciplinary Proceeding Against Kagele*, 72 P.3d 1067 (Wash. 2003) (delay not a mitigating factor despite passage of three to six years because lawyer failed to demonstrate that delay was inexcusable or undue); *Lawyer Disciplinary Bd. v. Barton*, 690 S.E.2d 119 (W. Va. 2010) (delay of two years between filing of ethics complaint against lawyer and filing of formal charges by disciplinary counsel was not unreasonable so as to warrant dismissal of disciplinary proceeding, absent showing of prejudice or disadvantage to lawyer; law license annulled for lawyer's misappropriation of funds).

Similarly, a delay may be found not to be mitigating if a lawyer is not harmed by it. *See, e.g., In re Crossen*, 880 N.E.2d 352 (Mass. 2008) (ten-year delay in bar counsel's prosecution of case not mitigating despite lawyer's claim that he was harmed by delay; lawyer did not show that testimony of witnesses who had died would have aided his defense and his conduct was worthy of disbarment); *In re Disciplinary Proceeding Against Carmick*, 48 P.3d 311, 323 (Wash. 2002) (when record did not indicate lawyer was harmed by delay, delay in timing of disciplinary hearing had only "very slight" effect as mitigating factor; sixty-day suspension for lawyer who misrepresented ex parte order to court and negotiated directly with adverse party); *In re Disciplinary Proceeding Against Juarez*, 24 P.3d 1040 (Wash. 2001) (two-year delay by bar in prosecuting matter not mitigating when lawyer not prejudiced and partly responsible for delay).

As is evident from the cases cited above, the duration of a delay found as mitigating varies, but is generally several years or more in length. Courts stress that when that delay has been significant and caused by either the disciplinary agency or the tribunal itself, mitigation is found appropriate. *See, e.g., In re Schonland*, 21 Vet. App. 428 (Vet. App. 2007) (two-year suspension imposed due to panel's own delay in disciplinary proceeding, among other mitigators, for lawyer who failed to prosecute clients' appeals and made misrepresentations to them, among other misconduct); *In re Friedman*, 23 P.3d 620 (Alaska 2001) (delay mitigating when bar counsel ended the investigation of misconduct in June 1994 but did not file petition until December 1995); *In re McGraw*, 217 P.3d 25 (Kan. 2009) (delay mitigated discipline when administrator filed formal complaint about two years and eleven months after respondent's criminal conviction; indefinite suspension imposed); *In re Miller*, 147 P.3d 150, 157 (Kan. 2006) (delay mitigated respondent's discipline when the matter "languished" in disciplinary administrator's office for almost three years; two-year suspension appropriate); *In re Belz*, 258 S.W.3d 38 (Mo. 2008) (finding among other factors that five years in disciplinary process before argument in court was mitigating under Standard 9.32(j); indefinite suspension for misappropriating client funds even though disbarment is usual result in such cases); *In re Wyatt's Case*, 982 A.2d 396 (N.H. 2009) (delay given significant weight when due, in part, to backlog by professional conduct committee and, if anything, minimized by lawyer's cooperative attitude; while disbarment appropriate baseline sanction, two-year suspension for lawyer who violated conflict-of-interest rules while representing ward); *In re Lawrence*, 98 P.3d 366 (Or. 2004) (ninety-day rather than six-month suspension for misconduct including concealment of details from court when delay in disciplinary proceedings under Standard 9.32(j) found as mitigating factor; more than five years had elapsed between events that gave rise to charges and trial panel's decision and substantial part of delay attributable directly to panel, which took nineteen months to issue opinion); *In re McDonough*, 77 P.3d 306 (Or. 2003) (lawyer's criminal acts that occurred between 1983 and 1985 given diminished weight because of lengthy delay between time respondent committed those offenses and bar's pursuit of disciplinary proceedings; eighteen-month suspension); *In re Disciplinary Proceeding Against Haley*, 126 P.3d 1262 (Wash. 2006) (mitigating factor of delay in disciplinary proceedings under Standard 9.32(j) was significant enough to justify altering presumptive sanction for conflict of interest from suspension to reprimand; delay between the grievances and formal complaint spanned about four years, and substantial delay between lawyer's violations and the grievance resulted in nearly fifteen-year delay in resolving case); *In re Disciplinary Proceeding Against Tasker*, 9 P.3d 822, 827 (Wash. 2000) (two-year suspension rather than presumptive sanction of disbarment for lawyer who knowingly misused client trust funds in light of disciplinary board's three-and-a-half-year delay before filing formal charges, among other mitigators; lawyer demonstrated delay was "the result of administrative understaffing and slack prosecution on the part of the [state bar] association," among other reasons); *cf. In re Parker*, 815 So.2d 794, 798 (La. 2002) (more than two-year delay because of state supreme court's "lengthy deliberations over the permanent disbarment rule" presented a factor that must be considered, but currently disbarred lawyer disbarred for misconduct that included failing to refund unearned fees, deceiving client, and undertaking representation in new matter after disbarment). *But see In re Wolterbeek's Case*, 886 A.2d 990 (N.H. 2005) (rejection of lawyer's argument that ten-year passage of time since his misconduct was mitigating factor, given lack of authority, and on facts of the case; disbarment warranted for failing to warn client of conflict of interest in regard to acquisition of client's property by partnership of which lawyer was member).

A lawyer's ability to establish this mitigating factor is more difficult to meet when he or she has played some role in causing the delay or extending its length of time. *See, e.g., In re Fowler*, 642 A.2d 1327, 1331 (D.C. 1994) (approximately five years elapsed between bar counsel's petition instituting formal charges and case coming before court but much of the delay attributable to lawyer; thirty-day suspension imposed); *Fla. Bar v. Varner*, 992 So.2d 224 (Fla. 2008) (counsel for lawyer twice filed motions for extension of time and grievances were filed against both lawyer and former partner so it took bar additional time to complete its investigation and lawyer had not previously objected to length of time it had taken to process case; no basis to find that his misrepresentation to court and opposing counsel was mitigated by unreasonable delay; one-year suspension appropriate); *In re Douglas' Case*, 937 A.2d 891 (N.H. 2007) (no mitigation for delay when lengthy discovery process was complicated by factors including committee's difficulty contacting lawyer, time spent on medical evaluation of her fitness to practice law, and overlapping disciplinary investigation and prosecution of her misconduct in separate disciplinary matter; disbarment warranted for converting client trust funds and withdrawing funds for disputed fee); *In re Paulson*, 216 P.3d 859, 885 (Or. 2009) (only potential mitigation factor of delay is "not such a factor here, because of the accused's role in contributing to the delay"; disbarment for lawyer whose misconduct included unreasonable delay in settling client's estate, withdrawal from representation without notice, and practicing law after suspension); *In re Summer*, 105 P.3d 848 (Or. 2005) (significant seven-year delay in bringing disciplinary proceeding not considered mitigating because lawyer contributed to delay by choosing to focus on criminal trial and appeal that led to conviction for theft by deception; 180-day suspension warranted); *In re Discipline of Babilis*, 951 P.2d 207 (Utah 1997) (at least some of the delay apparently for lawyer's benefit so he could resolve other pressing concerns; reversing lower court's finding that four-year delay was mitigating factor as delay not prejudicial and did not harm lawyer's reputation; disbarment appropriate); *In re Disciplinary Proceeding Against Preszler*, 232 P.3d 1118 (Wash. 2010) (no mitigating factor for delay in disciplinary proceedings because lawyer's motions and petition for review protracted the proceeding as much as anything the state bar did); *In re Disciplinary Proceeding Against Cohen*, 67 P.3d 1086, 1095 (Wash. 2003) (lawyer contributed to delay of more than three years between formal complaint and hearing by failing to respond to clients' grievance for more than nine months and, after formal complaint was filed, delayed filing answer for nearly two months after deadline; when balanced against numerous aggravating factors, delay falls short of being mitigator and did not justify departure from presumptive sanction of suspension).

### *Imposition of Other Penalties or Sanctions*

When a lawyer already has been assessed other penalties for misconduct, ranging from fines to criminal sentences, disciplinary sanctions may be mitigated under Standard 9.32(k). *See, e.g., In re Abrams*, 257 P.3d 167 (Ariz. 2011) (resignation from the bench upon the filing of sexual harassment charges, imposition of censure, and permanent injunction against former judge from serving as a judicial officer in the state for violating the Code of Judicial Conduct served as mitigators under Standard 9.32(k) in imposing two-year suspension from the practice of law); *In re Levine*, 847 P.2d 1093 (Ariz. 1993) (lawyer previously had personally paid thousands of dollars of sanctions imposed by courts against him; imposition of other sanctions and fees by the court, to extent that lawyer had paid them or will pay them, should be considered in mitigation); *In re Cardwell*, 50 P.3d 897, 902 (Colo. 2002) (mitigation under Standard 9.32(k) for severe penalties lawyer already had suffered, including a four-year sentence, for crimes he committed while assisting his client in pleading guilty in a DUI case but failing to disclose his client had previously been convicted of driving while ability impaired); three-year suspension rather than disbarment warranted); *People v. Evanson*, 223 P.3d 735 (Colo. O.P.D.J. 2009) (federal prison sentence of 120 months for conspiracy to commit tax fraud, tax evasion, and aiding and assisting in preparation of false income tax return was mitigating factor under Standard 9.32(k) but not sufficiently mitigating to deviate from presumed sanction of disbarment); *People v. D'Acquisto*, 146 P.3d 1041 (Colo. O.P.D.J. 2006) (mitigating factor under Standard 9.32(d) for lawyer who spent several days in jail for failure to appear and show cause why he should not be held in contempt of court and who had been administratively suspended for failing to cooperate in disciplinary investigation; three-year suspension rather than presumptive sanction of disbarment due to this and other mitigators); *In re McGraw*, 217 P.3d 25 (Kan. 2009) (one-year probation served following conviction for possession of methamphetamine considered in mitigation); *In re Lovelace*, 182 P.3d 1244 (Kan. 2008) (the one year in prison lawyer spent as a result of misdemeanor tax conviction considered in mitigation; indefinite suspension imposed in light of this and other factors); *In re Bilbe*, 841 So.2d 729 (La. 2003) (lawyer's suspension from practice before the Executive Office for Immigration Review and the Immigration and Naturalization Service because of misrepresentations to immigration judge was mitigating factor; three-year suspension rather than disbarment); *In re Pless*, No. 12#00117 (Wash. 2013) *available at* http://mcle.mywsba.org/DisciplineFiles/1748/0081.pdf (in imposing reprimand, resignation of his position by former assistant law school dean was one of the factors considered in mitigation); *Bd. of Prof'l Responsibility v. Custis*, 348 P.3d 823 (Wyo. 2015) (previous $500 sanction by Wyoming Supreme Court for brief containing material misrepresentations was the only mitigating factor present; public censure and imposition of other fees ordered by the court).

In some cases, however, courts will not apply this Standard even though the lawyers have had penalties or other sanctions imposed against them. *See, e.g., People v. Hill*, 71 P.3d 1023 (Colo. O.P.D.J. 2003) (lawyer's completion of other penalties or sanctions not considered in mitigation under Standard 9.32(k) insofar as he did not abstain from alcohol consumption during one-year period of probation nor seek out or complete formal anger management courses, both terms of his sentence upon conviction for third-degree assault of stepson); *In re Rumsey*, 71 P.3d 1150 (Kan. 2003) (county district court assessment of $250 in fees as sanction for filing false pleadings not persuasive mitigating factor given offenses and aggravation); *In re Disciplinary Proceeding Against Day,* 173 P.3d 915 (Wash. 2007) (no error in finding by hearing officer and board that criminal sentence for child molestation of former client did not mitigate sanction under Standard 9.32(k)).

Not every negative consequence of misconduct that a lawyer faces is considered a penalty or other sanction under this subsection, nor is a penalty or sanction found to constitute mitigation when the impact of it on the lawyer has been minimal. *See, e.g., In re Hanlon,* 110 P.3d 937 (Alaska 2005) (potential negative effect of penalty of suspension on lawyer's practice, reputation, or personal life not mitigating factor); *People v. Robbins,* 869 P.2d 517, 519 n.3 (Colo. 1994) (fact that respondent replaced some of misappropriated trust funds with funds from his pension and profit-sharing program, subjecting him to additional taxes and penalties, "is not in our view 'the imposition of other penalties or sanctions,'" for purposes of mitigation under Standard 9.32(k)); *Att'y Grievance Comm'n v. Spery,* 810 A.2d 487, 494 (Md. 2002) (exorbitant payments exacted as blackmail or extortion by lawyer's partners based on his misappropriation of $47,000 in partnership funds was not "other penalties or sanctions" under Standard 9.32(k); noting that other courts had found "other penalties or sanctions" as mitigation justifying lesser sanctions only when they were disciplinary or punitive in nature, court ruled that, in contrast, "any 'punishment' incurred by respondent at the hands of his partners is not discipline for his misconduct"; disbarment imposed); *In re Richmond's Case,* 872 A.2d 1023 (N.H. 2005) (corporate counsel's financial losses due to poor investment decisions while also operating business in violation of conflicts of interest rule did not constitute the type of non-disciplinary penalty or sanction that would warrant mitigation); *In re Fitzhenry,* 162 P.3d 260 (Or. 2007) (no weight given to fact that respondent's conduct was also punished by Securities and Exchange Commission investigation through cease-and-desist order when lawyer acknowledged that Securities and Exchange Commission's order had no real effect on his day-to-day work and he incurred no expense defending himself in either that proceeding or the disciplinary proceeding); *In re Disciplinary Proceeding Against Trejo,* 185 P.3d 1160 (Wash. 2008) (rejecting argument that lawyer's voluntary waiver of attorney's fees constituted self-imposed penalty); *cf. In re Ballinger,* 211 A.D.2d 6 (N.Y. App. Div. 1995) (rejecting as mitigation respondent's admission of guilt and other obligations to which he was committed as part of bargain for lighter federal sentence for felony convictions).

Jurisdictions differ on whether to consider reciprocal discipline—discipline imposed by another jurisdiction—as penalty or other sanction for purposes of mitigation under this Standard. *See, e.g., In re Van Dox,* 152 P.3d 1183, 1190 (Ariz. 2007) (hearing officer improperly considered potential effects of discipline on respondent's livelihood and reciprocal discipline in Florida and Virginia in determining sanction; "effects of sanctions on an attorney's practice and livelihood are not mitigating factors that may be considered in determining sanctions"); *In re Summer*, 105 P.3d 848 (Or. 2005) (Idaho's past and pending imposition of other criminal penalties and disciplinary sanctions found mitigating factor under Standard 9.32(k)); *In re Page*, 955 P.2d 239, 243 (Or. 1998) ("A mitigating factor, which always will exist in a reciprocal discipline proceeding, is that the accused already has been disciplined in another state for the same misconduct at issue here.").

## *Remorse*

A lawyer's remorse for misconduct can be considered in mitigation. *See, e.g., In re Wilson*, 982 P.2d 840, 841 (Colo. 1999) (lawyer's remorse and admission that his attempted discussion of sexual matters with client was "stupid and wrong" found mitigating under Standard 9.32(l); public censure warranted); *People v. Fei Qin*, 2016 Colo. Discipl. LEXIS 111 (Colo. O.P.D.J. 2016) (finding respondent's remorse genuine for the effect that his actions had on his family, this mitigating factor given significant weight in suspending lawyer for three months after he physically attacked his wife, who was holding their young child in her arms); *Iowa Supreme Court Atty. Disciplinary Bd. v. West*, 901 N.W.2d 519 (Iowa 2017) (lawyer expressing remorse to everyone involved and accepting responsibility considered mitigating factor for misconduct in connection with probate court and closing of an estate; sixty-day suspension imposed); *In re Schneider*, 404 P.3d 388 (Kan. 2017) (lawyer expressed genuine remorse for having failed to timely respond to motions and for having failed to fully advise his client); *Att'y Grievance Comm'n v. Adams*, 109 A.3d 114 (Md. 2015) (lawyer's remorse was considered a mitigating factor and resulted in a reprimand for delaying to file documents on behalf of a client resulting in a monetary loss to the client); *In re Bonner*, 896 N.W.2d 98 (Minn. 2017) (lawyer's remorse for misconduct was a mitigating factor resulting in indefinite suspension with no petition for reinstatement for nine months); *In re Koch*, 198 P.3d 910 (Or. 2008) (finding remorse mitigating when lawyer's brief statement to trial panel clearly indicated she regretted mistakes).

In some instances, courts have given significant weight to a lawyer's apology. *See, e.g., United States v. Koubrii*, 305 F. Supp. 2d 723, 759 (E.D. Mich. 2003) (placing "great weight and significance" on U.S. Attorney General John Ashcroft's personal apology and assurance that such incidents would not occur in the future made to court and counsel for his public comments about pending prosecution for aiding terrorists, in violation of court order prohibiting public disclosures); *Disciplinary Counsel v. Tomasky*, No. MMXCV054001846S, 2006 WL 3409101, at *5 n.6 (Conn. Super. Ct. Aug. 28, 2006) (remorse was a mitigating factor when lawyer mishandling foreign adoptions stated at hearing: "I understand that my client's [sic] disappointment in the adoption process have caused them real heartache. For that I am deeply sorry, especially in those cases when my own shortcomings have contributed to my client's disappointment. Your Honor, I would like to apologize to my clients. To each of you I say I'm sorry that I could not make your dream of adoption real, I'm sorry."); *Stevens v. Ky. Bar Ass'n*, 186 S.W.3d 744 (Ky. 2006) (public reprimand appropriate for assistant commonwealth's lawyer who had sexual contact with defendant in criminal matter handled by commonwealth attorney's office but expressed regret and remorse and apologized for his actions to Kentucky Bar Association, Hardin County Bench and Bar, and citizens of Hardin County); *In re Wyatt's Case*, 982 A.2d 396, 414 (N.H. 2009) (lawyer apologized to court, client, professional conduct committee, and bar at oral argument and, although disputing the findings of misconduct, "he recognized that reaching this point in the disciplinary process evidenced some fundamental failure on his part"). *But see In re Augenstein*, 871 P.2d 254, 258 (Ariz. 1994) (no finding of remorse based on lawyer's late apology, standing alone; agreeing with commission "that '[t]hose seeking mitigation relief based upon remorse must present a showing of more than having said they are sorry. . . . [T]he best evidence of genuine remorse is affirmative and, if necessary, creative efforts to make the injured client whole.'").

The timing of the apology can be a factor in determining the extent to which remorse will be deemed a mitigating factor. *See, e.g., In re Clark*, No. 06-62407-aer13, 2009 WL 936666, at *7 n. 19 (Bankr. D. Or. Mar. 26, 2009) (finding lawyer's "last minute remorse to be suspect"; while respondent's remorse, if sincere, was commendable, it came only after the U.S. trustee and case trustee were forced to intervene and then only at the sanctions hearing itself and might have carried more weight had it been at earlier stage of proceedings); *cf. In re Coe*, 903 S.W.2d 916, 918 (Mo. 1995) (court addressed the timing of a lawyer's apology and promise not to repeat the conduct, finding lawyer's "profuse public apology" a factor in mitigation, even when made only after an absence of remorse was noted by two members of the court).

Courts may question the genuineness of an assertion of remorse and when actual demonstration of remorse is lacking or diminished by the lawyer's other responses. *See, e.g., In re Abrams*, 257 P.3d 167 (Ariz. 2011) (rejecting former judge's assertion of remorse as a mitigating factor under Standard 9.32(l), court said the record did not clearly reflect he was remorseful, noting he earlier claimed that one of the female lawyers he sexually harassed did not object to his sexual comments and that he did not feel he was harassing her); *In re Moak*, 71 P.3d 343, 351 (Ariz. 2003) (rejecting argument that mitigating factors of remorse and repayment sufficiently demonstrate rehabilitation when lawyer failed to show commitment to remedying his serious ethical deficiencies: "We are unsure whether [respondent] fully understands and appreciates the duties imposed by the Rules of Professional Conduct and the magnitude of his transgressions. As a result, we are unpersuaded by this record that similar violations will not occur in the future."); *People v. Beecher*, 224 P.3d 442 (Colo. O.P.D.J. 2009) (little weight given to remorse as mitigating factor for lawyer who expressed remorse for harm caused by carrying on intimate relationship with client and engaging in tactics to harass witnesses in that he blamed others for hostility in case and failed to recognize that his conduct violated rules); *People v. Johnson*, 35 P.3d 192 (Colo. O.P.D.J. 1999) (expression of remorse, as opposed to conduct reflecting remorse, not significant factor in mitigation; lawyer expressed remorse for failing to make child support payments and violating both court's orders and his agreement to pay arrearages, but evidenced no effort to reduce arrearages owed); *In re Murray*, 47 A.3d 972, at *32 (Table) (Del. 2012) (finding respondent "did not appear remorseful" albeit stating an apology since he did not "appear to understand why his actions were subject to this disciplinary proceeding"; public reprimand for wasting judicial resources in seeking to withdraw from cases after his appointment and making statements disparaging the judges who appointed him); *In re Stull*, 985 A.2d 391 *9 (Table) (Del. 2009) (although lawyer testified he was "very concerned" about misleading court, he also testified that he did not think there were any material problems or violation of the rules since he did not take client funds; mitigating factor of remorse existed to small degree); *In re Silva*, 29 A.3d 924, 943 (D.C. 2011) (accepting recommendation of three years' suspension and affirming hearing board's finding that lawyer failed to express genuine remorse, court noted his expression of remorse "rings hollow" and was not sufficient to warrant lesser sanction); *In re Klotz*, 909 N.W.2d 327 (Minn. 2018) (finding of remorse tempered by lawyer's long deception and attempt to hide full scope of misconduct; fact that remorse came only after lawyer's misrepresentations and dishonesty were known resulted in indefinite suspension with no petition for reinstatement for eighteen months); *State ex rel. Okla. Bar Ass'n v. Kinsey*, 212 P.3d 1186 (Okla. 2009) (rejecting mitigating factor of lawyer's remorse because court not convinced it was genuine; while lawyer confessed wrongdoing when confronted with billing irregularity and reimbursed $2,072.70 in false travel expenses to law firm, she did nothing regarding nearly $14,000 of falsely billed attorney's fees).

As with other mitigating factors, remorse is insufficient to outweigh very serious underlying misconduct. *See, e.g., People v. Gustafson*, 128 P.3d 788 (Colo. O.P.D.J. 2005) (disbarment warranted for knowing conversion of $80,000 although lawyer clearly sorry, repeatedly testifying about how he felt remorse, shame, and professional embarrassment); *Atty. Grievance Comm'n v. Peters-Hamlin*, 136 A.3d 374 (Md. 2016) (evidence that lawyer showed some remorse for misconduct insufficient to overcome the seriousness of violations; lawyer's remorse was not sincere, warranting disbarment for instructing associate to claim deposition transcript as work-product and knowingly making false statements to the court); *In re Richmond's Case*, 872 A.2d 1023, 1031 (N.H. 2005) (expression of remorse not adequate to warrant mitigation when referee "found that '[respondent] has shown little appreciation for the conflicts that could arise from his multiple representation of parties'" and that a risk of harm was presented by his position that he may continue to offer legal services in areas in which he is not competent); *In re Feld's Case*, 815 A.2d 383, 92 (N.H. 2002) (in cases involving dishonesty, a lawyer must admit to professional misconduct to truly demonstrate remorse; here court rejected remorse as mitigating when no evidence that lawyer accepted responsibility for his ethical violations; court added that litigation's alleged "battlefield atmosphere" does not excuse respondent's misconduct); *Maddux v. Bd. of Prof'l Responsibility*, 288 S.W.3d 340 (Tenn. 2009) (lawyer's acknowledgment of wrongdoing and expression of sorrow at having missed the statute of limitations was insufficient for sanction reduction given numerous aggravating factors).

## *Remoteness of Prior Offenses*

Courts may consider the remoteness of a prior offense mitigating. *See, e.g., People v. Smith*, 136 P.3d 279 (Colo. O.P.D.J. 2006) (noting in mitigation under Standard 9.32(m) that three of lawyer's prior disciplinary matters occurred before 1994); *In re Odo*, 375 P.3d 320 (Kan. 2016) (finding mitigating that one of lawyer's prior offenses, a 2006 admonition, was remote in both time and nature to current misconduct); *In re Sutton*, 959 P.2d 904 (Kan. 1998) (construction traffic incident was remote in time and settled in 1995 so, therefore, mitigating); *In re Gastineau*, 857 P.2d 136 (Or. 1993) (in nineteen years of practice, lawyer had only one private admonition that was related to first dissolution case he handled and so, therefore, mitigating). *But see In re Moity*, Misc. No. 07-001, 2008 WL 104209 (W.D. La. Jan. 9, 2008) (remoteness of prior offenses not mitigating factor when they occurred only three years before current misconduct and supreme court's formal reprimand was only one and a half years earlier); *In re Beauregard*, 189 A.3d 1236 (Del. 2018) (less emphasis placed on remoteness of prior discipline as mitigating factor when only four years separated lawyers' completion of prior disciplinary probation and the misconduct leading to the violations in the current proceeding); *Fla. Bar v. Dopazo*, 232 So.3d 258 (Fla. 2017) (remoteness of prior disciplinary offenses not mitigating when they occurred less than three years before current misconduct and involved rule violation similar to the instant case).

The remoteness of a prior disciplinary offense is often considered when a court is weighing the significance of a prior disciplinary offense as an aggravating factor under Standard 9.22(a). *See, e.g., In re Malik*, 167 A.3d 1189 (Del. 2017) (most recent admonition occurred in 2013, less than a year before respondent's current misconduct, and therefore could not be considered remote in time; however, admonitions from 1990, 1993, and 1994 were remote in time, and an admonition from 2006 was remote in time but less so); *In re Thompson*, 911 A.2d 373, 376 n.9 (Del. 2006) (aggravating factor found in respondent's prior disciplinary record including private admonitions in 1985 and 1997, public reprimand and three-year probation in 2003; board assigned "considerably less weight" to 1985 private admonition and only "some limited weight" to 1997 private admonition because of their remoteness in time); *In re Ketter*, 992 P.2d 205 (Kan. 1999) (finding three misdemeanor convictions in North Carolina in 1988, approximately eleven years before present complaint, too remote to be considered in aggravation of punishment and, in fact, mitigating factor under Standard 9.32(k); but 1996 informal admonition properly considered as aggravating factor); *In re Wilson*, 149 P.3d 1200 (Or. 2006) (while lawyer's prior offenses are remote in time, in Oregon remoteness in time does not serve as mitigating factor but can serve to lessen significance of prior misconduct in aggravation); *In re Dugger*, 54 P.3d 595, 610 (Or. 2002) (remoteness in time diminishes significance of prior offense as aggravating factor, but does not function as mitigating factor; lawyer's prior offense of misrepresentation, which resulted in a sixty-three-day suspension in 1985 disciplinary action, "is entitled to some, but not considerable, weight" as aggravating factor); *In re Disciplinary Proceeding Against Cramer*, 225 P.3d 881, 890 (Wash. 2010) (rejecting lawyer's argument that prior discipline from 1991 and 1994 was "too remote" and should be mitigating factor and noting that court had considered misconduct more remote than this as an aggravating factor). *See also* discussion under Annotation to Standard 9.22(a); *People v. Dalton*, 367 P.3d 126 (O.P.D.J. Colo. 2016) (little weight applied in aggravation to prior discipline due to their remoteness when lawyer received a public censure in 1992 and was privately admonished in 1981).

## *Other Mitigating Factors*

Standard 9.32 sets forth a non-exhaustive list of mitigating factors to be considered that may justify a reduction in the sanction to be imposed. Courts occasionally have considered factors offered in mitigation other than those enumerated in Standard 9.32. For example, several courts view as mitigating the fact that no person was harmed by the lawyer's misconduct. *See, e.g., In re Farry*, 909 P.2d 1096, 1098 (Colo. 1996) (public reprimand appropriate when lawyer engaged in negligent conflict of interest, mitigating factors present "and the lack of actual harm to any client"); *In re Melvin*, 807 A.2d 550 (Del. 2002) (fact that lawyer's violation of protective order that he not contact ex-wife and destruction of wife's documents with potential evidentiary value did not result in harm to any client recognized as mitigating in evaluation of length of suspension); *In re Weier*, 994 S.W.2d 554 (Mo. 1999) (in evaluating mitigating circumstances for imposition of sanction for lawyer's failure to disclose financial involvement in client's partnership, court noted there was no discernible financial harm to partners); *In re Cupples*, 979 S.W.2d 932 (Mo. 1998) (lack of harm to any clients found as one circumstance in mitigation; no other mitigating circumstances in Standard 9.32 applied); *Bd. of Prof'l Responsibility v. Daniel*, 549 S.W.3d 90 (Tenn. 2018) (court found that the hearing panel did not abuse discretion when as a mitigating factor it considered that no client was deprived of any money); *cf. People v. Snyder*, 418 P.3d 550 (O.P.D.J. Colo. 2018) (although lawyer's misconduct caused little actual harm to his client's legal proceeding, there was a potential to cause great harm when lawyer neglected his clients' immigration matter).

In other instances, courts have taken into account possible benefits resulting from a lawyer's behavior. *See, e.g., In re Kearns*, 991 P.2d 824 (Colo. 1999) (lawyer's voluntary reporting to police and to office of disciplinary counsel of serious traffic accident that he caused while driving under the influence was deemed as additional mitigation by board); *In re Gibson*, 991 P.2d 277 (Colo. 1999) (thirty-day suspension for misrepresenting case status to client for four years in order to cover up neglect; short suspension adequate because of "[t]wo unusual aspects" of this case, i.e., that client suffered no harm and likely received more money from the lawyer than he would have from a judgment and fact that client had failed to pay lawyer any fees in four additional separate legal matters in which respondent represented client competently); *In re Disciplinary Proceeding Against Schafer*, 66 P.3d 1036 (Wash. 2003) (even though lawyer wrongfully used client's confidential information to expose corrupt judge, mitigation found because public served by respondent's actions in exposing corrupt judge and judge's removal from office; concurring opinions offer spirited debate as to appropriateness of mitigating factor of public good by whistleblower). *But see Fla. Bar v. Maurice*, 955 So.2d 535 (Fla. 2007) (approving referee's finding rejecting as mitigating factors items including: complaining client did not pay or lose any money during representation; lawyer paid bar's costs within two weeks of referee's decision; lawyer was never in violation of CLE requirements and always took more CLE than necessary; lawyer did not expressly tie these facts to any of the mitigating factors and even if these were interpreted as relating to mitigating factors under Florida Standard 9.32, she failed to demonstrate that referee's failure to find that these mitigating factors applied was clearly erroneous or without support in the record); *Mahoning Cnty. Bar Ass'n v. Sinclair*, 822 N.E.2d 360, 367 (Ohio 2004) (noting lawyer's cooperation in prosecution's case against U.S. congressman to whom he paid kickbacks "of little mitigating effect").

Lawyers sometimes ask courts for leniency based on how the discipline may unfairly impact the lawyer, his or her family, or even clients. *See, e.g., In re Lassen*, 672 A.2d 988, 1000 n.13 (Del. 1996) (while effect of public discipline upon lawyer's wife and young children is a factor tending toward mitigation, court stated that "[i]t is Respondent, however, who is responsible for the public scrutiny this sanction will bring upon his family [and] [t]he Court may not temper its treatment of Respondent to protect the interests of those peripherally affected if to do so would undermine the interests of the lawyer discipline system"); *Lawyer Disciplinary Board v. Plants*, 801 S.E.2d 225 (W. Va. 2017) (public reprimand was enough for former prosecutor who was now private lawyer when the goal of discipline is to restore public confidence in ethical standards of legal profession).

In some cases, lawyers have asked the court to consider in mitigation their self-imposed suspension or removal from the practice of law at the time of the misconduct, with varying degrees of success. *See, e.g., State ex rel. Okla. Bar Ass'n v. McMillen*, 393 P.3d 223 (Okla. 2017) (that lawyer self-suspended herself from the practice of law for five months accepted by the court as mitigating factor resulting in lifting of interim suspension); *State ex rel. Okla. Bar Ass'n v. Kinsey*, 212 P.3d 1186, 1193, 1195 (Okla. 2009) (in rejecting lawyer's argument that she should be given credit for "self-suspension" following her resignation as associate in law firm when an investigation revealed her false billings, the court called the term a "misnomer" and stated that a lawyer's self-suspension is not a substitute for court-imposed discipline; noting court order required a lawyer to give notice to clients of the suspension and here, respondent "may have refrained from practicing law, but she provided no proof that she was suspended from the practice of law or that she complied with [the rule] by giving notice"; concluding that the court may consider a lawyer's withdrawal from the practice "in its total consideration of mitigating evidence"); *cf. In re Soininen*, 853 A.2d 712, 714, 727 (D.C. 2004) (lawyer not entitled to credit for time served on "self-suspension" since she neither "complied with the notice requirements applicable to suspended attorneys nor demonstrated the existence of 'unique' or 'compelling' circumstances on which a successful request for such favorable treatment would have to be based"; court noting that "lack of a public record of self-suspension prevents the disciplinary system from monitoring the activities of an attorney who, like [respondent] claims to have suspended herself"). *But see Miss. Bar v. Caldwell*, 890 So.2d 855 (Miss. 2004) (in reciprocal discipline proceeding, recognition given to lawyer's voluntary withdrawal from the practice in the state while reciprocal proceeding was pending; identical discipline of ninety-day suspension imposed but suspension completed as of court order due to lawyer's voluntary withdrawal); *Office of Disciplinary Counsel v. Alderman*, 734 S.E.2d 737 (W. Va. 2012) (consideration given to evidence presented at mitigation hearing that lawyer voluntarily withdrew from the practice of law to enter rehabilitation treatment program for drug addiction; two-year suspension with credit for twelve of the fifteen months lawyer withdrew and remaining year held in abeyance pending two years supervised practice for two misdemeanor drug convictions).

Courts have also found the role that the client, coworkers, or other counsel may have played in a lawyer's misconduct is not mitigating. *See, e.g., In re Griffith*, 800 N.E.2d 259 (Mass. 2003) (in case of intentional material omission, court rejected as mitigating lawyer's obsession with case and contentious nature of proceedings, opposing counsel's independent failure to discover requested information and novel issues regarding possible statutory protection against disclosure; although a close point, some mitigation existed by reason of publicity surrounding the published opinion of federal judge sanctioning lawyer and significant monetary fine paid by him); *In re Disciplinary Action Against Nassif*, 504 N.W.2d 311, 314 (N.D. 1993) (rejecting lawyer's argument that his "client's lack of telephone, numerous moves, and volume of other work performed for the client" should have been considered in mitigation of lawyer's neglect and lack of diligence); *In re Knappenberger*, 108 P.3d 1161 (Or. 2005) (rejecting as mitigating lawyer's characterization of prohibited communication as being brief and transitory and justified by understandable emotional reaction to being sued by his employees; also rejecting as mitigating lawyer's quick withdrawal after learning of conflict of interest); *cf. In re Att'y D.*, 57 P.3d 395 (Colo. 2002) (conduct of other lawyers in similar circumstances is rarely if ever relevant to establishing either occurrence of a violation or propriety of sanction; fact that particular or numerous lawyers may have engaged in same practice as respondent neither justifying nor mitigating).

Humiliation can be considered in mitigation, but lawyers will find it difficult to establish. *See In re Peasley*, 90 P.3d 764 (Ariz. 2004) (public humiliation not mitigating factor for prosecutor accused of intentionally presenting false testimony in two separate capital murder trials). *But see In re Walker*, 24 P.3d 602 (Ariz. 2001) (lawyer who sexually harassed a client and attempted to enter into consensual sexual relationship with her warranted censure; his public and personal humiliation was important mitigating factor in that he was arrested at his office and taken to jail in handcuffs, charges against him were made public by local press, he was prosecuted for sexual indecency and prostitution and forced to participate in a diversion program, he was subject to malpractice allegations, and agreed to $50,000 settlement).

Ignorance is not a mitigating factor. *See, e.g.*, *In re Crossen*, 880 N.E.2d 352, 385 (Mass. 2008) (contention that lawyer acted in good faith in face of "murky" ethics rules failed as basis for mitigation when rules were not murky and lawyer's lack of good faith was amply supported in record); *In re Kersey's Case*, 842 A.2d 121 (N.H. 2004) (rejecting as mitigating lawyer's asserted belief that he was not required to comply with court order to turn over client files because he believed the court lacked jurisdiction to require him to surrender files). *But see In re McDermitt*, No. 05-11710, 2006 WL 1582390 (Bankr. D. Vt. May 30, 2006) (no sanction imposed and vacating prior disgorgement order against bankruptcy lawyer who filed 141 cases during sixteen days prior to effective date of new bankruptcy law and either missed deadlines for timely filing schedules or failed to timely file motions to extend deadlines for schedules in majority of cases; finding it appropriate to characterize substantial substantive changes in the law, looming effective date for changes in legal rights of persons seeking bankruptcy relief, and extraordinary number of individuals seeking to file bankruptcy in six-month period between enactment and effective date of new law as relevant mitigating factors).

Courts have looked favorably upon a lawyer seeking expert advice prior to taking action, though seeking such advice has not prevailed as a factor in mitigation when the lawyer failed to disclose relevant information at the time. *See, e.g.*, *People v. Casey*, 948 P.2d 1014, 1017 (Colo. 1997) (evidence that subordinate lawyer sought good faith consultation from senior partner not mitigating due to lack of detail regarding advice, if any, given to lawyer; court suggested, however, that good faith effort by subordinate to seek supervision can be mitigating factor, favorably citing article asserting that point, i.e., Irwin D. Miller, *Preventing Misconduct by Promoting the Ethics of Attorneys' Supervisory Duties,* 70 Notre Dame L. Rev. 259, 302–04 (1994)); *In re Phillips,* 107 P.3d 615 (Or. 2005) (recognizing reliance on timely ethics advice may provide mitigating factor but giving little weight here to consultation with ethics specialist regarding conflicts of interest situation because lawyer had entered into questionable joint venture prior to seeking ethics advice and failed to provide critical fact regarding the joint venture); *In re Benett,* 14 P.3d 66 (Or. 2000) (seeking ethics advice from bar not accorded weight as mitigating factor; even assuming seeking advice may provide mitigation, lawyer failed to present any definitive evidence of nature or extent of any communications with the bar).

## *Interim Rehabilitation*

The ABA House of Delegates deleted interim rehabilitation as a mitigating factor in February 1992 when it adopted amendments to Standard 9.32, and now the issue of rehabilitation is addressed only in Standard 9.32(i)(3), regarding recovery from mental disability or chemical dependency. In keeping with this change, most courts no longer consider interim rehabilitation to be mitigating. *See, e.g., In re Peasley,* 90 P.3d 764, 776 (Ariz. 2004) (acknowledging that interim rehabilitation is no longer a factor under the Sanctions Standards, but one that still can be considered because purpose of discipline is not to punish but protect the public; refusing to give any weight to this factor since no evidence of causal connection between misconduct involving the presentation of false testimony in murder prosecution with interim rehabilitation of reduced workload and additional preparation; it would not have prevented misconduct); *In re Knappenberger,* 135 P.3d 297, 304 n.4 (Or. 2006) (rejecting lawyer's assertion that trial panel erred in failing to consider extensive evidence of interim rehabilitation because, "in 1992, 'interim rehabilitation' was deleted from the ABA Standards list of factors that the court should consider in mitigation"); *In re Disciplinary Proceeding Against Marshall,* 157 P.3d 859 (Wash. 2007) (recognizing interim rehabilitation only in instances of recovery from mental disability or chemical dependency per 1992 amendments to Sanctions Standards). *But see People v. Rhodes,* 107 P.3d 1177 (Colo. O.P.D.J. 2005) (although lawyer suffering from depression presented no evidence of complete rehabilitation, mitigating credit given for interim rehabilitation when depressed lawyer sought professional help and continued to take depression medication prescribed for him by Lawyer's Assistance Program); *Fla. Bar v. Brutus,* 216 So.3d 1286 (Fla. 2017) (interim rehabilitation found to be mitigating factor for lawyer who failed to properly manage trust account); *Atty. Griev. Comm'n v. Barton,* 110 A.3d 668 (Md. 2015) (finding only mitigating factor was interim rehabilitation, hearing judge credited lawyer for taking over fifty cases pro bono involving clients of the office manager that lawyer failed to properly supervise); *Ohio State Bar Ass'n v. Jacob*, 80 N.E.3d 440 (Ohio 2017) (interim rehabilitation, including seeking assistance from the lawyers' assistance program and serving criminal sentence considered mitigating factor for a judge who solicited prostitute and falsified court record).

## *Presence of Multiple Mitigators*

While a single mitigating factor in a case may not be sufficient to reduce a lawyer's discipline, a court may find the presence of multiple mitigating factors warrants a reduced sanction. *See, e.g., In re Youn*, 793 S.E.2d 379 (Ga. 2016) (several significant mitigating factors including: lack of disciplinary history, cooperation with bar, professional reputation for integrity, efforts on behalf of civic organizations, and remorse supported issuance of requested eighteen-month suspension for lawyer federally convicted of counseling non-Georgia resident into possessing a Georgia driver's license); *In re Mintz*, 317 P.3d 756 (Kan. 2014) (lawyer who engaged in dishonest conduct that interfered with law enforcement investigation involving the another's death received indefinite suspension due to multiple mitigating factors, including absence of a prior disciplinary record, personal or emotional problems, full and free disclosure to the disciplinary board and cooperative attitude toward proceedings, impeccable reputation as a lawyer, and remorse for misconduct); *In re Rooney*, 709 N.W.2d 263 (Minn. 2006) (although no mitigating factor alone would suffice to avoid disbarment in intentional misappropriation of client funds, 18-month suspension warranted when numerous mitigating circumstances existed including lack of prior disciplinary history, full and timely restitution, remorse, cooperation with disciplinary authorities, evidence of good character and significant contributions to the community through pro bono legal work and other volunteer activities, extraordinary stress in lawyer's personal life at time of misconduct and fact that lawyer is receiving counseling for his problems); *In re Wenz*, 87 P.3d 376 (Mont. 2004) (in imposing public censure on lawyer who represented clients with adverse interests, commission considered several mitigating factors including lack of selfish motive, fact that both clients actively sought representation by firm, fact that lawyer was not directly involved in prosecution of one of the matters, lawyer's good reputation, thirty-five years of practice without disciplinary record, and delay in disciplinary proceeding); *In re Carpenter*, 95 P.3d 203 (Or. 2004) (mitigating factors included fact that lawyer had no prior disciplinary record (although this accorded little weight because respondent had been admitted to practice for only five months), he made full and free disclosure and had a cooperative attitude toward the disciplinary proceeding, he was inexperienced in the practice of law, he showed genuine remorse, and a police officer testified that he had good character and a good reputation with law enforcement and the local court; mitigating factors in this proceeding outweigh the aggravating factors; public reprimand warranted); *In re Cope*, 2018 LEXIS 210, at *10–11 (Tn. 2018) (multiple mitigating factors including absence of a prior disciplinary record, full and free disclosure to the Board, character and reputation of the attorney, and remorse justified imposition of twenty-five-month suspension rather than disbarment); *In re Pope*, 101 A.3d 1284 (Vt. 2014) (two-year suspension sufficient to protect public and deter other lawyers from engaging in misconduct for lawyer who had no prior disciplinary record, was generally cooperative, and had record of community service); *Lawyer Disciplinary Bd. v. Campbell*, 807 S.E.2d 817 (W. Va. 2017) (seven mitigating factors contributed to lawyer being admonished for sexual relationship with a client, including no prior disciplinary record, little experience in the practice of law, and remorse); *Lawyer Disciplinary Bd. v. Blyler*, 787 S.E.2d 596 (W. Va. 2016) (sixty-day suspension when several mitigating factors present, including significant personal, emotional, and financial toll of caring for wife as she suffered through early onset Alzheimer's; other mitigating factors included good character and reputation, cooperation in disciplinary process, and absence of selfish motive); *In re Ardent*, 877 N.W.2d 364 (Wis. 2016) (several mitigating factors including absence of dishonest or selfish motive, personal or emotional problems, and being subject to other penalties, including jail time, warranted public reprimand for misusing trust account, and taking loan from client without proper disclosures).

Sometimes a finding of multiple mitigating factors is insufficient to overcome egregious conduct. *See Fla. Bar v. Gilbert*, 246 So.3d 196 (Fla. 2018). Gilbert was disbarred for failing to supervise an employee who had embezzled more than $2 million from the firm. He asserted eight grounds for mitigation. They included absence of prior discipline, no dishonest or selfish motive, a timely good faith effort to make restitution, full and free disclosure to and cooperation with disciplinary counsel, good character or reputation, interim rehabilitation, imposition of other sanctions, and remorse. The Florida Supreme Court held such evidence in mitigation was insufficient to outweigh the egregiousness of the misconduct, including that Gilbert knew of his employee's history of wire fraud and embezzlement and had been warned of risks from the employee's probation officer.

## 9.4 Factors That Are Neither Aggravating Nor Mitigating

**The following factors should not be considered as either aggravating or mitigating:**

**(a) forced or compelled restitution;**
**(b) agreeing to the client's demand for certain improper behavior or result;**
**(c) withdrawal of complaint against the lawyer;**
**(d) resignation prior to completion of disciplinary proceedings;**
**(e) complainant's recommendation as to sanction;**
**(f) failure of injured client to complain.**

# Annotation

While courts on occasion have considered each of the six factors listed above as aggravating or mitigating in disciplinary proceedings, the purposes of lawyer discipline are best served by viewing them as irrelevant to the imposition of a sanction.

### *Forced or Compelled Restitution*

Courts generally find that lawyers who make restitution only after a court order has been issued compelling restitution or a disciplinary proceeding has been instituted against them are not acting out of a sense of responsibility for their misconduct. As such, their restitution is not considered in aggravation or mitigation under Standard 9.4(a). *See, e.g., In re Augenstein*, 871 P.2d 254 (Ariz. 1994) (forced or compelled restitution constitutes neither aggravating nor mitigating factor—at most, it is neutral under Standard 9.4(a); in this case indifference to making restitution was additional aggravating factor when settlement by lawyer whose misconduct included neglect of client matters was prompted by malpractice claim filed by client; two-year suspension imposed); *People v. Robbins*, 869 P.2d 517 (Colo. 1994) (restitution that is forced or compelled following discovery is not mitigating under Standard 9.4(a); disbarment warranted for lawyer who converted client's funds because restitution occurred after detection and he knew that misconduct would be reported to grievance committee); *People v. Benight*, 2016 WL 7856476 (Colo. O.P.D.J December 8, 2016) (lawyer would not be credited with mitigating factor for making payment to victim assistance fund as ordered by court as part of terms of probation for guilty plea to unlawful sexual contact with teenage girl; under Standard 9.4 such court ordered payment was neither aggravating nor mitigating); *People v. Kleinsmith*, 407 P.3d 1229 (Colo. O.P.D.J. 2016) in conversion case where lawyer was disbarred, one small garnishment of funds used to make restitution was neither mitigating nor aggravating under Standard 9.4); *People v. Brown*, 161 P.3d 1286, 1293 (Colo. O.P.D.J. 2007) (lawyer's payment on second day of hearing for immediate suspension was not timely and was "more akin to a 'forced or compelled' restitution," not considered either aggravating or mitigating under Standard 9.4(a); disbarment warranted for conversion of some $18,000 taken from six clients); *In re Thomson,* 464 S.E.2d 818 (Ga. 1996) (restitution made by lawyer only after ordered by bankruptcy court not considered mitigating factor; forced or compelled restitution neither aggravating nor mitigating under Standard 9.4(a)); *In re Brown,* 636 N.E.2d 1249 (Ind. 1994) (restitution after disciplinary proceeding initiated does not qualify as mitigating factor for lawyer who failed to personally pay discovery expenses as ordered by court; public reprimand imposed); *In re Hanley,* 627 N.E.2d 800 (Ind. 1994) (public reprimand warranted for lawyer who negotiated payment from client while representing client as public defender; in accord with Standard 9.4(a), no mitigating factor for refunding $200, plus interest, because restitution occurred more than six years after receipt and only after disciplinary proceedings were initiated); *In re Swisher,* 41 P.3d 847 (Kan. 2002) (citing former commentary to Standard 9.4(a), court found lawyer's letters of apology to complainants and refund to one client during week preceding disciplinary hearing not mitigating; two-year suspension imposed for lawyer who repeatedly provided false information regarding status of client representations and repeatedly failed to provide competent and diligent representation); *In re Scheurich,* 871 So.2d 1104 (La. 2004) (lawyer's payment of outstanding bills to third-party medical providers was restitution that appeared either forced or compelled and therefore was neither aggravating nor mitigating; three-year suspension for converting client funds to his own use, among other misconduct); *In re Kersey's Case,* 842 A.2d 121 (N.H. 2004) (fact that lawyer who continued to practice law after suspension and refused to turn over client files surrendered them under protest was not mitigating, as he asserted; citing Standard 9.4(a) that forced or compelled restitution as a factor is not aggravating or mitigating, court imposed disbarment); *In re Obert,* 282 P.3d 825 (Or. 2012) (per Standard 9.4(a), "forced" restitution of $1,200 fee by client's credit card company after she contested transaction does not weigh in lawyer's favor; six-month suspension imposed for misconduct including collecting excessive fee); *Bd. of Prof'l Responsibility v. Maddux,* 148 S.W.3d 37 (Tenn. 2004) (payments to former partners made by lawyer who, over three-year period, converted $92,500 for personal use from law firm of which he was a partner were neither aggravating nor mitigating under Standard 9.4(a) when restitution compelled by court order; thirty-day suspension); *In re Disciplinary Proceeding Against Cramer,* 225 P.3d 881 (Wash. 2010) (citing former commentary to Standard 9.4(a), court found restitution was compelled by Department of Revenue garnishment proceedings and compelled restitution is not a mitigating factor; lawyer disbarred for criminal acts and disciplinary violations in misrepresenting that he would not be practicing law in attempt to circumvent state taxes). *But see People v. Tidwell,* 35 P.3d 624, 630 (Colo. O.P.D.J. 2001) (lawyer's refund of advance fees to clients after disciplinary complaint filed "was not 'forced' or 'compelled'" under Standard 9.4(a) and could be construed as limited mitigating factor, although timing bore upon weight to be accorded restitution; disbarment for pattern of neglect and conversion of client funds); *In re Comish*, 889 So.2d 236 (La. 2004) (citing former commentary to Standard 9.4 that restitution should be considered in mitigation, even if made after complaint is filed, so long as it is made before formal disciplinary proceedings are instituted; here lawyer paid unearned fee to client in April 2000 while formal charges against lawyer not instituted until more than two years later; three-year suspension appropriate with all but a year and a day deferred due to mitigating factors).

## *Agreeing to Client's Demand for Improper Behavior or Result*

Unethical conduct is much less likely to be deterred if lawyers can lessen or avoid the imposition of sanctions by blaming the client for their actions. *See, e.g., In re Wiederholt*, 877 P.2d 765 (Alaska 1994) (agreeing to client's demand for certain improper behavior is specifically not a mitigating factor under Standard 9.4(b); even if it were, evidence in this case showed that client was less of a motivating factor than lawyer who intentionally misled court and other parties into believing that no execution sale had occurred and forging another client's name on joint check; disbarment appropriate sanction); *Fla. Bar v. Calvo*, 630 So.2d 548, 550 (Fla. 1993) (though scheme primarily originated with client, not lawyer, "[i]t is especially incumbent upon attorneys to use their legal expertise to discourage rather than further the type of flagrant fraud on the public involved in this case"; disbarment for misconduct involving securities offering); *Iowa Supreme Ct. Bd. of Prof'l Ethics & Conduct v. Vinyard*, 656 N.W.2d 127 (Iowa 2003) (in rejecting claim of lawyer whose license was revoked for participating with brother in money laundering and mail fraud that scheme was brother's idea, court observed that fact that lawyer did not initiate idea or set criminal conduct into motion does not work as a mitigating factor); *Att'y Grievance Comm'n v. Glenn*, 671 A.2d 463, 489 (Md. 1996) (citing former commentary to Standard 9.4, court said lawyer's misconduct, including engaging in dishonest conduct, warranted indefinite suspension: "We note that 'the client made me do it' is not a mitigator'"); *In re Smith*, 848 P.2d 612 (Or. 2003) (thirty-five-day suspension for lawyer who prepared letter threatening litigation in course of representing workers' compensation claimant; even assuming that the client was constitutionally privileged to make the same comments and that he induced the lawyer to prepare the letter, his conduct was not justified and neither aggravating nor mitigating under Standard 9.4(b).

## *Withdrawal of Complaint Against the Lawyer*

The mere fact that a complainant may have decided to withdraw a complaint should not be considered a mitigating factor. *See, e.g., People v. Vsetecka*, 893 P.2d

1309, 1310 (Colo. 1995) (when request for investigation of a lawyer is filed, "nothing short of deliberate misrepresentation by the complaining witness could affect grievance proceedings once they have been initiated"); *Att'y Grievance Comm'n v. Lee*, 903 A.2d 895, 905 (Md. 2006) (affidavit from the complainant stating satisfaction with lawyer's services subsequent to the conduct mentioned in the complaint was not sufficient to prevent imposition of an indefinite suspension; "Even though an individual complainant may believe that he or she was recompensed adequately as a result of the attorney's post-complaint gestures, allowing an attorney to avoid a pending investigation and potential disciplinary actions in such a manner would be contrary and detrimental to the purpose of the Maryland Rules of Professional Conduct 'to protect the public and the public's confidence in the legal profession'") (citation omitted).

## *Resignation Prior to Completion of Disciplinary Proceedings*

A lawyer's resignation before the disciplinary proceeding is complete is also neither an aggravating nor mitigating factor. *See, e.g., In re Schonland*, 21 Vet. App. 428 (Vet. App. 2007) (tendering of resignation, which court declined to accept, served as neither aggravating nor mitigating factor under Standard 9.4(d); suspension from practice before Court of Appeals for Veterans Claims for two years was appropriate sanction for lawyer's misconduct, which consisted of failing to prosecute appeals of his clients, misrepresenting the reason for dismissal of their appeals, and failing to cooperate with disciplinary investigation); *People v. Woodford*, 81 P.3d 370 (Colo. O.P.D.J. 2003) (Standard 9.4(d) provides that resignation from practice prior to completion of disciplinary proceedings is irrelevant for purposes of imposing sanction; here lawyer wrote letter to regulation counsel that he had permanently closed his law practice but fifteen-month suspension imposed for misconduct including preparing unenforceable trust documents, neglecting legal work, charging excessive fee, and failing to file tax returns, along with aggravating factors); *In re Perez*, 688 N.W.2d 562, 567 (Minn. 2004) (Minnesota does not allow lawyers to resign with charges pending, namely violations justifying disbarment; to permit such a practice "would not serve the ends of justice nor deter others from legal misconduct") (citations omitted); disbarment appropriate for lawyer convicted of mail fraud in California); *In re Disciplinary Action Against Crary*, 638 N.W.2d 23 (N.D. 2002) (fact that, after hearing panel issued report, lawyer tendered resignation from bar was neither mitigating nor aggravating factor and did not halt pending disciplinary proceedings under North Dakota Standard 9.4(d); lawyer disbarred for obtaining $3,500 unpaid loan and annuity purchases from ill elderly client, without advising client to seek independent counsel or disclosing receipt of annuity commissions, and drafting codicil to client's will, naming lawyer's wife as beneficiary).

## *Complainant's Recommendation as to Sanction*

The complainant's recommendation as to a sanction is a factor that should be neither aggravating nor mitigating. The consistency of sanctions cannot be assured if any individual's personal views concerning an appropriate sanction can either increase or decrease the severity of the sanction imposed by the court. Although the court should not consider the complainant's recommendation as to sanction, the complainant's feelings about the lawyer's misconduct need not be completely ignored. The complainant should be afforded the right to make a statement to the trier of fact in the disciplinary case concerning the lawyer's actions and the effect of the alleged misconduct on the complainant.

## *Failure of Injured Client to Complain*

The fact that an injured client has not complained about a lawyer's conduct should serve as neither aggravation nor mitigation. The disciplinary system is designed to protect all members of the public. That an injured person, for whatever reason, chooses not to complain about a lawyer's conduct should not relieve or excuse the lawyer. It may be that the complainant chose to "forgive and forget" or the complainant may have been unaware of the existence of the lawyer disciplinary agency, but courts generally will not take this factor into consideration when imposing discipline. *See, e.g., People v. Shields,* 905 P.2d 608 (Colo. 1995) (failure of client to complain to grievance committee or disciplinary counsel is neither aggravating nor mitigating factor under Standard 9.4(f); whether Social Services was satisfied with the work respondent actually performed or with his billing practices as to that work (and the record contains evidence supporting such conclusions) was not significant for purposes of assessing appropriate discipline; suspension for one year and one day warranted); *In re Dennis,* 188 P.3d 1 (Kan. 2008) (citing former commentary to Standard 9.4(f), court found that lawyer's argument—that indefinite suspension is inappropriate since neither disciplinary complaint was filed by a client—failed to recognize that his conduct has had an adverse effect on opposing parties, the court, and the judicial system); *In re Montpetit,* 528 N.W.2d 243 (Minn. 1995) (no complaint from clients about lawyer's trust account shortages among the mitigating factors considered by hearing referee but not accepted by the court in rejecting recommendation of stayed six months' suspension; four-month suspension imposed); *In re Disciplinary Action Against Hellerud,* 714 N.W.2d 38, 43–44 (N.D. 2006) (court reiterating, "client's failure to complain and the district court's ability to lower fees does not prevent the Disciplinary Board from hearing a complaint. Nor does it prevent this Court from imposing sanctions"; North Dakota Standard 9.4(f) cited); *In re Kluge,* 66 P.3d 492, 508 (Or. 2003) (in finding no mitigating factors applicable, court stated that "although the accused has stressed that his client has not complained about his representation, the absence of complaint from the client is not a mitigating factor" under Standard 9.4(f)); *In re Disciplinary Proceeding Against Schwimmer,* 108 P.3d 761, 766 (Wash. 2005) (in imposing disbarment, court stated that "it is of no importance that none of [respondent's] clients complained about his misappropriation of their funds"; Standard 9.4(f) cited); *cf. In re Belz,* 258 S.W.3d 38 (Mo. 2008) (imposing three-year suspension on lawyer for misappropriating funds over four years; although the failure of an injured client to complain is considered neither aggravating nor mitigating under Standard 9.4(f), the court noted that the client from whose account the funds were taken not only did not complain, but had chosen to remain the lawyer's client even after learning of the misconduct).

# Table of Cases

**F**

**H**

**I**

**K**

**L**

**M**

**Q**



**R**

**S**

**Y**



**Z**

# Index